Marxism after Marx

Also by David McLellan

THE YOUNG HEGELIANS AND KARL MARX
MARX BEFORE MARXISM
KARL MARX: the Early Texts
MARX'S GRUNDRISSE
KARL MARX: His Life and Thought
MARX
ENGELS
KARL MARX: Selected Writings
SIMONE WEIL: Utopian Pessimist
UNTO CAESAR: the Political Relevance of Christianity

Marxism after Marx

Fourth Edition

David McLellan

palgrave
macmillan

First published 1979 by
Macmillan Press Ltd

Second edition published 1980
by Macmillan Press Ltd

Third edition published 1998
by Macmillan Press Ltd

This edition published 2007 by
PALGRAVE MACMILLAN
Houndmills, Basingstoke, Hampshire RG21 6XS and
175 Fifth Avenue, New York, N.Y. 10010
Companies and representatives throughout the world.

PALGRAVE MACMILLAN is the global academic imprint of the Palgrave Macmillan division of St. Martin's Press, LLC and of Palgrave Macmillan Ltd. Macmillan® is a registered trademark in the United States, United Kingdom and other countries. Palgrave is a registered trademark in the European Union and other countries

ISBN-13: 978–1–4039–9727–2 hardback
ISBN-10: 1–4039–9727–6 hardback
ISBN-13: 978–1–4039–9728–9 paperback
ISBN-10: 1–4039–9728–4 paperback

This book is printed on paper suitable for recycling and made from fully managed and sustained forest sources.

A catalogue record for this book is available from the British Library.

Library of Congress Cataloging-in-Publication Data

McLellan, David.
    Marxism after Marx / David McLellan. —4th ed.
        p. cm.
    Includes bibliographical references and index.
    ISBN-13: 978-1–4039-9727-2 (cloth)
    ISBN-10: 1-4039-9727-6 (cloth)
    ISBN-13: 978–1–4039-9728-9 (pbk.)
    ISBN-10: 1-4039-9728-4 (pbk.)
        1. Communism – History. I. Title.

HX36.M4 2007
355.4309—dc22   2006047819

10 9 8 7 6 5 4 3 2 1
16 15 14 13 12 11 10 09 08 07

Transferred to Digital Printing in 2011

For Gabrielle and Stephanie

Contents

Preface to the First Edition

The varieties of Marxism over the last 100 years are so manifold and, at times, so subtle that any survey that aims to be fairly comprehensive is bound also to be fairly superficial. What I have tried to do is to describe the development of Marxist ideas. In order to make sense of this development, a minimum of reference to their political, social and economic context is necessary; but I have not attempted to give a history of Marxism as a movement. I hope to have provided the basic information for any reader interested either in the evolution of Marxist doctrine as a whole or in the specific ideas of, say, Gramsci or Althusser. Since my text is intended only to be introductory, I have added to each section a substantial further reading list divided into a commentary section (to give the reader some, albeit subjective, guide as to the content of the books) and a larger section of purely bibliographical references.

Gay Sharp has improved the style of the book on virtually every page; Tony Trivelli helped me substantially with the chapter on Gramsci; Nick Caswell and Jacqui Powell did the groundwork for the bibliography; and Joyce Macrae and Mary Nash prepared the final typescript splendidly.

D.M.
Canterbury
September 1978

Preface to the Third Edition

I have added substantially to the bibliographical material for each chapter and expanded both the final chapter and the conclusion.

D.M.
Canterbury
May 1998

Preface to the Fourth Edition

This edition is thoroughly revised and expanded. Books on various aspects of Marxism continue to appear as regularly as ever. I have therefore expanded all the bibliographies. I have also added, at the end of the book, a list of dictionaries of Marxism and, in particular, relevant journals. Most chapters contain minor additions; there are substantial additions to the chapters on Latin America, theories of underdevelopment, the Frankfurt School, Italian Marxism, and British Marxism. The chapter on Marxism in the United States and the Conclusion have been considerably expanded. There is also a new chapter on Marxism and Postmodernism. My aim has been to provide as comprehensive a guide as possible to Marxist thought since the death of Marx.

D.M.
Canterbury
Easter 2006

Introduction: The Legacy of Marx

At first sight, Marx would seem to have bequeathed a firm body of doctrine to his followers. In what he called the 'guiding thread' of his studies, Marx considered himself to have shown that the sum total of relations of production – the way men organised their social production as well as the instruments they used – constituted the real basis of society on which there arose a legal and political superstructure and to which corresponded definite forms of consciousness. Thus the way men produced their means of subsistence conditioned their whole social, political, and intellectual life. But at a certain stage in their evolution the forces of production would develop beyond the relations of production and these would then act as a fetter. Such a stage inaugurated a period of social revolution. These productive forces had to develop to the fullest extent possible under the existing relations of production before the old social order would perish. It was possible to pick out the Asiatic, ancient, feudal and modern bourgeois modes of production as progressive epochs in the economic formation of society. These bourgeois relations of production were the last ones to create a divided society and, with their end, the prehistory of human society would be brought to a close. For bourgeois society would end with a period of revolution that would culminate in the proletariat, through the agency of its own political party, gaining power and, after a period of dictatorship, creating a classless, communist society.

But the passage of time revealed serious ambiguities in Marx's thought. One obvious reason for this was the chaotic state in which Marx left his manuscripts at his death. Not only was his work unfinished, but the rough drafts that went beyond what he had actually published implied – at least in the minds of many – a thorough reassessment of his message. At the time of his death, Marx's thought was

1

known mainly through the rather simplistic *Communist Manifesto* and the difficult *Capital*. The publication of Marx's early writings around 1930 and the *Grundrisse* in 1941 are the most striking examples of the influence of unpublished material. Indeed, the history of the development of Marxist thought could almost be written in terms of the rediscovery of aspects of Marx's ideas that had either been neglected or unknown – or at least as far as Western Marxism is concerned.

A slightly less fortuitous reason for the ambivalence of Marx's legacy was that his way of thinking did not allow itself to be encapsulated in easy formulas. In his youth, Marx had detected an ambivalence in his master Hegel, and the same ambivalence was present – not surprisingly – in the disciple. For each was a dialectical thinker, and the Marxian dialectic in particular was open-ended: being a unity of subjective and objective factors, both the theory and the practice were constantly interacting and evolving. Marx himself had changed and developed his views, both political and economic, during his lifetime.

Thirdly, Marx had urged his followers not to interpret the world, but to change it. But the more successful they were in this the more Marxism tended to become the doctrine of a mass movement. Mass political parties were born in the second half of the nineteenth century and socialism was the most radical of them, appealing to all who were excluded from, or not getting enough of, the benefits of the new industrial society. What distinguished Marxism in this context was its rare ability to link revolutionary fervour and desire for change with a historical perspective and a claim to be scientific. Almost inevitably, therefore, the inherited ideas were simplified, rigidified, ossified. Marxism became a matter of simple faith for its millions of adherents, to whom it gave the certainty of final victory. But this entailed an ever-growing distance from the original ideas of Marx and their transformation into a dogmatic ideology with the correlative concept of heresy (or revisionism, as it was often called).

Lastly – and most evidently – the world has changed so much, and in so many places to which Marx paid little attention, that it would be idle to expect many specific points of his work to be still applicable. Marx certainly had views on the nature of socialist policy in Germany, and even, towards the end of his life, considered the possibility of revolution in Russia. But it remains paradoxical that Marx, a Victorian thinker who saw Europe and North America as the centre of the world's stage and the arena for future revolutions, is apparently now more widely respected as a mentor by the populations of Third World countries. It is most important to bear in mind in this connection that Marx envisaged a communist revolution taking place in countries where a certain degree of

economic well-being would permit considerable post-revolutionary political freedom. In the event, however, Marxist doctrines have proved most
successful in those countries where scarcity of resources means that political freedom is a luxury that cannot be afforded. Thus, in many developing countries a version of Marxism combined with nationalism has
functioned as an ideology for mass participation in the modernisation
process.

The difficulties contained in Marx's legacy – at least in the minds of its
recipients – can be shown by outlining briefly the ambivalences of his
views in the key fields of economics, sociology, politics, and philosophy.

In *economics*, the very foundations were unclear at the time of Marx's
death. Whether the labour theory of value could prove a useful tool in
analysing real economic movements had to await the posthumous publication of *Capital* Volume Three and Marx's solution to the question of
the transformation of values into prices. And his answer seemed unsatisfactory to many of his followers. On more immediately practical matters, Marx was clear that the collapse of the capitalist system was
inevitable – but the exact mechanism was unclear. Was the key to be
found in the tendency of the rate of profit to fall? Or was it a question
of overproduction and consequent underconsumption? Or a combination of both? Marx left the question sufficiently open for it to be a subject of considerable debate to this day. Moreover, Marx's economic
studies dealt primarily with the competitive stage of capitalism.
Although he correctly predicted the growth of monopoly, he was not in
a position to analyse its laws of motion and still less those of imperialism, which was peripheral to Marx's vision but is quite central to most
modern Marxist accounts of the world economic system.

In *sociology*, the *Communist Manifesto* had talked of the simplification
of class antagonisms and declared that 'society as a whole is more and
more splitting up into two great hostile camps, into two great classes
directly facing each other: Bourgeois and Proletariat'.[1] Yet Marx's
researches in the *Theories of Surplus Value* on the growth of the middle
class and of the unproductive service sector seemed to supply a much
more subtle view that even Bernstein would have found congenial. These
problems were not clarified, as Marx's attempt to define class was notoriously left unfinished at the end of *Capital* Volume Three. But the great
lacuna in this respect in Marx was his treatment of the peasantry. Given
the generally conservative attitude of the Western European peasantry, it
is not surprising that Marx could talk discouragingly of 'the idiocy of
rural life', and allot to the peasantry at the most a subordinate role in any
revolutionary movement. With the centre of gravity in Marxism moving

eastwards and the success in China of a peasant-based revolution that was in no sense proletarian, it was obvious that the connection with Marx's own ideas was becoming increasingly tenuous.

But the largest gap in Marx's writings was in *politics*. The continued existence, and indeed growth, of nationalism was evidently a phenomenon to which he paid far too little attention. Although strong on the analysis of contemporary political events (*Eighteenth Brumaire, Class Struggle in France, Civil War in France*), Marx left no coherent theory of the state, a topic to which he had intended to devote a whole book. This was the only part of his theoretical legacy that, according to him, only he could satisfactorily complete. The result was that only in the last few years have Marxists gone much beyond Marx himself in their work on the capitalist state. More importantly, from the practical point of view, Marx had not had to deal with the problem of the relationship between leadership, party and masses. The only organisations in which Marx was active were the Communist League, which was a propaganda group only several hundred strong, and the First International, which was a loose federation of sects and trade unions. The era of the mass party came only after Marx's death. Although he had declared that the emancipation of the working class would be achieved by the workers themselves, it was clear that their leaders, beginning with Marx himself, would be almost exclusively of bourgeois origin. Thus anyone – from a Leninist proposing a highly centralised 'vanguard' party to lead workers (who would otherwise have the most inadequate views about politics) to a libertarian socialist who believed that political power should be vested directly in workers' assemblies – could claim, without fear of refutation, that they were in the true Marxist tradition.

Finally, there was the question of Marx's *philosophical* legacy. In his early writings, Marx had talked of the abolition of philosophy, by which he meant that, in so far as philosophy posed ideal principles or essences, it would lose its function after a socialist revolution which embodied these principles or essences in socio-economic reality. However, with the revolution still a long way off, the 'footnotes to Plato' had to be dealt with and the growing membership of Marxist parties required a 'philosophy' in the sense of a coherent system of principles giving a total explanation of the universe. Given the cultural climate of the late nineteenth century, this had to be couched in scientific – and even positivist – terms. Although the later Marx certainly had traces of such attitudes in his work, it was given systematic form by Engels and culminated in the philosophy of dialectical materialism propagated by Communist orthodoxy. The re-emphasis of the Hegelian (and therefore anti-scientific in the crude sense) elements in Marx's thought was led by Lukács and given a firm foundation by the publication of Marx's early works. The notions of humanism and alienation were given unwonted prominence by many Marxists after 1930 and a long controversy ensued as to whether the 'young' or the 'old' Marx was the real one. This division is exemplified in Western Marxism by the opposition between the Frankfurt School and the Structuralist Marxists.

Note

1. K. Marx, *Selected Writings*, ed. D. McLellan (Oxford, 2000) p. 246.

Further reading

A reasonably full critical bibliography of Marx's writings and of the secondary literature can be found in D. McLellan, *Karl Marx: A Biography* (London and New York, 2006).

Part One

The German Social Democrats

Orthodoxies have an elastic quality to cover very different social groups, to unite them within a common terminology, but inevitably the version of orthodoxy held by different social groups will be different, incorporating each group's specific perspective.

Nigel Harris, *Beliefs in Society*

1
The Contribution of Engels

The most influential interpreter of Marx's thought after his death was undoubtedly Friedrich Engels. As a constant companion and collaborator of Marx he was regarded as having a privileged insight into the meaning and importance of Marx's writings. Always a keen correspondent, he acted as mentor to the nascent socialist parties and placed his astoundingly broad knowledge at the disposal of the socialist movement as a whole. In general, Engels developed Marx's ideas in two distinct directions that were both, to a noticeable extent, at variance with the original thrust of Marx's thought. Firstly, Engels took the initial steps along the path that was to end with the portrayal of Marxism as a dogmatic metaphysical system embodied in Soviet (and other) textbooks on dialectical materialism. Secondly, Engels was forced to come to terms with the problem facing the SPD as an allegedly revolutionary party operating on an increasingly successful scale in a parliamentary democracy.

Of course, these trends in Marxian doctrine had been developing well before Marx's death. In particular, Marx and Engels had operated a conscious 'division of intellectual labour' (with Marx concentrating on history and economics while Engels looked after military strategy and natural sciences): from their earliest meeting, there had always been a slight difference of approach between them. Engels, an autodidact, lacked the profound academic training in classical German philosophy and most of his working life was spent in the very practical management of a factory. Even in their respective drafts of the *Communist Manifesto*, Engels was slightly more evolutionist and determinist than Marx;[1] and his later spheres of special interest inevitably brought about a different methodological emphasis.[2] It must, however, be remembered that two out of the three major writings in which Engels developed his philosophical views were composed during Marx's lifetime: the drafts from which the *Dialectics of Nature* was eventually published (in 1925) were begun in 1873; and Engels actually read out to Marx the instalments of *Anti-Dühring* as he wrote them for the German Social Democrat newspaper *Volkstaat*.[3] Only *Ludwig Feuerbach and the End of Classical German Philosophy* was actually written after Marx's death.

Philosophy

There were two general factors that influenced Engels's development of a general world outlook strongly orientated towards science. The more widespread the socialist movement became, the more need there was of a clear philosophical statement orientating the party members – particularly as there were already rival systems in the field. And, quite naturally, the systematic orientation provided by Engels was strongly influenced by the growing preoccupation with scientific methodology in England and Germany. There was also the fact that Engels devoted a considerable portion of his time during the last two decades of his life to the study of natural science. After Engels retired from business in 1870, 'I went through as complete as possible a "moulting", as Herr Liebig calls it, in mathematics and the natural sciences, and spent the best part of eight years on it.'[4] This research was carried on in close contact with a circle of scientific friends such as Karl Schorlemmer, Professor of Chemistry at Manchester. What struck Engels as of particular importance were the discovery of the transformation of energy, the discovery of the cells as the basic unit of biological transformation, and the evolutionary theory of Darwin. These interests inevitably influenced Engels's presentation of his 'world view' and his emphasis on a materialist conception of nature rather than of history. In particular, the work of Darwin made a profound impression on Engels,[5] who came in for considerable criticism from fellow-Marxists for applying to society concepts drawn from biology.[6] A corollary was that some of Engels's writings were directed just as much at scientists as at educated members of the working class; indeed he believed that 'the more ruthlessly and disinterestedly science proceeds the more it finds itself in harmony with the interests and aspirations of the workers'.[7] In addition to this general influence, Engels was also led – paradoxically – to adopt some of the positions of his opponents, particularly in his *Anti-Dühring* (though the *Dialectics of Nature* was also originally conceived of as an 'Anti-Büchner'). Both Dühring and Büchner were thoroughgoing, if rather simplistic, materialists. In spite of his contempt for Dühring's 'system-creating', Engels said in his *Preface* that 'the polemic was transformed into a more or less connected exposition of the dialectical method and of the communist world outlook'.[8] Given the increasing popularity in socialist circles of the naively materialist evolutionary concepts propounded by such thinkers as Dühring, Büchner, Vogt and Haeckel (Dühring's work had been greeted enthusiastically on publication by Bernstein and Bebel), Engels was tempted to outbid them 'in order to prevent a new occasion for sectarian divisions and confusion from developing within the Party',[9] and thus merely offer a 'superior' form of materialist monism.

It is indicative of the difference between the approaches of Marx and Engels that Engels made constant use of the concept of 'matter' which was entirely foreign to Marx's work.[10] In *Anti-Dühring* Engels talked of 'the materiality of all existence' and said that 'both matter and its mode of existence, motion, are uncreatable and ... therefore their own final cause'.[11] At the same time, however, Engels claimed that his materialism differed from the 'simple metaphysical and exclusively mechanical materialism of the eighteenth century ... In opposition to this conception, modern materialism embraces the more recent advances in natural science ...'[12] In the *Dialectics of Nature*, however, Engels went further in his efforts to differentiate himself from mechanistic materialism and flirted with a view of matter that had affinities with German romantic philosophers such as Schelling and contemporary 'life-force' theorists. This involved investing matter with what looked like a covert spiritualisation. For although Engels talked about his views being 'not a philosophy at all any more, but simply a *Weltanschauung* which has to establish and prove itself in the real sciences', he yet introduced a profoundly teleological element into his thinking by claiming that it lay in the essence of matter to evolve into thinking beings.[13]

Central to Engels's materialism was his understanding of Hegel. For the later Engels, Hegel was a thinker 'of the greatest genius' who stood 'in the same relation to consciously dialectical natural science as the utopians to modern communism'.[14] And there was indeed a certain similarity between the system-building of the older Hegel and Engels's tendency to systematise Marxism on a natural-scientific basis. Engels, like Marx, 'inverted' Hegel, but the result was not the abolition-plus-realisation of philosophy so characteristic of their thinking in the 1840s. There was no notion that philosophy might have a content to be realised and put into practice; for Engels anticipated a time when 'what still survives of all former philosophy is the science of thought and its laws – formal logic and dialectics. Everything else is merged in the positive science of Nature and History.'[15] What Engels aimed at was the construction of a systematic materialism as all-embracing as Hegel's own system; and it is scarcely an oversimplification to say that this centrally involved the replacement of 'spirit' by 'matter' as the Absolute.

For Engels, Hegel's most significant contribution had been that he was the first thinker clearly to formulate the principal laws of the dialectic which 'can be reduced in the main to three: the law of the transformation of quantity into quality and vice versa; the law of the interpenetration of opposites; the law of the negation of the negation'.[16] It is obviously only in the vaguest sense that these could be called 'laws'. (It may be significant that they are not given the typical formulation of laws, i.e. 'all quantities when sufficiently increased undergo a qualitative change'.) There is difficulty, for example, in identifying what would count as a thesis and antithesis.[17] And Engels is ambivalent as to the heuristic quality of the laws: sometimes he gives the impression that dialectical thinking is little more than the realisation that there are no hard and fast lines of demarcation in nature,[18] and he defends Marx against Dühring's charge of having deduced the origin and destiny of capitalism by recourse to dialectical laws. 'On the contrary', he said, 'after he has proved from history that in fact the process has partially already occurred, and partially must occur in the future, he then also characterises it as a process which develops in accordance with a definite dialectical law.'[19] Yet at the same time Engels could talk of the 'proofs' of these laws (he seems to mean examples) and described the dialectic as 'a method of arriving at new results'[20] as opposed to simply a set of very general (and some would say therefore almost superfluous) categorisations of the results of natural science.[21]

Integral to Engels's material conception of nature was his epistemology. For Engels, man's knowledge of the external world were 'reflections'[22] or 'more or less abstract pictures of actual things and processes',[23] and concepts were 'merely the conscious reflex of the dialectical motion of the real world'.[24] At the same time Engels was far from wishing to abandon entirely the doctrine of the unity of theory and practice: indeed, somewhat paradoxically, the pithiest formulation of this doctrine – Marx's *Theses on Feuerbach* – was first published by Engels as an appendix to his own *Ludwig Feuerbach*. Engels's idea of what was involved in *praxis*, however, was sometimes rather anaemic, as when he summarised it as 'experimentation and industry'.[25]

History

Engels's second main contribution to the evolution of Marxist ideas lay in his interpretation of historical materialism and his historical studies.

Like most Second International theorists, Engels was stronger in history than in philosophy. Although it would be too neat to say that whereas Marx wished to change the world, Engels aimed to interpret it, this formulation does contain some truth. Engels's historical studies tended, unlike Marx's, to have no immediate political reference. Marx certainly became interested in primitive societies towards the end of his life and made extensive extracts from Lewis Morgan's book *Primitive Society*, but it was Engels who turned these notes into a full-scale work on *The Origin of the Family, Private Property and the State*.[26]

Engels's book was strikingly original in turning the attention of socialists to the possibility that sexual and production relations had in some respects been superior in primitive society. More specifically, the book constituted a substantial contribution to the study of the emancipation of women, considerably aided by Bebel's continuation of these themes in his popular *Woman under Socialism* (1883). It suffered, however, from its dependence on Morgan, whose Darwinist evolutionary perspective led him to posit a much too general scheme of evolution (particularly considering his almost total disregard for Asia and Africa). Given also that Morgan's ideas on primitive sexual promiscuity, group marriage, and the chronological priority of the matrilinear over the patrilinear *Gens* are extremely dubious, it is not surprising that the section on the family is the weakest part of Engels's book. More curious is his strict dichotomy between the production of the species on the one hand and the production of the means of existence on the other. This is exemplified in his view that monogamy was the first form of family to be based not on natural but on economic conditions and in his contrast of natural selection in savage and barbaric society with new *social* forces that only emerged later, all of which seem to posit a most un-Marxist division between the economic and the social.[27] Thus Engels seemed to conceive of primitive society as not subject to the influence of economic factors in the same sense as civilised societies, and had a noticeably more unilinear account of social development than Marx.

It is, of course, true that in his formulation of historical materialism Engels, if anything, underemphasised the role of the economic factor. This was partly because he was writing to Marxists who had run into difficulties by applying to history too simplistic an interpretation of Marx, and was thus trying to combat the trenchant criticisms being directed by non-Marxists at the crude version of the theory then available.

Engels admitted that he and Marx 'are ourselves partly to blame for the fact that the younger people sometimes lay more stress on the economic side than is due to it'.[28] His own position was that

> according to the materialist conception of history, the ultimately determining element in history is the production and reproduction of real life. More than this neither Marx nor I have ever asserted. Hence if somebody twists this into saying that the economic element is the only determining one, he transforms that proposition into a meaningless, abstract, senseless phrase. There is an interaction of all these elements in which, amid all the endless host of accidents (that is, of things and events whose inner interconnection is so remote or so impossible of proof that we can regard it as nonexistent, as negligible) the economic movement finally asserts itself as necessary.[29]

In general, Engels's statements amounted to this: that the superstructure had evolved out of, and occasionally alongside, the economic basis; that the superstructure could have a relative autonomy and a structure and laws peculiar to itself; that there was reciprocal interaction between superstructure and basis; and even that, in some circumstances and for a limited period, the superstructure could determine the evolution of the basis; but that nevertheless, in the long term, the superstructure was determined by the basis. What was novel in Engels's formulation was the theory of reciprocal interaction. This theory was expressed in terms that are analogous to the interaction of chemical particles and there are interesting parallels with passages in the *Dialectics of Nature*.[30] Engels considered that 'history has proceeded hitherto in the manner of a natural process and is essentially subject to the same laws of motion'.[31] His talk of an economic 'factor' as opposed to other factors tended to compartmentalise the social process and prepare the theoretical framework for the subsequent revisionist debate.

Politics

This less than dialectical approach to theory had its corollary in more practical matters: a technological approach illustrated at its most extreme in Engels's article *On Authority*, where he compares the discipline necessary in post-revolutionary society to that currently obtaining in factories. The emphasis on the non-subjective factors that had been present in his thought at least since the *Principles of Communism* of 1847 led him often to adopt a relatively mild attitude to the bourgeois state.

Engels tended to avoid emphasising the idea that the state needed to be smashed and considered the republic to be the 'ready-for-use political form for the future role of the proletariat'.[32] His view of the transition to communism is worth quoting at length:

> As soon as there is no longer any class of society to be held in subjection; as soon as, along with class domination and the struggle for individual existence based on the former anarchy of production, the collisions and excesses arising from these have also been abolished, there is nothing more to be repressed which would make a special repressive force, a state, necessary. The first act in which the state really comes forward as the representative of society as a whole – the taking possession of the means of production in the name of society – is at the same time its last independent act as a state. The interference of the state power in social relations becomes superfluous in one sphere after another, and then ceases of itself. The government of persons is replaced by the administration of things and the direction of the process of production. The state is not 'abolished', it withers away.[33]

This view of the state as 'withering away' is plainly a metaphor drawn from biology, with all that that implies.[34]

Engels's general leanings towards scientific study produced a dichotomy between science and politics: 'When one is a man of science, one does not have an ideal; one works out scientific results and when one is a party man to boot one fights to pull them into practice. But when one has an ideal, one cannot be a man of science ...'[35] Circumstances prevented Engels from exercising his very considerable gifts as a practical politician, living as he did in enforced isolation from the leaders of the SPD. Towards the end of his life, the growing electoral success of the Social Democrats led Engels to stress the evolutionary rather than the revolutionary side of Marxism and declare the tactics of 1848 to be outmoded in every respect. In his Preface to a new edition of Marx's *Class Struggles in France*, written in 1895 shortly before he died, Engels stated that the growth of Social Democracy 'proceeds as spontaneously, as steadily, as irresistibly, and at the same time as tranquilly as a natural process', and continued:

> We can count even today on two and a quarter million voters. If it continues in this fashion, by the end of the century we shall conquer the greater part of the middle strata of society, petty bourgeois and small peasants, and grow into the decisive power in the land, before

which all other powers will have to bow, whether they like it or not. To keep this growth going without interruption until it of itself gets beyond the control of the prevailing governmental system, not to fritter away this daily increasing shock force in vanguard skirmishes, but to keep it intact until the decisive day, that is our main task. And there is only one means by which the steady rise of the socialist fighting forces in Germany could be temporarily halted, and even thrown back for some time: a clash on a big scale with the military, a blood-letting like that of 1871 in Paris. In the long run that would also be overcome. To shoot a party which numbers millions out of existence is too much even for all the magazine rifles of Europe and America. But the normal development would be impeded, the shock force would, perhaps, not be available at the critical moment, the decisive combat would be delayed, protracted and attended by heavier sacrifices.[36]

Such passages, regarded as Engels's political 'testament', certainly played a role in influencing the leaders of the SPD, though it should be noted that Engels agreed (very reluctantly) to excise certain more revolutionary passages under pressure from the Berlin leaders.[37] In any event, it can readily be appreciated that Engels's rather ambivalent position provided ammunition for both sides in the great debate on whether Marx's political doctrines needed to be revised in the light of changing circumstances.

Notes

1. Cf. H. Bollnow, 'Engels' Auffassung von Revolution und Entwicklung in seinen "Grundsätzen des Kommunismus", 1847', *Marxismusstudien* (Tübingen, 1954).
2. For discussions of the differences between Marx and Engels, see D. Hodges, 'Engels's Contribution to Marxism', *Socialist Register*, ed. R. Miliband and J. Savile (London, 1965); A. Gamble and P. Walton, *From Alienation to Surplus Value* (London, 1971) pp. 51ff.; I. Fetscher, *Marx and Marxism* (New York, 1971) pp. 162ff.; R. DeGeorge, *Patterns of Soviet Thought* (Ann Arbor, 1966) pp. 77f.; and especially M. Rubel, Introduction to K. Marx, *Oeuvres*, vol. 3 (Paris, 1975).
3. The evidence for this is contained in the *Preface* to the second edition of *Anti-Dühring* published in 1885 after Marx's death.
4. F. Engels, *Anti-Dühring* (Moscow, 1954) p. 15.
5. See E. Lucas, 'Marx' und Engels' Auseinandersetzung mit Darwin', *International Review of Social History*, vol. 9, 1964.
6. Cf. L. Krader, 'The Works of Marx and Engels in Ethnology Compared', *International Review of Social History*, 1973, p. 243.
7. F. Engels, *Ludwig Feuerbach ...* (Moscow, 1946) p. 60.
8. F. Engels, *Anti-Dühring* (Moscow, 1954) p. 13.
9. Ibid., p. 99.

10. But not to Joseph Dietzgen, with whom the expression 'dialectical materialism' originates and to whose work Engels makes generous acknowledgement.
11. F. Engels, *Anti-Dühring*, pp. 71ff.
12. Ibid., p. 31.
13. Cf. F. Engels, *Dialectics of Nature* (Moscow, 1954) p. 209. Engels also thought that this process was cyclical in that all the planets were due to fall back into the sun as the sun got colder. But this would not be the end of the universe as matter would again evolve its finest flowering – 'a thinking mind' (op. cit., p. 39).
14. Ibid., p. 17.
15. Ibid., p. 32.
16. Ibid., p. 62.
17. See R. Cooper, *The Logical Influence of Hegel on Marx* (Washington, 1925) pp. 103ff., for an under-appreciated treatment of this question on a historical plane.
18. Cf., for example, F. Engels, *Anti-Dühring*, p. 19. See further: G. Stedman Jones, 'Engels and the End of Classical German Philosophy', *New Left Review*, 79 (1973) pp. 28ff.
19. F. Engels, *Anti-Dühring*, p. 152.
20. Ibid., p. 153.
21. For a lengthy analysis of the meaning and possible import of Engels's dialectics, see S. Hook, *Reason, Social Myths and Democracy* (New York, 1940) pp. 183ff. For an attempt to defend and apply Engels's approach, see M. Kosok, 'Dialectics of Nature', in *Towards a New Marxism*, ed. B. Grahl and P. Piccone (St Louis, 1973).
22. F. Engels, *Anti-Dühring*, p. 30.
23. Ibid., p. 47.
24. F. Engels, *Ludwig Feuerbach ...* , p. 54. Cf. also, for example, Engels to C. Schmidt, K. Marx, F. Engels, *Selected Correspondence* (hereafter MESC) (Moscow, 1965).
25. F. Engels, *Ludwig Feuerbach ...* , p. 24. See, however, for a rather different version, *Dialectics of Nature*, p. 231.
26. For evidence that Marx was more interested in the political aspects of primitive societies, see E. Lucas, 'Die Rezeption Lewis H. Morgans durch Marx and Engels', *Saeculum*, 1964. In general, see L. Krader, Introduction to *The Ethnological Notebooks of Karl Marx* (Assen, 1972).
27. In general see the Introduction to the edition by E. Leacock (New York, 1973). For the deleterious influence of Engels's views on the state, see L. Colletti, *From Rousseau to Lenin* (London and New York, 1972) pp. 105ff.
28. Engels to Bloch, MESC, p. 418.
29. Engels to Bloch, MESC, p. 417.
30. F. Engels, *Dialectics of Nature* (Moscow, 1972) p. 231, where he says that 'reciprocal action is the first thing that we encounter when we consider matter in motion as a whole from the standpoint of modern science ... reciprocal action is the true *causa finalis* of things.'
31. Engels to Bloch, MESC, p. 418.
32. Engels to Lafargue, MESC, p. 472. See also Engels to von Patten, MESC, p. 363, where Engels specifically refers to the passage at the end of the second section of the *Communist Manifesto* which he and Marx had declared to be outmoded in their Preface to the second German edition of 1872.

33. F. Engels, *Anti-Dühring* (Moscow, 1954) p. 315.
34. Marx never used this expression (*absterben*), preferring the more direct 'abolish' (*abschaffen*).
35. F. Engels, *Correspondence with Paul and Laura Lafargue* (Moscow, 1959) vol. 1, p. 234.
36. F. Engels, in Karl Marx–Frederick Engels: *Selected Works* (hereafter *MESW*) (Moscow, 1962) vol. 1, pp. 135f.
37. See further H.-J. Steinberg, 'Revolution und Legalität. Ein unveröffentlichter Brief Engels an Richard Fischer', *International Review of Social History* (1967); and C. Elliot, '*Quis custodiet sacra?* Problems of Marxist Revisionism', *Journal of the History of Ideas*, 28 (1967) pp. 73ff.

Further reading

Texts

There is a 50-volume edition of the works of Marx and Engels in English, published by Lawrence & Wishart in London and International Publishers in New York, completed in 2005.

The only selection of Engels's work in English is Engels: *Selected Writings* edited by W.O. Henderson. There are several selections of Marx and Engels's works together. Perhaps the most accessible is the Moscow *Selected Works*. This selection has the advantage of reproducing excerpts *in extenso*, including the whole of the *Origin* and *Ludwig Feuerbach* and a substantial extract from *Anti-Dühring*. Lesser extracts are contained in the selections edited by Feuer and by Tucker. There are also numerous selections, published by Moscow, of Marx and Engels's *On Religion, On Ireland, On Britain, On Literature and Art*, etc.

Anti-Dühring, Ludwig Feuerbach, Dialectics of Nature and *Origin* have been translated in separate editions by Lawrence & Wishart and International Publishers, the latter with a substantial introduction by Eleanor Leacock. Engels's articles on the German Revolution of 1849–9 have been edited by Eleanor Marx under the title *Revolution and Counter-Revolution in Germany in 1848*, as have Engels's writings on military matters: *Engels as Military Critic*, edited by W.O. Henderson and O. Chaloner. The same editors produced a new translation and edition of *The Condition of the Working Class in England*. The commentary of this edition is very critical of Engels. For the other side, see the Panther edition with an introduction by Hobsbawm, and also McLellan.

Commentaries

There is a commentary on Engels's *The Condition of the Working Class in England* from a literary and psychological point of view by S. Marcus,

Engels, Manchester, and the Working Class. Of biographies, there is the abridged Gustav Mayer, *Friedrich Engels* – no more than a pale shadow of Mayer's splendid two-volume biography in German, which is the best so far available. Grace Carlton's *Friedrich Engels: The Shadow Prophet* is rather thin. The Russian biography in English, *Frederick Engels: A Biography*, contains a lot of details – but is also an extreme example of hagiography. The same is true of the East German *Frederick Engels: A Biography*. Recently there has appeared W.O. Henderson's two-volume *Life of Friedrich Engels*. This is strong on the personal side and also on the factual historical, but is uniformly unsympathetic to Engels and has virtually no assessment of him as a theorist. For the personal side of Engels's later years, see also Y. Kapp, *Eleanor Marx: The Crowded Years*. There is a short treatment in McLellan's Modern Masters *Engels*. Chris Arthur's centenary volume is excellent, as is the collection by Steger and Carver.

Bibliography

Texts

Karl Marx – Frederick Engels: Collected Works (London, 1975).
Karl Marx – Frederick Engels: Selected Works, 2 vols (Moscow, 1962).
Marx and Engels: Basic Writings on Politics and Philosophy, ed. L. Feuer (New York, 1959).
Marx-Engels Reader, ed. R. Tucker (New York, 1972).
Engels: *Selected Writings*, ed. W.O. Henderson (London, 1967).
Engels as Military Critic, ed. W.O. Henderson and O. Chaloner (London, 1959).
Frederick Engels, *Anti-Dühring* (Moscow, 1954).
—— *The Condition of the Working Class in England*, ed. W.O. Henderson and O. Chaloner (Oxford, 1958).
—— *The Condition of the Working Class in England*, Introduction by Eric Hobsbawm (London, 1969).
—— *The Condition of the Working Class in England*, ed. D. McLellan (Oxford, 1996).
—— *Dialectics of Nature* (Moscow, 1972).
—— *Ludwig Feuerbach and the End of Classical German Philosophy* (Moscow, 1946).
—— *The Origin of the Family, Private Property and the State*, ed. with an Introduction by Eleanor Burke Leacock (London, 1972).
—— *The Peasant War in Germany* (Moscow, 1965).
—— *Revolution and Counter-Revolution in Germany in 1848*, ed. Eleanor Marx (London, 1971).

Commentaries

Chris Arthur, *Engels Today: A Centenary Appreciation* (London, 1996).
Grace Carlton, *Friedrich Engels: The Shadow Prophet* (London, 1965).
T. Carver, *Engels* (Oxford, 1981).
Heinrich Gemkow *et al.*, *Friedrich Engels: A Biography* (Dresden, 1972).

W.O. Henderson, *The Life of Friedrich Engels*, 2 vols (London, 1976).

L.F. Ilyichov *et al.*, *Friedrich Engels: A Biography*, trans V. Schneierson (Moscow, 1974).

Yvonne Kapp, *Eleanor Marx*, vol. 2, *The Crowded Years* (London, 1976).

David McLellan, *Engels* (London and New York, 1977).

Steven Marcus, *Engels, Manchester and the Working Class* (New York, 1974).

Gustav Mayer, *Friedrich Engels: A Biography*, trans. G. and H. Highet and ed. R.H.S. Crossman (London, 1936).

Fritz Nova, *Friedrich Engels: His Contribution to Political Theory* (London, 1967).

John Plamenatz, *German Marxism and Russian Communism* (London, 1954).

S. Rigby, *Engels and the Formation of Marxism: History, Dialectics, and Revolution* (Manchester, 1992).

J. Sayers *et al.* (eds), *Engels Revisited: New Feminist Essays* (London, 1987).

Gareth Stedman Jones, 'Engels and the End of Classical German Philosophy', *New Left Review*, 79 (1973).

—— 'Engels and the Genesis of Marxism', *New Left Review*, 106 (1977).

M. Steger and T. Carver (eds), *Engels after Marx* (Philadephia, 1999).

2
The Revisionist Controversy

The spread of Marxism outside Germany

The boundaries of the revisionist controversy were set by the boundaries of the spread of Marxism. Thus the controversy was largely confined to Germany, with Austria and Russia in second place. Kautsky's comment on the Belgian socialist leader Vandervelde could apply equally to France and Italy:

> the talk about their revisionism leaves me cold. They have nothing to revise, for they have no theory. The eclectic vulgar socialism to which the revisionists would like to reduce Marxism is something beyond which they [the Belgians] have not even begun to advance. Proudhon, Schäffle, Marx – it is all one to them; it was always like that, they have not retrogressed in theory, and I have nothing to reproach them with.[1]

In Italy, the workers' movement had been largely anarchist from the 1860s onwards: Marxism had only begun to make an impact in the 1890s with the formation of an increasingly successful socialist party. Nevertheless, the party remained 'very weak and confused',[2] lacking a firm industrial base and continually threatened by the anarchosyndicalists. The party managed to attract several intellectuals in the 1890s, among them Antonio Labriola, a professor of philosophy, who after a period of youthful Hegelianism, became a Marxist in 1894. In spite of a tendency to regard Marxism as merely a method (and thus compatible with several different sorts of philosophy), Labriola was probably the best interpreter of Marx in any country during the years immediately following Engels's death.[3] In his classic work *Essays on the Materialist Conception of History* he opposed materialistic interpretations of Marxism and, a forerunner of Gramsci and Lukács, made an anti-positivist and historicist Marxism welcome in Italy. But he was alone. The only other Italian socialist of international eminence – Benedetto Croce – was not a socialist at all: he remained all his life a liberal Hegelian. Croce was interested in what he considered to be Marxism's insights but not in viewing it as a theory predicting a given development of society. He therefore rejected the idea of Marxism as a science, criticised Marx's economics and particularly his theory of value and laid emphasis on the ethical side of socialism.[4]

In France, there were three main factors militating against the emergence of a revisionist movement. Firstly, the key opposition was between socialism and syndicalism rather than between different varieties of Marxism. In Germany, the trade unions had been suppressed during the anti-socialist legislation of 1878–90 whereas the party had been allowed to function electorally and thus became dominant; in France, the trade unions escaped from such political control. Secondly, the leadership of the French movement as a whole was never Marxist: France – like Italy and Spain – was only growing slowly economically and lacked the modern industrial working-class base that characterised Germany. Thirdly, none of the French Marxists were really interested in economics, which was one of the central points of the revisionist controversy.

The only organised Marxists were the followers of Jules Guesde grouped in the small Parti Ouvrier Français. Although initially strong on revolutionary principles, they were weak on theory and had to rely largely on Lafargue to propagate Marx's ideas in an exceptionally superficial manner.[5] Marx's well-known remark that he himself was not a Marxist[6] was inspired by his would-be French followers and certainly his work was very little read there in the original or even in translation. Guesde's Parti Ouvrier Français had only six out of the thirty-seven socialist deputies elected in 1893; the rest were shared among four other parties with a considerable number of independents. But with the parliamentary success of 1893, the POF promptly became 'revisionist': it was committed to parliamentary collaboration with the other socialist parties, to the achievement of socialism by peaceful means, and even (in an effort to attract votes) modified its programme to make it acceptable to medium-sized farmers. With the foundation of the unified SFIO in 1905, all the 'Marxist' leaders had become reformist socialists. An additional reason that prevented the emergence of an orthodox versus revisionist debate was the role played by Jean Jaurès who dominated the French political left for the twenty years before his assassination in 1914. Jaurès tended to subordinate theory to the tactical needs of the moment. He is best characterised as a revolutionary democrat: he certainly had more Marxist revolutionary 'spirit' than almost all his 'Marxist' contemporaries. But intellectually, Jaurès was an idealist who had no particular class reference for his ideas, which did not go beyond a Republican form of government inspired by a unity of idealism and historical materialism (by which he meant no more than French eighteenth-century materialism) on a moral basis.

The origins of German revisionism

Indeed, it can be shown that even in Germany the spread of Marxist ideas was not very far advanced in the 1880s: of the two parties which united to form the *Sozialistische Partei Deutschlands* (SPD) at Gotha in 1875, one held strongly to the state socialism preached by its founder, Ferdinand Lassalle, whose ideas were still the predominant influence in socialist circles in Germany during the 1870s and 1880s; the other party – the so-called Eisenach Party led by Marx's followers Liebknecht and Bebel – had very little Marxism in it, in spite of Marx's optimistic opinion to the contrary. Marx's views made such slow progress initially that it has been calculated that by 1880 there were only five men in Germany who had a well-founded understanding of his economics.[7] With the rather dubious exceptions of Eccarius and Dietzgen, *Capital* made no impression on the German working class. There were two factors that helped Marxism become the dominant view of the SPD by the end of the 1880s. Firstly, the anti-socialist law of 1879–90 inevitably radicalised the left opposition to the government, but at the same time seemed to give the lie to Lassallean socialism which evidently lacked the support from the state that it relied on for its socialist schemes. The experience of the 1880s appeared rather to support the Marxist view of the state as an instrument of the ruling class. Secondly, the expanding party had the need for an ideology and there was simply no systematic alternative to Marxism. Marxists also occupied key positions in the party's theoretical debates: Bernstein was editor of the party's official newspaper *Sozialdemokrat* from 1881 and Kautsky's *Neue Zeit*, founded in 1883, the year of Marx's death, consistently publicised the views of Marxists in all questions of interest to the party; Bebel, whose gifts as a practical politician and organiser were outstanding, exercised considerable influence as a Reichstag deputy. By the end of the 1880s there was a growing consensus that Lassalleanism and the previously popular economics of Rodbertus had been discredited by their Marxist critics. The right wing of the party broke away in 1887, leaving the way open for a simplified form of Marxism to be enthroned as the

Party's official ideology at the first Congress after the repeal of the anti-socialist law, held in 1891 at Erfurt. Prefiguring the future split in the Party's approach, the Erfurt Programme was divided into two very different halves: one on theory, for which Kautsky was responsible, and one on practice drawn up by Bernstein. The first half reiterated the traditional doctrines of the drive to monopoly, the decline of the middle class, the impoverishment of the proletariat and the inevitability of the socialisation of the means of production in a classless society; the second half contained such immediate demands as universal suffrage, freedom of expression, free schooling and a progressive income tax. But no sooner has this rather simplified version of Marxism triumphed in the SPD than the suggestion was made that it needed to be revised. As Otto Bauer said: 'The revisionist theory is nothing but the counterpart of vulgar Marxism, the necessary impoverishment of the doctrine of Marx during its first penetration into larger and larger sections that are not yet prepared for it.'[8] The leading proponent of this revisionism was Edward Bernstein.

Bernstein, the son of a Berlin railway engineer, had joined the party in 1872 and soon became one of its leading journalists. The anti-socialist law compelled him to emigrate to England in order to be able to continue his activities. Bernstein's stay in England was decisive for his view of Marxism.[9] Although Bernstein himself maintained that the idea of his being influenced by the Fabians was 'completely mistaken',[10] almost all the leaders of the SPD, including Engels and Bebel, thought it self-evident that, to quote Rosa Luxemburg, 'Bernstein has constructed his theory upon relationships obtaining in England. He sees the world through English spectacles';[11] and this was a view shared by the Fabians themselves. Bernstein was naturally critical of many Fabian doctrines when he first moved to England, but during the 1890s his views moved very close to theirs.

Bernstein was plainly evolving towards some sort of revisionism in the years 1891–3 but it was not until Engels's death that the controversy really broke out. In 1895 Bernstein wrote an article on the 1849 revolution in France. (Socialists of the time were accustomed to comment on, and situate themselves in regard to, the 1848 revolution in much the same way as contemporary Marxists do with the 1917 revolution.) Bernstein took a view that was almost diametrically opposed to Marx's view in *The Class Struggles in France*: for Bernstein, the June days were unnecessary adventurism and he preferred Louis Blanc to Blanqui; and this contrast contained lessons for 1895. These lessons Bernstein worked on systematically in a series of articles entitled *Probleme des Sozialismus* (Problems of Socialism) published between 1896 and 1898 in *Die Neue*

Zeit. These articles were later expanded into Bernstein's most important book, published in 1899 under the cumbersome title *Die Voraussetzungen des Sozialismus und die Aufgabe der Sozialdemokratie* ('The Presuppositions of Socialism and the Tasks of Social Democracy'). Of course, the SPD had had its reformist tendencies, articulated by such writers as Vollmar and David, well before Bernstein began to work out his ideas: what aroused opposition in the SPD's intellectual leadership was the fact that Bernstein's revisionism was self-proclaimed, systematic and fundamental – at least in intention.[12] Bernstein was also seen (together with Kautsky) as the heir of Marx and Engels – the person on whom fell the duty of safeguarding the tradition. (He was, together with Bebel, Engels's executor.) It is therefore surprising how slow was the reaction to Bernstein's novel views. Kautsky felt a personal loyalty to Bernstein and did not openly criticise him until the summer of 1898. Indeed, Kautsky agreed that some form of revision was necessary and even encouraged Bernstein to supply it: 'You have overthrown our tactics, our theory of value, our philosophy; now all depends on what is the new that you are thinking of putting in place of the old.'[13] It was only when it became clear how radical Bernstein's intentions really were that opposition began to harden. There was also the fact that, in spite of his desire to systematise, Bernstein was essentially an eclectic thinker. 'We were all more or less socialist eclectics',[14] wrote Bernstein in 1895 and this applied to him more than most. 'Systematic thought and logical progression sat heavily upon me',[15] he wrote, and this made it difficult to get a coherent picture of his ideas.

Before examining these views in detail, it is important to give a brief account of the socio-political context in which the revisionist controversy was fought out. The title of Bernstein's book is important, for he conceived himself to be reformulating the theoretical presuppositions of the SPD and bringing it into line with its already reformulated practice. In his view, the SPD's tactics were more or less reformist – and here he thought he could call for support on Engels's 1895 Introduction to *The Class Struggles in France* – and his task was to harmonise the theory with this reformism in practice. As the SPD grew ever larger, the administrative and bureaucratic elements grew in importance until at last they became the decisive factor.[16] Although the membership remained surprisingly proletarian, the deputies (who were mainly lawyers and journalists) were well to the right of the activists, the more conservative country districts were over-represented, and – most importantly – the enormous effort put into the highly successful vote-gathering machine inevitably deflected the party from more revolutionary objectives. The trade unions played no direct part in the revisionist controversy – they had little time for theory of any sort – but they undoubtedly sympathised with the gradualism of the revisionists. From this point of view, the SPD was never a very 'Marxist' party and the theoretical disputes tended to be confined to its leading intellectuals.

Given this state of affairs, it is not surprising that Bernstein's views gained fairly widespread support. Their main opponent was Karl Kautsky: born in Prague in 1854, he had known Marx and – together with Bernstein – was widely regarded as the direct 'successor' to Marx and Engels. With the defection of Bernstein, it was up to Kautsky to defend Marxist orthodoxy. Referred to half-ironically as 'the Pope of Marxism', Kautsky was the most influential socialist thinker during the two decades prior to 1914 – Luxemburg, Lenin, Trotsky and Stalin all sat at his feet. As editor of *Die Neue Zeit*, the party's theoretical monthly, for over thirty years, he occupied a central and predominant role among all Marxist intellectuals. In spite of their evident disagreements, Kautsky's worldview had many similarities with that of Bernstein and it makes sense to compare and contrast their respective positions before going on separately to discuss the radicals – and in particular Rosa Luxemburg.

Economics

Perhaps the most fundamental of Marx's doctrines that Bernstein wished to revise was his theory of value. From Fabians such as Shaw and Webb, Bernstein had learnt a lot about the marginalist doctrines of Jevons, who wished to equate value with utility and make it dependent on individual desires and the relationship of supply to demand. Bernstein had been disappointed by *Capital* Volume Three and this led him to question the whole of Marx's theory of value. The most influential critique of Marx at the time was *Zum Abschluss des Marxschen Systems* ('Karl Marx and the Close of his System') by the Austrian marginalist Eugen Böhm-Bawerk, who considered that the notion of value had no objective existence (as in Marx) but was simply a quantitative relation between use-values, an abstraction from them. This led Bernstein to view Marx's theory as some kind of abstract hypothesis, and here he was to some extent merely following Engels.[17]

For Bernstein, Marx's theory of value was 'a purely abstract concept'[18] and the labour theory of value 'can claim acceptance only as a speculative formula or a scientific hypothesis'.[19] He also considered that this theory could not give an account of the total value of social production and so was inadequate as a starting-point. This led the eclectic Bernstein to attempt a synthesis between Marxian and marginalist concepts of value.

On a less rarified level, Bernstein was a close observer of contemporary trends, and his very lack of interest in systematic theory meant that he was able to perceive some of these trends more clearly than his more 'Marxist' contemporaries. Whether he was able accurately to interpret them is not so evident. Thus Bernstein was quick to register the new sense of economic well-being that started in 1895: the last few years of the century saw a rapid rise in real wages and the creation of a 'labour aristocracy' who might have a lot to lose in a revolution. Bernstein saw that the growth of cartels, trusts and monopoly capital were important phenomena, as were the concomitant socialisation of production and the separation of ownership and control. From these factors, together with the increase in credit facilities and enormously improved communication and information services, Bernstein concluded that capitalism was gaining in ability to regulate itself. Nor did he draw the corollary that the ownership of capital was being concentrated: on the contrary, he believed (and backed up his views with a barrage of statistics) that property was being diffused by such institutions as joint stock companies, which meant that there were more capitalists than before. Moreover, small and medium-sized firms were not being eliminated but continued to flourish as numerously as ever. And from this there followed political consequences:

> It is thus quite wrong to assume that the present development of society shows a relative or indeed absolute diminution of the number of the members of the possessing classes. Their number increases both relatively and absolutely. If the activity and the prospects of social democracy were dependent on the decrease of the 'wealthy', then it might indeed lie down to sleep. But the contrary is the case. The prospects of socialism depend not on the decrease but on the increase of social wealth.[20]

So far, therefore, from thinking that crisis was inevitable, Bernstein believed that the existence of trusts, cartels, etc., enabled capitalism to survive almost indefinitely. Indeed, he even said that this harmonious development of capitalism could lead through uninterruptedly to socialism.

Kautsky, on the other hand, considered such ideas to be dangerous illusions. In particular, he considered Bernstein's critique of Marx's doctrine of concentration to be the key to his revisionism. Contesting the conclusions that Bernstein drew from his statistics, Kautsky maintained that, although the number of small enterprises was not necessarily less, their economic domain was decreasing as they were often little but the last refuge of the lower middle classes on the verge of proletarianisation. Kautsky believed that periodic depression would eventually squeeze small businesses out of existence and that, as ever-increasing resources were necessary for reinvestment, only the very wealthiest would be able to survive. Whereas Bernstein regarded cartels, etc., as a means of capitalist self-regulation, for Kautsky they were evidence of the final involution of the system, the end of 'free' competition and the imminence of a collapse. Although, in reply to Bernstein's criticisms, Kautsky denied that Marx had had a 'breakdown' theory, the Erfurt Programme certainly did seem to subscribe to such an idea and Kautsky himself took the view that crises would be ever more serious and that cyclical depressions were inevitable under capitalism. He admitted later (as against Rosa Luxemburg) that domestic consumption could absorb increased production. But in his argument with Bernstein he maintained that an increase in production was inevitable with the further introduction of machinery and that the consumption capacity of the working class would not rise concomitantly, since the system tended to depress wages as far as possible. The resulting surplus produce could not be absorbed by the capitalists, who had to re-invest more and more, and an eventual collapse was inevitable.

Although the question of imperialism did not enter directly into the revisionist debate, it was clearly linked to Kautsky's underconsumptionist views and also explained why he did not expect capitalism to evolve in a liberal, cooperative direction. Whereas Bernstein was driven on occasion to defending German colonial expansion, the analysis of imperialism was one of Kautsky's chief theoretical innovations in Marxist doctrine.[21] As early as the mid-1880s, Kautsky had connected the annexation of over-seas territories with his underconsumptionist views: the home market being insufficient, new markets would have to be found in colonies. Later he emphasised the importance for groups outside the industrial capitalists – the military, the bureaucracy, and, above all, the finance capitalists – of a colonial expansion that enabled not only the export of surplus goods but also the capital to buy them. In his *Sozialismus und Kolonialpolitik* (considered by Bebel to be his best book) he argued that capital was now being exported as an effort to limit productivity and stabilise the system. Kautsky also emphasised the imbalance in expansion between the industrial and the agricultural sectors of the world market, the slow expansion of the latter being unable fully to supply the market or raw materials for the former. Originally he had held war to be a necessary outcome of imperialism. But by 1912, under the influence of a more cooperative international climate, and the appearance of Hilferding's *Finanzkapital*,[22] Kautsky was asserting that colonies were in the long run detrimental even to the capitalist system. Capitalism needed peace to develop and therefore capitalists sufficiently aware of their own interest could prevent both the arms race and war by inaugurating a phase of 'ultra-imperialism'. Imperialism was thus neither inevitable nor the 'last' stage of capitalism – a view strenuously attacked by Lenin.

Sociology

This fundamental disagreement in economics had consequences for the respective views of Bernstein and Kautsky on the way society was evolving and in particular on the impoverishment of the proletariat and class polarisation. Bernstein rejected the idea of impoverishment that had been so clearly enunciated in the Erfurt Programme. In this he was (ironically) following the lead given by Engels.[23] Impressed (perhaps too much so) by the prosperity of the Reich in the late 1890s, Bernstein confidently denied that real wages were sinking – though it is far from clear that Marx ever subscribed to the view that such a tendency was inevitable.[24] There is little doubt that real wages did rise during the 1890s, particularly among the labour aristocracy; there is also little doubt that the process was short-lived, and that relative impoverishment was a fact by the early 1900s. Kautsky never held a doctrine of absolute impoverishment.[25] But he did claim that the surplus value produced by capitalism was larger than ever and that, however much the workers might force better conditions from their employers and from the state, increased technology necessarily meant increased exploitation; and therefore the proportion of the gross national product accruing to the working class would decline.

The second corollary of Bernstein's central assertion was that, although the control of capital might be being concentrated, this involved a diffusion of ownership. Bernstein had a much looser definition of class than Marx: he considered it to be simply a social stratum which was largely formed by similarity of living conditions. He considered the middle class to be increasing in size – and had income statistics etc. to prove it. He also supported his view by asking: 'where does this mass of commodities go which is not consumed by the magnates and their stooges?', and replied (neglecting the obvious answer that the surplus was reinvested): 'If it does not go to the proletarians in one way or another, it must be absorbed by other classes. Either a relative decrease in the number of capitalists and an increasing wealth in the proletariat, or a numerous middle class – these are the only alternatives which the continuous increase of productivity allows.'[26] But, according to Bernstein, the middle class was not only increasing but also changing in composition with the advent of white-collar workers employed in the ever-growing industrial concerns and governmental bureaucracy. True to his optimistic view of the possibility of non-antagonistic political development, Bernstein considered that this middle class would eventually side with the workers, but only when the workers had become members of bourgeois society in the sense of an ordered and civilised social system. Kautsky also realised that a 'new middle class' was coming into existence, but he always maintained the view that, however bourgeois their life-style might be, they would eventually become proletarianised and enter the class struggle. For their economic position was essentially proletarian and, under the impact of automation, their political attitudes would come to reflect this. Although Kautsky sometimes realised the potentially reactionary motives of many middle-class groupings in Germany, both he and Bernstein were tragically mistaken in the faith they placed in their eventual political attitudes.

As usual in the question of class polarisation, the peasantry presented a difficult problem. Bernstein confined himself to remarking briefly that 'in the world of Western Europe ... the small and medium-sized agricultural holding is growing in numbers, while the large or very large holding is declining'.[27] South German reformists such as Eduard David drew the obvious political conclusion by advocating collaboration with the peasantry whose votes were all-important to the SPD in those areas. The question of how far the party could go in modifying its policies in order to attract the votes of the small peasants was the central political question behind the revisionist controversy. In his book *Die Agrarfrage* ('The Agrarian Question'), published in 1899 and much admired by Lenin, Kautsky argued that the interests of the peasantry – in particular for protective tariffs and the maintenance of private ownership – were directly opposed to those of the proletariat. Hence the peasantry could never become socialist – at least in Germany, for Kautsky was more optimistic about Russia. He maintained, further, that the peasantry were doomed to disappear: their smallholdings were not economically viable as they lacked the necessary capital investment and adaptability, and they were, in fact, being eliminated: 'the growth in the number of small agricultural holdings is but a particular form of the growth in the number of proletarian households which goes hand in hand with the increase of large capitalist exploitation in industry and sometimes even in agriculture.'[28] This thesis of the proletarianisation of the peasantry was implausible when faced with statistics and Kautsky later abandoned it; but he maintained both his opposition to collaboration with the peasantry and his view that the abolition of smallholdings was necessary for agrarian progress and the creation of the surplus necessary for socialism.

Politics

The impression is often given that the revisionist debate was purely theoretical, but in fact the theoretical issues discussed above had severely
practical implications. For to orthodox Marxists such as Kautsky, their
interpretation of the labour theory of value, of impoverishment and of
polarisation meant that the interests of capital and labour were irrecon-
cilable, that there was no such thing as the 'national interest', and that
the proletariat must preserve its isolation in the political arena. For the
revisionists, on the other hand, who wished to abandon the labour theory
of value, had ceased to believe in the breakdown of capitalism, and
pointed to the growth of the middle class as evidence of non-polarisation,
capitalism had shown itself to be sufficiently adaptable for there to be
hope of its gradual transformation into socialism. Socialism was seen as
the more or less peaceful inheritor of a fully developed capitalism.

In his *Probleme des Sozialismus* ('Problems of Socialism') of 1898,
Bernstein wrote: 'Although no doubt social catastrophes could and no
doubt also would very much hasten the process of development, they
could still never create overnight the homogeneity of relationships that
would be necessary for a simultaneous transformation of economics and
today at least are not yet present.'[29] This was Bernstein's case for a rejection of any revolutionary approach to politics: the economic prerequisites for socialism were just not there. Thus the political struggle should
be a gradual one for the inauguration of democracy – by which Bernstein
meant a society 'where no one class possesses political privilege that is
opposed to the whole community'[30] – a kind of system of class equilibrium. This democracy was 'the form for the realisation of socialism',
which would 'raise the worker out of the social position of a proletarian
into that of a bourgeois'[31] or citizen. In view of this continuity, there was
no place in Social Democracy for diatribes against liberalism. For Social
Democracy was not only the chronological, but also the intellectual successor to liberalism: 'there is actually no really liberal conception that
does not also belong to the elements of the ideas of socialism'.[32] Hence
Bernstein's political gradualism: socialism was being realised. In 1898,
he declared, in a summary of his *credo*:

> It is my firm conviction that the present generation will already see
> realised a large part of socialism, if not in official form, at least in con-
> tent. The constant enlargement of social duties, i.e. of the duties and
> corresponding rights of the individual against society and of the duties
> of society to the individual, the extension of the right of society, as

organised in the nation or the state, to supervise economic life, the construction of democratic self-government at village, district and provincial levels, and the extension of the tasks of these associations – and that for me is development towards socialism.

The transfer of economic enterprises from private to public control will naturally accompany this development, but it will only be able to proceed slowly ... There can be more socialism in a good factory law than in the nationalisation of a whole group of factories. I admit it openly: I have for what is commonly called 'the final goal of social- ism' extraordinarily little feeling and interest. This goal, whatever it may be, is nothing to me, the movement is everything.[33]

The central point of Kautsky's difference from Bernstein was his insis- tence on the reality of class conflict and the consequent impossibility of forging links with the bourgeoisie. Kautsky correctly realised that sec- tions of the bourgeoisie were in fact becoming more reactionary and he even consistently rejected the notion of alliance with the peasantry. Reforms could not deal with the fundamental reality of class conflict and the granting of democratic rights could never provide a substitute for revolution. He even argued that parliamentary democracy with its electoral battles heightened class consciousness and conflict.

This policy of proletarian isolation was partly the result of a belief in the imminence of capitalist breakdown common to many social democ- rats in the 1890s. As early as 1881, Bebel had written that the condition for the capitulation of the ruling classes was 'that the development can ripen and not be destroyed by an unforeseen interruption and be driven to explode too early'.[34] In 1897 he still believed it possible to calculate the end of capitalism 'with mathematical certainty'.[35] Engels, too, in 1895, foresaw the possibility of the downfall of capitalism 'by the end of the century', and, according to the *Daily Chronicle* Engels possessed a graph to predict when the SPD would be able to take power.[36] Hence the emphasis on organisation so that the party would be able to use the rev- olutionary situation that it could not itself bring about.

Paradoxically, therefore, the generally deterministic attitude of the SPD and the belief in the inevitability of a proletarian victory became an argu- ment for inaction as the conditions were never thought to be 'mature' enough for intervention. Kautsky did, of course, often emphasise the need for organisation, for propaganda and the eventual taking of politi- cal power, but these principles were often glossed over in practical cir- cumstances. Indeed, Kautsky's fundamental position is well summed up in the following passage from one of his replies to Bernstein: 'The task of

Social Democracy consists, not in bringing about the inevitable catastrophe, but in delaying it as long as possible, that is to say, in avoiding with care anything that could resemble a provocation or the appearance of a provocation.'[37] For Kautsky, the SPD was a revolutionary party, but not a party preparing a revolution. Even in his most radical publication *Der Weg zur Macht* ('The Road to Power'), 1909, which was much admired at the time, there was an underlying passivity – though it is a curious fact that the SPD executive thought it *too* radical and tried to censor it. With its emphasis on unity at all costs, the SPD tended to gloss over ideological differences and the importance attached by its leaders to organisation led, after 1907, to the growth of bureaucratic elements in the party.[38] A good example of this concealed passivity was Kautsky's view on the mass strike. Kautsky claimed to be one of the first to advocate this tactic and was an ardent defender of it, particularly in 1905–6. Yet he never advocated a mass strike in any specific situation and appended a long string of preconditions that would have to be met before it could be successful: participation of all workers, general disaffection of all members of society, weak government, etc., etc. For Kautsky, unlike Rosa Luxemburg, the mass strike was never more than a defensive weapon only to be used in the last resort if the democratic privileges of the working class were attacked. This passive stance of Kautsky was reinforced by consideration of the immense power at the disposal of the Prussian state, including the most powerful army in the world.

But Kautsky's views on politics were far from being mechanistic. He always emphasised the importance of class consciousness and, further, anticipated something of Lenin's doctrine of 'consciousness from without'. As early as 1901 he wrote: 'Knowledge is still today a privilege of the property-owning classes: the proletariat cannot create out of itself a strong and living socialism. It must have it brought to it.'[39] For scientific socialism was a theory derived from observation and then applied by skilled scholars in a kind of social technology. Thus the ever-present duty of a well-organised party was to spread class consciousness and provide the proletariat with a coherent political theory. Piecemeal reformist demands were never enough: Kautsky held the classical Marxist view of the state as an instrument of class domination and rejected it as a possible source of salvation for the working class. Thus trade union struggles could never of themselves be sufficient and he rejected 'economism' just as decisively as Lenin. His aim was always (and here he differed fundamentally from Bernstein) the conquest of political power by the proletariat and the consequent subjection of the state to a radical change. But when Kautsky talked of the state he usually had in mind the German military

monarchy which was – at best – semi-democratic. It was one of the
tasks of the proletarian revolution to make Germany fully democratic.
Thus by 'dictatorship of the proletariat' Kautsky did not mean a situation of class war or the 'Jacobin anarchy'[40] so feared by Bernstein. He
merely meant the majority rule of the proletariat under fully democratic –
and parliamentary – institutions.[41] Although this only became clear in
his critique of the Bolshevik revolution, it was a view implicit in his
earlier works.

Philosophy and historical materialism

In his views on historical materialism, Bernstein quoted with approval
Engels's letter of 1890 to Bloch.[42] According to him, Engels's remarks
implied that the materialist conception of history was 'in fact not purely
materialist, much less purely economic'.[43] For Bernstein, the Marxism of
his day was too materialist and too determinist. Hence his dubbing of
the materialists as 'Calvinists without God'.[44] 'It is by no means always
easy', he declared,

> to lay bare the relations which exist so exactly that it can be deter-
> mined with certainty where in given cases the strongest motive
> power is to be sought. The purely economic causes create, first of all,
> only a disposition for the reception of certain ideas, but how these
> then arise and spread and what form they take, depends on the co-
> operation of a whole series of influences. More harm than good is
> done to historical materialism if at the outset one rejects as eclecti-
> cism an accentuation of the influences other than those of a purely
> economic kind, and a consideration of other economic factors than
> the technique of production and their foreseen development.
> Eclecticism – the selecting from different explanations and ways of
> dealing with phenomena – is often only the natural reaction to the
> doctrinaire desire to deduce everything from one thing and to treat
> everything according to one and the same method. As soon as such
> desire is excessive the eclectic spirit works its way again with the
> power of a natural force. It is the rebellion of sober reason against the
> tendency inherent in every doctrine to fetter thought.[45]

Too sharp a distinction was being made between base and superstructure: intellectual understanding and ethical ideals were also important
impulses to action and Bernstein wished to afford 'the ideological, and
especially the ethical, factors greater space for independent activity than

was formerly the case'.[46] The Erfurt Programme had laid too much stress on laws of capitalism that were universally valid and akin to natural laws, and Bernstein criticised Kautsky's 'habit of presenting as absolute something that has only a relative force'.[47]

These interpretations of historical materialism stemmed from a fundamental philosophical divergence which had to do with the meaning of materialism, the importance of the dialectic, and the growth of Kantian influence in Marxism. Bernstein later declared himself to have been 'an adherent of the school of positivist philosophy and sociology'.[48] Yet he was very concerned to reject 'materialism' – by which he meant the view that 'from any given point in time onwards all further events are determined beforehand by the whole of existing matter and the direction of force in its parts'.[49] This view was identical to the mechanical materialism of the eighteenth century and very little to do with Marx. Bernstein was, of course, influenced by Darwin, but in a manner entirely akin to his economic and sociological views. In an unpublished manuscript of 1898, he wrote: 'A study of biology yields the proposition that the more developed, i.e. the more complicated and functionally differentiated an organism is, the less is its development accomplished by absolutely contradictory changes of the whole body. Within certain limits, the same is true of human society.' And later in the same manuscript: 'A political revolution is plainly the most unsuitable time for the socialisation of industry.'[50] Evolution could plainly be opposed to revolution. The reason for the crudeness of Bernstein's view of materialism was his rejection (and ignorance) of Hegel and his abhorrence of the dialectic. In *Evolutionary Socialism* he wrote: 'Every time that we see the theory which starts from the economy as the basis of social development capitulate before the theory which overemphasises the cult of force we will come across a Hegelian sentence ... Every great achievement of Marx and Engels was achieved not by means of the Hegelian dialectic but in spite of it.'[51] It was, moreover, their attachment to the Hegelian dialectic that was responsible for Marx and Engels's Blanquism.

Yet for all his rejection of materialism and of Marxism as a science, Bernstein had an extremely empiricist bent to his thought – largely due to his rejection of Hegel and any dialectical approach to these matters. The very barrenness of his positivist approach led him to seek a separate moral basis for his socialism; and his belief that economic forces of themselves would not bring about socialism led him to seek for other possible impulses. He found one ready-made in the revival of neo-Kantianism which, from the 1860s onwards, had become the dominant philosophy taught in German universities and impeded an adequate appreciation of the dialectic for a whole generation of Marxists. F.H. Lange's *History of Materialism* (1866) was the basic text and Bernstein was also strongly influenced by Schmidt, Vorländer, Cohen and Woltmann, who were all leading Social Democrats as well as neo-Kantians.[52] Kantian views were attractive on two counts: Kant's doctrine that it was impossible to know the 'thing in itself' and that we cannot get behind the categories our minds impose upon the world could give any materialism an ultimately idealist slant. Secondly, and more importantly, Kant's distinction between statements of fact and statements of value meant that his ethics was intended to be self-contained since it was thought to be independent of any descriptive statements. Thus it could logically co-exist with a vulgar Marxism supposedly devoid of any value judgements. It was in this field that Bernstein's eclecticism became a mere muddle.

But Bernstein was not alone: even Kautsky felt the attraction of neo-Kantianism. Kautsky admitted (quite correctly) in 1898 that 'philosophy was never my strong point', but maintained that 'the economic and historical standpoint of Marx and Engels is capable of being integrated, if necessary, even with neo-Kantianism'.[53] But Kautsky did not continue this line of thought. He was more systematically influenced by Darwin than was Bernstein: Kautsky was a Darwinian before he was a Marxist and remained one, to some extent, all his life, his conception of social evolution being always tied to that of natural evolution. Hence his excessive emphasis on productive forces and objective necessity. Kautsky's book on *Ethik und materialistische Geschichtsauffassung* ('Ethics and Historical Materialism'), 1907, attempted to demonstrate, in rather a crude way influenced by Darwinian evolution, that ethical ideas varied according to class. By contrast, however, his book *Ursprung des Christentums* ('The Origins of Christianity') was an original and impressive application of historical materialism to that period.[54] Kautsky could not work up any enthusiasm for Hegel, of whom he was profoundly ignorant: for him, Hegel was an evolutionary determinist with unfortunate speculative and conservative bents. He could have echoed the startling declaration of the revisionist Conrad Schmidt at the Hanover Congress of 1899: 'In our agitation let us rather replace "dialectic" by the much more precise and richer concept of "evolution" which is more intelligible to the workers. Bebel has invoked the spirit of the great Darwin. We stand nearer to him than to Hegel.'[55] Where Kautsky differed from Bernstein was in emphasising the struggle of opposites in nature and applying this directly and remorselessly to the class struggle. But in spite of his almost endless reiteration of 'natural necessity' Kautsky could not avoid, when pressed, according to ethics virtually the same status as did some of the revisionists. At the end of his book on ethics he stated:

Neither can social democracy as the organisation of the proletariat in its class struggle do without the moral ideal, without moral revulsion against exploitation and class domination. But this ideal can gain no assistance from scientific socialism ... Of course, in socialism the researcher is also a fighter ... Thus, for example, in Marx the working of a moral ideal breaks through in his scientific research but he is always at pains, and rightly so, to banish it from his work, in as far as it is possible ... Science has only to do with the knowledge of necessity.[56]

Conclusion

Bernstein and Kautsky shared many points in common, their separation was only gradual, and the controversy sharpened as it progressed. When pushed into a declaration of faith, Kautsky wrote:

But if once the materialist conception of history and the conception of the proletariat as the motive force of the coming social revolution were abandoned, then I would have to admit that I was through, that my life no longer had any meaning.[57]

Kautsky is often portrayed as having a vacuous theory that was able to gloss over any tactical compromise. But this is unfair: although it may apply to some of his more rambling works of the 1920s, the earlier Kautsky made important contributions to Marxist theory with its ideas on class consciousness, on imperialism, and on the application of Marxist principles to specific historical areas – quite apart from his exceptional talents as a propagandist as shown in his *Commentary* on the Erfurt Programme and his *Economic Doctrines of Karl Marx*. Nor is it true that Kautsky became progressively conservative: his thought – at least pre-1914 – is remarkably consistent. His theory certainly served to hold the party together for many years, although that should not be seen as its main function.[58] For Kautsky was quite ready to split the party when an important issue of principle was involved. Nor would it be right to contrast his theory with his practice: in a fundamental sense, the theory was no more revolutionary than the practice. This is true of the SPD as a whole, which was never, even at its inception, as radical as is often thought. The party was concerned primarily to implement the purely democratic ideas that had failed to gain acceptance in 1848. In many ways, therefore, Bernstein and Kautsky were part of the same world: however much they might differ on the question of proletarian isolation, they were both fully committed to parliamentary tactics. As the most distinguished historian of the period has said: 'The distinction between the contenders remained largely a subjective one, a difference of ideas in the evaluation of reality rather than a difference in the realm of action.'[59] Bernstein and Kautsky were also akin in their ignorance of Hegel and enthusiasm for Darwin which resulted in their common simplistic approach which failed to accord any genuinely dialectical dimension to social reality. Bernstein's ideas were thus merely the mirror of contemporary ossified Marxism. But by the early 1900s the intellectual currents in Europe rejecting positivism were already on the increase.[60] And in Marxism this trend found its initial expression in the writings of radicals such as Rosa Luxemburg.

Notes

1. Kautsky to Victor Adler, in the latter's *Briefwechsel* (Vienna, 1954) p. 401.
2. Engels to Sorge, in Marx, Engels, *Werke* (Berlin, 1957) (hereafter *MEW*) vol. 39, p. 213.
3. The best account of Labriola in English is L. Kolakowski, *Main Currents of Marxism* (Oxford, 1978) vol. 2, pp. 175ff.
4. See further H. Stuart Hughes, *Consciousness and Society* (London, 1959) ch. 2, and A. Davidson, *Antonio Gramsci* (London, 1977) pp. 94ff.
5. See further: N. MacInnes, 'Les débuts du Marxisme théorique en France et en Italie (1880–1897)', *Cahiers de l'ISEA*, vol. 102, 1960, and L. Derfler, *Paul Lafargue* (Cambridge, 1998).
6. Quoted in Engels to Bernstein, *MEW*, vol. 35, p. 388. See also Marx's reservations on Longuet and Lafargue in *MEW*, vol. 35, p. 110.
7. Cf. H.-J. Steinberg, *Sozialismus und deutsche Sozialdemokratie*, 3rd edn (Bonn, 1972) p. 16.
8. Quoted by Y. Bourdet in his Introduction to R. Hilferding, *Le Capital financier* (Paris, 1970).
9. For well-documented evidence, see B. Gustaffsson, *Marxismus und Revisionismus* (Frankfurt, 1972) vol. 1, pp. 129ff.
10. Quoted in ibid., p. 128.
11. R. Luxemburg, *Gesammelte Werke* (Berlin, 1925) vol. 3, pp. 104f.
12. See the advice of the Party Secretary Ignaz Auer to Bernstein: 'People *do* things like that, but they don't *say* them!', E. Bernstein, *Entwicklungsgang eines Sozialisten* (Leipzig, 1925) p. 35.
13. Kautsky to Bernstein, quoted in H.-J. Steinberg, *Sozialismus und deutsche Sozialdemokratie*, 3rd edn (Bonn, 1972) p. 78.
14. E. Bernstein, *Die Neue Zeit*, vol. 13, p. 103.

15. Quoted in J.P. Nettl, *Rosa Luxemburg* (Oxford, 1966) vol. 1, p. 204.
16. Cf. J.P. Nettl, 'The German Social-Democratic Party 1890–1914 as a Political Model', *Past and Present*, 30 (1965).
17. See Engels's preface to his edition of *Capital*, vol. 3 (Moscow, 1971) pp. 8ff.
18. E. Bernstein, *Evolutionary Socialism* (New York, 1961) p. 29.
19. Ibid., p. 30.
20. Ibid., p. 48.
21. See further H.-C. Schröder, *Sozialismus und Imperialismus* (Hanover, 1968).
22. See below, pp. 63ff.
23. F. Engels, 'Zur Kritik des sozialdemokratischen Programmentwurfs 1891', *MEW*, vol. 22, p. 231.
24. See T. Sowell, 'Marx's "Increasing Misery" Doctrine', *American Economic Review*, 1960.
25. See G. Herre, *Verelendung und Proletariat bei Karl Marx* (Düsseldorf, 1973) pp. 14f.
26. E. Bernstein, op. cit., p. 50.
27. Ibid., p. 71.
28. K. Kautsky, *Die Agrarfrage* (Stuttgart, 1899) p. 174.
29. E. Bernstein, 'Allgemeines über Utopismus und Eklektizismus', *Die Neue Zeit*, vol. 15, p. 167.
30. E. Bernstein, *Evolutionary Socialism*, p. 142.
31. Ibid., pp. 147f.
32. Ibid., p. 151.
33. E. Bernstein, 'Die Zusammenbruchstheorie und die Kolonialpolitik', *Die Neue Zeit*, vol. 16, pp. 555f.
34. A. Bebel, *Briefwechsel mit F. Engels* (The Hague, 1965) p. 106.
35. *Protokoll über die Verhandlungen des Parteitages zu Hamburg* (Berlin, 1897) p. 125.
36. Cf. the interview recorded in *MEW*, vol. 22, p. 547.
37. K. Kautsky, *Le Marxisme et son critique Bernstein* (Paris, 1900) p. xii.
38. For the thesis that the bureaucratic organisation of mass movements tends to make them oligarchical and conservative, see R. Michels, *Political Parties* (New York, 1959). Michels was himself a disillusioned ex-member of the SPD. See also J.P. Nettl's article in *Past and Present* cited above, n. 16.
39. K. Kautsky, *Die Neue Zeit*, vol. 19, p. 90. For further positive evaluation of Kautsky's views on this subject, see R. Larsson, *Theories of Revolution* (Stockholm, 1970) pp. 49ff., and 256ff.
40. Bernstein to Kautsky, 20 Feb. 1898, quoted in H.-J. Steinberg, *Sozialismus und deutsche Socialdemokratie*, 3rd edn (Bonn, 1972) p. 4. Cf. also *Evolutionary Socialism*, pp. 145f.
41. Cf. K. Kautsky, *The Dictatorship of the Proletariat* (Ann Arbor, 1964) *passim*, which emphasises Kautsky's view of Bolshevik rule as a dictatorship over society and the proletariat produced by the mistaken desire to overstep the laws of social development.
42. See above, p. 14.
43. E. Bernstein, *Evolutionary Socialism*, p. 17.
44. Ibid., p. 7.
45. Ibid., pp. 13f.
46. Ibid., p. 15.
47. Bernstein to Kautsky, 22 Jan 1886, quoted in H.-J. Steinberg, *Sozialismus und deutsche Sozialdemokratie* (Bonn, 1972) p. 60.

48. E. Bernstein, 'Entwicklungsgang eines Sozialisten', *Die Volkswirtschaftslehre der Gegenwart in Selbstdarstellungen* (Leipzig, 1925) p. 40.
49. E. Bernstein, *Evolutionary Socialism*, p. 7.
50. Quoted in B. Gustafsson, *Marxismus und Revisionismus* (Frankfurt, 1972) vol. 2, p. 389.
51. E. Bernstein, *Die Voraussetzungen des Sozialismus*, Rowohlt edition (Hamburg, 1972) pp. 62f. (The whole chapter on Marxism and the Hegelian dialectic is unaccountably missing from the English translation.)
52. The basic account of the influence of Kantianism on the Revisionist movement is K. Vorländer, *Kant und Marx* (Tübingen, 1926).
53. Kautsky to Plekhanov, *Der Kampf*, vol. 18 (1925) p. 1.
54. See the re-evaluation in the last chapter of D. McKown, *The Classical Marxist Critique of Religion* (The Hague, 1975).
55. *Protokoll über die Verhandlungen des Parteitages zu Hannover* (Berlin, 1899) p. 148.
56. K. Kautsky, *Ethik und Materialistische Geschichtsauffassung* (Stuttgart, 1906) p. 141. For an even more extreme statement, see Hilferding's Preface to his *Finanzkapital*.
57. Kautsky to Bernstein, 30 Aug 1897, quoted in H.-J. Steinberg, *Sozialismus und deutsche Sozialdemokratie*, 3rd edn (Bonn, 1972) p. 77.
58. See E. Matthias, 'Kautsky und der Kautskyanismus', *Marxismusstudien* (Tübingen, 1957), whose influential and insightful account goes too far in this direction.
59. C. Schorske, *German Social Democracy, 1905–1917* (Cambridge, Mass., 1955) p. 29.
60. See H. Stuart Hughes, *Consciousness and Society* (London, 1959) ch. 2.

Further reading

General books on the period

A good book on the European intellectual scene during the Second International is H. Stuart Hughes' *Consciousness and Society*. On the origins of the SPD, see Lidtke's *The Outlawed Party*. Geary's article is good on the grass-roots basis of the Party, and Nettl's short study embodies insights from modern political analysis. Hunt is a reliable overview, but the basic text remains Schorske's excellent *German Social Democracy*.

On the Second International as a whole Joll is a good introduction. Volume Three of Cole's *History of Socialist Thought* and Volume One of Braunthal are slightly more detailed. Haupt is an excellent study of the events leading up to its demise in 1914. See also Pierson's scholarly study *Marxist Intellectuals and the Working Class Mentality in Germany 1887–1912*, and Chapter 4 of Howard and King's *History of Marxian Economics*.

The revisionist debate

Bernstein's major work is best available in the edition by Tudor. See also Steger's *Selected Writings*. Two commentaries in English are Peter Gay's

The Dilemma of Democratic Socialism, and, more recently, Steger's *The Quest for Evolutionary Socialism*. See also the articles by Gneuss and Elliot. There is a good collection of contributions to the revisionist debate in Tudor and Tudor.

Kautsky's major works have been translated: see *The Road to Power* for his politics, *The Dictatorship of the Proletariat* for his view of the Bolshevik Revolution, and *The Foundations of Christianity* for his strengths as a historian. Lichtheim's *Marxism* has a good, though short, chapter on Kautsky. See also Kolakowski's *Main Currents of Marxism*, Volume Two, Chapter Two, and Salvadori's lengthy study. The best general work is by Steenson.

Bibliography

General books on the period

Evelyn Anderson, *Hammer or Anvil: The Story of the German Working-class Movement* (London, 1945).
A. Bebel, *My Life* (London, 1912).
Max Beer, *Fifty Years of International Socialism* (London, 1935).
A. Joseph Berlau, *The German Social Democratic Party: 1914–1921* (New York, 1950).
Julius Braunthal, *History of the International* vol. I, *1864–1914* (London, 1966).
G.D.H. Cole, *The Second International: 1889–1914* vol. III of *A History of Socialist Thought* (London, 1956).
B. Croce, *Historical Materialism and the Economics of Karl Marx* (London, 1966).
L. Derfler, *Paul Lafargue and the Flowering of French Socialism 1882–1911* (Cambridge, 1998).
M. Donald, *Marxism and Revolution: Karl Kautsky and the Russian Marxists 1900–1924* (New Haven, 1998).
R. Palme Dutt, *The Internationale* (London, 1964).
Richard Geary, 'The German Labour Movement: 1848–1919', *European Studies Review*, 6 (1976).
H. Goldberg, *Jean Jaurès* (Madison, 1966).
Georges Haupt, *Socialism and the Great War: The Collapse of the Second International* (Oxford, 1972).
M.C. Howard and J.E. King, *A History of Marxian Economics*, vol. I, *1883–1929* (Princeton, N.J., 1989).
H. Stuart Hughes, *Consciousness and Society: The Reorientation of European Social Thought, 1890–1930* (London, 1959).
Richard N. Hunt, *German Social Democracy: 1918–1933* (London, 1964).
James Joll, *The Second International* (London, 1955).
L. Kolakowski, *Main Currents of Marxism* (Oxford, 1978), vol. 2.
A. Labriola, *Essays on the Materialist Conception of History* (London, 1966).
—— *Socialism and Philosophy* (St Louis, Miss., 1978).
Veron L. Lidtke, 'German Social Democracy and German State Socialism', *International Review of Social History*, 9 (1964).
—— *The Outlawed Party: Social Democracy in Germany, 1878–1890* (Princeton, N.J., 1966).

William H. Maehl, 'August Bebel and the Development of a Responsible German Socialist Foreign Policy', *Journal of European Studies*, I. 6 (1976).

Harry J. Marks, 'Sources of Reformism in the Social Democratic Party of Germany: 1890–1914', *Journal of Modern History*, XI, 3 (1939).

J.P. Nettl, 'The German Social-Democratic Party 1890–1914 as a Political Model', *Past and Present*, 30 (1965).

Gerhart Niemeyer, 'The Second International: 1889–1914', in M.M. Drachkovitch (ed.), *The Revolutionary Internationals* (Stanford, 1964).

W. Pelz (ed.), *Wilhelm Liebknecht and German Social Democracy* (Westport, 1994).

Stanley Pierson, *Marxist Intellectuals and the Working Class Mentality in Germany 1887–1912* (Cambridge, 1993).

D. Renton, *Classical Marxism: Socialist Theory and the Second International* (Cheltenham, 2002).

H. Rogers, *Before the Revisionist Controversy: Kautsky, Bernstein and the Meaning of Marxism* (New York, 1992).

Günter Roth, *The Social Democrats in Imperial Germany* (Totowa, N.J., 1963).

Bertrand Russell, *German Social Democracy* (London, 1965).

Carl K. Schorske, *German Social Democracy, 1905–1917: The Development of the Great Schism* (Cambridge, Mass., 1955).

J. Stanley (ed.), *From Georges Sorel: Essays in Socialism and Philosophy* (Oxford, 1977).

G. Steenson, *After Marx, before Lenin: Marxism and Socialist Working-Class Parties in Europe 1884–1914* (Pittsburgh, 1991).

Hans-Josef Steinberg, *Sozialismus und deutsche Sozialdemokratie: zur Ideologie der Partei vor dem Weltkrieg* (2nd edn, Hanover, 1969; 3rd edn, Bonn, 1972).

Bernstein: texts

Edward Bernstein, *Cromwell and Communism* (London, 1930).

—— *Evolutionary Socialism: A Criticism and Affirmation*, introduced by Sidney Hook (New York, 1961).

—— *The Preconditions of Socialism*, ed. H. Tudor (Cambridge, 1993).

—— *Ferdinand Lassalle as a Social Reformer* (London, 1893).

—— *My Years of Exile: Reminiscences of a Socialist* (London, 1921).

—— *Selected Writings 1900–1921*, ed. M. Steger (Atlantic Highlands, 1996).

H. Tudor and J.M. Tudor (eds), *Marxism and Social Democracy: The Revisionist Debate, 1890–1896* (London, 1988).

Bernstein: commentaries

Sydney D. Bailey, 'The Revision of Marxism', *The Review of Politics*, 16 (1954).

Charles F. Elliot, 'Quis custodiet sacra? Problems of Marxist Revisionism', *Journal of the History of Ideas*, 28 (1967).

Peter Gay, *The Dilemma of Democratic Socialism: Edward Bernstein's Challenge to Marx* (New York, 1962).

Christian Gneuss, 'The Precursor: Edward Bernstein', in L. Labedz (ed.), *Revisionism: Essays in the History of Marxist Ideas* (London, 1962).

M. Steger, *The Quest for Evolutionary Socialism: Edward Bernstein and Social Democracy* (Cambridge, 1997).

Kautsky: texts

Karl Kautsky, *Bolshevism at a Deadlock* (London, 1931).
—— *The Class Struggle* (Chicago, 1910).
—— *Communism in Central Europe in the Time of the Reformation* (London, 1897).
—— *The Dictatorship of the Proletariat*, introduced by John H. Kautsky (Ann Arbor, 1964).
—— *The Economic Doctrines of Karl Marx* (London, 1925).
—— *Ethics and the Materialist Conception of History* (Chicago, 1907).
—— *The Foundations of Christianity: A Study in Christian Origins* (London, 1925).
—— *Ireland* (Belfast, 1974).
—— *The Road to Power* (Chicago, 1909).
—— *Socialism and Colonial Policy: An Analysis* (Belfast, 1975).
—— *Terrorism and Communism* (London, 1920).
—— *Thomas More and His Utopia* (London, 1927).

Kautsky: commentaries

R. Geary, *Karl Kautsky* (Manchester, 1987).
L. Kolakowski, *Main Currents of Marxism* (Oxford, 1978) vol. 2, ch. 2.
G. Lichtheim, *Marxism* (London, 1964) part 5, section 5.
M. Salvadori, *Kautsky and the Socialist Revolution* (New York, 1979).

3
The Radicals

Introduction

By 1905, the revisionist controversy had virtually ended; and in this controversy those who were to emerge later as 'left radicals' held positions not very different from that of Kautsky. The real break came about 1910 when the gradual process that the party had been undergoing began to be transparent. This process has been well described as follows:

> Ideology, the same old outward-going ideology of revolution, served more and more exclusively as a means of internal cohesion. With the continuation of 'practical' politics at all levels – participation in elections, trade-union activity, attempts to form blocs with bourgeois parties in the Reichstag – the gulf between theory and practice inevitably widened; hence increased ideological assertion became all the more necessary to sublimate the uselessness of practical politics – the uselessness which was all that was permitted. In turn, the lower echelons of party work became a desert in which one served to obtain one's promotion – instead of the grass roots of a vital struggle; the party congresses ceased to be the law-making and policy-making sovereign assembly and became an annual ritual where ideology was enthroned and from which participants dispersed full of moral satisfaction – to illuminate their comrades accordingly. The structure remained unaltered, except for the growth of the executive and its bureaucracy, but its functions, and with them the foci of power, underwent a considerable change.[1]

Yet the radicals never (until the founding of the Communist Party at the very end of 1918) formed a separate political party, and remained merely a pressure group inside the SPD. Moreover, most of the radicals were outsiders, mainly of Jewish origin, who hovered uneasily between the German and more peripheral socialist movements. The only two prominent 'insiders' were Mehring and Liebknecht. Franz Mehring was a brilliant political journalist who applied the principles of historical materialism to Germany, particularly in studies of the German Social Democratic Party and of Prussia. He also pioneered historical materialism in the field of literary criticism, drawing attention to the relationship between the greatness of writers and their class aspirations and claiming that the best literature came from emergent classes. His studies of eighteenth and nineteenth-century German literature – and especially his *Lessing Legende* of 1893 – were admired by Engels. Mehring also edited several of Marx's early works and wrote the classic biography of Marx. Karl Liebknecht, the only SPD deputy to vote against the war credits in 1914, was above all known for his *Militarism and Anti-Militarism*, one of the best Second International analyses of the role of the bourgeois state apparatus. For the rest, the strength of the radicals lay in non-Germans. Parvus (his real name was Israel Helphand), the sharpest critic of revisionism within the party and the originator of the term 'opportunism', was a Russian Jew from Odessa.[2] Anton Pannekoek, who regularly contributed to debates in the German party press, was a Dutch astronomer.[3] Karl Radek, who was active as a journalist on the left of the SPD in the years preceding 1914, before moving to Russia, came from Galicia.[4] And finally, Rosa Luxemburg, the most outstanding of the radicals, came from South East Poland.

Luxemburg: social reform or revolution

The radicals were – naturally – vociferous in their opposition to Bernstein, though their ideas at this stage were not distinct from those of Kautsky. Parvus was the first to launch an attack on Bernstein in the *Sachsische Arbeiterzeitung* of January–March 1898. His main point was that 'At the source of all opportunistic errors inside the socialist workers' movement can be found a common trait: the incapacity to connect in an organic plan the present work of the party with its social revolutionary goal. In their eyes this splits in two: here "goal" there present tasks. The most they recognise is a parallelism: agitation for social revolution and activity inside the capitalist state.'[5] But the strongest attack on Bernstein was by Rosa Luxemburg in the pages of the *Leipziger Volkszeitung* of the same year, reissued as a book in 1899 under the title *Social Reform or Revolution*. This tightly-written, vigorous polemic has become one of the minor classics of radical Marxism. Luxemburg's initial thesis was that 'there exists an indissoluble tie between social reform and revolution'.[6] Bernstein, she continued, had admitted that he was only concerned with the means (social reforms) and not with the end (revolution). But Bernstein's notion of reform meant abandoning the theory of capitalist breakdown – the cornerstone of scientific socialism – and 'if one admits, with Bernstein, that capitalist development does not move in the direction of its own ruin, the socialism ceases to be objectively necessary'.[7]

More specifically, Luxemburg attacked Bernstein's conclusions in the three related fields of economics, sociology and politics. In economics she claimed that the credit and cartelisation which Bernstein had said were stabilising capitalism had the opposite effect: credit increased the contradiction of capitalist society by accentuating the separation of production from ownership; and cartelisation increased contradictions between producer and consumer, between organised capital and the working class, between the international character of the capitalist world economy and the national character of the capitalist state. From this it followed that, in spite of the recent period of calm, a severe crisis was inevitable.

With regard to Bernstein's social theories, Luxemburg claimed that he was wrong in denying the disappearance of the middle class. The apparent resilience of middle-size enterprises did not undermine Marx's theory of breakdown:

> The struggle of the average-size enterprise against big capital cannot be considered a regularly proceeding battle in which the troops of the weaker party continue to melt away directly and quantitatively. It should rather be regarded as a periodic mowing down of small capital, which rapidly grows up again only to be mowed down once more by large industry. The two tendencies play catch with the middle capitalist layers. As opposed to the development of the working class, the descending tendency must win in the end. The victory of the descending tendency need not necessarily show itself in an absolute numerical diminution of middle-size enterprises. It shows itself, first, in the progressive increase of the minimum amount of capital necessary for the functioning of the enterprises in the old branches of production; second, in the constant diminution of the interval of time during which the small capitalists conserve the opportunity to exploit the new branches of production. The result, as far as the small capitalist is concerned, is a progressively shorter duration of his economic life and an ever more rapid change in the methods of production and of investment; and, for the class as a whole, a more and more rapid acceleration of the social metabolism.[8]

Joint stock companies, by creating large concentrations of capital, merely separated production from ownership. In probably the key passage in the whole polemic, she wrote:

> By transporting the concept 'capitalist' from the relations of production to property relations, and by speaking of 'men' instead of speaking of 'entrepreneurs' Bernstein moves the question of socialism from the realm of production into the realm of relations of fortune – from the relation between capital and labour to the relation between rich and poor.[9]

Luxemburg also contested the hopes that Bernstein placed in cooperatives and trade unions. Cooperatives were, for her, no more than a hybrid form in the midst of capitalism. As for trade unions, their function of increasing the proportion of social wealth accruing to the working class was doomed to frustration by the twin processes of the proletarianisation of the middle class which threatened increasing unemployment, and the growth of the productivity of labour. The trade union struggle became a 'sort of labour of Sisyphus'[10] – a phrase which earned Rosa Luxemburg the immediate and continued enmity of the trade union leaders.

Thirdly, Luxemburg claimed that Bernstein's confidence in political democracy was misplaced. This for two reasons: firstly, democratic institutions had 'largely played out their role as aids in bourgeois development'.[11] She did not deny the importance of parliamentary struggle, but her reasons were rather back-handed: the very ineffectiveness of parliamentary struggle would convince the proletariat that, for any fundamental change, the conquest of political power was essential. More importantly, Luxemburg insisted that 'the structure of capitalist property and the capitalist state develop in entirely different directions'.[12] Capitalist society was characterised by the fact that wage labour was not a juridical but only an economic relation: 'in our whole juridical system, there is not a single legal formula for the present class domination'.[13] But this meant that the kind of political and legal reforms advocated by Bernstein could not possibly tackle the problem.

In short, Luxemburg concluded, Bernstein's views were mechanical and undialectical:

> Legal reform and revolution are not different methods of historical progress that can be picked out at pleasure from the counter of history, just as one chooses hot or cold sausages. They are different moments in the development of class society which condition and complement

each other, and at the same time exclude each other reciprocally as, e.g., the north and south poles, the bourgeoisie and the proletariat.[14]

Luxemburg's pamphlet was by no means innovatory – except perhaps in her idea that bourgeois domination was extra-legal.[15] On the contrary, she claimed to be defending the traditional tactic of the SPD against the innovations of Bernstein. Her defence of the traditional themes of historical materialism and the objective necessity of revolution was much the same as that of Kautsky, although she was quicker to attack Bernstein as Kautsky was initially held back by ties of friendship. In supporting the parliamentary struggle she still wanted to unite a reformist practice with a revolutionary theory. It was only Lenin at this time who advocated a different approach.

Luxemburg: consciousness and activity

Although *Social Reform or Revolution* did not mark Rosa Luxemburg off from the SPD leadership, her writings immediately before and after the Russian Revolution of 1905 showed a very distinctive emphasis. The rising cost of living and the contracting market of these years caused a great increase in working-class activity and it was in this context that Rosa Luxemburg began to develop her ideas on class consciousness. Already in *Social Reform or Revolution* she had talked of the importance of trade union activity and political struggle in that 'through them the *awareness*, the consciousness, of the proletariat becomes socialist, and it is organised as a class'.[16] It was from this point of view that she criticised Lenin's *One Step Forwards, Two Steps Backwards* in her article on 'Organizational Questions of Russian Social Democracy' published in *Die Neue Zeit* of 1904. Here Luxemburg was at pains to emphasise the 'dialectical' relationship between leaders and masses as against what she saw as mechanical control by a Central Committee. Lenin's ideas seemed to her 'a mechanistic transfer of the organisational principles of the Blanquistic movement of conspiratorial groups to the Social Democratic movement of the working masses'.[17] Luxemburg praised the 'spontaneous' nature of Russian working-class demonstrations in recent years. For her, centralism 'can be nothing but the imperative summation of the will of the enlightened and fighting vanguard of the working class as opposed to its individual groups and members. This is, so to speak, a "self-centralism" of the leading stratum of the proletariat; it is the rule of the majority within its own party organisation.'[18] In Germany decentralisation had certainly helped the revisionist movement, but that was no argument for centralism in Russia.

Luxemburg tended to see Lenin's views as the left-wing mirror of Bernstein: a sectarianism that separated the party from the masses in the same way as Bernstein separated the movement from its goal. Neither was Lenin right to glorify the disciplinary influence of the factory on the proletariat: the next revolution in Russia would be bourgeois and soon bureaucratic discipline would simply facilitate the exploitation of the proletariat by the bourgeoisie. Finally Luxemburg insisted that opportunism could not be eradicated by the elaboration of a party *constitution* – however perfect – and concluded:

> Moreover, in this anxious attempt of a part of Russian Social Democracy to protect the very promising and vigorously progressing Russian labour movement from error through the guardianship of an omniscient and omnipresent central committee we see the same subjectivism which has already played more than one trick on the socialist movement in Russia ... But now the 'ego' of the Russian revolutionary quickly turns upside down and declares itself once again as the all-powerful directors of history – this time as his majesty the central committee of the Social Democratic labour movement. However, the nimble acrobat fails to see that the true subject to whom this role of director falls is the collective ego of the working class, which insists on its right to make its own mistakes and to learn the historical dialectic by itself. Finally, we must frankly admit to ourselves that errors made by a truly revolutionary labour movement are historically infinitely more fruitful and more valuable than the infallibility of the best of all possible 'central committees'.[19]

Of course, much of the emphasis of Rosa Luxemburg on the party as agitator rather than organiser springs from her experience of the German situation, where she considered the masses to be more radical than the leadership.[20]

Central to Luxemburg's conception of revolution was the notion of 'spontaneity'. This later became a term of abuse when used by orthodox Communists: for if a revolution were automatically produced by the progress of capitalism and the workers' rising was spontaneous, there was little room for the intervention of a 'vanguard party'.[21] Looked at from another point of view, the notion of spontaneity bears a striking resemblance to Marx's idea on consciousness and revolution of the 1840s – a context in which fatalism played no part. It should also be noted that Luxemburg's idea of spontaneity became more pronounced the more unsatisfactory she found the SPD leadership, and that it was a spontaneity of action, never of theory.[22] She never denied the necessity for creative leadership.

The embodiment of spontaneity, for Luxemburg, was the mass strike. The mass strike had previously been viewed with suspicion by the German Social Democrats owing to its anarchist origins; but the relative success of mass strikes in 1903/4 – particularly in Belgium – led to growing attention being paid to the idea; even Bernstein advocated a mass strike as a possible reply to attacks on universal suffrage. Kautsky also gave a cautious welcome on the idea which gained considerable impetus from the Russian Revolution of 1905. The Jena Congress of 1905 – perhaps the most radical of all the SPD Congresses – adopted Bebel's rather ambivalent resolution on the mass strike as, above all, a defensive tactic. But no more than defensive: efforts to use the mass strike later the same year in face of attempts to impose suffage restrictions petered out owing both to the failure of the Russian Revolution and the coolness of the Party Executive. The trade union leaders were strongly opposed to talk of a mass strike which, they considered, endangered their gradual gains, careful organisation, financial provision and centralised leadership. At their Cologne Congress of 1905 they condemned the idea of the mass strike, and with it, the radical wing of the party.

It was in this context that Rosa Luxemburg wrote her pamphlet on *Mass Strike, Party and Trade Unions*, as an effort to bridge the gap between the economic reformism of the trade unions and political action. She was concerned to make clear that the mass strike was no longer an anarchist tool and therefore that the previous criticisms of Engels along those lines were now misplaced. As for the trade union opposition, this was largely beside the point as the principal lesson of the Russian Revolution was that 'the mass strike is not artificially "made", not "decided" out of the blue, not "propagated", but rather that it is an historical phenomenon which at a certain moment follows with historical necessity from the social relations'.[23] She then analysed the role of the mass strikes in Russia in 1905 and drew three main conclusions. Firstly, the mass strike was not an isolated action: it was rather 'the sign, the totality-concept of a whole period of the class struggle lasting for years, perhaps decades'.[24] Secondly, the economic and political elements in the mass strike were inseparable:

The economic struggle is that which leads the political struggle from one nodal point to another; the political struggle is that which periodically fertilizes the soil for the economic struggle. Cause and effect here continually change places. Thus, far from being completely separated or even mutually exclusive, as the pedantic schema sees it, the economic and political moments in the mass strike period form only two interlacing sides of the proletarian class struggle in Russia. And *their unity* is precisely the mass strike.[25]

Thirdly, instead of the mass strike leading to revolution, it was the other way round: it was the revolution which created conditions enabling the fusion of the economic and political elements in the mass strike. In a passage summarising her views she wrote:

If the mass strike does not signify a single act but a whole period of class struggles, and if this period is identical with a period of revolution, then it is clear that the mass strike cannot be called at will, even if the decision to call it comes from the highest committee of the strongest Social Democratic party. As long as Social Democracy is not capable of staging and countermanding revolutions according to its own estimation of the situation, then even the greatest enthusiasm and impatience of the Social Democratic troops will not suffice to call into being a true period of mass strikes as a living, powerful movement of the people.[26]

According to Luxemburg, the element of spontaneity placed a great role in all Russian strikes. This was not because of the 'unschooled' nature of the Russian proletariat, but because 'revolutions allow no one to play schoolmaster to them'.[27] This did not mean that leadership was unnecessary. Luxemburg catalogued its role as follows:

To give the slogans, the direction of the struggle; to organise the tactics of the political struggle in such a way that in every phase and in every moment of the struggle the whole sum of the available and already released active power of the proletariat will be realised and find expression in the battle stance of the party; to see that the resoluteness and acuteness of the tactics of the Social Democracy never fall below the level of the actual relation of forces but rather rise above it – that is the most important task of the 'leadership' in the period of the mass strike.[28]

In the final sections of her pamphlet Luxemburg attempted to demonstrate that the relative success of the mass strikes in Russia was not due to Russia's backwardness: the economic and social situation of the Russian and German workers was much more alike than was generally realised. Neither could the German trade unions argue that they were insufficiently organised to attempt a mass strike. Organisation and struggle were dialectically united. What the trade unions had strikingly neglected was class consciousness:

> The class consciousness implanted in the enlightened German worker by Social Democracy is theoretical and latent: in the period of domination of bourgeois parliamentarism it cannot, as a rule, become active as direct action of the masses ... In the revolution, where the masses themselves enter the political arena, class consciousness becomes practical and active.[29]

Lastly, Luxemburg attacked the idea of the 'equal authority' of the trade unions and the Party. The trade unions were a part of the whole movement, but in a very specific sense: the trade union movement was not to be identified with its leaders, but was what 'lives in the consciousness of the masses of proletarians who have been won for the class struggle'.[30]

Luxemburg was not alone in advocating the mass strike: Bernstein worried his trade union allies by advocating it for specific reforms; for Bebel and the SPD leadership it was a defensive measure of the last resort and ultimately even Kautsky did not go beyond this position.[31] For Luxemburg it was far more: it came to stand for her whole political strategy. Although originally to be supplemented by the traditional parliamentary tactic, she began to move to a position (connected with her developing views on imperialism) that consigned parliamentary activity to an obsolete phase of the struggle. In this sense, Radek was accurate in saying that Luxemburg's *Mass Strike* marked the beginning of the separation of the Communist movement from Social Democracy in Germany.[32] In the context of the current German situation her views were plainly over-optimistic and, in the short term, Kautsky was right. Germany bore little resemblance to Russia. Lenin certainly thought Kautsky's views were realistic and even the impatient Parvus considered that Luxemburg took no account of the realities of the political situation. The Jena Congress had marked the apogee of radicalism in the SPD. The trade union leaders were opposed to the whole mass strike idea and shared the view attributed to the Party Secretary Auer that 'general strikes are general nonsense'.[33] During 1906 they began a counter-offensive and at the Mannheim Congress (the very Congress that Luxemburg's *Mass Strike* pamphlet had been written to influence) it was made clear, in spite of Kautsky's opposition, that the trade unions were equal, and not subordinate, to the Party and that no mass strike could be launched without their – extremely improbable – agreement. The spirit of Jena was reversed and revisionism reintroduced into the Party by the more intractable means of trade union influence.

Luxemburg: imperialism

The doctrine of the mass strike was closely connected with the idea of imperialism. It was a common view among left-wing radicals that imperialism and its attendant militarism meant more power to the bureaucracy and less to parliament; hence the necessity to resort to direct action. From the early 1900s Eisner, Liebknecht and Kautsky had all pointed to imperialism increasing *pari passu* with the rise of socialism.[34] The most important work in this field was Rosa Luxemburg's *Accumulation of Capital*. Her original studies had been in economics and in 1907 she obtained a job teaching mainly economics at the Party school in Berlin. She wrote up her lectures almost immediately into the short *Introduction to Political Economy*. In 1911 she became particularly interested in the problems of the reproduction of capital and in 1913 she published her greatest work, *The Accumulation of Capital*. She began with Marx's models for simple reproduction and extended reproduction as set out in *Capital* Volume Two. Her main criticism of Marx was that, once technical change was introduced into his model for expanded reproduction, there was no explanation as to how the consequent surplus product could be absorbed within the closed system: there was no reason for there to be any demand for the accumulation of surplus value. After an extended discussion of the treatment of the question in the classical economists and the Russian Legal Marxists, Luxemburg propounded her own solution. It was necessary to abandon the idea of a closed system: the surplus was realised by sales to non-capitalist countries. 'The decisive fact is that the surplus value cannot be realised by sale either to workers or capitalists, but only if it is sold to such social organisations or strata whose mode of production is not capitalistic.'[35] Hence the phenomenon of colonial expansion; and Luxemburg had some excellent passages on the destruction of peasant societies and a strong emphasis on the economic function of militarism. Thus capitalism could grow just as long as there were precapitalist societies to be exploited. When all these societies had been absorbed into the process of capitalist accumulation, the capitalist system would collapse since 'it proceeds by assimilating the very conditions which alone can ensure its own existence'.[36] Thus:

> the more ruthlessly capital sets out the destruction of non-capitalist strata at home and in the outside world, the more it lowers the

standard of living for workers as a whole, the greater also the change in the day-to-day history of capital. It becomes a string of political and social disasters and convulsions, and under these conditions, punctuated by periodical economic catastrophes or crises, accumulation can go on no longer ... At a certain stage of development there will be no other way out than the application of socialist principles.[37]

No Marxist economist of the time agreed with the conclusions of *The Accumulation of Capital*. It has been criticised on two main grounds. There was considerable contemporary criticism of its technical economic theses; and there is good general agreement that her criticism of Marx was misguided.[38] Secondly, there was considerable ambiguity as to how automatic Luxemburg thought the process of capitalist breakdown. She certainly seems to have believed a breakdown theory of some sort to have been essential for a correct socialist strategy. Lenin, of course, disagreed and Luxemburg's automatic views, together with the fatalism supposedly inherent in her views on spontaneity, were the target of a whole barrage of subsequent Leninist criticism.[39] Much of this criticism was completely misguided as Luxemburg was certainly no more 'fatalist' than Marx himself.[40] Whatever her confusions in the rather technical problems of reproduction, her broad account of economic imperialism and its devastating impact on underdeveloped societies continues to be of relevance.

The split in the SPD

From 1906 onwards the position of the radicals inside the party became increasingly difficult. During the revisionist controversy they had been more or less dominant, and had therefore been supporters of centralisation. But as the trade unions, with the tacit agreement of the Executive, made their influence felt, the radicals were more and more on the outside. As Schorske has put it in his classic work on the period:

> The unionists, with their anti-revolutionary attitude, may be presumed to have represented more accurately than the Social Democratic Party the mass of German workers in our period. By organising these masses where the party could not, the union leaders were able to transmit the subjective attitudes of the politically passive workers into the Social Democratic Party itself, with the party executive as their agent. In this sense, the trade-union conquest made the party more representative of German labor than it had been before 1906. Yet herein lay a fatal difficulty: the trade-union bureaucracy was anti-revolutionary

in Permanenz, by virtue of its corporate interest in the existing order. The working class was not similarly committed, and the party had heretofore represented the proletariat's revolutionary potential as well as its reformist actuality. By capitulating before the trade-unions in our period, the party surrendered its political flexibility, and this prepared the ground for its subsequent dissolution.[41]

This general conservative trend was reinforced by the organisation of the Party: by 1906 the bureaucratic element had a majority on the Executive and the administrative side became increasingly divorced from the political. By 1911 Ebert, the epitome of the new SPD bureaucrat, was the most influential man in the Party. The brief radicalisation of 1910 with waves of strikes and agitation for electoral reform led to a split between Kautsky and Luxemburg. Kautsky refused to publish her article *What Now?* in *Die Neue Zeit* due to its advocacy of the mass strike and republicanism. She outlined her general attitude to the Party leadership as follows:

> Even within the class party of the proletariat every great, decisive movement must originate not in the initiative of a handful of leaders but in the determination and conviction of the mass of party supporters. The decision to fight the present struggle for the right to vote in Prussia ...'by all means' – including that of the mass strike – can only be taken by the broadest groups in the party.[42]

The final victory of the revisionists was marked by the 1912 election campaign, which was designed to achieve maximum cooperation with bourgeois parties.[43]

Given this background, the decision of the Reichstag SPD delegates, with the single exception of Liebknecht, to vote for war credits in 1914 was not surprising. From the early 1900s both Liebknecht and Eisner had urged the party to take seriously the problems of militarism and imperialism. Nevertheless, at the Stuttgart Congress of the International in 1907, the SPD delegation took a noticeably conservative stance on militarism and war and even advocated a positive attitude to colonialism. Fear of the introduction of anti-socialist laws, fear of defeat by Tsarist Russia, the prior decision of the trade unions to cooperate with the government and, above all, fear of loss of working-class support all influenced the 4 August vote.

By 1912, the left radicals were beginning to emerge as a coherent force within the SPD with a twin emphasis on the mass strike (and mass action in general) and imperialism as the central political phenomenon. As the war progressed and opposition to it increased, the split in the SPD was consummated. By early 1917 both Spartacists (as the left radicals came to be called) and the oppositional Centrists were expelled from the party, and the *Unabhängige Sozialistische Partei Deutschlands* (Independent German Socialist Party) was formed to include everyone from the Spartacists to Kautsky and even the pacifist Bernstein. From the outset the left radicals would brook no compromise. Their attitude is best illustrated by Rosa Luxemburg's *Junius Pamphlet*, with its trenchant analysis of the collapse of the International, and her appropriately entitled *Either-Or*. Both were published by the Spartacus League, whose main views were: wholesale opposition to the war, which was viewed as a result of imperialist rivalry between the capitalist classes of different countries; a consequent emphasis on internationalism; and a reliance on mass action to achieve their objectives. A correlative of this last point was a critique of the Bolshevik Revolution that Luxemburg wrote in prison in 1918. Although more distrustful of the usefulness of bourgeois democracy than Lenin, and not sharing his enthusiasm for the peasantry, she had been broadly speaking in agreement with Lenin's views on the possibility of a bourgeois revolution in Russia spearheaded by the proletariat.[44] And she had considerable praise for the events of 1917:

> The party of Lenin was the only one which grasped the mandate and duty of a truly revolutionary party; with the slogan – 'all power in the hands of the proletariat and peasantry' – they ensured the continued move forward of the revolution. Thereby the Bolsheviks solved the famous problem of 'winning a majority of the people' which has always weighed on the German Social Democracy like a nightmare.[45]

However, she also had criticisms of what appeared to be necessary conditions of the Bolsheviks' success: for according to her, nationalisation of the land would have been preferable to its seizure and distribution to the peasants; the emphasis on national self-determination within Russia was misguided; the Bolsheviks were wrong to dissolve the Constituent Assembly; and finally

> freedom only for the supporters of the government, only for the members of one party – however numerous they may be – is no freedom at all. Freedom is always and exclusively freedom for the one who thinks differently. Not because of any fanatical conception of 'justice' but because all that is instructive, wholesome and purifying in political

freedom depends on this essential characteristic; and its effectiveness vanishes when 'freedom' becomes a special privilege ... Lenin is completely mistaken in the means he employs. Decree, dictatorial force of the factory overseer, draconic penalties, rule by terror, all these things are but palliatives. The only way to rebirth is the school of public life itself, the most unlimited, the broadest democracy and public opinion. It is rule by terror which demoralises.[46]

It is a matter of dispute to what extent Luxemburg changed or modified these views during the remaining months of her life.[47]

In the event, the impact of the Spartacus League on the turbulent events of November 1918–January 1919 was minimal. Up to the last days of 1918 it was a pressure group within the USPD, only transforming itself into the German Communist Party (KPD) on 1 January 1919. It consisted merely of small and isolated propaganda groups. When, in October 1918, the SPD finally had power put into its hands (typical of its all-pervasive passivity), the Spartacus League duly opposed the parliamentary form of government, but had little to propose in its place. In December it published its programme, with its formal commitment 'never to take over governmental power except in response to the clear, unambiguous will of the great majority of the proletarian mass of all of Germany'.[48]

When the SPD government tried to enforce order after large street demonstrations in the early days of January, there was an armed uprising which petered out in a few days. The revolt was neither initiated, nor controlled by the Spartacus League, nor did it agree with its aims. But it provided the government with the opportunity to crush the extreme left and both Luxemburg and Liebknecht were murdered. German socialism was then polarised between the subsequently Bolshevised German Communist Party and the SPD, where vestiges of Marxism became increasingly difficult to find.[49]

Notes

1. J.P. Nettl, *Rosa Luxemburg*, abridged edition (Oxford, 1969) p. 151.
2. Cf. Z. Zeman and W.B. Scharlau, *The Merchant of Revolution* (London, 1965). See further on Parvus, pp. 84ff. below.
3. See further, pp. 186ff below.
4. Cf. W. Lerner, *Karl Radek: The Last Internationalist* (Stanford, 1970).
5. Parvus, 'Der Opportunismus in der Praxis', *Die Neue Zeit*, vol. 19, p. 660.
6. R. Luxemburg, 'Social Reform or Revolution', in *Selected Political Writings*, ed. D. Howard (London and New York, 1971) p. 52.
7. Ibid., p. 58.

8. Ibid., pp. 70f.
9. Ibid., pp. 96f. Cf. also p. 107.
10. Ibid., p. 105.
11. Ibid., p. 110.
12. Ibid., p. 112.
13. Ibid., p. 116.
14. Ibid., p. 115.
15. See further: J.P. Nettl, *Rosa Luxemburg*, abridged edition (Oxford, 1969) p. 134.
16. R. Luxemburg, op. cit., p. 86.
17. R. Luxemburg, 'Organizational Questions of Russian Social Democracy', *Selected Political Writings*, p. 290. For a slightly more nuanced account of Lenin's views at the time, see below, pp. 94ff. See N. Geras, 'Rosa Luxemburg after 1905', *New Left Review*, 89 (1975) pp. 41f., for the way in which Luxemburg later modified her charge of Blanquism.
18. R. Luxemburg, op. cit., p. 290.
19. Ibid., pp. 305f.
20. Further on the contacts between German and Russian Marxists at this period, see P. Lösche, *Der Bolschewismus im Urteil der deutschen Sozialdemokratie* (Berlin, 1967) ch. 2; and C. Weill, *Marxistes russes et Social-democratie allemande 1898–1904* (Paris, 1977).
21. Cf. N. Geras, 'Luxemburg's Concept of Collapse', *New Left Review*, 82 (1973) p. 20.
22. Cf. J.P. Nettl, *Rosa Luxemburg*, abridged edition (Oxford, 1969) p. 154.
23. R. Luxemburg, 'Mass Strike, Party and Trade Unions', *Selected Political Writings*, p. 231.
24. Ibid., p. 237.
25. Ibid., p. 241.
26. Ibid., p. 244.
27. Ibid., p. 245.
28. Ibid., p. 247.
29. R. Luxemburg, *Politische Schriften* (Leipzig, 1969) p. 194.
30. R. Luxemburg, 'Mass Strike, Party and Trade Unions', p. 270.
31. See pp. 31ff. above.
32. K. Radek, *Rosa Luxemburg, Karl Liebknecht, Leo Jogiches* (Hamburg, 1921) p. 15, quoted in J.P. Nettl, *Rosa Luxemburg* (Oxford, 1969) p. 205.
33. *Protokoll über die Verhandlungen des Parteitages des SPD zu Mannheim* (Berlin, 1906) p. 246.
34. Cf. H.-C. Schröder, *Sozialismus und Imperialismus. Die Auseinandersetzung der deutschen Sozialdemokratie mit dem Imperialismusproblem und der 'Weltpolitik' vor 1914* (Hanover, 1968).
35. R. Luxemburg, *The Accumulation of Capital* (London, 1971) pp. 351f. The key chapter is 26.
36. Ibid., pp. 466f.
37. Ibid.
38. See her spirited reply, *The Accumulation of Capital – An Anti-Critique*, edited with a good introduction by K. Tarbuck (London and New York, 1972). See also P. Sweezy, *The Theory of Capitalist Development* (New York, 1942) pp. 202ff., and T. Kemp, *Theories of Imperialism* (London, 1967). A more sympathetic treatment is contained in Joan Robinson's Introduction to the English edition.

39. Cf. E. Stokes, 'Late Nineteenth Century Colonial Expansion and the Attack on the Theory of Economic Imperialism. A Case of Mistaken Identity?', *Historical Journal*, 12 (1969) pp. 297f.
40. Cf. N. Geras, 'Luxemburg's Concept of Collapse', *New Left Review*, 82 (1973).
41. C. Schorske, *German Social Democracy 1905–1917* (Cambridge, Mass., 1955) p. 110.
42. R. Luxemburg, 'The Next Step', *Selected Political Writings*, ed. R. Looker (London, 1972) p. 159.
43. On the way in which the Party came progressively to mirror the structure of the state that it opposed, see G. Ritter, *Die Arbeiterbewegung im Wilhelminischen Reich* (Berlin, 1959).
44. Cf. N. Geras, 'Rosa Luxemburg after 1905', *New Left Review*, 89 (1975) pp. 21ff.
45. R. Luxemburg, *The Russian Revolution*, ed. B. Wolfe (Ann Arbor, 1961) p. 38.
46. Ibid., pp. 69ff.
47. Cf. J.P. Nettl, *Rosa Luxemburg*, abridged edition (Oxford, 1969) pp. 444ff., and further P. Lösche, *Der Bolschewismus im Urteil der deutschen Sozialdemokratie* (Berlin, 1967) pp. 134ff. See also the reply of Lukács to Luxemburg in *History and Class Consciousness* (London, 1971) pp. 272ff.; and N. Geras's evaluation in *The Legacy of Rosa Luxemburg* (London, 1976) pp. 176ff.
48. 'What does the Spartacus League want?', in R. Luxemburg, *Selected Political Writings*, ed. D. Howard (New York, 1971) p. 376.
49. See further D. Authier, J. Barrot, *La Gauche communiste en Allemagne 1918–1921* (Paris, 1976). On German Marxism in the 1920s, see below, pp. 171ff.

Further reading

There are three good selections of Luxemburg, all with competent introductions, by Looker, Waters and Howard. There are also specialist selections on the national question by Davis, and on the Bolshevik revolution – under the misleading title of *Leninism or Marxism?* – by Wolfe. Her major work, *The Accumulation of Capital*, is available with a good introduction by Joan Robinson, as well as several minor works – *Social Reform or Revolution, The Mass Strike*, etc. – as pamphlets.

The best commentary on Luxemburg's ideas is Geras's *The Legacy of Rosa Luxemburg*. For the context, see Nettl's splendid biography, either in the two-volume original or the still substantial one-volume abridgement. Also useful are Basso's *Rosa Luxemburg: A Reappraisal*, Dunayevskaya's enthusiastic follow-up, and Bronner's *Rosa Luxemburg: A Revolutionary for Our Times*.

On the other radicals, there is a good biography of Parvus by Zeman and Scharlau, a less substantial treatment of Radek by Lerner and an even thinner account of Liebknecht by Meyer. For the abortive 1918 revolution, see the books by Mishark, Waldmann and Haffner.

Bibliography

Luxemburg

Texts

Dick Howard (ed.), *Selected Political Writings of Rosa Luxemburg* (London and New York, 1971).
R. Looker (ed.), *Rosa Luxemburg: Selected Political Writings* (London, 1972).
Horace B. Davis (ed.), *The National Question: Selected Writings by Rosa Luxemburg* (New York, 1976).
Rosa Luxemburg, *The Accumulation of Capital*, Introduction by J. Robinson (London, 1971).
—— *The Accumulation of Capital – An Anti-Critique* in Rosa Luxemburg and N. Bukharin, *Imperialism and the Accumulation of Capital*, ed. K. Tarbuck (London and New York, 1972).
—— 'The Belgian General Strike of 1902' (five articles) in *Permanent Revolution* (Journal of Workers' Fight), 1 (1973).
—— *The Mass Strike, The Political Party and the Trade Unions* (New York, 1971).
—— *The Russian Revolution and Leninism or Marxism?*, Introduction by B.D. Wolfe (Ann Arbor, 1961).
—— *Social Reform or Revolution?* (London, n.d.).
M.-A. Waters (ed.), *Rosa Luxemburg Speaks* (New York, 1970).

Commentaries

Hannah Arendt, 'Rosa Luxemburg: 1871–1919', in *Men in Dark Times* (London, 1970).
L. Basso, 'Rosa Luxemburg: The Dialectical Method', *International Socialist Journal*, 16–17 (1966).
—— *Rosa Luxemburg: A Reappraisal* (London, 1975).
Stephen Bronner, *Rosa Luxemburg: A Revolutionary for Our Times* (New York, 1987).
E.H. Carr, 'Red Rosa, 1917', in *1917: Before and After* (London, 1969).
F.L. Carsten, 'Freedom and Revolution: Rosa Luxemburg', in L. Lebedz (ed.), *Revisionism: Essays in the History of Marxist Ideas* (London, 1962).
Tony Cliff, *Rosa Luxemburg* (London, 1968).
Raya Dunayerskaya, *Rosa Luxemburg, Women's Liberation and Marx's Philosophy of Revolution* (Atlantic Highlands, 1982).
Paul Frölich, *Rosa Luxemburg: Her Life and Work* (London, 1940).
Norman Geras, *The Legacy of Rosa Luxemburg* (London, 1976).
G. Lee, 'Rosa Luxemburg and the Impact of Imperialism', *Economic Journal*, 81 (1971) 324.
George Lichtheim, 'Rosa Luxemburg', in *The Concept of Ideology and Other Essays* (New York, 1967).
George Lukács, 'The Marxism of Rosa Luxemburg', in *History and Class Consciousness* (London, 1971).
J.P. Nettl, *Rosa Luxemburg*, 2 vols (Oxford, 1966) (extensive bibliography, pp. 863–917); and abridged edition in one volume (Oxford, 1969).
E. Vollrath, 'Rosa Luxemburg's Theory of Revolution', *Social Research* 40, 1 (1973).

Other radicals

Charles B. Burdick and Ralph H. Lutz, *The Political Institutions of the German Revolution: 1918–1919* (London, 1966).
Sebastian Haffner, *Failure of a Revolution: Germany 1918–1919* (Chicago, 1986).
Warren Lerner, *Karl Radek: The Last Internationalist* (Stanford, 1970).
Richard Lowenthal, 'The Bolshevisation of the Spartacus League', *St Antony's Papers*, 9 (London, 1960).
Franz Mehring, *On Historical Materialism* (New York, 1975).
Karl W. Meyers, *Karl Liebknecht: Man Without a Country* (Washington, 1957).
John W. Mishark, *The Road to Revolution: German Marxism and World War I. 1914–1919* (Detroit, 1967).
Allan Mitchell, *Revolution in Bavaria – 1918–1919: The Eisner Regime and the Soviet Republic* (Princeton, 1966).
A.J. Ryder, *The German Revolution of 1918: A Study of German Socialism in War and Revolt* (Cambridge, 1967).
H. Schurer, 'Radek and the German Revolution', *Survey: A Journal of Soviet and East European Studies*, 53 (1964).
—— 'Alexander Helphand – Parvus: Russian Revolutionary and German Patriot', *Russian Review* (1959).
Eric Waldmann, *The Spartakist Uprising of 1919 and the Crisis of the German Socialist Movement* (Milwaukee, 1958).
Z. Zeman and W.B. Scharlau, *The Merchant of Revolution: The Life of Alexander Israel Helphand* [Parvus] (London, 1965).

4
Austro-Marxism

The term Austro-Marxism indicates a trend among Austrian socialists which began with the publication of the weighty *Marxstudien* in 1907. Austro-Marxism was not a political or a workers' organisation: it was an intellectual tendency. Its main adherents were Max Adler, Karl Renner, Otto Bauer and Rudolf Hilferding, all of whom had original minds eager to get to grips with new problems facing Marxism in fields as diverse as neo-Kantianism, marginalist economics, and the national question.

Max Adler produced by far the most sophisticated rendering of Marx from a neo-Kantian perspective. His primary emphasis was on epistemology: experience was a logical construct and thus prior to the division between spirit and matter. Adler treated Marx's methodology as, in a sense, Kantian: penetrating behind the appearances to the reality. Claiming to be following Kautsky, Adler asserted that Marxism was scientific, historical materialism, and thus nothing to do with any philosophy or *Weltanschauung*. Adler's aim was to complement historical materialism by providing it with a philosophy in the shape of neo-Kantianism. Where he differed from the German neo-Kantians such as Vorländer was in refusing to treat socialism as an ethical postulate. Marxism as such was scientific and thus nothing to do with ethics, which could itself be founded by a (Kantian) critical perception of human nature and society.[1] Although verging on idealism in philosophy, in politics Adler was in the radical wing of the Austrian party (a combination found in an even more extreme form in the Kantian Karl Liebknecht) and continued after the war to be a strong advocate of workers' councils rather than national parliaments.[2]

Karl Renner moved to the right wing of the Austrian party (the only one not to split after the war) having lost faith in the revolutionary potential of the proletariat. His chief contribution to Marxist theory was a pioneering study of the relationship of law to economics as a particular example of historical materialism. But the central contribution of Austro-Marxism lay in the political and economic works of Bauer and Hilferding. Bauer was the leading political thinker of the Austro-Marxists. In his major work on the national question[3] – obviously a question of prime concern to the inhabitants of the multinational Austro-Hungarian Empire – Bauer put much emphasis on the psychological and cultural factors in the constitution of nations and proposed a form of federation as a half-way house to national self-determination. Unlike Lenin and Rosa Luxemburg, he considered that the national community embodied values which were quite compatible with socialism. At the end of his book on the national question Bauer had a section on imperialism which, for its time was extremely original. According to Bauer, the cyclical depressions under capitalism made capitalists seek further spheres of influence in underdeveloped countries where the profit rate was higher. Cartels and banks made this process easier as they could get their investments protected by tariffs. Bauer then drew attention to the connection between monopoly capitalism and imperialism.[4] He later developed a critique of the Russian Revolution, admitting the necessity for a temporary minority dictatorship only as a defensive measure justifiable on condition of its evolving into a majoritarian democracy.[5] Bauer was a sharp critic of 'state capitalism' in the Soviet Union around 1930. His views became predominant in the so-called '2 1/2 International' founded in 1920 by the Austrian Social Democrats, the Mensheviks, and other European Labour Parties.

Bauer's remarks on imperialism were taken up at greater length in Hilferding's *Finanzkapital*, the greatest work of the Austro-Marxists, described by Kautsky as 'a veritable continuation of the second and third volumes of *Capital*'.[6] Hilferding had already gained prominence by offering, in his reply to Böhm-Bawerk's attack on Marx, the clearest definition of the distinction between the marginalist and the Marxist approach to economics.[7] He began with an analysis of the growing control of credit institutions over industry leading to a growing corporate ownership. This was enhanced by the necessity of capital-intensive industries to protect themselves against the falling rate of profit. There was a narrowing of the number of decision-makers in society, more conscious control and planning, and increasing control of cartels and trusts by banks: 'an ever-increasing part of the industrial capital belongs no longer to the industrialists who employ it. They only dispose of capital thanks to the banks who remain its owner. On the other hand, the bank must immobilise an ever greater part of its capital in industry. Thus the bank becomes an industrial capitalist on an ever greater scale. Bank capital, that is, capital in the form of money, which is in reality thus transformed into industrial capital – that is what I call finance capital.'[8]

Hilferding (together with Tugan-Baranowsky and the contemporary American Marxist Robert Brenner) saw competition as the Achilles heel of capitalism. In his interpretation of Marx's reproduction schema, crises occurred because the two sectors of the economy which produced respectively the means of production and the means of consumption were not coordinated. In the (in his view impossible) event of such a coordination, an 'organised capitalism' could continue to expand indefinitely. But the most capitalism could achieve was a generalised cartel to attempt to regulate crisis tendencies. Once internal competition had been eliminated, there was pressure for tariff protection against external competition in order to be able to enforce a monopolistic price policy. The consequence was a strong state power thoroughly opposed to classical liberal principles. In passages which have not lost their insight and power over the decades, Hilferding wrote:

> Finance capital does not aim at freedom but at domination; it has no feeling for the independence of the individual capitalist, but requires his subordination; it avoids the anarchy of competition and aims at organisation – though, of course, only in order to be able to take up competition again at an even higher level. But in order to achieve this, in order to maintain and increase its domination, it needs the State whose function it is to guarantee it the internal market through its customs and tariff policies and make easier the conquest of external markets. It needs a politically powerful State which in its trade policies is not obliged to take account of the opposed interest of other States. Finally, it needs a strong State which can enforce its financial interests abroad, and use its political power in order to enforce on smaller States suitable treaties of supply trade, a State which can intervene everywhere in the world in order to be able to transform the whole world into a sphere for the implantation of its finance capital. Finance capital needs a State which is strong in order to conduct a policy of expansion and incorporate new colonies in its sphere of influence.[9]

The increasingly powerful and aggressive nature of the capitalist states, supported by the ideologies of nationalism, racialism and militarism, led to heightened international tension through growing competition to monopolise markets and sources of raw materials. There was also an increase in the practice of dumping abroad goods unsaleable at home at the 'monopolistic' high prices and a tendency to export capital by founding businesses abroad. This led to economic warfare between nations and armed expansion into underdeveloped regions to enlarge the potential market, in a process in which freedom, democracy and equality were the first casualties:

> Finance capital has no concern for the harmony of capitalist interests: it knows that the competitive struggle is turning more and more into a struggle for political power. As the ideal of peace grows pale, in the place of the idea of humanity comes the ideal of the greatness and power of the State ... Although founded on economics, finance capital is ideologically justified through the extraordinary distortion of the idea of a nation, which no longer recognises the right of every nation to political self-determination and independence and which is no longer the expression, at the national dimension, of the democratic belief in the equality of everything that is human. Rather the economic predominance of monopoly is reflected in the predominant position which one's own nation must acquire. This nation appears as predestined before all others. Because the subjugation of foreign nations occurs by force, and thus apparently in a very natural manner, the dominant nation appears to owe this domination to its particular natural qualities, thus to its racial qualities. This racial ideology thus constitutes a justification, dressed up as science, for the striving after power of finance capital which attempts to prove the scientific determination and necessity of its operations. In the place of the democratic ideal of equality comes an ideal of oligarchical domination.[10]

Finally, the whole process tended to end in armed conflict: 'in the violent conflict of hostile interests the dictatorship of the magnates of capital finally turns into the dictatorship of the proletariat'.[11] Thus the capitalist system would not collapse for strictly economic reasons but because of the revolutionary prospect opened up by imperialist wars.

Hilferding was criticised for attributing too great an importance to finance capital, whose dominant role was of short duration; and also for concentrating on the sphere of circulation rather than that of production (whence his view of crisis as simply the effect of disproportionality between different spheres of production). But in general, Hilferding was the first to give a serious economic analysis of imperialism which was the foundation for Lenin's work in this area. As a study of monopoly and its imperialist consequences, Hilferding's book was the most impressive work on economics produced by any thinker of the Second International.

Notes

1. See further T.B. Bottomore's Introduction to the collection entitled *Austro-Marxism* (Oxford, 1978) pp. 11ff.
2. See particularly his *Staatsauffassung des Marxismus* (Berlin, 1922) and below, p. 188.
3. O. Bauer. *Die Nationalitätenfrage und die Sozialdemokratie* (Vienna, 1907).
4. See further G. Lichtheim, *Marxism* (New York and London, 1964) pp. 307f.
5. See Y. Bourdet (ed.), *Otto Bauer et la Révolution* (Paris, 1968).
6. K. Kautsky, 'Finanzkapital und Krisen', *Die Neue Zeit*, vol. 29, p. 883.
7. Böhm-Bawerk's work and Hilferding's reply have been republished with an Introduction by P. Sweezy (New York and London, 1975).
8. R. Hilferding, *Das Finanzkapital*, ed. E. März (Frankfurt, 1968) vol. 2, p. 309.
9. Ibid., pp. 456f.
10. Ibid., pp. 457f.
11. Ibid., p. 507.

Further reading

Literature in English on the Austro-Marxists is sparse. See, nevertheless, the articles by Leser and Croan, Chapter 12 of the second volume of Kolakowski's *Main Currents of Marxism*, and, above all, the selection *Austro-Marxism* and its Introduction by Bottomore; also the first volume of Howard and King's *A History of Marxian Economics*, Chapters 5 and 6. Works by Böhm-Bawerk and Renner have been translated into English, both with introductions. An English translation of *Finanzkapital* is available, and there are good studies of Hilferding by Smaldone and by Wagener.

Bibliography

Austro-Marxism, texts selected and edited by T. Bottomore and P. Goode (Oxford, 1978).

E. Böhm-Bawerk, *Karl Marx and the Close of his System*, ed. P. Sweezy (New York, 1949).

M. Croan, 'Prospects for the Soviet Dictatorship: Otto Bauer', in *Revisionism*, ed. L. Labedz (London, 1972).

Rudolf Hilferding, *Finance Capital* (London, 1980).

M.C. Howard and J.E. King, *A History of Marxian Economics*, vol. 1, *1883–1929* (Princeton, 1989).

L. Kolakowski, *Main Currents of Marxism* (Oxford, 1978) vol. 2, ch. 12.

N. Leser, 'Austro-Marxism: A Reappraisal', in *The Left-Wing Intellectuals between the Wars 1919–1939*, ed. W. Laqueur and G. Mosse (New York, 1966).

K. Renner, *The Institutions of Private Law and their Social Functions*, ed. G. Kahn-Freund, 2nd edn (London, 1976).

W. Smaldone, *Rudolf Hilferding: The Tragedy of a German Social Democrat* (Dekalb, 1998).

P. Wagener, *Rudolph Hilferding: The Theory and Politics of Democratic Socialism* (Atlantic Highlands, 1996).

Part Two
Russian Marxism

People who boast that they made a revolution always see the day after that they had no idea what they were doing, that the revolution *made* does not in the least resemble the one they would like to make. That is what Hegel calls the irony of history, an irony which few historical personalities escape.

Engels to Vera Sassoulitch

5
Origins

Marx, Engels and Plekhanov

At first sight, Russia would not seem the most promising land for revolution. In the mid-nineteenth century Russia had been a by-word for reaction and was still basically medieval; and even after the emancipation of the serfs in 1861, Russia continued to be an underdeveloped agrarian society. Certain sections of Russia society nevertheless enjoyed a lively intellectual life much influenced by developments in Western Europe, which were viewed as a model for Russian progress. But the stubborn conservatism of the government made these intellectual movements invariably oppositional. The autocratic, centralised nature of the state and the lack of industrial development (and thus of any concomitant bourgeois class) meant that the revolutionary movement in Russia tended to be composed exclusively of intellectuals who relied more on moral fervour and rhetoric than on systematic, critical, detailed analysis.

The most radical of these revolutionary movements was that known as Populism. As the name suggests, their most powerful attachment was to the people of Russia and the people's power to regenerate the nation. The Populists were eclectic in drawing on Western philosophy: Hegel, materialist trends, and various forms of socialism were all grist to their mill. Central to their concern was the defence of the Russian peasant commune, firstly against the capitalism so vigorously criticised by Western Europe socialists, and secondly as a basis for a socialist society in Russia. When it came to tactics, there were two schools of Populist thought: those who believe in the self-emancipation of the people and tried to achieve this by peaceful propaganda, and those who believed in the necessity of attacking the autocracy directly through small groups of terrorists. When the movement to propagandise among the peasantry in the mid-1870s had failed, a more close-knit organisation – *Zemlya y Volya* (Land and Liberty) – was formed but soon split into those favouring agrarian reform, who called themselves *Chernyi Peredel* (General Redivision), and those who put the accent on terrorist activity – *Narodnaya Volya* (People's Will). The latter achieved one of its aims in the assassination of the Tsar in 1881 but found that this in itself accomplished nothing except the decimation of the group.

The 1880s saw the first appearance, in any force, of Marxist ideas on the Russian scene, ideas that were evolved in the context of constant debate with the Populists. Marx's thought was known in Russia relatively early: his *Poverty of Philosophy* had been translated into Russian, Tkatchev – one of the leading Populist revolutionaries – had read Marx in the 1860s, and the Russian translation of *Capital* in 1872 was the first to appear in any foreign language. But the Populists' reading of Marx was very partial: they accepted (by and large) his sociological analysis and critique of bourgeois society, but not his materialist outlook or belief in proletarian revolution. For them, Marx's politics had no direct application to Russia – the grounds on which, after all, the Russian censor had originally allowed *Capital* to be published.

The views of Marx and Engels themselves on Russia were strikingly ambivalent. They had studied Russian development in some depth. The central question was the fate of the peasant commune. Writing in 1875 against Tkatchev, Engels said:

> It is clear that communal ownership in Russia is long past its flourishing period and to all appearances is moving towards its dissolution. Nevertheless, the possibility undeniably exists of transforming this social form into a higher one ... This, however, can happen only if, before the complete breakup of communal ownership, a proletarian revolution is successfully carried out in Western Europe.[1]

In the early 1870s Engels had seen the Russian Revolutionaries as in some way implicated with Bakunin, but by the late 1870s, with the growth of the revolutionary movement and the foundation of *Zemlya y Volya*, Marx became more sympathetic to the Populists. In his letter to Mikhailovsky of 1877, Marx suspended his judgement on Chernyshevsky's view that a rural commune could serve as a basis for Communism and declared only: 'if Russia continues to pursue the path she has followed since 1861, she will lose the finest chance ever offered by history to a people and undergo all the fatal vicissitudes of a capitalist regime'.[2] Pressed again on this point in 1881 by Vera Sassoulitch, Marx replied:

> The analysis given in *Capital* assigns no reasons for or against the vitality of the rural community, but the special research into this subject which I conducted, the materials for which I obtained from original sources, has convinced me that this community is the mainspring of Russia's social regeneration, but in order that it might function as such one would first have to eliminate the deleterious influences which assail if from every quarter and then to ensure conditions normal to spontaneous development.[3]

Thus paradoxically, Marx was moving nearer to the Populists just at the time when Plekhanov and his followers in Geneva were establishing a Marxist anti-Populist position.[4] In 1882 Marx and Engels declared in the preface to the Russian edition of the *Communist Manifesto* that: 'if the Russian Revolution becomes a signal for a proletarian Revolution in the West, so that both complement each other, the present Russian common ownership of land may serve as the starting point for a Communist development'.[5] By 1894, however, Engels believed that the development of capitalism in Russia had destroyed the revolutionary possibilities of the Commune: a revolution in Russia would only 'hasten the victory of the modern industrial proletariat, without which contemporary Russia cannot achieve a socialist transformation arising either out of the village community or out of capitalism'.[6]

But this ambivalence on the part of Marx and Engels (the evidence for which was largely unpublished at the time)[7] failed to affect the first Russian Marxists. Although Marxism as an active force inside Russia only emerged with the reawakening of social and political activity following the disastrous famine of 1890, a cohesive group of Russian Marxists had been established in Geneva as early as 1883. Calling itself the *Group for the Emancipation of Labour*, they comprised only three members: Gregory Plekhanov, Pavel Axelrod and Vera Sassoulitch. Plekhanov was the son of an army officer and had been an active Populist for several years before accepting Marxism in the early 1880s. He was not only the first Russian completely to embrace Marxism: he was also the undisputed intellectual leader of the Russian Marxists until the turn of the century and educator of a whole generation of revolutionaries.

For Plekhanov, in the opening words of his last substantial publication, 'Marxism is a complete theoretical system'.[8] He possessed both

a cool, logical, systematic mind which set great store by doctrinal orthodoxy and, at the same time, a personal aloofness symbolised by his
remaining outside Russia for the four decades preceding 1917.
Plekhanov first reached a wide audience with his *Monist View of History*,
published in Russia under a pseudonym in 1884. It was the first systematic exposition of historical materialism in Russia and also established
Plekhanov's reputation in the West – a reputation which he enhanced
by offering the first detailed criticism of Bernstein's revisionist views.
The *Monist View* presented Marxism as the inheritor of all the positive
tendencies inherent in French eighteenth-century materialism, Utopian
socialism and German idealism. In this and other subsequent works, he
opposed his monist view to the idea of mutually interacting 'factors'.
Plekhanov was distinctive in attributing a considerable role to purely
geographical influences on historical development,[9] and in applying
historical materialism to the study of aesthetics. Along with Mehring
and Lafargue, Plekhanov elaborated the view that art depended on class
values and thus that the ultimate criterion of judgement was the content and not the form.

But these views did little more than popularise Engels: Plekhanov's
most important contribution was the laying down of an orthodox
Marxist perspective for the development of the revolution in Russia.
As the most 'Westernising' of the Russian Marxists, Plekhanov saw no
fundamental difference between Russia and the West. His two lengthy
pamphlets – *Socialism and the Political Struggle* and *Our Differences* – written
immediately after his conversation to Marxism, established (in spite of
their cool reception by Engels)[10] the orthodox doctrine in this domain
until the end of the century. Plekhanov's views may be summarised in
three basic points:

Firstly, Russia was in some sense already a capitalist country and
becoming more so. The emancipation of the serfs had meant the introduction of a commodity market and wage-labour. Drawing on the
seventh chapter of *Capital* Volume One, Plekhanov declared Russia to
be already in the system of manufacturing capitalism.

Secondly, this demonstrated that, as far as political tactics were concerned, Russia was about to enter the stage of factory production and the
proletariat was the oppositional class of the future. The proletariat
would become the leader in the democratic revolution because it had
emerged as a political opposition *before* the bourgeoisie and had a superior
organisation. The experience of Western Europe – and particularly
Germany in 1848 – had demonstrated the unreliability of the bourgeoisie
as a revolutionary class.

Thirdly, their appreciation of the above two points conferred upon the radical intelligentsia the right and duty of leading the proletariat in a political party which would fight for (a) the overthrow of the autocracy and the establishment of a liberal democracy, and (b) the subsequent seizure of power by the proletariat in a dictatorship. The idea that the first stage would be 'under proletarian hegemony' was elaborated by Plekhanov's colleague Axelrod.[11]

The founding of the RSDLP

The 1880s was a period of stagnation for Marxism in Russia. It was the famine of 1891 which eventually galvanised the Marxist circles there and impelled them towards less theoretical activity. Plekhanov himself was one of the first to suggest the transition from broad propaganda to more direct agitation. In this respect the lead was set by the Marxists in Vilna, which was unique in having a large population of better-organised Jewish workers.[12] Their principal document was the brochure *On Agitation*, which put more emphasis on purely economic aims – albeit as the starting-point to raise working-class consciousness to a political level – and thus tended to minimise the importance of political literature. The ideas of the Vilna group proved influential among the oppositional groups which, usually of Populist origin, existed all over central European Russia. They included the group in St Petersburg which from 1895 onwards agitated in local factories on specific issues and called itself the Union of Struggle for the Emancipation of the Working Class. Their ideas were given force by the successful St Petersburg textile strike in 1896.[13]

But the Group for the Emancipation of Labour found it difficult to accommodate itself to these new developments. Plekhanov wished to devote himself to broad theoretical problems, not day-to-day worker agitation. Axelrod took on most of this work, but there was at best an uneasy co-existence between the two groups in the Union of Russian Social Democrats Abroad founded in 1895. There were also difficulties within the intelligentsia groups inside Russia with pressure from certain workers to join them and break down the rigid worker/intellectual separation that had existed hitherto – a view fostered by the very success of the strikes of the mid-1890s. The old stagers felt increasingly that the insistence on economic objectives was to the detriment of a clear political perspective and Axelrod subjected 'Economism' to an extended critique in 1897.[14] Nevertheless the infant Russian Social Democratic Labour Party was founded in Minsk in March 1898.

But all was not plain sailing: the Union Abroad fell into the control of younger revolutionaries who, while not disagreeing with Plekhanov, resented his claim to control; and inside Russia the 'Economists', who wished to separate the workers' struggle from the struggle for political emancipation, continued to enjoy success. By 1900, Plekhanov, shocked by Kautsky's tolerant attitude to Bernstein, urged that a definitive break be made with the Economists. There were two basic trends by this time in Russia: firstly there were the clear Economists led by Kuskova and Prokopovitch; secondly, Marxist intellectuals such as Tugan-Baranovsky and Struve who sympathised with Bernstein but supported anti-Tsarist political action and were sometimes known as Legal Marxists. In opposition to both these groups, Plekhanov complained that the Economists denied the necessity to organise for political ends. He wished to maintain the independence of the Party from the working class and preserve the level of its consciousness. The Party, according to Plekhanov, should be *ahead* of the proletariat and the orthodox theoreticians should control the Party – an idea that was to be developed with even greater force by Lenin.

Lenin was born in Samara in 1870. Like almost all other Russian Marxists, he had initially been attracted by Populist ideas (his elder brother was executed in 1882 for participating in a Populist attempt to assassinate the Tsar) but had become a full Marxist by the time of his three-year stay in St Petersburg during the early 1890s.[15] There he participated in the Union, attacking the ideas of *On Agitation*, and emerged as one of the most important Marxist leaders. These experiences led Lenin to a close study of organisational tactics and of the developmental view of working-class consciousness from industrial struggles to political struggles. In 1895 he produced his first major work, entitled *What the Friends of the People Are*, the fruit of his previous arguments with the Populists. Its basic ideas were fully in line with Russian Marxist orthodoxy. Lenin argued, firstly, that it was necessary to combat the Populists (the 'Friends of the People') when they tried to speak for socialism, though to accept them as subordinate allies in so far as they struggled against the autocracy and for a radical democratic programme. Secondly, he claimed that the peasantry were more and more open to the ideas of the Russian Marxists as they were increasingly being split into a rural proletariat and a rural bourgeoisie. Thirdly, he insisted on the role of the proletariat as 'the sole and natural representative of Russia's entire working and exploited population. Natural because the exploitation of the working people in Russia *is everywhere capitalist in nature* – but the exploitation of the mass of producers is on a small scale, scattered and underdeveloped, while the exploitation of the factory proletariat is on a large scale, socialised and concentrated'.[16] Lenin differed from his colleagues here only in having a slightly more optimist view of the vanguard role of the proletariat and the revolutionary nature of the peasantry than, for example, Plekhanov.

In 1896 Lenin was arrested and went into exile. Because he held that the development of working-class consciousness and of the Social Democratic Party went hand in hand with the economic development of Russia, he studied this subject in great detail in his exile and produced a much underrated work, *The Development of Capitalism in Russia*. This book was a clearly documented study of the emergence of capitalism out of feudalism in Russia, filling out some of the details that Marx would no doubt have put in his unfinished Volume Three of *Capital*. In opposition to the Populists, who argued that capitalist development was impossible in Russia, because wages were too low to allow the home market to expand, Lenin argued that Russia was already capitalist. The stage of usury capital and merchant capital outlined by Marx had already been superseded in some places by manufacturing capital – capital applied directly to the productive system – and the next stage of industrial capital was already on the horizon. From this detailed analysis Lenin concluded that the proletariat held a unique position in that they were the only class fully to appreciate and be able to articulate the exploitation of all Russian labourers, including the artisans and rural proletariat. *The Development of Capitalism in Russia* gave the economic evidence for the conclusion that he had already arrived at in *What the Friends of the People Are*: with the factory proletariat,

> exploitation is fully developed and emerges in its pure form, without any confusing details. The worker cannot fail to see that he is oppressed by *capital*, that his struggle has to be waged against the bourgeois *class* ... That is why the factory worker is none other than the foremost representative of the entire exploited population.[17]

This perspective – with its idea of the proletariat leading the population in the revolutionary struggle – governed Lenin's political thinking up to 1914.

On his return from his Siberian exile in early 1900 Lenin, together with his former colleagues in the St Petersburg Union Martov and Potresov, gave Plekhanov his support in the struggle to establish a clear orthodox line. But, for Lenin, the moment for this would only be opportune when the orthodox had gathered their strength, and he thought that this would best be attained through a journal – *Iskra* – which would not only establish an orthodox line but, through its distribution network, create the party organisation that had so long been lacking. When *Iskra*, largely due to Lenin's driving force, had firmly established itself inside Russia, he broke with the Union Abroad, who were complaining of the *Iskra* committee's authoritarian and separatist attitudes over the mass movement of the working class. This split foreshadowed that two years later between Bolsheviks and Mensheviks. The principles of the *Iskra* organisation were summed up in Lenin's long pamphlet *What is to be Done?*[18]

The Bolshevik–Menshevik split

There had been disputes among the *Iskra* editorial board over a programme for the Russian Social Democratic Labour Party. This involved a disagreement over whether capitalism was yet the dominant mode of production in Russia (and therefore over the Party's attitude to the Liberals), over future relationships with the peasantry, in whose support for proletarian aims Lenin had far less confidence than Plekhanov, and also over the relationship of the Party to the proletariat.[19] Nevertheless, on the eve of the Congress of July 1903, the leadership appeared united. The Congress was the crowning success of *Iskra's* long struggle to build an all-Russian Social Democratic Party. The Congress began well with an overwhelming condemnation of the 'Economists' and a rejection of the Federalist principle advocated by the separately organised Jewish *Bund*. But with the debate on the Party's rules this unanimity disappeared. Lenin and Martov proposed different drafts of Article 1. Lenin's read that a Party member was one 'who accepts the Party's programme and supports the Party both financially and by personal participation in one of its organisations';[20] whereas Martov preferred to say that a member 'accepts the Party's programme and supports the Party both financially and by regular work under the control and direction of one of the Party organisations'.[21] Lenin maintained that his early draft 'narrows this concept while Martov's expands it, for (to use Martov's own correct expression) what distinguishes his concept is its "elasticity". And in the period of party life that we are now passing through it is just the "elasticity" that undoubtedly opens the door to all elements of confusion, vacillation, and opportunism'.[22] Martov later claimed that Lenin's draft

> eliminated not only numerous intellectuals who sympathised with the Party and rendered it assistance while finding themselves

incapable of joining an illegal organisation, but also a large part of social democratic workers who constituted a link between the Party and the masses but who for reasons of expediency refused to join its ranks.[23]

Although the difference in wording seems almost insignificant it was indicative of a wide gulf between the two sides. To compensate for his defeat on this issue (Martov's draft obtained a small majority) Lenin was all the keener to have a small Central Committee and a reduced editorial board for *Iskra* – only three members for each. This involved the retirement of the 'old guard' of Sassoulitch, Axelrod and Potresov. Although this could be justified in terms of efficiency (the three had never contributed much to the running of the paper), it caused a lot of ill-feeling. Lenin was able to get his way, however, when the *Bund* delegates walked out of the Congress and his own followers were thus in the majority – Bolsheviks as opposed to the followers of Martov, who came to be known as 'Minoritarians' or Mensheviks.

The dispute at the beginning undoubtedly owed a lot to personalities and Martov wrote to Karl Kautsky that the dispute was personal rather than one of principle. Almost a year later Axelrod admitted that there were 'still no clearly defined differences concerning either principles or tactics. Even concerning the question of organisation, the divergences are not at the level of principle, but on the area of utilisation, in the application of the organisational principle that we all accept.'[24] Indeed, at the Fourth Party Congress, which temporarily united the Bolsheviks and the Mensheviks, Lenin's draft was accepted without opposition. Organisationally the Mensheviks were not noticeably more democratic than the Bolsheviks, and rather less so in 1905/6 when Lenin was revising the structure set out in *What is to be Done?* And the Mensheviks were just as revolutionary as the Bolsheviks in the 1905 revolution. It was after 1905 that differences began to emerge clearly, with the Mensheviks favouring a closer alliance with the radical Liberals and distrusting the peasantry, while the Bolsheviks tended to adopt the opposite view. On both these scores Lenin's violent polemic against the Mensheviks for abandoning the old orthodox view of 'proletarian hegemony in the democratic revolution' had a certain justification. His charge, however, of wishing to 'liquidate' the Party was for the most part ungrounded: the Mensheviks merely wished to build up a mass party by engaging in legal (as well as illegal) activities – a policy which the Bolsheviks themselves followed after 1912.

Notes

1. K. Marx, F. Engels, *Basic Writings on Politics and Philosophy*, ed. L. Feuer (New York, 1959) p. 473.
2. K. Marx, F. Engels, *Selected Correspondence* (Moscow, 1965) p. 312.
3. K. Marx, *Selected Writings*, ed. D. McLellan (Oxford and New York, 2000) pp. 576ff.
4. Cf. Marx's tart remarks on the Geneva group as opposed to the Populist activists in *Selected Correspondence*, p. 333.
5. K. Marx, *Selected Writings*, ed. D. McLellan, p. 584.
6. F. Engels, *MEW*, vol. 22, p. 435.
7. Marx's reply to Vera Sassoulitch and his lengthy drafts were not published until 1924 and 1926 respectively.
8. G. Plekhanov, *Fundamental Problems of Marxism* (London, 1937) p. 1.
9. See, for example, section 6 of *Fundamental Problems*.
10. Cf. Engels to Sassoulitch, 23 Apr. 1885, in Marx-Engels, *Selected Correspondence* (Moscow, 1965) pp. 383ff.
11. Cf. A. Ascher, *Pavel Axelrod and the Development of Menshevism* (Cambridge, Mass., 1972) pp. 134ff.
12. See especially A. Patkin, *The Origins of the Russian-Jewish Labour Movement* (London and Melbourne, 1947) pp. 101ff.
13. On the Union, see R. Pipes, *Social Democracy and the St Petersburg Labour Movement 1885–1897* (Cambridge, Mass., 1963), and the criticism of Pipes in A. Wildman, *The Making of a Workers' Revolution* (Chicago, 1967) pp. 73ff.
14. 'Economism' is a very vague term: see the discussion in J. Keep, *The Rise of Social Democracy in Russia* (Oxford, 1963) pp. 58ff.
15. For a rebuttal of the view that elements of Populist or Jacobin thinking had a lasting effect on Lenin's thought, see N. Harding, 'Lenin's Early Writings – the Problem of Context', *Political Studies*. Dec. 1975.
16. V. Lenin, *What the Friends of the People Are, Collected Works*, vol. 1, p. 299.
17. V. Lenin, *The Development of Capitalism in Russia, Collected Works*, vol. 1, p. 299.
18. See below, pp. 92ff.
19. See, in particular, J. Frankel's Introduction to *Vladimir Akimov on the Dilemmas of Russian Marxism* (Cambridge, 1969) pp. 60ff.
20. V. Lenin, 'Draft Rules of the RSDLP', *Collected Works*, vol. 6, p. 474.
21. Quoted in V. Lenin, 'Account of the Second Congress of the RSDLP', *Collected Works*, vol. 7, p. 27.
22. V. Lenin, 'Speech on Party Rules', *Collected Works*, vol. 6, p. 500.
23. L. Martov, *Geschichte der russischen Sozialdemokratie* (Berlin, 1925) p. 84.
24. Axelrod to Kautsky, 22 May 1904, quoted in C. Weill, *Marxistes russes et Socialdemocratie allemande* (Paris, 1977) p. 131.

Further reading

Soviet Union (general)

Although consistently anti-Bolshevik, Schapiro's *The Communist Party of the Soviet Union* contains much well-researched material. McAuley's

Politics and the Soviet Union is a good introduction, though its bias is towards the contemporary and the sociological. Nettl's *The Soviet Achievement* is a readable short overview. Carr's *History* is monumental. More recently, see Malia's *History*, Lewin's interestingly idiosyncratic Overview, and the literature on the nature of the Soviet socio-economic formation detailed on pp. 363 f. below. Sandle provides a reliable short introduction.

Origins of Bolshevism and Menshevism

There are general books by Haimson and, better, by the Menshevik Dan. Venturi is excellent on the Populist background. Mendel and Kindersley deal with Legal Marxism. Frankel's introduction to Akimov sheds a lot of light on Economism; Pipes gives the St Petersburg background; and Patkin examines the role of the Jewish *Bund*. Keep's *The Rise of Social Democracy in Russia* is the basic text. Best of all is Wildman's *The Making of a Workers' Revolution*. See also Bergman's biography of Zasulich, and Burbank's study of the intelligentsia.

Plekhanov's early works can be found in Volume One of his *Selected Philosophical Works*. His most important books – *Development of the Marxist View of History* and *Fundamental Problems of Marxism* – are available in English. A *Selected Philosophical Works* is currently being issued. Baron's work is the main commentary. See also Walicki's *Marxism and the Leap to the Kingdom of Freedom*, Chapter 3, and White's *Karl Marx and the Origins of Dialectical Materialism*, Chapters 7 and 8.

The best short survey of the Mensheviks is Ascher's collection *The Mensheviks in the Russian Revolution*, with an excellent introduction. Ascher had produced a splendidly detailed biography of Axelrod; and Getzler a workmanlike study of Martov. Harding's collection of *Key Documents* is very useful.

Bibliography

Soviet Union (general)

J. Arnason, *The Future that Failed: Origins and Destinies of the Soviet Model* (London, 1993).

Alexander Baykov, *The Development of the Soviet Economic State* (New York, 1948).

Nicolas Berdyaev, *The Russian Idea* (New York, 1948).

J.M. Bochenski, *Soviet Russian Dialectical Materialism* (Dordrecht, 1963).

B. Byely, *Marxism-Leninism on War and Army* (Honolulu, 2002).

E. Carr, *A History of the Soviet Union*, 11 vols (London, 1950–74).

Maurice Cornforth, *Dialectical Materialism and Science* (London, 1949).

R. Davies, *Soviet Economic Development from Lenin to Khrushchev* (Cambridge, 1998).

Maurice Dobb, *Soviet Economic Development Since 1917*, 6th edn (New York, 1966).
Merle Fainsod, *How Russia is Ruled*, rev. edn (Cambridge, Mass., 1963).
Jerome Gilison, *The Soviet Image of Utopia* (Baltimore, 1975).
Loren R. Graham, *Science and Philosophy in the Soviet Union* (New York, 1966).
John Hazard, *The Soviet System of Government*, 3rd edn (Chicago, 1965).
History of the Communist Party of the Soviet Union [Bolsheviks] (Moscow, 1943).
R. Hudelson, *The Rise and Fall of Communism* (Boulder, 1993).
David Joravsky, *Soviet Marxism and Natural Science* (London, 1961).
John Keep (ed.), *Contemporary History in the Soviet Mirror* (London, 1964).
D. Lane, *State and Politics in the USSR* (Oxford, 1985).
M. Lewin, *The Soviet Century*, ed. G. Elliot (London, 2005).
M. Malia, *A History of Socialism in Russia 1917–1991* (New York, 1994).
Ernest Mandel, 'On the Nature of the Soviet State', *New Left Review*, 108 (1978).
Mary McAuley, *Politics and the Soviet Union* (London, 1977).
P.E. Mosley, *The Kremlin and World Politics* (New York, 1960).
J.P. Nettl, *The Soviet Achievement* (London, 1967).
Martin Nicolaus, *Restoration of Capitalism in the USSR* (Chicago, 1975).
Alec Nove, *An Economic History of the USSR* (London, 1969).
Alexander Philipov, *Logic and Dialectic in the Soviet Union* (New York, 1952).
Myron Rush, *Political Succession in the USSR* (New York, 1965).
M. Sandle, *A Short History of Soviet Socialism* (London, 1999).
Leonard Schapiro, *The Communist Party of the Soviet Union*, 2nd edn (London, 1970).
Howard J. Scherman, *The Soviet Economy* (New York, 1969).
Derek Scott, *Russian Political Institutions* (London, 1965).
A Short History of the Communist Party of the Soviet Union (Moscow, 1970).
John Somerville, *Soviet Philosophy: A Study of Theory and Practice* (New York, 1946).
Rudolf L. Tökes (ed.), *Dissent in the USSR: Politics, Ideology and People* (Baltimore, 1977).
Robert C. Tucker, *The Soviet Political Mind* (New York, 1963).
Gustav Wetter, *Dialectical Materialism: A Historical and Systematic Survey of Philosophy in the Soviet Union* (London, 1958).
P.J.D. Wiles, *The Political Economy of Communism* (Oxford, 1962).
Karl Wittfogel, 'The Marxist View of Russian Society and Revolution', *World Politics*, xii (1960).

Origins of Russian Marxism

N. Berdyaev, *The Origins of Russian Communism* (London, 1937).
Jay Bergman, *Vera Zasulich: A Biography* (Stanford, 1983).
J. Burbank, *Intelligentsia and Revolution* (Oxford, 1986).
Theodore Dan, *The Origins of Bolshevism* (New York, 1964).
David Footman, *Red Prelude: A Life of A.I. Zhelyabov*, 2nd edn (London, 1968).
Jonathan Frankel, *Vladimir Akimov on the Dilemmas of Russian Marxism: 1885–1903* (Cambridge, 1969).
Shmuel Galai, *The Liberation Movement in Russia: 1900–1905* (Cambridge, 1973).
L.H. Haimson, *The Russian Marxists and the Origins of Bolshevism* (Cambridge, Mass., 1955).
J.L.H. Keep, *The Rise of Social Democracy in Russia* (Oxford, 1963).

Richard Kindersley, *The First Russian Revisionists: A Study of 'Legal Marxism' in Russia* (Oxford, 1962).

David Lane, *The Roots of Russian Communism: A Social and Historical Study of Russian Social Democracy, 1898–1907* (Assen, 1969).

A.P. Mendel, *Dilemmas of Progress in Tsarist Russia: Legal Marxism and Legal Populism* (Cambridge, Mass., 1961).

A.L. Patkin, *The Origins of the Russian-Jewish Labour Movement* (London and Melbourne, 1947).

Richard Pipes, *Social Democracy and the St Petersburg Labour Movement: 1885–1897* (Cambridge, Mass., 1963).

L.B. Schapiro, 'The Role of the Jews in the Russian Revolutionary Movement', *Slavonic and East European Review*, 4 (1961).

J. Schneiderman, *Sergei Zubatov and Revolutionary Marxism: The Struggle for the Working Class in Tsarist Russia* (Ithaca, New York, 1977).

S.V. Utechin, *Russian Political Thought: A Concise History* (London, 1963).

Franco Venturi, *Roots of Revolution: A History of the Populist and Socialist Movements in Nineteenth Century Russia*, Introduction by I. Berlin (London, 1960).

Allen K. Wildman, *The Making of a Workers' Revolution: Russian Social Democracy – 1891–1903* (Chicago, 1967).

Plekhanov: texts

G.V. Plekhanov, *Anarchism and Socialism* (London, 1906).

—— *In Defense of Materialism: The Development of The Monist View of History* (London, 1947).

—— *Fundamental Problems of Marxism* (London, 1937).

—— *Materialismus Militans: Reply to Mr. Bogdanov* (London, 1973).

—— *The Materialist Conception of History* (London, 1940).

—— *The Role of the Individual in History* (London, 1940).

—— *Selected Philosophical Works*, 5 vols (London and New York, 1978–80).

Plekhanov: commentaries

Samuel H. Baron, 'Between Marx and Lenin: George Plekhanov', in L. Labedz (ed.), *Revisionism Essays on the History of Marxist Ideas* (London, 1962).

—— 'Plekhanov and the Revolution of 1905', in J.S. Curtiss (ed.), *Essays in Russian and Soviet History* (Leiden, 1963).

—— *Plekhanov: The Father of Russian Marxism* (London, 1963).

Andrej Walicki, *Marxism and the Leap to the Kingdom of Freedom* (Stanford, 1995) ch. 3.

James White, *Karl Marx and the Origins of Dialectical Materialism* (London, 1996) chs 7 and 8.

Mensheviks

Abraham Ascher, 'Axelrod and Kautsky', *Slavic Review*, XXVI (1967).

—— *The Mensheviks in the Russian Revolution* (London, 1976).

—— *Pavel Axelrod and the Development of Menshevism* (Cambridge, Mass., 1972).

Anna Bourguina, *Russian Social Democracy: The Menshevik Movement. A Bibliography* (Stanford, 1968).

Israel Getzler, *Martov: A Political Biography of a Russian Social Democrat* (Melbourne, 1967).
—— 'The Mensheviks', *Problems of Communism* xvi (1967).
Leopold Haimson (ed.), *The Mensheviks: From the Revolution of 1917 to the Second World War* (Chicago, 1974).
N. Harding (ed.), *Marxism in Russia: Key Documents 1879–1906* (Cambridge, 1983).
Geoffrey A. Hosking, *The Russian Constitutional Experiment: Government and Duma, 1907–1914* (Cambridge, 1973).
J.L.H. Keep, 'Russian Social Democracy and the First State Duma', *Slavonic and East European Review*, 34 (1955).
Maureen Perrie, *The Agrarian Policy of the Russian Socialist-Revolutionary Party from its Origins through the Revolution of 1905–1907* (Cambridge, 1976).

6
Trotsky

One of Lenin's chief opponents in 1903 was Trotsky. Born in 1879 into a family of fairly prosperous Jewish farmers, Trotsky had early developed an enthusiasm for revolution and a talent for journalism. He had been a member of the *Iskra* group and a close collaborator of Lenin but after 1904 evolved positions that were independent of both the Bolsheviks and of the Mensheviks. Trotsky's optimism about mass working-class consciousness and activity led him to reject Lenin's emphasis on the organisation of a revolutionary vanguard party. Indeed, Trotsky was as virulent in his opposition to Lenin's views on the Party as any Menshevik. In his *Report of the Siberian Delegation on the Second Congress*, Trotsky castigated Lenin who 'with the talent and energy characteristic of him, assumed the role of the party's disorganiser'.[1] Trotsky wanted a party whose organisation was adapted to the working-class movement and which allowed the maximum participation of the workers. In his pamphlet *Our Political Tasks* (1904) – which has been called 'the most cogent analysis of the Bolshevik phenomenon'[2] – Trotsky sees Lenin's ideas as sharing with the 'Economists' a despair in the potential of the Russian proletariat to act politically:

> If the Economists have sought to flee from the enormity of their task by assigning themselves the humble role of marching *at the tail* of history, the 'politicists' have resolved the problem by striving to transform history *into their own tail*.[3]

Lenin was, according to Trotsky, a Russian Robespierre who wished to assign a supremacy of politics characteristic of the Jacobins. The Bolsheviks therefore wished to substitute themselves for the proletariat.

Comparing the Bolshevik and Mensheviks, he wrote:

> The difference between the systems ... is decisive in defining the charac-
> ter of our party's work. In one case we have a system of *thinking for* the
> proletariat, of the political substitution of the proletariat; in the other a
> system of *educating* politically the proletariat, *mobilising* it, so that it may
> exercise its effective pressure on the will of all groups and parties. These
> two systems produce the results which are, objectively, totally different.[4]

It was against this background that Trotsky made one of his most
famous predictions:

> In inner-party politics, these methods lead, as we shall yet see, to this:
> the party organisation substitutes itself for the party, the central com-
> mittee substitutes itself for the organisation, and, finally, a 'dictator'
> substitutes himself for the central committee.[5]

His experience of the Soviets in 1905 only served to reinforce this view,
which remained unmodified in spite of his attempt to act as concilia-
tor between the two wings of Russian Social Democracy. It was only in
the crisis of 1917 that Trotsky came to the conclusion that the
Bolshevik party was a necessary vehicle for the success of his revolutionary aims.

Trotsky's views on the party were by no means unique. But his analysis
of Russian society and his conclusions for the future of the revolution
were just that. Decisive for the development of these ideas was his meeting in Munich in the spring of 1904 with Parvus, an émigré Russian Jew
prominent on the left wing of the German party. In a series of articles entitled *War and Revolution*, published in *Iskra* in 1904, Parvus had outlined
the following propositions. The nation state was fast becoming obsolete
owing to the drive for overseas markets, and the continuous industrial
expansion that led capitalist powers into conflict with each other and
would eventually result in war. Russia would be compelled to join in such
a war, but since her social structure was obsolescent, this would aid social
disintegration and make the possibilities of revolution more likely:

> The world process of capitalist development brings about a political
> upheaval in Russia. In turn, this will affect political development in
> all capitalist countries. The Russian revolution will shake the political
> foundations of the capitalist world and the Russian proletariat will
> assume the role of the *avant-garde* of the social revolution.[6]

Owing to the weakness of the Russian bourgeoisie and Russia's rapid industrialisation, the proletariat was the only really revolutionary force. The conclusion was that Russian Social Democracy should aim for an immediate workers' government.

According to Trotsky, Parvus 'brought me closer to the problems of the Social Revolution, and, for me, definitely transformed the conquest of power by the proletariat from an astronomical "final" goal to a practical task for our own day'.[7] Trotsky took over these ideas, found them confirmed in the events of 1905, in which he himself played the leading role, and gave them a theoretical framework by means of a detailed social and political analysis of contemporary Russia. This was in two parts: a socio-economic theory of combined and uneven development, and its political counterpart of permanent revolution. Together, they were 'the most radical restatement, if not revision, of the prognosis of Socialist revolution undertaken since Marx's *Communist Manifesto'*.[8] In his socio-economic analysis, Trotsky started from the phenomenon of Russia's backwardness: 'we can say that the main characteristic of Russian social development is its comparative primitiveness and slowness'.[9] But added to this there was the fact that 'Russian social life, built up on a certain internal economic foundation, has all the time been under the influence, even under the pressure, of its external social-historical milieu'.[10] The Russian state had to swallow more of the surplus product to defend itself, as it was less developed than those exerting pressure on it (Poland, Sweden, and Lithuania). Thus:

> From a certain moment – especially from the end of the seventeenth century – the state strove with all its power to accelerate the country's natural economic development. New branches of handicraft, machinery, factories, big industry, capital, were, so to say, artificially grafted on the natural economic stem. Capitalism seemed to be an offspring of the state.[11]

This meant that there was no internally self-sufficient capitalist class investing their own surplus, but the state investing what it could borrow abroad from the European bourgeoisie – an artificial and precarious arrangement. Its artificiality (as opposed to slow organic growth) meant that it could be all the more rapid. And, indeed, the pace of industrialisation about 1900 was enormous. The relatively few capitalists who ran this expansion were dependent on the foreign capital, which was channelled through the state, and thus lacked an independent and wide social basis. Parallelly, the working class was created very rapidly and came straight from the land – unlike the West. Thus Russia could skip over stages in economic development, but this created at the same time a curious social structure: a centralised, autocratic government with aristocratic privilege and a large peasantry, combined with advanced industrialisation and a cohesive, if small, working class. This combination of the old and the new with no mediating factor such as a strong middle class made for social and political instability. Trotsky's conclusion was:

> The administrative, military and financial power of absolutism, thanks to which it could exist in spite of social development, not only did not exclude the possibility of revolution, as was the opinion of the liberals, but, on the contrary, made revolution the only way out; furthermore, this revolution was guaranteed in advance on all the more radical character in proportion as the great might of absolutism dug an abyss between itself and the nation.[12]

What was later to become known as the theory of 'permanent revolution' flowed from this analysis. For, according to Trotsky, the working class had a significance in Russia that was out of proportion to its size in that a worker in a large-scale industry was more important than a worker in a smaller enterprise – and Russian industry was nothing if not large-scale. And this industry was more exposed than in the West as it was not encompassed by a long-standing and all-pervasive capitalist socio-cultural ethos. The working class was in a position to paralyse industry and control urban centres as in few other countries. Trotsky asserted, therefore, that 'it is possible for the workers to come to power in an economically backward country sooner than in an advanced country'.[13] He also asserted that Russia combined the three factors of an economically low level of capitalist development, a politically insignificant capitalist bourgeoisie, and a powerful revolutionary proletariat. And he quoted Kautsky to the effect that 'the struggle for the interests of all Russia has fallen to the lot of the only now-existing strong class in the country – the industrial proletariat'.[14] Of course, a certain level of working-class consciousness was necessary for the seizure of power but Trotsky claimed that a determined minority was sufficient. (Here we see in embryo the domination of the political over the social and economic that was to be so characteristic of post-revolutionary Russia.) The support of the peasantry would be necessary and they would see that their problems could only be solved by revolutionary means – but the proletariat must nevertheless remain dominant. Yet as divisions among the peasantry emerged following the redistribution of land the proletariat would be forced to adopt socialist attitudes. (Here Trotsky went far *beyond* Parvus.) The proletarian government would find that increasingly radical measures would be forced upon them:

Immediately that power is transferred into the hands of a revolutionary government with a socialist majority, the division of our programme into maximum and minimum loses all significance both in principle and in immediate practice. A proletarian government under no circumstances can confine itself within such limits.[15]

Therefore

there can be no talk of any sort of *special* form of proletarian dictatorship in the bourgeois revolution, of *democratic* proletarian dictatorship (or dictatorship of the proletariat and the peasantry). The working class cannot preserve the democratic character of its dictatorship without refraining from overstepping the limits of its democratic programme. Any illusions on this point will be fatal. They would compromise social democracy from the very start.[16]

This was 'the idea of uninterrupted revolution ... an idea which connected the liquidation of absolutism and feudalism with a socialist revolution'.[17] But these same socialist measures would assure such violent internal opposition (particularly given the disparate and backward social structure) that the very existence of the proletarian government would become doubtful without external support.

Without the direct state support of the European proletariat the working class of Russia cannot remain in power and convert its temporary domination into a lasting socialist dictatorship.[18]

And it was, of course, precisely this support from the European proletariat that was not forthcoming for the Russian Bolsheviks once they had come to power in 1917.

Notes

1. L. Trotsky, *Vtoroi Syezd RSDRP (Otchet Sibirskoi Delegatsii)* (Geneva, 1903), p. 11, quoted in B. Knei-Paz, *The Social and Political Thought of Leon Trotsky* (Oxford, 1978) p. 180.
2. B. Knei-Paz, op. cit., p. 193.

3. L. Trotsky, *Nashi Politicheskye Zadachi* (Geneva, 1904) p. 54, quoted in B. Knei-Paz, op. cit., p. 197.
4. L. Trotsky, op. cit., p. 50.
5. Ibid., p. 54.
6. N. Parvus, *Rossiya y revolyutsiya* (St Petersburg, 1906) p. 133, quoted in A. Zeman and W. Scharlau, *The Merchant of Revolution* (London, 1965) p. 64.
7. L. Trotsky, *My Life* (London, 1930) p. 147. See also L. Trotsky, *Stalin* (London, 1947) pp. 429f.
8. L. Deutscher, *The Prophet Armed. Trotsky 1879–1921* (Oxford, 1954) p. 150.
9. L. Trotsky, *The Permanent Revolution and Results and Prospects*, 3rd edn (New York, 1969) p. 37.
10. Ibid., p. 38.
11. Ibid., p. 41.
12. Ibid., p. 44.
13. Ibid., p. 63.
14. Ibid., p. 66.
15. Ibid., p. 78.
16. Ibid., p. 80.
17. Ibid., p. 81.
18. Ibid., p. 105.

Further reading

Texts

The works of Trotsky's exile are collected into the Pathfinder multi-volume edition (New York, 1972ff.). The best single volume anthology is by Deutscher. Of Trotsky's early works *Results and Prospects* is available in a work with the title *Permanent Revolution*. For his gifts as a contemporary historian, see 1905 and, of course, *The History of the Russian Revolution*. For his views in the 1920s, *The Lessons of October, The New Course*, and *Towards Socialism or Capitalism?* are all available in separate editions. For his views on Stalinism, see *The Revolution Betrayed* and his biography *Stalin*. *Literature and Revolution* demonstrates his gifts as a literary critic.

Commentaries

For long Deutscher's splendid three-volume biography was the only extended commentary. However, Day's *Leon Trotsky* and the *Politics of Economic Isolation* sheds much light on Trotsky's policies in the 1920s and Howe's Modern Masters *Trotsky* is a good short introduction from a democratic socialist viewpoint. But the fundamental work is undoubtedly Knei-Paz's *The Social and Political Thought of Leon Trotsky* which is meticulously researched and comprehensive. There are also collections of much smaller pieces by Krasso and by Smith. Mavrakis's *On Trotskyism* is a disappointing polemic from a Maoist viewpoint, while Molyneux's

Leon Trotsky's Theory of Revolution is a good exposition by a follower. See also Ali's lively introduction and Volkogonov's biography.

Bibliography

Texts

Leon Trotsky, *The Writings of Leon Trotsky 1929–1940*, ed. G. Breitman and S. Lovell (New York, 1972ff.), 11 volumes.
—— *The Bolsheviki and World Peace* (New York, 1918).
—— *The Case of Leon Trotsky* (London, 1937).
—— *Diary in Exile – 1935* (London, 1959).
—— *The First Five Years of the Communist International*, 2 vols (New York, 1953).
—— *The History of the Russian Revolution*, 3 vols (London, 1945).
—— *In Defense of Marxism* (New York, 1973).
—— *The Lessons of October* (London, 1937).
—— *Literature and Revolution* (Ann Arbor, 1960).
—— *The Living Thoughts of Karl Marx* (London, 1940).
—— *My Life* (New York, 1960).
—— *The New Course* (Ann Arbor, 1965).
—— *1905* (London, 1972).
—— *On Lenin: Notes Towards a Biography* (London, 1971).
—— *Problems of the Chinese Revolution* (London, 1969).
—— *The Real Situation in Russia* (New York, 1928).
—— *Results and Prospects*, in *The Permanent Revolution and Results and Prospects* (London, 1962).
—— *The Revolution Betrayed: What is the Soviet Union and Where is it Going?* (London, 1937).
—— *Stalin: An Appraisal of the Man and His Influence* (London, 1941).
—— *The Stalin School of Falsification* (New York, 1937).
—— *Terrorism and Communism: A Reply to Karl Kautsky* (Ann Arbor, 1961).
—— *The Third International After Lenin* (New York, 1936).
—— *Towards Socialism or Capitalism?* (London, 1976).
—— *The Trotsky Papers: 1917–1922*, 2 vols, ed. J.M. Meijer (The Hague, 1964, 1971).
—— *Where is Britain Going?* (London, 1926).
—— *The Young Lenin* (London, 1972).

Anthologies

Leon Trotsky, *The Age of Permanent Revolution: A Trotsky Anthology*, ed. Isaac Deutscher (New York, 1964).
—— *Basic Writings*, ed. Irving Howe (London, 1964).
—— *The Essential Trotsky* (London, 1963).
—— *Leon Trotsky on Britain* (New York, 1973).
—— *Leon Trotsky on the Jewish Questions* (New York, 1970).
—— *Leon Trotsky on Literature and Art*, ed. Paul N. Siegel (New York, 1970).
—— *Leon Trotsky on the Trade Unions* (New York, 1969).
—— *Leon Trotsky Speaks* (New York, 1972).

Leon Trotsky, *Marxism and Military Affairs, 1921–1924* (Colombo, 1969).
—— *Marxism and Science* (Colombo, 1973).
—— *Military Writings* (New York, 1969).
—— *Problems of Everyday Life and Other Writings on Culture and Science* (New York, 1973).
—— *The Spanish Revolution: 1931–1939* (New York, 1973).
—— *The Struggle Against Fascism in Germany*, Introduction by Ernest Mandel (New York, 1971).
—— *Whither France?* (New York, 1936).

Commentaries

T. Ali, *Introducing Trotsky and Marxism* (Oxford, 2000).
Siegfried Bahne, 'Trotsky on Stalin's Russia', *Survey* (1962).
P. Beilharz, *Trotsky, Trotskyism and the Transition to Socialism* (Beckenham, 1987).
Joel Carmichael, 'Trotsky's Agony', *Encounter*, 5–6 (1972).
—— *Trotsky: An Appreciation of His Life* (London, 1975).
Richard B. Day, *Leon Trotsky and the Politics of Economic Isolation* (Cambridge, 1973).
—— 'The Theory of Long Waves: Kondratiev, Trotsky, Mandel', *New Left Review*, 99 (1976).
Isaac Deutscher, *The Prophet Armed: Trotsky 1879–1921* (Oxford, 1954).
—— *The Prophet Unarmed: Trotsky 1921–1929* (Oxford, 1959).
—— *The Prophet Outcast: Trotsky 1929–1940* (Oxford, 1963).
Max Eastman, *Leon Trotsky: The Portrait of a Youth* (New York, 1925).
Norman Geras, 'Political Participation in the Revolutionary Thought of Leon Trotsky', in G. Parry (ed.), *Participation in Politics* (Manchester, 1972).
Louis Gottschalk, 'Leon Trotsky and the Natural History of Revolutions', *American Journal of Sociology* (1938).
Joseph Hanson *et al.*, *Leon Trotsky: The Man and His Work* (New York, 1969).
Geoff Hodgson, *Trotsky and Fatalistic Marxism* (Nottingham, 1975).
Irving Howe, *Trotsky* (London and New York, 1978).
Baruch Knei-Paz, *The Social and Political Thought of Leon Trotsky* (Oxford, 1978).
—— 'Trotsky, Marxism and the Revolution of Backwardness', in Shlomo Avineri (ed.), *The Varieties of Marxism* (The Hague, 1977).
Nicolas Krasso (ed.), *Trotsky: The Great Debate Renewed* (St Louis, 1972).
Lee Chen-Chung, 'Trotsky's Theory of "Permanent Revolution" and Mao Tse-tung's Theory of the "Continuous Revolution" ', *Issues and Studies* (1972).
Steven Levine, 'Trotsky on China: The Exile Period', *Papers on China*, 18 (Harvard, 1964).
George Lichtheim, 'Reflections on Trotsky' in Lichtheim, *The Concept of Ideology* (New York, 1967).
Alasdair MacIntyre, 'Trotsky in Exile', *Encounter* (1963).
Robert H. McNeal, 'Trotsky's Interpretation of Stalin', *Canadian Slavonic Papers*, 5 (1961).
L. Maitan, 'The Theory of Permanent Revolution', in E. Mandel (ed.), *Fifty Years of World Revolution* (New York, 1968).
André Malraux, 'Leon Trotsky', in Trotsky, *Writings 1933–34* (New York, 1972).
Kostas Mavrakis, *On Trotskyism: Problems of Theory and History* (London, 1976).

John Molyneux, *Leon Trotsky's Theory of Revolution* (London, 1981).
Nicholas Mosley, *The Assassination of Trotsky* (London, 1972).
Joseph Nedava, *Trotsky and the Jews* (Philadelphia, 1972).
Giuliano Procacci, 'Trotsky's View of the Critical Years: 1929–1936', *Science and Society* (1963).
Heinz Schurer, 'The Permanent Revolution: Leon Trotsky', in L. Labedz (ed.), *Revisionism; Essays in the History of Marxist Ideas* (New York, 1962).
Louis Sinclair, *Leon Trotsky: A Bibliography* (Stanford, 1972).
Irving H. Smith (ed.), *Trotsky* (Englewood Cliffs, N.J., 1973).
M.S. Venkaturamani, 'Leon Trotsky's Adventure in American Radical Politics: 1935–1937', *International Review of Social History*, IX (1964).
Robert D. Warth, 'Leon Trotsky: Writer and Historian', *Journal of Modern History* (1948).
Fred Weinstein, 'Trotsky and the Sociological Dimension: An Analysis of Social Action', *Social Forces* (1961).
D.Volkogonov, *Trotsky: The Eternal Revolutionary* (London, 1996).
Bertrand D. Wolfe, 'Leon Trotsky as Historian', *Slavic Review* (1961).

7
Lenin

The Party

What Is to be Done? was Lenin's fundamental work on the Party although, as is indicated below, its importance should not be overestimated. The sub-title to Lenin's pamphlet – *Burning Questions of our Movement* – is particularly important as an indication of the historical context.

So far from being innovatory, Lenin was out to reassert the Plekhanov orthodoxy of the pre-1894 period against later developments;[1] and so far from revealing a break of confidence in the masses, the book was designed to remedy 'the lag of the leaders behind the spontaneous upsurge of the masses'.[2] The first three chapters criticised the 'Economists' and terrorists, and described the disarray of the movement in the late 1890s, and so on. Lenin attacked the *Credo* of Kuskova and the two Russian workers' newspapers *Rabochaia Mysl* and *Rabochee delo* as typical of 'Economism'.[3] His main point was that these groups showed inadequate leadership and inability to articulate the role of the proletariat as leader of all classes in the struggle against the autocracy. Basing himself on his conclusions in *The Development of Capitalism in Russia*, Lenin declared that they could not produce the initial organisation of the Party necessary to parallel politically the transition from *Kustar* (handicraft) production to national capitalism. The Economists could only duplicate the proletariat's isolated and local efforts. In subsequent chapters and in line with Plekhanov and Axelrod, Lenin elaborated his ideas on Social Democratic consciousness. This involved an intensive knowledge of the socio-economic situation and prospects of every class. It was therefore impossible for the proletariat, whose 'economic' struggle was too narrow, to achieve this consciousness. (Lenin never talked of 'class consciousness' with regard to the proletariat.) Echoing Plekhanov and Axelrod, Lenin maintained that the proletariat, left to itself, would inevitably follow bourgeois ideology. In this connection, Lenin quoted Kautsky at length and then continued in the key passage:

> Since there can be no talk of an independent ideology formulated by the working masses themselves in the process of their movement, the only choice is – either bourgeois or socialist ideology. There is no middle course (for mankind has not created a 'third' ideology, and, moreover, in a society torn by class antagonisms there can never be a non-class or an above-class ideology). Hence, to belittle the socialist ideology in any way, to turn aside from it in the slightest degree means to strengthen bourgeois ideology. There is much talk of spontaneity. But the spontaneous development of the working-class movement leads to its subordination to bourgeois ideology, to its development along the lines of the Credo programme; for the spontaneous working-class movement is trade-unionism, is *Nur-Gewerkschaftlerei*, and trade-unionism means the ideological enslavement of the workers by the bourgeoisie. Hence, our task, the task of Social-Democracy, is to combat spontaneity, to divert the working-class movement from this spontaneous, trade-unionist striving to come under the wing of the bourgeoisie, and to bring it under the wing of revolutionary Social-Democracy.[4]

In Chapter Four, Lenin moved to his proposals. Given the Party's task of assuming the role of leading *all* exploited classes in the democratic revolution (the 'hegemony of the proletariat in the democratic revolution' to use Plekhanov's phrase), it must have an all-Russian organisation. This was best centred on an all-Russian newspaper such as *Iskra* aspired to be. Such an organisation could maintain contacts and doctrinal cohesion on an all-Russian basis, ensure specialisation and non-duplication, and maintain the hegemonic position of the proletariat. Such an organisation would also have the attributes of secrecy, centralisation, specialisation and exclusivity. But all these attributes would be dependent on Lenin's fundamental idea, which was the real point at issue in the Bolshevik-Menshevik split: that the organisation should be composed of professional revolutionaries. They would be professional in two senses: they would devote themselves full time to party work and they would be fully trained: 'the struggle against the political police requires special qualities; it requires professional revolutionaries'.[5] Lenin was not against mass organisations – on the contrary – but he insisted that they must be quite separate from the party elite:

> We must have such circles, trade unions, and organisations every-where in as large a number as possible and with the widest variety of functions; but it would be absurd and harmful to confound them with the organisation of revolutionaries, to efface the border-line between them, to make still more hazy the all too faint recognition of the fact that in order to 'serve' the mass movement we must have people who will devote themselves exclusively to Social-Democratic activities, and that such people must train themselves patiently and steadfastly to be professional revolutionaries.[6]

Neither was Lenin against inner-party democracy, but this implied full publicity and election to all offices, and only an 'incorrigible utopian' could advocate this under present conditions in Russia. The leadership would therefore have to be chosen through the oligarchical principle of co-option.[7]

It should be stressed that Lenin's views represented the whole of the Emancipation of Labour Group, including Plekhanov and Axelrod: *What Is to be Done?* was therefore the last major publication carrying the assent of all the orthodox Marxists. After the split at the Second Congress, Plekhanov and Martov both accused Lenin of 'dictatorship'. Luxemburg published a biting critique of Lenin's ideas,[8] and, as we have seen, so did Trotsky. Yet, at least until 1905, there was not much difference between Bolsheviks and Mensheviks as regards internal party democracy.[9] The dif-ference between Lenin and his critics was not one of principle but of approach, and certainly accusations of Blanquism were quite misplaced: influence over, and support of, the masses, were absolutely essential to his theory.

It would, in any case, be wrong to overemphasise the importance of *What Is to be Done?* Lenin wrote later that his pamphlet 'should not be treated apart from its connection with the concrete historical situation of a definite, and now long past, period in the development of our Party'.[10] 'The Economists,' he said at the 1903 Congress, 'have gone to one extreme. To straighten matters out somebody had to pull in the other direction – and that is what I have done.'[11] He never republished the book after 1917 – though it was canonised, for obvious reasons, by Stalin.

The wave of strikes and unrest that swept Russia in 1905 rendered much of *What Is to be Done?* completely out of date: Lenin's pessimism was refuted by the revolutionary spontaneity of the masses.[12] Whereas in *What Is to be Done?* Lenin had been against a Party that was open to mass membership, the changed conditions of 1905 brought floods of new members. Party membership increased ten times and the distinction between an elitist party and mass organisation became less rigid. Although Lenin did not abandon the idea of a clandestine party, he did concede that 'our party has stagnated while working underground'.[13] He urged his followers 'to extend your bases, rally all the worker social democrats round yourselves, incorporate them in the ranks of the party organisation by hundreds and thousands',[14] and stated that 'the new form of the basic organisation or nucleus of the workers' party must be definitely much broader than were the old circles. Apart from this, the new nucleus will most likely have to be less rigid, more free, more loose organisation.'[15] This entailed changes in party structure: Lenin committed himself to the introduction of the elective principle and the curtailment of the powers of the Central Committee and even advocated the principle of referendum.[16]

The new Party structure was summed up in the phrase 'democratic centralism'. The phrase was of Menshevik origin and, on Lenin's proposal, was incorporated into the statutes of the Party at the Stockholm Congress of 1906 which temporarily reunited the two factions.[17] In his *Report* on the Congress, Lenin explained that the principle of democratic centralism consisted in 'working tirelessly to make the local organisations the principal organisational units of the party in fact, and not merely in name, and to see to it that all the highest standing bodies are elected, accountable, and subject to recall'.[18] The rights of a minority within the party were also guaranteed. Lenin stated his principle as 'freedom of discussion, unity of action'[19] – and the call to action could only be issued by the Congress, not the Central Committee.

It is, of course, true that the new democratic centralism of 1905–6 was not only due to the revolutionary fervour of the times: Lenin cannot have been uninfluenced by the fact that the Bolsheviks were in a minority at the Stockholm Unity Congress of 1906 and that the Central Committee there elected was under Menshevik control. With the failure of the revolution, the renewed split between the Bolsheviks and the Mensheviks, and the period of reaction from 1908 to 1912, the sectarian spirit inside the Bolshevik party came back in force. Under Lenin's impulsion, the Party, persecuted inside Russia and internally divided abroad, became increasingly monolithic. Lenin came to insist on the 'party' line.[20]

Once again, however, as 1905 had swept away the rigid organisation of the Bolshevik Party, so 1917 inaugurated the most open and 'liberal' period in the Party's life. Once again, the Party membership increased

tenfold in a few months and the monolithic, highly centralised structure of the Party could not survive the heady atmosphere of new-found
liberty. Different tendencies operated inside the Party, whose organisation was 'necessarily somewhat loose and fluid',[21] and vigorous debates
on policy options occurred at every level. Trotsky, previously vilified by
Lenin, but now welcome as a comrade in arms, went as far as to declare
the party to be 'de-Bolshevised'.[22]

But this state of affairs did not, and could not, last long. The civil war
and severe dislocation that confronted the Bolsheviks from 1918 to 1921
necessitated a clamp-down on previous liberties. There had been a very
open debate on the sort of peace to be concluded with the Germans, and
until 1921 there was much discussion of economic policies and relationships to the Soviets and trade unions, with Bukharin and Lenin on opposite sides. But the end of the civil war found the country completely
exhausted. The proletariat had been decimated and the majority of the
population were hostile to the Communist Party (as it had been
renamed). The Central Committee found itself contested by the Workers'
Opposition, led by Shliapnikov and Kollontai, who demanded the uninhibited right for the workers to elect their own trade union leaders and
an independence *vis-à-vis* the Party. Almost as much opposed to the current Party tendencies were the Democratic Centralists, who wished for
more internal democracy in the Party and real powers for local Soviets.
Their opposition were based on all too real grievances,[23] and Lenin had, as
late as the end of 1920, reiterated the right of all tendencies within the
Party to free expression and their proportional representation in the Party
Congress. But the Tenth Party Congress, meeting in March 1921 only weeks
after the brutal repression of the Kronstadt rising,[24] marked the definite
break with this tradition. On Lenin's proposal two resolutions were
adopted; the first ordered 'the immediate dissolution of all groups without exception formed on the basis of one platform or another (such as the
Workers' Opposition Group, the Democratic Centralists Group etc.)',[25]
with a two-thirds majority to expel members from the Party. The second
resolution specifically condemned the Workers' Opposition and declared,
in a spirit quite alien to the confidence in the masses expressed in 1917,
that 'only the political party of the working class, i.e. the Communist
Party, is capable of uniting, training and organising a vanguard of the proletariat and of the whole mass of the working people that alone will be
capable of withstanding the inevitable petty-bourgeois vacillations of this
mass, and the inevitable traditions and relapses of narrow craft unionism
or craft prejudices among the proletariat'.[26] Expulsions duly followed and
shortly afterwards Stalin became the Party's General Secretary.

Revolution

Lenin's ideas on revolution started from the orthodox tradition which he inherited from Plekhanov and more specifically from his examination of Russia's economic development in his book *The Development of Capitalism in Russia*. In his 1894 polemic against the Populists, *What the Friends of the People Are*, Lenin formulated his conclusion that Russia was already basically capitalist in its economic structure and that (the bourgeoisie being too weak) the proletariat would have to lead the struggle for democracy. Some commentators have read *What the Friends of the People Are* as advocating, in a voluntarist, Jacobin manner, an immediate *socialist* revolution. Although Lenin talked of a 'victorious communist revolution', the number of preconditions specified show that he believed this to be in the distant future. He never talked of an immediate socialist revolution until his 1916 studies of imperialism had changed his fundamental framework. Until then, his basic perspective was that of the proletariat leading a bourgeois revolution in a basically capitalist Russia.

This idea that the immediate aim was the overthrow of the autocracy and the establishment of a bourgeois democracy was common to almost all Russian Marxists at the turn of the century: one of the major points of subsequent disagreement was the means to achieve this aim and specifically the problem of alliances. Both Bolsheviks and Mensheviks agreed that an alliance with the liberals was necessary but the Mensheviks viewed the possibilities of this alliance with optimism, whereas Lenin viewed it with systematic mistrust which became accentuated during the 1905 revolution. From their defeat in this revolution, the Mensheviks drew the conclusion that socialism could only triumph by means of initial reforms gained by an alliance with the liberals; Lenin drew the opposite conclusion – that the liberals were totally unreliable allies in any revolutionary struggle. This disagreement was typified by their respective attitudes to the Duma: the Mensheviks were keen on participation and subsequent alliance with the Cadet liberal party; Lenin initially imposed a boycott on his followers, in spite of strong opposition – a view which he later changed and admitted to be mistaken.

But it was on the subject of the role of the peasantry in the coming revolution that Lenin demonstrated the flexibility and originality of his thought. His growing intransigence *vis-à-vis* the liberals led Lenin to view the peasantry more optimistically and he can claim to be the first Marxist who proposed associating the peasantry in political power, thus placing them in the position of the liberals in the classical West-European Marxist schema. The events of 1905 convinced him that the fate of the revolution depended on the attitude of marginal groups and particularly the peasantry. Whereas the Mensheviks considered the peasantry to be too disorganised to be reliable allies, Lenin, in his *Two Tactics* written in the summer of 1905, proposed a 'revolutionary democratic dictatorship of the proletariat and peasantry'. The peasantry were included because, according to the conclusion of *Two Tactics*,

> it is not only by the prospect of radical agrarian reform that the peasantry is attached to the revolution, but by all its general and permanent interests as well. Even when fighting with the proletariat, the peasantry stands in need of democracy, for only a democratic system is capable of accurately expressing its interests and ensuring its predominance as a mass, as the majority. The more enlightened the peasantry becomes the more consistently and resolutely will it stand for a thoroughgoing democratic revolution; for, unlike the bourgeoisie, it has nothing to fear from the people's supremacy, but on the contrary stands to gain by it.[27]

At the Fourth Party Congress in 1906, Lenin proposed the nationalisation of land and its distribution to the peasants in order to prise the peasantry away from the big bourgeoisie and create the economic basis for a democratic republic along American as opposed to Prussian lines – small independent landowners rather than a Junker system. The revolution would be 'democratic', on the other hand, because Lenin was quite clear about the bourgeois nature of the revolution: 'the democratic forms in the political system, and the social and economic reforms that have become a necessity for Russia, do not in themselves imply the undermining of capitalism, the undermining of bourgeois rule; on the contrary, they will, for the first time, really clear the ground for a wide and rapid, European and not Asiatic, development of capitalism; they will, for the first time, make it possible for the bourgeoisie to rule as a class'.[28] But the idea of a revolution that was bourgeois in its social and economic form while socialist in its political form may seem rather ambivalent.

How different were Lenin's ideas from Trotsky's 'permanent revolution'? This has been a subject of much controversy: orthodox Communists have wanted to claim that Lenin had a single coherent theory that embraced both 1905 and 1917. Trotsky's followers (and Trotsky himself) wanted later to minimise his differences with Lenin, while Stalinists have tried to argue the opposite in order to justify their view of Trotsky's pristine 'treachery'. The debate is also clouded by the imprecision of a lot of the terminology used. What is clear is that Trotsky was by no means as hostile to the peasantry as has often been claimed and that Lenin himself was often unclear about the relationships of the two revolutions and even, on an often-quoted occasion, stated:

> From the democratic revolution we shall at once and precisely in accordance with the measure of our strength, the strength of a class-conscious and organised proletariat, begin to pass to the socialist revolution. We stand for uninterrupted revolution. We shall not stop halfway.[29]

And Lenin talked on many occasions of the *Perastanie* or 'growing over' of one stage into another.

However, this should not obscure the differences between Trotsky and Lenin. Lenin had first studied economics in the context of his polemics against the Populists, and any suggestion of immediate socialism in Russia reminded him too much of his erstwhile adversaries. Although Lenin was clear that the struggle for socialism would begin immediately on the victory of the 'bourgeois' revolution, he strongly criticised Trotsky for 'mixing up different historical periods and comparing Russia, which is going through her bourgeois revolution, with Europe, where these revolutions were completed long ago',[30] and characterised his 'major error' as 'ignoring the bourgeois character of the revolution and having no clear conception of the transition from this revolution to the socialist revolution'.[31] And this remained his fundamental view until 1917.

Just as in 1905, the Bolshevik leaders were surprised once again in February 1917 and followed the mass upheavals rather than led them. Until the arrival of Lenin in St Petersburg early in April 1917, the Bolsheviks vacillated and tended to align with the Mensheviks in giving conditional support to the Provisional Government – which is not surprising in that, as orthodox Marxists, they considered themselves to be in the middle of a *bourgeois* revolution. In his *Letters from Afar* of March 1917 Lenin had already toyed with the idea that the passage from bourgeois revolution to some sort of proletarian revolution might already be possible. This idea was taken up again in his famous *April Theses* which made at least one Bolshevik exclaim that 'Lenin has just made himself a candidate for a throne that has been vacant for the last thirty years – that of Bakunin'.[32] Lenin declared that

> the specific feature of the present situation in Russia is that the country is *passing* from the first stage of the revolution – which, owing to the insufficient class-consciousness and organisation of the proletariat,

placed power in the hands of the bourgeoisie – to its *second* stage, which must place power in the hands of the proletariat and the poorest sections of the peasants.[33]

The Party should therefore deny support to the Provisional Government, give up its idea of reuniting with the Mensheviks, and agitate among the masses for an end to war, nationalisation of all land, and power to the Soviets. Lenin claimed that the revolutionary democratic dictatorship that he had advocated since 1905 had already been realised and that

> the person who *now* speaks of only a 'revolutionary – democratic dictatorship of the proletariat and peasantry' is behind the times, consequently he has in effect *gone over* to the petty bourgeoisie against the proletarian class struggle; that person should be consigned to the archive of Bolshevik prerevolutionary antiques (it may be called the archive of 'old Bolsheviks').[34]

Lenin was nevertheless insistent on the need to carry mass support in any overthrow of the provisional government. Any other course, any attempts to act in the name of a minority, would be 'senseless Blanquism'.[35] But in July a series of massive demonstrations that the Bolsheviks had not supported nevertheless led to the suppression of the Bolsheviks by the Provisional Government supported by the Mensheviks and Social Revolutionaries. Lenin drew the conclusion that

> All hopes for a peaceful development of the Russian revolution have vanished for good. This is the objective situation: either complete victory for the military dictatorship, or victory for the workers' armed uprising ... The slogan 'All Power to the Soviets!' was a slogan for peaceful development of the revolution which was possible in April, May, June, and up to July 5–9, i.e. up to the time when actual power passed into the hands of the military dictatorship. This slogan is no longer correct, for it does not take into account that power has changed hands and that the revolution has in fact been completely betrayed by the S.R.s and Mensheviks.[36]

But Lenin did not pursue these ideas immediately. During the rest of July and August he was composing *State and Revolution* in his Finnish exile. But by September the failure of the coup by General Kornilov led to a reaction in favour of the Left. Both the Soviet of St Petersburg, with

Trotsky (who had just formally joined the Bolsheviks) as its president, and the Soviet of Moscow fell under Bolshevik influence. Unorganised revolt was widespread in the countryside. By mid-September Lenin – still in Finland – wrote to the Central Committee: 'The Bolsheviks, having obtained a majority in the Soviets of workers and soldier deputies of both capitals, can and *must* take State power into their own hands.'[37] Most of the Party leaders still in Russia, mindful of the July defeat, were loath to take Lenin's suggestion seriously and he went as far as threatening to resign from the Central Committee and appeal to the ordinary members in order to stir them to the decisive action which he only finally managed to implement by coming to St Petersburg in person in mid-October. Even so, such influential members as Zinoviev and Kamenev (and they were not alone) continued to oppose insurrection and even publicised the split (and thus Lenin's intentions) in print. But the plans for insurrection meticulously prepared and supervised by Trotsky, had their own momentum and when the Provisional Government attempted to close certain Bolshevik papers on 24 October the Bolshevik seizure of power began, a seizure which, at least in its initial stages, must be one of the easiest and least bloody in all history.

Imperialism

According to Lenin, the phenomenon of imperialism was tied to a change in the nature of capitalism: the growth of monopoly capitalism. This form of capitalism superseded competitive capitalism at the beginning of the twentieth century when the advanced economies came to be dominated by finance controlled by banks which were themselves concentrated in cartels or trusts. The former type of capitalism was typified by the export of goods: monopoly capitalism exported capital. The surplus capital could not be used at home (for this would mean a decline in profits for the capitalists) but 'for the purpose of increasing profits by exporting capital abroad to the backward countries. In these backward countries profits are usually high, for capital is scarce, the price of land is relatively low, wages are low, raw materials are cheap.'[38] This in turn led to the *de facto* division of the world into the various spheres of influence of international cartels. Although it was a common criticism of Lenin that in fact colonial expansion preceded the high point of monopoly capital,[39] his formulations are vague and do not involve, in fact, a causal thesis.[40]

This much was common to several Marxist thinkers of the time, including Kautsky who had changed his mind about the future of imperialism in the years immediately preceding the outbreak of the war and considered that there might develop an 'ultraimperialism' in which the leading capitalist nations would divide up the world peacefully in some kind of international cartel. For Lenin, this was an impossibility, for

> the more capitalism is developed, the more strongly the shortage of raw materials is felt, the more intense the competition and hunt for sources of raw materials throughout the whole world, the more desperate the struggle for the acquisition of colonies.[41]

Moreover, according to Lenin, Kautsky was only concerned with industrial capital and had not realised that it was financial capital that gave imperialism its inevitable characteristics. The capitalist system could not achieve equilibrium, for

> financial capital and the trusts do not diminish but increase the differences in the rate of growth of the various parts of the world economy. Once the relation of forces is changed, what other solution of the contradictions can be found under capitalism than that of force?[42]

In the eighth chapter of his pamphlet, Lenin pointed to two internal effects of imperialism. First, monopoly – the foundation of imperialism – created a tendency for technical progress to retard and stagnate. Secondly – and more importantly – the super-profits of imperialism made it possible 'to bribe the upper strata of the proletariat, and therefore foster, give shape to, and strengthen opportunism'.[43] Here lay the explanation for the politics of the Second International. Lenin did not go into the question of how many workers had been bought off or why the whole proletariat of the relevant countries should not be affected, or what effect this would have on revolutionary possibilities.[44]

Although Lenin called imperialism the 'moribund' stage of capitalism, on the whole his view was far less optimistic. 'It is a mistake', he said,

> to believe that this tendency to decay precludes the rapid growth of capitalism. It does not. In the epoch of imperialism, certain branches of industry, certain strata of the bourgeoisie, and certain countries betray, to a greater or lesser degree, now one and now another of these tendencies. On the whole, capitalism is growing far more rapidly than before; but this growth is not only becoming more and more uneven in general, its unevenness also manifests itself, in particular, in the decay of the countries which are the richest in capital.[45]

The sub-title of Lenin's pamphlet was *A Popular Outline* and, as such, did not claim to be a work of outstanding originality. Lenin made specific references to the English Liberal Hobson (who had claimed that colonial expansion was due to a lack of home investment opportunities) and to Hilferding: but his most immediate source was Bukharin's *Imperialism and the World Economy*, which was completed a few months before Lenin's pamphlet. Bukharin took as his starting-point Hilferding's analysis of imperialism in terms of the necessary demands of financial capitalism;[46] and he went on to describe the extent to which monopoly had developed in the few years since Hilferding's book. The increasing intervention of the State had led to the national economy as a whole being organised in the form of a capitalist trust or state capitalism. He stressed, however, as against the prevailing view in the German Social Democratic Party, that imperialism was a necessary feature of contemporary capitalism and that it inevitably led to war and revolution.[47] From Luxemburg, on the other hand, Lenin borrowed little, as her views tended to shift the emphasis too much to underdeveloped countries and involved an 'imperialist economism' which left little room for political activity.

For the development of Lenin's revolutionary perspectives, his analysis of imperialism was crucial. The imperialist war had brought world financial capitalism to its final stage and introduced the objective and subjective preconditions for worldwide socialist revolution. Already in 1915, Lenin was writing that 'the task confronting the proletariat of Russia is the consummation of the bourgeois-democratic revolution in Russia in order to kindle the socialist revolution in Europe'.[48] Before leaving Switzerland in 1917, he had come to the conclusion that 'the objective circumstances of the imperialist war make it certain that the revolution will not be limited to the *first* stage of the Russian revolution, that the revolution will *not* be limited to Russia'.[49] The era of proletarian revolution for Russia had dawned and Lenin devoted himself to reflecting on what form the proletarian state should adopt.

The state

Lenin's most important work on the state was his *State and Revolution*; indeed, it has been called by Colletti far and away 'Lenin's greatest contribution to political theory'.[50] It is a sort of practical counterpart to his ideas on imperialism.

The book had its origin in Lenin's argument with Bukharin in the summer of 1916 over the existence of the state after a proletarian revolution. Bukharin had emphasised the 'withering' aspect, whereas Lenin insisted on the necessity of the state machinery to expropriate the expropriators. In fact, it was Lenin who changed his mind, and many of the ideas of *State and Revolution*, composed in the summer of 1917 – and particularly the anti-statist theme – were those of Bukharin.[51]

Lenin's direct and simple definition of the state is that 'the State is a special organisation of force: it is an organisation of violence for the suppression of some class'.[52] Hence his denigration even of parliamentary democracy, which was influenced by what he saw as the recent increase of bureaucratic and military influences:

> To decide once very few years which member of the ruling class is to repress and crush the people through parliament – this is the real essence of bourgeois parliamentarism, not only in parliamentary-constitutional monarchies, but also in the most democratic republics.[53]

Thus, following Marx's conclusions on the Paris commune, which Lenin took as his model,[54] Lenin declared that the task of the revolution was to smash the state. Although for a period under Communism 'there remains for a time not only bourgeois right but even the bourgeois State without the bourgeoisie',[55] Lenin believed that after a successful proletarian revolution the state had not only begun to wither, but was in an advanced condition of decomposition. But Lenin also called the state 'the armed and ruling proletariat'. Did this, too, wither? Yes, it did, in so far as it was in any way a power separate from, and opposed to, the masses. (The influence on Lenin of his recent experience of the Soviets is clear here.) He had little to say of the institutional form of this transition period. There was a strong emphasis on the dictatorship of the proletariat:

> A Marxist is solely someone who *extends* the recognition of the class struggle to the recognition of the *dictatorship of the proletariat*. This is what constitutes the most profound distinction between the Marxist and the ordinary petty (as well as big) bourgeois. This is the touchstone on which the *real* understanding and recognition of Marxism is to be tested.[56]

But there was little analysis of the shape this dictatorship might take, which is all the more tantalising as Lenin's strong insistence on the withering of the state *immediately* after the revolution has libertarian or even anarchist overtones. His general view seemed to embody the classic socialist formula that the government of people could give way to the administration of things:

> *We ourselves*, the workers, will organise large-scale production on the basis of what capitalism has already created, relying on our own experience as workers, establishing strict, iron discipline backed up by the State power of the armed workers; we will reduce the role of the State officials to that of simply carrying out our instructions as responsible, revocable, modestly paid 'foremen and accountants' (of course, with the aid of technicians of all sorts, types and degrees). This is *our* proletarian task, this is what we can and must *start* with in accomplishing the proletarian revolution. Such a beginning on the basis of large-scale production will of itself lead to the gradual 'withering away' of all bureaucracy, to the gradual creation of an order without quotation marks, an order bearing no similarity to wage slavery, an order in which the functions of control and accounting – becoming more and more simple – will be formed by each in turn, will then become a habit, and will finally die out as the *special* functions of a special section of the population.[57]

In the political sphere, what is most striking is the absence of reference to the agent of revolution: the Party itself. In his one serious reference to the Party Lenin said:

> By educating the workers' Party, Marxism educates the vanguard of the proletariat which is capable of assuming power and *of leading the whole people* to Socialism, of directing and organising the new order, of being the teacher, the guide, the leader of all the workers and exploited in the task of building up their social life without the bourgeoisie, and against the bourgeoisie.[58]

It is ambiguous here whether it is the vanguard or the proletariat which 'is capable of assuming power and leading ...'. Lenin's general cast of thought would tend to the former, but Lenin nowhere enlarged on the apparent clash which this entailed with his more liberal statements.

The optimism inherent in *State and Revolution* did not, however, long survive the success of the October Revolution. The difficulties were enhanced by the isolation of the Soviet State among hostile powers, the failure of the revolutionary movement abroad and the consequent necessity for the Soviet government to sign a separate and humiliating peace with the Germans at Brest-Litovsk – a policy which Lenin had the greatest difficulty in getting adopted in the face of strong opposition from such Left Communists as Trotsky and Bukharin. Already a different emphasis was present in Lenin's reply to Bukharin at the Seventh Party Congress in March 1918. 'Just when will the State wither away?', he asked, and answered, 'We shall have managed to convene more than two congresses before the time comes to say: see how our State is withering away. It is too early for that. To proclaim the withering away of the State prematurely would distort the historical perspective.'[59] The gradual shift from dictatorship of the proletariat to dictatorship of the Party and the equivalence of Party and state was aided and abetted by three main factors: the fact that the Party found power thrust into its hands; the growth of bureaucracy; and the lack of an effective workers' voice.

In late 1917 the Bolshevik Party was small and its organisation ineffective. Some Bolsheviks, such as Preobrazhensky, even suggested that the Party be dissolved in the Soviets. But, as Liebman says,

> in proportion as the popular basis of the new regime got smaller and Soviet democracy became more formal, the Party, which offered a firmer resistance to social and political difficulties thanks to its greater cohesion, reinforced its authority and reestablished to its own advantage the previous disequilibrium.[60]

By 1919 the Party and the state were inextricably linked and the dictatorship of the proletariat became equated with the dictatorship of the Party and Lenin was able to talk of class relationships being exercised 'under the leadership of the Party'.[61]

This Party domination was enhanced by the suppression of opposition, beginning with dissolution of the Constituent Assembly in January 1918. Before the revolution, Lenin had been in favour of the convocation of the Constituent Assembly, not apparently realising the inevitable clash with the slogan of 'all power to the Soviets'. The decision to dissolve the Constituent Assembly, for which the Bolsheviks had only obtained 25 per cent of the votes, was unavoidable for a Party that claimed to be pursuing the proletarian socialist revolution. For the largest party in the Constituent Assembly represented peasant interests and the whole structure of the Assembly was much more appropriate to a bourgeois democracy.

But neither did the Soviet last long as an expression of popular will: the Civil War and the militarisation of public life soon led to the eclipse of Soviet power. The very existence of opposition parties was also gradually threatened. Before 1917, Lenin had never suggested a single-party state and the subsequent inability of the Bolsheviks to arrive at a coalition with their socialist opponents was due just as much to their opponents' intransigence as to their own. But pressure of Civil War and the tendency to equate anti-Bolshevism with the counter-revolution led to the eventual suppression of all opposition parties. The Social Revolutionaries, representing as they did the better-off peasantry, were basically hostile to the Bolshevik programme; but this was not the case with the Mensheviks, whose popular support (despite the Bolshevik harassment) tended to grow. In June 1918 they were excluded from the Pan-Russian Congress of Soviets and systematically suppressed at the end of 1920.

This tendency towards monolithism was increased by the growth of bureaucracy.[62] Bureaucracy was encouraged by the increased nationalisation programme caused by confiscations and the war effort. There was also the influence of the traditional bureaucratic methods of Russian autocracy, and the desire to find work for the increasing number of unemployed by absorbing them into the state machine. By the end of 1920 this administrative machine had swollen to almost six million employees, a growth that was in inverse proportion to the productive capacity of the economy. Although Lenin was in favour of recruiting bourgeois technicians and specialists and indeed giving them special privileges, he was incessant in his conflict with bureaucracy. 'All of us', he wrote, 'are sunk in the rotten bureaucratic swamp of "departments".'[63] By early 1921 Lenin characterised the Soviet Union as 'a worker state with bureaucratic distortion'.[64] And a year later, at the last Party Congress he attended, Lenin admitted:

> If we take that huge bureaucratic machine, that gigantic heap, we must ask: who is directing whom? I doubt very much whether it can truthfully be said that the Communists are directing that heap. To tell the truth, they are not directing, they are being directed.[65]

Even the famous Rabkrin, designed to be a popular watchdog over the administration, became yet another body with all the deficiencies which it was supposed to combat. Lenin's remarks on the subject during the last months of his active life are akin to despair.

The growth in the power of the Party and of the bureaucracy necessarily precluded the effective expression of grass-roots working-class opinion. Workers' control had been introduced in principle in November 1917, but was not an economic success and began to be abandoned after a few months. Under pressure of economic circumstances, Lenin called for piecework wages and even for Taylorism. The 'war communism' in 1918–21 necessitated a highly centralised control and the subsequent NEP meant an (albeit necessary) step backwards. Strikes were seen as illogical in a state 'belonging' to the workers. On the crucial question of the status of trade unions there were two diametrically opposed views. Firstly, there were the views of the so-called Workers' Opposition, represented by Kollontai and Shliapnikov, that the trade unions should have a decisive vote in the administration of economic matters. Secondly, there was the view of Trotsky that the trade unions should be simply an arm of political authority. Lenin accorded the trade unions a certain independence in the struggle against bureaucracy, but his view did not ultimately prevail.[66] The general inability of the Soviet government to put into practice the principles of *State and Revolution* filled Lenin's last years with gloom and pessimism.

The national question

Lenin supported the right of national self-determination: but he subjected this right to conditions which eventually led to its extinction in practice. In one of his earliest formulations, Lenin wrote:

> We on our part concern ourselves with the self-determination of the proletariat in each nationality rather than with self-determination of peoples or nations ... As to support of the demand for national autonomy, it is by no means a permanent and binding part of the programme of the proletariat. This support may become necessary for it only in isolated and exceptional cases.[67]

Thus Lenin could only give conditional recognition to the demand for national independence. The crucial case here was Poland, the largest of the subjugated nations of Europe and a subject of long-standing debate among socialists. Marx had given his unconditional support to demands for Polish independence, but Lenin criticised the Polish Socialist Party for unconditionally demanding the independence of their country. This is not to say that the national question was a minor one for Lenin. Rather the contrary: he was fully aware of the importance of harnessing national aspirations to the proletarian cause. Indeed, he expressed himself more forcibly in favour of the principle of national self-determination than almost any other social democratic leader of the time. But he had no time for talk of patriotism or 'national' culture. (His article of December 1914 'On the National Pride of the Great-Russians', where he seems to attribute an intrinsic worth to a Great-Russian national culture, must be viewed as an exception, possibly influenced by the desire to show that the Bolsheviks were not completely anti-Russian in their attitude to the war.) For Lenin, the question of national autonomy was purely one of tactics, for self-determination was always subordinate to the Party's interest.

Lenin was firmly opposed, therefore, to the Austro-Marxists' support for the federal principle and for national cultural autonomy. He did indeed proclaim his belief in 'full equality of all nations and languages, which recognises no compulsory official language ...' and 'a fundamental law that prohibits any privileges whatsoever to any one nation and any encroachment whatsoever upon the rights of a national minority', which 'particularly calls for a wide regional autonomy and fully democratic local self-government'.[68] Yet he did not go as far as Rosa Luxemburg (who saw nationalism as based on the reactionary intelligentsia and petty bourgeoisie who feared the growth of capitalism[69]) and wrote very specifically in 1913:

> We do not advocate secession, in general we are opposed to secession. But we stand for the right to secede owing to reactionary, Great-Russian nationalism, which has so besmirched the idea of national co-existence that sometimes *closer* ties will be established *after* free secession! The right to self-determination is an exception to our general premise of centralisation. This exception is absolutely essential in view of reactionary Great-Russian nationalism; and any rejection of this exception is opportunism (as in the case of Rosa Luxemburg).[70]

The outbreak of war in 1914 did nothing to alter these views. Although accepting Hilferding's and Luxemburg's basic thesis about the advent of a new stage of international monopoly capitalism, Lenin did not accept Luxemburg's conclusion that this had now rendered all national groupings obsolete. For the pace of capitalist development was uneven and less advanced in the areas of Eastern Europe with which he was most concerned.

Lenin's enthusiasm for self-determination was naturally somewhat lessened with the success of the revolution. The Bolsheviks were caught in the uneasy dilemma of having to negotiate with existing governments while fostering the cause of revolution abroad. In his *Theses* on the Brest-Litovsk peace, for example, he wrote that 'no Marxist without renouncing the principles of Marxism and of socialism generally, can deny that the interests of socialism are higher than the interests of the right of nations to self-determination'.[71] And once the Bolshevik Party was established as the representative of the interests of the proletariat in a multinational state, there was little room for national autonomy. Lenin approved of the Red Army's subjugation of Georgia in 1921, although he was dismayed by the excessive brutality of Stalin and Orjonikidze. It was on this occasion that he made his well-known remark:

> If matters had come to such a pass that Orjonikidze could go to the extreme of applying physical violence, as comrade Dzerzhinsky informed me, we can imagine what a mess we have got ourselves into.[72]

In fact, compared with many of his fellow Bolsheviks – Bukharin, Radek and Stalin, for example – Lenin was extremely 'liberal' in his national policy. But his efforts to put his ideas into effect were hindered by the Civil War and by the inevitable centralising tendencies of the military situation and of the drive towards industrialisation.

Philosophy

In his early years as a Marxist, Lenin did not believe that Marxism required a specifically philosophical component. In his *What the Friends of the People Are*, for example, written in 1894, Lenin said that 'insistence on dialectics ... is nothing but a relic of Hegelianism out of which scientific socialism has grown, a relic of its manner of expression'.[73] Indeed, it was a common idea at the end of the nineteenth century that Marxism had no philosophical content. Bourgeois critics saw this as an objection, orthodox Marxists (Franz Mehring, for example) saw it as a quality, while still other Marxists tried to supplement their Marxism with the views of Kant or Mach. In his Siberian exile, however, Lenin read Plekhanov and decided that Marxism did need a philosophy along the lines of Plekhanov's own thought. But even after the founding of the Bolshevik Party, he still believed that there should be no specific 'party line' in philosophy, and he was content to leave discussion of these questions to the brilliant group of professional philosophers and intellectuals, such as Bogdanov, Lunacharsky and Gorki, who had joined the Bolsheviks in 1905.

Bogdanov was much influenced by the latest developments in the philosophy of physics and in particular by the ideas of Ernst Mach. Around the turn of the century there had developed among scientists a critical attitude to the rather crude materialism of their immediate predecessors. This was epitomised by the shift from Dalton's long-standing view of the solid atom as the basic building block of the world to viewing the atom as a cloud of negatively charged electrons. To put it crudely, 'matter' seemed to have disappeared. Anticipating the line of scientific advance, Mach attempted to construct a view of the world which consisted entirely in sensations: what we call objects (including the self) were merely groupings of sensations classified in the most economical and coherent manner.[74] These views were taken up by Bogdanov, who, in the system which he termed Empiriomonism, attempted to go further and show that physical and mental phenomena were the same experience, although differently organised. Central to Bogdanov's view was the idea of experience as organised: mental phenomena were organised individually, physical phenomena were organised socially.

Even in 1908 Lenin viewed Machism as a matter of individual choice not only within the Party but also within each faction. But he himself reacted vigorously to oppose it inside his own faction. There were two main reasons for this. Firstly, the dispute between Lenin and the Otzovists – fellow-Bolsheviks led by Bogdanov, who wished to boycott the elections to the third Duma – became acute from 1907 onwards. Lenin was in a small minority and Bogdanov was chosen as spokesman for the faction. Bogdanov and his friends then began to extend their influence outside Russia and established a Bolshevik school for Party activists at Gorki's house in Capri. Lenin was thus forced to undermine Bogdanov's authority – and with it his Left opponents – in order to reassert his own control. Secondly, *Die Neue Zeit* printed a translation of Bogdanov's article on *Ernst Mach and the Revolution* with a short preface informing the Germans that the Bolsheviks had made Mach's philosophy the basis of their faction while the Mensheviks upheld the philosophy of Spinoza and Holbach. The recent publication of the *Essays on the Philosophy of Marxism*, which constituted the most audacious publication of the Machists to date (particularly considering Lunacharsky's remarks on 'religious atheism'), gave support to this view. Thus Lenin was afraid that the Bolsheviks would be considered to be philosophical revisionists and the Mensheviks orthodox philosophers. The aim of Lenin's *Materialism and Empiriocriticism*, therefore, was not to join together the issues of philosophy and politics, but rather to separate them: it was the Mensheviks who were trying to join the issues together and argue from the Bolsheviks' revisionism in philosophy to their revisionism in politics. Even as Lenin was composing his book, Deborin wrote in the Menshevik newspaper that

> the stamp of subjectivism and voluntarism lies in all tactics of so-called Bolshevism – the philosophical expression of which is Machism. Our Machist-shaped Marxists are conscious Bolsheviks who give meaning to the practice and tactics of the latter. And Bolshevik tacticians are practical people who are unwitting Machists and idealists.[75]

Thus the real importance of Lenin's *Materialism and Empiriocriticism* lies not so much in its philosophical arguments as in his view that on practical political grounds it was the only philosophy that benefited the proletariat. Contemporary philosophical trends such as Machism were regarded as ideologies that were incorrect from the standpoint of Party work; and it was the practical work of the Party that was all-important. The central philosophical views expressed in *Materialism and Empiriocriticism* were of secondary and transitory importance.

Materialism and Empiriocriticism was an extended and very polemical critique of Mach and Bogdanov. In a passage which demonstrated his equation of epistemology with ontology, Lenin said:

> The question here is not of this or that formulation of materialism but of the antithesis between materialism and idealism, of the difference between the two fundamental *lines* in philosophy. Are we to proceed from things to sensation and thought? Or are we to proceed from thought and sensation to things?[76]

And matter he defined as: 'A philosophical category denoting the objective reality which is given to man by his sensations and which is copied, photographed and reflected by our sensations, while existing independently of them'.[77] These two doctrines – the external reality of the world and the 'copy' theory of knowledge – formed the central themes of Lenin's materialism. The basic conception in the book was that two philosophical schools confronted each other: materialism and idealism. The slightest concession to idealism would objectively give aid and succour to the bourgeoisie by ending up in fideism and religion. And he attempted to show not only that those who have denied the reality of an objective world existing independently of sense perception had in fact been religious believers, but also – and much more implausibly – that there was a necessary connection between agnosticism about the existence of an external world and religion.

There is little of abiding philosophical interest in *Materialism and Empiriocriticism*. Lenin's (quite mistaken) view was that 'Marx and Engels scores of times termed their philosophical views dialectical materialism'.[78] It is true that Lenin's book was little more than a simplified version of the theses of Engels's later writings which were constantly quoted.[79] (There were only four quotations from Marx, none of which bear on the main points.) In general Lenin's version of materialism was pre-Marxian. Even his accounts of Mach's positions were a travesty on several points. But it is perhaps slightly unfair to judge Lenin's book on its philosophical content. Its aim was primarily a political one – and here it largely succeeded. In more general terms, Lenin's harking back to certain crude forms of eighteenth-century materialism is understandable given Russia's backward economic situation. The materialism of the eighteenth century was part of the bourgeoisie's revolt against aristocratic privilege and its religious underpinnings. Since Russia had no strong bourgeoisie, materialism became a proletarian weapon in its struggle against the feudalism of the Tsarist regime. In short, Lenin's backwardness in philosophy was a function of Russia's backwardness in economic development.[80]

After the débâcle of 1914, Lenin turned his attention again to philosophy – and in a much less instrumental manner. It is an amazing fact that in order to reorientate his perspective in face of the catastrophe that had overtaken European socialism, Lenin spent an enormous amount of time studying Hegel in great detail. This is in sharp contrast with *Materialism and Empiriocriticism*, where there are only two remarks on Hegel – both of them superficial – and little on dialectics.[81] His notes (which extend to some 300 printed pages) were only published in 1929 to support the Party in its struggle against 'mechanist' deviations.[82] The most important part of these *Philosophical Notebooks* is Lenin's study of Hegel's *Logic*. His intention here was to invert Hegel's idealism and thus give a correct account of Marx's materialism. But the accent shifted from critical comments on Hegel to the enthusiastic acceptance of the dialectical elements in Hegel's thought. At the end of his notes Lenin wrote that 'in this most idealistic of Hegel's works there is the least idealism and the most materialism'.[83]

Lenin's best-known remark in the *Philosophical Notebooks* was on the relation of Hegel to *Capital*:

> It is impossible completely to understand Marx's *Capital* and especially its first chapter, without having thoroughly studied and understood the whole of Hegel's *Logic*. Consequently, half a century later none of the Marxists understood Marx!![84]

This was in fact a self-criticism – as was also his comment on his former philosophical mentor Plekhanov, who 'wrote on philosophy about one thousand pages' but 'about dialectics *proper* ... nil!!'[85] The *Philosophical Notebooks* insisted that the 'copies' in the reflection theories of knowledge were incomplete and partial and that we never know everything. But the divergence from *Materialism and Empiriocriticism* was most marked in the view that idealism was not an error but a one-sided exaggeration: 'intelligent idealism', he said, 'is closer to intelligent materialism than stupid materialism'.[86] The contrast between materialism and idealism was replaced by that between dialectical and non-dialectical thinking. Lenin praised paragraph 25 of Hegel's *Encyclopaedia*, 'where "cognition" (theoretical) and "will" (practical activity) are depicted as two sides, two methods, two means of abolishing the "one-sidedness" both of subjectivity and of objectivity'.[87] He talked of the unity of subject and object and of Marx's introducing the criterion of practice into the theory of knowledge in his *Theses on Feuerbach*. 'Man's consciousness', he concluded, 'not only reflects the objective world but creates it.'[88] Lenin emphasised continually the conflict and unity of opposites as the main dialectical law. Indeed, he occasionally got carried away into a sort of 'irrationalist vitalism'.[89] It is, of course, impossible to demonstrate any precise link between Lenin's reading of Hegel and his subsequent political attitudes,[90] but it is clear that Lenin's philosophical response to the 1914 débâcle – the *Philosophical Notebooks* – is paralleled by his work on imperialism in the sphere of economics. And some commentators have claimed to see the influence of Lenin's reading of Hegel in parts of his *State and Revolution*, in his political view of the relationship of Party and masses during the revolution, and in his 1920–1 discussion of trade unions.[91]

Notes

1. See above, pp. 72f.
2. V. Lenin *What Is to be Done? Selected Works* (Moscow, 1960) vol. 1, p. 211.
3. On how Lenin in fact misrepresents the Economists, see A. Wildman, *The Making of a Workers' Revolution* (Chicago, 1967) pp. 118ff.
4. V. Lenin, *What Is to be Done?*, op. cit., pp. 156f.
5. Ibid., p. 215.
6. Ibid., pp. 228f.
7. See further, V. Lenin, *Collected Works*, vol. 6, pp. 229ff., spelling out the details of this centralisation.
8. See R. Luxemburg, *Organizational Questions of Russian Social Democracy* (1904). Further, see pp. 48f. above.
9. For the difficulties that, for example, Kautsky had in appreciating what points of principle could be involved in the split., see C. Weill, *Marxistes russes et Social-democratie allemande 1898–1904* (Paris, 1977) pp. 123ff.
10. V. Lenin, 'Preface to the Collection *Twelve Years'*, *Collected Works*, vol. 13, p. 101.
11. V. Lenin, *Speech on the Party Programme*, *Collected Works*, vol. 6, p. 489.
12. See, in general, S. Schwarz, *The Russian Revolution of 1905* (Chicago, 1967) ch. 4.
13. V. Lenin, 'The Reorganisation of the Party', *Collected Works*, vol. 10, p. 32.
14. Ibid.

15. Ibid. p. 34.
16. Cf. V. Lenin, 'The Social Democrats and the Duma Elections', *Collected Works*, vol. 11, p. 434.
17. Cf. V. Lenin, 'A Tactical Platform for the Unity Congress', *Collected Works*, vol. 10, p. 163.
18. V. Lenin, *Report on the Unity Congress, Collected Works*, vol. 10, p. 376.
19. Ibid., p. 381.
20. See, for example, V. Lenin, 'Resolution Adopted by the Second Paris Group', *Collected Works*, vol. 17, pp. 221ff.
21. L. Schapiro, *The Communist Party of the Soviet Union*, 2nd edn (London, 1970) p. 174.
22. Quoted in I. Deutscher, *The Prophet Armed: Trotsky, 1879–1921* (Oxford, 1954) p. 258. For a view stressing the radical alterations in the Bolshevik party in 1917, see R. Daniels, *The Conscience of the Revolution* (New York, 1969) first two chapters.
23. R. Daniels, *The Conscience of the Revolution*, chs 5 and 6.
24. See P. Avrich, *Kronstadt 1921* (Princeton, N.J., 1970).
25. V. Lenin, 'Preliminary Draft Resolution of the Tenth Congress', *Collected Works*, vol. 32, p. 244.
26. Ibid., p. 246.
27. V. Lenin, *Two Tactics, Collected Works*, vol. 9, pp. 98f.
28. Ibid., p. 48.
29. V. Lenin, 'Social Democracy's Attitude Towards the Peasant Movement', *Collected Works*, vol. 9, pp. 236f.
30. V. Lenin, 'The Historical Meaning of the Inner-Party Struggle in Russia', *Collected Works*, vol. 16, p. 376.
31. V. Lenin, 'The Aim of the Proletarian Struggle in our Revolution', *Collected Works*, vol. 15, p. 371.
32. N. Sukhanov, *The Russian Revolution, 1917* (London and New York, 1955) vol. 1, p. 287.
33. V. Lenin, 'The Tasks of the Proletariat in the Present Revolution', *Collected Works*, vol. 24, p. 22.
34. V. Lenin, 'Letters on Tactics', *Collected Works*, vol. 24, p. 45. On the view that Lenin's *April Theses* marked a radical break from his previous theories, to which he then returned by his emphasis on the role of the Soviets, see J. Frankel, 'Lenin's Doctrinal Revolution of April 1917', *Journal of Contemporary History*, Apr. 1969.
35. V. Lenin, 'The Seventh All-Russia Conference', *Collected Works*, vol. 24, p. 263.
36. V. Lenin, 'The Political Situation: Four Theses', *Collected Works*, vol. 41. p. 442.
37. V. Lenin, 'The Bolsheviks must Assume Power', *Collected Works*, vol. 26, p. 19.
38. V. Lenin, *Imperialism, The Highest Stage of Capitalism, Collected Works*, vol. 22, p. 241.
39. See, for example, D. Fieldhouse, *The Theory of Capitalist Imperialism* (London, 1967) pp. 187ff.
40. Cf. E. Stokes, 'Late Nineteenth Century Colonial Expansion and the Attack on the Theory of Economic Imperialism: A Case of Mistaken Identity?', *Historical Journal*, vol. 12 (1969), pp. 289ff.
41. V. Lenin, *Imperialism* ... , op. cit., p. 260.
42. Ibid., p. 274.

43. Ibid., p. 281.
44. See further E. Hobsbawm, 'Lenin and the "Aristocracy of Labour" ', *Monthly Review*, Apr. 1970, pp. 47ff.
45. V. Lenin, *Imperialism* ... , op. cit., p. 300.
46. See above, pp. 64ff.
47. For Lenin's considerable debt to Bukharin, see S. Cohen, *Bukharin and the Bolshevik Revolution* (New York, 1973) pp. 25ff.
48. V. Lenin, 'Several Theses', *Collected Works*, vol. 21, p. 402.
49. V. Lenin, 'Farewell Letter to Swiss Workers', *Collected Works*, vol. 23, p. 373.
50. L. Colletti, *From Rousseau to Lenin* (London and New York, 1972), p. 224.
51. See S. Cohen, *Bukharin and the Bolshevik Revolution* (New York, 1973) pp. 39ff.
52. V. Lenin, *Selected Works* (Moscow, 1960), vol. 2, p. 320.
53. Ibid., p. 338.
54. Cf. his very different view of the Commune as 'a government such as ours should not be' in *Two Tactics, Collected Works*, vol. 9, p. 81.
55. V. Lenin, *Selected Works*, vol. 2, p. 381.
56. Ibid., p. 328.
57. Ibid., p. 341.
58. Ibid., p. 322.
59. V. Lenin, 'Speech against Bukharin's Amendment', *Collected Works*, vol. 27, p. 148.
60. M. Liebman, *Le Léninisme sous Lénine* (Paris, 1973), vol. 2, p. 109.
61. V. Lenin, *Left-Wing Communism – An Infantile Disorder, Collected Works*, vol. 31, p. 48.
62. See Bukharin and Preobrazhensky's comments on this problem in *The ABC of Communism* (Harmondsworth, 1969) pp. 237ff.
63. V. Lenin, Letter to A. Tsyurupa, *Collected Works*, vol. 36, p. 566. See also his letter to Bogdanov of December 1921, *Collected Works*, vol. 38, p. 557.
64. V. Lenin, 'The Party Crisis', *Collected Works*, vol. 32, p. 48.
65. V. Lenin, 'Report of the Central Committee to the Eleventh Congress', *Collected Works*, vol. 33, p. 288.
66. See p. 127 below and, for detail, R. Daniels, *The Conscience of the Revolution* (New York, 1969) pp. 119ff.
67. V. Lenin, 'On Manifesto of Armenian Social Democrats', *Collected Works*, vol. 6, p. 327.
68. V. Lenin, 'Resolution on the National Question', *Collected Works*, vol. 19, p. 427.
69. For the differences between Lenin and Luxemburg here, see H. Davis, Introduction to Rosa Luxemburg, *The National Question: Selected Writings* (New York, 1976) pp. 8ff.
70. V. Lenin, Letter to S. Shahumyan, *Collected Works*, vol. 19, p. 501.
71. Lenin, 'Theses on the Question of a Separate Peace', *Collected Works*, vol. 26, p. 449.
72. V. Lenin, 'The Question of Nationalities', *Collected Works*, vol. 36, p. 605.
73. V. Lenin, *What the Friends of the People Are, Collected Works*, vol. 1, p. 164.
74. Further on Mach, see J. Blackmore, *Ernst Mach* (Berkeley, 1972) ch. 15.
75. Quoted in D. Joravsky, *Soviet Marxism and Natural Science* (London, 1961) p. 34.
76. V. Lenin, *Materialism and Empiriocriticism, Collected Works*, vol. 14, p. 42.
77. Ibid., p. 130.

78. Ibid., p. 19.
79. This was mainly *Anti-Dühring*. *The Dialectics of Nature* was not yet published.
80. This theme is elaborated in A. Pannekoek, *Lenin as Philosopher* (London, 1975) pp. 92ff.
81. For a contrary interpretation, see D.H. Ruben, *Marxism and Materialism* (Atlantic Highlands, 1977) particularly chs 5 and 6.
82. See below, pp. 139f.
83. V. Lenin, *Philosophical Notebooks, Collected Works*, vol. 38, p. 234.
84. Ibid., p. 180.
85. Ibid., p. 277.
86. Ibid., p. 276.
87. Ibid., p. 208
88. Ibid., p. 212. See also pp. 195, 201, 293, 211, 213.
89. Cf. L. Colletti, *Marxism and Hegel* (New York and London, 1973) pp. 162f.
90. For a more positive view, see M. Lowy, 'From the *Great Logic* of Hegel to the Finland Station in Petrograd', *Critique*, 6 (spring 1976), pp. 8ff.
91. See, for example, H. Lefebvre, *La Pensée de Lénine* (Paris, 1957) pp. 189ff; M. Liebman, *Le Léninisme sous Lénine* (Paris, 1973), vol. 2, pp. 349ff.

Further reading

Lenin: texts

Lenin's *Collected Works* are available in a 45-volume edition published in Moscow.

Lenin: commentaries

Two detailed biographies, both by men who had met Lenin, are Shub's *Lenin* and Fischer's *The Life of Lenin*. Wolfe's account in *Three Who made a Revolution* is good, but unfortunately stops in 1914. On Lenin's early life there is Deutscher's fragment of his projected biography. Rather dubious psychological interpretation is offered by Possony's *Lenin: The Compulsive Revolutionary* and Theen's *Lenin: Genesis and Development of a Revolutionary*. A good, short introduction is Morgan's *Lenin*. On the disillusion of Lenin's last years, see Lewin's *Lenin's Last Struggle*. Of his contemporaries, the most valuable book on Lenin as a person is Krupskaya's *Memories of Lenin*. This can be supplemented by the accounts of Balabanoff, Trotsky, Valentinov and Zetkin, but the most authoritative account is now Service's three-volume *Lenin: A Political Life*. Lenin's more ruthless activities are documented by Pipes's collection and Read's *Life* provides a good short introduction.

On Lenin's thought in general, Fischer's *The Essential Lenin* is a reliable, though very short, introduction and Shukman's *Lenin and the Russian Revolution* is a slightly longer one. Meyer's *Leninism* is still well worth reading. Rather too hostile to Lenin are Conquest's Modern Masters *Lenin* and Ulam's *The Bolsheviks*, although the latter contains a lot of detailed research. Lukács's *Lenin* is a short philosophical interpretation. There are very useful collections on various aspects of Lenin's thought by Sweezy and Magdoff, and by Reddaway and Schapiro. More recently, we have Cliff's thorough-going apologia in his three-volume *Lenin*. Liebman's *Leninism under Lenin* is an excellently insightful book, although unfortunately abridged from the original French. Best of all is Harding's two-volume *Lenin's Political Thought*, which reconstructs Lenin's different political strategies before and after 1914 with masterly scholarship. See also his useful synthesis *Leninism*, the books by Besancon and Lovell, both strongly critical of Lenin, and Polan's thought-provoking *Lenin and the End of Politics*.

In more specialised areas, Mandel contains a defence of Lenin's concept of the Party. On Lenin's change of tactics in 1917, see the excellent article by Frankel. On the international aspects of Lenin's strategy, see the works of Page. On Lenin's contributions to philosophy, see the critiques of Paul, Jordan and, above all, Pannekoek – and the defence of Lenin in the last two chapters of Ruben's *Marxism and Materialism*. On Lenin's rather functional attitude to culture, see Claudin-Urondo's *Lenin and the Cultural Revolution*.

1905 and 1917

On 1905, there is Trotsky's enthralling account with the same title. The best modern analysis is Schwarz's *The Russian Revolution of 1905*. As will be seen from the bibliography below, the books on 1917 are legion. The best compact account is Liebman's *The Russian Revolution*. Daniels and Ferro are both extended accounts of October, while Chamberlain's two volumes continue until 1924. Katkov and Kochan are both stimulating in their different ways. The most fundamental work is undoubtedly Carr's *The Bolshevik Revolution*. From the anarchist point of view, see the consistently anti-Bolshevik critique of Brinton.

Of eye-witness accounts, Trotsky's masterpiece – *The History of the Russian Revolution* – is in a class by itself. Sukhanov's *The Russian Revolution* is a very full account of his observations by a political journalist; similarly Reed's exhilarating *Ten Days that Shook the World*. Kerensky has defended his position in numerous memoirs. Pethybridge's *Eye-Witnesses of the Russian Revolution* is a useful collection, and Laqueur provides a history of the changing interpretations of 1917 (and after). See also Pipes's recent overview *The Russian Revolution*, and the two good studies by Read and by Wade.

Bibliography

Lenin: texts

V.I. Lenin, *Collected Works*, 45 vols (Moscow, 1960–70).
—— *Selected Works* – in one volume (Moscow, 1968); in three volumes (Moscow, 1960–1).
—— *The Essential Works of Lenin*, ed. M. Christian (New York, 1966). *The Lenin Anthology*, ed. R. Tucker (New York, 1975).

Lenin: commentaries

Angelica Balabanoff, *Impressions of Lenin*, Foreword by B.D. Wolfe (Ann Arbor, 1964).
Alain Besancon, *The Rise of the Gulag: The Intellectual Origins of Leninism* (New York, 1981).
M. Brinton, *The Bolsheviks and Workers' Control* (London, 1970).
Fernando Claudin, 'Democracy and Dictatorship in Lenin and Kautsky', *New Left Review*, 106 (1977).
C. Claudin-Urondo, *Lenin and the Cultural Revolution* (Hassocks, Sussex, 1977).
Tony Cliff, *Lenin*, 3 vols (London, 1975–8).
Lucio Colletti, 'Lenin's *State and Revolution*', in R. Blackburn (ed.), *Revolution and Class Struggle: A Reader in Marxist Politics* (London, 1977); and L. Colletti, *From Rousseau to Lenin: Studies in Ideology and Society* (London and New York, 1972).
R. Conquest, *Lenin* (London, 1972).
Isaac Deutscher, *Lenin's Childhood* (Oxford, 1970).
Ernst Fischer, *The Essential Lenin* (New York, 1972).
Louis B. Fischer, *The Life of Lenin* (London, 1965).
Jonathan Frankel, 'Lenin's Doctrinal Revolution of April 1917', *Journal of Contemporary History* (Apr 1969).
Maxim Gorky, *Days With Lenin* (New York, 1932).
Thomas Hammond, *Lenin On Trade Unions and Revolution: 1893–1917* (New York, 1957).
Neil Harding, *Leninism* (London, 1996).
—— *Lenin's Political Thought*, 2 vols (New York and London, 1977f.).
Christopher Hill, *Lenin and Russian Revolution* (London, 1947).
Z.A. Jordan, 'The Dialectical Materialism of Lenin', *Slavic Review*, XXV, 2 (1966).
N. Krupskaya, *Memories of Lenin*, with an Introduction by Andrew Rothstein (London, 1970).
Vladimir Ilyich Lenin: A Biography (Moscow, 1965).
Moshe Lewin, *Lenin's Last Struggle* (London, 1969).
M. Liebman, *Leninism Under Lenin* (London, 1975).
David Lovell, *From Marx to Lenin: The Evaluation of Marx's Responsibility for Soviet Authoritarianism* (Cambridge, 1984).
George Lukács, *Lenin: A Study on the Unity of his Thought* (London, 1970).
Ernest Mandel, 'The Leninist Theory of Organisation', in R. Blackburn (ed.), *Revolution and Class Struggle: A Reader in Marxist Politics* (London, 1977).
—— *The Leninist Theory of Organisation* (London, 1971).
A.G. Meyer, *Leninism*, 2nd edn (New York, 1962).
M.C. Morgan, *Lenin* (London, 1971).

S.W. Page, 'Lenin and Self-Determination', *Slavonic and East European Review* (1950).
—— 'Lenin: The National Question and the Baltic States, 1917–1919', *The American Slavic and East European Review*, VII, 1 (1948).
—— *Lenin and World Revolution* (New York, 1959).
—— 'The Role of the Proletariat in March 1917: Contradictions Within the Official Bolshevik Version', *Russian Review*, IX (1950).
Anton Pannekoek, *Lenin as Philosopher* (London, 1975).
G.A. Paul, 'Lenin's Theory of Perception', *Analysis*, vol. 5 (1938).
R. Pipes (ed.), *The Unknown Lenin* (New Haven and London, 1996).
A.J. Polan, *Lenin and the End of Politics* (London, 1984).
Stefan T. Possony, *Lenin: The Compulsive Revolutionary* (London, 1966).
C. Read, *Lenin: A Revolutionary Life* (London, 2005).
D. Ruben, *Marxism and Materialism* (Hassocks, 1977).
L. Schapiro, 'Putting the Lid on Leninism', *Government and Opposition*, II, 2 (1967).
L. Schapiro and P. Reddaway (eds), *Lenin. The Man, the Theorist, the Leader: A Reappraisal* (London, 1967).
R. Service, *Lenin: A Biography* (Basingstoke, 2000).
Robert Service, *Lenin: A Political Life*, 3 vols (London, 1985–94).
David Shub, *Lenin: A Biography* (New York, 1948).
Harold Shukman, *Lenin and the Russian Revolution* (New York, 1968).
Peter Struve, 'My Contacts and Conflicts with Lenin', *The Slavonic and East European Review*, XII, 36 (1934).
Paul M. Sweezy and H. Magdoff (eds), 'Lenin Today: Eight Essays on the Hundredth Anniversary of Lenin's Birth', *Monthly Review*, XXI, 11 (1970).
Rolf Theen, *Lenin: Genesis and Development of a Revolutionary* (London, 1974).
Leon Trotsky, *On Lenin: Notes Towards a Biography* (London, 1971).
Adam Ulam, *Lenin and the Bolsheviks* (New York, 1964).
Nikolai Valentinov, *The Early Years of Lenin*, ed. R. Theen (Ann Arbor, 1969).
—— *Encounters with Lenin* (Oxford, 1968).
D. Volkogonov, *Lenin: Life and Legacy* (London, 1994).
J. White, *Lenin: The Practice and Theory of Revolution* (London, 2001).
B. Williams, *Lenin* (Harlow, 2000).
Edmund Wilson, *To the Finland Station* (London, 1960).
Bertram D. Wolfe, 'Leninism' in M.M. Drachkovitch (ed.), *Marxism in The Modern World* (Stanford, 1965).
—— *Three Who Made a Revolution* (New York, 1948).
Clara Zetkin, *Reminiscences of Lenin* (New York, 1934).

1905

Sydney Harcave, *First Blood: The Russian Revolution of 1905* (London, 1965).
H. Schurer, 'The Russian Revolution of 1905 and the Origins of German Communism', *The Slavonic and East European Review* 39 (1960–1).
Solomon M. Schwarz, *The Russian Revolution of 1905: The Workers' Movement and the Formation of Bolshevism and Menshevism* (Chicago, 1967).
Leon Trotsky, *1905* (London, 1972).

1917 and its aftermath

Raphael R. Abramovitch, *The Soviet Revolution: 1917–1939* (London, 1962).
Arthur Adams (ed.), *The Russian Revolution and Bolshevik Victory: Causes and Processes* (Lexington, Mass., 1972).
Peter Arshinov, *History of the Makhnovist Movement: 1918–1921* (Chicago, 1974).
Abraham Ascher, 'Russian Marxism and the German Revolution: 1917–1920', *Archiv für Sozialgeschichte*, 6–7 (1966–7).
N. Berdyaev, *The Russian Revolution* (London, 1935).
The Bolsheviks and the October Revolution: Minutes of the Central Committee of the Russian Social-Democratic Labour Party (Bolsheviks) August 1917–February 1918 (London, 1974).
R.P. Browder and A.F. Kerensky (eds), *The Provisional Government: 1917*, 3 vols (Stanford, 1962).
J. Bunyan and H.H. Fisher, *The Bolshevik Revolution 1917–1918: Documents and Materials* (Stanford, 1934).
E.H. Carr, 'The Background of the Russian Revolution', in Heinz Lubasz (ed.), *Revolutions in Modern European History* (London, 1966).
—— *1917: Before and After* (London, 1969).
—— *The Bolshevik Revolution: 1917–1923*, 3 vols (London, 1950–3).
William H. Chamberlain, *The Russian Revolution: 1917–1921*, 2 vols (London, 1935).
V. Chernov, *The Great Russian Revolution* (New Haven, Conn., 1936).
Robert V. Daniels, *Red October: The Bolshevik Revolution of 1917* (New York, 1967).
—— 'The Russian Revolution Runs its Course', in H. Lubasz (ed.), *Revolutions in Modern European History* (London, 1966).
Marc Ferro, *The Russian Revolution of February 1917* (London, 1973).
O. Figes, *A People's Tragedy: The Russian Revolution 1891–1924* (London, 1996).
O.H. Gankin and H.H. Fisher, *The Bolsheviks and the World War: The Origins of the Third International* (London, 1940).
George Katkov, *Russia 1917: The February Revolution* (London, 1969).
—— 'German Foreign Office Documents on Financial Support to the Bolsheviks in 1917', *International Affairs*, XXXII (1956).
Alexander F. Kerensky, *The Catastrophe: Kerensky's Own Story of the Russian Revolution* (New York, 1927).
—— *The Kerensky Memoirs* (London, 1966).
—— *The Prelude to Bolshevism* (London, 1919).
Lionel Kochan, *Russia in Revolution* (London, 1970).
R. Kowatski, *The Bolshevik Party in Conflict. The Left Opposition of 1918* (Basingstoke, 1991).
Walter Laqueur, *The Fate of the Revolution: Interpretations of Soviet History* (London, 1967).
Marcel Liebman, *The Russian Revolution* (London, 1970).
Roger Pethybridge (ed.), *Eye-witnesses of the Russian Revolution* (London, 1964).
Richard Pipes, *The Formation of the Soviet Union* (Cambridge, Mass., 1954).
—— *The Russian Revolution* (New York, 1990).
M. Phillips Price, *My Reminiscences of the Russian Revolution* (London, 1921).
Alexander Rabinovitch, *Prelude to Revolution: The Petrograd Bolsheviks and the July 1917 Uprising* (Bloomington, Ind., 1968).

O.H. Radkey, *The Election of the Russian Constituent Assembly of 1917* (Cambridge, Mass., 1950).

—— *The Agrarian Foes of Bolshevism: Promise and Default of the Russian Socialist Revolutionaries, February to October 1917* (New York, 1958).

C. Read, *From Tsar to Soviets: The Russian People and their Revolution* (London, 1996).

J. Reed, *Ten Days that Shook the World* (New York, 1935).

John L. Snell, 'The Russian Revolution and the German Social Democratic Party in 1917', *The American Slavic and East European Review*, XI, 1 (1956).

N.N. Sukhanov, *The Russian Revolution, 1917: Eye-witness Account*, 2 vols (London and New York, 1955).

Leon Trotsky, *The History of the Russian Revolution*, 3 vols (London, 1967).

R. Wade, *The Russian Revolution 1917* (Cambridge, 2000).

Rex A. Wade, *The Russian Search for Peace: February–October 1917* (Stanford, 1969).

8
Russian Marxism in the 1920s

War Communism

There were two main problems facing the victorious Bolsheviks: a political one – the role and function of the Party and the state; and an economic one – how to lay the foundations of a socialist economy. The economic problem was basic and formed the substance of the major controversies among Russian Marxists, who, particularly after the failure of revolution in Western Europe in 1921 and 1923, turned their attention more to internal problems. War Communism, the New Economic Policy (NEP) and finally the doctrine of Socialism in One Country were all different responses to the problem of how to develop an industrialised socialist economy in a backward peasant country. The almost total lack of previous thinking about post-revolutionary economic problems meant that the Bolsheviks had to start from scratch and the ravages of the Civil War involved an even more radical reconstruction. There was little in Marx himself to guide. The October victory had taken the Bolsheviks by surprise and, most importantly, they had relied on the supposedly international nature of the revolution and consequent help from a victorious West European proletariat to overcome the problems created by their own backwardness.

The first economic measures of the Bolsheviks were relatively moderate: selective nationalisation, an eight-hour working day, a redistribution of nationalised land among the peasants on a more equitable, though still individual, basis, and the sporadic and semi-spontaneous institution of workers' control.

By the spring of 1918, however, the economic situation worsened. Workers' control further dislocated an economy already exhausted by years of war and, in face of the threatened chaos, Lenin proposed what he called a 'state capitalism' explicitly modelled on the German war economy, a brief forerunner of the kind of retreat embodied in the NEP. It consisted in a dual effort to gain greater central control over the economy by the reinforcement of labour discipline, wage incentives and managerial authority, and to arrive at a compromise with larger financial interests; in other words, 'to suspend the offensive against capital'[1] and try to establish a *modus vivendi* with the old economic order.

By the summer of 1918, the onset of the Civil War rendered Lenin's 'state capitalism' (which had already come under fire from the Left Communists) untenable. The extreme state control known as 'War Communism' was instituted in order for the Soviet Government simply to survive. War Communism had three main aspects. Firstly, there was a huge increase in nationalisation, beginning with the Decree of General Nationalisations of June 1918 which brought almost all large-scale enterprises under state control. Crippling shortages of fuel and raw materials caused by the war blockade and enemy occupation of the economically most advanced areas of Russia made government intervention even more essential. The state monopolised exchange and government bureaucracy necessarily increased. Secondly, the runaway inflation which ruined the moneyed classes and large sections of the peasantry (the workers were partially protected by payment in kind) meant that the government could not increase its resources by issuing more money and had to requisition supplies from the peasantry. This alienated the support of the middle peasantry and resulted in a lowering of peasant productivity. Thirdly, as the pressure of the Civil War ended, demobilised units of the Red Army were assigned to particularly urgent tasks and there was a partial militarisation of the labour force under the discipline of Trade Union officials who were appointed from above.

These harsh policies had the support of all the Bolshevik leaders. One of the most optimistic was Trotsky, who was able to turn his attention from military matters at the beginning of 1920 and became one of the strongest advocates of the militarisation of labour as being necessary in a backward country and hastening the necessarily painful birth of a socialist economy. But Trotsky was not alone. Bukharin wrote the classical theoretical defence of War Communism in his *Economics of the Transition Period* published in 1920. After analysing the growth in state monopoly capitalism and the World War as a sign of its collapse, Bukharin departed from the classical Marxist tradition by proclaiming that a revolutionary period implied an initial disintegration of productive forces. Taking issue with Hilferding, who had said that a takeover of the six major banks in Berlin would enable the proletariat to control the

German economy, Bukharin insisted that 'the Communist revolution of the proletariat is accompanied, as in every revolution, by a *reduction* in productive powers'[2] a view which was comforting for a backward country like Russia. Bukharin also stated that the science of political economy would not exist under socialism and thereby gave the impression that post-revolutionary Russia was less subject to objective constructions than other countries.[3] And this fitted well with his blunt view of the necessity of compulsion:

> Proletarian compulsion in all its forms, from institutions to compulsory labour, constitutes, as paradoxical as this may sound, a method of the formation of a new Communist humanity from the human material of the capitalist epoch.[4]

This view was combined with a strong emphasis on the all-encompassing role of the state:

> The 'nationalisation' of the trade unions and the effectual nationalisation of all mass organisations of the proletariat result from the internal logic of the process of transformation itself. The minutest cells of the labour apparatus must transform themselves into agents of the general process of organisation, which is systematically directed and led by the collective reason of the working class, which finds its material embodiment in the highest and most all-encompassing organisation, in its state apparatus. Thus the system of state capitalism dialectically transforms itself into its own inversion, into the state form of workers' socialism.[5]

Lenin read Bukharin's book carefully and made critical comments on it.[6] Although disapproving of some of the terminology, Lenin basically did approve of Bukharin's views and in particular of his grim chapter on 'Extra-economic compulsion in the transition period'.[7]

The New Economic Policy

But War Communism could not last. It was to find a more lasting reincarnation in certain aspects of Stalin's policy of Socialism in One Country, but by the beginning of 1921 it was clear that it was simply exacerbating the country's economic problems rather than solving them. Unless drastic changes were made, the government itself would be in jeopardy. It was no coincidence that the Kronstadt rebellion occurred just as the New

Economic Policy (NEP) was being adopted at the Tenth Party Congress; and the approaching end of the Civil War removed the immediate justification for extreme measures. The NEP, which was to last seven years, began in March 1921 when the requisitioning system was replaced by a tax in kind which enabled the peasants to keep a fixed share of their surplus. This in turn led to the abolition of restrictions on free trade and the restoration of market relations between agriculture and industry. There was a certain amount of denationalisation, but only of small-scale enterprises, and industry was organised in trusts enjoying a limited market independence. In November 1921 the state bank was reopened, hard currency policies adopted, and the rouble stabilised in 1923.

The change from War Communism to the NEP was adopted on Lenin's initiative. Although rather apologetic about it in his speeches at the Tenth Party Congress,[8] Lenin soon presented the NEP as a return to the state capitalist policies of early 1918 after the aberration of War Communism. Concerning the last three years, he wrote: 'it was the war and the ruin that forced us into war communism. It was not, and could not be a policy that corresponded to the economic tasks of the proletariat. It was a makeshift.'[9] Some months later he said that War Communism was 'in complete contradiction to all we had previously written concerning the transition from capitalism to socialism'.[10] At the same time, Lenin continually referred to NEP as a 'retreat', implying a temporary regrouping of forces before a new offensive. On the other hand, Lenin did not regard NEP as simply a short-time expedient: 'the policy is a long-term one and is being adopted in earnest'.[11] The aim was to build an economically stable union with the peasantry and he even hinted at a ten-year span.[12] The hallmark of this transitional mixed system or state capitalism was its gradualism: 'what is new at the present moment for our Revolution is the need to resort to a "reformist", gradualist, cautious and roundabout approach to the solution of the fundamental problems of economic development'.[13] Or again: 'Compared with previous, revolutionary, approaches this is a reformist approach (revolution is a change which breaks the old order to its very foundations, and not one that cautiously, slowly, and gradually, remodels it, trying to break as little as possible).'[14]

After some initial hesitation Bukharin became one of the chief exponents of NEP. He admitted that his conception of War Communism had been adequate for the destruction of the old order, but not for the construction of the new. He justified the gradualism of the NEP on the grounds that the proletariat (unlike the revolutionary bourgeoisie) had to be backward at the moment of revolution and could only ripen toward revolutionary maturity in a post-revolutionary society; and this society would be controlled by a party guided, at least initially, by bourgeois intellectuals. (Bukharin was alive to the dangers that this involved and even talked of the possible emergence of a 'new class'.)

Although he had urged the change to a tax in kind a year before the inauguration of the NEP, Trotsky did not go along with the policy. He voiced opposition to it at its inception and could not accept the view that War Communism was an aberration forced on Russia by external circumstances. He admitted the success of NEP in agriculture but did not think it of any use in tackling the main problem of industrialisation. Indeed, the onset of NEP marked a decline in the general influence of Trotsky. An instance of this is the major debate on the role of the trade unions that occupied the party at the beginning of 1921. Whereas the Workers' Opposition argued for full proletarian democracy and the restoration of workers' control over industry, Trotsky – after his experience of the recalcitrant trade unions towards the end of the Civil War – argued that they should be deprived of their autonomy and integrated into the machinery of government. Lenin opposed what he called Trotsky's 'bureaucratic harassment' of the trade unions and sought for a compromise which guaranteed a measure of autonomy to them. In spite of support from Bukharin, Trotsky's views were decisively rejected at the Tenth Congress.

The Tenth Congress was also notable for its enthusiasm for making the Party increasingly monolithic. In March 1919 a five-man Political Bureau (Politburo), which had had a brief existence before the seizure of power, was reconstituted. The Civil War had meant that many major decisions could only be taken by a few, and the Central Committee of twenty-seven members was too unwieldy. An organisational Bureau and a Secretariat were established at the same time. Only Stalin was a member of all four bodies. As economic policy became more liberal, so the need for tighter political control increased. The Congress violently denounced the Workers' Opposition and banned factions inside the Party. Nevertheless, with the illness and death of Lenin some form of collective leadership was necessary although it was inherently unstable. The increasingly monolithic nature of the Party made it easier for those in control to enforce their own domination. With Lenin incapacitated it was natural that Stalin, Zinoviev and Kamenev should form a bloc to oppose Trotsky, who was still the most prestigious of the Bolshevik leaders. Trotsky singularly failed to react to his threatened exclusion from power: he did not exploit Lenin's criticisms of Stalin with the ruthlessness that would have been necessary; and he failed to champion the cause of inner party democracy before it was too late. It was only at the end of 1923, when Lenin lay dying and the balance of power had tipped decisively against Trotsky, that he spoke out. In his pamphlet *The New Course* (which contained all the major themes later elaborated in his critique of Stalinism) he called for the democratisation of Party organs and for free speech within the Party, while denouncing the trend to personal rule and bureaucratism. But the waning of Trotsky's influence was determined by larger factors than internal rivalries in the Politburo. With the Civil War at an end, the Commissariat of War was no longer at the centre of attention and Trotsky's particular administrative *élan* no longer in demand. Alone of the Politburo members Trotsky, a late recruit to Bolshevism, had no independent power base in a party organisation. The possibilities of revolution in Europe (to which Trotsky attached particular importance) were receding and the country in general – exhausted by the 'heroic' age of which Trotsky was a symbol – longed for a respite and a period of reconstruction. More prosaic economic questions began to dominate party discussions.

The NEP was an unsatisfactory policy in many respects. As Trotsky pointed out, it did not solve the fundamental problem of industrialisation in a backward country. There appeared to be a contradiction between the need to raise capital and expand the economy – for which agriculture was the only source – and the need to expand industry, which could only be done at the expense of agriculture. Should agriculture or industry play the leading role in economic development? Bukharin and Zinoviev took the view that an increase in purchasing power in the agricultural sector was a necessary condition for an increase in industrial productivity. Trotsky, on the other hand, thought that without an increased flow of industrial goods the production of grain and raw materials would decline. These two views went back to the division of opinion over War Communism, which had been viewed by those more pragmatically inclined as a temporary expedient dictated by military necessity and by others, more inspired by the heroic traditions of Bolshevism, as a correct, although premature, drive to socialism that was to be resumed as soon as circumstances permitted.

These two opposing viewpoints were first clearly expressed in response to the so-called 'scissors' crisis which emerged in 1923. This involved a rise in industrial prices and a simultaneous fall in agricultural prices, which was largely caused by the monopolistic position of state industry and its ability to turn the terms of trade with the agricultural sector in its own favour. Bukharin, as spokesman for the anti-Trotsky bloc, held to the view that a prosperous peasant economy was the prerequisite for industrial recovery and that any other policy would prejudice the historic alliance with the peasantry. Low industrial prices were necessary to expand the present peasant production and make industry itself more efficient. This would yield capital for investment through the growing profitability of state industry, taxes on the prospering agricultural sector, and the savings of the rich peasants or *kulaks*. The contrary view found its chief exponent in Preobrazhensky. Putting the emphasis clearly on production rather than circulation, Preobrazhensky considered that only the private sector – the peasants – could supply the capital necessary for industrial development. In his *New Economics* of 1924 he declared the necessity for 'primitive socialist accumulation' which was of necessity opposed to private accumulation. Its 'law' he defined as follows:

> The more a country which is changing to a socialist organisation of production is economically backward, petty bourgeois and peasant-orientated, and the smaller the contribution that the proletariat of the country concerned can contribute to the stock of socialist accumulation when the socialist revolution takes place, the more (proportionally) will socialist accumulation be compelled to rely on obtaining a portion of the surplus product of the pre-socialist economic sector and the smaller will be the relative importance of accumulation on the basis of its own production, that is, the less will it be nourished by the surplus product of workers in socialist industry.[15]

The underdeveloped industrial sector could not provide the necessary capital: the state would have to extract it from the peasantry, just as primitive capitalist accumulation had extracted it from non-capitalist sectors. The scissors crisis was thus to be welcomed and perpetuated by state intervention. Speed was of the essence in the critical transition period when the economy had neither the advantages of capitalism nor those of socialism: the very nature of the economic situation would require intensive industrialisation by means of a massive movement of surplus value from the agricultural to the state-owned sector irrespective of the wishes of the Party leadership. Trotsky was basically sympathetic to Preobrazhensky's analysis, although he denied that he wished to exploit the peasantry and obviously disagreed with Preobrazhensky's view that accumulation could proceed in an isolated economy. Stalin did not initially come down on either side in this controversy – although he was eager to exploit the left's apparently anti-peasant bias for political ends – and only after gaining a position of unassailable ascendancy did he inject his doctrine of Socialism in One Country with elements borrowed from Trotsky and Preobrazhensky.

Socialism in One Country

There were several reasons for the success of the doctrine of Socialism in One Country. The international climate was not favourable to revolution: the failure of the abortive risings in Saxony and Hamburg in 1923, in particular, lent force to the view in Russia that the European proletariat was not to be relied on and even to a certain extent disdain for the inefficiency of European Communists as compared to the victorious Bolsheviks. The country as a whole was exhausted by years of repulsing external aggression and of civil war and eager now for some policy of economic progress. Socialism in One Country seemed to present a clear and optimistic framework in which to pursue economic goals. And there was also the temptation of harnessing nationalistic sentiments and a proud feeling of independence to further the pursuit of economic aims.

Socialism in One Country had its origin in Bukharin's defence of NEP as an isolationist doctrine which guaranteed Russia's ability to 'grow into' socialism through her own resources. Stalin's conversion to the doctrine was sudden. As late as April 1924 he was saying that

> overthrowing the power of the bourgeoisie and establishing the power of the proletariat in one country does not yet ensure the complete victory of socialism. The principal task of socialism – the organisation of socialist production – has still to be fulfilled. Can this task be fulfilled, can the final victory of socialism be achieved in one country without the joint efforts of the proletarians in several advanced countries? No, it cannot.[16]

The doctrine was first enunciated by Stalin in an article of December 1924. Here he drew from Lenin's remarks on combined and uneven development a conclusion that

> the victory of socialism in one country, even if this country is less developed in the capitalist sense, while capitalism is preserved in other countries, even if these countries are more highly developed in a capitalist sense – is quite possible and probable.[17]

Trotsky's idea of permanent revolution, by contrast, because of its alleged pessimism about the success of a socialist revolution in Russia, was branded as 'a variety of Menshevism'.[18] Stalin admitted that for the 'complete' victory of socialism the support of the world proletariat was indeed necessary. But in *Problems of Leninism* (January 1926) he formulated his doctrine more forcefully as follows:

> We mean the possibility of solving the contradictions between the proletariat and the peasantry with the aid of the internal forces of our country, the possibility of the proletariat assuming power and using that power to build a complete socialist society in our country, with the sympathy and the support of the proletariat of other countries, but without the preliminary victory of the proletarian revolution in other countries.[19]

And the rider to it was toned down in that the 'complete, final' victory of socialism required the success of the world proletariat only in the sense that without it there would still exist 'the impossibility of having full guarantees against intervention, and consequently the restoration of the bourgeois order'.[20]

Stalin constantly referred to Socialism in One Country as a Leninist doctrine. He introduced it with a quotation from Lenin's statement in 1915 – when opposing Trotsky's slogan of a United States of Europe – that

> the victory of socialism is possible first in several or even in one capitalist country alone. After expropriating the capitalists and organising their own socialist production, the victorious proletariat of that country would arise *against* the rest of the world – the capitalist world – attracting to its cause the best classes of other countries.[21]

Stalin also referred to Lenin's article 'On Cooperation' of 1923, in which he said that 'the power of the state over large-scale means of production, political power in the hands of the proletariat, the alliance of this proletariat with many millions of very small peasants' was 'all that is necessary to build a complete socialist society out of cooperatives alone'.[22]

It is obvious, nevertheless, that Stalin was hard pressed in plausibly attributing his own innovations to Lenin, who had declared categorically that 'the complete victory of the socialist revolution in one country alone is inconceivable and demands the most active cooperation of at least several advanced countries',[23] a statement that he repeated many times and was in tune with the whole tenor of his thought.[24]

Undoubtedly the major theorist of Socialism in One Country was Bukharin. Basing himself on Lenin's later statements he argued that 'we *can* build socialism even on this wretched technical base ... we shall creep at a snail's pace, but ... all the same we are building socialism and we shall build it'.[25] The NEP would lead to socialism for, in Soviet society, the superstructure regulated the base. Possession of the commanding heights of the economy (and particularly control of credit) would cause the non-socialised elements of the economy – including agriculture – to evolve towards socialism. Western European capitalism had stabilised without the benefit of the Russian market and therefore Russia was obliged to develop in isolation. Expansion through more intensive use of the existing capital would lead to the reduction of industrial goods and benefit the agricultural sector. And it was on the agricultural sector that Bukharin placed more emphasis. The rich and efficient peasants – the *kulaks* – would be enabled through cooperatives to grow into socialism. Whence his much criticised call to the entire peasantry: enrich yourselves!

Trotsky's views on Socialism in One Country are somewhat obscure as they were caricatured by Stalin, who counterposed his doctrine of Socialism in One Country to Trotsky's doctrine of permanent revolution and portrayed permanent revolution as pessimistic about the internal possibilities in the Soviet Union and putting more emphasis on unreliable adventures abroad. Trotsky in vain protested that his previous ideas on permanent revolution were irrelevant to present circumstances and nothing to do with the debate. Indeed, Trotsky's early writings had not excluded the possibility of some sort of Socialism in One Country. With the end of the Civil War, Trotsky advocated policies based on economic isolation which were very close to Socialism in One Country: Stalin's views as expressed in 1925 can be seen as a regression to the self-sufficiency that Trotsky had been advocating in 1920. It was not until 1926 that Trotsky challenged Stalin's position, although Zinoviev had done so much earlier. One important reason for his challenge was his conviction, born of his service on various economic missions, that Russia could only expand her capital stock by a reintegration with the world economy.[26] Abandoning his views of 1921 to 1923, Trotsky argued that the decline of Europe and its struggle for new exports could be turned to Russia's advantage as she could easily import machinery for grain: Russia should encourage applications for concessions and welcome foreign investment. Thus Russia's economy would not be slowed to Bukharin's 'snail's pace'. In his *Towards Socialism or Capitalism?* Trotsky pinpointed his basic disagreement with Stalin's protectionism:

> If we were suddenly to shift our resources ... to the making of new machinery we would either destroy the necessary proportion between the different branches of the economy, and between the basic and circulating capital in a given branch, or, if we maintained

the proportion we should be greatly decreasing the whole coefficient of development. And for us, a decrease in the rate of development is infinitely more dangerous than the import of foreign machinery and of the foreign goods we require in general.[27]

Trotsky saw no reason why the political division of the world into two camps should imply an economic one: Russia should be prepared to benefit from the international division of labour. In other words, what Trotsky objected to was not Socialism in One Country so much as socialism in a separate country which pretended to develop in disregard for the world economy in general. But Trotsky's position was not only an economic one. Basing himself on the whole thrust of the Marxist tradition from the *Communist Manifesto* onwards, he did not abandon his view that socialism could only be achieved in Russia through world revolution. The building of socialism was in any case a very lengthy process and the view of Stalin and Bukharin seemed to him to prejudice the entire international orientation of the Party and to despair of the revolutionary potential of the world proletariat. The Anglo-Soviet Council, which fostered cooperation with the reformist trade unions of Great Britain and directly opposed revolution, was a case in point. Equally symptomatic was the disastrous collaboration with the Kuomintang in China. However, the views of Trotsky and the Left Opposition in general found less and less acceptance in the Party. Trotsky was hampered by his self-proclaimed view that 'in the last instance, the party is always right',[28] and his virtual assimilation of right to might in his anti-Kautsky polemic of 1920, *Terrorism and Communism*. He was increasingly isolated and, in spite of a last-minute attempt by Zinoviev and Kamenev to rally a United Opposition against Stalin in 1926, Trotsky was expelled from the Party in 1927, from Moscow in 1928, and from Russia in 1929.

Art and philosophy

Prior to the October Revolution, there had been no clear Party view on the relationship between art and Bolshevism. In 1905 Lenin had written that

> literature must become a *part* of the common cause of the proletariat, 'a cog and a screw' of one great single Social-Democratic mechanism set in motion by the entire politically-conscious vanguard of the entire working class.[29]

But this referred exclusively to those inside the Party and did not advocate censorship of those who were not Party members. In reaction against nineteenth-century literature, the main schools at the time of the revolution put their emphasis on form rather than content. They were thus not immediately compatible with Marxism although some of them – and particularly the Futurists and their leading poet Mayakovsky – were enthusiastic about the revolution. An attempt to fill this gap was the founding in 1917 of the Proletkult organisation. This organisation was independent of the Bolshevik Party: its moving spirit was Lenin's old philosophical enemy Bogdanov and it had the support of the new Commissar for Education, Lunacharsky, and of Bukharin, editor of *Pravda*. Proletkult conceived itself to be leading the cultural (as opposed to the political or economic) revolution by fostering specifically proletarian forms of art. In 1920 it sponsored an all-Russian Association of Proletarian Writers (VAPP).

Although Proletkult fitted well with the pioneering spirit of War Communism, the arrival of NEP brought it to a close. Lenin sharply criticised the views of the Proletkult leaders:

Only a precise knowledge and transformation of the culture created by the entire development of mankind will enable us to create a proletarian culture. The latter is not clutched out of thin air; it is not an invention of those who call themselves expert in proletarian culture. This is all nonsense. Proletarian culture must be the logical development of the store of knowledge mankind has accumulated under the yoke of capitalist, land-owner and bureaucratic society.[30]

1922 saw the extension of a general censorship of open challenges to the official line. Lunacharsky wrote:

We in no way shrink from the necessity of applying censorship even to belleslettres since under this banner and beneath this elegant exterior poison may be implanted in the still naive and dark soul of the great mass of the people, which is constantly ready to waver and, owing to the too great hardships of the journey, to throw off the hand which is leading it through the wilderness to the promised land.[31]

The most sophisticated critique of Proletkult came from Trotsky, by far the most talented of the Bolshevik leaders in literary matters. In his *Literature and Revolution* Trotsky denied the existence of 'Marxist' art just as he had repudiated the notion of a specifically 'proletarian' military strategy that some had advocated during the Civil War. Equally, there could be no rejection of past cultural achievements. 'The proletariat', Trotsky declared, 'cannot begin the building of a new culture without first absorbing and assimilating elements of the old cultures.'[32] As against those who wished to replace bourgeois culture by proletarian culture, Trotsky wrote:

> It is fundamentally incorrect to place in opposition to bourgeois culture and bourgeois art proletarian culture and proletarian art. These latter will never exist, because the proletarian regime is temporary and transitional. The historical significance and the moral greatness of the proletarian revolution derives from the fact that it is laying down the foundations of a culture which is above classes and which will be the first truly human culture.[33]

The main task under the dictatorship of the proletariat was therefore the 'imparting to the backward masses of the essential elements of the culture which already exists'.[34] In artistic matters the Party should in general be reticent, for the 'domain of art is not one in which the Party is called upon to command'.[35] It was nevertheless impossible to tolerate those actively opposed to the revolution and therefore 'we should have a watchful revolutionary censorship and a broad flexible policy in the field of art, free from petty, partisan maliciousness'.[36] With the success of the doctrine of Socialism in One Country Trotsky's views came under attack, particularly from Lunacharsky and Bukharin, mainly on the grounds that Trotsky's denial of proletarian culture left a cultural vacuum between pre-revolutionary culture and the establishment of socialism. Debate about the relationship of Marxism to art continued to be lively until 1929, when the tightening-up of Party control over literature, coinciding with Stalin's 'Left Turn', brought about the end of independent literary production symbolised by the suicide of Mayakovsky in early 1930.

Although Marxism had no traditional doctrine on art, with philosophy it was a different matter. Ever since Engels, Marxism had possessed a philosophy – dialectical materialism – the importance of which had been re-emphasised by Lenin in his *Materialism and Empiriocriticism*. At the time of the revolution, vulgar materialism was the dominant philosophy among the Bolsheviks, but by the mid-1920s two sophisticated interpretations of dialectical materialism had established themselves. Both could claim to be pursuing Lenin's final instructions on philosophy as laid down in his short article 'On the Significance of Militant Materialism'. Here Lenin argued both that philosophers should create a materialist alliance with the natural scientists and that they should found a 'Society of Materialist Friends of the Hegelian Dialectic'.[37] The two schools in question came to be known as Mechanists and Deborinists according to whether they emphasised the dialectical or materialist part of dialectical materialism. The Mechanists had as chief spokesmen Bogdanov and Bukharin, whom Lenin in his testament had criticised for 'never having made a study of dialectics and, I think, never fully understood it'.[38] They held that philosophy was not a separate science, but rather the method of all sciences. They believed, secondly, that all motion was external, from without. Each thing was a unity and had no internal contradictions. Bukharin said that motion came from without and advanced an equilibrium theory to explain relationships:

> The world consists of forces, acting in many ways, opposing each other. These forces are balanced for a moment in exceptional cases only. We then have a state of 'rest', i.e., their actual 'conflict' is concealed. But if we change only one of these forces, immediately the 'internal contradictions' will be revealed, equilibrium will be disturbed, and if the new equilibrium is again established, it will be on a new basis, i.e., with a new combination of forces, etc. It follows that the 'conflict', the 'contradiction', i.e., the antagonism of forces acting in various directions, determines the motion of the system.[39]

Thirdly, the mechanists downgraded the idea of qualitative leaps in nature. According to them all higher phenomena could in principle be reduced to simpler, lower ones. In the case of Bukharin these philosophical views fitted well with his determinist, gradualist position in economics, and with the outlook of NEP in general – though it should be noted that Trotsky, in his rare incursions into philosophy, was also a mechanist.[40]

The Deborinists took their name from Abram Deborin, an academic professor of philosophy. Their main views were that philosophy had an independent status as a discipline and that nature was dialectical and contradiction inherent in the very essence of things. They therefore emphasised the existence of dialectical leaps and denied that mind was reducible to matter. The Deborinists were helped by the publication, for the first time, of Engels's *Dialectics of Nature* in 1925 and Lenin's *Philosophical Notebooks* in 1929. They were also assisted by the political eclipse of Bukharin, whose Mechanism was officially condemned in 1929. However, if Mechanism was a 'Right' deviation, Deborinism was soon linked with 'Left' deviationism, accused of political neutrality in philosophy, of separating theory from practice, underestimating Lenin, overestimating Hegel and Plekhanov, and finally condemned in 1930 as 'Menshevising idealism'. Stalin's voice became supreme in philosophical matters, as elsewhere.

Notes

1. V. Lenin, 'The Immediate Tasks of the Soviet Government', *Collected Works*, vol. 27, p. 245.
2. N. Bukharin, *Economics of the Transformation Period* (New York, 1971) p. 58.
3. Mention should be made in this context of Bukharin and Preobrazhensky's *ABC of Communism*, published in 1919, which, while containing little of theoretical interest, was immensely popular and epitomised the heroic optimism of War Communism.
4. Bukharin, op. cit., p. 160.
5. Ibid., p. 79.
6. These fascinating comments, first published in 1929 as part of the Stalinist campaign to discredit Bukharin, are reprinted in an appendix to the above edition, pp. 212ff.
7. For a different view of the state, written in 1924, see the highly original work by E. Pasukanis, *General Theory of Law and Marxism* (London and New York, 1978), which went much further than its ostensible subject of legal theory. Pasukanis maintained that legal forms were connected with commodity production and saw the fetishism of the legal subject in bourgeois society as parallel to Marx's fetishism of commodities.
8. Cf. V. Lenin, *Collected Works*, vol. 32, pp. 402ff.
9. V. Lenin, 'The Tax in Kind', ibid., p. 343.
10. V. Lenin, 'The NEP and the Tasks of the Political Education Departments', *Collected Works*, vol. 33, p. 62.
11. V. Lenin, 'Speech on the Tax in Kind', *Collected Works*, vol. 32, p. 429.
12. Cf. ibid., p. 431.
13. V. Lenin, 'The Importance of Gold', *Collected Works*, vol. 33, p. 109.
14. Ibid., p. 110.
15. E. Preobrazhensky, *La Nouvelle Economique* (Paris, 1966) p. 180.
16. J. Stalin, *Leninism* (London, 1940) p. 153.
17. Ibid., pp. 94f.
18. Ibid., p. 93
19. Ibid., p. 156
20. Ibid.
21. V. Lenin, 'On the Slogan for a United States of Europe', *Collected Works*, vol. 21, p. 342.
22. V. Lenin, 'On Cooperation', *Collected Works*, vol. 33, p. 468.
23. V. Lenin, 'Speech to the Sixth Congress of Soviets', *Collected Works*, vol. 28, p. 154.
24. For a contrary view, which finds more support in Lenin for Socialism in One Country than Stalin was able to find, see K. Radjavi, *La Dictature du Prolétariat et Le Dépérissement de L'Etat de Marx à Lénine* (Paris, 1975) pp. 148ff.
25. Quoted in S. Cohen, *Bukharin and the Bolshevik Revolution* (New York, 1975) p. 187.

26. See R. Day, *Leon Trotsky and the Politics of Economic Isolation* (Cambridge, 1973) chs 1–3.
27. L. Trotsky, *Towards Socialism or Capitalism?* (London, 1976) pp. 43f.
28. Quoted in I. Deutscher, *The Prophet Unarmed, Trotsky 1921–1929* (Oxford, 1959) p. 139.
29. V. Lenin, 'Party Organisation and Party Literature', *Collected Works*, vol. 10, p. 45.
30. V. Lenin, 'The Tasks of the Youth League', *Collected Works*, vol. 31, p. 287.
31. Quoted in E.H. Carr, *The Bolshevik Revolution*, vol. 3 (London, 1953) p. 65.
32. L. Trotsky, *Literature and Revolution* (Ann Arbor, 1969) p. 226.
33. Ibid., p. 14.
34. Ibid., p. 193.
35. Ibid., p. 218.
36. Ibid., p. 221.
37. V. Lenin, 'On the Significance of Militant Materialism', *Collected Works*, vol. 33, p. 234.
38. V. Lenin, 'Letters to Congress', *Collected Works*, vol. 36, p. 595.
39. N. Bukharin, *Historical Materialism* (New York, 1925) p. 74.
40. See Trotsky's comments in 1925 on the chemist Mendeleyev (*Sochineiya*, vol. 21, pp. 268ff.) and his *In Defense of Marxism* (New York, 1973) particularly pp. 44f and 73ff.

Further reading

Russia in the 1920s

The basic text is Carr's multi-volume *History*. Bettelheim's two volumes on *The Class Struggles in the USSR* offer a neo-Maoist interpretation. Lewin's *Russian Peasants and Soviet Power* is the most fundamental treatment of the peasantry. On the industrialisation issue, see the books by Erlich and Jasny, Preobrazhensky's *The New Economics*, and Day's revealing *Leon Trotsky and the Politics of Economic Isolation*. The growing monolithism of the Bolshevik Party is well described in Schapiro's *Origin of the Communist Autocracy* and Daniels's *The Conscience of the Revolution*. For the fate of the workers in whose name the revolution had been made, see Kaplan's *Bolshevik Ideology and the Ethics of Soviet Labour* and Brinton's *The Bolsheviks and Workers' Control*. Avrich's book deals fully with the turning-point of Kronstadt, and Fitzpatrick's *The Commissariat of Enlightenment* is good on cultural questions. Bukharin's major works – *The Economic Theory of the Leisure Class, Imperialism ... , Economics of the Transformation Period,* and *Historical Materialism* – are all available in separate editions. Cohen's extensive biography, *Bukharin and the Bolshevik Revolution*, will be the major commentary for a long time to come. For works by and on Trotsky relevant to this period, see above, pp. 88ff.

Bibliography

Russia in the 1920s

Paul Avrich, *Kronstadt 1921* (Princeton, N.J., 1970).

Charles Bettelheim, *Class Struggles in the USSR: First Period, 1917–1923* (Hassocks, Sussex, 1977).

—— *The Class Struggles in the USSR: Second Period, 1923–1930* (Hassocks, Sussex, 1978).

C.E. Black (ed.), *Transformation of Russian Society* (Cambridge, Mass., 1960).

F. Borkenau, *World Communism* (Ann Arbor, 1962).

Maurice Brinton, *The Bolsheviks and Workers' Control, 1917–1921: The State and Counter-Revolution* (London, 1970).

N. Bukharin, *The Economic Theory of the Leisure Class* (New York, 1927).

—— *Economics of the Transformation Period* (New York, 1971).

—— *Historical Materialism: A System of Sociology* (New York, 1925).

—— *Imperialism and World Economy* (New York, 1929).

—— *Philosophical Arabesques* (London, 2005).

N. Bukharin and E. Preobrazhensky, *The ABC of Communism* (London, 1924).

E.H. Carr, *The Interregnum: 1923–1924* (London, 1954).

—— *Socialism in One Country: 1924–1926*, 3 vols (London, 1958–64).

E.H. Carr, *The Russian Revolution from Lenin to Stalin, 1917–29* (London, 1979).

E.H. Carr and R.W. Davies, *Foundations of a Planned Economy: 1926–1929*, 3 vols (London, 1969–78).

Stephen F. Cohen, *Bukharin and the Bolshevik Revolution* (New York, 1975).

Robert V. Daniels, *The Conscience of the Revolution: Communist Opposition in Soviet Russia* (Cambridge, Mass., 1960).

R.W. Davies, *The Industrialisation of Soviet Russia*, 2 vols: Vol. 1 *The Socialist Offensive, 1929–1930*; Vol. 2 *The Soviet Collective Farm, 1929–1930* (London, 1979).

R. Day, *Leon Trotsky and the Politics of Economic Isolation* (Cambridge, 1973).

J. Degras (ed.), *The Communist International 1919–1943* (London, 1956).

Alexander Erlich, *The Soviet Industrialisation Debate, 1924–1928* (Cambridge, Mass., 1960).

Sheila Fitzpatrick, *The Commissariat of Enlightenment: Soviet Organisation of Education and the Arts under Lunacharsky* (Cambridge, 1970).

David Footman, *Civil War in Russia* (London, 1961).

Sidney Heitman, 'Between Lenin and Stalin: Nikolai Bukharin', in L. Labedz (ed.), *Revisionism* (London, 1962).

N. Jasny, *Soviet Economists of the Twenties* (New York, 1972).

Frederick I. Kaplan, *Bolshevik Ideology and the Ethics of Soviet Labour, 1917–1920: The Formative Years* (London, 1968).

Adam Karfwan, 'The Origin of the "Political Economy of Socialism": An Essay in Soviet Economic Thought', *Soviet Studies, 3 (1953)*.

Moshe Lewin, *Russian Peasants and Soviet Power – A Study of Collectivisation* (Evanston, Ill., 1968).

Richard Pipes, *The Formation of the Soviet Union: Communism and Nationalism 1917–1923* (Cambridge, Mass., 1964).

E.A. Preobrazhensky, *From New Economic Policy to Socialism: A Glance into the Future of Russia and Europe* (London, 1962).

—— *The New Economics* (Oxford, 1965).

W.W. Rostow, *The Stages of Economic Growth* (Cambridge, 1971).
Leonard Schapiro, *Origin of the Communist Autocracy: Political Opposition in the Soviet State, First Phase, 1917–1922* (London, 1955).
Robert Service, *The Bolshevik Party in Revolution* (London, 1979).
Jay B. Solenson, *The Life and Death of Soviet Trade Unionism: 1917–1928* (New York, 1969).
Nicolas Spulber, *Soviet Strategy for Economic Growth* (Bloomington, Ind., 1964).
A.S. Whiting, *Soviet Policies in China: 1917–1924* (London and New York, 1954).

9
Stalinism

Industry, agriculture and party

Stalin's innovation was to subordinate everything (including the inter-national dimension of Bolshevism and the structure of the Party itself) to the goal of rapid heavy industrialisation at the expense of the agri-cultural sector. In the mid-1920s, Stalin had poured scorn on the 'super-industrialisers' such as Trotsky, who suggested that Russia's output would be increased by almost 20 per cent per annum. But in the middle of 1929 the appropriation of the capital investment was suddenly increased by as much as five times and the decision taken to go for mass collectivisation of agriculture. This mammoth effort could only be achieved by a united Party and the two years preceding were occupied by the last great debate in the Bolshevik Party between those who advo-cated a development of the Soviet economy based on the principles of the New Economic Policy, whose leading spokesman was Bukharin, and those who put absolute priority on increasing industrial production, the policy of Stalin, although how extreme it would prove to be only became clear very slowly. The crisis inside the party was precipitated by two factors: firstly, by 1929 the pre-1914 levels of productivity in indus-try had been attained and a plan for expansion had to be agreed on. The first Five Year Plan, which was to be promulgated in the spring of 1929, was in its embryonic stages. Secondly, the supply of grain at the end of 1927 and the beginning of 1928 began to drop drastically – largely as a result of the growing dearth of production goods, which meant that the peasants had less for which they could exchange their surpluses.

Urgent action was required in the face of the crisis and the Politburo was divided. Bukharin defended what had become the NEP (and anti-Trotskyist) orthodoxy of progress through agricultural expansion on the

United States model. Reluctantly in January 1928 he agreed to temporary measures of a punitive sort to wrest their surpluses from the *kulaks*.
In fact, since these measures were carried out by the Party apparatus
under Stalin's control, Stalin could make them much more drastic than
the Politburo decision had warranted and at the same time himself
complain later of 'excesses'.

In the power struggle that followed, Bukharin and his followers were
doomed from the start. In vain did he quote incessantly from Lenin's
later articles on cooperatives and emphasise how vital Lenin considered
the preservation of the alliance with the peasantry. Bukharin was in reality opposed neither to collectivisation – only insisting that it was a long-
term aim that presupposed a certain stock of machinery, etc. – nor to
planned industrialisation – provided it was gradual and flexible. But the
'Right Opposition' – as Stalin cleverly managed to dub them – were hampered by the fact that the struggle was fought out in the top Party organs
where Stalin was firmly entrenched. They had strong support among the
rural masses and even urban workers, but were precluded from appealing
to it by their previous condemnation of factionalism and the insistence
on unity and conformity to Party decisions that they themselves had
used with such effect against the Trotskyists two years earlier. Stalin's
control of the Party machine was overwhelming and, indeed, the very
nature of the Party had changed radically with a threefold increase of
membership between 1924 and 1928. More generally, the Right was associated with pessimism whereas Stalin right through until mid-1929 could
present himself as a man of the centre equipped with forceful solutions
to the country's problems such as would appeal to the growing mass of
pragmatic administrators. By July 1928 the Rightists had failed to convince the Central Committee and lost their potential majority on the
Politburo. The dismissal of the leaders of the Moscow Party Organisation
who sympathised with Bukharin and the ousting of Tomsky from leadership of the Trade Union marked the total eclipse of the Right. With
Bukharin's description of Stalin's policies as a reversal to the 'military-
feudal' exploitation of the Tsarist regime, the split was irreparable.

Now more than ever in control of the Party, Stalin radicalised his policies. Throughout 1928 the problem of grain supplies continued and,
although in the summer of 1928 he had still rejected the notions of class
war in the countryside and expropriation of the *kulaks* (the first Five Year
Plan provided for collectivisation of only 20 per cent of farming by 1933),
a rapid change was evident during the last six months of 1929, presaging
his 'revolution from above'. Decisions were increasingly taken by Stalin
alone, relations with peasantry worsened, the anti-Right campaign grew

in violence, and there was a building-up of the 'cult of the personality' to counteract the obvious difficulties facing the government in its collectivisation campaign. In the Comintern, too, the policy of alliance with non-Communist socialists (so strongly criticised earlier by Trotsky) was jettisoned; Social Democrats were regarded as social Fascists and even as greater enemies than the Fascists themselves.

The gathering storm broke in December 1929. Stalin declared in a speech to the Marxist agrarians that the Party had 'recently passed from the policy of *restricting* the exploiting proclivities of the *kulaks* to the policy of *eliminating the kulaks as a class*'.[1] He continued: 'It is ridiculous and fatuous to expatiate today on the expropriation of *kulaks*. You do not lament the loss of the hair of one who has been beheaded',[2] and concluded, in a statement that spelt death for millions: 'there is another question which seems no less ridiculous: whether the *kulak* should be permitted to join the collective farms. Of course not, for he is a sworn enemy of the collective farm movement. Clearly, one would think.'[3] From October 1929 to March 1930 the percentage of those in collective farms rose from 4 to 58 per cent. The chaos and abuses were widespread and Stalin ordered a halt. By September 1930 the percentage had dropped to 21. But by the end of 1930 it had risen again to more than half and to three-quarters by 1934. This enormous upheaval led to some ten million people being deported and bitter resistance by large sections of the peasantry which was not confined to the *kulaks* (itself a vague description which did not exceed 4 per cent of the peasantry). Party cadres were almost totally unprepared for the rapid change of policy. Famine was widespread and millions died as the government – now at last firmly in control of the agricultural sector – insisted on retaining, and even increasing, the grain procurements for the cities. Agricultural production took many years to recover to the levels of the late 1920s (over half the livestock had been slaughtered by the desperate peasantry) but foundations for the rapid industrial expansion of the 1930s had been firmly laid.[4]

Although the decision to extend state control to agriculture was rapid and its result catastrophic, the prerequisites for such a move had been building up for some time. Throughout 1929 food supplies for the towns had been in a parlous state and provoked widespread unrest. Agricultural prices rose as the opposition of the peasantry to government demands increased. The harsh measures of, for example, cutting the supply of manufactured goods to those who could not or would not fulfil their quotas only increased the tension. The reasons Stalin gave for what he described as 'the great turn' were the recent improvements of labour productivity in the industrial sector, and particularly in industrial construction, combined with the improving supply of grain from the small collectivised agricultural sector as compared with the recalcitrant private holdings. Ideologically, Stalin stressed the view that class struggle intensified as socialism approached. More practically, he felt that the fragile momentum of industrialisation could only be preserved by a frontal assault on agriculture. The old Bolshevik mistrust of the peasantry as an alien barrier was still strong and it was easy to re-create the atmosphere of Civil War and War Communist policies. With the collectivisation of agriculture, the framework for a planned economy with emphasis on the development of heavy industry was firmly established.

The repercussions of Stalin's policies on the Party were equally drastic. The purges of the late 1930s can be seen as the political counterpart of Stalin's economic policy. Although the Party had been weakened by the expulsion of the Bukharinists, many Trotskyists were lured back in time to support Stalin's 'Left Turn'. The assassination of Kirov in late 1934 gave the signal for the beginning of the purges: Zinoviev and Kamenev were among the first to be tried and executed for political opposition. The great show trials, culminating with that of Bukharin in 1938, effectively obliterated the possibility of any alternative government. As Deutscher has succinctly put it:

> Among the men in the dock at the trials were all the members of Lenin's Politburo, except Stalin himself and Trotsky, who, however, though absent, was the chief defendant. Among them, moreover, were one ex-premier, several vice-premiers, two ex-chiefs of the Communist International, the chief of the trade unions (Tomsky, who committed suicide before the trial), the chief of the General Staff, the chief political Commissar of the Army, the Supreme Commanders of all important military districts, nearly all Soviet ambassadors in Europe and Asia, and, last but not least, the two chiefs of the political police.[5]

The government personnel was renewed from top to bottom. Some three million died, only 3 per cent of the delegates to the 1934 Party Congress reappeared in 1939, and, of the Central Committee elected in 1934, 70 per cent were shot. A wave of new administrators filled the spaces left by the purges and, in spite of a new 'democratic' constitution in 1936, even the trappings of formal democracy were neglected: during the long years of Stalin's ascendancy there were only four Party Congresses and only three of the Comintern.

Stalin as theoretician

It would be putting it mildly to say that Stalin was no very subtle mind when it came to Marxist theory. Nevertheless, he was responsible for several innovations in Marxist doctrine that have gained wide currency. The elaboration of the doctrine of Socialism in One Country has already been mentioned. The main text summing up Stalinist theory was the *History of the Communist Party of the Soviet Union (Bolshevik): Short Course*, which appeared in 1938 and continued to be the main authority for Communist doctrine for almost twenty years. The *History* contained several innovations. Firstly, reversing Engels's order, Stalin discussed dialectical *method* before *philosophy*. Leaning heavily on Engels's later writings and on Lenin's *Materialism and Empiriocriticism*, the dialectical method (which Stalin contrasted with metaphysics) was defined as the view that all phenomena in nature were interconnected, that all phenomena were in a state of movement, that movement could be abrupt and changes in quantity give rise to changes in quality, and finally that contradiction was inherent in all things. And of Marxist philosophical materialism (which was contrasted with idealism) the principal features were said to be that the world was by its very nature material, that matter was a primary objective reality existing outside the independent of our minds, while mind was a secondary reflection of matter, and that the world and its laws were fully knowable. It is noteworthy that Stalin reduced Engels's Laws of the Dialectic to two: although talking of the interpenetration of opposites and the transformation of quantity into quality, Stalin omitted all mention of the law of the negation of the negation, the political implications of which are obvious.

Dialectical materialism was rigidly separated from historical materialism. In dealing with the latter, Stalin attributed a significance to the role of ideas that was not reducible to their origin and went out of his way to emphasise their importance. Although new ideas had to await the appropriate material development yet

as regards their role in history, historical materialism, far from denying them, stresses the role and importance of these factors in the life of society in its history ... they become a most potent force which facilitates the carrying out of the new tasks set by the development of the material life of society, a force which facilitates the progress of society.[6]

This emphasis was carried even further in 1939 when Stalin declared that

> the community of interest between worker, peasant and intellectual in the Soviet Union has formed the basis for the development of such motive forces as the moral and political unity of Soviet society, and the mutual friendship of the nations of the U.S.S.R., and Soviet patriotism.[7]

Concerning the Soviet Union, Stalin introduced the novel concept of 'Revolution from above'. Talking of the expropriation of the *kulaks*, Stalin wrote that 'the distinguishing feature of this revolution is that it was accomplished from above, on the initiative of the state, and directly supported from below by millions of peasants'.[8] With the advent of socialism in the USSR, moreover, although classes continued to exist, they were defined as 'non-antagonistic' since none of them oppressed the others. The new doctrine of Socialism in One Country also helped to explain the failure of the state to wither away. Stalin stated that the state would remain even in the period of Communism (which the Soviet Union had not yet reached) 'unless the Capitalist encirclement is liquidated, and unless the danger of foreign military attack has been eliminated'.[9]

Interest in philosophical questions revived after the war with a wide-ranging 'philosophical discussion' which ended with condemnation of Alexandrov's *History of Western European Philosophy* for being too 'objectivist'. This was largely on the initiative of Zhdanov, Stalin's spokesman on all intellectual matters. Stalin also intervened personally in support of Lysenko's anti-Mendelian views on genetics, which became thereafter *de rigeur* in academic circles. But the most striking example of Stalin's innovation was his pronouncement on the linguistics controversy in 1950 in which he condemned the views of Marr, the most distinguished of Soviet linguistic theoreticians. Marr had maintained that language was part of ideology, that there were sharply separated qualitative distinctions between language systems in that they were connected with class development, and that formal, logical thinking was due to be superseded by dialectical materialism, until, finally,

> thought gains the upper hand over language, and will continue to gain it, until in the new classless society not only will the system of spoken language be done away with, but a unitary language will be created, as far, then even further, removed from articulate language as the latter from gesture.[10]

Stalin, on the contrary, maintained that language was a creation of the whole people, and not of a class, that it developed gradually, and not by leaps, and that Marr was an idealist, in that language could never be separated from thought. More broadly, Stalin opened the way for discussions of the relative independence of ideas. Once again he stated that

> the base creates the superstructure precisely in order that it may serve it, that it may actively help it to take shape and to consolidate itself, that it may actively strive for elimination of the old, moribund base and its old superstructure.[11]

He reiterated his doctrine of non-antagonistic classes and practically denied the application of the law of quantity and quality to the Soviet Union.

> It should be said in general for the benefit of comrades who have an infatuation for such explosions that the law of transition from an old quantity to a new by means of an explosion is inapplicable not only to the history of the development of languages; it is not always applicable to some other social phenomena of a basal or superstructural character. It is compulsory for a society divided into hostile classes but it is not at all compulsory for a society which has no hostile classes.[12]

Specifically, Stalin declared that 'a Marxist cannot regard language as a superstructure on the base' and 'to confuse language and superstructure is a serious error'.[13] More generally, Stalin elaborated the idea that the correctness of Marxist doctrines was limited to the period in which they were expressed. It might seem that some of Stalin's own doctrines contradicted earlier Marxist views. But

> the two different formulas correspond to two different epochs in the development of society, and precisely because they correspond to them the two formulas are correct, each for its own epoch. To demand that these formulas should not be mutually contradictory, that they should not exclude each other, is just as absurd as it would be to demand that there should be no contradiction between the epoch of domination of capitalism and the epoch of the domination of socialism, that socialism and capitalism should not exclude each other.[14]

The correlation between these theoretical innovations and Stalinist political practice is evident.

Trotsky's critique of Stalinism

Although the advent of Stalinism in the Soviet Union stifled original thinking about Marxist theory, it did provoke one highly original contribution: Trotsky's critique of the Soviet Union which, along with his insightful analysis of Fascism, was his main preoccupation in exile. It is true that Stalin had borrowed several of the ideas that Trotsky (or more accurately Preobrazhenski) had espoused from 1920 onwards: Bukharin even went as far as to call Stalin's policies 'a complete ideological capitulation to Trotskyism'.[15] But Trotsky did not share Stalin's economic isolationism, or his nationalist view that downgraded revolution in the West, or his equation of nationalisation with socialism. He was therefore faced with the problem of how to categorise the Soviet Union in Marxist terms. In the centre of his analysis he placed the phenomenon of bureaucracy, about which Marx himself had had several things to say.[16] Unlike Lenin, who had implied in *State and Revolution* that the problem could be overcome by political and administrative measures, Trotsky saw bureaucracy as rooted in Russia's social and historical circumstances. It was the product of backwardness. In *The Revolution Betrayed* – his major work on the subject, written in 1936 – he wrote:

> The basis of bureaucratic rule is the poverty of society in objects of consumption with the resulting struggle of each against all. When there are enough goods in the store the purchasers can come whenever they want to. When there are little goods the purchasers are compelled to stand in line. When the lines are very long, it is necessary to appoint a policeman to keep order. Such is the starting point of the power of Soviet bureaucracy.[17]

The consequent problem, however, of how the rise of a bureaucracy in a backward country like Russia could be avoided was never clearly answered by Trotsky.

In his account of Soviet society, Trotsky refused to equate nationalised property with social property: this could only come into existence when the transitional form of state property had disappeared. The change in proprietorship in the Soviet Union did not of itself mean anything, particularly when accompanied by huge Stakhanovite wage differentials and a bureaucratic hierarchy. Could the Soviet Union therefore be called a State Capitalist Society? In the crucial ninth chapter of *The Revolution Betrayed* Trotsky rejected this description. The bureaucracy did not constitute a new class. They did not own the means of production or accumulate and pass on their wealth like capitalists. The bureaucracy was recruited and had no independent property roots in the economic structures. Their role was therefore not an example of class exploitation but of social parasitism.

What, then, *was* the character of the Soviet regime? According to Trotsky, it was characterised by a contradiction between the increasing socialisation of the productive forces and the increasingly bourgeois norms of distribution. It was therefore a *transitional* society, but not necessarily in transition towards socialism. It would evolve in two – but only two – ways: towards socialism or towards capitalism. The prolonged rule of the bureaucracy would only lead to the restoration of capitalism.

One of the central themes of *The Revolution Betrayed* was the parallelism between the French and Russian revolutions, and Trotsky was at pains to find the equivalent in Russia of Thermidor, which marked the final fall of the Jacobins and was the prerequisite for the rise of Bonaparte. In the late 1920s, he had identified the danger of Thermidor as coming from Bukharin and the Right Opposition since he then interpreted the French Thermidor as being the restoration of the bourgeoisie. The rise of Stalin could be fitted into such analysis as it did not imply a transfer of power between classes. Trotsky nevertheless wished to call Stalin the Russian Bonaparte and by 1934–5, after the assassination of Kirov, Trotsky was regarding Thermidor as the transfer of power *inside* the revolutionary movement from the mass of the bourgeoisie to a small rich minority. The parallel of the Soviet Union had been the transfer of power, from 1924 onwards, from the mass of the proletariat to the bureaucracy and the workers' aristocracy. This was not a counter-revolution, but a reaction inside a revolution. Socialism in One Country was the doctrine of Thermidor which led to bureaucratic domination. It was in this context that Trotsky drew the analogy with Bonapartism:

> Carrying the policies of Thermidor further, Napoleon waged a struggle not only against the feudal world but also against the 'rabble' and the democratic circles of the petty and middle bourgeoisie; in this way he concentrated the fruits of the regime born out of the revolution in the hands of the new bourgeois aristocracy. Stalin guards the conquests of the October Revolution not only against the feudal-bourgeois counterrevolution but also against the claims of the toilers, their impatience and their dissatisfaction; he crushes the left wing that expresses the ordered historical and progressive tendencies of the unprivileged working masses; he creates a new aristocracy by means

of an extreme differentiation in wages, privileges, ranks, etc. Leaning for support upon the topmost layer of the new social hierarchy against the lowest – sometimes vice versa – Stalin has attained the complete concentration of power in his own hands. What else should this regime be called if not Soviet Bonapartism?[18]

There were strong similarities with Fascist forms of Bonapartism in terms of both being crisis regimes in which politics had gained a certain autonomy over society by the personification of power. The crucial difference, for Trotsky, was that Stalinism was the Bolshevik Bonapartism of a young class, Fascism that of an old and dying class.

Nevertheless, Trotsky did not break with the Soviet Union. For him, it was still in some sense the country of the revolution and an inspiration to the world proletariat. For the Soviet Union alone had the nationalised property that was a basic precondition for socialism. It was still a workers' state, albeit degenerated, and required a *political revolution*, but not a *social* one. Trotsky was also influenced by his belief in the inevitability of war with Fascists, in which the Soviet Union would need support. These views began to be opposed by certain Trotskyists inside the Fourth International, which Trotsky had founded in 1934 to oppose Stalinism. They could not so easily separate Stalin from the Soviet Union and began to doubt the validity of the whole October Revolution. This view was particularly prevalent among the American section of the Fourth International, where writers such as James Burnham and Max Schachtman began to argue that the bureaucratisation of the Soviet Union was the beginning of a world bureaucratisation which would supersede both capitalism and socialism in the name of rational, efficient, production.[19] Trotsky himself was affected by these ideas and, towards the very end of his life, conceived of a third alternative for the Soviet Union. Posing the question of whether the coming epoch was one of social revolution or decline into totalitarian bureaucracy, Trotsky declared:

It is absolutely self-evident that if the international proletariat, as a result of the experience of our entire epoch and the current new war, proves incapable of becoming the master of society, this would signify the foundering of all hope for a socialist revolution, for it is impossible to expect any other more favourable condition for it.[20]

He talked also of the possible 'congenital incapacity of the proletariat to become a ruling class' and the possibility that 'in its fundamental traits the present USSR is the precursor of a new exploiting regime on an international scale'.[21] Trotsky never envisaged that the very reasons for the rise of Stalinism might also be those which made for Bolshevik success in 1917 – the poverty of Russia's social institutions and economic foundations, and the consequent existence of politics in a vacuum where radical measures and planned industrial expansion concentrated power and increased bureaucracy. His final speculations did not represent the main theme of Trotsky's thought (and he angrily repudiated those who extrapolated from them) but they did show how very tentative his conclusions had become by the end of his life.

Notes

1. J. Stalin, *Leninism* (London, 1940) p. 325.
2. Ibid., pp. 325f.
3. Ibid., p. 326.
4. It is somewhat ironical to recall that in the 1902 debate on the Party programme Lenin had said that if the peasantry would not accept the proletarian proposals, then 'when the dictatorship comes, we shall say about you: "it's no use wasting words when you have got to use force".' Vera Sassoulitch had commented on this in the margin: 'Upon millions of people! Just you try!' See L. Schapiro, *History of the Communist Party of the Soviet Union* (London, 1970) p. 47.
5. I. Deutscher, *Stalin: A Political Biography* (Harmondsworth, 1966) pp. 368f.
6. J. Stalin, *History of the CPSU: Short Course* (Moscow, 1943) p. 116.
7. *The Essential Stalin*, ed. B. Franklin (New York, 1972) p. 367.
8. J. Stalin, *History of the CPSU: Short Course*, p. 305.
9. *The Essential Stalin*, p. 387.
10. Quoted in G. Wetter, *Dialectical Materialism* (London, 1958) p. 196. For by far the most original Soviet contribution to linguistics, written in 1929, see V. Volosinov, *Marxism and the Philosophy of Language* (New York, 1973).
11. *The Essential Stalin*, p. 408f.
12. Ibid., p. 425.
13. Ibid., p. 412.
14. Ibid., p. 443f.
15. Quoted in S. Cohen, *Bukharin and the Bolshevik Revolution* (New York, 1975) p. 311.
16. Cf., for example, I. Fetscher, 'Marxism and Bureaucracy', in *Marx and Marxism* (New York, 1971) p. 204ff.
17. L. Trotsky, *The Revolution Betrayed* (London, 1937) p. 110. This theme had already been outlined in Trotsky's *The New Course*, published in 1923.
18. 'The Workers' State, Thermidor and Bonapartism', *Writings of Leon Trotsky, 1934–35* (New York, 1971) p. 181.
19. See B. Rizzi, *La bureaucratization du monde* (Paris, 1939) and its sequel, J. Burnham, *The Managerial Revolution* (New York, 1941).
20. 'The USSR in War', in L. Trotsky, *In Defense of Marxism* (New York, 1973) p. 15.
21. Ibid., p. 9.

Further reading

Texts

Stalin's collected *Works* stopped publication, on his fall from grace, with volume 13. There are separate editions of his major works: *Marxism and the National and Colonial Question, Leninism, Economic Problems of the USSR*, etc. There is a useful collection, with an introduction defending Stalin, in Franklin's *The Essential Stalin*.

Commentaries

Of biographies, in many ways still the best are the two studies by participants in the events they described: Souvarine and Trotsky. Fischer is sound: most accessible is Deutscher's eminently readable attempt to do some justice to Stalin's achievement. More recently, we have a thorough account by Ulam, a more psychological study by Tucker, and an over-hostile one by Hingley.

There are many studies of the Stalinist era, some of them stronger on polemic than on analysis. On the origins of Stalinism, Carr's *Socialism in One Country* and *Foundations of a Planned Economy* are exhaustive and reliable. See also Lewin's *The Making of the Soviet System* and Medvedev's *Let History Judge: The Origins and Consequences of Stalinism*. On the purges of the 1930s Conquest's *The Great Terror* is fascinatingly detailed. Deutscher's *The Unfinished Revolution* is probably the best reflective introduction. For the atmosphere of Stalin's later years, see Djilas's *Conversations with Stalin*. Seton-Watson has a good survey of the international aspects, and, for the measured reflections of a contemporary Communist, see Ellenstein's *The Stalin Phenomenon*. See also Lacqueur's *Stalin: The Glasnost Revelations*, Stites's *Revolutionary Dreams: Utopian Visions and Experiment Life in the Soviet Union* and, especially good on Stalinism as an ideology, Walicki's *Marxism and the Leap to the Kingdom of Freedom*, Chapter 5. The surveys by Litvin and Keep and by Ward are useful and van Ree claims some Marxist consistency for Stalin's thought.

Bibliography

Texts

Joseph Stalin, *Works*, 13 vols (Moscow, 1952–5).
—— *The Essential Stalin: Major Theoretical Writings, 1905–1952*, ed. Bruce Franklin (New York, 1972).
—— *Leninism* (London, 1940).
—— *Marxism and the National and Colonial Question* (London, 1936).
Robert H. McNeal (ed.), *Stalin's Works: An Annotated Bibliography* (Stanford, 1967).

Commentaries

Victor Alexandrov, *The Tukhachevsky Affair* (London, 1963).

Svetlana Alliluyeva, *Twenty Letters to a Friend* (London, 1967).

John A. Armstrong, *The Politics of Totalitarianism: The Communist Party of the Soviet Union from 1934 to the Present* (New York, 1961).

Abdurakham Avtorkhanov, *Stalin and the Soviet Communist Party: A Study in the Technology of Power* (New York, 1959).

Henri Barbusse, *Stalin: A New World Seen Through One Man* (London, 1935).

Nikolaus Basseches, *Stalin* (London, 1952).

Max Beloff, *The Foreign Policy of Soviet Russia: 1929–1936* (London, 1962).

Conrad Brandt, *Stalin's Failure in China* (Cambridge, Mass., 1958).

E.H. Carr, *Socialism in One Country: 1924–1926*, 3 vols (London, 1958–64).

E.H. Carr and R.W. Davies, *Foundations of a Planned Economy: 1926–1929*, 3 vols (London, 1969–78).

Dudley Collard, *Soviet Justice and the Trial of Radek and Others* (London, 1937).

Lucio Colletti, 'The Question of Stalin', in R. Blackburn (ed.), *Revolution and Class Struggle: A Reader in Marxist Politics* (London, 1977); and *New Left Review*, 61 (1970).

Robert Conquest, *The Great Terror: Stalin's Purge of the Thirties* (New York, 1968).

Robert V. Daniels (ed.), *The Stalin Revolution – Fulfillment or Betrayal of Communism?* (Boston, 1965).

Theodore Denno, *The Communist Millennium: The Soviet View* (The Hague, 1964).

Isaac Deutscher, *Soviet Trade Unions* (London, 1950).

—— *Stalin: A Political Biography* (Harmondsworth, 1966).

—— *The Unfinished Revolution: Russia 1917–1967* (London, 1967).

Milovan Djilas, *Conversations with Stalin* (London, 1962).

M.M. Drachkovitch and Branko Lazitch, *The Comintern: Historical Highlights* (New York, 1966).

J. Ellenstein, *The Stalin Phenomenon* (London, 1976).

Alexander Erlich, 'Stalin's Views on Soviet Economic Development' in Ernest J. Simmons (ed.), *Continuity and Change in Russian and Soviet Thought* (Cambridge, Mass., 1955).

D. Filtzer, *Soviet Workers and Stalinist Industrialization* (Cambridge, 1992).

Louis Fischer, *The Life and Death of Stalin* (London, 1953).

Ruth Fisher, *Stalin and German Communism* (Cambridge, Mass., 1948).

Valentino Gerratana, 'Stalin, Lenin and Leninism', *New Left Review*, 103 (1977).

Zaga Golubovic, 'The History of Russia under Stalin', *New Left Review*, 104 (1977).

Elliot R. Goodman, *The Soviet Design for a World State* (New York, 1960).

A.V. Gorbatov, *Years of My Life: The Memoirs of a General of the Soviet Army* (London, 1964).

Loren R. Graham, *The Soviet Academy of Sciences and the Communist Party: 1927–1932* (Princeton, N.J., 1967).

Chris Harman, *How the Revolution was Lost* (London, 1969).

R. Hingley, *Joseph Stalin: Man and Legend* (London, 1974).

G.F. Hudson, *Fifty Years of Communism: Theory and Practice 1917–1967* (London, 1968).

George D. Jackson, *Comintern and Peasant in East Europe: 1919–1930* (London, 1966).

Julius Jacobson (ed.), *Soviet Communism and the Socialist Vision* (New Brunswick, N.J., 1972).

Naum Jasny, *Soviet Industrialisation: 1928–1952* (Chicago, 1961).

George Katkov, *The Trial of Bukharin* (London, 1969).

Arthur Koestler, *Darkness at Noon* (New York, 1961).

Walter Lacqueur, *Stalin: The Glasnost Revelations* (New York, 1990).

Isaac Don Levine, *Stalin* (London, 1931).

Moshe Lewin, *The Making of the Soviet System* (New York, 1985).

A. Litvin and J. Keep, *Stalinism: Russian and Western Views at the Turn of the Millennium* (New York, 2005).

Kermit E. McKenzie, *Comintern and World Revolution, 1928–1943: The Shaping of Doctrine* (New York, 1964).

Roy A. Medvedev, *Let History Judge: The Origins and Consequences of Stalinism* (New York, 1971; revised edn, 1989).

Barrington Moore, *Soviet Politics – The Dilemma of Power: The Role of Ideas in Social Charge* (New York, 1965).

Olga A. Narkiewicz, *The Making of the Soviet State Apparatus* (Manchester, 1970).

Alec Nove, *An Economic History of the USSR* (New York, 1984).

—— *Economic Rationality and Soviet Politics: or, Was Stalin Really Necessary?* (New York, 1964).

Thomas H. Rigby (ed.), *Stalin* (Englewood Cliffs, N.J., 1966).

Arthur Rosenberg, *A History of Bolshevism* (Garden City, New York, 1967).

Hugh Seton-Watson, *From Lenin to Krushchev: The History of World Communism* (New York, 1960).

Max Shachtman, *The Bureaucratic Revolution: The Rise of the Stalinist State* (New York, 1962).

Edward Ellis Smith, *The Young Stalin: The Early Years of an Elusive Revolutionary* (New York, 1967).

Boris Souvarine, *Stalin: A Critical Survey of Bolshevism* (London, 1939).

—— 'Stalinism', in M.M. Drachkovitch (ed.), *Marxism in the Modern World* (Stanford, 1965).

Richard Stites, *Revolutionary Dreams: Utopian Vision and Experimental Life in the Soviet Union* (New York, 1989).

Julian Towster, *Political Power in the USSR, 1917–1947: The Theory and Structure of Government in the Soviet State* (Oxford, 1948).

Leon Trotsky, *Stalin: An Appraisal of the Man and his Influence* (London, 1941).

Robert C. Tucker, *Stalin as Revolutionary, 1879–1929: A Study in History and Personality* (New York, 1973).

—— *Stalin in Power: The Revolution from Above, 1928–1941* (New York, 1990).

—— (ed.), *Stalinism: Essays in Historical Interpretations* (New York, 1977).

Robert C. Tucker and S.F. Cohen (eds), *The Great Purge Trial* (New York, 1965).

Adam B. Ulam, *The Unfinished Revolution* (London, 1970).

—— *Stalin: The Man and His Era* (London, 1974).

Alexander Uralov, *The Reign of Stalin* (London, 1953).

E. van Ree, *The Political Thought of Joseph Stalin: A Study in Twentieth Century Revolutionary Patriotism* (London, 2002).

Andrej Walicki, *Marxism and the Leap to the Kingdom of Freedom: The Rise and Fall of Communist Utopia* (Stanford, 1995).

C. Ward, *Stalin's Russia*, 2nd edn (London, 1999).

Sidney and Beatrice Webb, *Soviet Communism: A New Civilisation?* (New York, 1938).

10
Post-Stalin Communism

The denunciation of Stalin by Krushchev at the 20th Party Congress in 1956 had profound repercussions over the whole Communist world. Stalin was declared to have

> sanctioned in the name of the Central Committee of the All-Union Communist Party [Bolsheviks] the most brutal violation of socialist legality, torture and oppression, which led as we have seen to the slandering and self-accusation of innocent people.[1]

Krushchev condemned the 'cult of the individual' and called for a restoration of the Leninist principles of Soviet socialist democracy. In early 1960s, Krushchev implemented proposals for a limited degree of economic decentralisation associated with the name of the Russian economist Libermann. But above all he concentrated on improving the agricultural sector, which had been so neglected under Stalin. Material incentives were restored, investment improved, collective farms were allowed to control their own mechanised power, and a great drive was launched to bring under cultivation the Virgin Lands of Kazakhstan.

In keeping with the new spirit, the 22nd Party Congress in 1961 adopted a revised programme which superseded the two previous programmes of 1903 and 1919. New elements in the programme were the declaration that 'peaceful coexistence of the socialist and capitalist countries is an *objective necessity* for the development of human society',[2] and that capitalism had entered a new crisis, 'the principal feature of which is that its development is not connected with a world war'.[3] The USSR, on the other hand, would lay the material and technical bases for Communism in the next decade and by 1980 '*a communist society will be in the main built in the USSR'.*[4] Even more striking in terms of orthodox Marxism was the claim that the Party was no longer the vanguard of the proletariat but of the whole people. The programme also called for the inculcation of a Communist morality based on the principles of socialist humanism – a concept long absent from the orthodox Leninist tradition. However, with the fall of Krushchev in 1964, a more positive attitude to Stalin began to emerge together with a lessening of the emphasis on peaceful coexistence. This was reflected in the basic political textbook *Foundations of Scientific Communism*, published in 1967. This was accompanied on the international scene by the appearance (about the time of the invasion of Czechoslovakia) of Brezhnev's doctrine of 'limited sovereignty'. This involved the idea that the paths towards socialism could not be all that different, that the defence of socialism was a matter for the world socialist system, and the transformation of the concept of national dictatorship of the proletariat into that of an international dictatorship. The new constitution to replace the Stalin constitution of 1936 was decided on in 1961 but did not emerge until 1977. It reinforced the power of the Party – uniting both the General Secretaryship of the Party and the Presidency of the state in the person of Brezhnev – and, in line with the 22nd Congress, dropped talk of 'the dictatorship of the proletariat' in favour of the 'state of the whole people'.

Although the Soviet Union did not contribute much to the development of Marxist ideas in the post-Stalin era the situation in her Eastern European neighbours was different. In Poland, one of the government's chief economic advisers, Oskar Lange, attempted to integrate such 'bourgeois' disciplines as econometrics into a socialist system that was decentralised, allowed for a certain amount of self-management and permitted prices to be established according to the law of value. The philosophical renaissance in Poland was led by Leszek Kolakowski, who, in a series of lively essays, claimed that Marxism was no closed system, rejected the traditional Marxist conception of ideology and argued for an epistemology based on the notion of *praxis* rather than on the theory of reflection.[5] Kolakowski's humanism contained a strong moral element:

No one is relieved of either positive or negative responsibility on the grounds that his actions formed only a fraction of a given historical process. A soldier is morally responsible for a crime committed on the orders of his superior; an individual is all the more responsible for acts performed – supposedly or in fact – on the orders of an anonymous history ... we profess the doctrine of total responsibility of the individual for his deeds and of the amorality of the historical process.[6]

Kolakowski eventually went into exile, and more influential inside the country was the work of Adam Schaff. A member of the Party's Central Committee, Schaff was a specialist in linguistics and in his *Introduction to Semantics* (1962) produced the best attempt to integrate modern linguistic theory into Marxism.[7] Although strongly opposed to Kolakowski's 'young Marxism' and defending a modified form of reflection theory, Schaff did appeal to the notion of alienation and, dubious as to the rate at which socialism could proceed in abolishing the state, the family and community production, declared:

> It is possible to explain the persistence of alienation in socialist countries. But it is unconvincing, or at any rate ill-advised, to deny its existence, as, unfortunately, is often done even in books which claim to be scientific. It is disingenuous to imagine that men's consciousness, attitudes, and social institutions can be changed overnight simply as a result of the abolition of private ownership of the means of production.[8]

In Czechoslovakia, the loosening of Moscow's influence implied by the 20th Congress of the CPSU led the Czechs to rejuvenate their Marxism by drawing on their long democratic and cultural tradition, a process which culminated in the 'Prague Spring' of 1968. These reforms were especially noticeable in economics and in philosophy. In economics, the dominant figure was Ota Sik, whose *Plan and Market under Socialism* supplied the theoretical basis for many of the 1968 reforms. Sik wished to emphasise the importance of market relations even under socialism and the equal importance of leaving considerable initiative to workers' collectives. In an analysis that paralleled Weber's critique of bureaucracy, Sik explained Czechoslovakia's poor economic performance by the excessive centralisation of the planning system:

> The administrative system of management restricts the enterprises' independence and undermines the optimum development of their initiative. Management bodies in the enterprises could seldom decide independently and flexibly on any economic process according to the rapidly changing economic conditions, but were primarily compelled to keep formal records to carrying out the administratively prescribed quantitative indicators.[9]

Sik did not deny the need for planning, but insisted on the necessity for feedback from the bottom:

> There must be economic relationships among the producers that will continually force them to take account of the consumers' interests as they make decisions on production. Here, any producer who makes a one-sided decision at the expense of consumers, should feel the negative effect on himself as consumer, just as the optimum decision should bring a positive effect. And economic relationships where there is a constant confrontation and direct mutual balancing of people's interests as producers and as consumers furthering a socially necessary expenditure of labour – these relationships are what we mean by *socialist commodity-money relationships*.[10]

This was tantamount to admitting that the law of value would continue to exist under socialism.

The most original Czech philosopher in the 1960s was Karel Kosik, who drew upon the work of Lukács, Marcuse and Sartre to restate what he saw as the fundamental bases of Marx's philosophy. Kosik's basic proposition was:

> Man does not live in two different spheres, nor does he inhabit history with one part of his being and nature with his other part. *Man is at all times at once in nature and in history.* As an historical, and thus as a social being, he humanises nature but also knows it and recognises it as the absolute totality, as the self-sufficient *causa sui*, as a precondition and prerequisite of humanisation.[11]

Therefore man's central activity was human *praxis*, which was

> the arena for the metamorphosis of the objective into the subjective and the subjective into the objective. It is the 'active centre' in which human intentions are realised and laws of nature discovered. Human *praxis* unites causality and purposiveness.[12]

Kosik paid unwanted attention to art and even drew on Heidegger's concept of *Sorge* to illuminate the human condition.

By far the greatest departure from Moscow orthodoxy was made by Yugoslavia. With the political break from Moscow in 1948 and the rejection of the Soviet Union as a model, Yugoslavian Marxists developed a strong critique of the Soviet Union. Some held that Bolshevism as such was progressive but that the Soviet Union had ceased to move towards Communism, being now governed by an entrenched bureaucratic ruling class.[13] More radical Yugoslavs rejected the Leninist party as a betrayal of Marx. According to them, the direct result of Leninism was 'statism' defined as a system in which

> the state apparatus completely coalesced with those of the Communist Party and other political organisations constituting its transmission mechanisms. As the *collective* owner of the means of production, this apparatus employs the labour force and exploits it. The personal share of each representative of the ruling class in the distribution of surplus value is proportional to his position in the state hierarchy. With respect to the statist class, as well, we must speak in the true Marxist spirit of the prospect for expropriating the expropriators and for socialising the means of production.[14]

This critique of the Soviet Union was backed up by a revival of Marxist humanist philosophy centring upon the University of Belgrade and the review *Praxis*, founded in 1967. In one of the early numbers one of its editors, Gaio Petrovic, stated:

> One of the basic achievements of our postwar philosophical development is the discovery that man, who was excluded from the Stalinistic version of Marxist philosophy as an obstruction, is in the centre of authentic Marxist philosophical thought.[15]

This concentration on the problems of alienation and freedom in socialist society led to a return to the ideas of the young Marx. As the historian of the *Praxis* group has written:

> It became clear that the problems with which the young Marx was grappling – *Praxis*, the conflict of human existence and essence, the question of what constitute true needs and basic human capacities, alienation, emancipation, labour and production, and other concerns expressed at that time – far from being sins of youth underlay all his mature work, and furthermore, remain even now the living crucial issues of our time and indeed of the whole epoch of transition.[16]

The group was, however, suppressed in 1975, with many of its leading members being dismissed from their posts.

The most striking aspect of the Yugoslav model was their emphasis on workers' self-management (which dates from 1949) in the context of a considerably decentralised economy and a strongly market-orientated socialism. Beginning with the need to find a method by which the partisans could govern liberated areas during the war, Yugoslav self-management became increasingly pragmatic in the pursuit of economic growth and technical development based on legitimate self-interest and strong material incentives.

In the post-Stalin era of Western European Communism the central figure is the Italian communist leader Palmiro Togliatti, who had been a close friend and collaborator of Gramsci. Togliatti had always maintained a fairly independent line, but the Krushchev speech of 1956 gave him the opportunity of broadening his position by declaring, firstly, that the mere criticism of Stalin as a person was too superficial an approach to the phenomenon of Stalinism; secondly, that the construction of socialism was possible in a multi-party state; and thirdly that the whole Communist movement had become a poly-central system in which Moscow no longer held the unique place. In line with these views, Togliatti's Yalta *Memorandum* of 1964 took issue with the positions taken up by the Chinese Communist Party but equally opposed their formal condemnation by the Soviet Union. Togliatti claimed that 'any proposal to create once again a centralised international organisation'[17] was unacceptable, and stated firmly:

We always start from the idea that socialism is the regime in which there is the widest freedom for the workers, that they in fact participate in an organised manner in the direction of the entire social life. Therefore, we greet all positions of principle and all facts showing us that this is the reality in all the Socialist countries and not only in the Soviet Union. On the other hand, events that sometimes disclose the contrary to us damage the entire movement.[18]

Togliatti's ideas, buttressed by an interpretation of Gramsci favourable to their policies, were given wide currency by the Communist Party of Italy in recent years, and led to the famous 'historic compromise' in which the PCI, in the hope of extending its own power base, was willing to give qualified support to parties whose basic orientation was not socialist.

The French and Spanish Communist parties, in the 1970s, followed the Italian lead and thus gave rise to the concept of 'Eurocommunism'. The French Party decided, in 1976, to drop the aim of 'dictatorship of proletariat' from its programme, and its tactics in the 1978 elections gave rise to unprecedented criticism of the lack of open debate inside the Party, led by prominent Party intellectuals such as Althusser and Ellenstein. The most outspoken was the Spanish Communist Party. Its general secretary, Santiago Carillo, in his controversial book *Eurocommunism and the State*, laid stress on the achievement and extension of democratic liberties and human rights and saw the gaining of an electoral mandate as an essential step in the struggle to transform capitalism. In a passage which obviously refers to the Soviet Union, Carillo goes as far as to say:

> In actual fact the lack of democratic 'credibility' of us communists among certain sections of the population in our countries is associated – rather than with our own activity and policy – with the fact that in countries where capital ownership has disappeared, the dictatorship of the proletariat has been implanted, with a one-party system, as a general rule, and has undergone serious bureaucratic distortions and even very grave processes of degeneration.[19]

At its 1978 Congress, the Party even decided, in spite of strident opposition from Moscow, to abandon specific reference to Leninism in its self-definition, thus heralding the breakup of most of the European parties following the collapse of the Soviet Union.

This collapse of the Communist regimes in the USSR and Eastern Europe came as a surprise. In the early and mid-1980s these regimes has looked to most commentators as stable as ever. By the end of the 1990s, however, Communist parties had lost effective power in all the countries of Eastern Europe, though the old elite still held important positions of power in Bulgaria, Serbia, Romania and Albania. In Poland, widespread strikes led to elections and a Solidarity government in September 1989. In Hungary where a market economy had been slowly expanding during the 1980s, the Communist Party liberalized from within and was defeated in elections held in the spring of 1990. In the German Democratic Republic, Honecker tried to cling on to power but, undermined by Gorbachev's *Perestroika*, conceded elections in March 1990 and was roundly defeated. In Czechoslovakia, large-scale popular unrest caused the Communist Party to liberalise from within and a non-Communist government led by Dubcek and Havel emerged in December 1989. By 1991 Yugoslavia had been dissolved, with only Serbia, turning under Milosevic to an increasingly xenophobic nationalism, retaining its continuity while in Romania an internal coup ended in violence and the ending of Ceausescu's dictatorship.

This profound transformation was strongly influenced by the policy of the Soviet leadership under Gorbachev and his reversal of the Brezhnev doctrine of legitimate interference in neighbouring socialist states. *Perestroika*, as his policy came to be known, involved a thorough-going reform of the economic system with a greater role for market transactions and more autonomy for economic enterprises together with administrative reforms lessening central control and giving more freedom to the republics. In an attempt to enhance his economic reforms, Gorbachev sought to increase the power of the Soviets as a counterweight to the Communist Party which he saw as controlled by the entrenched interests of the economic bureaucracy.[20] But the economic reforms failed to deliver, criticism and dissident political activity increased, and independence movements in the regions and the republics gained strength. In August 1991, Gorbachev was placed under house arrest by his own political elite and Yeltsin, already head of the Russian Republic, took control, in what was effectively a counter-coup, of the USSR as a whole. And the USSR itself was formally dissolved on 31 December 1991.

As far as Marxist thought is concerned, the transformation of Eastern Europe and the USSR prompts two areas of concern, which are intimately bound together. What explanation can be offered for these events and what effect does all this have for the status of Marxism? Some have drawn a straight line from Marx to Brezhnev and drawn the conclusion that the collapse of Communism is the ultimate refutation of Marxism. Others such as Trotsky (see above) have seen in the Soviet Union experiment a kind of degenerate bureaucratic autocracy. Still others have seen the Soviet Union as a state capitalist society and thus as a necessary precursor to any possible socialism. Since almost all these analyses are produced by Marxists in the West,[21] and in particular in Anglo-Saxon countries, they are dealt with in the chapter on Marxism in the United States[22] and the more general question of the meaning of the collapse of Communism for Marxism as a whole in the Conclusion.

Notes

1. *Krushchev Remembers*, ed. E. Crankshaw (New York, 1971) p. 530.
2. *The Road to Communism, Documents of the 22nd Congress of the CPSU* (Moscow, 1961) p. 506.
3. Ibid., p. 470.
4. Ibid., p. 512.
5. See particularly, L. Kolakowski, 'Karl Marx and the Classical Definition of Truth', in *Towards a Marxist Humanism* (New York, 1968).
6. L. Kolakowski, *Towards a Marxist Humanism*, pp. 140f.

7. See particularly pp. 140ff.
8. A. Schaff, *Marxism and the Human Individual*, ed. R. Cohen (New York, 1970) pp. 128f.
9. O. Sik, *Plan and Market under Socialism* (White Plains and Prague, 1967) p. 98.
10. Ibid., p. 167.
11. K. Kosik, *Dialectics of the Concrete* (Dordrecht, 1978) p. 151.
12. Ibid., p. 71.
13. Cf., for example, M. Djilas, *The New Class* (London and New York, 1962).
14. S. Stojanovic, *Between Ideals and Reality* (London and New York, 1973).
15. *Praxis*, Vol. 1 (1967) p. 64.
16. M. Markovic and R. Cohen, *Yugoslavia: The Rise and Fall of Socialist Humanism* (Nottingham, 1975) p. 18.
17. P. Togliatti, *Memorandum*, in W. Griffith (ed.), *Sino-Soviet Relations 1964–1965* (Cambridge, 1967) p. 380.
18. Ibid., p. 383.
19. S. Carillo, *Eurocommunism and the State* (London, 1977) p. 155.
20. See further S. Whitefield, *Industrial Power and the Soviet State* (Oxford, 1993).
21. But see the works of Boris Kagarlitsky detailed below.
22. See below pp. 363 ff.

Further reading

USSR

Krushchev's own account – if it be his – is contained in *Krushchev Remembers*, which has the 1956 denunciation of Stalin as an appendix. The best accounts of the Krushchev era are Crankshaw's *Krushchev*, Linden's *Krushchev and the Soviet Leadership*, and, more recently, the Medvedevs' *Krushchev: The Years in Power*. On the boring subject of contemporary Soviet doctrine, see Wetter's *Soviet Ideology Today*, and De George's *The New Marxism*. The best short introductions are the second half of McAuley's *Politics and the Soviet Union*, and chapter 4 of Leonard's *Three Faces of Marxism*. See also the commentaries by Rothberg and Tatu. On the collapse of the Soviet system, see White's *Gorbachev and After*, Hill's *Communist Politics under the Knife*, Kagarlitsky's *The Disintegration of the Monolith*, and Ticktin's *Origins of the Crisis in the USSR*. Evans describes significant changes under various leaders and chapter 6 of Kagarlitsky's *Russia under Yeltsin and Putin* gives an account of the post-Soviet Left there. Brown's collection is a good overview.

Eastern Europe

Two good general introductions are Ionescu's *The Politics of the European Communist States* and Pelikan's *Socialist Opposition in Eastern Europe*. On the ideas, see De George's *The New Marxism*. For a Left critique, see Bahro's *The Alternative in Eastern Europe*. For two accounts of socialist economics in this area, see Horvat's *The Political Economy of Socialism* and Brus and Laski's *From Marx to the Market: Socialism in Search of an Economic System*. There is a useful collection in Stokes's *From Stalinism to Pluralism: A Documentary History of Eastern Europe Since 1945*.

On *Poland* see in general Jordan's *Philosophy and Ideology*, also the books by Schaff and Kolakowski.

On *Czechoslovakia* the best account of the context of the Prague Spring is Kusin's *The Intellectual Origins of the Prague Spring*. See also the books of Pelikan, Sik and Kosik.

On *Yugoslavia*, see Auty's biography *Tito*, which can be supplemented by Ross Johnson's *The Transformation of Communist Ideology* and Clissold's collection, *Yugoslavia and the Soviet Union*. An excellent assessment, by a sociologist, of the realities of self-management, is Zukin's *Beyond Marx and Tito*. A short history of the *Praxis* group is contained in Markovic and Cohen's *Yugoslavia: The Rise and Fall of Socialist Humanism*. The best critique by an 'insider' is Stojanovic's *Between Ideals and Reality*. See also Petrovic's *Marx in the Mid-twentieth Century*.

Fowkes's book compares and contrasts different Communist regimes. Taras's collection examines the role of dissident Marxists in undermining Communist power. Swain and Swain provide a reliable general history.

Western Europe

On the Italian version of Eurocommunism see Sassoon's *The Italian Communists Speak for Themselves* and Hobsbawm's interview with Napolitano, *The Italian Road to Socialism*. On Spain, see Carillo's *Eurocommunism and the State*. In general, see Claudin's *Eurocommunism and Socialism*, which is critical but still sympathetic, and Mandel's outright attack, *From Stalinism to Eurocommunism*.

Bibliography

USSR (general)
Paul Bellis, *Marxism and the USSR* (London, 1979).
Robert Conquest, *Power and Policy in the USSR* (New York, 1961).
Isaac Deutscher, *Russia After Stalin* (London, 1953).
Wolfgang Leonard, *The Kremlin Since Stalin* (Oxford, 1962).
—— *Three Faces of Marxism* (New York, 1974).
M. Lewin, *Political Undercurrents in Soviet Economic Debates* (Princeton, N.J., 1974).
Sidney Ploss, *Conflict and Decision Making in Soviet Russia: A Case Study of Agricultural Policy, 1953–1963* (Princeton, N.J., 1965).
Gustav A. Wetter, *Soviet Ideology Today* (New York, 1966).

Krushchev: texts

Nikita Krushchev, *The Crimes of the Stalin Era* (New York, 1956).
—— *Krushchev Speaks* (Ann Arbor, 1963).
—— *Krushchev Remembers*, 2 vols (London, 1972–4).

Krushchev: commentaries

E. Crankshaw, *Krushchev* (London, 1966).
Merle Fainsod, 'Krushchevism', in M.M. Drachkovitch (ed.), *Marxism in the Modern World* (Stanford, 1965).
Mark Frankland, *Krushchev* (Harmondsworth, 1966).
Carl A. Linden, *Krushchev and the Soviet Leadership: 1957–1964* (Baltimore, 1966).
Richard Loewenthal, 'The Nature of Krushchev's Power', *Problems of Communism*, IX (1960).
R. and Z. Medvedev, *Krushchev. The Years in Power* (Oxford, 1977).
Roger Pethybridge, *A Key to Soviet Politics: The Crisis of the Anti-Party Group* (New York, 1962).
Lazar Pistrak, *The Grand Tactician: Krushchev's Rise to Power* (New York, 1961).
Myron Rush, *The Rise of Krushchev* (Washington, 1958).
Adam B. Ulam, *The New Face of Soviet Totalitarianism* (Cambridge, Mass., 1963).
Bertram D. Wolfe, *Krushchev and Stalin's Ghost* (New York, 1957).

Post-Krushchev

A. Brown (ed.), *The Demise of Marxism-Leninism in Russia* (Basingstoke, 1994).
Archie Brown and Jack Gray (eds), *Political Culture and Political Change in Communist States*, 2nd edn (London, 1979).
Robert Conquest, 'After Krushchev: A Conservative Restoration?', *Problems of Communism*, XII (1963).
—— *Russia after Krushchev* (New York, 1965).
Alexander Dallin and Thomas Larson, *Soviet Politics since Krushchev* (Englewood Cliffs, N.J., 1968).
Isaac Deutscher, *Russia, China and the West* (London, 1970).
John Dornberg, *The New Tsars: Russia under Stalin's Heirs* (Garden City, New York, 1971).
A. Evans, *Soviet Marxism-Leninism: The Decline of an Ideology* (Westport, 1993).
Ronald Hill, *Communist Politics under the Knife: Surgery or Autopsy* (London, 1990).
B. Kagarlitsky, *Russia under Yeltsin and Putin: Neo-Liberal Autocracy* (London, 2002).
Boris Kagarlitsky, *The Disintegration of the Monolith* (London, 1992).
D. Lovell (ed.), *The Transition: Evaluating the Post-Communist Experience* (Aldershot, 2002).
Boris Meissner, *The Brezhnev Doctrine* (Kansas City, 1971).
Abraham Rothberg, *The Heirs of Stalin: Dissidence and the Soviet Regime, 1953–1970* (Ithaca, New York, 1972).
Daniel Tarschys, *The Soviet Political Agenda* (London, 1979).
Michel Tatu, *Power in the Kremlin from Krushchev to Kosygin* (New York, 1970).
Hillel Ticktin, *Origins of the Crisis in the USSR: Essays on the Political Economy of a Disintegrating System* (Armonk, NY, 1992).
Stephen White, *Gorbachev and After* (Cambridge, 1991).

Sino-Soviet conflict

Edward Crankshaw, *The New Cold War: Moscow vs. Peking* (Baltimore, 1963).
Leopold Labedz and G.R. Urban (eds), *The Sino-Soviet Conflict: Eleven Radio Discussions* (London, 1965).
Robert C. North, *Moscow and Chinese Communists* (Stanford, 1953).
Donald S. Zagoria, *The Sino-Soviet Conflict: 1956–1961* (Princeton, N.J., 1962).

Eastern Europe (general)

Rudolf Bahro, *The Alternative in Eastern Europe* (London, 1978).
Wlodzimier Brus and Kazimierz Laski, *From Marx to the Market: Socialism in Search of an Economic System* (Oxford, 1989).
Richard T. De George, *The New Marxism: Soviet and East European Marxism since 1956* (New York, 1968).
B. Fowkes, *The Rise and Fall of Communism in Eastern Europe* (Basingstoke, 1995).
Chris Harman, *Bureaucracy and Revolution in Eastern Europe* (London, 1974).
Branko Horvat, *The Political Economy of Socialism: A Marxist Social Theory* (New York, 1982).
G. Ionescu, *The Politics of the European Communist States* (London, 1967).
G.D. Jackson, *Comintern and Peasant in East Europe: 1919–1930* (New York, 1966).
L. McFalls, *Communism's Collapse, Democracy's Demise? The Cultural Context and Consequences of the East German Revolution* (Basingstoke, 1995).
Jiri Pelikan, *Socialist Opposition in Eastern Europe* (London, 1976).
H. Seton-Watson, *The East European Revolution*, 3rd edn (London, 1957).
H.G. Skilling, *The Government of Communist East Europe* (New York, 1966).
Gale Stokes (ed.), *From Stalinism to Pluralism: A Documentary History of Eastern Europe since 1945* (New York, 1991).
G. Swain and N. Swain, *Eastern Europe since 1945* (London, 1993).
R. Taras (ed.), *The Road to Disillusion: From Critical Marxism to Postcommunism in Eastern Europe* (New York, 1992).
R. Tökés, *Opposition in Eastern Europe* (London, 1979).

Poland

Peter Green, 'The Third Round in Poland', *New Left Review*, 101–2 (1977).
Z. Jordan, *Philosophy and Ideology: The Development of Philosophy and Marxism-Leninism in Poland since the Second World War* (Dordrecht, 1963).
Leszek Kolakowski, *Marxism and Beyond: On Historical Understanding and Individual Responsibility* (London, 1968).
Adam Schaff, *A Philosophy of Man* (New York, 1963).
—— *Marxism and the Human Individual* (New York, 1970).

Czechoslovakia

Vladimir Fisera (ed.), *Workers' Councils in Czechoslovakia* (London, 1978).
K. Kosik, *Dialectics of the Concrete* (Dordrecht, 1976).
Vladimir Kusin, *The Intellectual Origins of the Prague Spring: The Development of Reformist Ideas in Czechoslovakia, 1956–1967* (Cambridge, 1971).
Jiri Pelikan, *The Secret Vysocany Congress of the Czech Communist Party* (New York, 1971).

—— 'The Struggle for Socialism in Czechoslovakia', in R. Blackburn (ed.), *Revolution and Class Struggle: a Reader in Marxist Politics* (London, 1977).
Ota Sik, *Plan and Market Under Socialism* (White Plains and Prague, 1967).

Yugoslavia

Phyllis Auty, *Tito: A Biography* (London, 1970).
—— *Yugoslavia* (London, 1965).
I. Avakumovic, *History of the Communist Party of Yugoslavia* (Aberdeen, 1964).
R. Bicanic, *Economic Policy in Socialist Yugoslavia* (Cambridge, 1973).
Stephen Clissold (ed.), *Yugoslavia and the Soviet Union: 1939–1973* (Oxford, 1976).
Milovan Djilas, *The New Class* (London and New York, 1962).
J.C. Fisher, *Yugoslavia: A Multi-national State* (San Francisco, 1966).
G. Hoffman and W.F. Neal, *Tito's Yugoslavia* (California, 1960).
A. Ross Johnson, *The Transformation of Communist Ideology: The Yugoslavia Case, 1945–1953* (Cambridge, Mass., 1973).
Mihailo Markovic and Robert S. Cohen, *Yugoslavia: The Rise and Fall of Socialist Humanism* (Nottingham, 1975).
Gajo Petrovic, *Marx in the Mid-twentieth Century* (New York, 1967).
Svetozar Stojanovic, *Between Ideals and Reality: A Critique of Socialism and its Future* (London and New York, 1973).
J.B. Tito, *Selected Speeches and Articles* (Zagreb, 1963).
Adam B. Ulam, 'Titoism' in M.M. Drachkovitch (ed.), *Marxism in the Modern World* (Stanford, 1965).
W. Vucinic (ed.), *Contempoary Yugoslavia* (Berkeley, 1969).
S. Zukin, *Beyond Marx and Tito: Theory and Practice in Yugoslav Socialism* (Cambridge, 1975).

Western Europe

Giorgio Amendola, 'The Italian Road to Socialism' (interview), *New Left Review*, 106 (1977).
Santiago Carillo, Regis Debray and Max Grallo, *Dialogue on Spain* (London, 1976).
Santiago Carillo, *Eurocommunism and the State* (London, 1977).
F. Claudin, *Eurocommunism and Socialism* (London and New York, 1978).
Paolo Flores d'Arcais and Franco Moretti, 'Paradoxes of the Italian Political Crisis', *New Left Review*, 96 (1976).
E. Hobsbawm and G. Napolitano, *The Italian Road to Socialism* (London, 1977).
Maria-Antonietta Macciocchi, *Letters from Inside the Italian Communist Party to Louis Althusser* (London, 1973).
Ernest Mandel, *From Stalinism to Eurocommunism* (London, 1978).
D. Plotke and C. Boggs (eds), *Eurocommunism* (Berkeley, 1979).
D. Sassoon (ed.), *The Italian Communists Speak for Themselves* (Nottingham, 1978).
G. Urban (ed.), *Eurocommunism* (London, 1978).

Part Three

European Marxism between the Wars

[W]e must try to understand every change, development and revision of Marxist theory, since its original emergence from the philosophy of German Idealism, as a necessary product of its epoch [Hegel]. More precisely, we should seek to understand their determination by the totality of the historico-social process of which they are a general expression [Marx]. We will then be able to grasp the real origins of the degeneration of Marxist theory into vulgar-Marxism. We may also discern the meaning of the passionate yet apparently 'ideological' efforts of the Marxist theorists of the Third International today to restore 'Marx's genuine doctrine'.

Karl Korsch, *Marxism and Philosophy*

11
Lukács

The works of Lukács, Korsch, Gramsci and others considered in this section were formulated during the relatively brief period of capitalist instability inaugurated by the First World War. Following the collapse of the pre-1914 world order and of the systematic Marxism of the Second International that was to a large extent its mirror, central Marxist concepts such as class struggle, the dictatorship of the proletariat, the nature of proletarian democracy, the function of the state, and the role of philosophy all became subject to radical reformulation. Central Europe – Germany and the nation states emerging from the ruin of the Austro-Hungarian empire – played an important role in this change. With the growing rigidification of Marxist thought in the Soviet Union, the focus of originality shifted once more westwards. The work of Lukács is an idealised picture of the revolutionary movement and Communist parties that had led the risings during 1918–19 in Germany, in Austria and in his native Hungary. But the picture remained at some distance from reality as these revolutionary movements proved a failure and Lukács found himself theorising in a socio-political vacuum. He himself, in the Preface to *History and Class Consciousness*, talked of 'those exaggeratedly sanguine hopes that many of us cherished concerning the duration and tempo of the revolution'.[1]

Lukács was born in 1885 in Budapest into a wealthy Jewish family (his father was director of the largest Hungarian bank). Until the end of the First World War he studied and wrote in various universities in Germany and Austria-Hungary. Joining the Communist Party in 1918, he became Minister for Education in the short-lived Hungarian Soviet regime of 1919. Following its collapse, Lukács emigrated to Vienna where he wrote most of the essays he collected in his most important book – *History and Class Consciousness*. He moved to Moscow in 1929.

171

Lukács was in a rare position to appreciate the importance of classical German philosophy for Marxism. In the years before 1914 he had fully assimilated the debates surrounding the demise of the neo-Kantian school, the beginnings of phenomenology, and the growing influence of intuitionist and romantic tendencies, all of which currents were reacting against the primacy attached to the methodology of the natural sciences.[2] Largely inspired by Dilthey, this view of the world held the study of history to be central:

> The study of history disclosed the essential nature of man as it unfolded in the totality of human experience and the historian entered into the life of past generations by reliving in his own mind the thoughts and actions whereby men had once defined themselves. *Geisteswissenschaft* and *Lebensphilosophie*, 'science of spirit' and 'philosophy of life', were two aspects of one untiring search for a supra-empirical vision of the living and moving totality of world history.[3]

One of the main tools used by Lukács to conceptualise the problems of his time was the philosophy of Hegel. With the possible (and rather minor) exception of Labriola, Lukács was the first Marxist thinker seriously to evaluate the role of Hegel in the formation of Marx's thought and recapture the Hegelian dimension (in the *Phenomenology* just as much as the *Logic*) of Marxism. In this, Lukács strikingly anticipated the new light cast upon Marx's thought by the publication around 1930 of the *Economic and Philosophical Manuscripts*. Like the young Marx, Lukács had found his way to Marxism through Hegel. This approach involved Lukács in opposing the theoretical presuppositions both of the 'economism' practised by the socialist trade union leaders for the previous two decades and the emphasis on natural necessity so evident in the scientism of so many previous Marxist philosophers. He criticised the idea of a dialectics of nature, the reflection theory of knowledge,[4] and took *Anti-Dühring* to task for its deficient understanding of dialectics:

> Engels does not even mention the most vital interaction, namely the *dialectical relation between subject and object* in the historical process, let alone give it the prominence it deserves. Yet without this factor dialectics ceases to be revolutionary, despite attempts [illusory in the last analysis] to retain 'fluid' concepts. For it implies a failure to recognise that in all metaphysics the object remains untouched and unaltered so that thought remains contemplative and fails to become practical; while for the dialectical method the central problem is to *change reality*.[5]

All the central ideas of *History and Class Consciousness* – reification, dialectic of subject and object, and totality – had their roots in Hegel. The main thesis of the book was that the two terms of its title – history and class consciousness – were in fact one and the same. In his discussion of class consciousness, Lukács began where Marx left off. Notoriously, Marx's account of class was incomplete: but, in a famous passage of the *Eighteenth Brumaire*, Marx had distinguished the objective factor (common relationship to the means of production) and the subjective factor (consciousness of shared interests etc.).[6] Lukács went beyond the actual subjective consciousness of the proletariat and talked of 'ascribed' class consciousness, i.e. the consciousness a class *would* have if it were fully aware of its own interests. This class consciousness, for Lukács, 'has no psychological reality'.[7] In the crucial passage, he wrote:

By relating consciousness to the whole of society it becomes possible to infer the thoughts and feelings which men would have in a particular situation if they were *able* to assess both it and the interests arising from it in their impact upon immediate action and on the whole structure of society. That is to say, it would be possible to infer the thoughts and feelings appropriate to their objective situation. The number of such situations is not unlimited in any society. However much detailed research is able to refine social typologies there will always be a number of clearly distinguished basic types whose characteristics are determined by the types of position available in the process of production. Now class consciousness consists in the fact of the appropriate and rational reactions 'ascribed' to a particular typical position in the process of production. This consciousness is, therefore, neither the sum nor the average of what is thought or felt by the single individuals who make up the class. And yet the historically significant actions of the class as a whole are determined in the last resort by its consciousness and not by the thought of the individual – and these actions can be understood only by reference to this consciousness.[8]

Historically, Lukács gave an excellent account of the development and limitations of class consciousness over the previous four centuries and claimed that class consciousness proper only emerged with the Industrial Revolution because only then did classes become national entities and consciousness become 'purer' with the polarisation of the bourgeoisie and the proletariat, although the growing mobility and complexity of developed capitalist society would obviously create difficulties for this last conception. Lukács believed that his emphasis on consciousness was vital at the time at which he was writing, when the objective conditions were ripe for world revolution, whose success therefore depended on the less tangible element of proletarian consciousness:

> A *new* element is required: the consciousness of the proletariat must become deed. But as the mere contradiction is raised to a conscious-ness dialectical contradiction, as the act of becoming conscious turns into a *point of transition in practice*, we see once more in greater con-creteness the character of proletarian dialectics as we have often described it: namely, since consciousness here is not the knowledge of an opposed object but is the self-consciousness of the object *the act of consciousness overthrows* the objective form of the object.[9]

In his 1967 Preface to the work Lukács said that his distinction between actual and ascribed class consciousness corresponded to Lenin's distinc-tion in *What is to be Done?* between trade union consciousness and the socialist consciousness implanted 'from outside'.[10] And, according to Lukács, the 'bearer of the class consciousness of the proletariat and the conscience of its historical vocation'[11] was the Party.

Lukács believed that a developed class consciousness would enable the proletariat to become both the subject and the object of history:

> Only when the consciousness of the proletariat is able to point out the road along which the dialectics of history is objectively impelled, but which it cannot travel unaided, will the consciousness of the pro-letariat awaken to the consciousness of the process, and only then will the proletariat become the identical subject-object of history whose praxis will change reality.[12]

In a long and detailed analysis, Lukács attempted to show how previous thought had not been able correctly to perceive the world as it radically separated subject from object.[13] Only with Hegel was this separation overcome, albeit in an idealist fashion. The only class which could unite subject and object was the proletariat, which expressed in its subjective thought [at least in its 'ascribed' consciousness] what it was objectively doing in history. This historical interaction of subject and object was for Lukács the basic form of the dialectic:

> It is of the first importance to realise that the method is limited here to the realms of history and society. The misunderstanding that arises from Engels's account of dialectics can in the main be put down to the fact that Engels – following Hegel's mistaken lead – extended the

method to apply also to nature. However, the crucial determinant of dialectics – the interaction of subject and object, the unity of theory and practice, the historical change in the reality underlying the categories as the root cause of changes in thought, etc. – are absent from our knowledge of nature.[14]

In this context Lukács quoted several times from Marx's *Theses on Feuerbach* on the unity of theory and practice. For Lukács, as for Marx, practice was the concrete union of thought and reality.

Previously, understanding the world has been blocked by the phenomenon for which Lukács popularised the term 'reification'. Lukács started explicit from Marx's analysis of the fetishism of commodities in *Capital*, in which the social relations between persons became transformed – both subjectively and objectively – into relations between commodities. The world of things ruled men through objective laws that appeared to be independent of them. Men became objects, passive spectators of a process that structured their lives for them. Starting from the economic division of labour, Lukács traced the progress of this reification in the state and in modern bureaucracy (here borrowing from Max Weber's concept of 'rationality').

Linked to the notion of reification was that of totality. One of the results of reification was 'the destruction of every image of the whole'.[15] The specialisation of labour and the general atomisation of society meant that people and the world surrounding them were viewed as discrete, separate entities with no intrinsic connection. The bourgeoisie had necessarily to view things like this, for it was essential to their way of life. The central impetus of the reification process up till the present had been the all-pervasiveness of objectivity: in a reified world there were no subjects. However, the evolution of capital in society had now reached a point where the proletariat could destroy reification and become the subject of the historical process. The partial and static views of the bourgeoisie could never attain to *knowledge* of society:

> Only in this context which sees the isolated facts of social life as aspects of the historical process and integrates them in a *totality*, can knowledge of facts hope to become knowledge of *reality*.[16]

Lukács insisted on this point:

> It is not the primacy of economic motives in historical explanation that constitutes the decisive difference between Marxism and

bourgeois thought but the point of view of totality. The category of totality, the all-pervasive supremacy of the whole over the parts is the essence of the method which Marx took over from Hegel ... *The primacy of the category of totality is the bearer of the principle of revolution in science.*[17]

And later:

Reality can only be understood and penetrated as a totality, and only a subject which is itself a totality is capable of this penetration ... *only the class can actively penetrate the reality of society and transform it in its entirety.* For this reason 'criticism' advanced from a standpoint of class, is criticism from a total point of view and hence it provides the dialectical unity of theory and practice. In dialectical unity it is at once cause and effect, mirror and motor of the historical and dialectical process. The proletariat as the subject of thought in society destroys at one blow the dilemma of impotence: the dilemma created by the pure laws with their fatalism as by the ethics of pure intentions.[18]

It thus becomes clear why Lukács set great store by the correct methodology. Indeed – somewhat ignoring his own emphasis on totality and the fluidity of concepts – he posited a rigid dichotomy between the theses of Marx and his method:

Let us assume for the sake of argument that recent research has disproved once and for all every one of Marx's individual theses. Even if this were to be proved, every serious 'orthodox' Marxist would still be able to accept all such modern findings without reservation and hence dismiss all Marx's theses *in toto* – without having to renounce his orthodoxy for a single moment ... orthodoxy refers exclusively to *method.*[19]

According to Lukács, there was no contemporary problem – including war, crises, and the economic problems of Soviet Russia – that could not be solved by the dialectical method alone.

It has been pointed out that the historical context of Lukács's book was the October Revolution of 1917, of which Lukács's work could be said to be the idealised theory. Lukács did talk of Lenin's decisive influence on him, and as long as proletarian consciousness was ascribed rather than actual, there was a temptation to find it embodied in an elite of revolutionary intellectuals. Nevertheless, in general, Lukács was nearer to Luxemburg or

Trotsky in his faith in the organic growth of proletarian consciousness and its ability to control its leaders in face of the bureaucratic tendency to which the Leninist Party was subject.

It is not surprising that Lukács's book met with opposition from inside the Communist Party. Philosophically, it smacked of Left Hegelianism, and rejected the rather naive materialism that was the basis of the Soviet interpretation of the world. Indeed, it described such materialism as 'inverted Platonism' and the 'ideological form of the bourgeois Revolution'.[20] The Bolsheviks were engaged in transforming European Communist parties in their own image and the appearance of a major, and apparently innovatory, theoretician outside Russia was an embarrassment to them. Also, Lukács' enthusiasm for Rosa Luxemburg and workers' councils lent some support to the syndicalist tendencies which were the main obstacle to efforts at Bolshevising the Western Communist Parties. Lukács's book was condemned by the Fifth Comintern Congress in 1924. Lukács published a self-criticism which he later said was not to be taken seriously, but in 1967 he wrote an extended Preface to a re-edition of *History and Class Consciousness* in which he said that his book was an example of 'revolutionary Messianism'[21] and had 'no topical importance in the current controversies about the true nature of Marxism'.[22] He identified its central error as narrowing the basis of economics by disregarding the notion of labour as mediating between man and nature and denying the ontological objectivity of nature. This had led to an Hegelian equation of alienation with objectivation. These themes are continued in the massive *Ontology* on which he was working at the time of his death.

In the 1920s, Lukács published a short book on Lenin emphasising the dialectical elements in Lenin's approach. He also criticised Bukharin's mechanistic sociology, although he shared his political stance in the late 1920s. However, as Stalin's rule was consolidated, Lukács turned to less controversial matters – above all, to literary criticism. Carrying further Engels's contrast between realism and naturalism, he extolled the former, represented by Shakespeare, Balzac and Scott, who managed to unite the objective world with their own subjective appreciation of it. The naturalists (of whom Zola was his prime example) merely reflected their environment without achieving a full subject–object unity. Lukács devoted himself to expounding a critical realism and rational humanism which he found embodied in classical German literature (Goethe) and continued in his own time by Thomas Mann. He sharply contrasted the views of these writers with the later irrationalist romantic trends that were contained in various decadent bourgeois forms of modernism.

The culmination of Lukács's work in this field was his *Aesthetics*, in which he tried to maintain a position between what he considered the decadence of Western subjective idealism and the over-simplifications of Soviet socialist realism. Following Hegel and the early Marx, he portrayed art as a process of humanisation, a reflection and representation of man's essential nature and of the unity of mankind.[23]

Lukács has been criticised for his undue emphasis on consciousness: the proletariat is not its own creator, it is created by the capitalist mode of production. And Lukács had no theory of *how* the proletariat develops its own consciousness, except in the ultra-Left view that the party alone is capable of representing the proletariat's ascribed consciousness.[24] Nevertheless, despite his compromises with Moscow in the latter part of his life, Lukács's work was seminal. He revived interest in the Hegelian element in Marxism and his treatment of the concepts of alienation, reification, totality, etc., were fundamental to later Marxist critiques of bourgeois culture.

Notes

1. G. Lukács, Preface to 1967 edition, *History and Class Consciousness* (London, 1971) p. xli.
2. See further, H. Stuart Hughes, *Consciousness and Society* (London, 1959) ch. 2.
3. G. Lichtheim, *Lukács* (London, 1970) p. 27.
4. Cf. G. Lukács, *History and Class Consciousness*, p. 200.
5. Ibid., p. 3.
6. Cf. B. Ollman, 'Marx's use of "Class" ', *American Journal of Sociology* (Mar. 1968). For the debatable view that Lukács's views are implicit in Marx, see I. Meszaros, 'Contingent and Necessary Class Consciousness', in *Aspects of History and Class Consciousness*, ed. I. Meszaros (London, 1971) p. 94.
7. G. Lukács, op. cit., p. 75.
8. Ibid., p. 51.
9. Ibid., p. 178.
10. Cf. 1967 preface, ibid., p. xviii.
11. Ibid., p. 41.
12. Ibid., p. 197.
13. Ibid., pp. 110ff.
14. Ibid., p. 24.
15. Ibid., p. 103.
16. Ibid., p. 8.
17. Ibid., p. 27.
18. Ibid., p. 39.
19. Ibid., p. 1.
20. Ibid., pp. 202, 222.
21. Ibid., 1967 Preface, p. xiv.
22. Ibid., p. ix.

23. See further, G. Lichtheim, *Lukács*, ch. 8.
24. See for example, A. Callinicos, *Althusser's Marxism* (London, 1976) pp. 26ff.;
L. Colletti, *Marxism and Hegel* (London, 1972) pp. 175ff.

Further reading

Texts

Lukács's most important contribution to Marxist philosophy is undoubtedly *History and Class Consciousness*, and particularly the long article on reification. His important early essays are in *Political Writings*. See also his short study, *Lenin*. Of his philosophical works of less immediate political relevance, see *The Young Hegel*, which seeks to minimise the influence of religion on Hegel's early thought, and the recently translated *Ontology: Hegel* and *Ontology: Marx*. The best of Lukács's literary criticism is contained in his *Theory of the Novel* and *Essays on European Realism*. See also his very early *The Soul and its Forms*. There is a useful collection in Kadarky's *The Lukács Reader*.

Commentaries

The most accessible introduction is Parkinson's *Lukács*, together with the collection of essays he edited. Lichtheim's short book is dense and difficult but full of insights. Probably the best overall account is Lowy's *Georg Lukács: From Idealism to Bolshevism*, though it limits itself largely to pre-1930. Meszaros's collection, *Aspects of History and Class Consciousness*, is very useful and the same author's *Lukács's Concept of Dialectic* contains an excellent bibliography. Meszaros, a pupil of Lukács, is engaged on a full-length study of his teacher. On the early Lukács, Stedman-Jones's article is a well-founded critique. Zitta's study is highly idiosyncratic. On Lukács as a literary critic, see the third chapter of Jameson's *Marxism and Form*. Lukács's later philosophy is treated in Shafai's *The Ontology of Georg Lukács*, while his philosophical beginnings are dealt with in Congdon's *The Young Lukács*. There is a full biography in Kadarky's *Georg Lukács: Life, Thought and Politics*, and Gluck provides a good study of the intellectual background.

Bibliography

Texts

George Lukács, *Conversations with Lukács*, ed. T. Pinkus (London, 1973).
—— *The Destruction of Reason* (London, 1974)
—— *Essays on Thomas Mann* (London, 1964)

—— 'Existentialism or Marxism?' in R.W. Sellars and M. Farber (eds), *Philosophy for the Future* (New York, 1949), and George Novack (ed.), *Existentialism Versus Marxism* (New York, 1966).

—— *Goethe and His Age* (London, 1968).

—— *The Historical Novel* (London, 1962).

—— *History and Class Consciousness* (London, 1971).

—— *Lenin: A Study of the Unity of his Thought* (London, 1970).

—— *The Lukács Reader*, ed. A. Kadarky (Oxford, 1995).

—— *Marxism and Human Liberation*, ed. E. San Juan (New York, 1973).

—— *The Meaning of Contemporary Realism* (London, 1963).

—— *Ontology: Hegel. Hegel's False and His Genuine Ontology* (London, 1977).

—— *Ontology: Marx. Marx's Basic Ontological Principles* (London, 1977).

—— *Political Writings, 1919–1929: The Question of Parliamentarism and Other Essays* (London, 1972).

—— *Solzhenitsyn* (London, 1970).

—— *The Soul and the Forms* (London, 1973).

—— *Studies in European Realism* (London, 1950).

—— *The Theory of the Novel: A Historico-Philosophical Essay on the Forms of Great Epic Literature* (London, 1971).

—— *Writer and Critic and Other Essays* (London, 1970).

—— *The Young Hegel* (London, 1975).

Commentaries

Lee Congdon, *The Young Lukács* (Chapel Hill, 1983).

Andrew Feenberg, *Lukács, Marx and the Sources of Critical Social Theory* (New York, 1986).

Mary Gluck, *Lukács and His Generation 1900–18* (Cambridge, 1985).

Lucien Goldmann, *Lukács and Heidegger: Towards a New Philosophy* (London, 1978).

F. Jameson, *Marxism and Form* (Princeton, N.J., 1971).

Agnes Heller, *Lukács Revalued* (Oxford, 1983).

Arpad Kadarky, *Georg Lukács: Life, Thought and Politics* (Oxford, 1991).

George Lichtheim, *Lukács* (London, 1970).

Michael Lowy, *Georg Lukács: From Idealism to Bolshevism* (London, 1979)

Istvan Meszaros (ed.), *Aspects of History and Class Consciousness* (London, 1971).

—— *Lukács' Concept of Dialectic* (London, 1972).

G. Parkinson, *Georg Lukács* (London, 1977).

—— (ed.), *Georg Lukács: The Man, his Work and his Ideas* (London, 1970).

Fariborz Shafai, *The Ontology of Georg Lukács: Studies in Materialist Dialectics* (Aldershot, 1996).

G. Stedman Jones, 'The Marxism of the Early Lukács: an Evaluation', *New Left Review*, 70 (1971), and *New Left Review* (eds), *Western Marxism: A Critical Reader* (London, 1977).

Victor Zitta, *Georg Lukács' Marxism: Alienation, Dialectics, Revolution: A Study in Utopia and Ideology* (The Hague, 1964).

12
Korsch

Many of the themes broached in Lukács's work were also present in that of Karl Korsch. Korsch was the son of a Hamburg banker. He studied law and joined the USPD in 1917 and the KPD in 1920. Like Lukács, his writings were much influenced by his experience in the turbulent years of 1918–23 and emphasised theoretical questions. Korsch believed that the 1918–19 Revolution had failed for psychosocial reasons, and attempted to understand the previous evolution of Marxist theory by applying Marx's own ideas to Marxism. Korsch's major work was *Marxism and Philosophy*, which was published in 1923 and aroused an even more furious opposition than Lukács's work, of which he said in an afterword, 'so far as I have been able to establish, I am happily in basic accord with the themes of the author [Lukács], which relate in many ways to the question raised in this work, although based on a philosophical foundation'.[1] Korsch was one of the most prominent members of the KPD and briefly a minister in the Thuringian government. During the middle 1920s, he was a member of the extreme left faction in the KPD which opposed the official Soviet line of NEP and the thesis of the stabilisation of capitalism in Western Europe. Korsch was expelled from the KPD in 1926 and had to flee Germany in 1933, emigrating to America, where he continued his theoretical work.

The main question to which Korsch directed his attention in *Marxism and Philosophy* was the role of philosophy in the Marxist view of the world. Korsch was concerned to rehabilitate the Hegelian element in Marxism, although not as explicitly as Lukács. He summarised the main thesis of his work as follows:

> We have already mentioned that Marx and Engels themselves always denied that scientific socialism was any longer a philosophy. But it is

easy to show irrefutably, by reference to the sources, that what the revolutionary dialecticians Marx and Engels meant by the opposite of philosophy was something very different from what it meant to later vulgar-Marxism. Nothing was further from them than the claims to impartial, pure theoretical study, above class differences ... The scientific socialism of Marx and Engels, correctly understood, stands in far greater contrast to these pure sciences of bourgeois society (economics, history or sociology) than it does to the philosophy in which the revolutionary movement of the Third Estate once found its highest theoretical expression.[2]

However, bourgeois historians of philosophy did not perceive that German classical idealism lived on in scientific socialism. Both they and the prominent Marxist thinkers of the Second International considered Marxism to be primarily economics and thus robbed it of the philosophical element that gave it life. Korsch – more strongly than Lukács – was critical of Engels in this context.[3] Korsch's aim was to 'apply Marx's principle of dialectical materialism to the whole history of Marxism,[4] and, in so doing, he distinguished three phases of Marxism: from the beginnings up until 1848, from 1848 to the end of the century, and the twentieth-century phase. In the first phase, Marx and Engels produced their 'theory of social development comprehended and practised as a living totality'.[5] In the second phase, marked by their later works, they separated out the various components of the whole – the economic, political, scientific, etc. Korsch tended to use Marx's earlier writings, quoting a lot from the *German Ideology* or the *Theses on Feuerbach* rather than the *Communist Manifesto* or the *Critique of Political Economy*, which, according to him, 'present the materialist principle in a largely one-sided way'.[6] Their followers, however,

> despite all their theoretical and methodological avowals of historical materialism, in fact divided the theory of social revolution into fragments ... Later Marxists came to regard scientific socialism more and more as a set of purely scientific observations, without any immediate connection to the political or other practices of class struggle ... A unified general theory of social revolution was changed into criticisms of the bourgeois economic order, of the bourgeois state, of the bourgeois system of education, of bourgeois religion, art, science and culture.[7]

The example Karl Korsch quoted was that of Hilferding, whose economics seemed to him devoid of any practical political perspectives. But

Korsch extended his critique to the theories of the Second International in general:

The so-called orthodox Marxism of this period (now a mere vulgar-Marxism) appears largely as an attempt by theoreticians, weighed down by tradition, to maintain the theory of social revolution, which formed the first version of Marxism, in the shape of pure theory. This theory was wholly abstract and had no practical consequences – it merely sought to reject the new Reformist theories, in which the real character of the historical movement was then expressed as un-Marxist. This is precisely why, in a new Revolutionary period, it was the orthodox Marxists of the Second International who were inevitably the least able to cope with such questions as the relation between the State and proletarian revolution.[8]

The third phase was represented by such thinkers as Rosa Luxemburg or Lenin who revived original Marxist theory in, for example, *State and Revolution*. Korsch drew attention to 'the peculiar parallelism between the two problems of Marxism and philosophy and Marxism and the State'.[9] In the views of Marx and Engels the abolition of the state was a counterpart of their desire to overcome and supersede philosophy – and the continuation of both the state and the philosophy as separate spheres was characteristic of the theoreticians of the Second International.

In general, Korsch asserted – with Lukács – that Marx and Engels were dialecticians before they were materialists, and that the proletariat would have considerable tasks to accomplish in the ideological field. The emphasis on dialectics and totality reaffirmed the importance of the role of consciousness and had its political counterpart in support for workers' councils.

Notes

1. K. Korsch, *Marxismus and Philosophie* (Leipzig, 1923) p. 71.
2. K. Korsch, *Marxism and Philosophy* (London, 1970) p. 61f.
3. Cf. K. Korsch, op. cit., pp. 46f.
4. Ibid., p. 51.
5. Ibid., p. 54.
6. Ibid., p. 67.
7. Ibid., pp. 54ff.
8. Ibid., p. 58.
9. Ibid., p. 48.

Further reading

Texts

Korsch's major work *Marxism and Philosophy* is available in English. The collection edited by Kellner gives a wider perspective.

Commentaries

See the introduction by Halliday to the English translation of *Marxism and Philosophy*. Better is Kellner's introduction to his selection. For a thorough treatment, see Goode's intellectual biography.

Bibliography

Texts

D. Kellner (ed.), *Karl Korsch: Revolutionary Theory* (Austin, Texas, 1977).
Karl Korsch, *Karl Marx* (London, 1938).
—— *Marxism and Philosophy*, ed. F. Halliday (London, 1970).
—— *Three Essays on Marxism* (London, 1971).

Commentaries

P. Goode, *Karl Korsch: A Study in Western Marxism* (London, 1979).
Hedda Korsch, 'Memories of Karl Korsch', *New Left Review*, 76 (1972).
Paul Mattick, 'The Marxism of Karl Korsch', *Survey: A Journal of Soviet and East European Studies*, 53 (1964).
Telos, vol. 26 (1975). (Devoted to articles on Korsch.)

13
Council Communism

The most comprehensive ideological challenge to Soviet Leninism in the inter-war period was concentrated around the ideas that came to be known as 'Council Communism'. These thinkers took their inspiration from the years 1917–23 when workers' councils or Soviets had been prominent in the revolutionary struggle. They rejected the idea that parliamentary institutions or trade unions could be vehicles for the emancipation of the proletariat. The notion of a Party – particularly on Leninist lines – became increasingly suspect to them as the Russian Revolution progressed and they eventually came to view the Soviet regime as another variant of bourgeois rule.

Both Lukács and Korsch were advocates of workers' councils though the remarks of Lukács were limited to *History and Class Consciousness*, where he wrote:

Every proletarian revolution has created workers' councils in an increasingly radical and conscious manner. When this weapon increases in power to the point where it becomes the organ of state, this is a sign that the class consciousness of the proletariat is on the verge of overcoming the bourgeois outlook of its leaders. The revolutionary workers' council [not to be confused with its opportunist caricature] is one of the forms which the consciousness of the proletariat has striven to create ever since its inception. The fact that it exists and is constantly developing shows that the proletariat already stands on the threshold of its own consciousness and hence on the threshold of victory. The workers' council spells the political and economic defeat of reification. In the period following the dictatorship it will eliminate the bourgeois separation of the legislature, administration and judiciary. During the struggle for control its mission is twofold. On the one hand, it must overcome the fragmentation of the proletariat in time and space, and on the other, it has to bring economics and politics together into the true synthesis of proletarian praxis.[1]

The Council Communists saw themselves as returning to Marx in their assertion that the proletariat was the first class in history to be able to achieve *self*-emancipation. The capitalist process of production required large units of specialised and well-organised workers and thus equipped the proletariat with the capacity to become the initiators of historical change. They also went to some extent beyond Marx by drawing on anarcho-syndicalist views to say that Communism could be achieved without passing through a transitional state. Their views had been preceded by Rosa Luxemburg,[2] by such early Russian Marxists as Akimov, who was labelled an 'economist' by Lenin,[3] and by the Austro-Marxist Max Adler. All Council Communists found their greatest inspiration in the experience of the Soviets in the 1917 revolution: for them, the Soviets were the beginning of the dictatorship of the proletariat. Following the subordination of the Soviets to Party and state in Russia, the Council Communists developed a comprehensive critique of Bolshevism by drawing parallels between the political theories of the Second and Third Internationals – particularly with regard to their denial of the possibility of the proletariat's attaining of itself to a revolutionary class consciousness. The Council Communists also considered that the rise of Fascism was to some extent facilitated by the Bolsheviks themselves in that they not only often acted in a manner not easily distinguishable from the Fascists but also, by depriving the working class of their ability to act autonomously, weakened their capacity to resist Fascism.

The most important of the Council Communists was Anton Pannekoek, a Dutch Professor of Astronomy who had been prominent before 1914 on the left of the Dutch and German parties, advocating such doctrines as the mass strike and consciousness through struggle. Although no specialist in economics, Pannekoek devoted much time before 1917 to attacking Marxists whose economic theories seemed to leave little place for working-class initiative. He criticised Hilferding and Otto Bauer for saying that capitalism was capable of infinite expansion and also Rosa Luxemburg for having too 'automatic' a view of capitalist breakdown. The debate on Marx's models for the reproduction of capital and accumulation in general was renewed in the 1920s when Henryk Grossmann changed the emphasis to the sphere of production rather than circulation and claimed that the falling rate of profit would lead to the end of accumulation.[4] Pannekoek rejected these views, too, as portraying the working class as merely reacting to economic forces over which they could have had no control. Parallel with these views on economics was Pannekoek's idea that what he called the 'passive radicalism' of Kautsky merely aimed to conquer state power for the proletariat, whereas 'the struggle of the proletariat is not simply a struggle against the bourgeoisie *for* state power as an object, but on the contrary, a struggle *against* state power'. Proletarian revolution therefore consisted in 'the annihilation and dissolution of the instruments of state power by the instruments of power of the proletariat'.[5]

Pannekoek's faith in the potential of the working class to transform their own situation was inspired by the mass strikes in Holland, Belgium, Germany and Russia. Compared with these forms of spontaneous working-class self-organisation, he believed that parliamentary activity and trade union bureaucracy was unimportant and, indeed, misleading. He was therefore impressed by the Russian Soviets of 1917 and, like Luxemburg, expressed critical approval. He soon became disillusioned when the Bolsheviks advocated working through parliament and trade unions in the West, both of which institutions Pannekoek had by now come to consider to be positively counter-revolutionary. He had little sympathy with the Bolsheviks' evident desire to get support, in the difficult first few years of their regime, from the existing working-class institutions in the West.[6] According to Pannekoek, the Bolshevik government had evolved into a dictatorship *over* society, which could not do without the state. This was due ultimately to Russia's economic underdevelopment; Pannekoek therefore revised his earlier view that the Third World could liberate itself on the Russian model and thought that socialism was only capable of realisation in the industrially advanced West. The working class in East and West had been misled into confusing socialism with public property or nationalisation; and they were at a disadvantage as they were more traditional than the bourgeoisie and would thus take longer to abandon their inherited Marxist ideas. For Pannekoek, socialism in itself was not a science, a theory that leads to socialism, but simply the expression of the real movement of the working class. Equally, the ideas of trade unions, political parties, and the state, were essentially linked with capitalism and would disappear along with it. Working-class self-emancipation required absolutely new forms of organisation which would not allow the separation from the working-class activity and control of the various spheres of social life and thought. Pannekoek considered it significant that whenever the working class, in a revolutionary situation, were forced to protect their own interests against those of capital, their organisation took the form of workers' councils. He even sketched out a view of Communist society in which there would be no government, only a hierarchy of councils with factory councils as its controlling base:

> The councils are not a government; even the most central councils do not have a governmental character. They do not dispose of any means for imposing their wishes on the masses; they have no organ of power.[7]

These councils would organise a society in which distribution would first conform to labour expended until a stage had been reached in which social consumption would outweigh individual consumption and in which free sharing would ensure the implementation of the famous slogan from the *Critique of the Gotha Programme*: 'From each according to his ability, to each according to his need.'

Pannekoek was supported in his views by a fellow Dutchman, Hermann Gorter, a poet who founded an anti-Bolshevik Communist Party in 1926. Gorter argued against Lenin that the Russian experience was not necessarily applicable in advanced capitalist countries. In Western Europe the working class tended to be central to production and capable of self-organisation whereas the peasantry was reactionary. This meant that the proletarian masses should be the centre of attention and the Party less so. The progressive role of trade unions and parties was over. As Pannekoek wrote:

> The old forms of organisation, the Trade Unions and political parties, and the new forms of councils [Soviets] belong to different phases in the development of society and have different functions. The first has to secure the position of the working class among other classes within capitalism and belongs to the period of expanding capitalism. The latter has to achieve domination for the workers, to destroy capitalism and class divisions, and belongs to the period of declining capitalism.[8]

The emphasis of the raising of class consciousness in all spheres of everyday life was continued by the work of Wilhelm Reich, who emphasised the need to liberate the proletariat from repression in all spheres of life – particularly that of sex. Unlike most of the Council Communists, Reich placed his confidence in women and in the young, who, as more subjugated than the rest of society, had a better chance to see through the mechanism of repression. Like the other Council Communists, Reich thought Bolshevism prepared the way for Fascism by reinforcing in parties and trade unions authoritarian structures.[9]

The views of the Council Communists depended on the ability of the proletariat to react spontaneously to the political challenges of the inter-war period. Their ideas in fact met with little response among the workers and by the late 1930s the work of most of them – for example, Pannekoek, Korsch and Reich – tended therefore to become more abstract and removed from the immediate working-class struggle.

Notes

1. G. Lukács, *History and Class Consciousness* (London, 1971) p. 80.
2. See, for example, her 'Organizational Questions of Russian Social Democracy', *Selected Political Writings*, ed. D. Howard (London and New York, 1971) pp. 283ff.
3. See further, *Vladimir Akimov and the Dilemmas of Russian Marxism*, ed. J. Frankel (Cambridge, 1969).
4. Cf. H. Grossmann, *The Law of Accumulation and the Breakdown of the Capitalist System* (London, 1992).
5. A. Pannekoek, 'Massenstreik und Aktion', *Die Neue Zeit*, vol. 30, p. 544.
6. See Lenin's reply in *Left-Wing Communism – an Infantile Disorder, Collected Works*, vol. 31, pp. 21ff.
7. A. Pannekoek, *Workers' Councils* (Melbourne, 1950) p. 52.
8. A. Pannekoek, 'General Remarks on the Question of Organization', *Living Marxism*, vol. 4, p. 148.
9. See further on Reich: C. Rycroft, *Reich* (New York, 1971) chs 3 and 4.

Further reading

There is little readily available in English on other than major figures. Smart's collection has a good selection of the basic texts and Mattick has recently produced a long-needed presentation. Pannekoek's *Lenin as Philosopher* has recently been reissued in English.

Bibliography

S. Bricianer (ed.), *Pannekoek and the Workers' Councils* (St Louis, Miss., 1978).
R. Kuhn, 'Henryk Grossmann and the Regeneration of Marxism', *Historical Materialism*, vol. 13, no. 3, 2005.
Paul Mattick, *Anti-Bolshevik Communism* (London, 1977).
Anton Pannekoek, *Lenin as Philosopher* (New York, 1948).
—— *The Way to Workers' Control* (London, 1957).
D.A. Smart (ed.), *Pannekoek and Gorter's Marxism* (London, 1978).

14
Gramsci

Introduction

Antonio Gramsci (1891–1937) shared many of the concerns of the Council Communists. Like them, Gramsci believed that the revolutionary movement should start with the everyday life of the working masses. In other words, like Lukács, he stressed the notion of totality. In contrast to the fatalistic Marxism of the Second International, Gramsci rehabilitated the subjective, creative side of Marxist thought. Always a consistent revolutionary, he re-emphasised the political dimensions of Marxism and the importance of ideological struggle in the process of socialist transformation. Gramsci's life and thought may be divided into four periods. Until 1918, he was developing his own critique of traditional Marxism as a member of the Italian Socialist Party (PSI). During the two 'red years' of 1919–20, he was the main inspiration behind the movement for Factory Councils in Turin and editor of its newspaper *Ordine Nuovo*. From 1921 to 1926, after the foundation of the Communist Party of Italy (PCI), Gramsci, as one of its leaders, was involved in formulating its policies and conducting negotiations with the Comintern. Finally, while a prisoner from 1926 until his death in 1937, he produced his major theoretical work – the *Prison Notebooks*. But however varied his career, and however manifold his concerns, Gramsci's ideas on the revolutionary process in advanced capitalism represent some sort of continuity.

The Turin Council movement

Gramsci was born at Ales in Sardinia in 1891. Sardinia was a very backward area of the newly unified Italy, having been exploited by a succession of foreign conquerors and not having moved fully out of the feudal age. Gramsci's mother came from a well-to-do Sardinian family, but his father was an outsider, a minor civil servant from the mainland. An accident at the age of three, which caused him to grow up a hunchback, and his father's imprisonment for mishandling his affairs, meant that Antonio had a poor and lonely childhood. But he read voraciously, did well at school, in spite of his isolation, and eventually moved into local journalism. He then studied at the University of Turin, specialising in linguistics. In 1913 he joined the Italian Socialist Party (PSI) and in 1916 became a full-time journalist on its paper *Avanti*. Gramsci was much impressed by the passionate syndicalism of Sorel, but the main influence upon him at this time was the Hegelian historicism of Croce, who emphasised personal moral responsibility and progress towards socialism through the spreading of culture. Partly under the influence of Croce, Gramsci absorbed more history than any other Marxist since Marx. In 1917, inspired by the Russian Revolution, he began to engage actively in political organisation and become prominent in the emergent Factory Councils Movement.

After the war, Italy was faced with a huge economic crisis. Agriculture was still basic to the economy and much depleted because of the drafting of peasants into the army. There had been a large increase in the state debt to finance the war and inflation was rampant. Demobilised soldiers swelled the unemployment figures. Working-class militancy increased as a result of this economic crisis and the consequent lowering of living standards in a war out of which many capitalists had done very well and which the socialists had opposed. The trade unions were considered by many workers – particularly in the big metallurgical works of Turin – to be much too moderate and out of touch with grass-roots opposition. It was out of this unrest that the movement for Factory Councils began. These organisations had their germ in the 'internal commissions' elected by trade union members that had sprung up in these factories over the previous decade to handle small-scale matters of arbitration and discipline. They became increasingly seen during 1918 as bodies potentially capable of expressing and defending the workers' real interests.

Gramsci and *Ordine Nuovo* wanted the internal commissions to be turned into Factory Councils. 'Today', Gramsci wrote,

> the internal commissions limit the power of the capitalist in the factory and perform functions of arbitration and discipline. Tomorrow, developed and enriched, they must be the organs of proletarian power, replacing the capitalist in all his useful functions of management and administration.[1]

The first step towards achieving this was to ensure, firstly, that everyone in the company elected their representatives; and secondly, that the council was based firmly on the division of labour inside the factory. Gramsci later defined the council organisation as follows:

Every factory is subdivided into workshops and every workshop into crews with different skills; each crew carries out a particular part of the work process. The workers in each crew elect one of their number as delegate, giving him an authoritative and revocable mandate. The assembly of delegates from the entire factory makes up a Council, and this Council elects an executive committee from its own ranks. The assembly of political secretaries of the various executive committees forms in turn a central committee of the Councils, and this central committee selects from its own number an education committee for the whole city with the task of organising propaganda, drawing up work plans, approving projects and proposals from individual factories and even individual workers, and finally giving general leadership to the whole movement.[2]

For Gramsci, the councils were very different from the trade unions that they aimed to control and ultimately to replace. 'The actual process', he wrote,

of the proletarian revolution cannot be identified with the development and activity of revolutionary organisations of a voluntary and contractual nature, such as political parties and trade unions. These organisations arise in the sphere of bourgeois democracy and political liberty, as affirmations and developments of this political liberty ... The revolutionary process takes place in the sphere of production, in the factory, where the relations are those of oppressor to oppressed, exploiter to exploited, where freedom for the worker does not exist, and democracy does not exist.[3]

Trade unions, in other words, bureaucratic and elitist by nature, operated within the framework of bourgeois society. Significant, in this respect, was the great emphasis laid by *Ordine Nuovo* on improving technology and productivity within the factory. They aimed to enable the worker to control and expand a genuinely socialist process of production, rather than compete with the capitalists for a greater share of present profit.

The Factory Councils were central to Gramsci's conception at this time of the revolutionary transformation of Italy. The main task of the council was to change the attitude of the mass of the workers from an attitude of dependence to one of leadership. They could do this by drawing into their operations those workers who had no representatives, educating them in administrative and technical skills, and, by thus rejuvenating both unions and Party, lay the basis for a new workers' state. For the Factory Council was the new proletarian state in miniature:

> The socialist state already exists potentially in the institutions of social life characteristic of the exploited working class. To link these institutions, coordinating and ordering them into a highly centralised hierarchy of competencies and powers, while respecting the necessary autonomy and articulation of each, is to create a genuine workers' democracy here and now – a workers' democracy in effective and active opposition to the bourgeois State, and prepared to replace it here and now in all its essential functions of administering and controlling the national heritage.[4]

Gramsci's picture of the Factory Council reads like an idealised picture of the Russian Soviets and there is no doubt that their role as organs of dual power in 1917 made a great impression on him. However, the emphasis on technical efficiency in production and the conception of the councils as organs of political and economic self-government went far beyond the Russian Soviet models. As the course of the Russian Revolution unfolded and the power of the Soviets declined, Gramsci was led to emphasise the Party as the necessary complement to the council. Initially, Gramsci had characterised 1917 as 'the revolution against Karl Marx's *Capital*',[5] a spontaneous, libertarian outburst. Gramsci's sources on what was happening in Russia were very limited until 1921;[6] the information available to him stressed the role of the Soviets, and the only work of Lenin's that he seems to have fully absorbed was *State and Revolution*, in which the role of the Party was minimal. Thus it is not surprising that he considered Lenin, Luxemburg and Pannekoek to have very similar views.

But the failure of the Turin Council movement in late 1920, his growing acquaintance with the realities of the Soviet Union, and his concern over the rise of Fascism led Gramsci to modify his views. (A minor illustration of this was the increasingly favourable use by Gramsci of the term 'Jacobin', which before 1920 had invariably been pejorative.) Gramsci was one of the most enthusiastic advocates of leaving the PSI and founding the PCI in January 1921. Even before the founding of the Italian Communist Party Gramsci had declared, in an article of which Lenin approved, that there was a need for 'a homogeneous cohesive party with its own doctrine, tactics, and rigid and implacable discipline'. The council movement would be doomed to failure without a Communist Party that could 'co-ordinate and centralise in its central executive committee the whole of the proletariat's revolutionary action'.[7]

Indeed, in Gramsci's view, this had been the chief reason for the defeats of 1920. This change of emphasis is further illustrated by Gramsci's rather military description of the Party as containing three levels: the captains, who direct and establish strategy; the corporals, who transmit the views of captains; and the disciplined and faithful soldiers who lack 'any creative spirit or organisational ability'.[8] However, Gramsci always maintained that there was a dialectical relationship between leaders and masses. For example, he defined what he described as 'organic centralism' as follows:

> The consensus cannot be passive and indirect, but must be active and direct: it therefore necessitates the participation of individuals even if that brings about an appearance of disintegration and tumult. A collective consciousness, a living organism, does not get formed before multiplicity is united by the rubbing together of individuals.[9]

He emphasised, like Lukács, the moral qualities of the party, and, again like Lukács, had a position that often seemed to be midway between those of Luxemburg and of Lenin. He was equally opposed to spontaneity and to 'directionism'. Spontaneous feelings he defined as

> ones that are not the result of any systematic educational activity on the part of an already conscious leading group, but had been formed through everyday experience illuminated by 'common sense', i.e., by the traditional popular conception of the world – what is unimaginatively called 'instinct', although it too is in fact a primitive and elementary historical acquisition.[10]

Such feelings were not misguided but needed to be 'given a conscious leadership or raised to a higher plane by inserting them into politics'.[11] Directionism, on the contrary (which Gramsci associated with the advocacy of a narrow vanguard party by Bordiga, the other main theoretician of the PCI) did not regard

> the party as the result of a dialectical process in which the spontaneous movement of the revolutionary masses and the organisational and directive will of the centre converge, but only as something floating in

the air which develops in itself and for itself, and which the masses will reach when the situation is favourable and the revolutionary wave has reached its height, or when the party centre thinks that it must start an offensive and lowers itself to the masses to stimulate them and carry them into action.[12]

Thus, although Gramsci entered after 1920 what he called the 'realm of necessity' and referred very little to the conciliar movement, he did not abandon the lesson of his earlier experience in Turin. In spite of the need for compromise with Bordiga and his close involvement with the Comintern, Gramsci's emphasis still differed from that of Lenin. He did not put so much emphasis as Lenin on 'consciousness from the outside' – at least as expressed in *What is to be Done?* – as his remarks on spontaneity and directionism indicate. Also, Lenin seemed to be much more concerned with 'conjunctural' aspects of political strategy and questions of immediate political power than Gramsci was. But it was only in the *Prison Notebooks* that the real differences in emphasis were worked out in any detail.

The *Prison Notebooks*

The *Prison Notebooks*, written between 1929 and 1936, are undoubtedly Gramsci's major theoretical achievement. They are, however, notoriously difficult to interpret, for several reasons. As notes not intended for publication they are often elliptical and discontinuous; Gramsci is often expressing novel concepts in the language of Croce or Machiavelli; being written in prison, they are often intentionally vague and allusive in order to get past the censorship; and finally they have been subject to the most diverse interpretations as providing ammunition for both supporters and critics of the 'historical compromise' of the PCI. The main themes that emerge are the extended role assigned to intellectuals, the prominence of the concept of hegemony, and the resulting differential strategies for revolution in the East and in the West.

The intellectuals

Gramsci has been called the theoretician of the superstructure; and nothing illustrates the reason for this more clearly than the centrality of the role of intellectuals in his thought. In contrast to Marx, who used the term in its more restricted traditional sense, basing it on a distinction between manual and mental labour, Gramsci used the concept of an intellectual in a much wider manner. In his opinion, previous attempts to define the criterion of intellectual activity had become too narrow:

> The most widespread error of method seems to me that of having looked for this criterion of distinction in the intrinsic nature of intellectual activities, rather than in the ensemble of the system of relations in which these activities (and therefore the intellectual groups who personify them) have their place within the general complex of social relations.[13]

He continued: 'All men are intellectuals ... but not all men have in society the function of intellectuals.'[14] From this Gramsci drew the conclusion that

> each man, finally, outside his professional activity, carries on some form of intellectual activity, that is, he is a 'philosopher', an artist, a man of taste, he participates in a particular conception of the world, has a conscious line of moral conduct, and therefore contributes to sustain a conception of the world or to modify it, that is, to bring into being new modes of thought.[15]

According to Gramsci, each social class

> creates together with itself, organically, one or more strata of intellectuals which give it homogeneity and an awareness of is own function not only in economic but also in the social and political fields.[16]

Gramsci drew a distinction between 'traditional' and 'organic' intellectuals. Traditional intellectuals were intellectuals who – mistakenly – considered themselves to be autonomous of social classes and who appeared to embody a historical continuity above and beyond socio-political change. Examples would be writers, artists, philosophers, and, especially, ecclesiastics. They were those intellectuals who survived the demise of the mode of production that gave them birth. The fact that they were linked to historically moribund classes and yet pretended to a certain independence involved the production of an ideology, usually of an idealist bent, to mask their real obsolescence. While the notion of a traditional intellectual was primarily a historical one, that of an organic intellectual was much more sociological. The extent to which an intellectual was organic was measured by the closeness of the connection of the organisation of which he was a member to the class which that organisation represented. Organic intellectuals articulated the collective consciousness of their class in the political, social and economic sphere. At the same time, they had a certain autonomy:

> The relationship between the intellectuals and the world of production is not as direct as it is with the fundamental social groups but is, in varying degrees, 'mediated' by the whole fabric of society and by the complex of superstructures, of which the intellectuals are, precisely, the 'functionaries'. It should be possible to measure the 'organic quality' of the various intellectual strata and their degree of connection with the fundamental social group, and to establish a gradation of their functions, and of superstructures from the bottom to the top.[17]

Gramsci evolved the concept of traditional and organic intellectuals through a series of historical studies. Whereas, for example, in France and England the bourgeoisie managed to gain the upper hand against the clergy and aristocracy – though in England this was largely confined to economic domination – in Italy the traditional cosmopolitan intellectuals of the Church managed to suppress or assimilate the intellectuals of the bourgeoisie, which only produced their own 'organic' intellectuals at the Risorgimento. In America, on the other hand, there was an 'absence to the considerable degree of traditional intellectuals' and thus a development with

> an incomparably more rapid rhythm than in old Europe, where there exists a whole series of checks (moral, intellectual, political, economic, incorporated in specific sections of the population, relics of past regimes which refused to die out) which generate opposition to speedy progress and give to every initiative the equilibrium of mediocrity, diluting it in time and space.[18]

The problem now facing the working class was the production of its own organic intellectuals, which Gramsci sometimes talked of as being a necessary precondition for any successful revolutionary movement. The proletariat needed to convert to its cause bourgeois intellectuals, but this was not enough:

> One of the most important characteristics of any group that is developing towards dominance is its struggle to assimilate and to conquer 'ideologically' the traditional intellectuals, but this assimilation and conquest is made quicker and more efficacious the more the group in

question succeeds in simultaneously elaborating its own organic intellectuals.[19]

The task of these organic intellectuals – and Gramsci specifically refers to his experience in *Ordine Nuovo* – was to draw out and make coherent the latent aspirations and potentialities already inherent in working-class activity. The relationship of organic intellectuals and their class was thus a dialectical one: they drew their material from working-class experience at the same time as imparting to it a theoretical consciousness. The formation of organic intellectuals was much more difficult for the proletariat than for the bourgeoisie, which had enjoyed its own life and culture in the interstices of feudal society. Occasionally Gramsci even went as far as to say that the proletariat could only really produce its own intellectuals *after* the seizure of state power.[20]

One answer Gramsci had to this problem was the political party:

The political party for some social groups is nothing other than their specific way of elaborating their own category of organic intellectuals directly in the political and philosophical field and not just the field of productive techniques. These intellectuals are formed in this way and cannot indeed be formed in any other way, given the general character and conditions of formation, life and development of the social group.[21]

The Party was the organisation of intellectuals that was the most organically linked to its class: it was the 'collective intellectual', an expression first coined by Togliatti. The Party (which Gramsci called the 'Modern Prince' in allusion to Machiavelli)

can only be an organism, a complex element of society in which a collective will, which has already been recognised, and has to some extent asserted itself in action, begins to take concrete form. History has already provided this organism, and it is the political party – the first cell in which they come together – germs of a collective will tending to become universal and total.[22]

The political deviations of the Second International (and, some might add, of certain forms of Leninism) stemmed from a neglect of the necessarily organic link between leadership and masses.

Gramsci's emphasis on the role of intellectuals led him to a subtler presentation of historical materialism than many previous Marxist theoreticians. He was fond of quoting from Marx's *Theses on Feuerbach* and believed that the legacy of Hegel had still not been fully assimilated by a Marxism that tended to oppose crudely materialism to idealism.[23] This type of sociology, wrote Gramsci,

> has been an attempt to create a method of historical and political science in a form dependent on a pre-elaborated philosophical system, that of evolutionist positivism ... it became the philosophy of non-philosophers, an attempt to provide a schematic description and classification of historical and political facts, according to criteria built up on the model of natural science. It is therefore an attempt to define 'experimentally' the laws of evolution of human society in such a way as to 'predict' that the oak tree will develop out of the acorn. Vulgar evolution is at the root of sociology; and sociology cannot know the dialectical principle with its passage from quantity to quality.[24]

To Gramsci Marxism was a development of Hegelianism and

> a philosophy that has been liberated (or is attempting to liberate itself) from any unilateral and fanatical ideological elements; it is consciousness full of contradictions in which the philosopher himself, understood both individually and as an entire social group, not only grasps the contradictions but posits himself as an element of the contradiction and elevates this element to a principle of knowledge and therefore action.[25]

In this context, Gramsci suggested that it would be a mistake to confuse the ideas of Engels with those of Marx, rejected Plekhanov's 'vulgar materialism', and advocated a return to the original Marxian dialectical unity between materialism and idealism. In particular, he criticised at length Bukharin's *Historical Materialism* for its philosophical materialism and portrayal of Marxism as an evolutionary positivist sociology.[26]

Thus the centre of interest for Gramsci was less on the economic substructure of society than on the means by which the proletariat could attain to understanding of the socio-economic relations of capitalist society and on the political means necessary to overthrow it. Rejecting, in a manner similar to that of Korsch, the two tendencies he labelled as 'economism' and 'ideologism', Gramsci declared:

> It has been forgotten that in the case of historical materialism one should put the accent on the first term – 'historical' – and not on the

second – which is of metaphysical origin. The philosophy of praxis is absolute 'historicism', the absolute secularisation and earthliness of thought, an absolute humanism of history.[27]

It is in this context that Gramsci repeatedly emphasised the importance of 'will' in political activity,[28] outlined – albeit briefly – a humanism akin to that of Marx's *Paris Manuscripts*,[29] and asserted that in Communist society freedom would predominate over necessity.[30]

In general, Gramsci tended to analyse the base through the superstructure, and was well aware of the very mediated sense in which historical materialism should be interpreted. He was one of the most dialectical of Marxist thinkers, and his analyses – particularly in the *Prison Notebooks* – of the relationship of necessity and liberty, of the superstructure, of the connection of intellectuals to the working class, etc., were constantly informed by a dialectical approach.

Hegemony

One of the main functions of intellectuals, then, in addition to ensuring the economic organisation and political power of their class, was to preserve the hegemony of their class over society as a whole by means of a justifying ideology of which they were the agents. As with the concept of intellectuals, so with that of hegemony. Gramsci modified and enriched the Marxist tradition by extending a concept that had previously had rather a narrow application. The term had been much used by Plekhanov and his fellow Marxists around the turn of the century to describe the role of the proletariat in what they believed to be the coming bourgeois revolution in Russia, and re-emerged in various Comintern documents of the 1920s.[31] Gramsci specifically acknowledged his debt to Lenin, whose treatment of hegemony he considered to be his greatest theoretical contribution.[32] Gramsci continued to use the term in the sense of the process by which the proletariat gained leadership over all the forces (and particularly the peasantry) opposed to capitalism and welded them into 'a new, homogeneous politico-economic historical bloc, without internal contradictions'.[33] This notion of a 'historical bloc' in which economic, social, and ideological forces combined in a temporary unity to change society was central to many of Gramsci's analyses. A historical bloc implied something more than just alliance, for

> the dominant group is co-ordinated concretely with the general interests of the subordinate groups, and the life of the State is conceived of as a continuous process of formation and superseding of

unstable equilibria (on the juridical plane) between the interests of the fundamental group and those of the subordinate groups – equilibria in which the interests of the dominant group prevail, but only up to a certain point, i.e. stopping short of narrowly corporate economic interests.[34]

Drawing on his experience in the Turin Councils movement, Gramsci broadened the concept of hegemony to include in it an analysis of the means by which ruling classes obtained the consent of the subordinate group to their own domination:

> The intellectuals of the historically (and concretely) progressive class (he wrote), in the given conditions, exercise such a power of attraction that, in the last analysis, they end up by subjugating the intellectuals of the other social groups; they thereby create a system of solidarity between all the intellectuals, with bonds of a psychological nature (vanity, etc.) and often of a cast character (technical-juridical, corporate, etc.).[35]

The world view of the ruling class, in other words, was so thoroughly diffused by its intellectuals as to become the 'common sense' of the whole of society. The bureaucratic and technological rationalism analysed by Weber was part of the capitalist ideological hegemony which functioned to repress any creative or innovatory initiatives of the working class.[36] Gramsci considered this realisation that for the most part the ruling class did not have to resort to force to maintain its dominance to be the core of his theory: 'it is even possible to affirm that present-day Marxism in its essential trait is precisely the historical-political concept of hegemony'.[37]

As with this study of the intellectuals, Gramsci drew on historical research for his account of hegemony. The Jacobinism of the French bourgeoisie, for example, by its ability to appeal to the peasantry was a national-popular movement which had penetrated the mass of French people. Again, in the USA, the ruling class could exercise enormous ideological hegemony owing to its ability directly to apply capitalist values in the absence of any feudal tradition. The Renaissance in Italy, on the other hand, was confined to an intellectual elite and provided no basis for the unification of the country. The Northern liberalism of Piedmont had had to conquer Italy by force and could not exercise ideological hegemony over it: instead of penetrating the masses it had had to steal their intellectuals. 'If you study the whole history of Italy up to the present time', wrote Gramsci, 'you can see that a small group of leaders methodically succeeded in absorbing into itself the political personnel thrown up by movements of the masses, that were subversive in origin'.[38] More recently Gramsci saw the failure of the Second International as stemming from the inability of the working-class movement to resist the penetration of bourgeois ideological hegemony.

The concept of hegemony was thus the answer to the puzzle of capitalism's ability to survive in the bourgeois democracies of the West:

> The 'normal' exercise of hegemony on the now classical terrain of the parliamentary regime is characterised by the combination of force and consent, which balance each other reciprocally without force predominating excessively over consent. Indeed, the attempt is always made to ensure that force would appear to be based on the consent of the majority expressed by the so-called organs of public opinion – newspapers and associations – which therefore, in certain situations, are artificially multiplied.[39]

Whilst the bourgeoisie continued to exercise such a cultural hegemony, a proletarian revolution was impossible. Gramsci was fond of quoting Marx's remarks in his *Preface to the Critique of Political Economy* on the ideological forms in which men become conscious of social conflicts and fight them out. As long as capitalist hegemony persisted, the proletariat remained unaware of the contradictory nature of capitalist society and of the possibility of transforming it. For a necessary part of the ideological hegemony of the capitalists was their ability to represent their own interests as those of society as a whole. Gramsci thus had the great merit of being the first Marxist theorist seriously to analyse how the bourgeoisie managed to perpetuate its domination through consent rather than coercion, although Gramsci considered his views on this question to have been at least adumbrated by Lenin. Equally fatal to revolutionary success was any belief in an economic determinism and the inevitability of revolution which had characterised much previous Marxism. For, according to Gramsci.

> it may be ruled out that immediate economic crises of themselves produce fundamental historical events; they can simply create a terrain more favourable to the dissemination of certain modes of thought, and certain ways of resolving questions involving the entire subsequent development of national life.[40]

To establish its own hegemony the working class must do more than struggle for its own narrow sectarian interests: it must be able to present itself as the guarantor of the interests of society as a whole. The establishment of a proletarian counter-hegemony was impossible without the active participation of the intellectuals of the working class. The Party was also an essential element here. Gramsci had a broader view of the party than Lenin, since he conceived of it as deeply committed to an ideological and cultural struggle as well as to the seizure of state power. Gramsci was convinced that the Leninist strategy of neglecting the ideological hegemony of the bourgeoisie would not work in the advanced industrialised countries of the West. Thus he advocated a Party that was an educational institution offering a counter-culture whose aim was to gain an ascendancy in most aspects of civil society (as opposed to directly political institutions) before the attempt was made on state power. The party organisations – and also the Factory Councils – trained the workers in the assumption of control over their own lives and thus anticipated a post-revolutionary situation. Control of state power without hegemony in civil society was an insecure basis for a socialist programme. And in one rather isolated passage, Gramsci even stated:

> A social group can, and indeed must, already exercise 'leadership' before winning governmental power (this indeed is one of the principal conditions for the winning of such power); it subsequently becomes dominant when it exercises power, but even if it holds it firmly in its grasp, it must continue to 'lead' as well.[41]

Not, of course, that Gramsci neglected the necessary element of force, but he viewed it as dialectically linked with the struggle for hegemony in civil society: both persuasion and force were necessary in any revolutionary process. And particularly in the West, where capitalism had so long been permeating society with its own view of the world, a struggle for ideological hegemony was sometimes paramount. Gramsci realised that this struggle was extremely difficult without all the resources available to those who held economic and political power, and, as with the creation of organic working-class intellectuals, sometimes implied that hegemony in civil society could only properly be acquired *after* the assumption of political power.

The state, civil society and revolution

His analysis of the process by which the proletariat could gain hegemony in the West led Gramsci to pose the question of the relationship of civil society to the state and contrast here Russia and the West. Although both Gramsci and Marx claimed to be getting their concept of civil society from Hegel, their use of the term was, in fact, very different. Whereas Marx used the expression civil society to mean the totality of economic relationships,[42] Gramsci used civil society to refer to the superstructure. Civil society was 'the ensemble of organisms commonly called private' which 'corresponds to the function of hegemony which the dominant group exercises throughout society'.[43] Sometimes Gramsci did talk of civil society as fulfilling a mediation function between economics and politics: 'between the economic structure and the State with its legislation and its coercion stands civil society'.[44] Usually, however, civil society denoted for Gramsci all the organisations and technical means which diffuse the ideological justification of the ruling class in all domains of culture. And Gramsci's conception of ideology was both extremely wide – including even most aspects of natural science – and extremely varied – extending its appeal from philosophy to folklore. Thus civil society had above all a cultural function and, through the hegemony of the ruling class, presented the 'ethical content of the State'.[45]

The use of the term 'state' is also difficult in Gramsci. Sometimes it is used to cover both civil society and political society, although in Marx they are usually sharply distinguished.

> The general notion of State (wrote Gramsci) includes elements which need to be referred back to the notion of civil society (in the sense that one might say that State = political society + civil society, in other words hegemony protected by the armour of coercion).[46]

Elsewhere, Gramsci says that the state equals dictatorship and hegemony, and even says that 'civil society and State are one and the same'.[47] In 1931, talking of his notebooks on the intellectuals, he wrote:

> This study also leads to certain determinations of a concept of State, which is usually understood as political society (or dictatorship; or coercive apparatus to bring the mass of people into conformity with the specific type of production and a specific economy at a given moment) and not as an equilibrium between political society and civil society or the hegemony of a social group over the entire national society exercised through the so-called private organisations (like the church, the trade unions, the schools, etc.); it is precisely in civil society that intellectuals operate specially.[48]

Although Gramsci was aware of the close cooperation between civil society and the state – and even their fusion under Fascism – he does also contrast them. And this contrast was more marked in a liberal-capitalist regime than in a feudal-fascist or socialist regime.

One of Gramsci's most original conceptions was to draw a distinction in this context between the East (Russia) and the West. The most striking passage is as follows:

> In Russia the State was everything, civil society was primordial and gelatinous; in the West, there was a proper relationship between State and civil society, and when the State trembled a sturdy structure of civil society was at once revealed. The State was only an outer ditch, behind which there stood a powerful system of fortresses and earth works.[49]

This implied different revolutionary strategies in East and West. In primitive societies the state should be the object of frontal attack; in more developed societies, it should be civil society. Borrowing terms from recent studies of military science, Gramsci termed the first sort of attack 'a war of movement or manoeuvre' in which artillery could open up sudden gaps in defences and troops be rapidly switched from one point to another to storm through and capture fortresses, and the second a 'war of position' in which enemies were well balanced and had to settle down to a long period of trench warfare. The French bourgeoisie, for example, preceded its success in its 1789 Revolution by a war of position in the shape of a lengthy cultural assault on the ideological supports of aristocratic power. And Gramsci considered that the war of position became more important as capitalism developed. The war of movement was so costly to the working class that it should only be launched when absolutely necessary. Gramsci considered Rosa Luxemburg's pamphlet on the *Mass Strike* to be an attempt at a theoretical justification of the war of movement in the West. Luxemburg's view that an economic crisis could precipitate a general crisis leading to revolution was criticised by Gramsci as being both 'economistic' and spontaneist. In Luxemburg's view, he wrote, immediately economic factors had the following effects:

> 1. They breach the enemy's defences, after throwing him into disarray and causing him to lose faith in himself, his forces, and his future; 2. in a flash they organise one's own troops and create the necessary cadres – or at least in a flash they put the existing cadres (formed, until that moment, by the general historical process) in positions which enable them to encadre one's scattered forces; 3. in a flash they bring about the necessary ideological concentration on the common objective to be achieved. This view was a form of iron economic determinism, with

the aggravating factor that it was conceived as operating at lightning speed in time and in space. It was thus out and out historical mysticism, the awaiting of a sort of miraculous illumination.[50]

On the other hand, the war of manoeuvre could never be entirely abandoned:

> In politics, the war of manoeuvre exists so long as it is a question of winning positions which are not decisive, so that all the resources of the State's hegemony cannot be mobilised. But when, for one reason or another, these positions have lost their value, and only the decisive positions are at stake, then one passes over to siege warfare; this is concentrated, and requires exceptional qualities of patience and inventiveness.[51]

In other words, Gramsci was warning against the simplistic assumption that a Leninist strategy as exemplified in Russia could be applied unproblematically in the West. For

> war of movement increasingly becomes war of position, and it can be said that a State will win a war insofar as it prepares for it minutely and technically in peacetime. The massive structures of the modern democracies, both as State organisations and as complexes of associations in civil society, constitute for the art of politics as it were the 'trenches' and the permanent fortifications of the front in the war of position: they render merely 'partial' the element of movement which before used to be 'the whole' of war.[52]

Correlative to this distinction between wars of position and wars of manoeuvre Gramsci distinguished between crises that were organic and those that were conjunctural:

> It is necessary to distinguish [he wrote] organic movement (relatively permanent) from movement which may be termed 'conjunctural' (and which appears as occasional, immediate, almost accidental). Conjunctural phenomena too, depend on organic movements to be sure, but they do not have any very far-reaching historical significance; they give rise to political criticism of a minor, day-to-day character, which has as its subject top political leaders and personalities with direct governmental responsibilities. Organic phenomena on the other hand give rise to socio-historical criticism, whose subject is

wider social groups – beyond the public figures and beyond the top leaders.[53]

Whether a war of position or of manoeuvre was appropriate depended on the assessment of the crisis as organic or conjunctural. If the established ruling class was, over decades, confronted with incurable structural contradictions, then the organic nature of crisis might afford the opportunity for a war of manoeuvre. For an organic crisis involved a rupture between structure and superstructure and therefore a crisis in hegemony of the ruling class.

Gramsci foresaw that the hegemony of the proletariat would abolish the distinction between the state and civil society:

> Only the social group that poses the end of the State and its own end as the target to be achieved can create an ethical State – i.e. one which tends to put an end to the internal divisions of the ruled, etc., and to create a technically and morally unitary social organism.[54]

Gramsci realised that a period of transition might be necessary in which the proletariat would have to rely on state power during the transformation of civil society, thus producing the phenomenon that he called 'statolatry'.[55] However much Gramsci might have deviated from Marx in his use of the concept of civil society, they were both agreed that the final aim was a reabsorption of political society by civil society in a classless society.

The East/West and war of position/manoeuvre contrasts were to some extent informed by Gramsci's views of Communist politics in the 1920s. Although written during his enforced solitude in prison, Gramsci's ideas on the intellectuals, hegemony, etc., were closely connected with his experience over the previous decade both inside the Italian Party and in the international socialist movement. In Italy, Gramsci's views on the Party intellectuals and hegemony were codified by the Lyons Theses adopted under his direction in 1926. The central problem of the disparity between the North and the South and the need to win peasant support were the subject of a seminal article *On the Southern Question* on which Gramsci was working at the time of his arrest. On the international scene the main object of his criticism in the field of political tactics was Trotsky. Gramsci's adherence, at least in principle, to the Comintern's policies after 1923 was bound to lead to conflict with Trotsky. From 1921 to 1924 Gramsci tended, in fact, to oppose in Italy the Comintern's United Front policies. Nevertheless, when Bordiga, heartened by Zinoviev's brief 'left turn' at the Fifth Comintern Congress in 1924, began to defend Trotsky in Italy, Gramsci opposed Bordiga from a 'centrist' position and was forced to take a stand on Trotsky's policies. Gramsci opposed Trotsky's view of the relative stabilisation of capitalism in the West and the poor prospects for revolution, and Trotsky's political position and theoretical views were condemned by the Central Committee of the PCI (on which Gramsci and his supporters had a majority) as

> a pessimistic view of the development of world revolution and a conception of the revolutionary process which ignores correct relationships between the workers and peasants ... considering the defeat and degeneration of the proletarian revolution in a predominantly petty-bourgeois country inevitable if the victory of the working-class in the West does not ensure within a brief term the help of proletarian state power from the most advanced industrial countries.[56]

In 1929 the Comintern again changed its line: it declared a fresh collapse of capitalism to be imminent in the West, in which the Social Democrats would try to prop up the old order and thus should be regarded as the main enemy. Gramsci opposed this 'class against class' thesis but still maintained his objections to Trotsky's theory of permanent revolution.

It was in this context that the remarks in *The Prison Notebooks* were conceived. Here Gramsci showed little sympathy for either of the aspects of the theory of permanent revolution. Trotsky's ideas in *Results and Prospects* on the evolution of the Russian Revolution were described as 'inert and abstract'[57] and the Bolshevik insistence on revolutionary/democratic dictatorship in opposition to Trotsky's ideas was, for Gramsci, an example of the development of the concept of hegemony in practice.[58] He did grudgingly admit that Trotsky had been proved right in 1917. But it was the international aspect of Trotsky's ideas that Gramsci was chiefly concerned to criticise. Again, Gramsci admitted that Trotsky had outlined (in 1924) a revision of current tactics by drawing a distinction between Eastern and Western fronts, but he had only done it 'in a brilliant, literary form, without directives of a practical character'.[59] In the main, Gramsci viewed Trotsky as 'the political theorist of frontal attack in a period in which it only leads to defeats'. Here Gramsci drew a distinction between a rather narrow Trotsky who tried mechanically to apply to other countries methods that had, for very specific reasons, been successful in Russia, and Lenin, who was much more flexible. Permanent revolution was 'the political reflection of the theory of war of manoeuvre ... i.e., in the last analysis, a reflection of the general-economic-cultural-social conditions in the country in which the structures of national life are embryonic and loose, and incapable of becoming "trench or fortress". In this case one might say that Bronstein (Trotsky) apparently "Western", was in fact a cosmopolitan – i.e., superficially national and superficially Western or European. Ilitch (Lenin), on the other hand, was profoundly national and profoundly European.'[60] Gramsci was deeply opposed to what he saw as the mechanical internationalism of Trotsky:

> To be sure [he wrote] the line of development is towards internationalism, but the point of departure is 'national' ... It is in the concept of hegemony that these exigencies which are national in character are knotted together, one can well understand how certain tendencies either do not mention such concepts or merely skim over it.

Referring to the experience of the Second International and to Trotsky's views in the mid-1920s, he continued:

> That non-national concepts (i.e. ones that cannot be referred to each individual country) are erroneous can be seen *ab absurdo*: they have led to passivity and inertia in two quite distinct phases: 1. in the first phase, nobody believed that they ought to make a start – that is to say, they believed that by making a start they would find themselves isolated; they waited for everybody to move together, and nobody in the meantime moved or organised the movement; 2. the second phase is perhaps worse, because what is being awaited is an anachronistic and anti-natural form of 'Napoleonism' (since not all historical phases repeat themselves in the same form). The theoretical weaknesses of this modern form of the old mechanism are masked by the general theory of permanent revolution, which is nothing but a generic forecast presented as a dogma, and which demolishes itself by not in fact coming true.[61]

It is therefore not surprising that Gramsci came down in favour of Stalin in the controversy over Socialism in One Country.

One area, however, in which Gramsci did agree with Trotsky was his analysis of Fascism. More clearly than most, Gramsci analysed Fascism as a movement of the petty-bourgeoisie reacting to their loss of political influence. 'The characteristic aspect of Fascism', he wrote, 'consists in having succeeded in constituting a mass organisation of the petty bourgeoisie. This is the first time in history that this has occurred.'[62]

Initially a revolutionary movement fostering the collapse of the traditional bourgeois state, Gramsci saw it as later becoming reactionary. Fascism concentrated all means of diffusing ideology in the state and thus robbed civil society of its autonomy. But Fascism was incapable of suppressing private property and thus depriving the bourgeoisie of control of the means of production. Thus it could only be a transitory phenomenon and in the long term the bourgeoisie would regain political power.

With the exception of the Russian revolutionaries, Gramsci has been the most original Marxist thinker of the last fifty years. His contribution spanned the entire spectrum of Marxist politics in the decade following the October Revolution. He talked the same language as the Council Communists such as Pannekoek and Gorter and yet was active in the Third International. His work on the system of hegemony, and on the intellectuals as an organic link between base and superstructure, builds directly on the work of Marx and, to a lesser extent, that of Lenin. And, as the bibliography below shows, he has been the most influential of Western Marxist thinkers in the latter half of the twentieth century.

Notes

1. A. Gramsci, 'Workers' Democracy'. *Selections from Political Writings 1910–1920* (London, 1977) p. 66.
2. A. Gramsci, 'The Turin Factory Councils Movement', *Selections from Political Writings, 1910–1920* (London, 1977) p. 317. See also the programme adopted by the first meeting of Turin factory delegates in A. Gramsci, op. cit., pp. 114ff.
3. A. Gramsci, 'The Factory Council', *Selections from Political Writings*, pp. 260f.
4. A. Gramsci, 'Workers' Democracy', *Selections from Political Writings*, p. 65.
5. A. Gramsci, 'The Revolution against *Capital*', *Selections from Political Writings*, p. 34.
6. See further: A. Davidson, *Antonio Gramsci* (London, 1977), pp. 163ff.
7. A. Gramsci, 'Towards a Renewal of the Socialist Party', *Selections from Political Writings*, pp. 194f.
8. A. Gramsci, *Selections from Prison Notebooks*, ed. Q. Hoare and G. Nowell Smith (London, 1971) p. 152.
9. A. Gramsci, *Note sul Machiavelli* (Turin, 1949) p. 158, quoted in J.-M. Piotte, *La Pensée politique de Gramsci* (Paris, 1970) p. 244.
10. A. Gramsci, *Selections from the Prison Notebooks*, pp. 198f.
11. Ibid., p. 199.
12. Gramsci to Togliatti; 9 Jan. 1924, quoted in A. Davidson, *Antonio Gramsci*, p. 208.
13. A. Gramsci, *Selections from the Prison Notebooks*, p. 8.
14. Ibid., p. 9.
15. Ibid.
16. Ibid., p. 3.
17. Ibid., p. 12.

18. Ibid., p. 20.
19. Ibid., p. 10.
20. See particularly, J. Karabel, 'Revolutionary Contradictions: Antonio Gramsci and the Problem of Intellectuals', *Politics and Society*, vol. 6 (1976) pp. 123ff.
21. A. Gramsci, *Selections from the Prison Notebooks*, p. 15.
22. Ibid., p. 129.
23. Ibid., p. 402.
24. Ibid., p. 426.
25. Ibid., pp. 404f.
26. Cf. ibid., pp. 385ff., 396, 425ff.
27. Ibid., p. 465.
28. Cf. ibid., pp. 172, 175, 185, 345, 360.
29. Cf. ibid., pp. 351ff.
30. Cf. ibid., pp. 367, 405.
31. See further: C. Buci-Glucksmann, *Gramsci et L'Etat* (Paris, 1975) p. 19 and P. Anderson, 'The Antinomies of Antonio Gramsci', *New Left Review*, 100 (1976–7) pp. 15ff.
32. Cf. A. Gramsci, *Selections from the Prison Notebooks*, p. 365.
33. Ibid., p. 168.
34. Ibid., p. 182.
35. Ibid., p. 60.
36. See the section on 'scientific management' or Taylorism in *Selections from the Prison Notebooks*, pp. 301ff.
37. A. Gramsci, *Lettere dal Carcere* (Turin, 1965) p. 616. Quoted in A. Davidson, *Antonio Gramsci: Towards an Intellectual Biography* (London, 1977) p. 260.
38. A. Gramsci, *Lettere dal Carcere*, p. 633.
39. A. Gramsci, *Selections from the Prison Notebooks*, p. 80.
40. Ibid., p. 184.
41. Ibid., pp. 57f.
42. Cf., for example, K. Marx, 'On the Jewish Question', *Selected Writings*, ed. D. McLellan (Oxford, 2000) pp. 60ff.
43. A. Gramsci, *Selections from the Prison Notebooks*, p. 12.
44. Ibid., p. 208.
45. Ibid.
46. Ibid., p. 263.
47. Ibid., p. 160.
48. *Lettere dal Carcere*, p. 481.
49. Ibid., p. 238.
50. Ibid., p. 233.
51. Ibid., p. 239.
52. Ibid., p. 243.
53. Ibid., pp. 177f.
54. Ibid., p. 259.
55. Ibid., pp. 268f.
56. Quoted in A. Davidson, *Antonio Gramsci*, p. 219.
57. A. Gramsci, *Selections from the Prison Notebooks*, p. 34.
58. Cf. ibid., p. 165.
59. Ibid., p. 236.
60. Ibid. and f.

61. Ibid., p. 240f.
62. Quoted in J. Joll, *Gramsci* (London, 1977) p. 57.

Further reading

Texts

Gramsci's fundamental *Prison Notebooks* are available in an excellent selected edition. They can be supplemented by the two volumes of *Selections from Political Writings* covering the years up to his imprisonment, and the *Letters from Prison*. A good selection is provided by Forgacs.

Commentaries

The best all-round biography is Fiori's *Antonio Gramsci: Life of a Revolutionary*. Joll's Modern Masters book is an excellent short introduction, as is also, from a more philosophical angle, Boggs's *Gramsci's Marxism*. Lengthier treatments are Cammett's *Antonio Gramsci and the Origins of Italian Communism* and Davidson's *Antonio Gramsci: Towards an Intellectual Biography*. On Gramsci's revolutionary activities in Turin, see Clark's meticulous history, *Antonio Gramsci and the Revolution that Failed*, and the more partisan treatments in Williams's *Proletarian Order* and Spriano's *The Occupation of the Factories*. Specifically on the *Prison Notebooks*, see the Introduction to their edition by Hoare and Nowell Smith and the penetrating article on 'The Antinomies of Antonio Gramsci' by Anderson. Mouffe's collection *Gramsci and Marxist Theory* is useful, and Femia's *Gramsci's Political Thought* is a measured and precise analysis. Sassoon's books show Gramsci's contemporary relevance and Martin provides a good introduction.

Bibliography

Texts

P. Cavalcanti and P. Piccone (eds), *History, Philosophy and Culture in the Young Gramsci* (St Louis, 1975).
D. Forgacs (ed.), *A Gramsci Reader: Selected Writings 1916–1935* (London, 1999).
Antonio Gramsci, *Cultural Writings* (London, 1985).
—— *Letters from Prison* (New York, 1973).
—— *The Modern Prince and Other Writings*, ed. L. Marks (London, 1957).
—— *New Edinburgh Review*, three special Gramsci issues (1974).
—— *The Open Marxism of Antonio Gramsci*, ed. C. Marzani (New York, 1957).
—— *Pre-prison Writings*, ed. R. Bellamy (Cambridge, 1994).
—— *Selections from Political Writings: 1910–1920* (London, 1977).
—— *Selections from Political Writings: 1921–1926* (London, 1978).

—— *Selections from the Prison Notebooks*, ed. Q. Hoare and G. Nowell Smith (London, 1971).

Commentaries

Perry Anderson, 'The Antinomies of Antonio Gramsci', *New Left Review*, 100 (1976–7).
Thomas R. Bates, 'Gramsci and the Theory of Hegemony', *Journal of the History of Ideas*, 36 (1975).
R. Bellamy and D. Schechter, *Gramsci and the Italian State* (Manchester, 1993).
Carl Boggs, *Gramsci's Marxism* (London, 1976).
John M. Cammett, *Antonio Gramsci and the Origins of Italian Communism* (Stanford, 1969).
W.N. Clark, *Antonio Gramsci and the Revolution that Failed* (New Haven, 1977).
A.B. Davidson, *Antonio Gramsci: Towards an Intellectual Biography* (London, 1977).
—— 'The Varying Seasons of Gramsci Studies', *Political Studies*, 20 (1972).
Joseph Femia, *Gramsci's Political Thought: Hegemony, Consciousness and the Revolutionary Process* (Oxford, 1981).
—— 'Hegemony and Consciousness in the Thought of Antonio Gramsci', *Political Studies*, 23 (1975).
Giuseppe Fiori, *Antonio Gramsci: Life of a Revolutionary* (London, 1970).
R. Holub, *Antonio Gramsci: Beyond Marxism and Postmodernism* (New York, 1992).
P. Ives, *Language and Hegemony in Gramsci* (London, 2004).
James Joll, *Gramsci* (London, 1977).
V.G. Kiernan, 'Gramsci and Marxism', *Socialist Register (1972)*.
C. Levy, *Gramsci and the Anarchists* (Oxford, 1999).
J. Martin, *Gramsci's Political Analysis: A Critical Introduction* (Basingstoke, 1998).
J. Martin (ed.), *Antonio Gramsci: Critical Assessments of Leading Political Philosophers* (London, 2002).
Neil McInnes, 'Antonio Gramsci', *Survey*, 53 (1964).
John Merrington, 'Theory and Practice in Gramsci's Marxism', *Socialist Register* (1968) and *New Left Review* (eds), *Western Marxism: A Critical Reader* (London, 1977).
Chantal Mouffe (ed.), *Gramsci and Marxist Theory* (London, 1979).
T. Nemeth, *Gramsci's Philosophy: A Critical Study* (Brighton, 1980).
A. Pozzolini, *Antonio Gramsci: An Introduction to his Thought* (London, 1970).
P. Ransome, *Antonio Gramsci: A New Introduction* (Hemel Hempstead, 1992).
A. Sassoon, *Gramsci and Contemporary Politics: Beyond Pessimism of the Intellect* (London, 2000).
Anne Showstack Sassoon, *Approaches to Gramsci* (London, 1982).
—— *Gramsci's Politics* (London, 1987).
Paolo Spriano, *The Occupation of the Factories: Italy 1920* (London, 1977).
Palmiro Togliatti, *On Gramsci and other Articles* (London, 1977).
Gwyn A. Williams, 'The Concept of Egemonia in the Thought of Antonio Gramsci', *Journal of the History of Ideas*, 21 (1960).
—— *Proletarian Order: Antonio Gramsci, Factory Councils and the Origins of Communism in Italy* (London, 1975).

Part Four
China and the Third World

Today's China is an outgrowth of historic China. We are Marxist historicists; we must not mutilate history ... A communist is a Marxist internationalist, but Marxism must take on a national form before it can be applied.

Mao Zedong, 1939

15
The Making of the Chinese Revolution

Introduction

From the time of the establishment of the first united empire in China by the Han Dynasty in the second century BC, China had, in spite of dynastic changes, been an exceptionally stable society. With very little influence from the outside, China constituted a self-sufficient, fertile land mass bounded by desert, mountains and oceans, and nurturing a self-centred, independent, civilisation. The economy was dominated by an efficient agriculture and rural handicrafts, and the official philosophy of Confucianism sanctioned a hierarchical society which viewed change as degeneration. During the nineteenth century, however, this economic, political and doctrinal self-sufficiency was shattered when the Manchu dynasty, who had imposed their rule on China from the North in the seventeenth century, proved incapable of resisting Western encroachment. Events from the Opium War of 1840 to the defeat by the previously despised Japanese in 1895, and the suppression of the Boxer rebellion in 1900, revealed China to be almost completely defenceless in the face of economic and military pressure from the West.

In the face of these incursions, opinion inside China was divided between those who thought that the only salvation for their country lay in a wholesale adoption of Western culture, those who thought only Western technology was needed while Chinese culture and institutions could be preserved, and those who were opposed to any sort of importation from the West. The modernisers won to the extent that a Republic was proclaimed in 1912 but, while the Western powers continued to carve out for themselves lucrative trading concessions on the East China coast, any idea that a Western-type democracy could rejuvenate China proved misplaced. With no emperor to unify the country, only different centres of military remained, controlled by various warlords whose irregular troops battened on the peasantry, destroyed the economic equilibrium of the countryside, and swept aside for ever the imperial bureaucracy. It was during this chaotic period of 'warlord rule' from 1915 to 1925 that Mao Zedong formed his political opinions.

Mao Zedong was born in 1893 in Shaoshan in the Hunan province of South Central China. His father was a poor peasant who became relatively rich from trading in grain. Mao left school at the age of 13, and worked for his father, but in spite of family opposition enrolled in a nearby secondary school in 1909. Two years later he moved to the provincial capital at Changsha to continue his studies. When the Republic was proclaimed, Mao served in the Republican army for six months, before returning to his studies when the warlords gained control. The extent to which his upbringing and schooling left its mark on Mao's thought is obviously a matter of conjecture. The fact that Chinese thought is basically more empirical and pragmatic than its Western counterpart may well have influenced Mao's Marxism. There were also dialectical elements in Buddhism and Taoism, both of which tended to think in terms of opposites – everything being imbued by the contradiction of Yin and Yang. On a more immediate level, Mao was undoubtedly influenced by his reading of classical Chinese novels such as the *Water Margin* with their glorification of peasant revolts and military exploits. Mao entered the First Normal School in Changsha in 1913 and studied there until graduation five years later, by which time he had become a radical nationalist, though not yet a Marxist.

Mao encountered Marxism in Peking, where he obtained a job as an assistant librarian in 1918. Although Marxism was almost unknown in China before 1917 (very little of Marx or Lenin had been translated into Chinese), the success of the Bolsheviks in overthrowing the Russian autocracy persuaded many Chinese intellectuals that they could follow suit. Nationalism emerged as a real force in 1919 with the May Fourth Movement, in which there were widescale demonstrations and rioting when it was learned that the corrupt government had agreed to hand over to the Japanese the important province of Shantung (previously held by the Germans) in spite of the promises by the Western powers that it should revert to China. The general disillusion with Western ideals led the Chinese intelligentsia to turn increasingly to Marxism. The Chinese Communist Party (CCP) was founded in Shanghai in 1921 and Mao was one of thirteen members present.

From the start, the Chinese Communist Party was confronted with the traditional problem of what policies to adopt in what seemed to be a nationalist, republican, 'bourgeois' revolution. In early 1920, most revolutionary nationalist forces supported the Kuomintang (KMT) of Dr Sun Yat-sen which had succeeded in establishing itself with Russian aid, in South China based on Canton. In early 1926, under the leadership of Chiang Kai-shek, who had succeeded Sun, the Kuomintang mounted the Northern Expedition to drive out the warlords and the Western imperialists who abetted them. What should be the attitude of the Chinese Communist Party to the Kuomintang? The basic principles of Leninism absorbed by the tiny CCP indicated distrust of bourgeois parties, separate and independent organisation, and the reliance on the revolutionary potential of the working class in an uninterrupted movement of international dimension. At the Second Congress of the Comintern in 1920, Lenin had advocated that 'the Communist International must enter into a temporary alliance with bourgeois democracy in colonial and backward countries, but must not merge with it, and must unconditionally preserve the independence of the proletarian movement even in its most rudimentary form'.[1] This, however, left open the question of the precise nature of the KMT which Trotsky considered a bourgeois party, whilst Stalin thought it a coalition of different classes. The latter view prevailed and, under Russian pressure, the CCP formed a United Front with the KMT in 1923. The Communists joined KMT to form a block within it as its left wing.

Mao and the peasantry

Prior to the Northern Expedition Mao had been a bureaucrat in Shanghai, charged with coordinating the work of the CCP and the KMT. Given his antipathy to intellectuals and the ignorance of urban life, it is not surprising that he was not very successful. Before returning to Hunan in 1926, Mao had adopted an 'orthodox' Marxist position. In his article entitled *Analysis of Classes in Chinese Society*, remarkable for its lack of enthusiasm for the peasantry, he wrote:

> To sum up, it can be seen that our enemies are all those in league with imperialism – the warlords, the bureaucrats, the comprador class, the big landlord class, and the reactionary section of the intelligentsia attached to them. The leading force to our revolution is the industrial proletariat. Our closest friends are the entire semi-proletariat and petty-bourgeoisie. As for the vacillating middle bourgeoisie, their right wing may become our enemy and their left wing become our friend – but we must be constantly on our guard and not let them create confusion within our ranks.[2]

However, by September 1926, Mao had become convinced that the central role in the revolutionary movement would be played by the peasantry and that, at least for the moment, they were more progressive than the workers as they had political as well as economic aims. Recognised as the Party's expert on peasantry, he returned to Hunan in 1926 in the wake of the Northern Expedition which had begun well and overrun the whole of central China by the summer of 1926. The nine months he spent there from August 1926 to May 1927 were crucial to the development of his Marxist thinking. The peasants among whom Mao was working were, for the most part and in an increasing number, tenants. Their plots were very small and landowners took 50 per cent of the crop. The burden of debt was increased by inflation and the heavy taxation imposed by the warlords, often in advance. Those who became bankrupt provided ready recruits for the warlord army. It is therefore not surprising that there was a rapid growth in the peasant revolutionary movement following the success of the Northern Expedition. Prior to the activities of Mao, the Communists had had no clear agrarian programme, and the KMT's proposals were very moderate, involving simply rent reduction and no land confiscation.

The central role of the peasantry was brought out in Mao's famous *Report on an Investigation of the Peasant Movement in Hunan*, in which he explained and defended the anti-landlord measures taken by the Hunan Peasant Association. The beginning of the report is visionary:

The present upsurge of the peasant movement is a colossal event. In a very short time, in China's central, southern and northern provinces, several hundred million peasants will arrive like a mighty storm, like a hurricane, a force so swift and violent that no power, however great, will be able to hold it back. They will smash all the trammels that bind them and rush forward along the road to liberation. They will sweep all the imperialists, warlords, corrupt officials, local tyrants and evil gentry into their graves. Every revolutionary party and every revolutionary comrade will be put to the test, to be accepted or rejected as they decide.[3]

The actual measures that Mao reports the Association as taking are relatively moderate and closely follow the Comintern's instructions. But whereas the Comintern laid the emphasis on proletarian hegemony, Mao declared that 'the poor peasants have always been the main force in the bitter fight in the countryside. They have fought militantly through the two periods of underground work and of open activity. They are the most responsive to Communist Party leadership.'[4] He described the poor peasants as 'vanguards of revolution',[5] and failed to mention proletarian leadership. It was this emphasis on the leading role of the peasantry that constituted one of Mao's most original contributions, though what this meant in practice was only evident when the Chinese Communist Party came to control large rural areas.[6]

Revolutionary strategy

One of the reasons why Mao's views were not well received by the Party was the pressure from Moscow to preserve the alliance with the KMT which would have been jeopardised by too much rural agitation. However, Chiang Kai-shek had moved to the right and wished to gain the backing of big business interests at the expense, if necessary, of the alliance with the Communists. When the Communists organised a successful uprising in Shanghai (which held China's biggest concentration of industrial workers) Chiang turned ruthlessly against them. Hundreds of their members were killed and the Party as a whole proscribed. In spite of this disaster, Stalin still wanted cooperation with the 'left' KMT leaders who had split with Chiang Kai-shek, and this meant restraining the peasant revolutionary movement for fear, once more, of alienating KMT support. Stalin was concerned to avoid responsibility for the apparent failure of the Chinese revolution and he saw himself as vulnerable to criticism from Trotsky, with whom the final showdown was approaching. Stalin saw the KMT as a progressive revolutionary force which was resolutely anti-imperialist and capable of carrying out the bourgeois-democratic revolution that would mark China's definitive emergence from feudalism and, by means of economic reforms, prepare for socialism. The small nascent Communist Party could not aim at power on its own and should join the KMT in a 'block of four classes' – national bourgeoisie, petty bourgeoisie, peasants and workers. To Trotsky, this was Menshevism – a mechanistic belief in stages and confidence in the possibility of independent bourgeois action. He believed, on the contrary, that in China the KMT was just as beholden to landed interests and foreign capital as had been the Russian bourgeoisie before 1917. Thus the KMT was bound, in a crisis, to turn against the workers – and this duly happened in 1926. Trotsky was vindicated in his criticism of Stalin, though his view that a socialist revolution could not be founded on the peasantry, his scepticism about a movement based on rural vanguards and peasant guerillas, and his distrust of the nationalism so important to the Chinese revolution show that he was less insightful about events after 1926.[7]

But Trotsky's criticisms were not available to the Chinese Communist Party leadership, which was pressed by the Comintern to adhere to the incoherent policies advanced by Stalin in 1927: opportunistic alliance with the KMT, but, at the same time, continued armed uprising to show that the policies of 1926–7 had not been a failure. After the predictable failure of these armed uprisings, Mao retreated with the remnants of the Communist soldiery to the wild, mountainous region of the Chingkangshan on the Eastern borders of Hunan. Here, viewed with a certain suspicion by the Central Committee of the Party, he could put into practice some of his ideas on agrarian reform.

There had been no specific proposals for agrarian reform in Mao's 1927 *Report*, but his views as expressed in other documents were very radical: all holdings of over 30 *mous* should be confiscated, whether simply by paying no rent or by actively redistributing it through Peasant Associations. Once established on the Chingkanshan, he put this policy into effect, classifying all proprietors as enemies and even executing some of them. This was not enough for the Central Committee, who criticised him, so he said, for 'having leaned to the Right, for having done too little burning and killing, and for having failed to carry out the so-called policy of "turning the petty bourgeois into proletarians and then forcing them into the revolution" '.[8] However, the military control of the Communists was weak, as a large proportion of their forces consisted of bandits, beggars and members of the *lumpenproletariat*. Opposition from the peasantry was strong and it was essential for the army not to antagonise them. So in April 1929, at the time when the Communist base was moved from the Chingkanshan to the more hospitable area of South Kiangsi, Mao changed his policy to confiscating only the estates of landlords, which were redistributed according to the size of family. When the strength of the Communists grew and the Kiangsi Provincial Soviet was established in February 1930, Mao had moved considerably to the right by allowing even the rich peasants to keep their land.

At this stage social and economic reform was tailored to promote military survival. It was the Red Army's ability to survive and prosper that eventually ensured the triumph of Mao's ideals in the Party. In the late 1920s Mao was dubious about the Central Committee's ideas on the hegemony of the urban proletariat, their view that Party members should be exclusively peasants or proletarians, and their enthusiasm for all-out struggle rather than gradual expansion from base areas. But he was protected from undue interference by his geographical remoteness. In 1929, following the failures of the armed uprisings, the Central Committee, on which Li Li-san was the moving spirit, ordered Mao to split up his forces, as the cities were still expected to give the signal for revolution while the Red Army should simply prepare the masses in the countryside to support the proletariat. According to Li Li-san, the cities were the brains and heart of the ruling class while the villages were only the limbs. To attack the limbs was not radical enough: the heart was what mattered. Thus, all the talk of 'encircling the city with the country' or of 'relying on the Red Army to take the cities is sheer nonsense'.[9] Mao, however, took seriously the fact that, according to Chou En-lai, the proportion of proletarians in the Party had sunk from about two-thirds in 1926 to only 3 per cent by 1929. He argued that China's being a semi-colonial country for which several imperialist powers were contending and the consequent tangled warfare among the revolutionary classes meant that a Russian model of revolution could not be applied. Thus Li Li-san's policy

which merely calls for roving guerilla actions cannot accomplish the task of accelerating this nation-wide revolutionary high tide, while the kind of policy adopted by Chu Teh and Mao Zedong, and also by Fang Chih-min is undoubtedly correct – that is, the policy of establishing base areas; of systematically setting up political power; of deepening the agrarian revolution; of expanding the people's armed forces by a comprehensive process of binding up first the township Red Guards, then the district Red Guards, then the country Red Guards, then the local Red Army troops, all the way up to the regular Red Army troops; of spreading political power by advancing in a series of waves etc., etc.[10]

In the autumn of 1929, Moscow's policy on world revolution became more instantaneous and the Chinese party was urged to launch attacks on major urban centres. Mao, probably against his better judgement, participated. On their failure, Li was made the scapegoat by Moscow and accused, with some justification, of 'semi-Trotskyism'. The party Central Committee, more than ever under Moscow's control, moved from its semi-clandestine existence in Shanghai to the securer base of Kiangsi and disagreement with Mao became acute, not only on the question of proletarian hegemony, but also on military matters. Drawing on the classical Chinese tradition in such writers as Sun Tzu, Mao declared that 'our strategy is to "pit one against ten", and our tactics are to "pit ten against one" '.[11] In what has become a *locus classicus*, Mao summarised his tactics as follows:

Disperse the forces among the masses to arouse them and concentrate the forces to deal with the enemy.

> The enemy advances, we retreat; the enemy halts, we harass; the enemy tires, we attack; the enemy retreats, we pursue.
>
> In an independent regime with stabilised territory, we adopt the policy of advancing in a series of waves. When pursued by a powerful enemy, we adopt the policy of circling around in a whirling motion.
>
> Arouse the largest numbers of the masses in the shortest possible time and by the best possible methods.
>
> These tactics are like casting a net; we should be able to cast the net wide or draw it in at any moment. We cast it wide to win over the masses and draw it in to deal with the enemy. Such are the tactics we have applied in the past three years.[12]

However, this policy of luring the enemy into Communist territory in order to surround him was too defensive for the Central Committee. Mao's tactics proved successful in defeating the Encirclement campaigns of the KMT in the early 1930s. But during the fifth Encirclement campaign in 1933, following Mao's loss of influence in an increasingly Stalinised party, the policy of meeting the KMT head on led to disaster. The KMT had encircled the Communist area with blockhouses and the only course left was for the Red Army to break out and seek refuge elsewhere. They did so in 1934 and trekked for 6000 miles and twelve months over the most difficult terrain before finding a secure base in Yenan in Northwest China. It was during the Long March, at the Tsunyi conference in March 1935, that Mao became the undisputed leader of the Party.

The years 1935 to 1949 saw a steady expansion of Communist power, first in a United Front with the KMT against the Japanese invaders, then in a Civil War against the KMT itself. In the base area of Yenan a moderate agrarian policy was pursued: rents were limited to one third of the yield; there was no land confiscation; incentives of land reclamation helped the Communists to attain virtual self-sufficiency in food; and, to lessen the need for government finance, the army and the Party officials took part in farming and other productive activities. The embattled nature of the Communist enclave meant that more emphasis than ever was put on the army:

> Every Communist must grasp the truth, 'Political power grows out of the barrel of a gun'. Our principle is that the Party commands the gun, and the gun must never be allowed to command the Party. Yet, having guns, we can create Party organizations, as witness the powerful Party organizations which the Eighth Route Army has created in northern China. We can also create cadres, create schools, create

culture, create mass movements. Everything in Yenan has been created by having guns. All things grow out of the barrel of a gun.[13]

The Communists gained many supporters by being regarded as the most resolute opponent of the Japanese: the Long March had been justified in part as an anti-Japanese expedition. Cooperation with the KMT had been forced on the Communists by Moscow and by the Japanese invasion, and was never very real, both sides realising that eventual civil war was inevitable.

Mao's views on the future of the revolution were outlined in his article *On New Democracy* in 1940. In keeping with the Leninist doctrine – which was particularly emphasised by the Stalinist Popular Front policies of the Third International after 1935 – he now spoke of revolution by stages – a bourgeois, democratic revolution preceding the socialist revolution:

In the course of its history the Chinese revolution must go through two stages, first, the democratic revolution, and second the socialist revolution, and by their very nature they are two very different revolutionary processes.[14]

But this democracy was not of the old sort, it was a new democracy:

A change occurred in China's bourgeois-democratic revolution after the outbreak of the first imperialist world war in 1914 and the founding of a socialist state on one-sixth of the globe as a result of the Russian October Revolution of 1917.

Before these events, the Chinese bourgeois-democratic revolution came within the old category of the bourgeois-democratic world revolution, of which it was a part. Since these events the Chinese bourgeois-democratic revolution has changed, it has come within the new category of bourgeois-democratic revolutions and, as far as the alignment of revolutionary forces is concerned, forms part of the proletarian-socialist world revolution.[15]

Because of the phenomenon of imperialism, the world revolution, of which China was a part, was a socialist revolution, and therefore the Chinese revolution, although bourgeois, could be conducted under proletarian hegemony.

Although the Chinese revolution in this first stage (with its many sub-stages) is a new type of bourgeois-democratic revolution, and is not yet itself a proletarian-socialist revolution in its social character, it has long become a part of the proletarian-socialist world revolution and is now even a very important part and a great ally of this world revolution. The first step or stage in our revolution is definitely not, and cannot be, the establishment of a capitalist society under the dictatorship of a Chinese bourgeoisie, but will result in the establishment of a new democratic society under the joint dictatorship of all the revolutionary classes of China headed by the Chinese proletariat. The revolution will then be carried forward to the second stage, in which a socialist society will be established in China.[16]

Mao went beyond Lenin in stating that the dictatorship would be one of several revolutionary classes. He wished to emphasise the revolutionary character of the Chinese people as a whole. The emphasis on the bourgeois character of the revolution was satisfying to the peasantry which had no enthusiasm for socialism. And when he mentioned the proletariat what he really meant was the CCP, which was standing in for an 'absent' working class. The rapid transition to socialism and the China-centred nature of the post-1949 development were not yet part of Mao's thinking.

At the same time, Mao set out to strengthen and discipline the Party in the face of intense pressure from the KMT and the increase in membership following the expansion of the Communist areas. This was done in a Rectification Campaign of 1942 – the first of many such campaigns culminating in the Cultural Revolution of 1966. What particularly concerned Mao was that the Party should not be a simple replica of foreign models and particularly of the Soviet Union:

For the Chinese Communists who are part of the great Chinese nation, flesh of its flesh and blood of its blood, any talk about Marxism in isolation from China's characteristics is merely Marxism in the abstract, Marxism in a vacuum. Hence to apply Marxism concretely in China so that its every manifestation has an indubitably Chinese character, i.e., to apply Marxism in the light of China's specific characteristics, becomes a problem which it is urgent for the whole Party to understand and solve. Foreign stereotypes must be abolished, there must be less singing of empty, abstract tunes and dogmatism must be laid to rest; they must be replaced by the fresh, lively Chinese style and spirit which the common people of China love.[17]

Guerrilla warfare

In many ways, the most original contributions of Mao to the theory and practice of contemporary Marxism are his views on guerilla tactics and the strategy to be adopted in a lengthy struggle against a militarily superior opponent. His most important writings on this subject date from the 1930s.[18] During this decade Mao was faced with the problem of how to conduct a partisan war where sections of the countryside were in revolt against the Kuomintang government which controlled the cities, and, later, with the problem of tactics in an initially defensive war where large areas of the country were occupied by a militarily superior aggressor – Japan. Mao considered that guerrilla forces should be so organised that, through rapid concentration, they could mount local offensives with superior forces despite an overall inferiority. As soon as possible, they should operate in conjunction with regular troops, working behind the enemy's lines, disturbing his communications, etc. Most importantly, the guerrillas should control bases to which they could periodically retire. These should be areas that were geographically difficult of access (mountainous, bordered by swamps or deserts, etc.). In these areas, the troops themselves should work land and be active in production. They should help raise the productivity of the local inhabitants and, if possible, organise elementary social services. This would both avoid their being a burden on the locals and counter the boredom of periodic inactivity that sapped the morale of all traditional armies.

These tactics were later applied successfully by Tito's partisans in Yugoslavia, by the FLN in Algeria, during the Cuban revolution, and, of course, in Indo-China. Their most impressive vindication is Mao's *On Protracted War*, which outlined the course of the war against Japan with extraordinary foresight. Mao began by warning against either the hope of a quick victory or belief in inevitable defeat. The Japanese were certainly superior both military and economically, but they were engaged in an unjust war that had little international support. China, on the other hand, could rely on manpower resources vastly superior to Japan's and a growing national sense of progress and unity in a just cause that would gain increasing international recognition. These factors meant that the war would be protracted and had three stages: a defensive one of primarily mobile guerrilla warfare, a stage of stalemate when Japan would have too much to do in defending occupied territory to advance any further, and a final stage in which China could pass over into a regular military offensive. This was the pattern not only in the war against Japan but also in the subsequent Civil War. The continued emphasis on the importance of political consciousness and of morale, and the theme of men not weapons being the decisive factor, were, of course, characteristic of the Chinese Revolution as a whole.

In China the use of administrative force and of terror was much less than at any period in the Soviet Union. This was because of the optimism of the Chinese Communists concerning the reform of consciousness through – among other things – essentially moral appeals.

Mao's philosophy

At the same time, Mao devoted himself to giving the Party a philosophi-cal basis and produced two essays entitled *On Practice* and *On Contradiction*. In the first, Mao emphasised that 'above all, Marxists regard man's activity in production as the most fundamental practical activity, the determinant of all his other activities'.[19] In addition, 'class struggle in particular, in all its various forms, exerts a profound influence on the development of man's knowledge. In class society everyone lives as a member of a particular class, and every kind of thinking, without excep-tion, is stamped with the brand of a class.'[20] Mao continued the Marxian tradition as exemplified in Lukács, Gramsci, and the later Lenin. This emphasis on the unity of theory and practice was basic to Marx, though absent from Kautsky, the early Lenin and Stalin. *On Practice* married the *Theses on Feuerbach* with a crude, inductive, natural scientific method, and denied that Marxism had any ontological basis or underlying metaphysic. This chimed well with Mao's own aversion to book-learning and dogma-tism, and also his desire to give a theoretical justification for his own poli-cies. The very practical success of the Yenan regime – though unorthodox by Communist standards – was its own justification. For the Marxist phi-losophy of dialectical materialism 'emphasises the dependence of theory on practice and in turn serves practice. The truth of any knowledge or theory is determined not by subjective feelings but by the objective result in social practice. Only social practice can be the criterion of truth.'[21]

In his second essay, *On Contradiction*, Mao began by dividing current schools of thought into 'the metaphysical or vulgar evolutionist world outlook' which 'sees things as isolated, static and one-sided' and a world outlook which 'searches in an over-simplified way outside a thing for the causes of its development'.[22] Opposed to this view was 'the world outlook of material dialectics' which

> holds that in order to understand the development of a thing we should study it internally and in its relations with other things; in

other words, the development of things should be seen as their internal and necessary self-movement while each thing in its movement is interrelated with and interacts on the things around it. The fundamental cause of the development of a thing is not external but internal; it lies in the contradictoriness within the thing.[23]

Mao set aside talk of the 'laws' of the dialectic and put the notion of contradiction into the centre of his view of the world. In a statement that verges on the kind of talk about the essence of all that exists that he had rejected in *On Practice*, Mao declared that contradiction was universal and 'exists in the process of development of all things ... in the process of development of each thing a movement of opposites exists from beginning to end'.[24] This comes very near to establishing an ontological principle. Mao criticised the views of Deborin and his school for claiming that contradiction appears not at the beginning of the process but only at a certain stage in its development.

But more than the universality of contradiction, Mao was concerned to emphasise its particularity. Dogmatists 'do not understand that conditions differ in different kinds of revolution and so do not understand that different methods should be used to resolve different contradictions; on the contrary, they invariably adopt what they imagine to be an unalterable formula and arbitrarily apply it everywhere, which only causes setbacks to the revolutions or makes a sorry mess of what was originally well done'.[25] Different contradictions demanded different methods of resolving them. For example, 'in Russia, there was a fundamental difference between the contradiction resolved by the February Revolution and the contradiction resolved by the October Revolution'.[26] More specifically Mao wished to analyse what he termed a principal contradiction and a principal aspect of a contradiction. He wrote: 'there are many contradictions in the process of development of a complex thing, and one of them is necessarily the principal contradiction, whose existence and development determines or influences the existence and development of the other contradictions'.[27] The implications for current policies was evident: the war against Japan was the principal contradiction and the struggle against the KMT was for the moment secondary. With regard to the general principles of historical materialism, Mao's views led to a possible emphasis on the superstructural elements of politics and culture that he was to exploit later in full. He wrote:

The productive forces, practice and the economic base generally play the principal and decisive role; whoever denies this is not a materialist.

But it must also be admitted that in certain conditions, such aspects as the relations of production, theory and the superstructure in turn manifest themselves in the principal and decisive role. When it is impossible for the productive forces to develop without a change in the relations of production, then the change in the relations of production plays the principal and decisive role ... When the superstructure (politics, culture, etc.) obstructs the development of the economic base, political and cultural changes become principal and decisive.[28]

Mao's final point was that the elements in any contradiction were not only complementary – necessary conditions of each other's existence – but also identical in that they transformed themselves into each other. War transformed itself into peace, or, more specifically, 'by means of revolution the proletariat, at one time the ruled, is transformed into the ruler, while the bourgeoisie, the erstwhile ruler, is transformed into the ruled, and changes its position into that originally occupied by its opposite'.[29] The conclusion was that 'the struggle between opposites permeates the process from beginning to end and makes one process transform itself into another, it is ubiquitous, and is therefore unconditional and absolute'.[30]

Notes

1. Quoted in A.S. Whiting, *Soviet Policies in China 1917–1924* (New York and London, 1954) p. 50.
2. Mao Zedong, 'Analysis of the Classes in Chinese Society', *Selected Works* (Peking, 1965–77) vol. 1, p. 19. See further: S. Schram, 'Mao Tse-tung and the role of the various classes in the Chinese revolution', in *The Polity and Economy of China* (Tokyo, 1975) pp. 225ff.
3. Mao Zedong, 'Report on an Investigation of the Peasant Movement in Hunan', *Selected Works*, vol. 1, pp. 23f.
4. Ibid., p. 32.
5. Ibid., p. 30.
6. For the originality of Mao's views here, see B. Schwartz, *Chinese Communism and the Rise of Mao* (Cambridge, Mass., 1951) pp. 73ff. For a contrasting view, see K. Wittfogel, 'The Legend of "Maoism" ', *China Quarterly*, vols 1 and 2.
7. For Trotsky on China, see further: L. Trotsky, *Problems of the Chinese Revolution* (New York, 1966) and B. Knei-Paz, *The Social and Political Thought of Leon Trotsky* (Oxford, 1978) pp. 358ff.
8. Mao Zedong, 'The Struggle in the Chingkang Mountains', *Selected Works*, vol. 1, p. 98.
9. Quoted in B. Schwartz, *Chinese Communism and the Rise of Mao* (Cambridge, Mass., 1951) p. 139.
10. Mao Zedong, 'A Single Spark Can Start a Prairie Fire', *Selected Works*, vol. 1, p. 118.

11. Mao Zedong, 'Strategy in China's Revolutionary War', *Selected Works*, vol. 1, p. 237.
12. Mao Zedong, 'A Struggle Spark Can Start a Prairie Fire', *Selected Works*, vol. 1, p. 124.
13. Mao Zedong, 'Problems of War and Strategy', *Selected Works*, vol. 2, pp. 224f.
14. Mao Zedong, 'On New Democracy', *Selected Works*, vol. 2, pp. 341f.
15. Ibid., p. 343.
16. Ibid., p. 347.
17. Mao Zedong, 'The Role of the Chinese Communist Party in the National War', *Selected Works*, vol. 2, pp. 209f.
18. In particular, *Problems of Strategy in Guerrilla War Against Japan* and *On Protracted War*, both dating from 1938.
19. Mao Zedong, 'On Practice', *Selected Works*, vol. 1, p. 295.
20. Ibid., p. 296.
21. Ibid., p. 297.
22. Mao Zedong, 'On Contradiction', *Selected Works*, vol. 1, pp. 312f.
23. Ibid., p. 313.
24. Ibid., p. 316.
25. Ibid., p. 322.
26. Ibid.
27. Ibid., p. 331.
28. Ibid., p. 336.
29. Ibid., pp. 338f.
30. Ibid., p. 343.

Further reading

Mao Zedong: texts

Fundamental are the five volumes of the *Selected Works* which go as far as the end of 1957. There are several one-volume collections, of which the best is Schram's *The Political Thought of Mao Tse-tung*. This should be supplemented by the extremely revealing post-1956 collection, *Mao Tse-tung Unrehearsed*. Schram's 7 volume edition is indispensable. See also Knight's collection on Mao's philosophy and Cheng's good survey.

Mao Zedong: commentaries

A stimulating, though highly critical, introduction is Deutscher's article, 'Maoism: its Origins and Outlook'. A more favourable presentation of the background is Fairbank's rather mistitled *The United States and China*.

Two short accounts of Mao's life and thought are Fitzgerald's *Mao Tse-tung and China* and Smart's *Mao*. See also the more recent books by Lynch and by Terrill. The best larger account is Schram's biography *Mao Tse-tung*. Short is detailed and indispensable. This can be supplemented by Wilson's excellent collection on various aspects, *Mao Tse-tung in the Scales of History* and by Chang and Halliday's unremitting emphasis on Mao's crimes.

Chinese Communism pre-1945

Still fundamental is Snow's eye-witness account, *Red Star over China*. The international dimension is covered in d'Encausse and Schram's *Marxism and Asia* and a good collection of contemporary documents is Schurmann and Schell's *Republican China*. A reliable short introduction is Fitzgerald's *The Birth of Communist China*. Guillermaz's first volume contains a lot of useful information and Schwartz's *Chinese Communism and the Rise of Mao* is a basic study by one of the leading American scholars. An inspiring account is given in Suyin's *The Morning Deluge*, which takes the story up to 1935, of which year there is a full treatment available in Wilson's *The Long March, 1935*. In many ways, the most reliable and detailed account – particularly on the military side – is Ch'en's *Mao and the Chinese Revolution*. See also Fairbank's *The United States and China*. Wasserstrom's collection is a good guide to recent Western reappraisals and Dirlik's two books are stimulating.

Bibliography

Jerome Ch'en, *Mao Papers: Anthology and Bibliography* (Oxford, 1970).
P. Cheng *et al.* (eds), *The Search for Modern China: A Documentary Collection* (New York, 1999).

Mao Zedong: texts

Mao Zedong, *Selected Works*, 5 vols (Peking, 1965–77).
—— *Selected Works*, one volume, abridged by B. Shaw (New York, 1970).
—— *Quotations* (Peking, 1966).
Mao Tse-tung on Revolution and War, ed. M. Rejai (New York, 1970).
Mao Tse-tung: An Anthology of His Writings, ed. Anne Freemantle (New York, 1972).
Mao Tse-tung Unrehearsed, Talks and Lectures 1956–1971, ed. S. Schram (Harmondsworth, 1974).
Mao Tse-tung, A Critique of Soviet Economics (New York and London, 1977).
Mao's Road to Power, ed. S. Schram, 7 vols (Armonk, 1989–2005).
Mao Zedong on Dialectical Materialism: Writings on Philosophy 1937, ed. N. Knight (Armonk, 1990).
Stuart R. Schram, *The Political Thought of Mao Tse-tung*, 2nd edn (Harmondsworth, 1969).

Mao Zedong: commentaries

J. Chang and J. Halliday, *Mao: The Unknown Story* (New York, 2005).
Arthur Cohen, *The Communism of Mao Tse-tung* (Chicago, 1964).
—— 'Maoism' in M.M. Drachkovitch (ed.), *Marxism in the Modern World* (London, 1966).

P. Corrigan *et al.*, *For Mao* (New York and London, 1979).
Isaac Deutscher, 'Maoism: Its Origins and Outlook', in R. Blackburn (ed.), *Revolution and Class Struggle: A Reader in Marxist Politics* (London, 1977).
A. Dirlik *et al.* (eds), *Critical Perspectives on Mao Zedong's Thought* (Atlantic Highlands, 1997).
C.P. Fitzgerald, *Mao Tse-tung and China*, rev. edn (London, 1977).
Leo Goodstadt, *Mao Tse-tung: The Search for Plenty* (London, 1972).
R. Howard, *Mao Tse-tung and the Chinese People* (London, 1978).
M. Lynch, *Mao* (London, 2004).
R. Payne, *Portrait of a Revolutionary: Mao Tse-tung* (New York, 1961).
L. Pye, *The Man in the Leader* (New York, 1978).
Edward E. Rice, *Mao's Way* (Berkeley, 1966).
Stuart Schram, *Mao Tse-tung* (Harmondsworth, 1966).
P. Short, *Mao: A Life* (London, 1999).
Ninian Smart, *Mao* (London, 1974).
Richard H. Solomon, *Mao's Revolution and the Chinese Political Culture* (Berkeley, 1971).
R. Terrill, *Mao: A Biography* (Stafford, 2000).
Stephen Uhalley, *Mao Tse-tung: A Critical Biography* (New York, 1975).
Dick Wilson (ed.), *Mao Tse-tung in the Scales of History* (Cambridge, 1977).

Chinese Communism pre-1945

Lucien Bianco, *Origins of the Chinese Revolution: 1915–1949* (Stanford, 1971).
C. Brandt, B. Schwartz and J.K. Fairbank, *A Documentary History of Chinese Communism* (Cambridge, Mass., 1952).
H. Carrère d'Encausse and S. Schram, *Marxism and Asia: An Introduction with Readings* (London, 1969).
A. Chan, *Chinese Marxism* (London, 2003).
Lionel M. Chassin, *The Communist Conquest of China: A History of the Civil War, 1945–1949* (Cambridge, Mass., 1965).
T. Cheek (ed.), *Mao Zedong and China's Revolution: A Brief History with Documents* (Basingstoke, 2002).
Jerome Ch'en, *Mao and the Chinese Revolution* (Oxford, 1965).
A. Dirlik, *Marxism in the Chinese Revolution* (Lanham, 2005).
John King Fairbank, *The United States and China*, 3rd edn (Cambridge, Mass., 1972).
C.P. Fitzgerald, *The Birth of Communist China* (London, 1964).
Jacques Guillermaz, *History of the Chinese Communist Party: 1921–1949* (Folkestone, 1975).
Harold Isaacs, *The Tragedy of the Chinese Revolution* (London, 1938).
Chalmers A. Johnson, *Peasant Nationalism and Communist Power: The Emergence of Revolutionary China 1937–1945* (Stanford, 1953).
T. Kampen, *Mao Zedong, Zhou Enlai and the Evolution of the Chinese Communist Leadership* (Denmark, 2000).
Donald M. Lowe, *The Function of China in Marx, Lenin and Mao* (Berkeley, 1966).
A. Pantsov, *The Bolsheviks and the Chinese Revolution, 1919–1927* (Richmond, 2000).
John E. Rue, *Mao Tse-tung in Opposition: 1927–1935* (Stanford, 1966).
T. Saitch and H. Van de Ven (eds), *New Perspectives on the Chinese Communist Revolution* (Armonk, 1994).

Franz Schrumann and Orville Schell (eds), *Republican China: Nationalism, War and the Rise of Communism, 1911–1949* (London, 1967).

Benjamin Schwartz, *Chinese Communism and the Rise of Mao* (Cambridge, Mass., 1951).

M. Selden, *China in Revolution: The Yenan Way Revisited* (Armonk, 1995).

Edgar Snow, *Journey to the Beginning* (London, 1959).

——— *Red Star over China*, rev. edn (London, 1972).

Han Suyin, *The Morning Deluge: Mao Tse-tung and the Chinese Revolution 1893–1953* (London, 1972).

Dick Wilson, *The Long March, 1935: The Epic of Chinese Communism's Survival*, rev. edn (London, 1977).

16
Maoism in Power

The path of economic development

Inheritance and first measures

On the eve of its victory over the KMT, the Chinese Communist Party inherited an economy in ruins. High inflation had engendered currency collapse, communications had been destroyed (with the KMT fleet still blockading the East China coast), figures for industrial production were well below pre-war level, and there was threat of real famine in the cities. In the face of this disaster, the Party had several advantages: it could rely on the general goodwill of the populace, who were experiencing the first united government that China had enjoyed for forty years; there existed a well-organised and cohesive system of Party cadres with experience of administration through long years of Civil War, unlike the Soviet Union whose Civil War followed revolutionary victory rather than preceding it; and (also unlike the Soviet Union) China had a large and powerful ally of sorts and was not therefore as isolated on the world stage as was Bolshevik Russia. The new regime rapidly took a number of financial measures which unified and fairly distributed the taxes, brought inflation under control – largely by tying money values to units of basic commodities – and produced a balanced budget. At the same time, basic economic recovery was achieved by a moderate approach to industry and agriculture. Large capitalist enterprises that were closely associated with the KMT were nationalised, but the so-called national bourgeoisie who controlled the smaller businesses were left alone and even encouraged – in line with Lenin's policy in the months immediately following the Bolshevik Revolution. But the most important measure adopted by the Communists was the Land Law of June 1950. This implemented over two or three years a policy that was much more moderate than that adopted in the Communist-held areas during the Civil War. The new law guaranteed each individual, as his private property at the age of 16, a minimum land-holding such that a family of five had about one hectare. The reforms were carried out and organised under the guidance of Party cadres with help from the Peasant Associations – limited to poor and middle peasants – that the Party had established in the villages. The land thus redistributed (and it amounted to about half the land then under cultivation) was confiscated from religious institutions and landowners. This reform was not fundamentally egalitarian as land belonging to rich peasants was protected, though it was not as inegalitarian as the Russian NEP in that the rich peasantry were not permitted to increase their holdings. The reform was nevertheless fundamentally in accord with the views of Lenin and Stalin that mechanisation would have to precede collectivisation. Mao endorsed this programme, but its chief proponent was Liu Shao-ch'i, who declared: 'Only when the conditions are mature for the extensive application of mechanised farming, for the organisation of collective farms, and for the socialist reform of the rural areas, will the need for a rich-peasant economy cease, and this will take some time to achieve.'[1] This economic reform was backed up by a marriage law which was designed to ensure that free choice should be the basic principle of every marriage and that the feudal hold of the family over the individual, and in particular the power of parents over children and husbands over wives, should be abolished.

The First Five Year Plan

The end of the period of reconstruction marked the beginning of the First Five Year Plan of 1953–7. The Chinese economy progressed much faster towards socialism during these years than had been envisaged in 1949. This was due partly to the inevitable clash between planning and the existence of private property, whether in industry or agriculture, and partly to the Korean War which imposed strains on the Chinese economy and hastened the reduction in economic power of classes who were potentially hostile to the regime. In industry, the profits of the national bourgeoisie were first restricted, then expropriated with compensation that they were encouraged to invest in state bonds. Most of those expropriated stayed on as managers of the businesses concerned. By the end of 1956, state ownership of industry was virtually complete. The First Five Year Plan was very successful in industry and the output of many major sectors was doubled over the five years. Soviet aid was a necessary condition of the success, with thousands of Soviet technicians helping to install and operate plants, and facilities being made available in Russia for Chinese students of technology.

In the agricultural sector, the drive towards cooperatives and collectivisation was originally intended to halt a slide in the opposite direction. Mao declared, 'as everyone has seen over the last few years, the influence of forces tending spontaneously toward capitalism is developing day by day in the countryside. New rich peasants are appearing everywhere and many prosperous middle peasants are trying to become rich peasants.'[2] Rich peasants were busy consolidating and exploiting their positions. During 1952, mutual aid teams had been established to help in farming each other's land. Then 'semi-socialist' cooperatives were introduced in which income was distributed according to the initial input of land and capital that an individual or family had contributed, as well as according to the actual labour provided. In the much larger, fully socialist cooperatives, land, labour and capital were held in common and income allotted according to work done. By the end of 1956, virtually all peasants were in cooperatives and the vast majority in fully socialist ones – ten years ahead of the goal set in 1953. This haste involved a certain clumsiness in implementation and some resistance on the part of the peasantry, but nothing on the scale of the Soviet Union in the early 1930s. This haste was necessary for two reasons. The first was the need to increase agricultural production in order to promote industry. Mao's faith in the revolutionary potential of the Chinese countryside and his preference for men over machines led him eventually to think that a rise in agricultural production would have to precede or at least accompany a rise in industrial production, in opposition to the traditional view that mechanisation would have to precede collectivisation – the view consistently supported by Liu Shaoch'i. The second reason was the need to support the increase in population, which began to rise dramatically on economic recovery. By the middle 1950s it was evident that all the improvements possible under the traditional system of small plots had been achieved, and that a radical new departure was necessary. A certain basis for the cooperatives was already present in the common ownership of some land and collaborative production in the villages, and in the complicated and widespread systems of irrigation that had existed for centuries, both of which factors had made Chinese agriculture more efficient than in any other non-capitalist country. Thus the Chinese peasant was already much more socially minded than his individualist Western European counterpart so graphically described by Marx.[3] There was also the existence of the Soviet experience to which explicit reference was made at the beginning of the First Five Year Plan:

> If we cannot basically solve the problem of agricultural co-operation within roughly three five-year plans, that is to say, if our agriculture cannot make a leap from small-scale farming with animal-drawn farm implements to large-scale mechanized farming, along with extensive state-organized land reclamation by settlers using machinery (the plan being to bring 400 to 500 million *mou* of waste land under cultivation in the course of three five-year plans), then we shall fail to resolve the contradiction between the ever-increasing need for commodity grain and industrial raw materials and the present generally low output of staple crops, and we shall run into formidable difficulties in our socialist industrialization and be unable to complete it. The Soviet Union, which had to face the same problem in the course of building socialism, solved it by leading and developing the collectivization of agriculture in a planned way. And we can solve ours only by the same method.[4]

With an annual growth rate of around 8 per cent in the gross national product and an increase of 20 per cent in agricultural production, the First Five Year Plan was successful and China was moving towards a full Soviet system of planned economy.

The Great Leap Forward

However, it was evident that at the end of the First Five Year Plan the growth rate was slowing down. True to his view that economic development advanced in 'waves' rather than gradually, Mao pre-empted the Second Five Year Plan by launching the frenetic economic drive that came to be known as the Great Leap Forward. The Great Leap Forward was launched in early 1958, although Mao had been arguing for some time that there should be investment in light industry and agriculture to promote a market for heavy industrial goods. The leap consisted in the advancement, above all, of small-scale local industry and agriculture, and the adaptation of the industrialised sector to these needs. This was to be achieved by the all-out mobilisation of local surplus labour and the development of local sources of power and raw materials. The most striking aspects of the latter policy was the programme for producing steel in thousands of home-made furnaces across the country. On his return from an inspection trip, Mao wrote:

> During this trip, I have witnessed the tremendous energy of the masses. On this foundation it is possible to accomplish any task

whatsoever. We must first complete the tasks on the iron and steel front. In these sectors, the masses have already been mobilised. Nevertheless, in the country as a whole, there are a few places, a few enterprises, where the work of mobilising the masses has still not been properly carried out ... There are still a few comrades who are unwilling to undertake a large scale mass movement in the industrial sphere. They call the mass movement on the industrial front 'irregular' and disparage it as a 'rural style of work' and 'a guerilla habit'. This is obviously incorrect.[5]

This implied a radical decentralisation of economic planning and an abandonment of the Soviet model for investment.[6]

Alongside the proposals for industry went a direct expansion of agricultural production by extending the Commune system. The Commune movement was an attempt to achieve the growth of agriculture needed to sustain industry and increase exports. Like Bukharin, Mao believed that industry should serve agriculture and he promoted the Communes in order to foster peasant accumulation, not in order to extract the surplus for the benefit of heavy industry like Preobrazhensky and Stalin. The Communes combined several large cooperatives to form units of about 100,000 people, although the size was extremely variable. During 1958 26,000 Communes took the place of 74,000 advanced cooperatives. This enabled the work force to be directed according to the general need of the Commune: light industry and large-scale agricultural improvements (irrigation, for example) would be facilitated. Communal eating, laundry, nurseries, etc., would release a lot of labour, particularly female, and reduce to a minimum the private property of the peasant. The system of payment was a combination of regard for needs and work contributed. In addition, the Commune was to become the basic unit of local government.

According to official sources, production of coal, steel and grain more than doubled during 1958. While it is true that production during the Great Leap Forward reached levels unattained during the next ten years, the official statistics were soon drastically revised downwards: in the initial euphoria, both target and results had been more imaginary than real. During the three years 1959–61 there were natural disasters of drought and flood that were almost unprecedented. In July 1960 Russian aid and technical experts were withdrawn virtually overnight. More importantly, the efforts required to maintain the pace of growth could not be kept up, the hasty transition to collective property aroused resentment, and the lack of an overall plan meant many bottlenecks and shortages.

During 1960 to 1962 the Chinese economy went into a decline, though the extent is difficult to measure as official statistics were no longer produced, and many millions died in the subsequent famine. In particular, the Communes became mostly administrative units managing non-agricultural enterprises – public works, mines, fertiliser production – while the old cooperatives or 'production brigades' became much more the basic unit of ownership and accounting. Private landholding was admitted, rewards were in proportion to work done, and salaries were paid in cash rather than in kind.

The economic situation improved after 1962, but the Cultural Revolution of 1966–9 was intended, among other things, to combat the re-emergence of inequality. The importance of the private sector, incentive schemes, and profit as a measure of economic viability were all associated with Liu Shao-ch'i and the 'capitalist roaders'. After 1969 there was a certain re-emphasis on central planning in industry and a steady growth in the steel, oil, automotive, and nuclear sectors. However, in China's central problem area, that of grain, population increases meant that the per capita output was only slightly above pre-war levels and that average consumption and living standards increased only marginally.

Class and contradiction

In his report to the Seventh Party Congress in 1945, entitled *On Coalition Government*, Mao had stated:

> It is a law of Marxism that socialism can be attained only via the stage of democracy. And in China the fight for democracy is a protracted one. It would be a sheer illusion to try to build a socialist society on the ruins of the colonial, semi-colonial, and semi-feudal order without a united new-democratic state, without the development of the state sector of the new-democratic economy, of the private capitalist and the cooperative sectors, and of a national, scientific and mass culture, i.e., a new-democratic culture, and without deliberation and the development of the individuality of hundreds of million of people – in short, without a thoroughgoing bourgeois-democratic revolution of a new type led by the Communist Party.[7]

By the beginning of the First Five Year Plan in 1953, however, Mao was saying that the transition to socialism had actually begun in 1949. But did this mean that classes had been abolished? The answer was that class struggle continued to exist during the transition period,[8] but that the transition to socialism could nevertheless be peaceful, as the contradiction between the bourgeoisie on the one hand and the peasantry and the proletariat on the other were, or at least could be, non-antagonistic. Indeed, the bourgeoisie was often said positively to welcome socialism. The 1937 essay *On Contradiction* had insisted that, as contradictions were omnipresent, they would exist even under socialism. But this view was only seriously elaborated in Mao's essay of 1957 entitled *On the Correct Handling of Contradictions Among the People*. Here Mao stated that a socialist victory had been achieved in China and that socialism was in the process of being built, but that contradictions would still remain – contradictions with the enemy and those among the people. The enemy consisted of all social forces and groups who resisted socialist revolution and contradictions with them were antagonistic. Contradictions among the people, however, were more varied:

In the conditions prevailing in China today, the contradictions among the people comprise the contradictions within the working class, the contradictions within the peasantry, the contradictions within the intelligentsia, the contradictions between the working class and the peasantry, the contradictions between workers and peasants on the one hand and intellectuals on the other, the contradictions between the working class and other sections of the working people on the other hand, and the national bourgeoisie on the other, the contradictions within the national bourgeoisie, and so on. Our People's Government is one that genuinely represents the people's interest, it is the government that serves that people. Nevertheless, there are still certain contradictions between this government and the people. These include the contradictions between the interests of the State and the interests of the collective on the one hand and the interests of the individual on the other, between democracy and centralism, between the leadership and the led, and the contradiction arising from the bureaucratic style of work of some of the state personnel in their relations with the masses. All these are also contradictions among the people.[9]

These contradictions were not necessarily antagonistic: 'the contradiction between the national bourgeoisie and the working class is one between exploiter and exploited, and is by nature antagonistic. But in the concrete conditions of China, the antagonistic contradiction between the two classes, if properly handled, can be transformed into a non-antagonistic one and resolved by suitable methods.'[10] The reason for this was that 'contradiction in socialist society fundamentally differs from those in the old societies, such as capitalist societies. In capitalist society contradictions find expression in acute antagonisms and conflicts, in sharp class struggle; they cannot be resolved by the capitalist system itself and can only be resolved by socialist revolution. The case is quite different with contradiction in socialist society; on the contrary, they are not antagonistic and can be ceaselessly resolved by the socialist system itself.'[11]

The antagonistic contradiction – that with the counter-revolutionary enemies of the people – had been to a large extent eliminated in the initial violence when the Communists took power;[12] those that involved the peasantry, the national bourgeoisie, and the intellectuals were being dealt with in a more continuous manner. At the time of the Great Leap Forward, talk of stages in the revolutionary movement gave way to talk of 'permanent' or 'interrupted' revolution. This perspective was used to justify the introduction of institutions – Communes – that were proper to a Communist society. 'After winning one battle', Mao said, 'we must immediately put forward new tasks. In this way, we can maintain the revolutionary enthusiasm of the cadres and the masses and diminish their self-satisfaction, since they have no time to be satisfied with themselves, even if they wanted to.'[13] And later: 'the advanced and the backward are the two extremities of a contradiction, and "comparison" is the unity of opposites ... disequilibrium is a universal objective law. Things for ever proceed from disequilibrium to equilibrium, and from equilibrium to disequilibrium, in endless cycles ... , but each cycle reaches a higher level. Disequilibrium is constant and absolute equilibrium is temporary and relative.'[14] Even Communism itself was not exempt from such 'revolutions'. This general attitude of Mao became more pronounced in the 1960s when he summed up his view of philosophy as follows:

> Engels talked about three categories, but as for me, I don't believe in two of those categories ... there is no such thing as the negation of the negation. Affirmation, negation, affirmation, negation ... in the development of things, every link in the chain of events is both affirmation and negation ...
>
> Socialism, too, will be eliminated, it wouldn't do if it were not eliminated, for then there would be no Communism ...
>
> Mankind will also finally meet its doom. When the theologians talk about doomsday, they are pessimistic and terrify people. We say that the end of mankind is something which will produce something more advanced than mankind.[15]

This idea of 'permanent revolution' may sound akin to that of Trotsky, but is in fact very different. Mao had – perforce – to allot a much more important role to the peasantry in the revolutionary movement than Trotsky, who was even more pessimistic concerning the revolutionary potential of the peasantry than was Lenin. Consequently, Mao refused to adopt the emphasis on heavy industrial development at the expense of the peasantry that Stalin – in accordance with the previously expressed views of Trotsky – had implemented. Further, following the principles of his critique of the Soviet Union. Trotsky would have denied that a bureaucratised Party like the CCP was capable of making a revolution – quite apart from the absence of the proletariat in a leading role. For the defeat of the urban-based Communists in 1927 and the de-industrialisation of the East coast by the Japanese invaders had deprived the Communist Party of any appreciable working-class base. In 1949, Mao nevertheless laid emphasis on the cities, but with the movement away from the Russian model of development in the mid-1950s, the non-proletarian nature of Maoism became plain. The proletariat was still maintained as a reference point, but the real areas of focus were the Party and the peasantry. Thus, as Schwartz has written: 'The term "proletarian" had already acquired new connotations. It had already come to refer to a cluster of proletarian moral qualities which could be set before both Party and masses as a norm of true collectivist behaviour. To a considerable extent, it had already been disengaged from its concrete class reference.'[16] Indeed, Mao often talked vaguely of 'the masses' by which he meant an agglomeration of the lower ranks of the peasantry and the urban petty bourgeoisie. The absent proletariat could not fulfil a hegemonic role against these groups so the Party had to act as its substitute. This phenomenon of 'substitutism' – the Party playing the role of the proletariat in the face of the peasantry whose initial aspirations were not socialist – goes a long way to explaining the authoritarian nature of the Party.[17]

The Party and the masses

The mass line and democratic centralism

Lenin's doctrine of democratic centralism had been adopted by the Chinese Communist Party since its inception. Freedom of discussion was allowed, but decisions, once taken, were to be obeyed by all. All members were to be consulted, but there was a rigid subordination of lower to higher levels in the Party. The long military struggle in which it was engaged meant that the Party leant more to centralism than to democracy. In a speech of 1942, Mao said of certain comrades: 'they do not understand the Party's system of democratic centralism: they do not realise that the Communist Party not only needs democracy but needs centralisation even more. They forget the system of democratic central-ism in which the minority is subordinate to the majority, the lower level to the higher level, the part to the whole and the entire membership to the Central Committee.'[18] However, this view (which was consistently supported by Liu Shao-ch'i) was tempered by Mao's doctrine of the mass line. He expanded this in a classic passage, as follows:

All correct leadership is necessarily 'from the masses to the masses'. This means, take the ideas of the masses (scattered and unsystematic ideas) and concentrate them (through study turn them into concen-trated and systematic ideas), then go to the masses and propagate and explain these ideas until the masses embrace them as their own, hold fast to them, and translate them into action, and test the directness of these ideas in such action. Then once again concentrate ideas from the masses and once again go to the masses so that the ideas are per-severed in and carried through. And so on, over and over again in an endless spiral, with the ideas becoming more correct, more vital, and richer each time. Such is the Marxist-Leninist theory of knowledge.[19]

But the very backwardness of China (which meant that initiatives would have to come from the Party) was held by Mao to be an advantage. He believed strongly in the malleability of human nature and considered the Chinese people to be more malleable than most:

China's 600 million people have two remarkable peculiarities; they are, first of all, poor, and secondly, blank. That may seem like a bad thing, but it is really a good thing. Poor people want change, want to do things, want revolution. A clean sheet of paper has no blotches, and so the newest and most beautiful words can be written on it, the newest and most beautiful pictures can be painted on it.[20]

Good communication with the masses was essential in order to provide the leadership with the stuff on which they had to go to work. Just as a factory could not function without raw material so

without democracy you have no understanding of what is happening down below; the general situation will be unclear; you will be unable to collect sufficient opinions from all sides; there can be no commu-nication between top and bottom; top level organs of leadership will depend on one-sided and incorrect material to decide issues, and thus you will find it difficult to avoid being subjectivist; it will be impossible to achieve unity of understanding and unity of action, and impossible to achieve true centralism.[21]

But nevertheless the initiatives of the masses tended not to be well received if they were regarded as not being impregnated with Mao Zedong's thought – as in some aspects of the Cultural Revolution.

Party organisation

The most striking fact about the relationship of the Party to the masses is the huge power of the decision-making that resides in the upper echelons of the Party. Organs of state (as opposed to the Party) such as the National Peoples Congress lack any real power. In the Party itself the important decisions are taken by the Standing Committee of the Politbureau. The Politbureau is elected by the full Central Committee. But the Central Committee meets only infrequently: it did not meet at all for example, from September 1962 to August 1966 and is sometimes called upon to ratify retrospectively important decisions taken by the Politbureau that have been enforced for a long time. The same applies to Party Congresses: there was only one between 1945 and 1969. Any form of participatory democracy is rendered impossible by the immense cloak of secrecy surrounding all deliberations at the top of the CCP. Differences of opinion among the leadership are simply not revealed and much less is known about their varying views than about those of the top of the Soviet Party. The mysterious fall and rise of Deng Xiaoping is an example. Among the peasantry, there is some real freedom at the level of the production brigade, but the economic decisions of the Commune as a whole are taken by the Party Committees. In factories, too, participation from below is minimal, despite attempts to encourage it, and power remains in the hands of the Party. Trade unions are restricted to helping to increase levels of production and any sort of autonomy is denied them – a position strikingly dissimilar to Lenin's views in 1921 on the necessity of organisations to defend workers' interests – if necessary against their own state. Neither is there any organisation to press for women's rights.

The Party has thus never completely escaped from the influence of Stalinism in the 1930s that affected all Communist parties. This Stalinist influence was reinforced by the fact that the Party, cut off from the proletariat that it was supposed to be representing, was forced into the position of commanding rather than representing. This bureaucratic authoritarianism was reinforced by the position of Mao Zedong in the

Party hierarchy. The CCP did not enjoy the tradition of inner-party democracy that had initially been so strong among the Bolsheviks. Nevertheless, the Party was no monolith, as the deep divisions that accompanied the Great Leap Forward and the Cultural Revolution demonstrated. Mao himself was never simply a dictator: many of his Party colleagues enjoyed revolutionary reputations in their own right and Mao had sometimes to resort to playing one off against another or even to promoting extra-Party campaigns to get his point of view across. The high point in Mao's ascendancy seems to have been the 1950s. In 1955, for example, Mao was able to speed up the tempo of collectivisation in clear opposition to the resolutions of the Central Committee. But the relative failure of the Great Leap Forward, with which he was personally associated, brought heavy criticism which had, as its background, an uneasiness among many of the Chinese leaders at Mao's growing divergence with the Soviet Union. In reply to the criticism of the Great Leap Forward by P'eng Teh-huai, Minister of Defence, that 'putting politics in command is not a substitute for economic principles, still less for concrete measures in economic work,'[22] Mao stated:

> By doing away with planning, I mean that they [the Planning Commission] dispensed with overall balances and simply made no estimates of how much coal, iron and transport would be needed. Coal and iron cannot walk by themselves; they need vehicles to transport them. This I did not foresee. I and the Premier did not concern ourselves with this point. You could say that we were ignorant of it. I ought not to make excuses, but I shall too, because I am not the head of the Planning Commission. Before August of last year my main energies were concentrated on revolution. I am a complete outsider when it comes to economic construction, and I understand nothing about industrial planning ... but Comrades, in 1958 and 1959 the main responsibility was mine, and you should take me to task.[23]

Although, at the Lushan Plenum of the Central Committee in August 1959, Mao secured a condemnation of P'eng's views (at the same time as he drastically revised his own), his own position was much diminished. In December 1958 he had resigned the position of President of the Government and occupied himself much less with Party affairs. He began to see the People's Liberation Army, which was under the control of P'eng's successor Lin Piao, as a possible alternative power basis for his own influence. At the Politbureau some months before the Lushan Plenum Mao was even reputed to have threatened: 'I will lead the peasants to overthrow the government. If your liberation army will not follow me, I will raise a Red Army, but I think the liberation army will follow me.'[24]

Nevertheless, the pre-eminence accorded to Mao's thoughts as the only legitimate interpretation of Marxism-Leninism in the Chinese context did afford him immense power (as, for example, in the events surrounding the fall of Liu Shao-ch'i and Lin Piao). Mao's *Thoughts* – partly because of their more accessible style – superseded all other Marxist classics. The *People's Daily* declared at the beginning of the Cultural Revolution:

> The attitude adopted toward the thought of Mao Zedong, acceptance or resistance, support or opposition, affection or hatred, is the dividing line, the touchstone by which to distinguish authentic revolution from pseudo-revolution, revolution from counter-revolution. Marxism-Leninism from Revisionism.[25]

Mao himself claimed that he had only fostered the cult of his personality as a counterweight to the Party bureaucracy.[26] But the grotesque lengths to which this was taken only served to caricature the essentially authoritarian and paternalistic nature of the relationship of the charismatic leader to the masses: in accordance with the Confucian tradition, the people were regarded as essentially good, but their ignorance required an enlightened leadership to be responsible for their well-being. According to Isaac Deutscher, 'national history, custom and tradition (including the deep philosophical influences of Confucianism and Taoism) have been reflected in the patriarchal character of the Maoist government, the hieratic style of its work and propaganda among the masses, and the magic aura surrounding the leader'.[27]

These characteristics of the Party's attitude to the masses in China can be seen more clearly in the fate of two movements which seemed – temporarily – to negate the essential paternalism of the Party: the 'Hundred Flowers' movement of 1957 and the Cultural Revolution of 1966–9.

The 'One Hundred Flowers' campaign

In May 1956 Mao Zedong gave his support to a certain liberalisation in China by launching the slogan 'may a hundred flowers bloom and a hundred schools of thought contend'. The collectivisation of agriculture and the nationalisation of industry had been virtually completed with the First Five Year Plan. There was a growing need to gain the active cooperation of intellectuals for future development. 'You may ban the expression of wrong ideas', Mao said, 'but the ideas will still be there. On the other hand, if correct ideas are pampered in hothouses and never exposed to the elements and immunised against disease, they will not win out against erroneous ones. Therefore, it is only by employing a method of discussion, criticism, and reasoning that we can really foster correct ideas and overcome wrong ones, and that we can really settle issues.'[28] There was also the hope that the campaign would lead to diminution in excessive bureaucracy.

At the Eighth Party Congress on September 1956 (held only a few months after the denunciation of Stalin at the Soviet Twentieth Congress) there was a strong current of constructive criticism. Some of the collectivisation campaigns had been over-hasty and involved an unnecessary resort to force; more attention should be paid to the desires of the masses; the growth of bureaucracy should be countered by workers' participation – an experiment in workers' control had been started in the Peking Tram Company and there was even favourable mention of Yugoslavia. More cooperation with other parties was urged and the cult of the leader formally condemned. These views were opposed by a large selection of the Party leadership, including Liu Shao-ch'i, but were given support by Mao's speech *On the Correct Handling of Contradictions Among the People* of February 1957, which admitted the possibility of non-antagonistic contradictions between government and masses and encouraged criticism: 'People may ask, since Marxism is accepted as the guiding ideology by the majority of the people in our country, can it be criticised? Certainly it can. Marxism is scientific truth and fears no criticism. If it did, and if it could be overthrown by criticism, it would be worthless.'[29]

The resulting wave of criticism, however, particularly from the leaders of minority parties and from universities and intellectuals in general, alarmed the leadership. There was widespread unrest and even direct opposition to the Party. Consequently, the movement for reform was transformed into an anti-rightist campaign and when Mao's speech *On Contradictions Among the People* was published in June 1957 significant changes were introduced into the text. In particular, criteria were spelt out for distinguishing 'poisonous weeds' from 'fragrant flowers'. These were:

1. Words and deeds should help unite, and not divide, the people of all our nationalities.
2. They should be beneficial, and not harmful, to socialist transformation and socialist construction.
3. They should help to consolidate, and not undermine or weaken, the people's democratic dictatorship.

4. They should help to consolidate, and not undermine, or weaken, democratic centralism.
5. They should help to strengthen, and not shake off or weaken, the leadership of the Communist Party.
6. They should be beneficial, and not harmful, to international socialist unity and the unity of the peace-loving people of the world.[30]

The purpose of these criteria was described, without any apparent irony, as being 'to foster free discussion of questions among the people'. But the Hundred Flowers movement was at an end.

The Cultural Revolution

The same process of an attempted shake-up of the bureaucracy through mass participation later brought under strict Party control is visible in greater detail in the Cultural Revolution. Formally, the Cultural Revolution began in the summer of 1965 with a controversy over Wu Han's play *Hai Jui Dismissed From Office* which had as its hero a sixteenth-century civil servant who criticised the Emperor himself. The Maoists saw this as a reference to P'eng Teh-huai and the criticisms he had made of the Great Leap Forward. The campaign culminated in the dismissal of P'eng Chen, Mayor of Peking and Wu Han's superior, in June 1966. It demonstrated that Mao wished to increase the impact of his own ideas after his partial retreat in the early 1960s and that he had become disillusioned with some of the normal Party channels. The Cultural Revolution proper began in August 1966 in the universities with a mass campaign to eliminate what were seen as 'Rightists', to re-emphasise the importance of Mao's thought, to lessen specialisation, and substantially to restrict the role of examinations. The work teams sent out by the Party apparatus to direct these campaigns ran into difficulties from the staff on the one side and the students on the other. A good deal of chaos ensued and the work teams were withdrawn. Liu Shao-ch'i and Deng Xiaoping were later blamed for this failure.

At the Plenum of the Central Committee in August 1966 it became clear that Mao and Lin Piao were advocating a return to the policies of 1958–59 in the face of opposition from Liu and Deng. The Maoists won and a decision was taken to promote mass mobilisation outside the ordinary Party channels. The aim was to attack 'those within the Party who are in authority and are taking the capitalist road'.[31] The vehicle was to be the movement known as the Red Guards.

The Red Guard movement was launched in the context of a struggle at the top of the Party but gradually acquired its own momentum. The Red

Guards were students whose lack of experience of pre-Communist misery made them readier to criticise present policies and whose absence from the universities would not be immediately damaging to the economy. They organised huge demonstrations in Peking; they went on long journeys in teams to help in production and participate in the autumn harvest; and wherever they went they emphasised the importance of the masses who had to make themselves felt, freedom to criticise, opposition to all conservatives, and the right to rebel. The one guideline to all this ferment was loyalty to the Party and to Mao Zedong's thought.

The chief target of criticism was Liu Shao-chi'i, who was accused of having too monolithic a view of the Party, of not being sufficiently opposed to the Soviet Union, and of putting too much emphasis on 'expertness' and in general encouraging the profit motive and material incentives. Liu, referred to as 'China's Krushchev', was pictured as the embodiment of all the Cultural Revolution was opposed to and the polar opposite to Mao Zedong's thought.

Some of the Red Guard movement was spontaneous, but most could not have been effected without the Party's help in arranging free transport, providing board and lodging, and so on. However, when the Red Guards attacked the offices of Party officials and tried to involve the workers in their demands, the movement began to get out of control and there was widespread dissension over tactics among the Guards themselves.

Mao took the responsibility for this stage of affairs: 'I am responsible for this havoc', he told Party cadres, but reassured them that no one was intending their overthrow. Nevertheless, in January 1967, he added fuel to the movement by launching the slogan 'seize power'. This slogan implied the establishment of the new forms of political power to replace the old ones, although the references to Marx and Lenin were somewhat misleading, as what the Maoists had in mind was not the replacement of one *class* by another. The decisive turning-point occurred in China's largest industrial conurbation, Shanghai. Here the decisions of December 1966 to extend the Cultural Revolution to the workers led to widespread unrest. A wave of strikes and agitation for higher wages and better working conditions had broken out by the end of 1966. There had been talk of the Paris Commune as the model to be followed and in early February a Shanghai People's Commune was established. However, when its leaders journeyed to Peking they found that Mao had tempered his approval:

> Many places have not applied to the centre to establish People's Commune. A document has been issued by the Centre saying that no place, apart from Shanghai, may set up People's Commune. The

Chairman is of the opinion that Shanghai ought to make a change and transform itself into a revolutionary committee, or a city committee or a city people's committee. Communes are too weak when it comes to suppressing counter-revolution.[32]

An alternative version of the same comment was given as follows:

If all [of these organisations] are changed into communes, what will we do with the Party? Where will we put the Party? In the committees set up under a commune, there will be members who belong to the Party, and others who don't. Where will we put the Party committee? ... There has to be a nucleus. It doesn't matter what it's called, it is all right to call it a Communist Party, it is all right to call it a social-democratic party, it is all right to call it a social-democratic workers' party, it is all right to call it a Kuomintang, it is all right to call it the I-kuan-tao, but in any case there has to be a party. In a commune there has to be a party; can the commune replace the Party?[33]

The effect of the Maoists in the struggle against the Party apparatus was the establishment of Revolutionary Committees from the provincial level downwards. They were composed of representatives of the masses, of the People's Liberation Army, and of 'good' cadres. Their task was to channel the upsurge of popular feeling into political ends and curb the merely 'economist' demands of the workers. Mao described the Committees as follows:

The basic experience of Revolutionary Committee is this – they are threefold: they have representatives of revolutionary cadres, representatives of the armed forces, and representatives of the revolutionary masses. This forms a revolutionary 'three-in-one' combination. The Revolutionary Committee should exercise unified leadership, eliminate redundant or overlapping administrative structures, follow the policy of better troops and simpler administration and organise a revolutionised leading group which keeps in contact with the masses.[34]

The formation of these Committees throughout 1967 and 1968 was closely supervised by the Party's Central Committee and by the People's Liberation Army and occurred amidst the clashes of different Left groups which often resulted in fighting that was only contained by army intervention. The result was to guarantee a preponderance of the military and reliable cadres over the mass organisations. Although the mass organisations helped considerably to rejuvenate the Party administration, the Chairmen of the Provincial Committees were invariably military men or old party cadres. The PLA played an increasing role in setting up the new administration, sometimes in alliance with the Red rebels and sometimes against them. The shaking up of the old bureaucracy and the mutual hostility and transitory nature of many of the rebel groupings left a power vacuum that could only be filled by the PLA, which was a fairly cohesive and unified body. It almost always acted as a moderating force against the students and mass movements which were out of key with the PLA's sense of discipline and order. In Wuhan, for example, the army actively suppressed the group that enjoyed the support of the influential Central Committee of the Cultural Revolution – a state of affairs that was only resolved by the personal intervention of Chou En-lai. Nevertheless, under Lin Piao, the PLA generally enjoyed Mao's confidence. As early as 1960 he had held up the army as a model of ideology and purity. At the height of the crisis in December 1967 the Central Committee decided that 'all past directives concerning the army's non-involvement' should be annulled, and that 'when the proletarian revolutionaries are still unable to control the situation and the protection of the People's Liberation Army is called for, the armed forces should at once enforce military control'.[35] It is significant that the proportion of military members on the Provincial Party Committees increased during the subsequent two years to more than 50 per cent. Finally, in the summer of 1968, the Red Guards were disbanded and large numbers of students and intellectuals were dispersed through the countryside.

With the Cultural Revolution proper at an end, the Ninth Congress in 1969 re-established Party control. The delegates were appointed from above and not elected. The new Central Committee was increased to 279 members, only 53 of whom had belonged to previous Central Committees. Forty per cent of its members were military and there were very few from the Red Guards. The new constitution increased the period between Congresses to five years and thus placed more power in the hands of the Politbureau. The swift fall of Mao's officially designated successor Lin Piao in 1971 and the campaign against the Gang of Four in 1976 marked the re-emergence of many of the elements – Deng Xiaoping, for example – previously disgraced in the Cultural Revolution. The career of Deng and the dispute with the Gang of Four demonstrated how the resolution of inner party disputes is confined to the very top of the party apparatus and the masses only subsequently made aware of the issues in terms of the crudest sort of misrepresentation and vilification.

Historical materialism

One element in the Chinese version of Marxism that is emphasised by the Cultural Revolution is the importance attached by the Chinese to human and moral factors. As against the general underlining by Marx of the determining role of 'the economic' and the dependency of the base on the superstructure, Maoism involves a rehabilitation of the superstructure common to many variants of twentieth-century Marxism: Gramsci, Stalinism, and so on. Traditionally, there had been a very strong emphasis in China on moral and political attitudes. These sorts of views more than any other were held to define a society and give it its particular character. It is in keeping with this tradition that the events of 1966–9 should be described as a *Cultural* Revolution. The strong emphasis on ideology in the Cultural Revolution implied that the struggle was a superstructural one and that the attack on Liu Shao-chi'i and 'capitalist roaders' referred more to ideas and relations between people than any specific mode of production. In his criticism of Stalin's book *Economic Problems of Socialism in the USSR*, Mao wrote:

> From the beginning to the end of this book Stalin does not say a word about the superstructure. He gives no thought to man, he sees things but not people ... The Soviets are concerned only with the relations of production, they do not pay attention to the superstructure, they do not pay attention to politics, they do not pay attention to the role of the people. Without a Communist movement, it is impossible to reach Communism.[36]

Many Chinese Communists had taken the view that only the long and arduous development of the productive forces of China could afford an adequate basis for the subsequent development of socialist culture. Mao considered that a revolution in the sphere of ideas effected by an intense inculcation of socialist attitudes could hasten the speed of economic development. Developments in the superstructure, in other words, could not only proceed parallel to, they could also themselves condition, the development of the base. It is relations between people and the subjective side of the revolutionary process that are summed up in the Maoist slogan 'Politics in Command'. This attitude was strengthened by the necessity of arousing to an awareness of their condition and some coordinated action the vast mass of the peasantry sunk in a centuries-old passivity.

As far back as his experience in the late 1920s on the Chingkanshan, Mao had been faced with a lack of correspondence between society and

ideology: the kind of lumpenpeasantry that then composed the majority of his soldiers had to undergo intensive political training before the
Red Army proper emerged. This gave some basis to the view that 'class'
was a subjective notion in Mao's thought in that it referred more to a
person's attitude than to his or her social origin. This view was only reinforced by the fact that, although the Party constantly used the term
'proletariat', it had no specific class reference. The substitution of the
Party for an absent proletariat necessarily meant an emphasis on ideology
uncharacteristic of classic Marxism.

This ideological emphasis was often moral in tone. Confucianism had
always linked morality with politics in a unified and intolerant system
of thought. It is striking how moral criteria are intermingled in Maoist
documents with more strictly Marxist categories. As Schram has said:

> Consider the definition which Mao put forward in the 1950s for the
> so-called 'five bad elements', still used today. Landlords, rich peasant,
> counter-revolutionaries, bad elements and rightists. Two of these cat-
> egories are sociological, two political and one moral. Mao did not
> appear to see any contradiction or problem in lumping them all
> together. Did he not perhaps see the revolution as the work of pro-
> letarians, peasants *and* good men? Does not all the available evidence
> suggest that Mao in fact shared with Liu Shaoch'i the very Chinese
> and indeed Confucian notion that it is impossible to separate the
> inner moral world of the individual from his outward behaviour and
> from the political realm as a whole.[37]

Indeed, sometimes the subjective side is given pre-eminence. In a famous
passage written in 1938, Mao had said:

> Weapons are an important factor in war, but not the decisive factor,
> it is people, not things, that are decisive. The contest of strength is
> not only a contest of military and economic power, but also a contest
> of human power and morale. Military and economic power is neces-
> sarily wielded by people.[38]

Hence, particularly during the Cultural Revolution, class struggle was
said to take place in the individual's consciousness which veered between
collective and private interests. Hence, too, the incessant praise of the
spirit of self-sacrifice, the fanatical rejection of material incentives, and
the general asceticism and puritanism that pervaded Chinese society.

The Sino-Soviet dispute

A certain amount of tension had always characterised Sino-Soviet relations. The forty years of armed struggle and mass mobilisation of the Chinese peasantry was a very different prelude to revolutionary power from Russian pre-revolutionary experience. As the only successful Communist Party, the Soviet Union was the inevitable model for the Chinese Communists. But at the same time, the inconsistent and sometimes disastrous instructions coming from Moscow in the late 1920s and early 1930s instilled a distrust of the Comintern – particularly in Mao, who was one of its chief victims. Mao had come to power in 1935 in opposition to the '28 Bolsheviks' who had the support of the Comintern. Moreover, Stalin had underestimated the importance of the CCP in the 1930s and thus afforded it more possibilities for independence than most other Communist parties.

The Sino-Soviet Treaty of Friendship, Alliance and Mutual Assistance of February 1950 gave China the formal support of the centre of the world Communist movement together with considerable economic assistance. The First Five Year Plan followed the Soviet precedent fairly closely with regard to priorities and methods of management. The Russians gave technical assistance in a number of large-scale projects and also long-term credits. It was most useful in starting some sectors virtually from scratch – oil, electronics – and in training Chinese technical personnel in the Soviet Union.

The Twentieth Party Congress in the Soviet Union, with its condemnation of Stalin and the personality cult, and endorsement of peaceful co-existence had obvious implications for Sino-Soviet relations. However ambivalent Mao may have felt towards Stalin, the condemnation of the personality cult obviously affected Mao's own position. At first, Chinese reaction was moderate, Stalin was said to have been 'a great Marxist-Leninist, yet at the same time a Marxist-Leninist who committed several gross errors without recognising them for what they were'.[39] And on the personality cult, the Chinese conclusion was:

> Marxism-Leninism acknowledges that leaders play an important role in history. The people and their Party need outstanding personalities who can represent the interests and the will of the people and stand in the forefront of the historical struggles to lead them. To deny the role of the individual, the role of the vanguard and leaders, is completely wrong.[40]

The Chinese approved of Moscow's reconciliation with Tito and of the Russians' action in Hungary in 1956, and even received sample atomic bombs from Russia in 1957.

However, with the development of the Russian policy of *détente* – symbolised by the Krushchev–Eisenhower meeting at Camp David in September 1959 – a split became unavoidable. The Chinese were exceedingly sensitive to the issue of *détente*: the history of their revolution was one of international struggle much more than that of Russia. In general, the Russian policy of *détente* meant a lessening of pressure on the United States just when the Americans were extending their influence in the Pacific. More specifically, it meant severely limiting the assistance the Russians were prepared to give to the Chinese on the issue of Taiwan and admission to the United Nations. The Soviets also pursued a policy of neutrality in the Sino-Indian border dispute of 1959. The consequent diplomatic isolation of the Chinese and constant affront to national pride seemed destined to continue indefinitely. *Détente*, and the emphasis on peaceful coexistence, meant a lessening of China's influence in world affairs as nations tended to be evaluated in terms of their economic wealth. If the CPSU succeeded in its aim of enjoying a leadership proportional to its economic power then China would remain a very junior partner. No doubt also the Chinese feared that Soviet policies might lead to the growth of liberalisation in the Soviet camp, a liberalisation that China herself could ill afford after the comparative failures of the Hundred Flowers campaign and the Great Leap Forward.

The more significant origins of the Sino-Soviet split, however, lay in different models for the achievement of socialism. The First Five Year Plan had made the Chinese realise that Soviet aid was too costly and too concentrated on giant heavy industrial enterprises that were out of key with the rest of the Chinese economy. It was not only that the Russians were very tight-fisted in their aid (Mao talked of negotiations with Stalin on this issue as being like getting blood out of a stone): the Chinese felt that they were being kept in a position of economic inferiority and were not really benefiting from it. 'Soviet products', Mao said, 'are heavy, crude, high-priced, and they always keep something back.'[41] Beginning with the 1955 drive towards raising agricultural productivity by means of almost total cooperativisation, China had begun to move from the Soviet model – the only one available to them in 1949. In contrast to the Soviet Union, there was an emphasis on the peasants and the countryside that was equal to, and sometimes greater than, that on heavy industry. The continued application of the Soviet model would have meant creating an unacceptable gulf between city and country. The peasants were, after all, the makers of the revolution. They could not be relegated simply to a source of surplus to be invested in heavy industrial development. Therefore, in order to avoid the 'natural' alternative of a Bukharinist accumulation through small peasant plots, immense efforts were necessary to push the peasants towards socialism. Hence the campaigns for cooperatives and communes, and the Cultural Revolution itself. Sino-Soviet relations were not helped by the ridicule poured on the Commune experiment by, for example, Krushchev.

The increasing divergence in their respective paths of development led the Chinese to formulate a sustained critique of the Soviet Union in terms of the restoration of capitalism. The view of the Soviet Union as capitalist (first formulated in the mid-1960s) was particularly associated with Mao rather than, say, with Liu Shao-ch'i. (One of the main points of the Cultural Revolution was to get rid of those who favoured better relations with the Soviet Union.) Although the description 'capitalist' often amounted to little more than a term of abuse, what the Chinese had in mind seems to have been as follows. Firstly, a new privileged stratum had been allowed to emerge in post-Stalin Russia. It consisted of Party officials, civil servants, intellectuals, etc., who could even collectively be described as a 'bourgeois dictatorship'. This had been made possible by the restoration of the market as a criterion of profitability, material incentives, and huge wage differentials. There had been an accompanying encouragement of private plots in the countryside. Doctrinally, class anatagonism was said to be at an end (in that the relations of production were completely in tune with the development of the productive forces), the dictatorship of the proletariat was over, and there existed a 'state of the whole people' and 'Party of the whole people'. Immediately after the Soviet invasion of Czechoslovakia in 1968, the Chinese began to call the Soviet Union 'social-imperialists' as well as 'capitalists': a view exacerbated by the Sino-Soviet border dispute of 1969.

It is difficult to find in Chinese documents any sustained analysis supporting these views. They are open to obvious objections. Firstly, most of the phenomena under discussion had their origin in the 1930s and cannot be attributed to a post-Stalin degeneration. Secondly, the Marxist criterion for the existence of a social class is its relation to the means of production and not to distribution. The existence of privilege and large wage differentials did not give rise in the Soviet Union to a process of capitalist accumulation. It is one thing to say that state ownership of the means of production is only a necessary and not a sufficient condition for socialism, but quite another to say that the difference between capitalism and socialism lies in the relative control that various sections of the population exercise over the distribution of the surplus product. The same is true of the description of the Soviet Union as 'imperialist'. In the terminology of Marx and Lenin, this term refers to the economic domination of one country over another as dictated by the needs of a capitalist economy. Soviet 'imperialism' was more directly political and military, and certainly not subject to the same economic imperatives as in the West. It could be added that the idea of a peaceful transition from socialism *back* to capitalism is as little in keeping with Marxism as the reverse process.

One of the consequences of the Sino-Soviet split was that China's foreign policy underwent a radical transformation. The view that the Soviet Union was a greater enemy than the United States had far-reaching consequences. From the early 1970s the Chinese tended to view the world more in terms of two superpowers seeking world domination than in traditional Left/Right terms. Indeed, China had a foreign policy well to the right of the old Soviet Union. In the early 1970s it seemed that the more 'radical' the internal policies of the Chinese government, the less socialist was its foreign policy. Following Lin Piao's classic formula that the 'cities of the world' (North America and Western Europe) would be encircled and conquered by the 'countryside' of Asia, Africa, and Latin America, Chinese aid had been given to many revolutionary movements around the world during the 1960s. But with the emergence of the view that the Soviet Union was an imperialist power, Chinese foreign policy took on a novel form. China supported, both morally and economically, armed repression by the Pakistani military government of Leftist dissidents prior to the establishment of Bangladesh. In April 1971 they supported similar measures by the Bandaranaike government in Ceylon. This change in policy was symbolised by the visit of President Nixon to Peking only two months after the mining of Haiphong Harbour. Peking was quick to recognise the military junta that overthrew President Allende in Chile and even gave it limited moral support. During the Civil War in Angola the Chinese found themselves supporting the CIA-backed FNLA against the Moscow-orientated Marxists. These extraordinary attitudes can only be explained on the far-fetched assumption that Soviet 'social imperialism' was the greatest threat to socialist revolution the world over.

Maoism: a conclusion

Maoism is a synthesis of Leninism and China's economic backwardness with the addition of certain traditional Chinese ideas. For all its 'Sinification' Maoism remained imbued by central Marxist concepts of class analysis, working-class leadership, the idea of history moving through stages, and a social theory infused by the concepts of dialectical materialism and contradiction.

The most typical aspects of Maoism are:

Firstly, China has aimed to develop the agricultural sector in harmony with the industrial sector. The peasantry were thus not the victims of development policy, but mobilised in order to achieve it. China has therefore been able to be a model for most Third-World countries, as the Chinese Communist Party was indisputably a peasant party and the peasantry formed the vast majority of the population of Third-World countries.

Secondly, Maoism has emphasised the importance of consciousness. For Marxism is the doctrine of the *proletariat* and it has therefore been necessary to instil a proletarian or social consciousness *into* the peasantry. The telescoping of the capitalist phase – both of development and of ideology – into the socialist phase has meant the enhancement of this process. Hence the *Cultural* Revolution.

Thirdly, Mao's doctrines on guerrilla war, evolved in the 1930s, are based on the active cooperation of the peasantry and have had widespread influence in Third-World countries.

Fourthly, China has evolved forms of anti-bureaucratic struggle that were implicit in *On the Correct Handling of Contradiction Among the People* and put into practice in the Cultural Revolution, although always ultimately under Party control.

Lastly, Maoism involves a moral, puritanical emphasis on thrift and devotion to the common good that is reminiscent of Rousseau.

Of the more specifically Marxist elements in Mao's thought little remains in China – though it has not lost its power to inspire guerilla movements such as that operating in neighbouring Nepal. Those young intellectuals formed in the Maoism of the 1960s and 1970s and wishing to maintain a critical spirit tend to have split in two directions:

the first found its way from Marx through Hegel back to the Enlightenment and French Revolution, and from that starting point developed an independent path towards modern Western constitutional democracy and human rights. The second followed the thought of Marx and Lenin to trace out the original aspirations of the Paris Commune and the October Revolution, and then worked its way forward through the history of the labour movement, rediscovering Bernstein, Kautsky, Trotsky, Bukharin and Luxemburg, to the reformist currents in the Soviet Union and Eastern Europe whose 'revisionism' Mao had denounced, and subsequent Eurocommunists like Berlinguer and Carillo, and ended up – perhaps without much conscious intent – as a strain of social democratic thought.[42]

These ideas began to flourish during the 'cultural fever' of the 1980s, only to receive a severe setback with the Tiananmen massacre of 1989. They find themselves at odds with the central direction of the Chinese Communist Party (CCP) as it grapples with the economic and social dislocation produced by the rapid expansion of capitalist relations of production. The crucial turning point here was in 1992 when the 14th Congress of the CCP formally proclaimed the goal of establishing a 'socialist market economy' – while at the same time Deng Xiaoping, the architect of this policy, forbade any theoretical discussion of it for at least three years. In 2000 China's President Ziang Zemin proclaimed the theory of the 'three representatives' to be the official ideology of the CCP. According to this doctrine, the CCP 'represents' the most advanced productive forces, the most progressive culture, and the interest of the whole nation. With the welcoming of private entrepreneurs as members of the Communist Party, it was clear that the first was likely to take precedence over the third and the process has continued apace under the presidency of Hu Jintao.

Asian Marxism outside China

The success of the Chinese revolution meant that the Chinese Communists had the space to deploy their ideas even before their accession to power. The same is true, to an extent much more limited by war and international power politics, of Vietnam, North Korea and Kampuchea. Elsewhere, Marxists in Asia have devoted themselves to socio-economic analyses of their societies and developing (unsuccessful) strategies to gain political power.

The basic question confronting Marxists in Asia was how to adapt the Marxian doctrine of historical materialism to their societies. This doctrine had seen societies as moving through various stages of modes of production with Communism as the final result. Marx himself had talked of an 'Asiatic' mode of production: 'in broad outlines Asiatic, ancient, feudal, and modern bourgeois modes of production can be designated as progressive epochs in the economic formation of society'.[43] What Marx meant by this was that the necessity of providing vast public works to achieve satisfactory irrigation had led to a highly centralized government built on a sub-stratum of self-contained villages and the entire absence of private property in land. But however interesting such conception may be historically, it had little influence on Asian Marxism, which operated largely within the analytical parameters of historical development laid down by Lenin and Stalin. Thus the question confronting Asian Marxists was whether their societies were analysable as predominantly feudal in the European sense.

These rather broad considerations had more immediate political implications. Put simply, would one revolution or two be needed to achieve socialism? As noted above, this question was answered very differently by the Chinese Communists in the 1950s from the views they propounded in the 1930s. In Vietnam, the leading Party theoretician Truong Chinh held that the feudal landowners and the small indigenous bourgeoisie were dependent on the French colonial power, and that therefore the national liberation struggle could harmonise nationalism and socialism. In Japan the dispute over the nature of the Meiji Restoration led to a division between those who considered Japan already capitalist, and therefore in need of a single revolution, as argued by Yamakama, and the Japanese Communist Party which held that bourgeois democratic revolution was first necessary to overcome the 'feudal' elements still powerful in Japanese society. Marxist economics had become highly influential in post-war Japanese universities and in this context the most interesting work to come out of this controversy over stages of development was that of Kozo Uno. He elaborated what he called a 'pure' theory of the economic laws of capitalist production, drawn from Marx's *Capital*. The very abstract nature of these laws, however, meant that there were some aspects of any real economy to which they did not conform. In particular, they did not govern the specific nature of Japanese agriculture and class relations which had to be analysed empirically.[44] In Indonesia, which contained the biggest Communist Party in the non-Communist world and a relatively substantial proletariat, feudalism and proletarian revolution could be directly combined. As D.N. Aidit, the most prominent post-war leader of the PKI wrote: 'The Indonesian proletariat is exploited by three forms of brutal exploitation, that is, imperialism, capitalism and feudalism.'[45] Here the successive stages of orthodox Marxism are radically telescoped.

Historical periodisation and revolutionary strategy obviously depended on a class analysis of Asian society. Crucial was the role allotted to the peasantry. One of the reasons for the success in West Bengal and eventually in Kerala of the Communist Party (Marxist), which broke away from the Communist Party of India in 1964, was that it merged the thinking of Lenin and Mao to give equal prominence to the working class and poor peasants in its campaigns; and, in a more academic vein, Indian Marxists have produced an impressive literature debating the nature of the mode of production in agriculture.[46] In Vietnam, Ho Chi Minh highlighted the revolutionary potential of the peasantry before Mao did. And in Kampuchea the Communist Party actually emptied its urban areas of workers and set about transforming all its inhabitants into peasants. A corollary of this was a reluctance to describe post-revolutionary governments as dictatorships of the proletariat and a tendency in China pre-1949 and Vietnam to talk more vaguely of 'the people'. Opinions have also differed on the persistence of class struggle in post-revolutionary society. Vietnamese Communists – whose leadership has been remarkably consensual – disapproved of Mao's views on this, rejected the Cultural Revolution, and, on this point if on few others, sided with Deng Xiaoping and the post-1978 rejection in China of class struggle as a principal contradiction. Indeed, in North Korea class struggle was claimed to have been completely eliminated.

The role of the party has proved equally problematic. Since Asian Marxism has been of the Marxist-Leninist variety, the party was conceived as a vanguard leading the various interests that it represented. In this respect Vietnam has proved the most orthodox. In Indonesia, the Communist Party in the 1950s adopted a Gramscian stance and promoted itself as an ideological force. In China in the 1960s, by contrast, the Cultural Revolution produced a violent anti-party reaction, whereas in North Korea the party was said to be the creation of its individual leader Kim Il Sung.

The espousal of violence as the midwife of revolution has depended on political culture and the degree of economic development. In China, North Korea, Vietnam and Kampuchea, careful thinking about guerrilla warfare contributed to the success of revolution. Non-violent approaches failed to yield political power, except in the Indian states of Kerala and West Bengal. The attempt to transfer Maoist guerrilla tactics to India in the Naxalite movement of 1967, under the charismatic leadership of Mazumdar, was a failure.[47] The Naxalites never managed to draw on nationalist sentiments, and capitalism proved to be too firmly entrenched in the Indian countryside to be overturned by guerrilla action. The Communist Party of India itself had embraced the doctrine of peaceful transition to socialism as early as 1958, following their victory in Kerala the previous year. The preamble to the party's new constitution set as a goal the achievement of 'full democracy by peaceful means' and represented 'a deep bow to the non-violent and democratic traditions of India'.[48] Similarly the post-war Japanese Communist Party adopted the parliamentary road to socialism, and Indonesian Marxists in the years before their brutal suppression in 1965 evolved a strategy for infiltrating and transforming the state by peaceful means. With the biggest Communist Party in the non-Communist world, Indonesian Marxism could appear as the ideology of a counter-elite who, as well as being relatively hospitable to the more left-leaning elements in Islam, held that the state had a dual aspect – pro-people as well as anti-people. The struggle for ideological hegemony could emphasise the pro-people element in the state and gradually transform its nature.[49]

If there is one striking characteristic of Asian Marxism, it is the emphasis on the superstructure. It is, of course, true that Western Marxism typically re-evaluated the force of ideology and culture as compared with the Marxism of the Second International. But this happened in a context where the leading Marxist theoreticians were increasingly isolated from Marxist political movements.[50] In Asia, however, the theoretical re-evaluation of the superstructure was achieved within the Marxist movement itself. In Mao's China it was felt that the socialisation of the economic base of society had progressed faster than the consciousness of the people, which was still imbued with conservative attitudes inherited from pre-revolutionary society. Constant struggle was necessary to keep the ideological superstructure abreast of the economic base, in contrast to Mao's successors who have returned to the more traditional Marxist view on the development of the productive forces. In Vietnam, one of the major factors making for the success of the revolution was the ability of Ho Chi Minh and his followers to imbue their movement with strong feelings of patriotism. Indigenous landowners and the bourgeoisie had so compromised themselves with the colonial power that the anti-imperialist nationalist revolution and the social land-reforming revolution were identical. In North Korea, the emphasis was on the independence, creativity and consciousness of humankind – all factors necessary for the creation of a new society – and the inspired individual leadership of, for example, Kim Il Sung to guide this creativity in the right direction. Here the Marxist view of the centrality of material factors for understanding and transforming society has been abandoned.[51] Even more so was this the case in Kampuchea under Pol Pot, where two views combined to form a lethal cocktail.[52] The first, taken from a crude dialectical materialism, was that all things were interrelated; the second was an extreme form of voluntarism which held, given the correct consciousness, that any obstacle could be overcome. Thus no misfortune could ever really be an accident: things being interconnected, there was always a cause and this resided in the individual's refusal to effect the necessary change in his/her

consciousness. The added chauvinism and sectarianism which character-
ized the Community Party of Kampuchea produced an ideology which,
both in its substance and in the importance attributed to it, was very far
removed from the mainstream Marxism perhaps best displayed by the
gradualist Gramscian approach of the Communist Party in Indonesia.

As Marxism travelled east, it inevitably east, it inevitably underwent
a profound transformation. Marxism was originally devised as a critical tool for dealing with capitalist societies. In Asia, the societies in
which it was successful were far from capitalist. Revisions of the traditional Marxist periodisation of history were essential, as well as a most
un-Marxist emphasis on ideology and consciousness. From a Marxist
point of view, these revisions and distortions are connected with premature attempts to construct socialism. As a distinguished Chinese scholar
has recently claimed: 'According to Marx's theory of the social formation, the history of those so-called socialist countries is nothing but the
history of societies from pre-capitalism.'[53] Asian Marxism thus appears,
in a compelling example of Hegel's irony of history, as a modernizing
precursor of capitalism.

Notes

1. *The Agrarian Reform Law of the People's Republic of China* (Peking, 1952) p. 88.
2. Mao Zedong, 'On the Co-operative Transformation of Agriculture', *Selected Works*, vol. 5, pp. 201f.
3. See K. Marx, *The Eighteenth Brumaire*, in *Selected Writings* ed. D. McLellan (Oxford, 2000) pp. 346ff.
4. Mao Zedong, 'On the Co-operative Transformation of Agriculture', *Selected Works*, vol. 5, pp. 196f.
5. Cited in S. Schram, *The Political Thought of Mao Tse-tung*, 2nd edn (Harmondsworth, 1969) pp. 253f.
6. See further: Mao Zedong, *A Critique of Soviet Economics* (New York and London, 1977).
7. Mao Zedong, 'On Coalition Government', *Selected Works*, vol. 3, p. 283.
8. See, however, for Mao's earlier view that classes would disappear, *Mao Tse-tung Unrehearsed*, ed. S. Schram (Harmondsworth, 1974) p. 269.
9. Mao Zedong, 'On the Correct Handling of Contradictions Among the People', *Selected Works*, vol. 5, pp. 385f.
10. Ibid., p. 386.
11. Ibid., p. 393.
12. It is impossible to determine exactly how many lost their lives in the Communist victory. Estimates vary from 135,000 to several million. See S. Schram, *Mao Tse-tung* (Harmondsworth, 1966) p. 267.
13. Mao Zedong, 'Sixty Articles in Work Methods', quoted by S. Schram in *Mao Tse-tung in the Scales of History*, ed. D. Wilson (Cambridge, 1977) p. 57.
14. Ibid., p. 58.

15. Mao Zedong, 'Talk on Question of Philosophy', *Mao Tse-tung Unrehearsed*, ed. S. Schram (Harmondsworth, 1974) pp. 226ff.
16. B. Schwartz, 'The Philosopher', in *Mao Tse-tung in the Scales of History*, ed. D. Wilson, p. 24.
17. See further, I. Deutscher, 'Maoism: Its Origins and Outlook' in *Revolution and Class Struggle*, ed. R. Blackburn (London, 1977).
18. Mao Zedong, 'Rectify the Party's Style of Work', *Selected Works*, vol. 3, p. 44.
19. Mao Zedong, 'Some Questions Concerning Methods of Leadership', *Selected Works*, vol. 3, p. 119.
20. *The Political Thought of Mao Tse-tung*, ed. S. Schram (New York, 1963) p. 253.
21. *Mao Tse-tung Unrehearsed*, ed. S. Schram, p. 164.
22. *The Case of P'eng Teh-huai* (Union Research Institute, Hong Kong, 1968) p. 12.
23. Mao Zedong, 'Speech at the Lusan Conference', *Mao Tse-tung Unrehearsed*, pp. 142f.
24. Quoted in J. Guillermaz, *The Chinese Communist Party in Power 1949–1976* (Folkestone, 1976) p. 242.
25. Quoted in J. Guillermaz, op. cit., p. 380.
26. See S. Schram, 'The Cultural Revolution in Historical Perspective', in *Authority, Participation and Cultural Change in China*, ed. S. Schram (Cambridge, 1973) p. 104.
27. I. Deutscher, 'Maoism: Its Origins and Outlook', in *Revolution and Class Struggle*, ed. R. Blackburn (London, 1977) p. 213.
28. Mao Zedong, 'On the Correct Handling of Contradictions Among the People', *Selected Works*, vol. 5, p. 411.
29. Ibid., p. 410.
30. Ibid., p. 412.
31. Quoted in L. Maitan, *Party, Army and Masses in China* (London and New York, 1976) p. 105.
32. *Mao Tse-tung Unrehearsed*, ed. S. Schram, p. 278.
33. Quoted in S. Schram, 'The Marxist', *Mao Tse-tung in the Scales of History*, ed. D. Wilson, p. 48.
34. Quoted in L. Maitan, *Party, Army and Masses in China*, p. 249.
35. Quoted ibid., p. 178.
36. Quoted in S. Schram, 'The Marxist', *Mao Tse-tung in the Scales of History*, ed. D. Wilson, p. 57.
37. Ibid., p. 65.
38. Mao Zedong, 'On Protracted War', *Selected Works*, vol. 2, p. 143.
39. Quoted in: J. Guillermaz, *The Chinese Communist Party in Power, 1949–1976*, p. 187.
40. Ibid., p. 188.
41. *Mao Tse-tung Unrehearsed*, ed. S. Schram, p. 199.
42. Qian Lichun, 'Refusing to Forget', in *One China, Many Paths*, ed. Chaohua Wang (London, 2003), pp. 308 ff. This whole book provides a good overview of social problems confronting contemporary China.
43. K. Marx, *Selected Writings*, ed. D. McLellan (Oxford, 2000), p. 426.
44. See K. Uno, *Principles of Political Economy: Theory of a Purely Capitalist Society* (Atlantic Highlands, 1980), and also the work of his disciple M. Itoh, *The Basic Theory of Capitalism* (London, 1988). For interesting interpretations of

Marxism currently being elaborated in Japan, see H. Uchida, *Marx for the Twenty-First Century* (London, 2006).

45. D. Aidit, *Indonesian Society and the Indonesian Revolution* (Jakarta, 1958), p. 62.
46. See, for example, V. Patnaik, *Agrarian Relations and Accumulation: The Mode of Production Debate* (Bombay, 1989).
47. See further the comprehensive account of Mohan Ram, 1971.
48. S. Gupta, *Communism in Indian Politics* (New York, 1972), p. 52.
49. D. Aidit, *The Indonesian Revolution and the Immediate Tasks of the Communist Party of Indonesia* (Peking, 1964), pp. 42 f.
50. D. Aidit, op.cit., pp. 44 ff.
51. On the peculiarities of North Korea, see B. Cumings, *North Korea: Another Country* (Chicago, 2003).
52. See further Ben Kiernan, 'Kampuchea as Stalinism', in Mackerras and Knight, p. 232.
53. Z. Duan, *Marx's Theory of Social Formation* (Aldershot, 1996), p. 126.

Further reading

Note. For further reading and a bibliography on Mao Zedong, see pp. 231ff.

Chinese Communism in power

On the first decade and a half of Chinese Communism, there is an excellent collection of contemporary documents in Schurmann and Schell's *Communist China*. The initial impact of Communism on a single village is detailed in Hinton's now classic *Fanshen*. For an account of the early years in industry, see Brugger's *Democracy and Organisation in the Chinese Industrial Enterprise*. For Mao's break with Soviet economic policy, see his *Critique of Soviet Economics* and the commentary in the book by Corrigan *et al., For Mao*. The second volumes of Suyin's biography of Mao, entitled *Wind in the Tower*, and of Guillermaz's study of the Party deal with this period. Schurmann's lengthy *Ideology and Organisation in Communist China* is well worth the effort required. MacFarquhar's *China Under Mao* is a comprehensive collection of articles from the *China Quarterly*.

The Cultural Revolution

Two good short introductions, highly favourable to the Maoist point of view, are Robinson's *The Cultural Revolution in China* and Hinton's *Turning Point in China*. For a different point of view, see Maitan's semi-Trotskyist account in *Party, Army and Masses in China* and Halliday's substantial review of Maitan, 'Marxist Analysis and Post-Revolutionary China'. Milton and Schurmann's *People's China* contains a comprehensive collection of documents. The economic background is well dealt with in Wheelwright and MacFarlane's *The Chinese Road to Socialism*. See also

Van Ginneken's *The Rise and Fall of Lin Piao*. Finally, Schram's collection, *Authority, Participation and Cultural Change in China* is excellent, the editor's own hundred-page contribution being perhaps the best general introduction to the Cultural Revolution.

Asian Marxism outside China

Mackerras and Knight provide a good overall survey. Joshi is interesting on India. On Pol Pot see Short, and Cumings is informative on North Korea. The best theoretical work is being done in Japan: see Kuroda's recent survey and Uchida's excellent collection.

Bibliography

Chinese Communism in power

Jack Belden, *China Shakes the World* (New York, 1971).
William Brugger, *Democracy and Organisation in the Chinese Industrial Enterprise: 1948–1953* (Cambridge, 1976).
J. Chesneaux, M. Bastid and M.-C. Bergère, *China from the 1911 Revolution to Liberation* (Hassocks, Sussex, 1978).
P. Corrigan *et al.*, *Socialist Construction and Marxist Theory* (New York and London, 1978).
Jacques Guillermaz, *The Chinese Communist Party in Power: 1949–1976* (Folkestone, 1976).
William Hinton, *Fanshen* (New York, 1966).
—— *Iron Oxen: A Documentary of Revolution in Chinese Farming* (New York, 1971).
Christopher Howe, *Employment and Economic Growth in Urban China: 1949–1957* (Cambridge, 1971).
James Chieh Hsiung (ed.), *The Logic of 'Maoism': Critiques and Explication* (New York, 1974).
Chalmers A. Johnson, *Ideology and Politics in Contemporary China* (Seattle, 1973).
Stanley Karnow, *Mao and China: From Revolution to Revolution* (London, 1973).
Roderick MacFarquhar (ed.), *China Under Mao: Politics Takes Command* (Cambridge, Mass., 1966).
Franz Schurmann, *Ideology and Organisation in Communist China* (Berkeley, 1966).
Franz Schurmann and Orville Schell (eds), *Communist China: Revolutionary Reconstruction and International Confrontation, 1949–1966* (London, 1967).
Mark Selden, *The Yenan Way in Revolutionary China* (Cambridge, Mass., 1972).
Edgar Snow, *The Long Revolution* (New York, 1973).
Han Suyin, *Wind in the Tower: Mao Tse-tung and the Chinese Revolution, 1949–1975* (London, 1976).
Ezra Vogel, *Canton Under Communism: Programs and Politics in a Provincial Capital, 1949–1968* (New York, 1969).

The Cultural Revolution

Richard Baum, *Prelude to Revolution: Mao, the Party and the Peasant Question, 1962–1966* (New York, 1975).

P.H. Chang, *Radicals and Radical Ideology in China's Cultural Revolution* (New York, 1973).

Jaap Van Ginneken, *The Rise and Fall of Lin Piao* (London, 1976).

Fred Halliday, 'Marxist Analysis and Post-Revolutionary China', *New Left Review* 100, (1976–7).

William Hinton, *Turning Point in China: An Essay on the Cultural Revolution* (New York, 1972).

K.S. Karol, *The Second Chinese Revolution* (London, 1975).

Livio Maitan, *Party, Army and Masses in China: A Marxist Interpretation of the Cultural Revolution and its Aftermath* (London and New York, 1976).

Roderick MacFarquhar, *The Origins of the Cultural Revolution: 1, Contradictions Among the People, 1956–1957* (Oxford, 1974).

David Milton, Nancy Milton, and Franz Schurmann (eds), *People's China: Social Experimentation, Politics, Entry into the World Scene, 1966–1972* (London, 1974).

Jan Myrdal, *China: The Revolution Continues* (London, 1973).

Joan Robinson, *The Cultural Revolution in China* (London, 1969).

Stuart R. Schram (ed.), *Authority, Participation and Cultural Change in China* (Cambridge, 1973).

Edgar Snow, *Red China Today* (London, 1970).

E.L. Wheelwright and Bruce MacFarlane, *The Chinese Road to Socialism: Economics of the Cultural Revolution* (New York, 1970).

China after Mao

M. Blecher, *China against the Tides: Restructuring through Revolution, Radicalism and Reform* (London, 1997).

P. Cheng (ed.), *Marxism and Capitalism in the People's Republic of China* (Lanham, 1989).

M. Chossudovsky, *Towards Capitalist Restoration? Chinese Socialism after Mao* (Basingstoke, 1986).

J. Gittings, *The Changing Face of China: From Mao to Market* (Oxford, 2005).

E. and M. Goldman (eds), *Chinese Intellectuals between State and Market* (New York, 2004).

C. Wang (ed.), *One China, Many Paths* (London, 2003).

E. Wincler (ed.), *Transition from Communism in China* (Boulder, 1999).

Y. Wong, *From Deng Xiaoping to Jiang Zemin: Two Decades of Political Reform in the People's Republic of China* (Lanham, 2005).

B. Xu, *Disenchanted Democracy: Chinese Cultural Criticism after 1989* (Ann Arbor, 1999).

Asian Marxism outside China

R. Albritton, *A Japanese Reconstruction of Marxist Theory* (London, 1986).

A. Basu, *Marxism in an Indian State: An Analytical Study of West Bengal Leftism* (Kolkata, 2003).

G. Bernstein, *Japanese Marxist: Portrait of Kawakami Hajinie 1879–1946* (Cambridge, 1990).

D. Chandler, *Brother Number One: A Political Biography of Pol Pot* (Boulder, 1999).

B. Cumings, *North Korea: Another Country* (Chicago, 2003).

W. Duiker, *Ho Chi Minh* (New York, 2000).

M. Itoh, *The Basic Theory of Capitalism* (London, 1986).

P. Joshi, *Marxism and Social Revolution in India and Other Essays* (New Delhi, 2002).

H. Kuroda, *Studies in Marxism in Postwar Japan: Main Issues in Political Economy and Materialist Outlook of History* (Tokyo, 2002).

C. Mackerras and N. Knight (eds), *Marxism in Asia* (Beckenham, 1985).

B. Martin, *Under the Loving Care of the Fatherly Leader: North Korea and the Kim Dynasty* (New York, 2004).

V. Porritt, *The Rise and Fall of Communism in Sarawak* (Clayton, 2004).

S. Seth, *Marxist Theory and Nationalist Politics: The Case of Colonial India* (New Delhi, 1995).

P. Short, *Pol Pot: History of a Nightmare* (London, 2004).

H. Uchida (ed.), *Marx for the Twenty-First Century* (London, 2006).

K. Uno, *Principles of Political Economy: Theory of a Purely Capitalist Society* (Atlantic Highlands, 1980).

17
Latin America

Introduction

Latin America had been subject to a colonial domination far longer than China. The success of the national liberation struggles of the nineteenth and twentieth centuries – largely against Spain – was blunted by the proximity of the United States with its pervasive economic influence. This influence has worked both for the speedy development of a techno-logical capitalism and for the preservation of large landed property serv-iced by landless labourers. Side by side with this there has persisted a large number of artisans who are still more numerous than factory work-ers in most Latin American countries. Finally, there has emerged a huge urban sub-proletariat irregularly engaged in service occupations, who number more than all manufacturing workers, artisans included.

Marxist Communism entered the Latin American scene in the 1920s. But because of the uneven industrial development, Marxism tended to be seen as protecting the interest of the relatively small industrial proletariat whereas the masses were more open to populist or corporatist ideas such as Peronism. The official Communist parties have therefore become defenders of a particular interest group within the system rather than revolutionary parties of the Marxist-Leninist type. Less official ver-sions of Marxism draw on the legacy of José Carlos Mariátegui a Peruvian Marxist theoretician active in the 1920s. Mariategui has been called the Gramsci of Latin America, though his analysis of the peasantry and land reform recalls the ideas that Mao was proclaiming in China at the same time. Mariátegui developed a fluid Marxism adapted to national circumstances, particularly with regard to the indigenous ques-tion where he envisaged a kind of Indo-American socialism in Peru incorporating the communal values of the Incas.

Cuba

The Cuban revolution is an illustration of this state of affairs, in that the initiative for it came neither from the working class nor from the Communist Party. Castro and his followers drew their original inspiration from the traditional national liberation movements against Spain and the United States that had little to do with socialism. Castro's first attempt to overthrow Batista in 1953 and his subsequently successful guerrilla struggle starting with only a handful of men in 1956, did not depart from this tradition. Castro's emphasis on the support of the masses and the need for Cuba to control her own destiny were reactions to the corruption and violence that characterised the United States-backed Batista regime and Batista's middle-class allies. The manifesto of the 26 July Movement, issued in November 1956, declared:

> The 26 July Movement can be defined as guided by thinking that is democratic, nationalist, and dedicated to social justice ... By democracy, the 26 July Movement still considers the Jeffersonian philosophy valid and fully subscribes to the formula of Lincoln of a 'government of the people, by the people, and for the people'.[1]

In particular, Castro did not see the necessity for a party. He is quoted by Debray as saying that

> there is no revolution without a vanguard; that this vanguard is not necessarily the Marxist-Leninist party; and that those who want to make the revolution have the right and duty to constitute themselves a vanguard, independently of these parties.[2]

But this is not to deny that the Cuban working class and, indeed, the Communist Party were necessary to the success of the Cuban revolution. Even at the initial assault on the Moncada barracks, there was considerable working-class support.[3] Although the rebel army was composed largely of radical petty-bourgeois and peasant elements, its opposition to the ruling bourgeoisie drew strong support from the proletariat, whose general strike at the critical point in 1959 enabled Castro to take power. The Cuban Communist Party had publicly supported Batista's first government in 1940 and prominent Communists were members of his government even after the 1952 coup. The Communist Party opposed the Castro guerrillas as being 'putschists' and only gave them its overt support when it was clear that they would be successful. On the other hand, the organisation of a post-revolutionary government and the twin tasks of agrarian reform and mass education would have been impossible without the active participation of the trained and disciplined cadres of the Communist Party.

The fact, however, that the Cuban revolution took a socialist turn was due more to external pressure than to its internal momentum.[4] Initially, Cuba adopted a neutral foreign policy and a reformist internal policy which tried to attract private investment. The growing nationalisation measures and the starting of agrarian cooperatives were greeted with boycott and blockade from the United States, which mistakenly took them to be signs of Communism. This had the effect of encouraging a large section of the Cuban bourgeoisie to emigrate to the United States and the further radicalisation of Cuban politics, culminating in Castro's declaring the revolution to be 'socialist' following the abortive United States-backed invasion at the Bay of Pigs.

In July 1961 Castro announced the formation of a new revolutionary party – the Partido de la Revolucion Socialista (PRS) which incorporated the Communist Party, though tension between Castro's followers and the old-line Communists still persisted. These differences were fostered by the rejection of violent revolution by Communist parties in such countries as Brazil, Colombia, Venezuela, and Peru. In sharp distinction to the Cuban attitudes, the Soviet Union, which wished to increase diplomatic and commercial relations with these countries, supported the Latin American Communist parties in attacking any strategy of armed revolution.[5] Although immediately after the fall of Batista there had been a strong emphasis in the Cuban economy on the development of a heavy industrial sector along Russian lines, this was abandoned in the mid-1960s in favour of concentrating on raising the level of sugar production in order to generate the necessary surplus for subsequent diversification. Many of the economic projections for Cuba have been overoptimistic,[6] but the achievements in social equality and education were most impressive.

The anti-colonial guerrilla origins of the Cuban revolution and the realisation that Soviet external aid was unreliable had led to a greater emphasis on consciousness and the subjective element than in any other Communist movement, including the Chinese. According to Guevara,

Pursuing the chimera of achieving socialism with the aid of the blunted weapons left to us by capitalism (the commodity as the economic cell, profitability, and individual material interest as levers, etc.), it is possible to come to a blind alley.

To build communism, a new man must be created simultaneously with the material base. That is why it is so important to choose correctly the instrument of mass mobilization. That instrument must be fundamentally of a moral character, without forgetting the correct use of material incentives, especially those of a social nature.[7]

Alongside this emphasis on the moral dimension of Communism went the rejection of the idea of separate stages leading towards a Communist society and the attempts, by means of extended free public services, to bypass the commodity exchange economy.

These attempts have been relatively successful. The drawbacks have been an authoritarian bureaucracy and political repression – though on a scale far more limited than many of her neighbours. Nevertheless, Cuba has been able to preserve for decades high standards of health and education, even exporting its doctors and troops to help, for example, the MPLA in Angola and FRELIMO in Mozambique. The economy, being heavily dependent on the USSR, suffered a severe downturn in the years following 1991 but has seen a recovery over the last decade. This is in spite of the attempted isolation of Cuba by the United States through, for example, the Helms-Burton Act of 1995/96 and is partly dependent on an increased emphasis on tourism. Cuba's opposition to the United States has also served as an encouragement to the recent emergence of Leftist forces in neighbouring countries, with the Zapatista movement in Mexico and presidential election victories for Lulu da Silva in Brazil, Chavez in Venezuela, and Morales in Bolivia.

Regis Debray

The practice of Che Guevara and the theory of Regis Debray viewed the Cuban experience as providing a model for revolutionaries in the rest of Latin America. The views of Debray were in sharp contrast to the orthodox Communists, who adhered to the classical Marxist notion of stages. According to them, Latin America was undergoing a 'democratic' revolution led by the progressive bourgeoisie against feudal landowners and United States imperialism. The socialist revolution would follow up the success of this 'national-democratic' revolution. The duty of Communists was to aid the success of the first revolution by participating in the parliamentary and electoral process in order to establish Popular Front governments led by middle-class parties. This attitude is based on the mistaken assumption that there was a fundamental clash of interest between the urban capitalists on the one hand and either the feudal landowners or

American imperialists on the other. The evidently unsatisfactory nature of this strategy from a Marxist revolutionary point of view led to a distinctively Latin American development of Marxism in the shape of the *foco* theory of Regis Debray, who rejected not only the Moscow schema but also the 'four-group United Front' strategy of Mao and even Trotsky's theory of permanent revolution stemming from combined and uneven development.

Debray's answer to the question of revolutionary stages, in his popular *Revolution in the Revolution?*, was that

> the nub of the problem lies not in the initial progress of revolution but in its ability to resolve in practice the problem of state power before the bourgeois-democratic stage, and not after ... it seems evident that in South America the bourgeois-democratic stage presupposes the destruction of the bourgeois state apparatus.[8]

And the destruction of the bourgeois state apparatus required the creation of guerrilla *focos*, i.e. bases or centres of guerrilla operations. According to Debray, 'in Latin America today a political line which, in terms of its consequences, is not susceptible to expression as a precise and consistent military line, cannot be considered revolutionary'.[9]

The basic question for the revolutionary was how to overthrow the capitalist state; and the answer was: 'by means of the more or less slow building up, through guerrilla warfare carried out in suitably chosen rural zones, of a mobile strategic force, nucleus of a people's army and of a future socialist state'.[10] In turn Debray rejected the strategies of armed self-defence (as being too static and therefore vulnerable to governmental repression), of armed propaganda (as following successful military action rather than preceding it), and the Chinese notion of a guerrilla base (because it needed conditions that were lacking in Latin America such as an extensive territory, dense rural population, common borders with friendly countries, and numerical insufficiency of enemy forces).

Debray then turned to the central question of the relation of the guerrilla force to the political party: 'to subordinate the guerrilla group strategically and tactically to a party that has not radically changed its normal peace-time organisation, or to treat it as one more ramification of party activity brings in its wake series of fatal military errors'.[11] The necessity of maintaining contact with the city would lead to the isolation of a guerrilla leader from his troops and unnecessary exposure to risk of capture. Dependence on the city sapped the morale of guerrillas and often led to their abandonment by the city leadership which lived in a totally different environment and had different problems. For 'the mountain proletarianizes the bourgeois and peasant elements, and the city can bourgeoisify the proletarians'.[12] Moreover, it sacrificed the unity of command necessary for successful guerrilla operations, and led to the dispersal of guerrilla forces.

Debray's conclusion was that the subordination of the military to the political, symbolised by Mao's supremacy over Chu Teh in China, Ho Chi Minh over Giap in Vietnam, and Lenin and Trotsky's position during the Russian Civil War, was inappropriate for Latin America where the Communist parties had not been able to take root and develop in the same way as in Russia and China. Therefore,

> under certain conditions, the political and the military are not separate, but form one organic whole consisting of the people's army, whose nucleus is the guerrilla army. The vanguard party can exist in the form of the guerrilla *foco* itself. The guerrilla force is the party in embryo. This is the staggering novelty introduced by the Cuban Revolution ... The people's army will be the nucleus of the party, not vice versa. The guerrilla force is the political vanguard in *nuce* and from its development a real party can arise. That is why the guerrilla force must be developed if the political vanguard is to be developed. That is why, at the present juncture, the principal stress must be laid on the development of guerrilla warfare and not on the strengthening of existing parties or the creation of new parties. That is why insurrectional activity is today the number one political activity.[13]

Debray's whole conception of the *foco* sprang from his contrast between the mountain and the plain or city. He overestimated the effects of the supposedly *dolce vita* in cities on militants. His strict city–mountain dichotomy reads almost like a class dichotomy, as when he said that

> when a guerrilla group communicates with city leadership or its representatives abroad, it is dealing with 'its' bourgeoisie. Even if such bourgeoisie is needed – as an artificial lung is needed in moments of asphyxia – this difference of interests ... must not be lost sight of.[14]

Although the city–country approach was present in China, Debray in fact reversed the process:

> Whereas in Vietnam the military pyramid of the liberation forces is built from the base up, in Latin America ... it tends to be built

from the apex down – the permanent forces first (the *foco*), then the semi-regular forces in the vicinity of the *foco*, and lastly or after victory (Cuba) the militia.[15]

Debray's three golden rules – constant vigilance, constant mistrust, constant mobility – meant cutting off guerrillas from the rest of the population, in stark contrast to Mao's approach where the peasantry was the water in which the fish swam.

The *foco* theory involved the elevation of the military above the political in a manner quite uncharacteristic of mainstream Marxism. This was due to an implicit overestimation of the extent to which the social and political structure of Latin America was ripe for revolution. Nowhere did Debray spell out how a guerrilla band could develop into a mass political movement, and the experience of Algeria is there to show how it can lead to a stagnant bureaucracy. This tendency to despise politics was not just tactical. As Eqbal Ahmad has written:

> Debray's *foco* theory does not reject organic ties with the civilians simply for fear of exposing them to governmental repression, although this is undoubtedly the most attractive aspect of his position. Nor is it only a matter of concern with achieving maximum mobility and initiative. One senses something deeper and disturbing – an awareness of distance from, if not exactly a distrust of, the rural population, an unadmitted estimation that the objective conditions for revolution do not exist in Latin America, total disbelief in the political processes and existing political parties as possible instruments for independence and social revolution.[16]

Since, following the Cuban revolution, the Latin American bourgeoisie has tended to ally itself more and more with United States imperialism, the necessity for a mass movement to articulate demands is all the more necessary. Moreover, to suppose that the Cuban revolution succeeded without a political party is a mistake. Mass revolutionary organisations had long existed there, particularly in the Oriente province. It is quite understandable that the impression that the Castroites succeeded in making a revolution in spite of their having no party makes their views attractive to the guerrilla theorists of Latin America. However, there is much evidence that the Cuban revolution was highly specific and therefore unrepeatable. The aim of the Cuban revolution was, at its beginning, a democratic reformist government; the peasants had already largely been proletarianised by large mechanised capitalist farms; there was an absence of intervention by the United

States; and, finally, even the bourgeoisie was disaffected with the Batista regime. The general result of this lack of political analysis in theories such as Debray's is a combination of a Hispanic revolutionary ethic with an American concentration on the technical details of guerrilla war which are only linked by a military romanticism. This outlook has affinities with urban terrorist movements in Western Europe – the Baader-Meinhof group in Germany and the Red Brigades in Italy. It has a more direct, though degenerate, offspring in the Shining Path in Peru and the FARC in Colombia. The best contemporary instantiation is perhaps the Zapatista movement in Mexico which combines armed struggle, modern communication methods, and appeal to a nationalist/popular revolutionary tradition.[17]

Liberation theology

More long lasting than the guerrilla theories of Debray (who soon gave up all this and became an adviser to President Mitterrand) was the emergence in Latin America in the late 1970s of a growing number of Christians who not only professed themselves to be Marxists but also considered their Marxism to be an indispensable part of their Christianity.

Lenin is reported as saying that 'only Communism and Catholicism offered two diverse, complete and inconfusable concepts of human life'.[18] But he reckoned without the experience of Latin America which is the only continent to have been both Christian and colonised. Christian Europe was never colonised and other colonised continents have not, on the whole, been Christian. The Second Vatican Council (1961–65) appeared to give official blessing to aspirations for Church renewal – a process which reached its Latin American high point in 1968 when the Second Conference of Latin American bishops meeting at Medellin in Columbia proclaimed its 'option for the poor'. The countries who have made the biggest contribution to liberation theology are Argentina, Uruguay, Chile, Peru and Brazil – which has more Catholics than any other country in the world. And it will come as no surprise that, in such a continent-wide movement, there are very diverse currents. Liberation theology was supported by a significant – though definitely minoritarian – part of the episcopate including such notable figures as Helder Camara, Archbishop of Recife in Brazil. Its theologians vary from the Colombian Camillo Torres, who felt he could best fulfil his priestly vocation by joining the guerrillas, was killed by the security forces, and has become something of a martyr of the Left, to the decidedly more nuanced writings of the Peruvian Jesuit Gustavo Guttierez whose *Theology of Liberation* is the best-selling of liberation theology books – the most magisterial being the multi-volume works of Juan Luis Segundo, and the best informed about Marx being those of Ernesto Dussel. What unites all these currents is the use of apparently Marxist categories to achieve critical self-renewal. There is a striking parallel here with Trotsky's theory of permanent revolution, according to which the very backwardness of Russia and therefore the lack of a strong bourgeois ethos meant that it could bypass any prolonged period of capitalism and move rapidly towards socialism. Similarly the very under-development of Latin America provides a revolutionary transformation not open to the more staid societies of Europe, both east and west.

Latin American theology has therefore attempted to integrate into its reflection the whole tradition of historical materialism and develop a theology which is both critical and materialist. In the 1970s the general influence of structuralism made appeals to essential human nature seem old-fashioned and tame. Talk about 'man as such' was on the wane as an unreal intellectual concept to be replaced by reference to identity in terms of sex, class, race and language. This rejection of traditional humanism was typified by Sartre's revision of his earlier views and his attempts to come to terms with Marxism which he declared to be 'the philosophy of out time'.[19] What Aristotle had been to the twelfth and thirteenth centuries, Marx was to many contemporary theologians. The Marxist hypothesis seemed to be the most comprehensive approach to the human sciences and thus a necessary preliminary for a contemporary theology. And by the time this realisation took place, Marxist humanism was itself on the defensive in face of more structuralist versions. Indeed, the Althusserian reading of Marx can claim a longer lasting influence in Latin America than elsewhere. This is partly due to two factors. Firstly, the time when Marxism began to have a profound impact on theology was the same time that Althusser's ideas were at their most popular in Latin countries of Europe. Secondly, this interpretation, with its talk of 'relatively autonomous levels' and so on, explicitly left room (of a sort) for religious belief. The much vaunted 'scientificity' of Althusser also made it seem more neutral than other forms of Marxism. The essential passivity of this type of approach was less appreciated.

The emphasis on practice and experience is one of the main aspects of Marxism that Latin American Christians have used to evaluate and transform their religious heritage. As a leading exponent has put it:

Perhaps one of the deepest coincidences between a non-dogmatic Marxism and an authentically Biblical Christianity lies precisely in this, that both have an absolutely peculiar relation to truth. Both of them demand that their truth be 'verified', that it 'become true', that it be fulfilled. They demand to be confirmed by the facts. They conceive of truth as truth in the facts and it is precisely in this that they stand opposed to all forms of idealism, metaphysics or ideology that understand truth as something 'in itself', outside the facts, in a 'separate realm'.[20]

Here the impact of Marx's *Theses on Feuerbach* cannot be overestimated. From the Latin American point of view, much previous Western theology of the 'death of God' variety, with its concentration on humanism and the individual, derived its inspiration from Feuerbach and thus seemed static and ultimately conservative compared to the practical, revolutionary emphasis of Marx. The liberation theologians are convinced that basic revolutionary change is necessary. And their presupposition is that 'the socioanalytical tools, the historical horizon of interpretation, the insight into the dynamics of the social process, and the revolutionary ethos and programme which Marxism has either received and appropriated or itself created are, however corrected or reinterpreted, indispensable for revolutionary change'.[21]

It is as well to stress that the liberation theologians do not wish to demonstrate any straightforward congruence between Marxism and Christianity. Indeed, any idea of the assimilation of Marxism and Christianity on the basis of an alleged common moral stance, is explicitly rejected by liberation theology. Theirs is a much more critical enterprise – the reinterpretation of traditional Christian ideas through a rigorous application of the Marxist materialist conception of history which is more fruitful than Western Christian commentators on Marx have realised. The gospel of love may be the general framework of aspiration underlying all human activity; but what the gospel will require in practice – for example, class strife and violence – will be decided by theoretical analysis of a Marxist type. Thus there is no specifically *Christian* politics or society theory.

The most general impact of Marxism on liberation theology is the self-critical, self-reflexive attitude which they both share. Thus the first target of liberation theology self-criticism is the involvement of the Latin American Church in the social and political structures that have compounded the domination and oppression of the mass of the people. For 'an awareness of the need for self-liberation is essential to a correct understanding of the liberation process. It is not a matter of "struggling for others", which suggests paternalism and reformist objectives, but rather of becoming aware of oneself as not completely fulfilled and as living in an alienated society.'[22] This self-critical attitude rules out any dogmatic interpretation of the Christian faith. The immobility of dogma inevitably serves to sanctify the present order of things, whereas Christian faith is inherently critical and subversive.

More specifically, liberation theology has re-evaluated the Old Testament to which, as Ernst Bloch pointed out, all Christian rebels have appealed, and emphasised the similarities between their opposition to the idols of capitalism and Marx's critique of commodity fetishism. Talking of the Exodus in words that echo the master/slave dialectic of Hegel, Jean Cardonnel states: 'The concrete experience of liberation is the only way to discover the fact of creation. It is the only deeply lived experience of oppression that prompts man to work toward his radical liberation, in which process he can come to discover that the world is a creation.'[23]

Similarly in its interpretation of the Gospel narratives, liberation theology is concerned to discover themes that find in Jesus's political messianism suggestive symbols and signposts rather than specific examples to imitate. Unlike such commentators as Engels or Kautsky, they are not concerned to link Jesus directly with the contemporary revolutionary movement of the Zealots. The picture of Jesus as an armed guerrilla fighter is not essential for liberation theology. It is clear that Jesus was engaged in active opposition to political authority. But the main point is that, for Jesus, the liberation of the Jewish people was only part of a universal revolution with more profound and permanent consequences than could be encompassed by the political liberation of a single people.

More generally, liberation theology, under the impact of Marxist approaches, wishes to relativise the concepts in which the Bible is expressed and accord them no more permanent authority than it does to biblical cosmology. It seeks to give a social and political dimension to traditional Christian concepts which tend to have become 'privatised'. The injunction to love your enemy, for example, no longer involves a vague universal good will: 'Love does not mean that oppressors are no longer enemies, nor does it eliminate the radicalness of the combat against them. "Love of enemies" does not ease tensions; rather it challenges the whole system and becomes a subversive formula.'[24] Returning to the Marxist tradition which saw early Christianity as the religion of the oppressed, 'poverty' is not something spiritual or individual, but implies solidarity with the poor and a protest *against* poverty. And salvation is viewed, at least in the first instance, as liberation from specific social and political oppression. What is clearly evident in all these changes of perspective, is the influence of the Marxist criticism of any individual morality divorced from the social and economic framework.

With the demise of the Sandinista regime in Nicaragua – to which liberation theologians had made a considerable contribution – and the ousting of most of the more overtly oppressive and authoritarian regimes, liberation theology has become more muted in its enthusiasm for explicitly Marxist categories. But its basic stance on the causes of poverty and the struggle for self-emancipation, a stance incorporating Marxist inspired themes, continues to be influential across the world and has played its part in the current emergence of Left-leaning regimes.

Notes

1. Programme of the 26 July Movement, quoted in R. Scheer and M. Zeitlin, *Cuba: An American Tragedy*, rev. edn (Harmondsworth, 1964).
2. R. Debray, *Revolution in the Revolution?* (Harmondsworth, 1968) pp. 96f.
3. For further details, see J. Woodis, *New Theories of Revolution* (London, 1972) pp. 200ff.
4. See further, in support of this view, R. Scheer and M. Zeitlin, *Cuba: An American Tragedy, passim.*
5. See *Fidel Castro Speaks*, ed. M. Kenner and J. Petras (Harmondsworth, 1972) pp. 181ff.
6. Cf. C. Auroi, *La Nouvelle Agriculture Cubaine* (Paris, 1975) pp. 213ff.
7. C. Guevara, 'Man and Socialism in Cuba', in *Man and Socialism in Cuba: The Great Debate*, ed. B. Silverman (New York, 1971) pp. 342f.
8. R. Debray, *Strategy for Revolution*, ed. R. Blackburn (London, 1970) pp. 71f.
9. R. Debray, *Revolution in the Revolution?*, pp. 24f.
10. Ibid., p. 25.
11. Ibid., p. 65.
12. Ibid., p. 75.
13. Ibid., 105, 115.
14. Ibid., p. 69.
15. Ibid, p. 50.
16. E. Ahmad, 'Radical but Wrong', in *Regis Debray and the Latin American Revolution* ed. L. Huberman and P. Sweezy (New York, 1969) p. 77.
17. See the enthusiastic endorsement of J. Holloway and E. Pelaez (eds), *Zapatista!: Reinventing Revolution in Mexico* (London, 1998).
18. V. Lenin, quoted in J. Hellman, 'French "Left-Catholics" and Communism in the Nineteen-thirties', *Church History*, Vol. 45 (1976), p. 507.
19. J.-P. Sartre, *Search for a Method* (New York, 1968), p. 30.
20. J. Bonino, *Christians and Marxists: The Mutual Challenge to Revolution* (London, 1976), p. 18.
21. J. Bonino, op.cit., p. 8.
22. G. Guttierez, *A Theology of Liberation* (New York, 1973), p. 146.
23. J. Cardonnel, *Dieux est mort en Jesus-Christ* (Bordeaux, 1968), p. 123.

24. G. Guttierez, *A Theology of Liberation* (New York, 1973), p. 276.

Further reading

Cuba and Latin America

The classic on exploitation in Latin America is Frank's *Capitalism and Underdevelopment in Latin America* This can be supplemented by Petras's fine studies *Politics and Social Structure in Latin America* and *The Left Strikes Back*. See also Lowy's collection and Harris's analysis.

On the Cuban background, see Blackburn's recent *Slavery and Empire: The Making of Modern Cuba*. For Castro, see Bonachea and Valdes's *Selected Works of Fidel Castro*. A selection of Castro's speeches is available in Kenner and Petras's *Fidel Castro Speaks*. Silverman's collection, *Man and Socialism in Cuba*, reprints Cuban discussions from the mid-1960s. An excellent book on mass participation in Cuba is Fagen's *The Transformation of Political Culture in Cuba*. See also Zeitlin's *Revolutionary Politics and the Cuban Working Class*. O'Connor's *The Origins of Socialism in Cuba* demonstrates at length the international and economic pressures. On the Cuban economy, Boorstin's *The Economic Transformation of Cuba* is a study of the early years by someone personally involved; Huberman and Sweezy's *Socialism in Cuba* surveys economic development; and Fraginals provides a study of Cuba's staple product, sugar. Barkin and Manitzas have a useful collection of articles from a socialist perspective, and Valdes and Lieuwen provide an extensive bibliography. For more recent developments, see Perez-Stable's discussion, Horowitz's collection and Connolly's biography of Castro.

Guevara

The best two selections of Guevara's writings are Bonachea and Valdes's *Che: Selected Works of Ernesto Guevara* (which has a good bibliography) and Gerassi's *Venceremos! The Speeches and Writings of Che Guevara*. A good commentary is Lowy's *The Marxism of Che Guevara*. There is also Sinclair's Modern Masters *Guevara* and Lavretsky's hagiographical *Ernesto Che Guevara*. Luther and Henken's biography and the collection by Garcia and Sola are useful.

Debray

The basic text is the short and pithy *Revolution in the Revolution? Strategy for Revolution* which contains various essays on the lessons of Cuba for revolution in Latin America. *Prison Writings* show Debray in a more philosophical mood. See also his revisionist *Critique of Arms*. As for commentaries, there is Blackburn's short introduction to *Strategy for Revolution*, a critique from an orthodox Communist viewpoint in Woodis's *New Theories of Revolution*, and (best) Huberman and Sweezy's *Regis Debray and the Latin American Revolution*.

Bibliography

Cuba and Latin America

Robert J. Alexander, *Trotskyism in Latin America* (Stanford, 1973).

L.A. Anguilar, *Marxism in Latin America* (New York, 1968).

David P. Barkin and Nita R. Manitzas (eds), *Cuba: The Logic of the Revolution* (New York, 1973).

M. Becker, *Mariátigui and Latin American Marxist Theory* (Athens, 1993).

Robin Blackburn, *Slavery and Empire: The Making of Modern Cuba* (London, 1978).

Edward Boorstin, *The Economic Transformation of Cuba* (New York, 1969).

A. Boron, *State, Capital, and Democracy in Latin America* (New York, 1993).

B. Carr and S. Ellner (eds), *The Latin American Left: From the Fall of Allende to Perestroika* (Boulder, 1993).

J. Castenada, *Utopia Unarmed: The Latin American Left after the Cold War* (New York, 1993).

Fidel Castro, *Selected Works of Fidel Castro*, 3 vols, ed. R.H. Bonachea and N.P. Valdes (Cambridge, Mass., 1972f.).

—— *Fidel Castro Speaks*, ed. Martin Kenner and James Petras (New York, 1969).

S. Connolly, *Castro* (London, 2002).

A. Collier, *Christianity and Marxism: A Philosophical Contribution to their Reconciliation* (London, 2001).

Regis Debray, *Conversations with Allende* (London, 1972).

Theodore Draper, 'Castroism', in Drachkovitch (ed.), *Marxism in the Modern World* (London, 1966).

Richard R. Fagen, *The Transformation of Political Culture in Cuba* (Stanford, 1968).

V. Geoghan, *Ernst Bloch* (London, 1996).

Manuel Morino Fraginals, *The Sugarmill: The Socio-Economic Complex of Sugar in Cuba* (London, 1977).

A.G. Frank, *Capitalism and Underdevelopment in Latin America*, rev. edn (New York, 1969).

P. Freire, *The Pedagogy of the Oppressed* (New York, 1971).

R. Harris, *Marxism, Socialism and Democracy in Latin America* (Boulder, 1992).

J. Holloway and E. Pelaez (eds), *Zapatista!: Reinventing Revolution in Mexico* (London, 1998).

I. Horowitz (ed.), *Cuban Communism*, 7th edn (New York, 1989).

Leo Huberman and Paul M. Sweezy, *Socialism in Cuba* (New York, 1969).

K.S. Karol, *Guerrillas in Power: The Course of the Cuban Revolution* (New York, 1970).

M. Lowy (ed.), *Marxism in Latin America from 1909 to the Present: An Anthology* (Atlantic Highlands, 1992).

E. McCaughan, *Reinventing Revolution: The Renovation of Left Discourse in Cuba and Mexico* (Boulder, 1997).

Ralph Miliband, 'The Coup in Chile', in R. Blackburn (ed.), *Revolution and Class Struggle: A Reader in Marxist Politics* (London, 1977).

James O'Connor, *The Origins of Socialism in Cuba* (Ithaca, New York, 1970).

M. Perez-Stable, *The Cuban Revolution. Origins, Course and Legacy* (New York, 1993).

J. Petras, *The Left Strikes Back: Class Conflict in Latin America in the Age of Neoliberalism* (Boulder, 1999).

James Petras, *Politics and Social Structure in Latin America* (New York, 1970).

James Petras and Maurice Zeitlin, *Latin America* (London, 1968).

R. Quirk, *Fidel Castro* (New York, 1993).

Bertram Silverman (ed.), *Man and Socialism in Cuba: The Great Debate* (New York, 1971).

N. Valdes and E. Lieuwen, *The Cuban Revolution: A Research Study Guide (1959–1969)* (New Mexico, 1971).

H. Vanden (ed.), *Latin American Marxism: A Bibliography* (New York, 1991).

C. Vilas, 'Forward Back: Capitalist Restructuring, the State and the Working Class in Latin America', in *Whither Marxism?*, ed. Bernd Magnus and Stephen E. Cullenberg (New York, 1994).

G. Wilpert, *Changing Venezuela by Taking Power: The History and Policies of the Chavez Government* (London, 2006).

J. Ann Zammit (ed.), *The Chilean Road to Socialism* (Brighton, 1973).

Maurice Zeitlin, *Revolutionary Politics and the Cuban Working Class* (Princeton, N.J., 1970).

Guevara: texts

Che Guevara, *Reminiscences of the Cuban Revolutionary War* (New York, 1968).

Che Guevara on Revolution: A Documentary Overview, ed. J. Mallin (Miami, 1969).

Che Guevara Speaks, ed. G. Lanvan (New York, 1969).

Che: Selected Works of Ernesto Guevara, ed. R.E. Bonachea and N.P. Valdes (Cambridge, Mass., 1970).

Complete Bolivian Diaries of Che Guevara and Other Captured Documents, ed. D. James (New York, 1969).

Diary of Che Guevara, ed. R. Scheer (New York, 1968).

Venceremos! The Speeches and Writings of Che Guevara, ed. J. Gerassi (New York, 1968).

Guevara: commentaries

F. Garcia and O. Sola, eds., *Che: Images of a Revolutionary* (London, 2000).

I. Lavretsky, *Ernesto Che Guevara* (Moscow, 1976).

Michel Lowy, *The Marxism of Che Guevara: Philosophy, Economics and Revolutionary Warfare* (New York, 1973).

E. Luther and T. Henken, *The Life and Work of Che Guevara* (Indianapolis, 2001).

Andrew Sinclair, *Guevara* (London and New York, 1970).

Debray: texts

Regis Debray *A Critique of Arms*, 2 vols (London, 1977f.).

—— 'Marxism and the National Question' (interview), *New Left Review*, 105 (1977).
—— *Prison Writings* (London, 1973).
—— *Revolution in the Revolution?* (New York, 1967).
—— *Strategy for Revolution*, ed. R. Blackburn (London, 1970).

Debray: commentaries

Leo Huberman and Paul M. Sweezy (eds), *Regis Debray and the Latin American Revolution* (New York, 1969).
Keith Reader, *Regis Debray: A Critical Introduction* (London, 1996).
Jack Woodis, *New Theories of Revolution: A Commentary on the Views of Frantz Fanon, Regis Debray and Herbert Marcuse* (London, 1972).

18
Marxism and Underdevelopment

This chapter deals with neo-Marxist theories of imperialism and under-development which are primarily inspired by the Latin American experience. They share, in the economic sphere, the rejection of the classical Marxist approach that writers such as Debray exemplify in the political sphere. Marx in the *Manifesto* had declared:

> The bourgeoisie cannot exist without constantly revolutionising the instruments of production and thereby the relations of production, and with them the whole relations of society. Conservation of the old modes of production in an altered form, was, on the contrary, the first condition of existence for all earlier industrial classes. Constant revolutionising of production, uninterrupted disturbance of all social conditions, everlasting uncertainty and agitation distinguish the bourgeois epoch from all earlier ones ... The bourgeoisie ... draws all, even the most barbarian, nations into civilisation. The cheap prices of its commodities are the heavy artillery with which it batters down all Chinese walls ... It compels all nations, on pain of extinction, to adopt the bourgeois mode of production; it compels them to introduce what it calls civilisation into their midst, i.e. to become bourgeois themselves. In one word, it creates a world after its own image.[1]

His comments on the progressive nature of Britain's role in India are in the same vein: only in his remarks on Ireland's having been stunted in its development by the English does he come close to the idea that colonial capitalism might yield results different from those obtained in Western Europe. By contrast, much Marxist writing on development has emphasized how foreign capitalist penetration actively develops its victims. To take the most striking example: it is obvious that the peasantry play a central role in any revolutionary theory of development; yet, until the Chinese experience, the peasantry were seen as little more than a source of surplus to be invested in other sections of the economy. In Lenin's theory of imperialism, for example, the centre of attention was still the advanced capitalist countries: what happened in the rest of the world was of interest largely to explain the emergence of a labour aristocracy in the West or war between imperialist powers. Even in Trotsky's theory of combined and uneven development, the working class of the advanced industrialised countries still occupied the central role. Of all the classical writers, only Gramsci with his work on the Southern Question in Italy took the underdevelopment of the peasantry seriously. Traditional views of imperialism conceived it to be a necessary development of capitalist economy in its search for raw materials, finding outlets for investment abroad, and increasing the market for its industrial products. The fact that the last two supposed facets of imperialism seem to be decreasingly (if at all) applicable has completely revised much Marxist theory – to the extent, among some thinkers, of saying that the Third World has become redundant for the development of the advanced sector. This change in perspective is symbolised by the fact that the national bourgeoisie, from being a progressive and democratic class in Lenin, is viewed by most neo-Marxist development theorists as unprogressive and parasitic. The realisation of the essential role of nationalism, the re-evaluation of the function of the petty bourgeoisie, the rejection of the proletariat (as in Fanon), the centrality accorded to the peasantry, and the ecological threat of the disastrous depletion of world resources have radically altered the context of the discussion from that of Marx and Lenin. A programme which advocates deindustrialisation of the West and peasant self-sufficiency in the Third World has little in common with classical Marxism.

The seminal work for the neo-Marxist theorists of underdevelopment was Paul Baran's *The Political Economy of Growth* which expanded on the ideas of Lenin, Luxemburg, and Trotsky by linking them with the claim that the development of the West was directly at the expense of the less developed economies.[2] Baran's work was very influential in the 1960s and 1970s. Samir Amin, for example, used Baran's work to consider how, with capital internationalised and labour relatively immobile within the nation-state, surplus value was distributed on a world scale. With capitalism always tending to overproduction, Amin held that the creation of surplus value meant an increase in real wages, proportionate to the increase in labour productivity, in the centre but not in the periphery which, although containing three-quarters of the world's population, appeared to be merely overseas projections of the central economies.

The most prominent disciple of Baran was Andre Gunder Frank. While Baran emphasised the stagnation of capitalism at the centre, Frank was more interested in its effects on the periphery. He drew on many specific examples, particularly from Latin America, to provide a would-be refutation of the currently popular modernisation theories of such writers as Rostow according to which modernisation and development were forced on backward nations by competition in international trade. Fukuyama proposes an updated version of the same thesis. For Frank, however, globalisation, from the sixteenth century onwards, had altered for the worse both the internal nature of non-developed societies and the external context in which they could develop. The capitalist world system involved 'chains' in which surplus is transferred from 'satellites' to 'metropoles' which might themselves be satellites of further metropoles. In this continuum of exploitative relationships, the wealth of the metropole was a direct result of the extraction of surplus from the satellites. Frank called this 'the development of under-development'.

The world-systems theory of Immanuel Wallerstein is in the same vein, focusing on the material dynamics of the world market and the multicentric states' system. Influenced by Braudel, Wallerstein is interested in the long cycles of capitalist development extending back to the sixteenth century. Unlike Frank, Wallerstein is less concerned with underdevelopment than with the interdependence of all elements in the world economy. He describes a chain of centre, semi-periphery and periphery, but also recognises the possibility of mobility, particularly from the semi-periphery in either direction. In addition, and again unlike Baran and Frank, he sees the active role of the bourgeoisie of nation-states as importantly affecting development. The Russian and Chinese revolutions, for example, although in Wallerstein's view progressive, were bound to be re-incorporated into the world capitalist system. But the contradictions of a global capitalism will increase the unification of anti-systemic forces on a world scale which in turn will favour the emergence of an international socialism.

Both developments in the world economy over the last twenty-five years and theoretical criticism have deprived dependency and underdevelopment theories of much of their influence. Frank and Wallerstein regard production for profit realised in the market as fundamental. Indeed, Wallerstein refers specifically to the work of Arrighi Emmanuel to buttress his theory. Emmanuel in his major work *Unequal Exchange* claimed that 'all imperialisms are, in the last resort, mercantile in character':[3] their profits came from trade in commodities rather than foreign investment. This results from the international differences in the value of labour power which makes commodities produced in the West expensive and those in the Third World cheap. And the consequently uneven exchange between them is in turn responsible for the widening gap in development.

Critics of Emmanuel have argued that Third World poverty was due to the underdevelopment of the productive forces rather than low wages: the former was the cause of the latter.[4] Indeed those nearer to the mainstream of Marxist economic thought have stressed the importance of locating exploitation in the process of production rather than that of exchange. In addition, these critics see economic development in the Third World as being blocked by pre-capitalist relations of production. Thus economic backwardness is the result of factors internal to societies and not imposed externally by contact with advanced capitalism whose initial and continued development was not dependent on the exploitation of peripheral societies. Indeed, these societies have suffered less from the presence of capitalist exploitation than from its absence. The proponents of so-called articulation theory have stressed the importance of analysing actual economic systems which often consist of more than one mode of production whose 'articulation' gave a particular character to that society.[5] Although often expressed in difficult Althusserian terms, articulation theory has had the merit of concentrating on the mode of production, albeit in a highly theoreticised form.[6]

In a more accessible mode, several writers have followed Cohen's interpretation of Marx's 1859 Preface[7] and pursued the line of thought in Marx that saw the global development of capitalism as progressive and providing the material basis for the emergence of socialism on a world scale. Bill Warren, for example, in *Imperialism* took the theoreticians of underdevelopment to task for adopting the Narodnik position of the 1890s[8] and re-asserted Lenin's arguments against them,[9] and claimed, moreover, that capitalist development in the Third World brought increased freedom and equality. His approach was rather broad-brush and overoptimistic in this regard. He also disregarded the state-sponsored capitalism of the newly industrialising countries such as Japan, South Korea or Singapore which represented a new international division of labour which presented as many difficulties for his approach as it did to that of the underdevelopment theorists.

Perhaps the most trenchant and rigorous critic of underdevelopment theory is Robert Brenner. His work on the transition from feudalism to capitalism aims to demonstrate the importance of class struggle and not, as in Baran, Frank, Wallerstein, and Emmanuel, either the relationship between centre and periphery in the world market or the transfer of surplus between them. Brenner claims that it is the class structure of peripheral societies that explains their position in the world economy and that it is capitalist competition which generates economic development. Brenner's emphasis on the relations of production encounters difficulties with, for example, the monopolistic and protectionist expansion of German capitalism in the second half of the nineteenth century and more generally with Cohen's view of the primacy of production forces over production relations. But Brenner's emphasis on competition (and the instability that it entails) in an age dominated by transnational capital[10] presents a powerful antithesis to dependency theory.

Notes

1. K. Marx, *The Communist Manifesto*, in *Selected Writings*, ed. D. McLellan (Oxford, 2000) p. 248f.
2. See pp. 379ff. below.
3. A. Emmanuel, *Unequal Exchange* (New York, 1972) p. 187.
4. See, for example, C. Bettelheim, 'Theoretical Comments', in Emmanuel, *Unequal Exchange*, pp. 287ff.
5. See J. Taylor, *From Modernization to Modes of Production* (London, 1979).
6. See E. Laclau, 'Feudalism and Capitalism in Latin America', *New Left Review*, Vol. 67, 1971.
7. G. Cohen, *Karl Marx's Theory of History: A Defence*, 2nd edn (Oxford, 2000).
8. See pp. 69f above.
9. B. Warren, *Imperialism: Pioneer of Capitalism* (London, 1980).
10. See R. Brenner, 'Bourgeois Revolution and the Transition to Capitalism', in A. Beier *et al.* (eds), *The First Modern Society* (Cambridge, 1989). Also *The Economics of Global Turbulence* (London, 2006) and p. 395 below. For a sophisticated defence of the dependency theory, see C. Kay, *Latin American Theories of Development and Underdevelopment* (London, 1989). For an excellent collection of Marxist essays on world development and globalisation, see R. Albritton *et al.* (eds), *Phases of Capitalist Development: Booms, Crises, and Globalizations* (Basingstoke, 2001).

Further reading

For accounts of the background in Marx's own ideas, see Melotti's *Marx and the Third World* and Avineri's collection, *Karl Marx on Colonialism and Modernisation*. On the elaboration of the Marxist theory of imperialism, see the studies by Kemp, Sutcliffe and Owen, Kiernan, and Barratt-Brown. A good, non-technical overview is Worsley's *The Third World*, but the best short introduction to the whole subject is Foster-Carter's article 'Neo-Marxist Approaches to Development and Underdevelopment'. The basic texts are Baran's *The Political Economy of Growth* and Frank's *Capitalism and*

Underdevelopment in Latin America. Their work is continued in Amin's two major contributions, *Accumulation on a World Scale* and *Imperialism and Unequal Development*, and Emmanuel's *Unequal Exchange*. Kay provides the best defence of dependency theory. See also Arrighi's path-breaking study, *The Political Economy in Rhodesia*, and his recent general overview, *The Geometry of Imperialism*. On Africa, see Fanon's classic *The Wretched of the Earth*, together with Caute's commentary, Friedland and Rosberg's collection *African Socialism*, Nyerere's *Ujamaa*, and Ake's *Revolutionary Pressures in Africa*. The most interesting African analyst is Cabral. See also Zelig's forthright study.

Bibliography

Claude Ake, *Revolutionary Pressures in Africa* (London, 1978).
Samir Amin, *Accumulation on a World Scale* (New York, 1974).
—— *Imperialism and Unequal Development* (Hassocks, Sussex, 1978).
G. Arrighi, *The Geometry of Imperialism* (London, 1978).
—— *The Political Economy in Rhodesia* (The Hague, 1970).
Shlomo Avineri (ed.), *Karl Marx on Colonialism and Modernisation* (New York, 1968).
D. Banerjee (ed.), *Marxian Theory and the Third World* (New Delhi, 1985).
P. Baran, *The Political Economy of Growth* (New York, 1957).
Michael Barratt-Brown, *The Economics of Imperialism* (London, 1975).
H. Bernstein, 'Modernisation Theory and the Sociological Study of Development', *Journal of Development Studies*, 7, 2 (1971).
A. Cabral, *Revolution in Guinea: An African People's Struggle* (London, 1969).
A. Callinicos, *Between Apartheid and Capitalism* (London, 1992).
David Caute, *Fanon* (London, 1970).
Gérard Chaliand, *Revolutions in the Third World: From 1945 to the Present* (Hassocks, 1977).
Renato Coustantino, *Neocolonial Identity and Counter-Consciousness: Essays in Cultural Decolonization*, ed. I. Meszaros (London, 1977).
A. Emmanuel, 'Myths of Development versus Myths of Underdevelopment', *New Left Review*, 85 (1974).
—— *Unequal Exchange: A Study in the Imperialism of Free Trade* (London, 1972).
R. Fagen *et al.* (eds), *Transition and Development: Problems of Third World Socialism* (New York, 1986).
Frantz Fanon, *The Wretched of the Earth* (London, 1965).
Aidan Foster-Carter, 'Neo-Marxist Approaches to Development and Underdevelopment', in Emmanuel De Kadt and Gavin Williams (eds), *Sociology and Development* (London, 1974).
—— 'Modes of Production Controversy', *New Left Review*, 107 (1978).
A.G. Frank, *Capitalism and Underdevelopment in Latin America*, 2nd edn (New York, 1971).
—— 'The Development of Underdevelopment', *Monthly Review*, 8 (1966).
William H. Friedland and Carl G. Rosberg (eds), *African Socialism* (Stanford, 1964).
David Horowitz, *Imperialism and Revolution* (London, 1971).

Emmanuel de Kadt and G. Williams (eds), *Sociology and Development* (London, 1974).

C. Kay, *Latin American Theories of Development and Underdevelopment* (London, 1989).

John H. Kautsky, *Communism and the Politics of Development* (New York, 1968).

Tom Kemp, *Theories of Imperialism* (London, 1967).

V.G. Kiernan, *Marxism and Imperialism* (London, 1976).

George Lichtheim, *Imperialism* (New York, 1971).

—— 'Oriental Despotism', in Lichtheim, *The Concept of Ideology* (New York, 1967).

Umberto Melotti, *Marx and the Third World* (London, 1976).

Julius Nyerere, *Ujamaa: Essays on Socialism* (Oxford, 1968).

K. Post and P. Wright, *Socialism and Underdevelopment* (London, 1989).

Hugo Radice (ed.), *International Firms and Modern Imperialism* (London, 1975).

L. Senghur, *On African Socialism* (London, 1964).

Gareth Stedman-Jones, 'The History of US Imperialism', in Robin Blackburn (ed.), *Ideology in Social Science: Readings in Critical Social Theory* (London, 1972).

R.B. Sutcliffe and R. Owen, *Studies in the Theory of Imperialism* (London, 1972).

José Villamil (ed.), *Transnational Capitalism and National Development: Studies in the Theory of Dependence* (Hassocks, Sussex, 1978).

Peter Worsley, *The Third World* (London, 1967).

L. Zelig, *Marxism in Africa: The Class Struggle across the Continent* (Cheltenham, 2002).

Zhongqiao Duan, *Marx's Theory of Social Formation* (Aldershot, 1996).

Part Five

Contemporary Marxism in Europe and the United States

Will theoretical needs immediately become practical ones? It is not enough that thought should tend towards reality, reality must also tend towards thought.

Karl Marx, 1844

293

Introduction

The character of contemporary Marxism in Europe and the United States was profoundly marked by the collapse of the Second International in 1914 and by the defeat of the working-class movements in Western Europe in the two following decades. This collapse meant that the centre of gravity of Marxist thought moved East, where it was soon suppressed by the rise of Stalin. Unlike the previous generation of leading Marxist theoreticians, those under consideration in the last part of this book were not important figures in political parties. They were academics rather than activists, writing in a period of decline of working-class activity and therefore in comparative isolation from political practice. Thus philosophy, epistemology, methodology, even aesthetics bulk larger in their work than do politics or economics. In a period when parliamentary democracy became normal throughout the advanced capitalist countries and their economies enjoyed a long period of unprecedented growth, an atmosphere of resigned pessimism spread among many Marxist intellectuals – a pessimism that was not alleviated by considering the repressive nature of Soviet bureaucracy. Geographically, Marxist thought was concentrated in Germany, France and Italy, countries with large Communist parties. Whereas Marx started with philosophy and moved to economics, the typical thinkers of Western Marxism have moved in the opposite direction, and even, in some cases, sought to complement Marxism with a philosophy anterior to Marx himself: for example, Spinoza in the work of Althusser or Kant in that of Colletti.

19
The Frankfurt School

The school and politics

Nothing exemplified this change of perspective more than the work of the Frankfurt School. Whereas the major thinkers of the 1920s in Europe – Lukács, Korsch, and Gramsci – were all active in politics, the Frankfurt School had no formal political affiliation. The Institute for Social Research had been founded in Frankfurt in 1923 with a huge endowment from a wealthy grain merchant and provided the institutional basis for the work of the Frankfurt School. The rise of Hitler meant the emigration of the Institute's members (they were almost all Jews) and it was eventually re-established in New York in 1936, to return to Germany only after the war. The typical ideas of the Frankfurt School did not emerge until Max Horkheimer took over the Directorship in 1930. The original Director was the Viennese Carl Grünberg, who was primarily a historian of socialist thought with roots in the world of Austro-Marxism. He edited the *Archive of History of Socialism and the Workers' Movement* which was the vehicle for many of the Institute's first publications.

Although these included essays by Lukács and Korsch, they were mainly historical studies based on the rather mechanistic Marxism of the Second International. Karl Wittfogel produced positivistic analyses of Chinese economy and society; Franz Borkenau worked on the emergence of the bourgeois world view; and Henryk Grossmann defended in detailed analyses the view that capitalist over-accumulation would inevitably lead to the decline in the rate of profit and the collapse of the capitalist system.[1] All three were members of the Communist Party, looked with favour on the Soviet Union and were concerned to analyse the socio-economic basis of bourgeois society. With the appointment of Horkheimer as Director in 1930, there was a noticeable shift in policy.

Politically, members of the Institute tended to reject both the reformism of the Social Democrats and the increasingly ossified doctrines of Moscow-orientated Communism. Without any specific political affiliations, they attempted to re-examine the basis of Marxist thought, concentrating their attention above all on the cultural superstructure of bourgeois society.

In their disillusionment both with the West and with the Soviet Union, Horkheimer and his closest collaborator Theodor Adorno drew a certain amount of inspiration from the Council Communists of the 1920s such as Korsch and, above all, Lukács, both of whom had recovered the philosophical dimension in Marxist thought. Much of the work of the Frankfurt School centred on the idea of reification which was central to *History and Class Consciousness*, and Lukács's emphasis on the notion of totality helped the Frankfurt School to correct the comparative neglect of superstructural elements. But their work was more than a restatement of the Hegelian dimension of Marxism. For Horkheimer, for example, Hegel's all-embracing idealism had quietistic political implications and his tendency ultimately to reduce the contradictions between subject and object, mind and matter, etc., to some sort of fundamental identity reduced the critical aspect of thought and thereby the possibility of real change in the world. Moreover, the Frankfurt School was not only concerned to revitalise certain elements within the Marxist tradition; they were also interested in attempting to integrate into it such initially non-Marxist disciplines as psychoanalysis. Even in the realm of philosophy, Horkheimer (in common with most of the Frankfurt School) was early influenced by idealist philosophers such as Schopenhauer, Kant and the 'irrationalism' of such more recent thinkers as Nietzsche, Dilthey, and Bergson – an irrationality which he saw as a protest against the abstract uniformity that increasingly oppressed the individual in advanced capitalist society. Although perverted by the Fascists in the 1930s to justify their own irrationalist aims, these thinkers had given valuable emphasis to the subjective and psychological dimensions of human life that seemed to be effaced through the growing permeation of society by the technical mentality of monopoly capitalism. Of course, Horkheimer did not agree with their neglect of the material dimension of reality: however much they might revise Marx, the Frankfurt School never denied Marx's view of the crucial role played by the economy in capitalist society. What they signally failed to do was to integrate what interest they had in economics into their analysis of society as a whole.

This failure was reflected in their attitude to politics. In the early 1930s the Institute members had at least a notional commitment to political practice. Although they lacked a specific programme for social change, their general commitment to the cause of the proletariat and their emphasis on the importance of *praxis* was strong. They conceived their work to be a contribution to clarifying the opposing forces at work in society and therefore raising the (class) consciousness of the exploited and providing them with a weapon in their struggle for emancipation. In his most forceful statement of this position, Horkheimer wrote:

> If the theoretician and his specific object are seen as forming a dynamic unity with the oppressed class, so that his presentation of societal contradictions is not merely an expression of the concrete historical situation but also a force within it to stimulate change, then his real function emerges. The course of the conflict between the advanced sectors of the class and the individuals who speak out the truth concerning it, as well as of the conflict between the most advanced sectors with their theoreticians and the rest of the class, is to be understood as a process of interactions in which awareness comes to flower along with its liberating but also its aggressive forces which incite while also requiring discipline.[2]

This view was different from the Leninist conception where the intelligentsia and vanguard leadership was one and the same. Even so, the Frankfurt School did signally fail to come into any significant relationship with the political organisations of the working class. Horkheimer considered that the system of workers' councils as most recently exemplified in Germany in 1919 showed the way forward to a new society. He wrote:

> The modalities of the new society are first to be found in the course of its transformation. The theoretical conception, the council system, which according to its pioneers is supposed to show the way to the new society, arises from *praxis*. It goes back to 1871, 1905 and other events. The revolution has a tradition on whose continuation theory is dependent.[3]

And this point of view also found expression in Horkheimer's admiration for the thought and action of Rosa Luxemburg. Nevertheless, the Institute's emphasis on a general analysis of society precluded any attention to specifically political problems: they failed, for example, to maintain contact with Korsch, the political activist who most nearly approximated to their general viewpoint. In any case, they had no ready audience for their theories: their disillusionment with Stalinism meant that the KPD was equally unacceptable to them. As Marcuse wrote later:

> The decisions of the leadership have been increasingly dissociated from the class interest of the proletariat. The former no longer presuppose the proletariat as a revolutionary agent but are imposed upon the proletariat and the rest of the underlying population.[4]

Even the oppositional KPO under Brandler was unacceptable to them as it still approved of Stalinism, however much it might criticise the bureaucratic centralism of the Comintern. The rise of Fascism and the emigration to the United States reinforced this tendency. In America, the School was completely isolated from revolutionary working-class activity and its political pessimism and sense of impotence increased. In *The Eclipse of Reason* Horkheimer wrote:

> Is activism, then, especially political activism, the sole means of fulfilment, as just defined? I hesitate to say so. The age needs no added stimulus to action. Philosophy must not be turned into propaganda, even for the best possible purpose.[5]

Only Marcuse continued to urge the necessity of emancipation from affluent society: Horkheimer and Adorno eventually retreated completely from a revolutionary perspective.

Critical theory

The label preferred by the Frankfurt School for their views was 'critical theory'. Although equally opposed to what it saw as the excessive idealism of phenomenology, the critical theory of the Frankfurt School was aimed largely at positivism. A progressive force during the rise of capitalism, positivism had more recently become a source of reification and an endorsement of the *status quo*. This criticism even at times extended to the work of Marx himself, who was considered to have paid too little attention to the superstructural dimension of domination in his social analysis. Hence the growing interest of the Frankfurt School in psychoanalysis and the concentration on aspects of the human personality that could not be fulfilled simply by catering for economic well-being.

The Frankfurt School's view of critical theory is best summed up in Horkheimer's article *Traditional and Critical Theory*, published in 1937. Horkheimer began with the question: what is theory? His answer was that 'theory for most researchers is the sum total of propositions about a subject, the propositions being so linked with each other that a few are basic and the rest derive from these'.[6] In Descartes these basic propositions had been arrived at deductively, in J.S. Mill inductively, and the same approach was evident in current empirical sociology which attempted 'the laborious ascent from the description of social phenomena to detailed comparisons and only then to the formation of general concepts'.[7] Whether the primary principles were obtained by selection, intuition or mere stipulation, there was always the same division between conceptually formulated knowledge and the facts to be subsumed under it. In this traditional theory, 'the genesis of particular objective facts, the practical application of the conceptual systems by which it grasps the facts, and the role of such systems in action, are all taken to be external to the theoretical thinking itself'.[8]

Critical theory, on the other hand, refused these dichotomies. They were an 'alienation' which involved a separation of value and research, of knowledge and action. The thinker was always a part of the object of his studies and it would be a mistake either to see the intellectual as 'free-floating' above society (as in Mannheim) or as completely embedded in society (as in vulgar Marxism). The view of critical theory therefore was

not simply to eliminate one or other abuse, for it regards such abuses as necessarily connected with the way in which the social structure is organised. Although it itself emerges from the social structure, its purpose is not, either in its conscious intention or in its objective significance, the better functioning of any element in the structure. On the contrary, it is suspicious of the very categories of better, useful, appropriate, productive, and valuable, as these are understood in the present order, and refuses to take them as non-scientific presuppositions about which one can do nothing. The individual as a rule must simply accept the basic conditions of his existence as given and strive to fulfil them.[9]

As opposed to the traditional view,

in the materialist conception, the basic activity involved is work in society, and the class-related form of this work puts its mark on all human patterns of reaction, including theory. The intervention of reason in the processes whereby knowledge and its object are constituted, or the subordination of these processes to conscious control does not take place therefore in a purely intellectual world, but coincides with the struggle for certain real ways of life.[10]

In this enterprise, critical theory saw itself as the inheritor of the whole Western philosophical tradition. It was not philosophy that was to be abolished, as in Marx, but its scientistic degeneration. In their most extended essay on this philosophical tradition, the *Dialectic of the Enlightenment*, Horkheimer and Adorno defined their subject as 'the self-destruction of the Enlightenment',[11] and set out to investigate the paradox that 'the enlightenment has always aimed at liberating men from fear and establishing their sovereignty. Yet the fully enlightened earth radiates disaster triumphant.'[12] Central to their book was the contrast between two types of reason. The first was concerned to discover means for the liberation of human beings from external constraints and compulsions. The second was an instrumental reason whose function was to exercise a technical control over nature and which received its main impetus from the eighteenth-century Enlightenment. In its more recent manifestations, this type of reason had degenerated into totalitarianism:

> For the Enlightenment, whatever does not conform to the rule of computation and utility is suspect. So long as it can develop undisturbed by any outward repression there is no holding it. In the process, it treats its own ideas of human rights exactly as it does the older universals. Every spiritual resistance it encounters serves merely to increase its strength. Which means enlightenment still recognises itself even in myths. Whatever myths the resistance may appeal to, by virtue of the very fact that they become arguments in the process of opposition, they acknowledge the principle of dissolvent rationality for which they reproach the Enlightenment. Enlightenment is totalitarian.[13]

The culmination of this attitude lay in the contemporary 'culture industry'. For the Enlightenment, instead of creating a variegated and liberating culture following the breakdown of the constraints of precapitalist order, had in fact achieved the reverse. For even amusement itself had become industrialised:

> The original affinity of business and amusement is shown in the latter's specific significance: to defend society. To be pleased means to say Yes. It is possible only by insulation from the totality of the social process, by desensitisation and, from the first, by senselessly sacrificing the inescapable claim of every work, however inane, within its limits to reflect the whole. Pleasure always means not to think about anything, to forget suffering even when it is shown. Basically it is helplessness. It

is flight; not, as is asserted, flight from a wretched reality, but from the last remaining thought of resistance. The liberation which amusement promises is freedom from thought and from negation.[14]

By implication, Marx's thought, too, contained elements of instrumental reason: Marx's emphasis on labour (which had been viewed positively in *Traditional and Critical Theory*) and on nature as an object for human exploitation put him in the Enlightenment tradition. Thus class struggle and political economy took second place in the Frankfurt School to a broader account of the way in which the relationship between man and nature had become vitiated.

The impact of psychoanalysis and fascism

In its criticism of the Enlightenment tradition, the Frankfurt School broadened the basis for a critique of capitalist society. In attempting to assimilate the insights of psychoanalysis they at the same time narrowed it. The Frankfurt School referred to Engels's remark that

we all laid and *were bound* to lay, the main emphasis on the *derivation* of political, juridical and other ideological notions, and of actions arising through the medium of these notions, from basic economic facts. But in so doing we neglected the formal side – the ways and means by which these notions, etc. come about – for the sake of the content.[15]

As well as analysing the proliferation of mass culture, the other 'superstructural' problem on which they came to concentrate was the nature and development of authority. And essential to this investigation was some understanding of psychoanalysis, and particularly of Freud. Although Trotsky had expressed an interest in psychoanalysis, the notion that Freud's ideas with their conservative pessimism about social change (which the Frankfurt School later came to share) could have anything to say to Marxism was a novel one in the 1920s. Pioneering here was Wilhelm Reich who was both politically active in the German Communist Party and a practising member of the International Psychoanalytic Association, and had the distinction of being expelled from both. His aim was to show that Marxism and psychoanalysis were compatible in that they occupied separate spheres – that of the social and that of the individual. Reich agreed with Freud that instinctual life was regulated by the pleasure principle but limited by the reality principle. For the ruling class, the reality principle served the perpetuation of their power. So, 'if the proletarian is brought to accept this reality principle – if it is presented to him as absolutely valid, e.g., in the name of culture – this means an affirmation of the proletarian's exploitation and of capitalist society as a whole'.[16] The mediating structure here was the family, which he saw as 'the authoritarian state in miniature'[17] and connected with the rise of Fascism. For Reich the sado-masochistic basis for the middle class (and to a great extent working class) was the patriarchal relationship of the father to his wife and children:

> he is, as it were the exponent and representative of the authority of the state in the family. Because of the contradiction between his position in the production process (subordinate) and his family function (boss) he is a top sergeant type; he kowtows to those above, absorbs the prevailing attitudes (hence his tendency to imitation) and dominates those below; he transmits the governmental and social concepts and enforces them.[18]

Thus, in addition to a politico-economic revolution, sexual revolution was necessary: 'the abolition of the commodity economy necessarily brings about the elimination of sexual morality and ... is a precondition for the abolition of emotional disorder in individuals'.[19]

A rather different approach was taken by Erich Fromm who, unlike Reich, attempted to integrate Marxism and psychoanalysis. Although similar to Reich in that he argued that the sado-masochistic personality was the dominant character structure brought about by modern capitalist society, he tended to submerge the individual in his psychosocial analysis. Thus although starting off as an orthodox Freudian, he came to rob Freud of his vital core. Fromm was more interested in the emotional conflict produced by social interaction than in any theory of instincts. As he said in the introduction to his major work *Escape from Freedom*, 'the key problem of psychology is that of the specific kind of relatedness of the individual toward the world and not the satisfaction or frustration of this or that instinctual need *per se*'.[20] Fromm's main theme was the basis of authoritarianism in the feelings of powerlessness and aloneness provoked by the inability to live an authentic, spontaneous life under contemporary political and economic arrangements. As Marcuse later wrote: 'Fromm, who has demonstrated the repressive features of internalization as few other analysts have done, revives the ideology of internalization.'[21] In recommending such values as 'inner strength' and 'integrity' Fromm had abandoned the Freudian-Marxist critical element in his previous writing: 'it is not the values that are spurious, but the context in which they are defined and proclaimed: "inner strength" has the connotation of that unconditional freedom which can be practiced even in chains'.[22] By the late 1930s, Fromm had effectively left the Frankfurt School.

The main impact of Freud on the thinking of the Frankfurt School was shown in their two studies of authority: *Studies in Authority and Family* and the better-known *Authoritarian Personality.* The Frankfurt School had always been committed to empirical study, and psychoanalysis had persuaded them to view the family as an essential link between base and superstructure.

In the *Studies* the weakening of the ego and the consequent assumption of the role of super-ego by social forces was seen as a function of the declining of the family in late bourgeois society. In the more ambitious *Authoritarian Personality* the aim was 'not merely to describe prejudice, but to explain it in order to help in its eradication'.[23] And the subject of the investigation was the authoritarian personality described by Horkheimer as involving

a mechanical surrender to conventional values; blind submission to authority together with blind hatred of all opponents and outsiders; anti-introspectiveness; rigid stereo-typed thinking; a penchant for superstition; vilification, half-moralistic and half-cynical, of human nature; projectivity.[24]

Although the Institute employed American statistical techniques, they refused to have a methodology which involved a hypothesis that could be proved or disproved. They attempted to uncover the sociological basis for prejudice and here conversational in-depth interviews were held to be as important as statistics. The implicit values, however, were liberal rather than Marxist, with an emphasis on tolerance rather than revolution. Although the irrational social dimension was not denied, the whole bent of the study was psychological rather than socio-political.

This psychological dimension was important in the Frankfurt School's discussion of Fascism, which tended to stress the psychosocial mechanism of authority and violence at the expense of detailed examination of economic substructure. The Frankfurt School saw a direct connection between capitalism and Fascism: as the capitalist economy evolved in a monopolist direction, so liberalism evolved towards totalitarianism. In a famous aphorism Horkheimer said: 'He who does not wish to speak of capitalism should also be silent about Fascism.'[25] Ignoring the very real differences in the form of civil liberties, legal safeguards, etc., that separated the constitutional liberal state from the Fascist state, the Frankfurt

School tended to stress the continuity between liberalism and Fascism. Marcuse, for example, wrote:

> The turn from the liberalist to the total authoritarian state occurs within the framework of a single social order. With regard to the unity of this economic base, we can say it is liberalism that 'produces' the total-authoritarian state out of itself, as its own consummation at a more advanced stage of development.[26]

This approach saw Nazism as the culmination of the trend towards irrational domination inherent in the growing emphasis on instrumental reason and technological rationalisation that was the legacy of the liberal Enlightenment tradition in the West.

The major exception to this approach was Franz Neumann who, in his classic *Behemoth*, paid scant attention to the work of his colleagues on the authoritarian personality and the sado-masochistic elements in the Fascist mentality. Neumann began by contesting the position of Frederick Pollock that Nazism was a new order in which the private accumulation of capital was no longer the driving force. In Pollock's view national socialism was no longer an exchange economy: politics had taken command to such an extent that private property was no longer its basis. By contrast, Neumann stressed the economic difficulties caused by growing cartelisation in Weimar Germany and the necessity for state intervention in order to 'strengthen the monopolistic position, to aid the complete incorporation of all business activities into the network of industrial organisations'.[27] 'The German economy of today', he wrote, 'has two broad and striking characteristics. It is a monopolistic economy – and a command economy. It is a private capitalistic economy, regimented by the totalitarian state. We suggest as a name best to describe it, "Totalitarian Monopoly Capitalism".'[28] Those who benefited from the Nazi economic legislation were by and large the same as those who benefited from the old monopoly capitalism. The profit motive was still basic: it just needed totalitarian political power to support it. Unlike Horkheimer, Neumann analysed the Nazi state in class terms and saw its politics as 'accepting and strengthening the prevailing class structure of German society'.[29] And Neumann supported this view with a mass of detailed observation.

Aesthetics

The most impressive achievement of the Frankfurt School lay in the field of aesthetics. Their interest in culture was strengthened by their experience of the United States in the achievement there of conformism by the dissemination of mass culture rather than the use of terror. What mass culture had in common with Fascism, in their view, was an increasing abolition of the distinction between the private and public spheres by exploiting or creating needs in the individual in order to support a particular system of domination. In their treatment of arts the Frankfurt School differed from the Leninist tradition in which art and literature were judged primarily by the attitude they displayed towards the class struggle. Following the tradition of Engels (and indeed Marx, whose favourite authors were Shakespeare and the royalist Balzac), the Frankfurt School considered the social insights of a work more important than the political stance of the author. This view had inspired much of the work of Lukács on the nineteenth-century bourgeois novel although Lukács's rejection of most 'modern' art forms separated him from the Frankfurt School, who were extremely interested in contemporary art forms. As Marxists, they stressed the social limitations of both author and audience, but they allotted art a more autonomous role than in the Leninist tradition. In its negative aspect, art was a protest against prevailing conditions and transcended society in so far as it hinted at more humane values. Hence their critique of mass culture which they saw as 'affirmative', of which Marcuse offered the following definition:

By affirmative culture is meant that culture of the bourgeois epoch which leads in the course of its own development to the segregation from civilisation of the mental and spiritual world as an independent realm of value that is also considered superior to civilisation. Its decisive characteristic is the assertion of a universally obligatory, eternally better, and more valuable world that must be unconditionally affirmed: a world essentially different from the factual world of the daily struggle for existence, yet realisable by every individual for himself 'from within', without any transformation of the state of fact.[30]

But this opposition to affirmative culture did not imply a cultural elitism. They were entirely opposed to any cultural asceticism which divorced art from material needs. The trouble with mass culture was that it was not truly popular. It was foisted on people rather than created by them, serving the interest of domination and potentially of totalitarianism.[31]

The Frankfurt School's most gifted critic in this field was Adorno, whose main field of cultural interest from his early years was that of music. Most modern music, Adorno maintained, was orientated towards the market. Other sorts of music, therefore, tended to be difficult, but not therefore reactionary. On the contrary, Adorno praised Schönberg, whose atonal music expressed the disharmonies of contemporary society:

> Here and now, music can do no more than to present, in its own structure, the social antimonies which, amongst other things, carry the responsibility for music's isolation. It will succeed all the better, the more deeply it manages to form, within itself, the force of those contradictions and the need to resolve them in society, and the more precisely it expresses, in the antimonies of its own language and forms, the miseries of the status quo, emphatically calling, through the ciphered language of suffering, for change.[32]

This implied an opposition to such composers as Stravinsky who merely adapted pre-bourgeois music to current society. Adorno reserved particular scorn for jazz, which he saw as a commodity-orientated form of music abetting the reconciliation of the individual to his lot in capitalist society.

In his later works, particularly *Negative Dialectics* of 1966, Adorno produced a philosophy that some have seen as wholly pessimistic. His dialectic was negative in that society had become so completely reified that domination was complete and prevented the formation of any critical reaction. Adorno tried to show how the 'culture industry' with its standardisation of only marginally different versions of diversion and distraction served as a social cement: under the guise of offering relaxation, it served to reinforce and reproduce the structure of the world from which people were trying to escape and thus enhanced their feelings of dependence and fatalism. Pursuing themes from *Dialectic of Enlightenment*, history is here seen, in contrast to what Adorno sees as the rather blithe optimism of Lukács, as set on a consistently downward path. Adorno is almost as consistently anti-subjective as contemporary French structuralists such as Althusser. But he remained convinced that art could offer resisting insights that could occasionally illuminate the general gloom.[33] And dialectics itself was negative also in the sense that it was oppositional: it protested against any classificatory thinking or concept of identity: 'dialectics is the consistent sense of non-identity. It does not begin by taking a standpoint.'[34] The aphoristic, sibylline, and sometimes deliberately self-contradictory nature of Adorno's writing has made him difficult of access. There has, however, recently been a revival of interest in his thought – possibly in keeping with the gloomy nature of our times. Fredric Jameson has hailed him as 'one of the greatest of twentieth-century Marxist philosophers' whose originality 'lies in his unique emphasis on the presence of late capitalism as a totality within the very forms of our concepts or of the works of art themselves'.[35] Thus Adorno's Marxism, although neglected in previous periods, may now have been caught up with by history.

The other major cultural critic of the Frankfurt School was Walter Benjamin, a friend of, and close collaborator with, Adorno. Benjamin derived his theological – or, rather, mystical – attitudes from his aesthetics and developed a 'negative' theological position in which mysticism and materialism converged. The allusive nature of Benjamin's approach is exemplified in the passage which opened one of his last essays:

> A puppet in Turkish attire and with a hookah in its mouth sat before a chessboard placed on a large table ... Actually, a little hunchback who was an expert chess player sat inside and guided the puppet's hand by means of strings. One can imagine a philosophical counterpart to this device. The puppet called 'historical materialism' is to win all the time. It can easily be a match for anyone if it enlists the services of theology, which today, as we know, is wizened and has to keep out of sight.[36]

Although Benjamin called himself a historical materialist, his images and language were heavily imbued with theological themes such as redemption and messianism and, much to Adorno's annoyance, he was loath to mediate the theological with the secular. Benjamin's expressions were deliberately, as he put it, 'Janus-faced', simultaneously strongly religious and strongly revolutionary materialist. This dichotomy can be seen in the contrast between the pessimistically mystical 'Theses on the Philosophy of History' written just before his suicide in 1940 and his projected history of nineteenth-century French ideologies known as 'The Arcades Project'.[37] Here, particularly in the section entitled 'The Work of Art in the Age of Mechanical Reproduction', Benjamin developed a distinctively historical materialist account of the relation of art and culture to technological innovation and social class.[38]

Benjamin was closely associated with Brecht and much of Benjamin's work consisted in a theoretical discussion of Brecht's writing, and in particular of the 'alienation effect' designed to prevent the assimilation of his work by providing the audience with a mechanism for critically distancing themselves from it. Benjamin was interested in the levels of meaning hidden in language, had a messianic theme to most of his writing, and was more optimistic than Adorno about the effects of the mass reproduction of art.[39]

Marcuse

Herbert Marcuse is the best known of the Frankfurt School, the only one of the original members not to have renounced his early revolutionary outlook. Before he joined the Institute he had tried to combine Marxism with a Heideggerian form of existentialism.[40] He had also welcomed the publication in 1932 of Marx's early writings and particularly the analysis of alienated labour in the *Economic and Philosophical Manuscripts*, which remained a constant focus of Marcuse's thought. Throughout the 1930s he published a series of articles which contained the germs of his later works. But his major work in this period was a study of Hegel entitled *Reason and Revolution*. It was the first work to make available in English the views of the critical theorists. Like Horkheimer, Marcuse was concerned to stress the rational element in Hegel's thought. He wished thereby to present a reading of Hegel that was different both from the Nazis who saw him as a precursor of the irrational romanticism of the organic state, and from the Stalinists, who saw Hegel as an aristocratic and reactionary thinker. Marcuse contrasted the radicalism implicit in Hegel's thought with the conservative implications of many of his positivist successors such as Comte. Neglecting the theological aspects of Hegel's thought, Marcuse sought to show an underlying continuity between Hegel and Marx. Hegel was the first thinker in Germany to have gained the insight that

> the given social order, based upon the system of abstract and quantitative labour and upon the integration of wants through the exchange of commodities, is incapable of asserting and establishing a rational community. This order remains essentially one of anarchy and irrationality, governed by blind economic mechanisms.[41]

Although Hegel's demand for a strong state to cope with this anarchic situation may have been misguided, he had brought philosophy to a point where it passed over into social practice:

> The final culmination of philosophy is thus at the same time its abdication. Released from its preoccupation with the ideal, philosophy is also released from its opposition to reality. This means that it ceases to be philosophy. It does not follow, however, that thought must then comply with the existing order. Critical thinking does not cease, but assumes a new form. The efforts of reason devolve upon social theory and social practice.[42]

In Marcuse's interpretation, the transition from Hegel to Marx was a transition to a different order of truth – one that could not be interpreted in terms of philosophy. For 'all the philosophical concepts of Marxian theory are social and economic categories, whereas Hegel's social and economic categories are all philosophical concepts'.[43] Hegel had emphasised the category of labour, but it was Marx who altered the emphasis from philosophical labour to that of the alienated worker. Here Marcuse, expanding on passages in Marx's *German Ideology*, touched on questions that were to continue to preoccupy him. 'These amazing formulations in Marx's early writings', he wrote,

> all contain the Hegelian term *Aufhebung*, so that abolition also carries the meaning that a content is restored to its true form. Marx, however, envisioned the future mode of labour to be so different from the prevailing one that he hesitated to use the same term 'labour' to designate alike the material process of capitalist and of communist society. He uses the term 'labour' to mean what capitalism actually understands by it in the last analysis, that activity which creates surplus value in commodity production, or, which 'produces capital'. Other kinds of activities are not 'productive labour' and hence not labour in the proper sense. Labour thus means that free and universal development is denied the individual who labours, and it is clear that in this state of affairs the liberation of the individual is at once the negation of labour.[44]

Marcuse does, however, go even beyond Marx himself when he claims that, with the transition from philosophy to social practice, 'the idea of reason has been superseded by the idea of happiness'.[45]

The concept of happiness and its frustration in contemporary society was central to the next of Marcuse's major works – *Eros and Civilisation* – the impact of which led to the impression that the theories of Freud and Marx might indeed be reconcilable. The aim of the book was profoundly political:

> This essay employs psychological categories because they have become political categories. The traditional borderlines between psychology on the one hand and political and social philosophy on the other have been made obsolete by the condition of man in the present era: formerly autonomous and identifiable psychical processes are being absorbed by the function of the individual in the State – by his public existence.[46]

Marcuse opposed the Freudian revisionists who concentrated on therapy within the framework of contemporary society. These revisionists were, according to him, only a specific example of those who neglected theory for an essentially conformist *praxis*, as did Hegel's positivist successors that he had already criticised in *Reason and Revolution*. But whereas Horkheimer and Adorno's analysis of late capitalist society led them to pessimistic conclusions, Marcuse's study of the psychological obstacles to liberation led him to a utopian radicalism.

Unlike Wilhelm Reich (to whom Marcuse paid extraordinarily little attention) Marcuse welcomed the later doctrines of Freud. He insisted that Freud's theory of instincts was thoroughly materialist and endorsed the idea of the death instinct as capable of penetrating the ambivalent nature of modern society. But Marcuse was not pessimistic: in his view, the death instinct aimed at a kind of Nirvana, a state of non-desire. Desire was produced by tension and tension was endemic to class society. If this tension could be reduced, then so would the power of the death instinct. The limitation of the death instinct and the enhancement of Eros could be achieved only in a society which encouraged polymorphous sexual gratification and widespread libidinal release. This involved the abolition of monogamic genital supremacy. Marcuse rejected Freud's view that a non-repressive civilisation was impossible. In contemporary society the conflict of the pleasure principle and the reality principle was determined by the social organisation of labour which had subordinated instincts to reality by means of what Marcuse called the 'performance principle'. This, however, was specific to a society governed by the imperative of scarcity. As technology advanced, this repression became increasingly 'surplus'. The way was thus open for a society no longer based on the performance principle, a society which would be able to do away with surplus repression by abolishing alienated labour. In a utopian vein, Marcuse anticipated a society in which labour would be replaced by an aesthetic kind of play which would finally destroy the power of the death instinct. Thus Marcuse complemented (and at times almost seemed to replace) Marx's economic exploitation by the concept of instinctual repression.

The theme of *Eros and Civilisation* was set in a more social context in Marcuse's most influential work, *One-Dimensional Man*. At the same time the optimism of *Eros and Civilisation* gave way to a deep pessimism.[47] Marcuse's verdict on advanced industrial society, and much of his specific analysis, is fully in line with that of Horkheimer and Adorno in their *Dialectic of the Enlightenment*. *One-Dimensional Man* marked a fundamental change in the traditional Marxist perspective. Although Marcuse agreed that capitalists and proletarians were still the basic classes in industrial society:

> the capitalist development has altered the structure and function of these two classes in such a way that they no longer appear to be agents of historical transformation. An overriding interest in the preservation and improvement of the institutional status quo unites the former antagonists in the most advanced areas of contemporary society. And to the degree to which technical progress assures the growth and cohesion of communist society, the very idea of qualitative change recedes before the realistic notions of a non-explosive evolution.[48]

Building on his earlier view that 'the turn from the liberalist to the total-authoritarian state occurs within the framework of a single social order',[49] Marcuse declared that advanced industrial society was totalitarian:

> For 'totalitarian' is not only a terroristic political co-ordination of society, but also a non-terroristic economic-technical co-ordination which operates through the manipulation of needs by vested interests. It thus precludes the emergence of an effective opposition against the whole. Not only a specific form of government or party rule makes for totalitarianism, but also a specific system of production and distribution which may well be compatible with a 'pluralism' of parties, newspapers, 'countervailing powers', etc.[50]

This totalitarianism was all the more secure as it seemed to have no conscious economic or political direction.[51] Technological society appeared to have satisfied men's needs and thus offered no room for protest. Marcuse attempted to distinguish between true and false needs. But what men's real needs were could not be determined at present, for

> in the last analysis, the question of what are true and false needs must be answered by the individual themselves, but only in the last analysis: that is, if and when they're free to give their own answer.[52]

This obviously left unresolved the question of how a society which totally controlled the consciousness of its members could possibly change; and the bulk of *One-Dimensional Man* was devoted to demonstrating the all-pervasive nature of this control. What distinguished current society was

> a flattening out of the antagonism between culture and social reality
> through the obliteration of the oppositional, alien, and transcendent
> elements in the higher culture by virtue of which it constituted
> *another dimension* of reality.[53]

In the realm of art, the material advances of society had produced 'a harmonising pluralism where the most contradictory works and truths peacefully coexist in indifference'.[54] In sexual matters, too, an 'institutionalised desublimation' had taken place:

> Sex is integrated into work and public relations and thus is made
> more susceptible to (controlled) satisfaction. Technical progress
> and more comfortable living permit the systematic inclusion of libidinal
> components into the realm of commodity production and
> exchange.[55]

Even language itself was progressively becoming a closed system which precluded even linguistic expression of opposition.

In the face of such a society, what hope was there for change? Marcuse stated at the beginning of his work that he vacillated between two contradictory hypotheses. The first was that advanced industrial society was capable of containing qualitative change for the foreseeable future; and the second that forces and tendencies existed which might break this containment and explode society. Throughout *One-Dimensional Man* the emphasis was on the first tendency. The possibility that the second tendency might come to the fore was only raised very briefly at the end of the book. This tendency would have to be based on those who existed outside the 'democratic process': 'the substratum of the outcasts and outsiders, the exploited and persecuted of other races and other colours, the unemployed and the unemployable'.[56] But for Marcuse, this could only be an 'accident':

> The chance is that the historical extremes may meet again: the most
> advanced consciousness of humanity, and its most exploited force.
> It is nothing but a chance. The critical theory of society possesses no
> concepts which could bridge the gap between the present and its
> future: holding no promise and showing no success, it remains
> negative.[57]

Of all the Frankfurt School, Marcuse remained the least empirical. At the same time, and paradoxically, he is its clearest and most systematic exponent. His commitment to a radicalism that most of his colleagues had abandoned has ensured him a continuing place in the Marxist tradition.

Habermas

The most impressive of the 'second generation' of the Frankfurt School is undoubtedly Jürgen Habermas. His work to date has an enormous range to it: as well as discussing, as did his predecessors, the problems of methodology and the use of natural scientific models of reason for instrumental control, Habermas is also concerned to integrate the more modern disciplines of hermeneutics and systems theory with the traditional interpretation of historical materialism. Building on the work of Horkheimer and Adorno in the *Dialectic of the Enlightenment*, Habermas examined the philosophical presuppositions which had allowed the transformation of reason from an instrument of liberation to one of domination. Marx had tended to use natural science as a model for his society theory, which minimised the role of philosophy, whereas for Horkheimer and Adorno (and Habermas) Marxist theory could only remain critical if it restored the philosophical dimension in opposition to all forms of scientism. Habermas agreed that there was an unresolved dichotomy in Marx between his empirical theory of the capitalist economy and the critical appraisal of revolutionary practice: Marx's theoretical categories were at times reductionist and even positivist. But Habermas wished to avoid the pessimistic cultural critique of the late Frankfurt School, which has been accused of a relapse into Young Hegelianism.[58] He attempted to achieve this in *Knowledge and Human Interests* by a basic reformulation of historical materialism. He did not wish, like Horkheimer and Adorno, to reject labour as a fundamental category of human activity; but he considered that implicit in Marx was a distinction between labour and interaction. The first was purposive rational action on an external world: the second involved communication between subjects. These two spheres (which corresponded to some extent with the classical Marxist division between forces of production and relations of production) were separate though related dimensions of social evolution. Each dimension had its own mode of knowledge and its own criteria of rationality: in the sphere of instrumental action, this involved extending technical control, in that of cultural development it involved the extension of forms of communication free from distortion and domination. Habermas then attempted to provide a theoretical framework for ideal communication, declaring that 'today the problem of language has replaced the traditional problem of consciousness'.[59] Habermas stated that technological society could only be rational if its policies were subject to public control. But discussion and opinion had to be free from manipulation and domination. The very act of speech involved the supposition of the possibility of an ideal speech situation in which the force of the better argument alone would decide the issue. This was only possible if all members of society had an equal chance to participate in the discussion; and this involved the notion of the transformation of society in a direction that would enable such a communicative competence to characterise all members of society. The ultimate goal of social emancipation was therefore inherent in any and every speech act. It must be admitted, however, that Habermas was highly unspecific as to the realisation of this society.

Whereas the theory of communicative competence he expounded in *Knowledge and Human Interests* was 'superstructural', Habermas's *Legitimation Crisis*, examined the chances of social emancipation at all levels. Past history had involved a series of social formations of which each was 'determined by a fundamental principle of organisation, which delimits in the abstract the possibilities for alterations of social states'.[60] Habermas analysed briefly liberal capitalism in terms similar to those of Marx, i.e., as involving a basic contradiction between social production and private accumulation. Enquiring whether the same was true of late capitalism, Habermas outlined a typology of crises inherent in contemporary society: an economic crisis, a crisis of rationality, of legitimacy, and of motivation. In Habermas's view, an economic crisis in late capitalism was not inevitable. But the steps taken by the state to avert it entailed a crisis of rationality. For the conflict of interests inherent in late capitalism and the contradictory demands on state intervention tended to mean that state aid was dysfunctionally distributed. This, in turn, created a crisis of legitimacy, for state intervention meant opening up the question of control and choice. The only solutions were buying off the most powerful parties or the creation of a new legitimising ideology. In addition, growing public intervention involved lessening the scope of the private sphere which had motivated bourgeois society and thereby a crisis in motivation. Summarising his conclusions, Habermas declared:

> Economic crises are shifted into the political system through the reactive-avoidance activity of the government in such a way that supplies of legitimation can compensate for deficits in rationality and extension of organisational rationality can compensate for those

legitimation deficits that do appear. There arises a bundle of crisis tendencies that, from a genetic point of view, represents a hierarchy of crisis phenomena shifted upwards from below. But from the point of view of governmental crisis management, these crisis phenomena are distinguished by being mutually substitutable within certain limits. These limits are determined by, on the one hand, the fiscally available quantity of value – the shortage of which cannot be validly predicted within crisis theory – and on the other by supplies of motivation from the socio-cultural system. The substitutive relation between the scarce resources, value and meaning, is therefore decisive for the prediction of crisis.[61]

In the third and final part of *Legitimation Crisis*, Habermas could see no solution to these staggered crises apart from recourse to a new set of norms that would involve the communicative competence he had discussed earlier and the appropriate socio-economic organisation.

Habermas's subsequent work, centring around his massive two-volume *Theory of Communicative Action*, published in 1981, takes him outside the scope of anything that could be even broadly described as Marxism.[62] Here he analyses what he calls the 'colonization of the life-world' by an increasingly instrumental rationality and attempts to construct an account of language which stresses the way in which all engaged in communicative action commit themselves thereby to overcoming communicative distortions through a process of discursive validity-testing. From this core notion Habermas went on, in a liberal-legalistic turn, to construct theories of democracy, ethics, and law which aimed to develop the uncompleted project of modernity in realising certain universally justifiable Enlightenment values. Equally outside the confines of Marxism are members of the third generation of the Frankfurt School such as Albrecht Wellmer writing on philosophy, Claus Offe on political sociology, or Axel Honneth on political theory who take up the themes of critical theory to develop reflections on democracy and civil society.[63] But insofar as the original impetus of the Frankfurt School survives into the twenty-first century it is in its transatlantic reincarnation in the work of Fredric Jameson.[64]

Notes

1. See further, p. 186 above.
2. M. Horkheimer, *Critical Theory: Selected Essays* (New York, 1972), p. 215.
3. M. Horkheimer, 'The Authoritarian State' in A. Arato and E. Gebhardt (eds), *The Essential Frankfurt School Reader* (New York, 1978), p. 104.

4. H. Marcuse, *Soviet Marxism* (New York, 1958), p. 106.
5. M. Horkheimer, *The Eclipse of Reason* (New York, 1947), p. 184.
6. M. Horkheimer, *Critical Theory: Selected Essays* (New York, 1972), p. 188.
7. Ibid., p. 192.
8. Ibid., p. 208.
9. Ibid., p. 207.
10. Ibid., p. 245.
11. M. Horkheimer and T. Adorno, *Dialectic of Enlightenment* (New York, 1972; London, 1973), p. xiii.
12. Ibid., p. 3.
13. Ibid., p. 6.
14. Ibid., p. 144. For a slightly different view of the same question, see A. Sohn-Rethel, *Intellectual and Manual Labour: A Critique of Epistemology* (London, 1978).
15. Engels to Mehring, in K. Marx and F. Engels, *Selected Correspondence* (Moscow, 1965), p. 459.
16. W. Reich, *Sex-Pol: Essays 1929–934*, ed. L. Baxandall (New York, 1972), p. 20.
17. W. Reich, *The Mass Psychology of Fascism* (New York, 1970), p. 30.
18. W. Reich, *Sex-Pol: Essays 1929–1934*, ed. L. Baxandall (New York, 1972), p. 242.
19. W. Reich, *The Sexual Revolution* (London, 1972), p. 73.
20. E. Fromm, *Escape from Freedom* (New York, 1941), p. 12.
21. H. Marcuse, *Eros and Civilization* (London, 1972), p. 180.
22. Ibid., p. 181.
23. T. Adorno *et al.*, *The Authoritarian Personality* (New York, 1950) vol. 1, p. vii.
24. M. Horkheimer, 'The Lessons of Fascism', in *Tensions That Cause War*, ed. H. Cantril (Urbana, 1950), p. 230.
25. M. Horkheimer, 'Die Juden und Europa', *Zeitschrift für Sozialforschung*, vol. 8 (1939), p. 115.
26. H. Marcuse, *Negations* (London and Boston, 1968), p. 19.
27. F. Neumann, *Behemoth: The Structure and Practice of National Socialism 1933–1944*, rev. edn (New York, 1944), p. 260.
28. Ibid., p. 261.
29. Ibid., p. 366.
30. H. Marcuse, 'The Affirmative Character of Culture', in *Negations*, p. 95.
31. For the most extended presentation of this view, see M. Horkheimer and T. Adorno, *Dialectic of Enlightenment*.
32. T. Adorno, 'Zur gesellschaftlichen Lage der Musik', *Zeitschrift für Sozialforschung*, vol. 1 (1932) p. 106.
33. See here T. Adorno, *Aesthetic Theory* (Boston, 1984).
34. T. Adorno, *Negative Dialectics* (London, 1973), p. 5. See the careful discussion of Adorno's negativity in M. Jay, *Marxism and Totality* (Berkeley, 1984), pp. 264 ff.
35. F. Jameson, *Late Marxism: Adorno, or, the Persistence of the Dialectic* (New York, 1990), pp. 4, 9.
36. W. Benjamin, *Illuminations: Essays and Reflections* (New York, 1968), p. 225.
37. W. Benjamin, *The Arcades Project* (Cambridge, 1999).
38. Both the 'Theses' and the article on art can be found in *Illuminations*, ed. H. Arendt (London, 1973), pp. 255 ff. and the 'Theses' in *Critical Theory: A Reader*, ed. D. Tallack (Hemel Hempstead, 1995), pp. 278 ff. See further

M. Lowy, *Fire Alarm: Reading Walter Benjamin's 'On the Concept of History'* (New York, 2006).

39. See further ch. 2 of F. Jameson's *Marxism and Form* (Princeton, N.J., 1971). Jameson's book as a whole is the best recent contribution to the study of Marxist aesthetics.
40. See H. Marcuse, *Heideggerian Marxism*, ed. S. Wolin and J. Abromeit (Lincoln, 2005).
41. H. Marcuse, *Reason and Revolution: Hegel and the Rise of Social Theory*, 2nd edn (London, 1954) p. 60.
42. Ibid., p. 28.
43. Ibid., p. 258.
44. Ibid., p. 293.
45. Ibid. See further on this point his essay on hedonism in *Negations*, p. 159ff.
46. H. Marcuse, *Eros and Civilization* (London, 1969), p. 21.
47. This pessimism is retracted in some of Marcuse's more recent pronouncements. See, for example, his *Essay on Liberation* (London and Boston, 1969).
48. H. Marcuse, *One-Dimensional Man: Studies in the Ideology of Advanced Industrial Society*, 2nd edn (London, 1968), p. 11.
49. H. Marcuse, *Negations*, p. 19.
50. H. Marcuse, *One-Dimensional Man*, p. 20.
51. Although *One-Dimensional Man* was chiefly concerned with the United States, Marcuse had previously published a similarly pessimistic analysis of the Soviet Union; see his *Soviet Marxism* (New York, 1958).
52. Ibid., p. 22.
53. Ibid., p. 58.
54. Ibid., p. 61.
55. Ibid., p. 71.
56. Ibid., p. 201.
57. Ibid.
58. See, for example, A. MacIntyre, *Marcuse* (London and New York, 1970), pp. 22, 40, 61.
59. J. Habermas, *Zur Logik der Sozialwissenschaften* (Frankfurt, 1970), quoted by T. McCarthy in his Introduction to *Legitimation Crisis* (London, 1976).
60. J. Habermas, *Legitimation Crisis*, p. 7.
61. Ibid., p. 93.
62. But see the careful discussion in M. Jay, *Marxism and Totality*, pp. 462 ff. which aims to keep him within the fold.
63. See, for example, A. Honneth, *The Struggle for Recognition: The Moral Grammar of Social Conflicts* (Cambridge, 1995).
64. On Jameson, see pp. 389 ff. below.

Further reading

Western Marxism in general

A stimulating introduction is Anderson's *Considerations on Western Marxism*. An outstanding, though difficult, work, centring on aesthetics, is Jameson's *Marxism and Form*. See also McInnes's *The Western Marxists* and the collections of articles edited by Blackburn, by Howard and Klare, and by the *New Left Review*. Anderson's short book, *In the Tracks of Historical Materialism*, is consistently stimulating. From within the tradition, see also Jay's *Marxism and Totality* and the books by Kellner and Jacoby. For a more critical approach, see Merquior's *Western Marxism*.

The Frankfurt School: general texts

Two comprehensive collections are Connerton's *Critical Sociology* and Arato and Gebhardt's *The Essential Frankfurt School Reader*. Jameson has a more specialised collection on *Aesthetics and Politics*, and *The Positivist Dispute in German Sociology* by Adorno and others is good background to the contemporary scene.

The Frankfurt School: general commentaries

The best introduction is Jay's thorough and informative *The Dialectical Imagination*. This can be supplemented by Schroyer's more speculative *The Critique of Domination*. For a critique from a more fundamentalist Marxist perspective, see Therborn's article and Slater's *Origin and Significance of the Frankfurt School*. A recent comprehensive account is to be found in Wiggerhaus's massive history.

Adorno and Horkheimer

Adorno's brilliance as a essayist can be appreciated in his two collections, *Prisms* and *Minima Moralia*. His indictment of contemporary society is available in *Dialectic of Enlightenment*, his psychological studies in *The Authoritarian Personality*, and his more philosophical reflections in *Negative Dialectics*. Commentaries on Adorno are Buck-Morss's *The Origin of Negative Dialectics* and Rose's *The Melancholy Science*. See also Chapter One of Jameson's *Marxism and Form*.

For Horkheimer, see his *Eclipse of Reason* and the collection *Critical Theory*, with a short introduction by Aronowitz. See also the fifth chapter of Howard's *The Marxian Legacy*.

Marcuse

The most available and accessible of Marcuse's works is *One-Dimensional Man*. For Marcuse's attempt to marry Marx and Freud, see his *Eros and Civilization*. The Hegelian background is contained in *Reason and Revolution*. The collection *Negations*, which contains essays from the 1930s as well as the 1960s, probably gives the best general introduction to Marcuse's thought. A comprehensive bibliography of Marcuse's works can be found in Marks's *The Meaning of Marcuse*, which is a good short introduction. For a highly critical conceptual analysis, see MacIntyre's *Marcuse*. Mattick's *Critique of Marcuse* and Woodis's *New Theories of Revolution* are critiques from a Marxist perspective. See also *Critical Interruptions*, a series of articles edited by Breines.

Others

On Benjamin, see the collections of his essays entitled *Illuminations: Essays and Reflections;* also his *magnum opus, The Origins of German Tragic Drama.* For commentaries, see the Introduction to the latter by Steiner, and the articles by Arendt and Jameson. For Fromm's contribution, see particularly *The Fear of Freedom* and *The Sane Society,* and the commentary by Schaar. For Habermas, see his main works: *Knowledge and Human Interests; Legitimation Crisis;* the two volumes on *The Theory of Communicative Action;* and *Between Facts and Norms.* More accessible is Outhwaite's useful *The Habermas Reader.* For commentary, see McCarthy's *The Critical Theory of Jürgen Habermas* and White's *The Recent Work of Jürgen Habermas,* as well as his edition of *The Cambridge Companion to Habermas.* The best introduction is Outhwaite's *Habermas: A Critical Introduction.*

Bibliography

Western Marxism in general

Perry Anderson, *Considerations on Western Marxism* (London, 1976).
—— *In the Tracks of Historical Materialism* (London, 1983).
Robin Blackburn (ed.), *Ideology in Social Science* (London, 1972).
David Caute, *The Fellow-Travellers* (London, 1977).
D. Howard and K. Klare (ed.), *The Unknown Dimension: Post-Leninist Marxism* (New York, 1972).
Russell Jacoby, *Dialectic of Defeat: Contours of Western Marxism* (Cambridge, 1981).
Martin Jay, *Marxism and Totality: The Adventures of a Concept from Lukács to Habermas* (Berkeley, 1984).
Douglas Kellner, *Critical Theory, Marxism and Modernity* (Cambridge, 1990).
Nicolas Lobkowicz (ed.), *Marx and the Western World* (London, 1967).
Neil McInnes, *The Western Marxists* (London, 1972).
J.E. Merquior, *Western Marxism* (London, 1986).
New Left Review (eds.), *Western Marxism: A Critical Reader* (London, 1977).

The Frankfurt School: general texts

Theodor W. Adorno *et al., The Positivist Dispute in German Sociology* (London, 1976).
Andrew Arato and Eike Gebhardt (eds), *The Essential Frankfurt School Reader* (London, 1978).

Paul Connerton (ed.), *Critical Sociology: Selected Readings of Adorno, Habermas, Benjamin, Horkheimer, Marcuse and Neumann* (London, 1976).
Fredric Jameson (ed.), *Aesthetics and Politics: Adorno, Benjamin, Bloch, Brecht, and Lukács* (London, 1978).

The Frankfurt School: general commentaries

Donald Fleming and Bernard Bailyn (eds), *The Intellectual Migration: Europe and America, 1930–1960* (Cambridge, Mass., 1969).
F. Jameson, *Marxism and Form* (Princeton, 1971).
Martin Jay, *The Dialectical Imagination: A History of the Frankfurt School and the Institute of Social Research, 1923–1950* (London, 1973).
George Lichtheim, 'From Marx to Hegel: Reflections on Georg Lukács, T.W. Adorno, and Herbert Marcuse', *Tri-Quarterly*, 12 (spring 1968).
J. Orr, 'German Social Theory and the Hidden Face of Technology', *Archives européennes de sociologie*, 15 (1974).
A. Quinton, 'Critical Theory', *Encounter*, 10 (1974).
Paul Robinson, *The Freudian Left* (New York, 1969).
Trent Schroyer, *The Critique of Domination: The Origins and Development of Critical Theory* (New York, 1973).
—— 'The Politics of Epistemology: A Marxist Perspective on the Current Debates in German Sociology', *International Journal of Sociology* 1, 4 (winter 1971–72).
Phil Slater, *Origin and Significance of the Frankfurt School: A Marxist Perspective* (London, 1977).
Göran Therborn, 'Frankfurt Marxism: A Critique', *New Left Review*, 63 (1970), and *New Left Review* (eds), *Western Marxism: A Critical Reader* (London, 1977).
Albrecht Wellmer, *Critical Theory of Society* (New York, 1971).
Rolf Wiggerhaus, *The Frankfurt School: Its History, Theories and Political Significance* (Cambridge, 1994).

Adorno and Horkheimer: texts

Theodor W. Adorno *et al.*, *The Authoritarian Personality* (New York, 1950).
—— (with M. Horkheimer), *Dialectic of Enlightenment* (New York, 1972; London, 1973).
—— *Minima Moralia: Reflections from Damaged Life* (London, 1974).
—— *Negative Dialectics* (London, 1973).
—— *Prisms* (London, 1967).
Max Horkheimer, *Eclipse of Reason* (New York, 1947).
—— *Critical Theory: Selected Essays* (New York, 1972).

Adorno and Horkheimer: commentaries

J. Bernstein, *Adorno: Disenchantment and Ethics* (Cambridge, 2001).
Susan Buck-Morss, *The Origin of Negative Dialectics* (New York and Hassocks, 1978).
D. Howard, *The Marxian Legacy* (London and New York, 1977) ch. 5.
F. Jameson, *Late Marxism: Adorno, or, the Persistence of the Dialectic* (New York, 1990).
Fredric Jameson, 'T.W. Adorno or Historical Tropes', *Salmagundi*, 5 (spring 1967).
S. Jarvis, *Adorno: A Critical Introduction* (London, 1998).
S. Muller-Doohm, *Adorno: An Intellectual Biography* (London, 2005).

Gillian Rose, *The Melancholy Science: An Introduction to the Thought of Adorno* (London, 1979).

Marcuse: texts

Herbert Marcuse, *Counterrevolution and Revolt* (London, 1972).
—— R.P. Wolff and B. Moore, *A Critique of Pure Tolerance* (London, 1969).
—— *Eros and Civilization: A Philosophical Inquiry into Freud* (London, 1969).
—— *An Essay on Liberation* (London and Boston, 1969).
—— *Negations: Essays in Critical Theory* (London and Boston, 1968).
—— *One-Dimensional Man: Studies in the Ideology of Advanced Industrial Society* (Boston, 1964).
—— *Reason and Revolution: Hegel and the Rise of Social Theory*, 2nd edn (London, 1964).
—— *Soviet Marxism: A Critical Analysis* (New York, 1958).
—— *Studies in Critical Philosphy* (London, 1972).
—— *A Critical Reader*, eds J. Abromeit and W. Cobb (New York, 2004).
—— *Heideggerian Marxism*, ed. S. Wolin and J. Abromeit (Lincoln, 2005).

Marcuse: commentaries

Paul Breines (ed.), *Critical Interruptions: New Left Perspectives on Herbert Marcuse* (New York, 1970).
J. Cohen, 'Critical Theory: The Philosophy of Marcuse', *New Left Review*, 57 (1969).
D. Kellner, *Herbert Marcuse and the Crisis of Marxism* (Berkeley, 1984).
Alasdair MacIntyre, *Marcuse* (London and New York, 1970).
Robert W. Marks, *The Meaning of Marcuse* (New York, 1970).
Paul Mattick, *Critique of Marcuse: One-dimensional Man in Class Society* (London, 1972).
P. Sedgwick, 'Natural Science and Human Theory: A Critique of Herbert Marcuse', *Socialist Register* (London, 1966).
J. Woodis, *New Theories of Revolution* (London, 1974).

Others

H. Arendt, 'Walter Benjamin, 1892–1940', in *Men in Dark Times* (London, 1970).
Walter Benjamin, *Illuminations: Essays and Reflections*, ed. H. Arendt (New York, 1968).
—— *The Origins of German Tragic Drama*, ed. P. Osborne (New York and London, 1998).
—— *Reflections* (London, 1978).
—— *Selected Writings*, 4 vols (Cambridge, 1996–2003).
—— *The Arcades Project* (Cambridge, 1999).
M. Cohen, *Profane Illumination: Walter Benjamin and the Paris of Surrealist Revolution* (Berkeley, 1993).
F. Dallmayr, 'Habermas: Knowledge and Human Interests and its Aftermath', *Philosophy of the Social Science*, 2 (1972).
G. Floistadt, 'Social Concepts of Action: Notes on Habermas' Proposal for a Social Theory of Action', *Inquiry*, 13 (1970).

Erich Fromm, *Being and Having* (London, 1978).
—— *Beyond the Chains of Illusion: My Encounter with Marx and Freud* (New York, 1962).
Erich Fromm, *The Crisis of Psychoanalysis: Essays on Freud, Marx and Social Psychology* (London, 1973).
—— *The Fear of Freedom* (London, 1942).
—— *Man for Himself* (New York, 1947).
—— *Marx's Concept of Man* (New York, 1961).
—— *The Sane Society* (New York, 1955).
Jürgen Habermas, *Between Facts and Norms: Contributions to a Discourse Theory of Law and Democracy* (Cambridge, 1995).
—— *Knowledge and Human Interests* (London, 1972).
—— *Legitimation Crisis*, ed. T. McCarthy (London, 1976).
—— *The Theory of Communicative Action*, 2 vols (Boston, 1984, 1987).
—— *Theory and Practice* (Boston, 1973).
—— *Towards a Rational Society: Student Protest, Science and Politics* (London, 1972).
A. Honneth, *The Critique of Power: Reflective Stages in a Critical Social Theory* (Cambridge, 1991).
—— *The Fragmented World of the Social: Essays in Social and Political Philosophy* (Albany, 1995).
H. Stuart Hughes, 'Franz Neumann between Marxism and Liberal Democracy', in D. Fleming and B. Bailyn (eds), *The Intellectual Migration: Europe and America, 1930–1960* (Cambridge, Mass., 1969).
Fredric Jameson 'Walter Benjamin; or Nostalgia', *Salmagundi*, 10/11 (fall 1969–winter 1970).
E. Leslie, *Walter Benjamin, Overpowering Conformism* (London, 2000).
L. Marcus and L. Nead (eds), *The Actuality of Walter Benjamin* (London, 1998).
Thomas McCarthy, *The Critical Theory of Jürgen Habermas*, 2nd edn (Cambridge, 1982).
Franz Neumann, *Behemoth: The Structure and Practice of National Socialism, 1933–1944*, rev. edn (New York, 1944).
—— *The Democratic and Authoritarian State: Essays in Political and Legal Theory* (New York, 1957).
William Outhwaite, *Habermas: A Critical Introduction* (London, 1994).
Friedrich Pollock, *The Economic and Social Consequences of Automation* (Oxford, 1957).
R. Rochlitz, *The Disenchantment of Art: The Philosophy of Walter Benjamin* (New York, 1996).
John H. Schaar, *Escape From Authority: The Perspectives of Erich Fromm* (New York, 1961).
T. Schroyer, 'The Dialectical Foundations of Critical Theory: J. Habermas' "Metatheoretical Investigations" ', *Telos*, 12 (1972).
—— 'Marx and Habermas', *Continuum*, 8 (1970).
A. Sohn-Rethel, *Intellectual and Manual Labour: A Critique of Epistemology* (London, 1978).
Stephen White (ed.), *The Cambridge Comparison to Habermas* (Cambridge, 1995).
—— *The Recent Work of Jürgen Habermas: Reason, Justice and Modernity* (Cambridge, 1988).

20
Existentialist Marxism

Introduction

Unlike the situation in Germany, it was only around the time of the Second World War that Marxism began to be a major force on the French intellectual scene. This Marxism was enriched by the many socialist traditions indigenous to France, by the prestige gained by Communism in having played a prominent role in defeating Fascism (and the parallel discredit of the liberalism associated with the Third Republic), and by the many foreign intellectuals who had found Paris a congenial place of exile. Thus the scene was set for a rich development of a very variegated Marxist thought. The emergence of an 'existentialist' version of Marxism in France after the war was aided by the growing French interest in Hegel and the impact of the publication of Marx's early writings. The experience of the war had destroyed confidence in the clear analytical rationalism so deeply embedded in the French philosophical tradition. Hegel, with his philosophy of history, his concepts of alienation and dialectic, his phenomenology of consciousness, seemed to offer a deeper understanding of recent experience. The philosophy of Hegel also seemed to be at the origin of most progressive thought. As Merleau-Ponty wrote:

All the great philosophical ideas of the past century had their beginnings in Hegel: the philosophies of Marx and Nietzsche, phenomenology, German existentialism, and psychoanalysis; it was he who started the attempt to explore the irrational and integrate it into an expanded reason which remains the task of our century.[1]

Hegel was made available to French Marxists through the work of Alexandre Kojeve and Jean Hyppolite, Kojeve had lectured on Hegel from 1933 to 1939 at the Ecole Pratique des Hautes Etudes in Paris[2] and in his audience were many of the influential post-war thinkers. In Kojeve's brilliant – though highly idiosyncratic – account, Hegel appeared as a revolutionary social theorist whose dialectic of master and slave was the centrepiece of his *Phenomenology*: work was the fundamental human activity and, in the struggle for recognition inside the work process, the workers were destined to transform their current position as slaves into that of masters of a free society. Reason was thus not some abstract and eternal category but the perpetually evolving consciousness of a humanity which posited itself in and through the world in a constantly self-transcending process. The parallels with Marcuse's Marxified reading of Hegel in *Reason and Revolution* are obvious.

If Kojeve's interpretation was idiosyncratic, Jean Hyppolite's work stuck closer to Hegel's actual text by translating the *Phenomenology* and publishing an extended commentary. Hyppolite placed at the centre of his interpretation the idea of the unhappy consciousness: the state of mind in which man had become aware of the ideal but found it incapable of realisation. In Hyppolite's view, Hegel had shown that this separation of man from himself was a necessary step on the road to self-recognition, a road which consisted in a perpetual dialectical overcoming of 'alienation'. Hyppolite also directed his readers' attention to Hegel's early Jena writings, in which he concentrated on the contradictions of early bourgeois society and particularly its alienated labour.

The radical interpretation of Hegel offered by Kojeve and Hyppolite aided the rapid assimilation of Marx's early writings into the French Marxist tradition in the immediate post-war years. This assimilation had to be made in opposition to the French Communist Party, whose intellectuals were enclosed, both politically and philosophically, in a stultifying Stalinism until the mid-1950s. In politics, the French Communist Party was obliged to follow the interests of Moscow, which often dictated a conservative line in internal French politics, while in philosophy there was little more to be done than repeat the laws of dialectical materialism as formulated by Stalin. The translation of Marx's early writings – and particularly the *Economic and Philosophical Manuscripts* – gave the impression that a very different form of Marxism was available, one that could enter into fruitful dialogue with the increasingly popular philosophies of phenomenology, personalism and existentialism. What was, broadly speaking, attractive in Marx's early work was the picture he painted of the all-round individual freely developing his personality in cooperative production with his fellow-men. The increasing power of technology and the possibilities of manipulating man in society

induced many commentators to take up what Marx said of the alienation of man in capitalist society and conclude that he was part of the
existentialist protest. For these thinkers, the very complexity of highly
developed societies made Marx's analysis more significant than could
have been anticipated in the nineteenth century. This recovery by the
French of concepts such as alienation and *praxis* that had been lost under
Stalinism had widespread repercussions in Yugoslavia, Czechoslovakia,
and other East European countries.[3] At the same time as reading the
young Marx, French social theorists were turning back to the original
theorists of 'Western' Marxism: Lukács (whose *History and Class
Consciousness* had anticipated much of the *Economic and Philosophical
Manuscripts*), Korsch, and the Frankfurt School in general. Particularly
influential was the work of Lukács's pupil Lucien Goldmann, whose
literary criticism emphasised the elasticity of class consciousness:

> The great *representative* writers are those who express, in a more or less
> coherent way, a world-view which corresponds to the maximum of
> possible consciousness of a class; this is the case especially for philoso-
> phers, writers and artists.[4]

Any Frenchman interested in Marxism had to come to terms in some way
with the Communist Party, whose inert mass overshadowed the intellectual scene. Many of the most prominent Marxist thinkers started inside the
Party – only to be expelled when their ideas became too adventurous. Two
typical examples will illustrate this trend. Roger Garaudy was the most
prominent intellectual in the Party for the two decades after the war and a
member of its Politburo. Until the early 1960s his writings were fully in the
Stalinist tradition where Marxism was viewed as a positivist, scientific
materialism. It was only after the (rather belated) public criticism of
Stalinism by the French Communist Party in 1962 that Garaudy began to
question the neglect of the concept of *praxis*, the emphasis on a reflection
theory of knowledge, stereotyped dialectical laws, etc. At the same time as
criticising Stalin, it is significant that Garaudy wrote a book on Hegel and
an original study of Marx. The new position which Garaudy adopted was
best expressed in *Marxism in the 20th Century*, where he wrote that

> The Twentieth Congress, far from destroying our hopes and certain-
> ties, had the opposite effect of making possible a third flowering for
> Marxist philosophy. It is not, however, by turning over the page too
> quickly and so neglecting to expose all the roots of evil, nor by thus
> failing correctly to apportion responsibility or to demand a profound

analysis of the causes that produced the former blindness, that this fresh start can be made possible.[5]

'This fresh start', according to Garaudy, could only be achieved by showing that

> Marxism contains within itself, in its very principle, infinite possibilities of development and renewal ... In order to achieve this aim it was essential forcibly to stress – too forcibly, maybe, since it necessitated breaking with an ingrained habitual procedure – the aspect of dialectical transcendence, with all the break and discontinuity in relation to the past that it implies.[6]

A particularly long section in the book was devoted to Marxism and religion. Many progressive Catholics had been interested in the young Marx (the worker-priest movement began in 1944) and Garaudy played a leading role in the lively Marxist-Catholic dialogue that developed in the 1960s.[7] However, Garaudy's views eventually went beyond the bounds of even a reformed Marxism and he was expelled from the Communist Party in 1970.

Henri Lefebvre was a much more original thinker than Garaudy. Lefebvre published selections from Marx's writings, including many from the *Paris Manuscripts*, as early as 1934 and wrote what remains an excellent introduction to Marx under the rather misleading title of *Dialectical Materialism*. Basing himself on a thoroughgoing humanism and on the idea of *praxis* as the dialectical relationship of man and nature through which man realised himself by overcoming his opposite – nature, Lefebvre put in the forefront of his interpretation the concept of the total man as the counterpart to alienated man:

> The total man is both the subject and the object of the Becoming. He is the living subject who is opposed to the object and surmounts this opposition. He is the subject who is broken up into partial activities and scattered determinations and who surmounts this dispersion. He is the subject of action, as well as its final object, its product even if it does seem to produce external objects. The total man is the living subject-object, who is first of all torn asunder, dissociated and chained to necessity and abstraction. Through this tearing apart, he moves towards freedom; he becomes Nature, but free. He becomes a totality, like Nature, but by bringing it under control. The total man is 'de-alienated' man.[8]

Lefebvre's most original and important work was *Everyday Life in the Modern World*. Here he attempted to ground the phenomenon of alienation in an examination of everyday life. The book particularly angered the orthodox Communists as it suggested that alienation would persist even after a successful proletarian revolution and that post-revolutionary Communist society was not immune from many of the problems currently afflicting capitalist society. In the second volume of *Everyday Life* and in much of his work in the 1960s Lefebvre looked at the deficiencies of modern civilisation. He made a distinction between wishes and desires and insisted that any real socialist advance would have to be tested by its influence on everyday life. The alienation involved in the impact of television, mass housing, and the decline of collective activities posed problems for socialism just as much as for capitalism. This 'bureaucratic society of controlled consumption' was very different from that described by Marx. For both the self-confident individual of early bourgeois society and the revolutionary opposition of the proletariat had disappeared. There were similarities between Lefebvre's analysis of modernity and that of Marcuse. But whereas Marcuse (and the Frankfurt School in general) had recourse to psychoanalysis to explain the role of consumerism, Lefebvre interpreted it through linguistics: with the privatisation of consumption went a replacement of signs by signals and of symbols by images. These replacements robbed the individual of any possibility of connecting, still less of 'totalising', his experiences.[9]

Sartre

Like the Frankfurt School, existentialism protested at the increasing tendencies of modern technology to treat men as things. The efforts to combine existentialism and Marxism were best exemplified in the work of Jean-Paul Sartre. In his existentialist manifesto, Sartre had declared:

> Man simply is. Not that he is simply what he conceives himself to be, but he is what he wills, and as he conceives himself after already existing – as he wills to be after that leap towards existence. Man is nothing else but what he makes of himself.[10]

Sartre's most extended exposition of this view was in *Being and Nothingness*, written during the war, which drew heavily on Husserl's phenomenology and Heidegger's existentialism. The book presented freedom as the central category of human existence:

> Human freedom precedes essence in man and makes it possible; the essence of human being is suspended in his freedom. What we call freedom is impossible to distinguish from the being of 'human reality'. Man does not exist *first* in order to be free *subsequently*; there is no difference between the being of man and his *being-free*.[11]

Although such a completely non-materialist and ahistorical picture of human existence was a long way from Marxism, Sartre began to move close to Marxism in the immediate post-war period. in *Materialism and Revolution* (1946) he attacked Stalin's *Dialectical Materialism and Historical Materialism* as a metaphysical and positivistic materialism, and once again stressed that 'this possibility of *rising above* a situation in order to get a perspective on it ... is precisely that which we call freedom. No materialism of any kind can ever explain it.'[12] At the same time he praised the young Marx (as opposed to Engels) and sketched out a major theme of his later work:

> One never oppresses anything but a freedom, but one cannot oppress it unless it lends itself in some way to this oppression, unless, that is, it presents the appearance of a thing to the Other. The revolutionary movement and its plan – which is to make society pass through the violence of one state in which liberties are alienated to another state based on their mutual recognition – is to be understood in these terms.[13]

If Sartre had found Communist philosophy abysmal in *Materialism and Revolution*, in his 1952 article on *The Communists and the Peace*, provoked by the Korean war, he found their politics progressive and advocated unquestioning obedience on the part of the workers to a Party which was their only guarantee of freedom in the future. This 'ultra-Bolshevik' position led to a split between Sartre and his former colleague Merleau-Ponty, who was moving away from Marxism just as Sartre was approaching it. In his major work, *Phenomenology and Perception*, Merleau-Ponty had emphasised human interaction and the dialectical unity of subject and object as opposed to their radical separation in Sartre, the faithful Cartesian. 'What continues to distinguish Sartre from Marxism, even in recent times,' he wrote 'is his philosophy of the *cogito*.'[14]

Sartre attempted to deal with Merleau-Ponty's criticisms in his most serious effort to come to terms with Marxism – the *Critique of Dialectical*

Reason – of which the first volume was published in 1960.[15] At first sight, Sartre's view on Marxism appeared surprisingly positive. In the important first part of the *Critique of Dialectical Reason* (originally published in 1957 under the title *Search for a Method*), Sartre began with a brief conspectus of recent European intellectual history. This ran from the period of Descartes and Locke, through that of Kant and Hegel, to the twentieth century, whose most progressive philosophical expression was Marxism. But Marxism itself had its own difficulties:

> What has made the force and richness of Marxism is the fact that it has been the most radical attempt to clarify the historical process in its totality. For the last twenty years, on the contrary, its shadow has obscured history; this is because it has ceased to live with history and because it attempts, through a bureaucratic conservatism, to reduce change to identity.[16]

Nevertheless

> Far from being exhausted, Marxism is still very young, almost in its infancy; it has scarcely begun to develop. It remains, therefore, the philosophy of our time. We cannot go beyond it because we have not gone beyond the circumstances which engendered it.[17]

Sartre adopted unreservedly Marx's formula that 'the mode of production of material life conditions the social, political, and intellectual life process in general'.[18] What existentialism could do (and Sartre still considered himself an existentialist) was to restore the dialectical dimension to the theory of knowledge which was 'the weak point of Marxism'. This would avoid a conception of knowledge either as a simple observation of external reality or as a reflection of that reality, both of which Sartre thought to be opposed to Marx's original conception of knowledge as *praxis*.

Sartre then attempted to define his own position in opposition to that which he attributed to such writers as Engels and Garaudy, according to which the relationship of consciousness to the socio-economic base was defined by clear principles. Sartre expressed in lapidary form the 'heuristic insufficiency' of contemporary Marxism by saying that whereas for vulgar Marxism Valéry was just a petty bourgeois intellectual, an existentialist Marxism would like also to be able to account for the fact that not every petty bourgeois intellectual was a Valéry.[19] Sartre concluded that

> We reproach contemporary Marxism for throwing over to the side of chance all the concrete determinations of human life and for not

preserving anything of historical totalization except its abstract skeleton of universality. The result is that it has entirely lost the meaning of what it is to be a man; to fill in the gaps, it has only the absurd psychology of Pavlov.[20]

He aimed, therefore, at producing a concrete anthropology by means of an approach in which sociology and psychology would not 'sleep side by side' but be integrated within the framework of a genuinely dialectical Marxism. This did not involve – as it had in some of Sartre's earlier works – a third way or idealistic humanism: the point was 'not to reject Marxism in the name of a third path or an idealist humanism, but to reconquer man within Marxism'.[21]

In the final section of *Search for a Method*, Sartre defined the method by which he intended to explicate Marx's saying that men make their own history but only under predetermined conditions: it was a progressive-regressive method which he called, alternatively, dialectical reason as opposed to analytical reason. In the example of someone opening a window, an observer could understand the action *regressively* (by appreciating, for example, that the room was overheated) and *progressively* by understanding the intention to let in fresh air. This was the method of 'real Marxism and existentialism' which

> recognizes the existence of ends wherever they are found and limits itself to declaring that certain among them can be neutralized at the heart of the historical process of totalization. This is the position of true Marxism and of existentialism. The dialectical movement, which proceeds from the objective conditioning to objectification, enables us to understand that the ends of human activity are not mysterious entities added on to the act itself; they represent simply the surpassing and the maintaining of the given in an act which goes from the present toward the future. The end is the objectification itself inasmuch as it constitutes the dialectical law of a human conduct and the unity of its internal contradictions.[22]

It was in this context that Sartre could define the minor though crucial role of existentialism within the Marxist framework:

> Existentialism will attempt to clarify the givens of Marxist Knowledge by indirect knowing (that is, as we have seen, by words which regressively denote existential structures), and to engender within the framework of Marxism a veritable comprehensive knowing which

will rediscover man in the social world and which will follow him in his praxis – or, if you prefer, in the project which throws him towards the social possibles in terms of a defined situation. Existentialism will appear therefore as a fragment of the system, which has fallen outside of Knowledge. From the day that Marxist thought will have taken on the human dimension (that is, the existential project) as the foundation of anthropological Knowledge, existentialism will no longer have any reason for being.[23]

Having outlined his methodological principles, Sartre began the *Critique of Dialectical Reason* proper by taking up once again the question of the dialectic, contrasting dogmatic dialectic with critical dialectic. Sartre was insistent that the latter must start from individuals:

If we do not wish the dialectic to become a divine law again, a metaphysical fate, it must proceed from individuals and not from some kind of supra-individual ensemble. Thus we encounter a new contradiction: the dialectic is the law of totalisation which creates several collectivities, several societies, and one history – realities, that is, which impose themselves on individuals; but at the same time it must be woven out of millions of individual actions. We must show how it is possible for it to be both a resultant, though not a passive average, and a totalising force, though not a transcendent fate, and how it can continually bring about the unity of dispersive profusion and integration.[24]

This 'totalising' nature of human action was a living process, as opposed to a totality which was an inert, finished entity such as a painting or a machine. Totality was thus the object of an analytical reason. Totalisations, on the other hand, could only be comprehended by dialectical reason. For 'the dialectic is a totalising activity. Its only laws are the rules produced by the developing totalisation.'[25] This reading of the dialectic entailed the rejection of dialectical materialism and of a dialectic of nature which Sartre traced back to Engels and criticised in the same terms as he had used in *Materialism and Revolution*.[26] In a long section entitled 'From Individual Praxis to the Practico-Inert' Sartre then described the way in which the primary social relations of individuals emerged. Starting from the principle that 'the crucial discovery of dialectical investigation is that man is "mediated" by things to the same extent as things are "mediated" by man',[27] Sartre placed the concept of material scarcity at the centre of this mediation. Marx's theory of historical materialism 'points to a factual evidence which we cannot go beyond *so long as* the transformations of social relations and technical progress have not freed man from the yoke of scarcity'.[28] Quoting Marx's famous counterposition of the realms of freedom and necessity at the end of *Capital* Volume Three, Sartre declared: 'As soon as there will exists *for everyone* a margin of *real* freedom beyond the production of life, Marxism will have lived out its span; a philosophy of freedom will take its place.'[29] For Sartre, scarcity was 'the basic abstract matrix of every reification of human relations in any society'.[30] His society of scarcity was almost Hobbesian in its description of antagonistic social relations. For

> In pure reciprocity, that which is Other than me is also the same. But in reciprocity as modified by scarcity, the same appears to us as anti-human in so far as this same man appears as radically Other – that is to say, as threatening us with death.[31]

Sartre rejected Engels' view that primitive society had been harmonious. For

> the historical process cannot be understood without a permanent element of negativity, both exterior and interior to man. This is the perpetual possibility *in man's very existence* of being the one who sends Others to their deaths or whom Others send to his – in other words, of scarcity.[32]

But nature was never purely passive. When worked on by men it could strike back in unintended ways. Sartre gave the example of a Chinese peasant who felled trees on his land to improve his cultivable acreage and found – since his neighbours had done the same – that his land was now destroyed by unchecked floods. This was the power of the 'practico-inert', a state of alienation in which the result of the *praxes* of individuals escaped their control and frustrated their designs.

In the social world, the practico-inert was represented by the series as opposed in the group. In a series, such as a bus queue, individuals were juxtaposed, united only by the inert object of the bus. Their only distinguishing features were their positions in the line: they lacked any structure of intercommunication. A class, too, was a series, for dialectical investigation 'shows us class at the level of the practico-inert field as a collective, and class being as a statute of seriality imposed on the multiplicity which composes it'.[33] The rest of the *Critique of Dialectical Reason* described the dialectical laws governing the emergence of the group from the series and the general degeneration from fused group into statutory groups and finally institutionalised groups which externally manipulated a serial ensemble and became a seriality themselves in turn. Following this itinerary, as Gorz has written,

> dialectical experience has made intelligible the emergence from individual praxes of all practical ensembles, and their transformation into each other, given that no single one of them has any *historical* priority *vis-à-vis* the others. The series, collective, fused group, statutory group, institutionised group, etc., are not successive *stages* of historical development but exist, clash and coalesce in the elementary formal structures (partial totalities and totalizations) of which History is the totalization.[34]

As an example of the group in fusion, Sartre described how separate individuals united to storm the Bastille. Once their immediate object was attained, the group became aware of itself as such and attempted to preserve itself by an oath of loyalty – a first step in limiting its own freedom. This was followed by pressure to retain individuals within the group (including the use of terror), a division of tasks within the group (organisation) and the eventual emergence of authority with its correlative of obedience and the powerlessness of individual reduced to a series:

> Such ultimately, are the limits of its praxis: born to dissolve series in the living synthesis of a community, it is blocked in its spatiotemporal development by the untranscendable statute of organic individuality and finds its being, outside itself, in the passive determinations of inorganic exteriority which it had wished to repress in itself. It is formed in opposition to alienation, in so far as alienation substitutes the practico-inert field for the free practical field of the individual; but it cannot escape alienation any more than the individual can, and it thereby relapses into serial passivity.[35]

Although Sartre's critique was not directly based on history (any more than Hegel's *Phenomenology*, to which it has striking resemblances – including the parallel treatment of Stalin and Napoleon), it was strongly influenced by the French, Cuban, Algerian and, above all, Russian revolutions. For Sartre, the Bolshevik Revolution consisted in the dictatorship of

> a self-perpetuating group which, in the name of a delegation which the proletariat had not given it, exercised power over the bourgeois

class which was in the process of being destroyed, over the peasant class and over the working class itself.[36]

Further,

the reason why the dictatorship of the proletariat (as a real exercise of power through the totalisation of the working class) never occurred is that the very idea is absurd, being a bastard compromise between the active, sovereign group and passive seriality.[37*]

But Sartre did not thereby abandon the idea of class struggle, the importance of which he was concerned to emphasise. Any version of the automatic economic collapse of capitalism would 'end up by reducing men to pure anti-dialectical moments of the practico-inert'.[38] In a conclusion which indicated the unfinished nature of his enterprise, Sartre wrote:

The regressive movement of the critical investigation has demonstrated the intelligibility of practical structures and the dialectical relation which interconnects the various forms of active multiplicities. But, on the one hand, we are still at the level of synchronic totalisation and we have not yet considered the diachronic depth of practical temporalisation; and on the other hand, the regressive movement has ended with a question: that is to say, it has to be completed by a synthetic progression whose aim will be to rise up to the double synchronic and diachronic movement by which History constantly totalises itself.[39]

Sartre's *Critique* is made all the more difficult both by an obscure and tortuous style and by the failure to edit the disorganised mass of material. Its strength lies in the brilliant psychological insights and phenomenological descriptions that characterised Sartre's previous work. Whether Sartre has succeeded in integrating them into a viable form of Marxism is an open question. The lack of any empirical historical reference (for example, in the section on scarcity), the emphasis on beginning with individuals,[40] and the ontological definition of man, which seems to maintain a dualistic approach to man and nature reminiscent of Cartesianism, are only with great difficulty compatible with a Marxist approach.

Arguments and the theorists of the 'New Working Class'

Whereas Sartre's immense synthesis remained speculative, the main two French revisions of Marxism in the late 1950s and early 1960s followed a more empirical and social approach. Sartre approached Marxism as an existentialist: the *Arguments* group and the theorists of the 'New Working Class' were ex-Communist Party members who sought insight from existentialism. Influenced by the Frankfurt School and the work of Lefebvre, the first group, centred on the review *Arguments*, inquired into the relevance of Marx's ideas on the abolition of philosophy, and the nature of alienation in a society which emphasised leisure as much as work and the cultural superstructure as much as politics or economics. The leading thinker of the *Arguments* group was Kostas Axelos. In his most important work, *Alienation, Praxis and Techne in the Thought of Karl Marx* Axelos viewed Marx's concept of alienation as too limited to the work process and incapable of dealing with the alienation inherent in advanced technology whether organised along capitalist or socialist lines. Self-creativity, for Axelos, had other dimensions than that of productive labour. In a striking reformulation of Marx's first *Thesis on Feuerbach*, Axelos summarised his position as follows:

> The principal thought of all historico-dialectic materialism (including Marx's) is that the object, reality, the materials are taken only under the form of produced objects, material reality, materials of work; they are thus effectively grasped, but they lack a ground and a horizon. That is why the other side was developed, in a metaphysical way – in opposition to naive or sophisticated realism – by idealist philosophy which, naturally, neither knew or recognised the world we call real: the totality of forms, forces, and weaknesses of the constituted, concretised and fixed world – the mode of being of the constituting and open World, the other side of the same and unique World. Marx wanted sensible objects to be superior to ideal objects, but he did not grasp human activity itself as *problematic activity*. Thus he considered – in the *Contribution to the Critique of Political Economy* as much as in the *Poverty of Philosophy* – material life as the only true human one, while thought and poetry were grasped only in their conditional and ideological forms.[41]

The inability of an economic concept of alienation to come to terms with the problems of a technological society were further explored by other members of the *Arguments* groups such as Fougeyrollas, Morin, and Chatelet.[42] In a more radical vein, the problems of modern bureaucratisation were analysed by the ex-Trotskyist writers of the group *Socialisme ou Barbarie* such as Claude Lefort and Cornelius Castoriadis[43] who influenced the thought of Antonio Negri discussed in the next chapter.

The theoreticians of the 'New Working Class' were more in line with traditional Marxism. Rejecting both the liberal view that the revolutionary consciousness of the working class necessarily disappeared under advanced capitalism and the rigid Communist Party definition of the proletariat that had remained unchanged for decades, writers such as André Gorz and Serge Mallet attempted to redraw the boundaries of class struggle. Gorz, a disciple of Sartre, attempted to show in his book *Strategy for Labour* that the revolutionary movement could no longer be satisfactorily based on the concepts of immiserisation and economic exploitation. Rising living standards and the introduction of automation meant the increasing importance of white-collar mental workers, while oppression under capitalism could only adequately be encapsulated by a concept of alienation that put the emphasis on workers' self-creativity. Thus the programme of struggle for workers' self-management could undermine the capitalist enterprise from within and overcome the political blockage caused by the opposition of reform to revolution. This analysis was supported by Mallet, who argued[44] that highly skilled mental and technical workers of advanced capitalism, hitherto viewed as not central to the proletariat, constituted, on the contrary, its revolutionary vanguard. Unhampered either by traditional craft distinctions or by unwieldy trade union bureaucracy, with their material position assured by adequate income, these young industrial cadres could use their pivotal position to restructure the socio-economic base of society. This view gained substantial confirmation in the events of May 1968.

In his subsequent work, Gorz maintains his view that full-time employment for all is neither possible nor desirable, given the tendency for new technology to polarise society between secure well-paid professionals and those in insecure, part-time, service jobs – or none at all. But, given also the potential of new technology to reduce the amount of necessary human labour, what is now needed is a liberation *from* work in which free time and 'autonomous activities' can take on an even larger role.[45] Later Gorz revised his position somewhat by advocating the preservation of the private sphere through specifying limits to the market and insisting that all domestic labour and caring services should be withdrawn from economic rationalisation: 'we must rethink all the activities which require us to give of ourselves with a view to developing self-organized, voluntary services'.[46] These views were complemented by his suggestion that the struggle in the workplace centred on 'the development of people's autonomy irrespective of companies' need for it'[47] and proposals for a basic social income guaranteed to all citizens whether formally employed or not.

Notes

1. M. Merleau-Ponty, *Sense and Non-Sense* (Evanston, Ill., 1964) p. 63.
2. See A. Kojeve, *Introduction to the Reading of Hegel* (New York, 1969).
3. See above pp. 156ff.
4. L. Goldmann, *The Human Sciences and Philosophy* (London, 1969) p. 59.
5. R. Garaudy, *Marxism in the Twentieth Century* (London, 1970) p. 18.
6. Ibid., p. 211.
7. In general, see further: P. Hebblethwaite, *The Christian-Marxist Dialogue and Beyond* (London, 1977).
8. H. Lefebvre, *Dialectical Materialism* (New York and London, 1968) pp. 162f.
9. See further on this subject Lefebvre's book *Le Langage et la société* (Paris, 1966), *Position: contre les technocrates* (Paris, 1967) and *Everyday Life in the Modern World* (London, 1971).
10. J.-P. Sartre, *Existentialism and Humanism*, ed. P. Mairet (New York, 1948) p. 28.
11. J.-P. Sartre, *Being and Nothingness* (New York, 1966) p. 30.
12. J.-P. Sartre, 'Materialism and Revolution', *Literary and Philosophical Essays* (New York, 1967), pp. 235ff.
13. Ibid., p. 251.
14. M. Merleau-Ponty, *Adventures of the Dialectic* (Evanston, Ill., 1973) p. 158.
15. On the contents of the second volume, see R. Aronson, *Jean-Paul Sartre: the Politics of the Imagination* (New York, 1979) and the excerpt published in the *New Left Review*, 100 (1977), under the title 'Socialism in One Country'.
16. J.-P. Sartre, *Search for a Method* (New York, 1968) p. 29.
17. Ibid., p. 30.
18. K. Marx, Preface to *A Critique of Political Economy*, in *Selected Writings*, ed. D. McLellan (Oxford and New York, 2000) p. 389.
19. Cf. J.-P. Sartre, *Search for a Method*, pp. 53ff. See further how this works out in practice in Sartre's immense study of Flaubert, to which he turned after finishing the *Critique of Dialectical Reason*.
20. Ibid., p. 82f.
21. Ibid., p. 83.
22. Ibid., p. 158f.
23. Ibid., p. 181.
24. J.-P. Sartre, *Critique of Dialectical Reason* (New York and London, 1976) p. 36. See also the long and difficult footnote on pp. 47f.
25. Ibid., p. 47.
26. Cf. Ibid., pp. 26ff.
27. Ibid., p. 79.
28. J.-P. Sartre, *Search for a Method*, p. 34
29. Ibid.
30. Ibid., p. 132.
31. J.-P. Sartre, *Critique of Dialectical Reason*, pp. 131f.
32. Ibid., p. 148.
33. Ibid., p. 306.
34. A. Gorz, 'Sartre and Marx', in *New Left Review* (eds), *Western Marxism: A Critical Reader* (London, 1977) p. 195.
35. J.-P. Sartre, *Critique of Dialectical Reason*, p. 668.
36. Ibid., p. 661.

37. Ibid., p. 662. See further his article 'Masses, Spontaneity, Party' in *Socialist Register* 1970.
38. Ibid., p. 788.
39. Ibid., p. 817f.
40. See further here the criticisms of R. Aronson. 'The Individualist Social Theory of J.-P. Sartre', in *Western Marxism: A Critical Reader* (London, 1977).
41. K. Axelos, *Vers la pensée planétaire* (Paris, 1964) p. 172, quoted in M. Poster, *Existential Marxism in Post-War France* (Princeton, N.J., 1975) p. 225.
42. See works cited in the bibliography.
43. See further D. Howard, *The Marxian Legacy* (London, 1977) pp. 222ff.
44. See S. Mallet, *La Nouvelle Classe ouvrière* (Paris, 1963).
45. See A. Gorz, *Farewell to the Working Class: An Essay on Postindustrial Socialism* (London, 1982) and *Paths to Paradise: On the Liberation from Work* (London, 1985).
46. A Gorz, *Critique of Economic Reason* (London, 1989) p. 145.
47. A Gorz, *Reclaiming Work: Beyond the Wage-based Society* (Cambridge, 1999).

Further reading

General

Three good books are Hughes's *The Obstructed Path*, which deals with the intellectual background, Caute's *Communism and the French Intellectuals*, which deals with the role of the Party, and Lichtheim's wider-ranging *Marxism in Modern France*. See also the books by Burkhard and by Stuart. On more recent developments, see Poster's excellent overview, *Existential Marxism in Post-War France* and Kelly's *Modern French Marxism*.

Sartre: texts

Sartre's major work, *Critique of Dialectical Reason*, has recently been made available in English. Unfortunately, this edition does not contain the important prefatory essay, which was first published in 1963 under the title *Search for a Method*. Two useful collections of Sartre's essays are *Literary and Philosophical Essays* and *Between Existentialism and Marxism*.

Sartre: commentaries

Discussion of Sartre's Marxism means discussion of *The Critique of Dialectical Reason* and perhaps the best introduction is Desan's *The Marxism of Jean-Paul Sartre*, which is a close textual analysis of the *Critique* as is Catalano's *Commentary*. The best overall books on Sartre's politics are Aronson's sympathetically critical *Jean-Paul Sartre: The Politics of the Imagination* and Dobson's *The Politics of Reason*. For a more hardline Marxist approach, see Chiodi's *Sartre and Marxism*. Gorz's article 'Sartre and Marx' is a defence of the *Critique* as Marxist; Lichtheim's 'Sartre, Marxism and History' is a more detached review of the same work. On the development of Sartre's politics, see Part Four of Thody's *Jean-Paul Sartre: A Literary and Political Study*. Relatively short commentaries on the *Critique* are contained in Chapter Seven of Howard's *The Marxian Legacy* and Chapter Seven of Poster's *Existential Marxism in Post-War France*. For background, see Odajnyk's *Marxism and Existentialism*. For short introductions that deal more with Sartre's literary and philosophical views than with his politics, see the books by Greene, Warnock, Danto and – still the best – Murdoch. For excellent historico-political background, see the second half of Judt's *Marxism and the French Left*.

Others

For Merleau-Ponty, see the translations of the anti-Stalinist *Humanism and Terror*, the second section of *Sense and Non-Sense*, and, above all, *Adventures of the Dialectic*. For commentary, see Bannan's *The Philosophy of Merleau-Ponty* and Rabil's *Merleau-Ponty: Existentialist of the Social World*. Also the eighth chapter of Howard's *The Marxian Legacy*. The works of Garaudy, Goldman, Gorz and Lefebvre have been translated as detailed below. For commentary, see Poster's overview which also contains an extended bibliography, and the discussion of Gorz by Lodziak and Tatman, by Little and by Bowring.

Bibliography

General

F. Burkhard, *French Marxism between the Wars: Henri Lefebvre and the 'Philosophies'* (Amherst, 2000).

David Caute, *Communism and the French Intellectuals* (London, 1964).

H. Stuart Hughes, *The Obstructed Path: French Social Thought, 1930–1960* (New York, 1968).

Tony Judt, *Marxism and the French Left: Studies in Labour and Politics 1830–1981* (Oxford, 1986).

M. Kelly, *Modern French Marxism* (Baltimore, 1982).

George Lichtheim, *Marxism in Modern France* (London, 1966).

Mark Poster, *Existential Marxism in Post-War France: From Sartre to Althusser* (Princeton, N.J., 1975).

R. Stuart, *Marxism at Work: Ideology, Class, and French Socialism during the Third Republic* (Cambridge, 1992).

Sartre: texts

Jean-Paul Sartre, *Being and Nothingness* (New York, 1966).
—— *Between Existentialism and Marxism* (London, 1974).
—— *The Communists and the Peace* (New York, 1968).
—— *Critique of Dialectical Reason*, trans. A. Sheridan Smith, 2 vols (London, 2006).
—— *The Ghost of Stalin* (New York, 1968).
—— *Literary and Philosophical Essays* (New York, 1967).
—— *Sartre in the Seventies: Interviews and Essays* (London, 1978).
—— *Search for a Method* (New York, 1968).
—— 'Socialism in One Country', *New Left Review*, 100 (1976–77).

Sartre: commentaries

R.M. Alberes, *Jean-Paul Sartre: Philosopher Without Faith* (London, 1964).
Ronald Aronson, 'The Individualist Social Theory of Jean-Paul Sartre', *New Left Review* (eds), *Western Marxism: A Critical Reader* (London, 1977).
—— *Jean-Paul Sartre: The Politics of the Imagination* (London, 1979).
J. Catalano, *A Commentary on Jean-Paul Sartre's Critique of Dialectical Reason* (Chicago, 1986).
Pietro Chiodi, *Sartre and Marxism* (Hassocks, Sussex, 1976).
Maurice Cranston, *Sartre* (London, 1962).
Arthur C. Danto, *Jean-Paul Sartre* (London, 1975).
Wilfred Desan, *The Marxism of Jean-Paul Sartre* (New York, 1965).
A. Dobson, *Jean-Paul Sartre and the Politics of Reason* (Cambridge, 1993).
Andre Gorz, 'Sartre and Marx', *New Left Review* (eds), *Western Marxism: A Critical Reader* (London, 1977).
Norman N. Green, *Jean-Paul Sartre: The Existentialist Ethic* (Ann Arbor, 1960).
Marjorie Greene, *Sartre* (New York, 1973).
Klaus Hartmann, *Sartre's Ontology: A Study of Being and Nothingness in the Light of Hegel's Logic* (Evanston, Ill., 1966).
D. Howard, *The Marxian Legacy* (London, 1977) ch. 7.
F. Jameson, *Sartre: The Origins of a Style* (New York, 1984).
René Lafarge, *Jean-Paul Sartre: His Philosophy* (Indiana, 1970).
R.D. Laing and D. Cooper, *Reason and Violence: A Decade of Sartre's Philosophy* (New York, 1964).
J. Lawler, *The Existential Marxism of Jean-Paul Sartre* (Amsterdam, 1976).
George Lichtheim, 'Sartre, Marxism and History', *History and Theory*, III, 2 (1963–64).
Iris Murdoch, *Sartre: Romantic Rationalist* (London, 1953).
Walter Odajnyk, *Marxism and Existentialism* (New York, 1965).
M. Poster, *Sartre's Marxism* (London, 1987).
James Shewiden, *Sartre: The Radical Conversion* (Athens, Ohio, 1969).
Philip Thody, *Jean-Paul Sartre: A Literary and Political Study* (New York, 1961).
Mary Warnock, *The Philosophy of Sartre* (London, 1965).

Others

Raymond Aron, *Marxism and the Existentialists* (New York, 1969).
—— *The Opium of the Intellectuals* (London, 1957).

John F. Bannan, *The Philosophy of Merleau-Ponty* (New York, 1967).
F. Bowring, *André Gorz and the Sartrean Legacy* (Basingstoke, 2000).
Michael Foucault, *The Archaeology of Knowledge and the Discourse on Language* (New York, 1973).
Roger Garaudy, *Marxism in the Twentieth Century* (London, 1970).
Lucien Goldmann, *The Human Sciences and Philosophy* (London, 1969).
André Gorz, *Socialism and Revolution* (London, 1973).
—— *Strategy for Labour* (New York, 1967).
Jean Hyppolite, *Studies on Marx and Hegel* (London, 1969).
Dominique Lecourt, *Marxism and Epistemology* (London, 1975).
Henri Lefebvre, *Dialectical Materialism* (New York and London, 1968).
—— *The Sociology of Marx* (London, 1968).
—— *The Survival of Capitalism* (London, 1976).
A. Little, *The Political Thought of André Gorz* (London, 1996).
Conrad Lodziak and Jeremy Tatman, *André Gorz: A Critical Introduction* (London, 1997).
Maurice Merleau-Ponty, *Adventures of the Dialectic* (Evanston, Ill., 1973).
—— *Humanism and Terror* (Boston, 1969).
—— *Sense and Non-Sense* (Evanston, Ill., 1964).
Albert Rabil, *Merleau-Ponty: Existentialist of the Social World* (New York, 1967).

21
Italian Marxism

By drawing on existentialist thought, some Marxist writers have tried to recover the human, subjective dimension in the face of both the sclerosis of orthodox Marxism and the growing influence of technology. But other thinkers in Western Marxism offered interpretations of Marxism radically opposed to that put forward by the Hegelo-existentialists. In Italy, for example, Della Volpe and his followers rejected any attempt to read Marx as an Hegelian. Della Volpe was a lifelong member of the Italian Communist Party, but disliked intensely its increasingly tolerant post-war attitude and, writing mainly in the 1950s and 1960s, elaborated a theory whose angular sharpness contrasted with the fluidity which the Party displayed in Italian politics. Like the arch-Hegelian Lukács, he concentrated on philosophy and methodology rather than sociology and economics, but there the similarity ended. For Della Volpe, Hegel was a mystic and a romantic who confused conceptual processes with real processes by means of a dialectic that went from the abstract to the concrete to end up again in the abstract. Marxist methodology, on the other hand, involved an epistemology that was based on a scientific logic which went from the concrete to the abstract to return to the concrete in a manner akin to that of the Galilean hypothetic-deductive method. This method, which Della Volpe claimed informed all of Marx's writings from 1843 onwards, was a genuine materialism in that it separated thought from its object. In an approach reminiscent of Hume rather than Hegel, he rejected both dialectical materialism of the Soviet type (which he thought too idealistic) and bourgeois positivist empiricism. The concept of contradiction belonged to the realm of thought and not to that of matter where the principle of experimentation reigned supreme. The scientific dialectic, he wrote, consisted in 'the reciprocal functionality of induction and deduction, of matter and reason, of act (or "accidental") and hypothesis (or "necessary")'.[1] The result was what he called 'determinate abstractions' and laws in the materialist sense. This one and only scientific method applied to all human activities including art.[2]

In his more political writings Della Volpe emphasised the debt of Marx to Rousseau and upheld the need for formal legal guarantees of egalitarianism in a transitional society to socialism. A transitional society which abolished all the formal legality and representative institutions of bourgeois society would run the risk of arbitrary tyranny. Here again, Della Volpe is objecting to what he saw as the tendency in Western Marxism to subsume real oppositions in an overriding insistence on unity in which subjects would fully recognise themselves in their objects, and so on.

These themes of Della Volpe were taken further by his pupil Lucio Colletti whose writings were more immediately influential in part because they were much clearer. Like Della Volpe, Colletti emphasised the importance of Rousseau as developing a critique of the separation of the citizen from the bourgeois in the capitalist state and a conception of popular democracy that was a direct precursor of the Paris Commune. In the realm of philosophy, Colletti was chiefly opposed to the Frankfurt School for their denial of materialism and of the scientific character of Marxism. But Colletti was equally opposed to the dialectical materialism of Engels and Lenin which he read as a denial of any genuine materialism by a simplistic transcribing of Hegel's version of a dialectic of matter. For 'materialism, in fact, is inconceivable without the principle of non-contradiction: the "dialectic of matter", contrarywise, is the negation of this principle'.[3] By contrast, Colletti reserved the dialectic for the field of thought (claiming that reality is non-contradictory) and emphasised the theme of alienation as central to all of Marx's work including the abstraction of labour under capitalism as analysed in *Capital*.[4] Despite his enthusiasm for the concept of alienation, Colletti was resolutely opposed to Hegel whose thought had infected Western Marxism from Engels to Sartre with an anti-scientific idealist strain with its culmination in the Frankfurt School.[5] Hegel's concept of an all-inclusive totality was incompatible with genuine science which separated thought from its object. In place of Hegel, Colletti considered Kant to be the 'one great modern thinker who can be of assistance to us in constructing a materialist theory of knowledge'.[6] The evident difficulty of reconciling his attachment to Marx's theory of alienation to his equally strong attachment to scientific method *à la* Della Volpe led to Colletti's abandoning Marxism in the mid-1970s.

No such problem confronted Colletti's contemporary Sebastiano Timpanaro in whose view Marx was more indebted to the straightforward eighteenth-century materialism of Holbach and La Mettrie than to either

Kant or Hegel. Timpanaro was an expert on philology and comparative linguistics, gained his living as a proof-reader, and remained a revolutionary socialist until his death in 2000. Timpanaro saw the late Engels as the inheritor of eighteenth-century materialism. In his book *On Materialism*, Timpanaro claimed that 'perhaps the sole characteristic common to virtually all contemporary varieties of Western Marxism is their concern to defend themselves against the accusation of materialism'.[7] This 'purification' of Marxism was typically symbolised by a devaluation of Engels. By materialism Timpanaro meant 'above all the acknowledgement of the priority of nature over mind, or if you like, the priority of the physical level over the biological level, and of the biological level over both the socioeconomic and cultural level'.[8] This priority Timpanaro meant both in a chronological sense and also in the way in which mind was still conditioned by matter. In particular Timpanaro rejected any attempt to accommodate Marxist materialism to psychoanalysis or structuralism which were both 'deeply permeated with anti-materialist ideology'.[9] Such attempts might culturally enrich Marxism but would always compel it to remain subaltern.

During the late 1970s, Marxism in Italy underwent a rapid decline. More recently, writers such as Badaloni and Lusurdo have produced innovating work, the former using Marx and Gramsci to produce a radical theory of democracy, the latter building on his critical history of liberal thought and practice to reformulate Marx's political theory. But the most striking offshoot of Italian Marxism was the emergence of the autonomista movement which emerged in opposition to the CP and Trade Union bureaucracy. Workers were seen not as passive but as powerful – if not betrayed by their leaders as in the summer of 1968. Tronti and others had, in the 1970s, attacked the orthodoxy of development of the forces of production through determined stages and the gradualism of the PCI. They claimed that the expansion of service jobs meant that the regime of the factory had been extended to society as a whole with the proletarianisation of whole swathes of white-collar workers. Antonio Negri built on this to elaborate a theory of history whereby not the logic of profit but class struggle was the motor force of capitalism: Fordism was designed to overcome the resistance to capital of skilled workers and artisans; but the organized resistance of factory labour to capital led to technological innovation which permitted it to restructure labour away from factories (or overseas) into flexible, part-time, service sectors. This involved the unwaged and Third World workers and the possibility of resistance on a global scale. With the arrival of immaterial labour and mass intellectuality, the time would soon be ripe for workers to revolt in such a manner as to rupture the self-reproduction of capital and liberate work from it.[10] The development of these ideas into a theory of the world-wide dissolution of capitalism is briefly discussed below.[11]

Notes

1. G. Della Volpe, *Logic as Positive Science* (London, 1980), p. 200.
2. See here his *Critique of Taste* (New York, 1978).
3. L. Colletti, *Marxism and Hegel* (New York, 1973), p. 192.
4. See his Introduction to the Pelican edition of *Karl Marx: Early Writings* (1971).
5. Colletti described *Dialectic of Enlightenment* as 'the last "Flowers of evil" of the old spiritualism and its desire to destroy things'. See his *From Rousseau to Lenin* (New York, 1972), p. 137.
6. L. Colletti, 'A Political and Philosophical Interview', *New Left Review*, 86 f., 1974, p. 10.
7. S. Timpanaro, *On Materialism*, in D. Tallack (ed.), *Critical Theory: A Reader* (Hemel Hempstead, 1995), p. 330.
8. Op. cit., p. 331.
9. Op. cit., p. 337.
10. See further here H. Cleaver, *Reading Capital Politically* (Brighton, 1979), pp. 51 ff., P. Virno and M. Hardt (eds), *Radical Thought in Italy* (Minneapolis, 1996), and S. Wright, *Storming Heaven: Class Composition and Struggle in Italian Autonomist Marxism* (London, 2002).
11. See below, pp. 392 ff.

Further reading

The best introduction is Fraser's *Introduction to the Thought of Galvano Della Volpe*. Della Volpe's major work, *Critique of Taste*, is available in English, as is his *Rousseau and Marx*. For Colletti, see particularly his collections *Marxism and Hegel* and *From Rousseau to Lenin*, and the chapter in Jay's book. For Timpanaro, see Anderson.

Bibliography

P. Anderson, *Spectrum* (London, 2006).
L. Colletti, *From Rousseau to Lenin* (New York and London, 1972).
—— *Marxism and Hegel* (New York and London, 1973).
J. Fraser, *An Introduction to the Thought of Galvano Della Volpe* (London, 1977).
G. Della Volpe, *Critique of Taste* (London and New York, 1978).
—— *Rousseau and Marx* (London, 1980).
M. Jay, *Marxism and Totality* (Berkeley, 1984), ch. 14.
P. Piccone, *Italian Marxism* (Berkeley, 1983).
S. Wright, *Storming Heaven: Class Composition and Struggle in Italian Autonomist Marxism* (London, 2002).

22
Structuralist Marxism

Equally opposed to Hegelo-Marxism, but much more influential, was the structuralist version of Marxism which arose in France in the mid-1960s. Structuralist Marxism sought to harmonise Marxist thought with the apparently organised and passive nature of advanced industrial society in which both the working class and the bourgeois ego had lost their self-confident sense of mission. Structuralism in general had its origin in the linguistic studies of Saussure or Jacobson who investigated the structure underlying language in general rather than its specific developments. Lévi-Strauss used the concept of structure to illuminate primitive societies, and Lacan and Foucault did the same in psychology and epistemology. For these thinkers, what was vital for our understanding of human society was not the conscious activities of the human subject, but the unconscious structure which these activities presupposed. Given the immense influence of structuralism in the 1960s, it is not surprising that a structuralist reading of Marx should emerge. The major figure here is Louis Althusser, a French philosopher who began elaborating his ideas around 1960. Althusser rejected both the humanist Marxism of the young Lukács, Sartre, and Gramsci with its emphasis on men as the subjects of history, and the simplistic economism that he considered inherent in traditional dialectical materialism.

Althusser started with the question of how to interpret Marx. In his view, Marx's work was not a coherent whole. It did indeed contain a scientific conception of history, but this needed to be extracted analytically by recognising the theoretical gaps, survivals of earlier modes of thinking, etc. In order to achieve this, a rigorous definition of the concepts involved and of their interrelation was essential. This was a task of philosophy. Althusser's basic question was: *'What is Marxist philosophy? Has it any theoretical right to existence? And if it does exist in principle, how can its specificity be defined?*[1] To answer this question, *Capital* was the basic text and Althusser aimed to uncover and display the philosophy inherent in it. Crucial to this effort was the realisation that Marx's work consisted of more than one sphere of discourse. Rejecting the humanism of Marx's early works, Althusser saw what he termed an 'epistemological break' between the young Marx and the mature Marx. The concept of an 'epistemological break' was borrowed from the French philosopher of science Gaston Bachelard, and was akin to the notion of scientific paradigm that Thomas Kuhn was elaborating at the same time. According to Althusser, Marx's early and late writing contained two distinct *problematics*. A problematic was '*the objective internal reference system of its particular themes*, the system of *questions* commanding the *answers* given'.[2] Marx's early, Hegelian writings, by concentrating on the concepts of alienation and species-being, displayed an ideological problematic of the subject; only his later writings contained a problematic that allowed the foundation of a science. But the break was not a clear one in Marx's texts. Some of the earlier ideological conceptions persisted in the *Grundrisse*, and even in *Capital*:

> When *Capital* Volume One appeared (1867), traces of the Hegelian influence still remained. Only later did they disappear *completely*: the *Critique of the Gotha Programme* (1875) as well as the *Marginal Notes on Wagner's 'Lehrbuch der politischen Okonomie'* (1882) are *totally and definitively exempt* from any trace of Hegelian influence.[3]

Hence the need for a *symptomatic* reading of Marx. It was impossible innocently and straightforwardly to grasp the meaning of a text. As Geras has well written

> the problematic, by determining what it includes within its field, thereby necessarily determines what is excluded therefrom. The concepts which are excluded (absences, lacunae), and the problems which are not posed adequately (semi-silences, lapses), or not posed at all (silences), are therefore as much a part of the problematic as are the concepts and problems that are present. And it cannot for that reason be grasped by a simple literal or immediate reading of the explicit discourse of a text. Rather it must be reached by a 'symptomatic' reading where the explicit discourse is read conjointly with the absences, lacunae and silences which, constituting a second 'silent discourse', are so many symptoms of the unconscious problematic buried in the text. Like all knowledge, reading, correctly

understood and correctly practised, is not vision but theoretical labour and production.[4]

There are obvious parallels here with Freud's theory of the unconscious. What did this symptomatic reading yield? It involved a rejection of humanism and of what Althusser saw as its corollary: empiricism. Empiricism, with its opposition of subject and object, abstract and concrete, was the view that the world could be grasped directly, a view which did not clearly separate concepts from their objects. According to empiricism, 'to know is to abstract from the real object its essence, the possession of which by the subject is then called knowledge'.[5] Empiricism opposes 'a given subject to a given object and calls knowledge the abstraction by the subject of the essence of the object. Hence the knowledge of the object is a part of the object itself'.[6] Althusser, on the contrary – in a distinctly neo-Kantian vein – saw the task of philosophy as the creation of concepts which were a precondition for knowledge. He insisted on the strict separation of the object of thought from the real object. 'Knowledge', he wrote,

> working on its 'object'... does not work on the real object but on the peculiar raw material which constitutes, in the strict sense of the term, its '*object*' (of knowledge) and which, even in the rudimentary forms of knowledge is distinct from the real object.[7]

Knowledge working on its object was a specific form of practice – theoretical practice:

> By practice in general I shall mean any process of *transformation* of a determinate given raw material into a determinate *product*, a transformation effected by a determinate human labour, using determinate means ('of production'). In any practice thus conceived, the *determinant* moment (or element) is neither the raw material nor the product, but the practice in the narrow sense: the moment of the labour of *transformation* itself, which sets to work, in a specific structure, men, means and a technical method of utilising the means.[8]

This theoretical practice consisted of three elements which Althusser called Generalities I, II and III. Generalities I were the raw materials of a given discipline – its ideas and concepts, partly scientific, partly ideological. These were worked over by the means of theoretical production (Generalities II) – the framework of concepts of a science which constituted its problematic. The production of this working over was Generalities III – the concrete-in-thought which provided knowledge of the real-concrete.[9] Marxist philosophy – dialectical materialism – was the theory of this theoretical practice.

The result of this epistemology when applied to society was the science of historical materialism. Parallelly to his strict separation of the object of thought from the real object, Althusser rejected Hegel's conception of totality in which the elements of the whole were merely phenomenal expressions of an inner essence, e.g. the essence of Rome expressed in Roman Law, Roman politics, etc. In contrast to this simple approach, what Marx did, according to Althusser, was to develop the concept of society as a totality

> whose unity is constituted by a certain specific type of *complexity*, which introduces instances, that, following Engels, we can, very schematically, reduce to three: the economy, politics and ideology.[10]

Each of these instances was a structure united in a structure of structures – causality was itself structural:

> The effects are not outside the structure, are not a pre-existing object, element or space in which the structure arrives to *imprint its mark*: on the contrary, it implies that the structure is immanent in its effects, a cause immanent in its effects in the Spinozist sense of the term, that *the whole existence of the structure consists of its effects*, in short that the structure, which is merely a specific combination of its peculiar elements, is nothing outside its effects.[11]

Each level had its own peculiar time, its own rhythm of development. This complex and uneven relationship of the instances or levels to each other at a specific time was called by Althusser a 'conjuncture'. Every conjuncture was said to be 'overdetermined' in that each of the levels contributed to determining the structure as well as being determined by it: determination was always complex. Thus Althusser rejected the idea that there was only one simple contradiction between forces and relations of production, between base and superstructure. Of course, the determining role of each level was not equal: their autonomy was only relative and the economy was always determining in the last instance. Althusser drew a distinction between instances which were dominant and those which were determinant. Under feudalism, for example, the political was the dominant instance but the fact that the political was dominant was itself determined by the economy.[12] Given that there was always a dominant element, Althusser called the structure a *structure in dominance*. But the determining role of the economy on this structure in dominance could never be isolated from the structure as a whole:

> The economic dialectic is never active in the *pure state*; in History, these instances, the superstructures, etc., are never seen to step respectfully aside when their work is done, or when the time comes, as his pure phenomena, to scatter before His Majesty the Economy as he strides along the royal road to the Dialectic. From the first moment to the last, the lonely hour of the 'last instance' never comes.[13]

The structure as a whole was decentred since its elements did not derive from a single essence or centre, as in Hegel.

From the notion of structural causality followed the conception of history as 'a process without a subject'. History was not the unilinear and homogeneous process of man's mastery over nature:

> To be dialectical-materialist, Marxist philosophy must break with the idealist category of the 'Subject' as Origin, Essence and Cause, *responsible* in its internality for all the determinations of the external 'Object', of which it is said to be the 'Subject'.[14]

In Hegel, this subject was the Absolute. According to Althusser, all Marx did in his early writings was to substitute the idea of human essence for the Absolute as the subject of history. It was only in 1845–46 that Marx came to see that human nature was 'no abstraction inherent in each single individual' but only 'the ensemble of the social relations',[15] and, with the aid of concepts such as the forces and relations of production, could understand history without the aid of the category of subject. This understanding of history was akin to the Althusserian 'reading' of a text: both had a structure but essentially no subject. Althusser expressed this forcefully as follows:

> The structure of the relations of production determines the *places* and *functions* occupied and adopted by the agents of production, who are never more than the occupants of these places, in so far as they are the 'supports' [*Träger*] of these functions. The true 'subjects' (in the sense of the constitutive subjects of the process) are therefore not these occupants or functionaries, are not, despite all appearances, the 'obviousnesses' of the 'given' of naive anthropology, 'concrete individuals', 'real'

men – but the *definition and distribution of these places and functions. The true 'subjects' are these definers and distributors: the relations of production* (and political and ideological social relations). But since these are 'relations', they cannot be thought within the category *subject.*[16]

This reading of history Althusser contrasted with what he called 'historicism' – the tendency to see man as the active subject of history (of which Sartre's *Critique of Dialectical Reason* would be an outstanding example) – and with the (ideological) humanism of Marx's early works in whose stead Althusser proposed a (scientific) theoretical anti-humanism.

Althusser's account of Marx, in particular its concept of the problematic and its insistence on the relative autonomy of the sciences, was a good antidote both to all types of reductionism and to extreme forms of Hegelian Marxism. Nevertheless, Althusser's theories met with criticism on three counts. Firstly, Althusser claimed that dialectical materialism was a science but offered no criterion of scientificity – of how we know its knowledge to be true knowledge. Any recourse to a 'real object' was ruled out by his rejection of empiricism. Secondly, Althusser declared ideology to be the realm of illusion, but still insisted that ideology was not restricted to class society but would also exist under Communism. For, thirdly, dialectical materialism, as Marxist science, was cut off from the influence of the conditions of social production, existed outside the social formation, and ultimately appeared as the preserve of an intellectual elite disconnected from the revolutionary activity of the working class. This failure to offer a satisfactory account of the relation of theory to practice was the weakest part of Althusser's Marxism. Critics have been quick to point out that, although Althusser's theories seem to stand above the class struggle, his counter-position of ideology and science in fact serves to justify the existence of the Party and bureaucracy: for scientific knowledge is necessarily open only to the few, while even under Communism the masses will have to make do with ideology. Althusser's attitude to Stalinism has been muted: he considered Stalinism only a 'deviation' and a superstructural error. In *For Marx*, for example, he wrote:

Everything that has been said of the 'cult of personality' refers exactly to the domain of the superstructure and therefore of State organisation and ideologies; further it refers largely to *this domain alone*, which we know from Marxist theory possesses a 'relative autonomy' (which explains very simply, in theory, how the socialist *infrastructure* has been able to develop without essential damage during this period of errors affecting the superstructure).[17]

The only critique of Stalinism that Althusser could propose was 'a concrete critique, one which exists in the facts, in the struggle, in the line, in the practices, their principles and their forms, of the Chinese Revolution'.[18] These criticisms led Althusser to modify his positions somewhat by agreeing that his assimilation of philosophy to science has been a 'theoreticist' deviation which had separated philosophy from the class struggle.[19]

As well as being possibly 'theoreticist', Althusser's work was highly theoretical, a tendency which reached its apogee in the work of Hindess and Hirst. The attempts of his followers to apply his ideas have concentrated on two main fields: contemporary politics and the study of history. In his early work Althusser had had almost nothing to say on the state. In his essay *Ideology and Ideological State Apparatuses*,[20] Althusser distinguished between Repressive State Apparatuses and Ideological State Apparatuses such as trade unions, churches, schools, etc., and analysed the role of the latter as important sites of class struggle. But the major attempt to apply Althusser's ideas to classes and state is contained in the work of Nicos Poulantzas. Poulantzas's work remained highly theoretical and concentrated on elaborating the correct problematic for analysing state and class. In *Political Power and Social Classes*, Poulantzas was trying to combat the economist reading of the contemporary state as simply the instrument of monopoly capital (which is the orthodox Communist view) and analyse its autonomy relative to the economy. The role of the state was 'a factor of cohesion between the levels of a social formation ... and the regulating factor of its global equilibrium as a system'.[21] Thus the contemporary capitalist state was a class state in that the social formation which it functions to maintain is one dominated, at the various levels, by the capitalist class – irrespective of what positions of political power, etc., may be held by representatives of this class. The result is an amalgamation of Marxism and structural-functionalism in which the chief difficulty remains the explanation of change in the structure. In *Classes in Contemporary Capitalism* Poulantzas rigorously excluded, along Althusserian lines, reference to consciousness in his analysis and rejected any form of economic reductionism. He described the structural determination of classes in contemporary society, i.e. the way in which their objective position within the social division of labour is reproduced. This reproduction is not only at the economic level but also at the political and ideological levels to which Poulantzas, in his effort to combat economism, gave great emphasis. He was particularly concerned, by a rather schematic and exclusive application of economic, political and ideological criteria, to limit the definition of working class to productive labourers and separate it off from the 'new working class' of white-collar, supervisory workers.[22]

More successful has been the application of Althusserian concepts to history and particularly to the 'new economic anthropology' of such writers as Rey, Terray, Meillassoux, and Godelier,[23] with their discussions of the relation between modes of production and social formations, and the consequences for development theory.[24] Thus Althusser's writings have proved very popular in Latin America where they have been used to analyse the existence of different modes of production interacting in the same society. More recently interest in Althusser has revived with the publication of his lurid autobiography and many of his unpublished manuscripts which show him to be constantly undermining, sometimes to the point of contradiction, his own writings.[25]

Notes

1. L. Althusser, *For Marx* (London and New York, 1970) p. 31.
2. Ibid., p. 67.
3. L. Althusser, *Lenin and Philosophy* (London, 1971) p. 90.
4. N. Geras, 'Althusser's Marxism: An Account and Assessment', in *New Left Review* (eds), *Western Marxism: A Critical Reader* (London, 1977) pp. 244f.
5. L. Althusser and E. Balibar, *Reading Capital* (London, 1970) pp. 35f.
6. L. Althusser, *For Marx* (London and New York, 1970) p. 251.
7. L. Althusser and E. Balibar, *Reading Capital*, p. 43.
8. L. Althusser, *For Marx*, p. 166.
9. See ibid., pp. 183ff. Althusser considers himself here to be explicating Marx's views in the third section of the 1857 Introduction to the *Grundrisse*.
10. Ibid., p. 232.
11. L. Althusser and E. Balibar, *Reading Capital*, pp. 188f.
12. See Balibar's elaboration of this point in *Reading Capital*, pp. 216ff.
13. L. Althusser, *For Marx*, p. 113.
14. L. Althusser, *Essays in Self-Criticism* (London, 1976) p. 96.
15. K. Marx, 'Theses on Feuerbach', in *Selected Writings*, ed. D. McLellan (Oxford and New York, 2000) p. 157.
16. L. Althusser and E. Balibar, *Reading Capital*, p. 180.
17. L. Althusser, *For Marx*, p. 240.
18. L. Althusser, *Essays in Self-Criticism*, p. 92.
19. See, in particular, ibid., pp. 105ff.
20. L. Althusser, *Lenin and Philosophy* (London, 1971) pp. 135ff.
21. N. Poulantzas, *Political Power and Social Classes* (London, 1973) pp. 44f.
22. See the critique of E.O. Wright, in *Class, Crisis and the State* (New York and London, 1978) ch. 2.
23. See works quoted in the bibliography.
24. See further here: A. Foster-Carter, 'The Modes of Production Controversy', *New Left Review*, vol. 107 (1978).
25. On the state of publication of Althusser's *Nachlass*, see G. Elliot, 'Ghostlier Demarcations: On the Posthumous Edition of Althusser's Writings', *Radical Philosophy*, vol. 90 (1998).

Further reading

Althusser: texts

See Althusser's earliest articles collected in *For Marx* and then his most basic text, *Reading Capital*. This can be supplemented by the collections *Lenin and Philosophy* and *Politics and History*. See also the *Essays in Self-Criticism*, which contains the polemic with John Lewis, and the *Reader* edited by Elliott.

Althusser: commentaries

For a book-length critique, see Callinicos's *Althusser's Marxism*. Similarly sympathetic and insightful is Geras's article of the same title. Chapter Five of Walton and Gamble's *From Alienation to Surplus Value* is more critical, as is Glucksmann's article 'A Ventriloquist Structuralism'. For a defence, see Anderson and Blackburn's article in *The Unknown Dimension*. The books by Benton and Elliott contain measured and careful discussions. See also the excellently sharp article by McCarney.

Others

Of Althusser's disciples, see particularly Poulantzas's work, *Political Power and Social Classes* and *Classes in Contemporary Capitalism*, and also his more empirical work on Fascism and the Mediterranean dictatorship. There is a critique of Poulantzas's view of the state in Miliband's article, and of his view of classes in Wright's book. Jessop has provided a full-length study of his politics.

Bibliography

Althusser: texts

Louis Althusser, *Essays in Self-Criticism* (London, 1976).
—— *For Marx* (London and New York, 1970).
—— *The Future Lasts a Long Time* (London, 1993).
—— *The Humanist Controversy and Other Writings*, introduction by G. Goshgarian (New York, 2003).
—— *Lenin and Philosophy and Other Essays* (London, 1971).
—— 'On the Twenty-Second Congress of the French Communist Party', *New Left Review*, 104 (1977).
—— *Philosophy of the Encounter: Later Writings 1978–1987*, trans. G. Goshgarian (London, 2006).
—— *Politics and History* (London, 1972).
—— *The Spectre of Hegel: Early Writings* (New York, 1997).
—— *Writings on Psychoanalysis: Freud and Lacan* (New York, 1996).
—— and Etienne Balibar, *Reading Capital* (London, 1970).

Etienne Balibar, *The Dictatorship of the Proletariat* (London, 1977).
—— 'Irrationalism and Marxism', *New Left Review*, 107 (1978).
—— *The Althusser Reader*, ed. G. Elliott (Cambridge, 1994).

Althusser: commentaries

P. Anderson and R. Blackburn, 'Louis Althusser and the Struggle for Marxism', in D. Howard and K. Klare (eds), *The Unknown Dimension* (New York, 1972).
Ted Benton, *The Rise and Fall of Structural Marxism* (New York, 1984).
Y. Boutang, *Louis Althusser: A Biography*, 2 vols (London, 2000).
A. Callari and D. Ruccio (eds), *Postmodern Materialism and the Future of Marxist Theory: Essays in the Althusserian Tradition* (London, 1996).
Alex Callinicos, *Althusser's Marxism* (London, 1976).
Simon Clarke, *One-Dimensional Marxism: Althusser and the Politics of Class* (London, 1980).
G. Elliott (ed.), *Althusser: A Critical Reader* (Oxford, 1994).
Gregory Elliott, *Althusser: The Detour of Theory* (London, 1987).
Norman Geras, 'Althusser's Marxism: An Account and Assessment', *New Left Review*, 71 (1972), and *New Left Review* (eds), *Western Marxism: A Critical Reader* (London, 1977).
Valentino Gerratana, 'Althusser and Stalinism', *New Left Review*, 101–2 (1977).
A. Glucksmann, 'A Ventriloquist Structuralism', in *Western Marxism: A Critical Reader* (New York and London, 1977).
P. Hirst, 'Althusser and Philosophy', *Theoretical Practice*, 2 (1971).
A. Kaplan and M. Sprinker (eds), *The Althusserian Legacy* (New York, 1993).
A. Levine, *A Future for Marxism? Althusser, the Analytical Turn and the Revival of Socialist Theory* (London, 2003).
W. Lewis, *Louis Althusser and the Traditions of French Marxism* (Lanham, 2005).
M. Macchiocchi, *Letters from Inside the Italian Communist Party to Louis Althusser* (London, 1973).
M. Majumdar, *Althusser and the End of Leninism?* (London, 1995).
R. Resch, *Althusser and the Renewal of Marxist Socialist Theory* (Berkeley, 1992).

Others

E. Balibar, *The Philosophy of Marx* (London, 1995).
S. Clarke, 'Marxism, Sociology and Poulantzas's Theory of the State', *Capital and Class*, 2 (1977).
Bob Jessop, *Nicos Poulantzas: Marxist Theory and Political Strategy* (New York, 1985).
Joseph McCarney, 'For and Against Althusser', *New Left Review*, 176 (1989).
R. Miliband, 'The Capitalist State: Reply to Nicos Poulantzas', *New Left Review*, 59 (1970).
Nicos Poulantzas, 'The Capitalist State: A Reply to Miliband and Laclau', *New Left Review*, 95 (1976).
—— *Classes in Contemporary Capitalism* (London, 1975).
—— *The Crisis of the Dictatorships: Portugal, Greece, and Spain* (London, 1976).
—— *Political Power and Social Classes* (London, 1973).
Steven Smith, *Reading Althusser: An Essay on Structural Marxism* (Ithaca, 1984).
E. Wright, *Class, Crisis and the State* (New York and London, 1978) ch. 2.

23
British Marxism

The fact that Marx lived and worked in Britain for more than thirty years did little to aid the implantation of his ideas on the British Left. Until 1880 Marx's doctrines were, with very few exceptions, unavailable to those who did not read German or French. In 1881 the Social Democratic Federation was formed to revivify Chartist ideas. The SDF was not formally Marxist, but its leader H.M. Hyndman did much in, for example, *England for All*, to publicise the ideas of Marx, to which he had been converted after reading *Capital*. The SDF was the leading British Marxist organisation until the First World War but never seems to have achieved an active membership of more than about one thousand. The Independent Labour Party, formed by Keir Hardie and his friends in 1893, avoided ideas of revolution and class confrontation and embodied a more ethical, non-conformist approach to socialism. The Labour Party, which grew out of the Labour Representation Committee formed at the instigation of the TUC in 1900, grew immensely in the pre-war years. But, unlike other workers' parties affiliated to the Second International, it was staunchly anti-Marxist in outlook.

By the time of the Bolshevik victory in Russia there were three main Marxist organisations in Britain, although all of them were minute compared with the Labour Party. The largest, the British Socialist Party, was formed in 1911 by a merging of the SDF with dissidents from the ILP. The Socialist Labour Party was an English version of its American namesake and propagated the Industrial Unionism of de Leon as interpreted by its main spokesmen, the Irish Marxist James Connolly, the Clydeside leader John Maclean, and J.T. Murphy. The smallest of the three was the Workers' Socialist Federation, inspired by Sylvia Pankhurst and particularly strong in the East End of London. All contributed members to the Communist Party of Great Britain which, after its foundation in 1920, became the leading Marxist organisation in Britain.

Unlike other European Communist Parties, the British Communist Party had not been formed as a result of a split in the majority Social Democratic Party. The Communist Party was therefore inclined to seek affiliation with the Labour Party, but found itself rebuffed. The attitude of Communists to the Labour Party was inherently ambivalent: they declared the reformism of Labour to be a betrayal of the working class but at the same time had to follow the Moscow line of United Front by presenting themselves as the left wing of the Labour Party. In spite of the widespread industrial unrest and the débâcle of the National Government, the Communist Party made little progress during the 1930s. It was, however, aided by the influx of considerable numbers of intellectuals who saw Communism as the best way of expressing their opposition to the rise of Fascism. Poets such as Auden, Day Lewis and Spender declared their adhesion to the proletarian cause. Gollancz's *Left Book Club*, founded in 1936, enjoyed the collaboration of such gifted exponents of Marxism as Laski and Strachey. But perhaps the only really original pre-war British Marxist was Christopher Caudwell, whose work was cut short by his death in the Spanish Civil War. In his two major works, *Illusion and Reality* and *Studies in a Dying Culture*, Caudwell produced, albeit in a disorganised manner, a treatment of the social function of literature that is full of suggestive insights.

After 1956, however, Marxism ceased to be equated simply with the orthodoxy of the small British Communist Party. With the Sino-Soviet split and the success of Castro in Cuba, even orthodox Communism was becoming widely differentiated. More importantly, Marxist thought had an increasing influence on the expanding university population of the mid-1960s. The main symbol of this was the founding in 1960 of the *New Left Review*, which has continued over the last twenty years to be the principal journal of the intellectual left in Britain. But this interest in Marxist theory has not been matched by any concomitant growth in numbers. The Communist Party remained small, adopted – in *The British Road to Socialism* – a far from revolutionary programme, and sought to move the Labour Party in a leftward direction. But it nevertheless remained the only Marxist organisation which enjoyed any real implantation in the labour movement. This means that in Britain the revolutionary left is almost synonymous with Trotskyism – from the largest of their groups, the Socialist Workers' Party (formally International Socialists), through the more theoretical International Marxist Group, to such extreme tendencies as the Workers' Revolutionary Party.

The fact that there was, compared to continental Europe, so little indigenous British Marxist thought goes hand in hand with the weakness of any indigenous Marxist political movement. In a famous thesis Perry Anderson and Tom Nairn argued that the seventeenth-century English revolution was not, as traditionally conceived, a struggle between a rising bourgeoisie and a declining aristocracy. It was, rather, the result of clashes within the landed class which 'left almost the entire social structure intact' with the result that, well into the nineteenth century, it was the aristocracy that formed 'the vanguard of the bourgeoisie'.[1] This incomplete character of Britain's bourgeois revolutions in which the capitalists were always prepared to make compromises with the aristocracy resulted, too, in a backward intellectual culture which produced no comprehensive analysis of society such as those of Durkheim in France or Weber in Germany – let alone any substantial Marxist critique.

Such a view was strongly contested.[2] In part, the argument reflected a generational gap and different intellectual traditions. Critics of the Anderson/Nairn thesis such as Edward Thompson belonged to a generation whose members – Ralph Miliband, John Saville, Stuart Hall, for example – had been influenced by the earlier British socialist thinkers and intellectuals inside, or close to, the Communist Party. Anderson, by contrast, belonged to a younger Marxist generation inspired by continental thinkers such as Sartre and, particularly, Gramsci. The latter was probably more discussed in Britain than in any other country outside his native Italy. It was one of the aims of the *New Left Review*, the principal journal of the intellectual Left in Britain and edited by Anderson from 1962 until 1983, to remedy, by assimilating European Marxism, the perceived insular backwardness of British culture.

This same contrast was evident in the field of history where Marxist influence has been strongest. An impressive body of work had been produced in the preceding decades by writers such as Gordon Childe, Maurice Dobb, Christopher Hill, Rodney Hilton and Eric Hobsbawm who had close links with the Communist Party. The younger generation, centred around the *New Left Review*, were, by contrast, more interested in viewing history through theories provided by continental European Marxism and, influenced by writers such as Deutscher, had, at least initially, a vaguely Trotskyist outlook which naturally put them at odds with those coming from a background more sympathetic to the Soviet Union. Hill's *The World Turned Upside Down*, Thompson's *The Making of the English Working Class* and his later *Whigs and Hunters* together with Hobsbawm's trilogy on the long nineteenth century were examples of detailed, empirical, narrative history 'from below'. Anderson's *Passages from Antiquity to Feudalism* and *Lineages of the Absolutist State*, on the other hand presented a history of European absolutism which concentrated more on institutions and yielded an analysis whose abstract character was designed to provide a comprehensive theory of the modern bourgeois state as it evolved in the West.

Whereas the American Left in the universities was more influenced by the Frankfurt School and in particular Marcuse (who had elected to stay there after the war), those around the *New Left Review* enthusiastically welcomed, albeit fairly briefly, the strongly theoretical, structuralist approach of Althusser and his disciples. 'Events', wrote Stedman-Jones in this vein, 'are only meaningful in terms of a structure that will establish them as such. In effect history is theory, and cannot logically be otherwise. It is the formulation of theoretical concepts with which to construct history that determines the greatness of the historian ... In England this has never been acknowledged.'[3] Although it was widely agreed that concepts such as relative autonomy, overdetermination, and ideology[4] could prove useful for historians, the Althusserian emphasis on theory also provoked a sweeping dismissal from Kolakowski and a bitter attack from Thompson.[5] The debate between the theoreticians and those who preferred a more native empirical approach was played out in the pages of the *History Workshop Journal*, but by the late 1970s the self-destructive theoreticism of many Althusserians had run its course. Hindess and Hirst's *Mode of Production and Social Formation* together with the short-lived journal *Theoretical Practice* were its most extreme examples. The equally (at times) theoretical approach employed by such analytical Marxists as Cohen and Elster has proved more fruitful.[6]

In the field of literature, and culture in general, the figure of Raymond Williams is central. His early work, together with that of Hoggart and Thompson, looked at culture as a whole way of life and the means by which social actors made sense of it. Although the rejection of what was seen as abstract theory and determinism tended to pull some forms of culturalism away from Marxism, with the publication of the works of Lukács and Gramsci in the 1960s, 'culturalism embraced those tendencies in Western Marxism which offered related ways of accounting for the "relative autonomy" of cultural phenomena while also welcoming the stress on the philosophical – as opposed to the scientific – reading of Marx'.[7]

This view of culture and ideology as the sites of domination and resistance found its main expression in the Birmingham Centre for Contemporary Cultural Studies directed by Stuart Hall. The major influence here was Gramsci, although the Centre did have a brief Althusserian period, and it concentrated on the ideological struggle around politics and institutions. This was in some contrast to Raymond Williams who (when not succumbing to the fashion for Althusser)[8] produced a libertarian version of Marxism which emphasised the cultural possibilities for social change and the capacity for individuals and groups to modify their conditions of existence. Williams is best known for popularising the term 'cultural materialism', a kind of materialist sociology of culture. Williams elaborated a concept of culture as a material social process creating specific and different ways of life. What concerned Williams most, and is best expressed in his *The City and the Country*, was what he called a 'structure of feeling', a concept as apparently paradoxical as cultural materialism itself. According to him, 'the term is difficult, but "feeling" is chosen to emphasize a distinction from more formal concepts of "world-view" or "ideology". It is not only that we must go beyond formally held and systematic beliefs, though of course we have always to include them. It is that we are concerned with meanings and values as they are actually lived and felt.'[9]

This emphasis on experience and feeling aroused some criticism. Terry Eagleton, Britain's leading Marxist critic, complained of Williams's 'consistent over-subjectivizing of the social formation'.[10] In Eagleton's view, Williams dissolved politics into culture and understated the importance of class struggle. His work belonged to a romantic populism which owed too much both to the anti-scientific attitude of Lukács, Goldmann, and the Frankfurt School and also the empiricist, liberal humanist values of the dominant culture. Eagleton later referred to his polemic against Williams as informed by 'the brisk impatience of relative youth'.[11] Indeed, he was then in a distractively Althusserian mode but his critique does illustrate both the sometimes ambiguous relation of Williams to Marxism[12] and, yet again, the division between those with their roots mainly in a native British socialism and those more influenced by continental European Marxism.

Although British political economy had been one of the major sources of Marx's thought, its contribution in the succeeding century was slight. In the 1930s Strachey had produced clear expositions such as *The Nature of Capitalist Crisis* or *The Coming Struggle for Power* and Dobb's *Political Economy and Capitalism* and later writings continued ably to defend Communist Party orthodoxy. The long post-war economic boom and the unresolved question of the relation of value to price in Marx's theory continued to present difficult problems. In particular, the publication in 1960 of Piero Sraffa's *The Production of Commodities by Means of Commodities*, an influential work of high intellectual rigour, not to say abstruseness, represented a wholesale undermining of neoclassical economics. And since Marx took over much of the conceptual framework of classical economics, and particularly Ricardo, Sraffa's work seemed to undermine much of traditional Marxian economics such as the labour theory of value, the relations of value to price, and falling rate of profit. Some Marxist economists, such as Rowthorn, objected to the reading of Marx as though he were a classical English economist.[13] Others accepted Sraffa's conclusions but claimed that by and large the main points of Marx's economics could be expressed purely in terms of price.[14] Much of this debate was highly technical.[15] Rowthorn himself produced more concrete analysis of, for example, the influence of British institutions on the British economy[16] and Armstrong, Glyn and Harrison stressed the importance of overaccumulation in explaining the crises of the 1970s.[17] But the most impressive contribution of Marxian political economy undoubtedly lay in its analyses of the more international dimensions of development theory.[18]

Although much Marxist writing had been devoted to discussing how to characterise the main representation of actually existing (alleged) Marxism, the collapse of the Soviet Union had been as little foreseen by its Marxist critics as it had been by non-Marxists. Trotsky had given his view[19] that the Soviet Union was a 'degenerate workers state', which, although the economy remained socialised, had suffered a bureaucratic deformation. This was challenged by Tony Cliff and his followers who claimed that the Soviet Union has developed into 'bureaucratic state capitalism'. On this view, the Soviet bureaucracy controlled both the economy and the state and, as such, was no different from any other exploiting class.[20] A different view from both Trotsky and Cliff was provided by Ticktin and the group around the journal *Critique* who are the only group of Marxist political economists who can fairly claim to be unsurprised by the rapid collapse of the Soviet Union. Ticktin examined in some detail the actual working of the Soviet system where, according to him the central government's pressure for increased output was resisted by bureaucrats lower down the chain of command concerned to safeguard their position. This conflict within the bureaucracy generated massive and increasing waste. This wastefulness was the result of low labour productivity, underutilisation of productive capacity, and slow technical progress. The Soviet elite was 'in a constant state of flux, insecurity and competition'[21] and thus in no position to control any surplus which might arise.[22] With the advent of capitalist relations of production in Russia and Eastern Europe, the work of Marxist political economists found itself on more familiar ground.[23]

Nearer home, the debate between Miliband and Poulantzas mirrored disagreements among Marxist historians and cultural critics. Miliband's *The State in Capitalist Society* viewed the British state as an instrument serving the interests of the bourgeoisie since it was dominated by them through a network of interpersonal relations that Miliband was at pains to analyse in some detail. Poulantzas, by contrast, adopted a structuralist approach whereby the capitalist state was seen as a system whose functioning was seen as independent of the mind-set of the ruling class – or indeed any one else.[24] Both protagonists later modified their positions. The whole area was taken further by the impressive work of Jessop who followed in the path of a revised Poulantzas. Jessop is concerned to theorise the transition from a Keynesian welfare state characteristic of a Fordist regime – that is, mass production, mass consumption, and massified semi-skilled labour – to a post-Fordist regime where permanent innovation and labour flexibility in an increasingly globalised economy mean the subordination of welfare to the discipline of the labour market. For Jessop, 'the state is located within a complex dialectic of structures and strategies'[25] which favours some strategies more than others. Nevertheless, 'there can be no guarantee that the state (and governments wielding state power) will act in the general interest of capital (whatever that might be). Indeed, insofar as the function of the capitalist state can be regarded as the expanded reproduction of capital, the specific form of the capitalist state at a particular stage in its historical development is always likely to problematize and eventually compromise this function.'[26] Thus, in spite of its structuralist pedigree, Jessop's approach strives to unite the different emphases of (continental) structure and (native) agency which have characterised the divisions within British Marxism.

Notes

1. T. Nairn, 'The British Political Elite', *New Left Review*, Vol. 23 (1964), p. 22.
2. See, for example, E.P. Thompson, 'The Peculiarities of the English', *Socialist Register* (1965).
3. G. Stedman-Jones, 'The Pathology of English History', *New Left Review*, Vol. 46 (1967), pp. 42f.
4. See pp. 351 ff. above.
5. L. Kolakowski, 'Althusser's Marx', *Socialist Register* (1971) and E.P. Thompson, *The Poverty of Theory* (London, 1978).
6. See below, pp. 386 ff.
7. C. McMahon, 'Marxism and Culture', in A. Gamble, D. Marsh and T. Tant (eds), *Marxism and Social Science* (London, 1999), p. 209.
8. For example in *Marxism and Literature* (Oxford, 1977).
9. Op. cit., p. 132.
10. T. Eagleton, *Criticism and Ideology: A Study in Marxist Literary Theory* (London, 1976), p. 32.
11. T. Eagleton (ed), *Raymond Williams: Critical Perspectives* (Oxoford, 1989), p. 4.
12. See the discussion in J. Higgins, *Raymond Williams: Literature, Marxism and Cultural Materialism* (London, 1999), ch. 5.

13. B. Rowthorn, 'Neo-Ricardianism or Marxism?', *New Left Review*, Vol. 86 (1974).
14. I. Steedman, *Marx after Sraffa* (London, 1971).
15. See B. Fine and L. Harris, 'Controversial Issues in Marxist Economic Theory', *Socialist Register* (1976).
16. B. Rowthorn, *Capitalism, Conflict and Inflation* (London, 1980).
17. P. Armstrong, A. Glyn and J. Harrison, *Capitalism since World War Two* (London, 1984).
18. See pp. 287 ff. above.
19. See pp. 148 ff. above.
20. See T. Cliff, *Russia: A Marxist Analysis* (London, 1964). See also the analysis of the USSR as extracting surplus value like Western capitalist states in S. Resnick and R. Wolff, *Class Theory and History: Capitalism and Communism in the USSR* (New York, 2002).
21. H. Ticktin, 'The Class Structure of the USSR and the Soviet Elite', *Critique*, Vol. 9 (1978).
22. For a careful discussion of these various views (and his own account) see D. Lane, *The Rise and Fall of State Socialism* (Cambridge, 1996), ch. 7.
23. See, for example, S. Clarke and others, *What about the Workers? Workers and the Transition to Capitalism in Russia* (London, 1993).
24. N. Poulantzas, 'The Problems of the Capitalist State', *New Left Review*, Vol. 58 (1969).
25. B. Jessop, *State Theory: Putting Capitalist States in their Place* (Cambridge, 1990), p. 129. See also his *The Future of the Capitalist State* (Cambridge, 2002).
26. C. Hay, *Marxism and the State*, in A. Gamble, D. Marsh and T. Tant (eds), *Marxism and Social Science* (London, 1999), p. 170.

Further reading

For the origins of the Left in Britain, see Beer's basic *History of British Socialism*. On the Social Democratic Federation, see Tsuzuki's biography of Hyndman and the second volume of Kapp's life of Eleanor Marx. On the origins of the Communist Party, see Kendall's excellent *The Revolutionary Movement in Britain* and Beckett's recent study. There is a Trotskyist account in Challinor's *The Origins of British Bolshevism*. For the early years of the Communist Party, see Macfarlane's balanced introduction *The British Communist Party* and Klugman's lengthy apologia. The articles by Sedgwick and by Williams contain short, reliable accounts of post-war Marxism. The books by Dworkin, Kenny, and Chun are later and longer accounts of the same. Widgery's lengthy selection, *The Left in Britain 1956–1968*, is edited from a Trotskyist perspective. An excellent guide to contemporary economic debates is the article by Fine and Harris. Jessop's *The Capitalist State* is a thorough discussion of recent work. Scruton's *Thinkers of the New Left* provides sharp polemic, while Inglis's biography of Williams provides an excellent overview of the period. The works of Anderson continue to inform: see the books by

Elliott and Blackledge. For recent work on analytical Marxism and market socialism, see the bibliography to the next chapter.

Bibliography

History

Perry Anderson, *English Questions* (London, 1992).
—— 'The Origins of the Present Crisis', in *Towards Socialism* (London, 1965).
W. Anderson, *James Connolly and the Irish Left* (Dublin, 1994).
F. Beckett, *Enemy Within: The Rise and Fall of the British Communist Party* (London, 1995).
Max Beer, *History of British Socialism*, 2 vols (London, 1919–21).
J. Callaghan, *The Far Left in British Politics* (Oxford, 1987).
Raymond Challinor, *The Origins of British Bolshevism* (London, 1977).
L. Chun, *The British New Left* (Edinburgh, 1993).
Henry Collins and Chimen Abramsky, *Karl Marx and the British Labour Movement* (London, 1965).
J. Connolly, *Selected Writings* (Harmondsworth, 1973).
D. Dworkin, *Cultural Marxism in Post War Britain: History, the New Left, and the Origins of Cultural Studies* (Durham, 1997).
John Bruce Glasier, *William Morris and the Early Days of the Socialist Movement* (London, 1921).
S.R. Graubard, *British Labour and the Russian Revolution: 1917–1924* (Cambridge, Mass., 1956).
Keir Hardie, *From Pit to Parliament* (London, 1913).
—— *Hardie's speeches and Writings: 1885–1915*, ed. Emrys Hughes (London, 1928).
E. Hobsbawm, *Age of Extremes: The Short Twentieth Century, 1914–1991* (London, 1994).
Bob Holton, *British Syndicalism, 1900–1914: Myths and Realities* (London, 1976).
H.M. Hyndman, *England For All: The Historical Basis of Socialism in England* (Hassocks, Sussex, 1977).
—— *The Record of an Adventurous Life* (London, 1911).
Fred Inglis, *Raymond Williams* (London, 1996).
Yvonne Kapp, *Eleanor Marx*, vol. II *The Crowded Years, 1884–1898* (London, 1976).
Walter Kendall, *The Revolutionary Movement in Britain, 1900–1921: The Origins of British Communism* (London, 1969).
M. Kenny, *The First New Left: British Intellectuals after Stalin* (London, 1995).
J. Klugman, *History of the Communist Party of Great Britain* (London, 1968ff.).
David Kynaston, *King Labour: The British Working Class, 1850–1914* (London, 1977).
Harold J. Laski, *Communism* (London, 1932).
L.J. Macfarlane, *The British Communist Party* (London, 1966).
S. Macintyre, *A Proletarian Science: Marxism in Britain 1917–1933* (Cambridge, 1980).
Norman and Jean MacKenzie, *The Fabians* (New York, 1977).
Paul Meier, *William Morris: The Marxist Dreamer*, 2 vols (Hassocks, Sussex, 1978).
Francis Mulhern, *The Moment of 'Scrutiny'* (London, 1978).
Tom Nairn, 'The English Working Class', in Robin Blackburn (ed.), *Ideology in Social Science: Readings in Critical Social Theory* (London, 1972).

M. Newman, *John Strachey* (Manchester, 1989).
Henry Pelling, *The Origins of the Labour Party: 1800–1900* (London, 1954).
Stanley Pierson, *Marxism and the Origins of British Socialism: The Struggle for a New Consciousness* (Ithaca, N.Y., 1973).
Peter Sedgwick, 'Varieties of Socialist Thought', *Protest and Discontent*, ed. B. Crick and W. Robson (Harmondsworth, 1970).
E.P. Thompson, *William Morris: Romantic to Revolutionary* (London, 1977).
C. Tsuzuki, *H.M. Hyndman and British Socialism* (Oxford, 1961).
Stephen White, *British and the Bolshevik Revolution* (London, 1979).
David Widgery, *The Left in Britain, 1956–168* (London, 1976).
Raymond Williams, 'Notes on British Marxism since the War', *New Left Review*, 100 (1976–7).
Michael Woodhouse and Brian Pearce, *Communism in Britain* (London, 1975).
Alex Zwendling, *Orwell and the Left* (New Haven, 1974).

Theory

P. Blackledge, *Perry Anderson, Marxism, and the New Left* (London, 2004).
T. Eagleton, *Marxism and Literary Criticism* (London, 2002).
J. Eldridge and L. Eldridge, *Raymond Williams: Making Connections* (London, 1994).
G. Elliott, *Perry Anderson: The Remorseless Laboratory of History* (Minneapolis, 1998).
B. Fine and L. Harris, 'Controversial Issues in Marxist Economic Theory', *Socialist Register*, 1976.
A. Glyn and R. Sutcliffe, *British Capitalism, Workers and the Profit Squeeze* (Harmondsworth, 1972).
I. Gough, 'Marx's Theory of Productive and Unproductive Labour', *New Left Review*, 76 (1972).
J. Higgins, *Raymond Williams: Literature, Marxism, and Cultural Materialism* (London, 1999).
E. Hobsbawm, *For a Rational Left: Political Writings 1977–88* (London, 1996).
—— Introduction to Karl Marx, *Pre-capitalist Economic Formations* (London, 1964).
—— *On History* (London, 1998).
G. Hodgson, 'The Theory of the Falling Rate of Profit', *New Left Review*, 84 (1974).
Bob Jessop, *The Capitalist State* (Oxford, 1982).
—— *The Future of the Capitalist State* (Cambridge, 2002).
—— *State Theory: Putting Capitalist States in their Place* (Cambridge, 1990).
Ralph Miliband, *Parliamentary Socialism* (London, 1973).
—— *The State in Capitalist Society* (London, 1973).
Tom Nairn, *The Break-up of Britain* (London, 1977).
Roger Scruton, *Thinkers of the New Left* (Harlow, 1985).
Ian Steedman, *Marx After Sraffa* (London, 1978).
E.P. Thompson, *The Making of the English Working Class* (London, 1963).
—— *The Poverty of Theory* (London, 1978).
R. Williams, *Culture and Society* (London, 1958).
—— *The Long Revolution* (London, 1961).
—— *Marxism and Literature* (Oxford, 1977).
—— *Politics and Letters* (London, 1978).
D. Yaffe, 'The Marxian Theory of Crisis, Capital and the State', *Economy and Society*, 2 (1973).

24
Marxism in the United States

History

Marx and Engels

Throughout their lives Marx and Engels showed considerable interest in the United States. Marx thought seriously of emigrating there in the early 1850s and was, for ten years, the best appreciated foreign journalist on the *New York Daily Tribune*; Engels visited New England in 1888. The United States represented, for Marx, 'the most modern of bourgeois societies'[1] in which, owing to the absence of a feudal past, 'the State, in contrast to all earlier national formations, was from the beginning subordinate to bourgeois society ... and never could make the pretence of being an end in itself'.[2] The result was a society in which

> though classes already exist, they have not yet become fixed, but continually change and interchange their elements in constant flux, where the modern means of production, instead of coinciding with a stagnant surplus population, rather compensate for the relative deficiency of heads and hands, and where, finally, the feverish, youthful movement of material production, which has to make a new world of its own, has left neither time nor opportunity for abolishing the old world spirit.[3]

Even by the middle of the nineteenth century, Marx had foreseen the tremendous economic development of America in which the discovery of gold in California, combined with the flow of population westwards, the incredible growth of the railway system, and the 'tireless energy of the Yankees'[4] would make the southern half of the north American continent 'the fulcrum of world commerce'.[5] Marx and Engels devoted long analyses to the Civil War, the outcome of which had cleared the path for proletarian struggle on the principle that 'labour cannot emancipate itself in the white skin where in the black it is branded'.[6] The abolition of slavery and huge industrial growth afforded the possibility – particularly after the chronic crisis of 1873–8 – of 'establishing a serious workers' party',[7] though Marx had early predicted that it would first take the form of a pro-capitalist radicalism.[8]

Weydemeyer and Sorge

The first implantation of Marxism in the United States had, in fact, begun well before Marx's death. This was largely the result of the immigration of skilled industrial workers following the failure of the 1848 revolutions in Europe. Largely of German origins, they made little impact on either the relatively small groups of organised labour in the East or the Populist agrarian movements of the West. Prominent among the first wave was Marx's friend Joseph Weydemeyer, the first Marxist in the United States. In 1853, Weydemeyer, with a few of his friends, founded the short-lived American Workers' League in New York City – a cross between a party and a trade union, whose aim was to agitate for the immediate improvement of workers' conditions on a socialist basis. Subsequently, Weydemeyer was active in Illinois and Missouri as a journalist and county auditor, fought in the Civil War, and died in 1866. As with the American Workers' League, the influence of the First International in America was largely limited to German-Americans. By 1870 the First International had several sections in America united under a Central Committee with Frederick Sorge as corresponding secretary. Always a peripheral movement, the International only survived the transfer of its seat to New York in 1872 by four years. Sorge was concerned to preserve Marxist principles in the International by insisting on the primacy of agitation for working-class demands until the development of a proletarian consciousness produced a viable basis for a political party. Thus he was led to combat both those who saw education as the major solution to proletarian misery and those who concentrated on the cause of women's suffrage, particularly the ambitious schemes of Victoria Woodhull. After the demise of the International, Sorge retired from active politics.

The SLP and De Leon

Immediately following the eclipse of the International, the Socialist Labour Party of North America was founded at a conference in Philadelphia attended by Sorge and by Weydemeyer's son Otto.

However, the Socialist Labour Party's attempts during the 1880s to imitate the electoral campaigns of the mighty German SPD were unsuccessful and the party stagnated in spite of the upsurge of trade union activity which resulted in the foundation of the American Federation of Labor in 1886. In particular the idealistic and basically reformist Knights of Labor mushroomed in the mid-1880s, leading the agitation for an eight-hour day and joining the new Independent Labor Party which ran Henry George in the New York mayoralty campaign of 1886. George, author of the popular *Progress and Poverty* (1879), advocated a single tax system in which land rents would be used for public purposes – a measure that had more to do with agrarian reform and small self-employed businessmen than with industrial capitalism.[9]

The SLP, almost exclusively composed of recent German immigrants, was unable to make any headway until the accession to its ranks of Daniel De Leon. Of Jewish and Caribbean origin, De Leon was educated in Holland and lectured at Columbia. He was at first an energetic supporter of George and then of the cooperative, collectivist nationalism of Bellamy before joining the SLP in 1890. As editor of the SLP paper *The People* – the only avowedly Marxist English-language paper in the United States – De Leon was the SLP's leading spokesman from 1890 until his death in 1914 and the most articulate and intransigent proponent of Marxism in America during those years.

De Leon firmly rejected compromising the Marxism of the SLP either with the populist movements for agrarian reform (the traditional form of American radicalism) or with the middle-class utopianism that had so bothered the previous generation. But De Leon's chief problem was the relationship of the SLP to the nascent trade union movement. His first strategy was that of infiltrating, which was abandoned when he failed to take over the Knights of Labor in the mid-1890s. More significant was the rejection by the American Federation of Labor (AFL) in 1894 of the famous Plank Ten proposing 'the collective ownership by all the people of all the means of production and consumption' (the eleven Planks were taken from the programme of the British ILP). Under the leadership of Samuel Gompers (who had originally been strongly influenced by Marx),[10] the AFL pursued, at least until the First World War, a philosophy of 'pure and simple Trade Unionism', which avoided all involvement in politics and preached a *laissez-faire* economics. The opposition of the AFL to De Leon's socialism was increased by his founding of a rival, but short-lived, Socialist Trades and Labor Alliance.

De Leon's opposition to non-political trade unionism was strengthened by his optimistic view of the possibilities for socialism in the

United States. He was somewhat disillusioned with what he saw as the reformist tendencies of the German Social Democratic Party, but he saw even less excuse for compromise in America. At the Amsterdam Congress of the International in 1904, he declared:

> The moment feudalism is swept aside, and capitalism wields the scep-
> tre untrammelled, as here in America – from the moment the ground
> is ready for revolution to step on; what is more, from that moment
> reform becomes a snare and a delusion.[11]

Thus economic development had made America readier for socialism than any other country: 'No other country is ripe for the execution of Marxian revolutionary tactics.'[12]

De Leon's strong stand led to a split in the SLP in 1899, when a large proportion of the membership who believed in more conciliatory attitudes to existing trade unions left the party and founded the Socialist Party. The comparative electoral success of the Socialist Party led De Leon to re-emphasise revolutionary trade union activity. Believing that the workers, in spite of their relative and absolute immiserisation, would otherwise follow a conservative trade union leadership, he joined in founding the International Workers of the World (IWW) in 1905, a movement which had its origin in the migrant lumber men and miners of the North West and was, according to Max Eastman, 'the only genuine *proletarian* or revolutionary organisation that ever existed in America'.[13] De Leon's theory was that the labour movement was temporarily divided into constructive and destructive wings. The task of the destructive wing, the SLP, was the transitory one of taking possession of the state in order to abolish it. (Like Marx, De Leon believed strongly in the possibility of a peaceful transition to socialism in the United States.) The task of the IWW, on the other hand, was the permanently constructive one of controlling, preserving and enlarging the means of production. Whereas the political movement had to be uncompromising in the class struggle, the economic movement could afford to be more gradual. By 1908, however, De Leon was excluded from the IWW, whose syndicalist leanings and belief in direct action and even sabotage brought them into conflict with the Marxists. His political career was at an end. Summing up, the year before his death, the main theme of his work, he wrote:

> Industrial Unionism bends its efforts to unite the Working Class
> upon the political as well as the industrial field – on the industrial

field because, without the integral organised Union of the Working Class, the revolutionary act is impossible; on the political field, because on none other can be proclaimed the revolutionary purpose without consciousness of which the Union is a rope of sand.[14]

Socialism and Communism

In the early 1900s the SLP was overshadowed by the Socialist Party, whose membership grew to over one hundred thousand by 1912 and whose President, Eugene Debs, obtained almost one million votes as presidential candidate in the same year. Ethnically pluralist, it benefited from the prestige enjoyed at the time by European socialism and from the influx of populist elements after its reversal of policy on land nationalisation. Unlike the SLP, the Socialist Party was only tangentially affected by Marxism. Ideologically very heterogeneous, it had three main tendencies: a right wing led by Victor Berger and composed of the municipal reformers of the Mid-West; a centre based on the Eastern seaboard, and led by Morris Hillquit who had left the SLP in 1899; and the left, drawing its strength from the West and led by Debs, who was the closest Socialist Party leader to De Leon, and the IWW leader Bill Haywood – though Haywood was expelled in 1912 following the Socialist Party's adoption of a resolution against sabotage. At the same time the Socialist Party produced a number of theorists who aided the popularisation of Marxism in America: Ernest Untermann, who translated *Capital*; Louis Boudin, whose *Theoretical System of Karl Marx* can be read even today with profit; and A.M. Simons, who edited the Party's theoretical journal *International Socialist Review*. The years immediately preceding the First World War saw a brief flowering of a 'lyrical left' when socialist ideas fused with all sorts of art forms, Greenwich Village was born, and the *New Review* began subtle discussions, from a Marxist angle, of feminism and the Negro question. However, the entry of America into the war and subsequent suppression of socialists who opposed it cut short this renaissance.

The Bolshevik victory of 1917, popularised by John Reed in his *Ten Days that Shook the World*, was hailed by the vast majority of socialists as a triumph, although the increasingly autocratic nature of the Bolshevik regime produced swift disillusion. Following the foundation of the Third International in 1919, the pro-Bolsheviks, largely drawn from the foreign-language federations, left the Socialist Party and formed the Communist Party led by Louis Fraina and Charles Ruthenberg. There was also a small Communist Labor Party consisting mainly of native Americans led by Benjamin Gitlow and John Reed. The two parties were driven underground by the application of wartime sedition laws. By the time they emerged in 1921, Lenin's 'right turn' instructed them to engage in electoral activity and to work within the existing trade union movement.[15] But, quite apart from the incubus of Stalinism they could make little headway in an America where Taylorism and the production line were squeezing out craft industries and the mass production of consumer goods caused a decline in traditional ethnic radicalism.

The Communist Party was further weakened in the late 1920s by splits over its orientation towards events in the Soviet Union. In 1929 the 'Right' Opposition, led by Jay Lovestone and Bertram Wolfe, was expelled. They were associated with the ideas and policies of Bukharin, believed America to be an 'exception' not immediately assimilable to Marxism-Leninism, and stressed the effects of American imperialism in tempering the revolutionary ardour of the masses. A year earlier, the 'Left' Opposition had been expelled. Followers of Trotsky, they formed two groups: the Workers' Party (later the Independent Socialist League) led by Max Schachtman, which later broke with Trotsky and eventually dissolved in 1958; and the Socialist Workers' Party, led by James Cannon, which consistently promoted Trotsky's views. The splintering of the non-Communist Left – the independently radical American Workers' Party was founded in 1934 by A.J. Muste – inaugurated a vigorous Marxist debate involving such intellectuals as James Burnham, Sidney Hook, Bertram Wolfe, and Max Eastman, and centring around the *Modern Quarterly* and the *Partisan Review*. However, it was the Communist Party which made most progress in the mid and late 1930s. The Socialist Party, now under its new leader Norman Thomas, declined throughout the 1930s, particularly through the influence of Roosevelt's New Deal: and the SLP remained a minor sect. The energetic and articulate Communist Party appeared as a solid, if small, bulwark against Fascism, expanded its influence in the newly-formed Confederation of Industrial Organisations, achieved a majority, within its own ranks, of native-born workers, and attracted a considerable number of literary intellectuals: by 1943 they had almost one hundred thousand members. However, the Party eventually rejected the conciliatory views of Earl Browder, its leader since 1934, and expelled him in 1945. Its new leader, William Z. Foster, rejected Browder's advocacy of peaceful coexistence and his talk of national interest. This hard line led to the isolation of the Communist Party in American society and a progressive decline. The impact of the Second World War, the subsequent economic boom, and the McCarthyite frenzy brought a period of stagnation and dissolution to Marxism which lasted from 1940 to 1960.[16]

The New Left

The revival of Marxism in the early 1960s took on a very different aspect. This 'New Left' looked backed in many ways to the 'Lyrical Left' of the 1900s. The resurgence of radicalism in the 1960s was galvanised by the increasing involvement of the United States in Vietnam. The Vietnam War acted as a catalyst, but the growth of the New Left was just as much a function of internal developments. Harrington's *The Other America* had revealed the widespread poverty and misery of white workers in America; the civil rights movement in the South had at length made plain to the nation at large the social and political discrimination suffered by the Blacks; and the large-scale permanent employment of women, encouraged by the necessity of the war effort, made possible the emergence on a wider scale of the feminism that had always been a part of the American radical tradition.[17] From the start, this New Left had an ambivalent relationship to Marxism. Traditionally, Marxism had been the theoretical expression of the reality and aspirations of the working class seen, potentially at least, as the majority of the population. In the United States, however – and here there is a difference from the situation in the United Kingdom – Marxism was not organically linked to the working class and tended, in its New Left form, to become the vehicle of protest for all oppressed minorities. Traditional Marxists of the Old Left rejected the New Left's sceptical humanism, its moralism, individualism, idealism, its vaguely 'existentialist' stances which they associated more with anarchy than with the class-based social and political analyses of Marxism. The increasingly anti-industrial, ecological bias of the New Left (in particular generated by sympathy for the Third World) seemed to the Old Left to be both romantic and reactionary. The unconventional life-style encouraged by the New Left – drugs, permissive sex, etc. – were seen as distractions from serious political commitment.

Given their heterogeneous minoritarian base, the theories of the New Left were very eclectic-anarchist and Ghandian as well as Marxist. The New Left had a student base: its main organisation was the Students for a Democratic Society (SDS) which was the new name taken by the Students' League for Industrial Democracy in 1959. Although the original demands of SDS were for more student power inside universities (as in, for example, the Free Speech Movement at Berkeley in 1964), these demands rapidly became political. American universities are so strongly influenced by the demands of the business world that any challenge to the university system almost necessarily has anti-capitalist overtones. Further SDS produced its own version of the 'New Working Class' theory discussed above: students were being trained in knowledge factories to fit the bureaucratic demands of advanced capitalism in which they would be as exploited and alienated as the industrial proletariat of the nineteenth century but at the same time possess a radical consciousness of that situation that would enable them to resist it more effectively.

In this respect, C. Wright Mills was perhaps more of an influence on the New Left than Marx. Indeed, it was Wright Mills who popularised the term 'New Left' in the United States. In his most influential book, *The Power Elite* (1956), Wright Mills rejected the idea of a ruling class and substituted a model of elite-masses. Although he criticised pluralism as deceptive (given the interlocking of the governmental, industrial and military elites), he did not reject it as such – as any Marxist class analysis would be bound to. His account of the role of the political/military establishment was without any direct reference to an economic basis and he rejected the idea that the working class of advanced capitalist society was 'the historic agency, or even the most important agency, in the face of the really impressive historical evidence that now stands against this expectation. Such a labour metaphysics, I think, is legacy from the Victorian Marxism that is now quite unrealistic.'[18] In as far as Marxism was influential in the early New Left it was in the form of the concept of alienation drawn from young Marx as interpreted by Erich Fromm.[19] The foundation document of the SDS – the Port Huron statement drawn up by Tom Hayden in 1962 – rejected Communism, which had 'failed, in every sense, to achieve its stated intentions of leading a world-wide movement for human emancipation',[20] and declared that 'Marx the humanist has much to tell us, but his conceptual tools are outmoded, and his final vision implausible'.[21] This Marxist humanism was made more influential by the work of Herbert Marcuse.

But this eclecticism did not last for long. As its historian has written, 'the three Rs of SDS began with reform, led to resistance, and have unofficially ended at revolution'.[22] The very ideological openness of the SDS meant a lack of common objectives in the movement and left it vulnerable to takeover by determined minorities. Further, it became increasingly felt that the vague humanitarian protest which had characterised the birth of the SDS could not get to grips with such complex phenomena as, for example, imperialism, and that serious radicalism would have to end in some form of Marxist theory and practice. The Communist Party and its youth wing, the DuBois clubs, began to revive in the early 1960s, but it was the Trotskyist and the Maoist versions of Marxism that made the most progress, particularly by means of their youth movements. The old Trotskyist Socialist Workers' Party produced the Young Socialist Alliance, which by the very early 1970s was the most active (and probably largest) Left-wing organisation, emphasising the problems of working-class struggle and proletarian consciousness. The same was true of the Johnson-Forrest (pseudonyms of Raya Dunayevskaya and C.L.R. James) tendency who rejected any Leninist conception of Party and claimed that the advance of technology presaged a world-wide workers' revolution independent of any party or union. This view, together with the *Socialisme ou Barbarie* group in France, can be seen as precursors of contemporary accounts of revolution *à la* Negri.[23] But it was the Maoist Progressive Labour Party, with its stress on violent anti-imperialist action, which benefited most from the growing involvement of America in Vietnam. They aligned themselves with black nationalists and the Panthers described themselves explicitly as 'Marxist-Leninist'. In the disastrous 1969 convention of the SDS, Progressive Labour gained control and the New Left was moribund. Those who refused the Progressive Labour line turned to an extremism of their own, forming short-lived guerrilla groups such as the Revolutionary Youth Movement and the Weathermen. With the decision to withdraw from Vietnam and the return of relative calm to university campuses, Left activism as a whole declined, though the economic crisis beginning in 1974 led to a limited resurgence and above all to a re-emphasis on the importance of a fuller understanding of the dynamics of the capitalist system and of the theoretical bases of classical Marxism.

Reasons for Marxism's lack of success

The above brief conspectus gives rise to the obvious question which formed the title of Werner Sombart's *Why is there no Socialism in the United States?* published in 1906. One obvious factor is that the United States, unlike Europe, had no feudal past. The American struggle for democracy was not conducted against a background of entrenched social privilege. In fact, the very openness of the American political system encouraged the incorporation of labour demands, in contrast to Europe where the working class, because of its exclusion from the political process, was forced into a socialist solidarity in order to express its democratic demands. The Americans, as de Tocqueville said, were 'born free' and, since the United States was founded as a reaction to intolerance in Europe, this freedom was essentially a negative one – a doctrine of individualism rather than communism. There was also the relative isolation of America from the violent upheavals provoked by wars in Europe. Yet this cannot be a sufficient answer, for the rapid industrial development of America produced a working class that would seem, on Marxist terms, as open to socialist ideas as, say, the Germans.

The existence of the Frontier was undoubtedly crucial. The possibility – however distant – of settling out West influenced many an urban immigrant. A the time of Sombart's writing, the United States was still primarily an agricultural country and radical protest was centred on the small farmers' populist opposition to monopolist industrial interests and Eastern banking, and advocacy of government control of railways, easier credit terms, and direct elections to the Senate. But although many of their demands could appear as anti-capitalist, the populist opposition to economic centralisation and their attachment to private property were based more on a traditional Protestant ethic than on any socialist principles. And since political radicalism was associated with populist proposals of no evident benefit to the working class, the incipient trade union movement, in asserting its independence, was imbued from the start with an opposition to political involvement and a dogged determination to stick to more mundane matters. More directly, of course, the existence of the Frontier limited the labour supply (and therefore unemployment) and slowed urban growth.

Of equal importance to the land question was the influence of immigration. Ethnic divisions held up working-class unity and the successive waves of immigrants provided a kind of hierarchy, with the newest arrived, particularly from Southern and Eastern Europe, at the bottom and a labour aristocracy developing among the more established skilled workers. Even when immigration was drastically reduced after the First World War, the internal migration into the cities of unskilled labour from the land meant the injection into the industrial workforce of the individualist, non-progressive attitudes bred in rural communities. By the time that organised labour emerged as a real force on the political scene, it could be assimilated into the reformist policies of the New Deal. Thus Sombart's answer to his own question – that socialism has 'foundered upon shoals of roast beef and apple pie'[24] – was not the major factor, even supposing his opinion of the affluence of the American worker at the time in question to be accurate.

Theory

During the 1960s and 1970s there was in the United States a most striking resurgence of interest in Marxist theory, particularly in academic circles. The most evident expression of this is not only a number of books published on Marxist themes but the number of subject journals, usually with the prefix 'radical' in their title, which present a more or less Marxist view of their subject as opposed to the 'establishment' journal.[25] The most distinctively American contributions to Marxist theory have, not surprisingly, been in the analysis of advanced capitalist society and its relation to imperialism. Any account of recent contributions must necessarily be extremely selective, but three areas stand out: the theories of the New Left about the nature of contemporary American society, the historiography of the United States from a Marxist standpoint, and, most importantly, the economic studies of American capitalism.

The New Left

With the publication of Marx's early writings and the commentaries on them of Erich Fromm and others,[26] Marx's ideas were no longer associated exclusively with the Soviet version of Communism and the view became widespread that Marx's concept of alienation was just as relevant to the twentieth century as the nineteenth – and possibly even more so. Max Horkheimer's *The Eclipse of Reason* (1949) had already taken a critical look at social and political liberalism in American society. But it was another product of the Frankfurt School – Marcuse's *One-Dimensional Man* – that became the epitome of New Left thinking in the mid-1960s.[27] Contemporary America was the most striking example for Marcuse of a society in which 'under the rule of a repressive whole, liberty can be made into a powerful instrument of domination'.[28] Marcuse's view was that

> the distinguishing feature of advanced industrial society is its effective suffocation of those needs which demand liberation – liberation also from that which is tolerable and rewarding and comfortable – while it sustains and absolves the destructive power and repressive function of the affluent society. Here, the social controls exact the overwhelming need for the production and consumption of waste; the need for stupefying work where it is no longer a real necessity; the need for modes of relaxation which soothe and prolong this stupefaction; the need for maintaining such deceptive liberties as free competition at administered prices, a free press which censors itself, free choice between brands and gadgets.[29]

And he specifically paid tribute to the studies of Wright Mills, Vance Packard, and William H. Whyte in providing the factual basis for his analysis. But the very breadth of New Left interest meant that their Marxism was diffuse, attempting to integrate into its theoretical framework such diverse problems as sexism and racism.[30]

American History

The supposed liberalism of American society has also come in for scrutiny from radical American historians. The doyen of this school is William A. Williams, who was particularly influential at the University of Wisconsin in the 1950s. He was concerned above all with foreign policy and its influence on social relations inside America. More specific than Williams is the work of Gabriel Kolko. In *The Triumph of Conservatism* (1963) Kolko looks at the period from 1900 to 1916 and sees the government of the time as aiming at 'the organisation of the economy and the larger political and social spheres in a manner that will allow corporations to function in a predictable and secure environment permitting reasonable profits over the long run'.[31] Thus many of the reforms seen as 'progressive' curbs on big business by the liberals involved were in fact merely the political rationalisation of business and industrial conditions 'on the assumption that the general welfare of the community could best be served by satisfying the concrete ends of business'.[32] Hence the 'triumph of conservatism' in the shape of the corporate elite bent on conserving the existing business interests. Kolko's views, which have as much affinity with Wright Mills as with Marx, have been extended in James Weinstein's *The Corporate Ideal in the Liberal State* (1968). Weinstein sees corporate liberal ideology as the ideology of the most advanced sectors of American business, created, in partnership with government, by the leaders of the giant corporations and financial institutions to achieve the integration of labour, small farmers and businessmen in a corporate state.

Economics

To date, however, the most original American contribution to Marxist theory has been in political economy. In many ways, the most important of these contributions was Paul Baran's *The Political Economy of Growth* (1957). After beginning with an account of the ideological components in previous economic theory, Baran broached his central theme: the role of the economic surplus in advanced capitalism. Here he distinguished between actual surplus (the difference between society's current output and its current consumption) and potential surplus which was 'the difference between the output that could be produced in a given natural and technological environment with the help of employable productive resources, and what might be regarded as essential consumption'.[33] In capitalist society potential surplus was larger than actual surplus for four reasons:

> *One* is society's excess consumption (predominantly on the part of the upper income groups, but in some countries such as the United

States also on the part of the so-called middle classes), the *second* is the output lost to society through the existence of unproductive workers, the *third* is the output lost because of the irrational and wasteful organisation of the existing productive apparatus, and the *fourth* is the output forgone owing to the existence of unemployment caused primarily by the anarchy of capitalist production and the deficiency of effective demand.[34]

Baran then looked back to the factors determining the change from competitive to monopoly capitalism and came to the view that monopoly, once progressive, was now a retrograde force. After examining the traditional Keynesian remedies for the problem of overproduction (with which he had some sympathy as short-term expedients), Baran came to the conclusion that, under capitalism, the surplus could only be absorbed by military expenditure with its corollary of imperialism and increased likelihood of war.

In the most important section of his book, Baran declared that the underdevelopment of most of the world was a direct result of the dynamics of monopoly capitalism which had blocked the primary accumulation of capital in underdeveloped regions and smothered their fledgling industries:

Although the expansion of commodity circulation, the pauperisation of large numbers of peasants and partisans, the contact with western technology, provided a powerful impetus to the development of capitalism, this development was forcibly shunted off its normal course, distorted and crippled to suit the purpose of Western imperialism.[35]

This is illustrated in the case of India, which was backward because of its incorporation in the Western capitalist system, and of Japan, which progressed because of its isolation. Baran refuted the idea that foreign investment could ultimately be beneficial to the Third World either financially or socially as the different types of state that it gave rise to in underdeveloped countries – directly colonial, *comprador*, or New Deal type – were all structurally incapable of using the large potential surplus for the benefit of their societies. Finally, economic development was only possible after a social revolution which would plan the use of the economic surplus with the emphasis, as in the Soviet Union, on the priority of heavy industrial development.

Baran's work was in many ways on the classical Marxist tradition. He built on Lenin's work on imperialism and the labour aristocracy, on

Luxemburg's theories of capitalist accumulation, and on Trotsky's conception of uneven development. What was strikingly new was the linking of these ideas to the problem of world development by the idea that the development of the West was directly at the expense of the underdeveloped countries. This view has had great influence on the modern school of development theorists,[36] and writers as diverse as André Gunder Frank and Guevara have acknowledged their debt to Baran. It also marked a change of emphasis in Marxist thought in viewing stagnation rather than crisis as the typical situation for advanced capitalism and shifting attention to the Third World whose future development was not simply to follow laboriously the steps already traced by the West.

The idea of surplus elaborated in the *Political Economy of Growth* and that of underconsumption as the cause of capitalism's crisis, which had been worked out in Paul Sweezy's *Theory of Capitalist Development* (1942), were combined in *Monopoly Capital*, co-authored by Baran and Sweezy and published in 1965. It is the most impressive Marxist overview of the United States economy. The book is organised around the central theme of 'the generation and absorption of the surplus under conditions of monopoly capitalism'.[37] The rise of monopoly capitalism, with the attendant elimination of competition, the disappearance of risk and the live-and-let-live attitude of the giant corporations to each other, means that the classical Marxist law of the tendency of the rate of profit to fall (which according to Baran and Sweezy, presupposes a competitive system) is no longer adequate to analyse contemporary capitalism:

> By substituting the law of rising surplus for the law of falling profit [they write], we are not therefore rejecting or revising a time-honoured theorem of political economy: we are simply taking account of the undoubted fact that the structure of the capitalist economy has undergone a fundamental change since that theorem was formulated. What is most essential about the structural change from competitive to monopoly capitalism finds its theoretical expression in this substitution.[38]

Thus Baran and Sweezy locate the cause of capitalist crisis in the realisation of surplus value rather than in its production.

The ever-increasing surplus finds some outlet in consumption, in investment, and simply in waste. But investigation shows that consumption, although rising in absolute terms, declines as a proportion of the rising surplus. Investment, whether domestic or foreign, as the amount that would be required to absorb the surplus, tends to rise above total income and thus make the investment pointless. The enormous sales effort of the modern corporation – advertising, packaging, planned obsolescence, etc. – absorbs a certain amount, but also has its limits:

> Twist and turn as one will, there is no way to avoid the conclusion that monopoly capitalism is a self-contradictory system. It tends to generate ever more surplus yet it fails to provide the consumption and investment outlets required for the absorption of a rising surplus and hence for the smooth working of the system. Since surplus which cannot be absorbed will not be produced it follows that the *normal* state of monopoly capitalist economy is stagnation.[39]

The government plays an even larger part in absorbing the surplus, but the uses to which the government can put the surplus are strictly determined by the nature of monopoly capitalist society and grow ever more irrational and destructive. The educational system is closely enmeshed with the needs of big capital and is structured to provide the suitable personnel for its different sections. Huge government spending on manifold facilities for the motor car epitomises the situation. But more striking – and dangerous – is the share of the surplus absorbed by the military and its whole influence on the American way of life.

Baran and Sweezy's work has been criticised by those writing from a more traditional Marxist standpoint – of whom the most outstanding thinker is the Belgian Trotskyist Ernest Mandel, whose huge *Marxist Economic Theory* is the best panoramic view of the subject. In later writings, Mandel criticises Baran and Sweezy for reasoning on the level of appearance by looking (with many insights drawn from Keynesian economics) at the crisis of monopoly capitalism from the point of view of markets and realisation without penetrating to the basis of Marx's value analysis of the production process. For Mandel, it is the process of capital accumulation that determines the progress of the capitalist mode of production. The tendency to concentration of capital gives rise both to monopoly and to an increase in the organic composition of capital (more spent on plant and raw materials than on wages). However the structure of the market may change, the basic problem is still how to raise the rate of exploitation so that production and accumulation remain profitable. Thus Baran and Sweezy are mistaken in their dismissal of the rate of profit as crucial. Mandel's own analysis of contemporary capitalism is contained in his important *Late Capitalism* where he outlines a theory of 'long wave cycles' to explain capitalist development and attempts to show why contemporary capitalism is at the end of a cycle and therefore unable to maintain the rate of surplus value.

Baran and Sweezy's book was written in the prosperous America of the late 1950s and early 1960s. The failure in Vietnam and growing international competition led Paul Mattick in *Marx and Keynes* (1970) to stress the inherent limits that the state experienced in dealing with the surplus. This theme is elaborated in James O'Connor's book *The Fiscal Crisis of the State* (1973). O'Connor, in common with the recent German School,[40] sees the state's authority relations as complex, semi-autonomous, and not reducible to an expression of the interests of the capitalist class. He develops a theory of why state intervention in the economic sphere has grown. To do this, he divides the economy into the competitive, monopoly and state sectors, and demonstrates how the monopoly and competitive sectors of the economy need each other and both require state intervention, sometimes of a contradictory nature. O'Connor's main thesis is that the state cannot, in the long term, raise enough revenue to meet the political demands of all three sectors. But the state needs to be a satisfactory provider of social benefits in order to secure its own legitimacy. In its attempt to achieve this, the state socialises more and more production costs. The state's function is to help accumulation by socialising the costs of private capital by investment in such things as roads and by providing such services as schools, medicare and the welfare costs of a hidden surplus labour force for the competitive sector. Thus the state is relatively autonomous in that it is not the instrument of a particular class but structures the political conflict between classes. The very growth of state intervention and competition for its favours leads to the endorsement by all parties of capitalist institutions: the state preserves the class structure of society by being seen to be independent of it. However, there is, according to O'Connor, an inherent contradiction between the state's economic function of accumulation and its political function of legitimisation – a contradiction which springs from that between the increasingly social nature of the productive forces and private appropriation of profit and, in some cases, of political power.

In contrast to the broad politico-economic perspective of O'Connor, Harry Braverman's *Labour and Monopoly Capital* (1974) looks in great historical detail at the effect of monopoly capital on the labour process. Braverman presents his work as being fully in harmony with the framework of Baran and Sweezy's *Monopoly Capital* – although, unlike them, he emphasises the role of the working class in the overthrow of capitalism and has a more traditionally Marxist conception of the surplus.

Braverman's aim is to investigate the structure of the working class and how it has changed. The beginning of his analysis is an apparent contradiction in recent research:

> On the one hand, it is emphasised that modern work, as a result of the scientific-technical revolution and 'automation', requires ever higher levels of education, training, the greater exercise of intelligence and mental effort in general. At the same time a mounting dissatisfaction with the conditions of industrial and office labour appears to contradict this view. For it is also said – sometimes even by the same people who at other times support the first view – that work has become increasingly sub-divided into petty operations that fail to sustain the interest or engage the capacities of humans with current levels of education; that these petty operations demand ever less skill and training and that the modern trend of work by its 'mindlessness' and 'bureaucratization' is 'alienating' ever larger sections of the working population.[41]

Leaning towards the second view, Braverman attacks the new working class theorists[42] and claims that, if the working class as a whole is studied, it will be seen that the growth in 'new' working-class occupations is no greater than that in other sectors.

In order to support these assertions, Braverman builds on Marx's discussion of the labour process in Volume One of *Capital*. Braverman denies the view, current both in the Second International theorists and in the Soviet Union, that the technological and administrative skills developed by capitalism are independent of class interest. Taylorism, for example, whose development of the separation of conception and execution Braverman describes in great detail, is essential to capitalist control of the production process and is still as influential as ever – job-enlargement schemes being only illusory fig-leaves. In Part Two of his book, Braverman traces the development of technological innovation and managerial techniques and their effect on the labour process – the increasing control of science over alienated labour. In Part Three, Braverman charts the progress of modern capitalism and the shifts of capital between industrial sectors that are involved in the rise of modern corporations; the universalisation of market relations; and growing state intervention. Part Four traces the growth in clerical and service sectors who are, according to Braverman, just as 'Taylorised' as any shop-floor worker in their function of monitoring the production process. The decline, with the growth of automative machinery, in the number of relatively well-paid operatives means that the low-paid clerical and service workers constitute a kind of modern 'reserve army of labour'. For, in fact,

the problem of the so-called employee or white-collar worker which so bothered earlier generations of Marxists, and was hailed by anti-Marxists as a proof of the falsity of the 'proletarianisation' thesis, has thus been unambiguously clarified by the polarisation of office employment and the growth at one pole of an immense mass of *wage-workers*. The apparent trend to a large non-proletarian 'middle class' has resolved itself into the creation of a large proletariat in a new form.[43]

In Part Five, Braverman looks at the ambiguous class position of the middle layers of society – junior executives, administrators, etc.; denies that the distinction between productive and unproductive labour has any significance for class analysis (because both sections are so intricately combined); and finally denies that mechanisation and education have resulted in the growth of skilled labour – both the average machine-minder and average service sector worker require very little training.

Braverman describes his work as being about class 'in itself' rather than 'for itself' and the absence of the theme of class struggle, and of reference to political and ideological factors so prominent in the work of, for example, Poulantzas – is notable. This view is due to Braverman's acceptance of Baran and Sweezy's view of capital's absolute domination over labour. Hence his blanket rejection of job-enrichment schemes and of demands for workers' participation. About the latter, for example, he writes:

The conception of a democracy in the workplace based simply upon the imposition of a formal structure of parliamentarism – election of directors, the making of production and other decisions by ballot, etc. – upon the existing organisation of production is delusory. Without the return of requisite technical knowledge to the mass of workers and the reshaping of the organisation of labour – without, in a word, a new and truly collective mode of production – balloting within factories and offices does not alter the fact that the workers remain as dependent as before upon 'experts', and can only choose among them, or vote for alternatives presented by them.[44]

Braverman's book, in contrast, again, with the work of Poulantzas, is characterised by a wealth of detailed observation – he was himself a metal worker for years. His forceful humanism, his direct style, and mastery of empirical studies make his treatment of the degradation of work in the twentieth century a worthy continuation of Marx.

This work has been continued by radical economists centring around reviews such as the *Review of Radical Political Economy* and the *Monthly Review*, the former being a product of the 1960s and the latter offering an independent Marxist viewpoint from the 1940s onwards. Building on the work of Baran and Sweezy and of Braverman, what these publications emphasised in the 1970s and 1980s were the long swings in capitalist accumulation and the social structures and segmentation of the workforce which accompanied them.[45] In what became known as the Social Structures of Accumulation approach, they stressed the ways in which politics influenced economics and the historically contingent nature of economic organisation. Here their approach was similar to that of the French 'regulation' school typified by writers such as Michel Aglietta which emphasised the political process of regulating the structural dimensions of capital accumulation. Bowles, Gordon and Weisskopf, for example, in their book *Beyond the Wasteland* attempted to measure the degree of waste generated by the capitalist system in the United States and proposed measures to overcome it such as full employment, higher wages, and democratic control of the workplace. With the reinvigoration of American capitalism during the Reagan years, however, many of the protagonists have veered towards mainstream economics and become more interested in whether and how the market could be combined with socialism.[46]

Market socialism and analytical Marxism

This idea of a socialism based upon market principles had its origin in highly theoretical debates in the 1930s between von Mises and Lange.[47] A practical impetus was given to the topic by the various attempts in Eastern Europe in the 1960s and 1970s to increase the role of the market, the brief *perestroika* period of Gorbachev, and the increasing marketisation of the Chinese economy. And the widespread influence of John Rawls's *A Theory of Justice* prompted socialists to produce their own equivalent while using a similar methodology. There are two main versions of market socialism of which one is based on the maximisation and equal distribution of profit while the other centres on workers' control of the means of production. In what is perhaps the most discussed of the first type of market socialism, John Roemer proposes a system in which all banks are nationalised, all corporations are run by representatives of the banks, the workers and the shareholders, the government lends at different interest rates to encourage growth in specific sectors, and – most significant of all – stocks and shares (which may be traded for other stocks but not sold for cash) are distributed equally to all citizens.[48] A good example of the second type of market socialism is the work of David Schweikart which puts workers' self-management (rather than egalitarian ownership of the means of production) at the heart of the system. In 'Economic Democracy', as Schweikart calls it, there are the three basic structures of worker self-management of enterprises, social control of investment, and a market for goods and services – but not for capital and labour. Other versions of this second type have been advanced by Weisskopf, by Fleurbaey, and by Andreani.[49] From a Marxist point of view, these attempts do not add much to the further-ance of Marx's own principles. Although market socialism is socialist in that it overcomes the division between capital and labour, it does not overcome capitalism's main contradiction between social production and private appropriation. Marx was no friend of the market: income according to need rather than desert was the principle of his communist society. And the best that he could have said of market socialism was that it represented a society 'which, is in every respect, economically, morally, and intellectually still stamped with the birthmarks of the old society from whose womb it emerges'.[50] Thus from Marx's point of view market socialism may be the best (or better than the best) at present available. But, as any final goal, it is strikingly jejeune in its conception of human motivation and potential.[51]

Many market socialists have linked their ideas with the more general approach known as 'analytical' or 'rational choice' Marxism. As the words imply, this approach combines the rigorousness of contemporary Anglo-Saxon analytical philosophy with a conception of society as con-sisting of self-interested individuals reminiscent of neoclassical econom-ics. In opposition to the structuralism of Althusser and reversing the insistence of Lukács that the specificity of Marxism resides in its method rather than its substantive theses, analytical Marxism has, like so many other twentieth-century versions of Marxism, tried to combine the Marxist tradition with the prevailing dominant ideology.

Analytical Marxism can be said to begin with the publication of Cohen's tour de force *Karl Marx's Theory of History: A Defence* in 1978. Cohen interpreted Marx's Preface to his 1859 *Critique of Political Economy* to mean that (1) the forces of production, including technical and scientific knowledge, have an innate tendency to develop over time, and that (2) the social relations of production are to be explained by these same forces and not vice versa. According to Cohen this constituted a functional explanation: just as the function of birds having hollow bones was to help them to fly, so the function of specific relations of production was to help the forces of production to develop.

Cohen's version of historical materialism was criticized by Jon Elster[52] whose approach to Marxism was strongly committed to a methodology of 'micro-foundations' which stressed the rational choice of individuals as the necessary basis for understanding all social and economic phenomena and even incorporated game theory in its approach.[53] While Elster remained interested in theory, other rational choice Marxists produced more applied social science. Adam Przeworski, for example, elaborated a Marxist political sociology of parliamentary democracies to explain the lack of success of socialist politics in the West.[54] Erik Olin Wright has produced an impressive body of work on the complexities of class politics in capitalist societies and particularly the contradictory position of some sections of the middle class.[55] And Robert Brenner has used the same sort of rational choice methodology in his account of the transition from feudalism to capitalism.[56] Perhaps the most impressively rational choice in his orientation is John Roemer whose *A General Theory of Exploitation and Class* attempts to rewrite Marxian economics in terms of rational choice. According to Roemer, productive forces, relations of production, class, and forms of exploitation can be isolated from each other and their combination needs to be explained in terms of individual rational choice. As against Braverman, Roemer claims that it is not domination within the labour process that is responsible for exploitation and class antagonism, but rather the unequal distribution of the means of production. He has consequently made significant contributions to the literature on market socialism along radically egalitarian lines.[57]

Naturally, rational choice Marxists have been criticised by other Marxists for their apparently excessive individualism and taking for granted what can only be explained by more structural concepts, that is, the very predominance of individualism in contemporary society.[58] Rational choice Marxism is in part a product of the Zeitgeist and particularly the rampant individualism of the Thatcher/Reagan years. The fact that Marxist social scientist borrowed methods employed in neoclassical economics such as game theory and general equilibrium theory was, to say the least paradoxical (though no more so than Sartre trying to reconcile his existentialism with Marxist principles) and it is not surprising that not much of Marx survived.

While interest in analytical Marxism has seen a decline, the emphasis on the political influence on economics, elaborated by radical economists of the *New Left Review*, has been carried forward by writers such as Ellen

Meiksens Wood and Robert Brenner. Influenced by the work of E.P. Thompson, Wood has outlined a contrast between the development of agrarian capitalism in Britain whose main exponent was Locke and which emphasises productivity and profit – and the non-capitalist ideology of the Enlightenment in pre-revolutionary France which offers a non-rational conception of modernity still relevant today. Unlike the rest of Europe where peasants owned the land, writes Wood, the economic process which 'eventually ended in a polarization between capitalist farmers and propertyless labourers' had 'to do with the new economic logic that subjugated English farmers to the imperatives of competition in unprecedented ways and degrees'.[59]

Jameson

A quite different approach to contemporary society is offered by Fredric Jameson, currently probably the most prominent American intellectual working within the Marxist tradition. Jameson has produced an impressive account of postmodernism in his *Postmodernism: The Cultural Logic of Late Capitalism*[60] and profound reflections on Western Marxism[61] which has been said to have reached its culmination in his own work.[62] But it is *The Political Unconscious* which represents Jameson's basic theoretical work. In the first half of the book, which precedes detailed discussion of writers such as Balzac and Conrad, Jameson outlines his Marxist approach to culture. Citing *Capital* and the *Communist Manifesto*, Jameson says that past cultural events can recover their original urgency for us only if they are retold within the unity of a single great collective story; only if, in however disguised or symbolic a form, they are seen as sharing a single fundamental theme – for Marxism, the collective struggle to wrest a realm of Freedom from a realm of Necessity; only if they are grasped as vital episodes in a single unfinished plot'[63] consisting in the history of class struggle. In order to uncover this 'political unconscious' Jameson argues that there are 'three concentric circles which mark out the sense of the social ground of a text'. The first is one in which 'history is reduced to a series of punctual events and crises in time'; the second is one of society seen as consisting of a constant tension and struggle between social classes; while a third all-encompassing circle is 'history now conceived in its vastest essence of the sequence of modes of production and the succession and destiny of the various human social formations, from prehistoric life to whatever far future history has in store for us'.[64] Jameson finishes his book with a discussion of ideology and utopia in which he sees 'all class consciousness of whatever type as utopian insofar as it expresses the unity of a collectivity' and claims that 'the achieved collectivity or organic group of whatever kind – oppressors fully as much as oppressed – is Utopian not in itself but only insofar as all such collectivities are themselves *figures* for the ultimate concrete collective life of an achieved Utopian or classless society'.[65] Jameson's sources are wide-ranging, from psychoanalysis to anthropology. The broad sweep of his approach succeeds in uniting them in the sort of 'grand narrative' that has currently gone out of favour. From a more strictly Marxist viewpoint, Jameson is obviously strongly influenced by Althusser yet manages, in a sort of Hegelian *Aufhebung*, to include him in a larger, totalising narrative.

Jameson's later work has included a striking reclamation of Adorno for the Marxist tradition[66] and a renewed emphasis on space as an essential ingredient in understanding the globalised world. Here Jameson builds on the fundamental work of the French Marxist Henri Lefebvre whose *The Production of Space* analyses space not as something neutral but as constituted through social and political practices.[67] Whereas traditionally space was seen as static and time as involving change and movement, Jameson rather reverses this: time has become static in that in spite of constant change and innovation, at a deeper level social life is standardised and 'the stream of human, social, and historical life has never flowed quite so homogeneously'.[68] The same is true of the compressed space of the global market: for all its emphasis on ethnic diversity and 'globalisation', it effectively produces a standardisation of space which is chaotic, depthless and atemporal. The political conclusions that Jameson draws from this analysis are pessimistic: the homogenising trends of postmodern society leave little room for conceiving of alternatives.

The main characteristic of Jameson's thought is therefore its ability to combine a Marxist framework containing such traditional concepts as class, reification or modes of production with an openness to some of the very different theoretical positions advanced in contemporary society. His intention is to reinvigorate Marxist thought by a critical engagement with alternative approaches, an engagement which aims to incorporate these approaches by historicising in true Hegelian manner their specific discourses.

Globalisation and empire

What is striking about recent work of Marxist inspiration is its global stretch. Brenner's work on the transition from feudalism to capitalism in

England leads to his view of competition as the motor of global capitalism; Jameson's work on Marxist aesthetics leads to later analyses of the spatial global logic of later capitalism and accounts for the enthusiasm for his work in China and Latin America; the collapse of Communism and the now global reach of US economic and military power has prompted new research on the world's political economy.

Books on globalisation abound, but it can be rather an elusive concept – indeed some doubt whether it exists at all.[69] Nevertheless, three aspects of recent socio-economic development seem undeniable. First, the most immediately striking characteristic is the volume of activity on the world financial markets. We are told that more than $1 trillion are sold in currency exchange transactions every day. More significantly, over the past 15 years the proportion of international financial dealing as opposed to trade has grown fivefold. The role of the financial speculator has increased as the power of national governments has decreased – consider the ignominious exit of the United Kingdom from the European Exchange Rate Mechanism on Black Monday in 1992. The second central aspect of globalisation is the increase in, and increasingly integrated nature of, world trade. There has been a massive growth in trade across the world, particularly in the service sector, over the last decades. And the production and distribution of the goods and services involved in this trade has become more and more integrated – cars and aeroplanes being produced in two or three different countries, assembled in a fourth, with distribution being controlled from a fifth. Both cause and effect of this process has been the growth in the power and influence of multinational corporations many of whose annual turnovers now exceed the GNP of smaller countries. Third, and perhaps even more fundamentally, globalisation is more than just an economic process. It is about the transformation and compression of time and space in the lives of those whom it affects. The mass availability of television, the rise of information technology, the fusion of satellites and computers, the impact of instantaneous electronic communication reaching into all corners of the globe has had a profound effect on the way we see both ourselves and our relation to others. The advent of global markets has tended to increase the inequality both within and between nations. Although the economy may be global, around two-thirds of the world's population are written off as far as foreign investment is concerned. Multinational corporations create overcapacity in industry after industry and trading blocks such as the EU and NAFTA engage in destructive competition while their workers find themselves threatened with redundancy or, at the least, lower incomes due to the availability of cheaper labour in poorer nations. Given such an uncertain outlook, it is not surprising that even those who initially welcomed globalisation have begun to have their doubts. Even those who had no time for Marx are beginning belatedly to recognise the accuracy of his predictions:

> Constant revolutionizing of production, uninterrupted disturbance of all social conditions, everlasting uncertainty and agitation distinguish the bourgeois epoch from all earlier ones. All fixed, fast-frozen relations, with their train of ancient and venerable prejudices and options, are swept away, all new-formed ones become antiquated before they can ossify. All that is solid melts into air, all that is holy is profaned, and the man is at last compelled to face with sober senses, his real conditions of life, and his relations with his kind ... In place of the old wants, satisfied by the productions of the country, we find new wants, requiring for their satisfaction the products of distant lands and climes. In place of old local and national seclusion and self-sufficiency, we have intercourse in every direction, universal interdependence of nations.[70]

In this context, the emergence, after the attacks on the United States in September 2001, of American political and military hegemony into an activist phase raises new questions. The so-called 'war on terror' is, in the eyes of American neo-conservatives, a truly global enterprise. Ideologically, this 'war' seems to present contradictory faces. On the one hand there is talk of spreading democracy and human rights. On the other, the primary vehicle for the international articulation of these rights, the United Nations, is sidelined. And the war itself, together with its aftermath, appears to abrogate, not least in the United States itself, many of the rights it is supposed to uphold. From this point of view, talk of democracy and the rights of man look suspiciously like an ideological product of the West which, while part of specifically Western culture, in its universalist ambitions acts as a cloak for Western economic and military imperialism. For global war itself is driven, at least in part, by depleting energy resources, particularly oil. The thirst for energy and economic advantage often involves attempts to impose alien political and legal concepts on societies perfectly capable of organising themselves on less individualistic and capitalist-inspired bases.

Perhaps the most globalised of all the accounts of globalisation is that of Michael Hardt and Antonio Negri. By the beginning of the twenty-first century, with increasing American military intervention abroad, the discussion of globalisation was supplemented by a fresh look at an older concept: imperialism. Striking here is the success of Hardt and Negri's books on *Empire* and *Multitude*. In a sense, Hardt and Negri are carrying the idea of globalisation to its extreme limits: they proclaim the end of the nation-state and thus the end of American imperial dominance – or possibly the extension of the American way to the whole globe. For empire, the political form of globalisation, has no centre and no limits.[71] Like Foucault's power, it is anonymously diffused through the whole of global society. Thus all war is civil war and all military intervention is police action. Unlike past empires, the emerging global empire has no 'other' to subjugate as Hardt and Negri, in a manner reminiscent of Fukuyama's 'end of history', believe that capitalism, and its political expressions, will soon inform the whole globe. A central theme in their work is the way in which the dominant form of capital is a network form and the ruling class has become bureaucratised as immaterial labour – labour which 'produces an immaterial good such as a service, a cultural product, knowledge, or communication'[72] – becomes hegemonic. The increasing importance of this immaterial, intellectual labour, particularly in sectors of the economy which add most value, is, according to Hardt and Negri, producing a collective labourer, a universal proletariat, a multitude with ever-growing powers of subversion. This multitude is conceived of as 'all those who work under the rule of capital and thus potentially as the class of those who refuse the rule of capital'.[73] And with the progressive immaterialisation of labour 'what the multitude produces is not just goods and services; the multitude also and most importantly produces co-operation, communication, forms of life, and social relationships. The economic production of the multitude, in other words, is not only a *model* for political decision-making, but also tends itself to *become* political decision-making.'[74] In this perspective, the bourgeoisie disappears and power is diffused into a universal proletariat.

Like its subject matter, Hardt and Negri's work is diffuse and difficult to get a grip on. It does not concentrate on specific politico-economic analysis but, anarchist more than Marxist, sees the power of government rather than economic relations as the main obstacle to human liberation. In the same vein, they borrow from Foucault and from Deleuze and Guattari, especially the latters' conception of desire as both constantly oppressed and hemmed in by constellations of power and at the same time continually undermining and outflanking them.[75] For all their postmodern credentials, however, Hardt and Negri accord to the historical process an optimistic inevitability reminiscent of the determinist tendencies of the Second International. Perhaps this goes some way to explaining the popularity of Hardt and Negri's books: they appeal to postmodern sensibilities; they chime with typical American can-do optimism; and to some extent this same historical optimism endorses both the global influence of America and of anti-state capitalism itself – deregulation being the basis of emancipation.

If Hardt and Negri are prone to concentrate on the political, juridical, cultural, and subjective dimensions of contemporary capitalism and talk up the utopian side of the Marxist project, others have stayed closer to the more mainstream Marxist activity of addressing the economic logic of capitalism. And they have drawn different conclusions on the economic basis of American imperialism and where it is headed. Wood, for example, draws on her historical work to point up the distinctive nature of US imperialism and thus the role of the military therein:

> the capitalist mode of economic imperialism is the first imperialism in history that does not depend simply on capturing this or that bit of territory, or dominating this or that subject people. It needs to oversee the whole global system of states and ensure that imperial capital can safely and profitably navigate throughout that global system. It has to deal not just with the problem of 'rogue' states or 'failed' states. It also has to keep subordinate states vulnerable to exploitation. Moreover, to be really effective, it has to establish the military and political supremacy of one power over all others, because if global capital needs an orderly system of multiple states, it is hard to see how it can tolerate a system in which power is more or less evenly distributed among various states.[76]

For Wood, globalisation is a response to the crisis of overcapacity and overproduction beginning in the 1970s. It is not concerned with free trade or integrating the world market: the different costs and conditions of production that result from social and economic fragmentation can increase profitability. The role of the nation-state is to perform the 'delicate balancing act between opening borders to global capital and deterring a kind of degree of integration that might go too far in levelling social conditions among workers throughout the world'.[77] In this process the nation-state plays an essential role in creating and maintaining the conditions of capital accumulation for 'no other institution, no transnational agency, has even begun to replace the nation state as an administrative and coercive guarantor of social order, property relations, stability of contractual predictability, or any of the other basic conditions required by capital in its everyday life'.[78] This dependency on other nation-states, combined with comparative economic decline, explains the renewed militarism of the United States and its pursuit of war without end and the threat of military intervention anywhere and anytime.

In the area of political economy the two major questions facing Marxists (and others) are the explanation for recurrent crises in the US economy and whether, as a result, it is in long-term decline. For Robert Brenner, the crises of post-war capitalism are due to overcompetition. He writes that 'given capitalism's unplanned, competitive nature, realization problems cannot be assumed away. The same cost-cutting by firms which creates the potential for aggregate profitability to rise creates the possibility for aggregate profitability to fall, leading to macro-economic difficulties'.[79] This amounts to a claim that the crises of capitalism are the direct effect of the market and not the pressure of wages on profit. It follows that class struggle to reform and go beyond capitalism can only better, and not worsen, the endemic vagaries of global capitalism.[80] Thus Brenner takes as his point of departure the decline of the manufacturing sector in the United States in contrast to 'stock-market Keynesianism' and its corollaries: 'the ever easier availability of cheap credit, the continued blowing up of asset-price bubbles, the impetuous and unending growth of debt, the credit-driven increase of consumer spending, and the dizzying rise of imports made cheap by the high dollar'.[81]

Whereas Brenner is primarily concerned with the effect of competition and the decline of US manufacturing which results from the uneven development of the global economy whereby those behind in capitalist development catch up with the leaders, others have emphasised the important of finance capital in understanding the global economy. Giovanni Arrighi, for instance, sees 'the financialization of capital rather than persistent "over-capacity and over-production" in manufacturing as the predominant capitalist response to the joint crisis of profitability and hegemony'.[82] Given the unprecedented increase in foreign indebtedness of the United States, 'it is hard', he writes, 'to see how this situation can be reproduced for any length of time without transforming into an outright tribute, or "protection payment", the $1 billion (and counting) that the United States needs *daily* to balance its current accounts with the rest of the world'.[83] For all America's military dominance, Arrighi sees its hegemony as unravelling. Given the massive buying of US government securities by Japan and China, he points to the fragility of the virtuous-but-potentially-vicious circle which depends on 'the US's capacity to present itself as performing the global functions of market of last resort and indispensable political-military power; and the capacity and willingness of the rest of the world to provide the US with the capital it needs to continue to perform these functions on an ever-expanding scale'.[84] The declining competitiveness of the US economy cannot for ever be offset by a depreciation of the dollar. This historical analysis of the successive rise and fall of economic empires from the Venetian through the Dutch and the British to the American leads Arrighi to see China, the real winner of the 'war on terror', as the current potential successor.

Arrighi's analysis is closely paralleled by that of David Harvey in his *The New Imperialism*. Building on his previous work on capitalist accumulation,[85] Harvey analyses what he calls 'the spatio-temporal fix' which is 'a metaphor for a particular kind of solution to capitalist crises through temporal deferral and geographical expansion'. But given that 'increasing quantities of fixed capital ... check uninhibited mobility ... the uneven geographical development of capitalism then assumes a form which is totally inconsistent with sustained accumulation either within the region or on a global scale'. One solution is the use of financial means 'to rid the system of overaccumulation by the visitation of crises of devaluation upon vulnerable territories'.[86] He continues: 'Like war in relation to diplomacy, finance capital intervention backed by state power frequently amounts to accumulation by other means. An unholy alliance between state powers and the predatory aspects of finance capital forms the cutting edge of a "vulture capitalism" that is as much about cannibalistic practices and forced devaluations as it is about achieving harmonious global development.'[87] He calls this process 'accumulation by dispossession'. Here 'the umbilical cord that ties together accumulation by dispossession and expanded reproduction is that given by finance capital and the institution of credit, backed, as ever, by state powers'.[88] The enormous foreign indebtedness of the United States increases the relevance of accumulation by dispossession and vulnerability to capital flight with drastic internal consequences.

The same gloomy conclusions are arrived at, though by a different route, by Dumenil and Levy. They also stress the financial character of ruling-class domination, but see its origin in the neo-liberal policies adopted in the 1980s. In the US these policies resulted in growing wealth for the rich, a decline in savings and increase in consumption of imported goods, foreign investment and capital flow out of the country. The consequence is that 'the United States is at the centre of a *system* in which capital is simultaneously exported and imported, to and from the rest of the world. A central feature of US imperialism is that, in Marx's terminology, it largely acts as an international "active capitalist", as opposed to a lender, on behalf of the holders of capital from other countries.'[89] But within this system its own position has deteriorated as the spending spree of the rich has increased dependency on foreign assets. Thus in their view it is neo-liberalism that is the problem, not imperialism which could continue its path if neo-liberal policies were adjusted. But while these authors, together with Brenner and Arrighi, see US finance as the source of the difficulties in the US economy, leading to a crisis of US hegemony, others are not so sanguine. They stress the strength of the state in protecting and managing capital, in acting as the world's banker, thus increasing the global surplus and promoting its distribution in a way that supports the management and reproduction of empire.[90]

Notes

1. K. Marx, Introduction to *Grundrisse, Selected Writings*, ed. D. McLellan (New York and Oxford, 2000) p. 355. See also Marx's comments on the United States Constitution as the epitome of Classical Liberalism in his *On the Jewish Question*, op. cit., pp. 59ff.
2. K. Marx, *Grundrisse*, ed. M. Nicolaus (New York and London, 1973) p. 884.
3. K. Marx, 'The Eighteenth Brumaire of Louis Bonaparte', *MESW*, vol. 1, p. 255. See also, for example, K. Marx, 'Results of the Immediate Process of Production', Appendix to *Capital*, vol. I, trans. B. Fowkes (New York and London, 1976) p. 1014.
4. K. Marx, F. Engels, *Werke* (Berlin, 1957ff.) vol. 7, p. 221.
5. Ibid.
6. K. Marx, *Capital*, vol. I (Moscow, 1954) p. 301.
7. Marx to Engels, *Werke*, vol. 34, p. 59. See also the remarks in the Preface to the Russian edition of the *Communist Manifesto* in *Selected Writings*, ed. D. McLellan, p. 583.
8. See the comments of Marx and Engels on Kriege in *Collected Works* (New York and London, 1976) vol. 6, pp. 41ff.
9. See Marx's comments on George in Marx to Sorge, *MEW*, vol. 35, p. 199.
10. See S. Gompers, *Seventy Years of Life and Labour* (London, 1925) vol. I, pp. 83ff. See further the first half of S. Kaufman, *Samuel Gompers and the Origin of the AFL* (Westport, 1973).
11. D. De Leon, *Flashlights of the Amsterdam Congress* (New York, 1929) p. 193.
12. Quoted in D. Herreshof, *The Origins of American Marxism* (New York, 1967) p. 136. For De Leon's view that America was riper for revolution than Germany, see his footnote to A. Bebel, *Woman Under Socialism* (New York, 1971) pp. 372f.
13. M. Eastman, *Love and Revolution: My Journey through an Epoch* (New York, 1964) p. 126.
14. D. De Leon, *Daily People*, 20 Jan 1913, quoted in S. Hook, *Marx and the Marxists* (Princeton, N.J., 1955) p. 176.
15. See pp. 126ff. above.

16. See, in particular, J. Starobin, *American Communism in Crisis, 1943–1957* (Cambridge, Mass., 1972) Part Three.
17. For a pioneering study, see B. Friedan, *The Feminine Mystique* (New York, 1963).
18. C. Wright Mills, *The Power Elite* (London, 1956) p. 212.
19. See E. Fromm, *Marx's Concept of Man* (New York, 1962).
20. Quoted in A. Adelson, *SDS* (New York, 1972) p. 208.
21. N. Young, *An Infantile Disorder?* (London, 1977) p. 138.
22. A. Adelson, *SDS* p. 203.
23. See H. Cleaver, *Reading Capital Politically* (London, 1979), pp. 45 ff. and E. Gogol, *Raya Dunayevskaya: Philosopher of Marxist-Humanism* (New York, 2005).
24. W. Sombart, *Socialism and the Social Movement* (London, 1909) p. 276.
25. Perhaps the most impressive of these is the *Review* published by the Union for Radical Political Economics in Ann Arbor.
26. See especially *Socialist Humanism*, ed. E. Fromm (New York, 1967).
27. On Marcuse, see further pp. 310f. above.
28. H. Marcuse, *One-Dimensional Man* (London, 1968) p. 23.
29. Ibid.
30. See, as examples, S. Firestone, *The Dialectic of Sex* (New York, 1970) and the June 1970 number (vol. 4) of *Radical America*, devoted to C.L.R. James.
31. G. Kolko, *The Triumph of Conservatism: A Reinterpretation of American History, 1900–1916* (Glencoe, Ill., 1963) p. 3.
32. Ibid.
33. P. Baran, *The Political Economy of Growth* (Harmondsworth, 1973) p. 133.
34. Ibid., p. 134.
35. Ibid., p. 276.
36. See pp. 286 ff. above.
37. P. Baran and P. Sweezy, *Monopoly Capital* (Harmondsworth, 1966) p. 21.
38. Ibid., p. 80.
39. Ibid., p. 113.
40. See particularly the work of Altvater, in *State and Capital*, ed. J. Holloway and S. Picciotto (London, 1978).
41. H. Braverman, *Labour and Monopoly Capital* (New York, 1974) pp. 3f.
42. See above pp. 336 ff.
43. H. Braverman, *Labour and Monopoly Capital* p. 355.
44. Ibid., p. 445.
45. See, for example, R. Edwards, D. Gordon and M. Reich, *Segmented Work, Divided Workers: The Historical Transformation of Labour in the United States* (Cambridge, 1982) and D. Gordon, *Fat and Mean: The Corporate Squeeze of Working Americans and the Myth of Managerial 'Downsizing'* (New York, 1996).
46. See S. Bowles and H. Gintis, *Recasting Egalitarianism: New Rules for Communities, States and Markets* (New York, 1998). For further discussion, see D. Kotz 'A Comparative Analysis of the Theory of Regulation and the Social Structure of Accumulation Theory', *Science and Society*, vol. 54, no. 1 (1990).
47. There is a good account in D. Lavoie, *Rivalry and Central Planning: The Socialist Calculation Debate Reconsidered* (Cambridge, 1985).
48. J. Roemer, *A Future for Socialism* (Cambridge, 1994).

49. See further *Market Socialism: The Current Debate*, ed. P. Bardhan and J. Roemer (Oxford, 1993).
50. K. Marx, *Selected Writings*, ed. D. McLellan (Oxford, 2000), p. 614. This 'lower phase of communist society' does not contain a market, but shares much of the ethical outlook of market socialism. For a different view see J. Lawler's contribution 'Marx as Market Socialist' to the Ollman (1998) collection. See also Trotsky's insistence on the role of the market in the Five-Year Plan: 'The Plan is checked and, to a considerable degree realised, through the market. The regulation of the market itself must depend upon the tendencies that are brought about through its mechanism', *Writings of Leon Trotsky (1932)* (New York, 1973).
51. See further B. Ollman (ed.), *Market Socialism: The Debate among Socialists* (New York, 1998).
52. See J. Elster, 'Further Thoughts on Marxism, Functionalism and Game Theory', in *Analytical Marxism*, ed. J. Roemer (Cambridge, 1986) and Cohen's response in his *History, Labour and Freedom: Themes from Marx* (Oxford, 1988).
53. See, for example, J. Elster, *Sour Grapes* (Cambridge, 1983).
54. See A. Przeworski, *Capitalism and Social Democracy* (Cambridge, 1985) and *Democracy and the Market* (Cambridge, 1991).
55. See, for example, E.O. Wright, *Classes* (London, 1985).
56. See T. Ashton and C. Philpin (eds), *The Brenner Debate* (Cambridge, 1985).
57. See pp. 386 f. above.
58. See, for example, the trenchant views of E. Wood, 'Rational Choice Marxism: Is the Game Worth the Candle?', in T. Carver and P. Thomas (eds), *Rational Choice Marxism* (Basingstoke, 1995).
59. E. M. Wood, *The Origin of Capitalism* (New York, 1999), p. 59.
60. See pp. 413 f. below.
61. F. Jameson, *Marxism and Form* (Princeton, 1971).
62. P. Anderson, *The Origins of Postmodernity* (New York, 1998), p. 71.
63. F. Jameson, *The Political Unconsicious* (Cornell, 1981), pp. 19f.
64. Op. cit., p. 75.
65. Op.cit., p. 291.
66. See F. Jameson, *Adorno, or, the Persistence of the Dialectic* (London, 1990).
67. See H. Lefebvre, *The Production of Space* (Oxford, 1991). For a different Marxist treatment of space, see the works of David Harvey, particularly *Spaces of Capital: Towards a Critical Geography* (Edinburgh, 2001).
68. F. Jameson, *The Seeds of Time* (New York, 1994), p. 17.
69. See, for example, J. Saul, *The Collapse of Globalism* (New York, 2005).
70. K. Marx, *Selected Writings*, ed. D McLellan (Oxford, 2000), p. 248.
71. M. Hardt and A. Negri, *Empire* (Boston, 2000), p. xii.
72. Op.cit., p. 290.
73. M. Hardt and A. Negri, *Multitude* (New York, 2004), p. 106.
74. Op. cit., p. 339.
75. See further below pp. 408 ff.
76. E. Wood, *Empire of Capital* (London, 2005), p. xi.
77. Op.cit., p. 136.
78. Op.cit., p. 139.
79. R. Brenner, 'The Economics of Global Turbulence', *New Left Review*, vol. 229 (May/June 1998), p. 24.

80. See E. Wood, 'The Politics of Capitalism', *Monthly Review* (September 1999).
81. R. Brenner, 'New Boom or New Bubble?', *New Left Review*, no. 5 (2004), p. 69. See also R. Brenner, *The Boom and the Bubble* (New York, 2002).
82. G. Arrighi, 'Tracking Global Turbulence', *New Left Review*, no. 20 (2004), p. 67. See further the same author's *The Long Twentieth Century: Money, Power and the Origin of Our Times* (London, 1994).
83. Arrighi, 'Tracking Global Turbulence', p. 70.
84. G. Arrighi, 'Hegemony Unravelling', *New Left Review*, no. 32 (2005), p. 65.
85. See D. Harvey, *Limits to Capital* (Oxford, 1982) and *Spaces of Capital: Towards a Critical Geography* (New York, 2001).
86. D. Harvey, *The New Imperialism* (Oxford, 2003), p. 134.
87. Op. cit., p. 136.
88. Op. cit., p. 152.
89. G. Dumenil and D. Levy, 'The Economics of US Imperialism at the Turn of the 21st Century', *Review of International Political Economy* (2004), no. 4, p. 665. See further the same authors' *Capital Resurgent. Roots of the Neoliberal Revolution* (Boston, 2004).
90. See, for example, L. Panitch and S. Gindin, 'Global Capitalism and American Empire' and 'Finance and American Empire', in *Socialist Register*, 2004 and 2005 respectively.

Further reading

The simplest short introduction is Diggins's *The American Left in the Twentieth Century*. See also Buhle's article in *Towards a New Marxism*. Bell's *Marxian Socialism in the United States* is short, brilliant and hostile. On De Leon and the Socialist Labour Party, see Herreshof's *The Origins of American Marxism*. On the origins and early years of the Communist Party, the two books by Draper are standard works; for later developments, see Starobin's *American Communism in Crisis*. Shannon's history of the Socialist Party is thorough and informative. On the New Left the best guide is Theodori's collection. On the SDS, see the excellent study by Sale. On contemporary dilemmas, see Jacoby's article. Buhle's *Marxism in the USA* is a good overview. See also Zinn's splendid history of America from the bottom up.

On market socialism, see Devine's *Democracy and Economic Planning*, Miller's *Market, State and Community*, and (nearest to Marx in perspective) Schweikart's *Against Capitalism*.

On analytical Marxism, see the bibliography below. A good example of analytical Marxism in practice is Roemer's *Free to Lose* which is an analysis of class and exploitation in non-technical language. Two good introductions are Mayer's *Analytical Marxism* and the collection by Carver and Thomas entitled *Rational Choice Marxism*.

Bibliography

History

E. Bacciocco, *The New Left in America: Reform to Revolution 1956–1970* (Stanford, 1974).
Daniel Bell, *Marxian Socialism in the United States* (Princeton, 1952).
W. Breines, *Community and Organization in the New Left 1962–1968*, 2nd edn (New Brunswick, 1989).
Paul Buhle, 'Marxism in the United States', in *Towards a New Marxism*, eds. B. Grahl and P. Piccone (St. Louis, Miss., 1973).
—— *Marxism in the USA* (New York, 1987).
P. Buhle, *Marxism in the US: Remapping the American Left* (London, 1991).
James Cannon, *The First Ten Years of American Communism* (New York, 1962).
—— *The History of American Trotskyism* (New York, 1944).
—— *The Struggle for a Proletarian Party* (New York, 1943).
John R. Commons, *History of Labour in the United States*, 2 vols (New York, 1921).
E. Debs, *Gentle Rebel: Letters of Eugene V. Debs*, ed. R. Constantine (Urbana, 1995).
J. Diggins, *The American Left in the Twentieth Century* (New York, 1973).
Theodore Draper, *The Roots of American Communism* (New York, 1957).
—— *American Communism and Soviet Russia: The Formative Period* (New York, 1960).
Max Eastman, *Love and Revolution: My Journey through an Epoch* (New York, 1964).
Donald D. Egbert and Stow Persons, *Socialism and American Life* (Princeton, 1952).
D. Fernandez-Morera, *American Academia and the Survival of Marxist Ideas* (Westport, 1996).
Philip Foner, *The Bolshevik Revolution: Its Impact on America, Radicals, Liberals and Labour* (New York, 1967).
A. Fried (ed.), *Communism in America: A History in Documents* (New York, 1997).
Albert Fried (ed.), *Socialism in America: From the Shakers to the Third International, A Documentary History* (New York, 1970).
Ray Ginger, *Eugene V. Debs: A Biography* (New York, 1970).
Benjamin Gitlow, *I Confess: The Truth about American Communism* (New York, 1929).
Vivian Gornich, *The Romance of American Communism* (New York, 1978).
D. Herreshof, *The Origins of American Marxism* (New York, 1967).
Morris Hillquit, *History of Socialism in the United States* (London, 1906).
Russell Jacoby, 'The Politics of Objectivity: Notes on the U.S. Left', *Telos*, 34 (1977/8).
E. Johanningmeier, *Forging American Communism* (New York, 1994).
H. Klehr, *The Heyday of American Communism: The Depression Decade* (New York, 1984).
H. Klehr and J. Haynes, *The American Communist Movement* (New York, 1992).
H. Klehr et al. (eds), *The Secret World of American Communism* (New Haven, 1995).
Harry W. Laidler, *Socialism in the United States* (New York, 1952).
Christopher Lasch, *The Agony of the American Left* (New York, 1968).
John H.M. Laslett, *Labour and the Left: Study of Socialist and Radical Influences in the American Labor Movement, 1881–1924* (New York, 1970).

S. Lipset and G. Marks, *It Didn't Happen Here: Why Socialism Failed in the United States* (New York, 2000).
Staughton Lynd, *Intellectual Origins of American Radicalism* (New York, 1969).
Constance Myers, *The Prophet's Army: Trotskyism in America, 1928–1941* (Westport, 1977).
B. Ollmann and E. Vernoff, *The Left Academy: Marxist Scholarship on American Campuses* (New York, 1982).
C. Pierson, *Socialism after Communism: The New Market Socialism* (Oxford, 1995).
Howard H. Quint, *The Forging of American Socialism* (New York, 1962).
C. Robinson, *Black Marxism: The Making of the Black Radical Tradition* (Chapel Hill, 2000).
Kirkpatrick Sale, *SDS* (New York, 1973).
David A. Shannon, *The Socialist Party of America: A History* (New York, 1967).
Werner Sombart, *Why is there no Socialism in the United States?*, trans. P.M. Hocking, Foreword by M. Harrington (London, 1976).
Joseph Starobin, *American Communism in Crisis: 1943–1957* (Cambridge, Mass., 1972).
W. Swanberg, *Norman Thomas: The Last Idealist* (New York, 1976).
Massimo Theodori (ed.), *The New Left: A Documentary History* (New York, 1969).
A. Wald, *The New York Intellectuals: The Rise and Decline of the Anti-Stalinist Left from the 1930s to the 1980s* (Chapel Hill, 1987).
F. Warren, *Liberals and Communism: The 'Red Decade' Revisited* (New York, 1994).
J. Weinstein, *The Decline of Socialism in America* (New York, 1969).
Tim Wolkfarth, *The History of American Trotskyism* (New York, 1968).
M. Young, *Harp Song for a Radical: The Life and Times of Eugene Victor Debs* (New York, 1999).
Nigel Young, *An Infantile Disorder? The Crisis and Decline of the New Left* (London, 1977).

Theory

Paul A. Baran, *The Political Economy of Growth*, 2nd edn (New York, 1962).
P. Baran and P. Sweezy, *Monopoly Capital* (New York, 1966).
Harry Braverman, *Labour and Monopoly Capital* (New York, 1974).
N. Castree and D. Gregory (eds), *David Harvey: A Critical Reader* (Oxford, 2006).
Rod Coombs, 'Labour and Monopoly Capital', *New Left Review*, 107 (1978).
E. Gogol, *Raya Dunayevskaya: Philosopher of Marxist-Humanism* (Lanham, 2000).
Michael Harrington, *Socialism* (New York, 1972).
—— *The Twilight of Capitalism* (New York, 1976).
D. Harvey, *Spaces of Hope* (Edinburgh, 2000).
—— *Spaces of Capital: Towards a Critical Geography* (Edinburgh, 2001).
—— *Spaces of Global Capital: A Theory of Uneven Geographical Development* (London, 2006).
F. Jameson, *Brecht and Method* (London, 1998).
—— *The Cultural Turn: Selected Writings on the Postmodern* (London, 1998).
—— *A Singular Modernity, Essays on the Ontology of the Present* (London, 2002).
—— and K. Weeks (eds), *Jameson Reader* (Oxford, 1999).
S. Homer, *Fredric Jameson: Marxism, Hermeneutics, Postmodernism* (New York, 1998).
—— and D. Kellner, *Fredric Jameson: A Critical Reader* (Basingstoke, 2004).

Gabriel Kolko, *The Triumph of Conservatism: A Reinterpretation of American History, 1900–1916* (Glencoe, Ill., 1963).

H. Marcuse, *One-Dimensional Man* (Boston, 1964).

S. McLemee and P. Le Blanc (eds), *C.L.R. James and Revolutionary Marxism: Selected Writings 1939–1949* (Amherst, 2000).

C. Nelson and L. Grossberg (eds), *Marxism and the Interpretation of Culture* (London, 1988).

J. O'Connor, *The Fiscal Crisis of the State* (New York, 1973).

A. Roberts, *Fredric Jameson* (London, 2000).

Paul M. Sweezy, *The Theory of Capitalist Development: Principles of Marxian Political Economy* (New York, 1942).

Paul M. Sweezy and Charles Bettleheim, *On The Transition to Socialism* (New York, 1971).

James Weinstein, *The Corporate Ideal in the Liberal State: 1900–1918* (Boston, 1968).

—— *The Decline of Socialism in America: 1912–1925* (New York, 1969).

William Appleman Williams, *The Great Evasion: An Essay on the Contemporary Relevance of Karl Marx and on the Wisdom of Admitting the Heretic into the Dialogue about America's Future* (New York, 1968).

B. Wise, *The Marxian Hermeneutics of Fredric Jameson* (New York, 1995).

E. Wood, *The Origin of Capitalism: A Longer View* (London, 2005).

—— *The Retreat from Class* (New York, 1986).

E. Wright, A. Levine and E. Sober, *Reconstructing Marxism: Essays on Explanation and the Theory of History* (New York, 1992).

Market Socialism and Analytical Marxism

Alan Carling, 'Rational Choice Marxism', *New Left Review*, 162 (1986).

Terrell Carver and Paul Thomas, *Rational Choice Marxism* (London, 1995).

G.A. Cohen, *Self-Ownership, Freedom and Equality* (Cambridge, 1995).

P. Devine, *Democracy and Economic Planning* (Cambridge, 1988).

Jon Elster, *Making Sense of Marx* (Cambridge, 1985).

Andrew Levine *et al.*, 'Marxism and Methodological Individualism', *New Left Review*, 123 (1980).

Tom Mayer, *Analytical Marxism* (London, 1994).

David Miller, *Market, State and Community* (Oxford, 1989).

Richard Miller, *Analyzing Marx: Morality, Power and History* (Princeton, N.J., 1984).

Alec Nove, *The Economics of Feasible Socialism* (London, 1983).

R.G. Peffer, *Marxism, Morality and Social Justice* (Princeton, N.J., 1990).

John Roemer (ed.), *Analytical Marxism* (Cambridge, 1986).

John Roemer, *Free to Lose: An Introduction to Marxist Economic Philosophy* (London, 1988).

David Schweikart, *Against Capitalism* (Cambridge, 1993).

Tony Smith, *Dialectical Social Theory and its Critics: From Hegel to Analytical Marxism and Postmodernism* (New York, 1993).

Ellen Wood, 'Rational Choice Marxism: Is the Game Worth the Candle?', *New Left Review*, 177 (1989).

Eric Wright *et al.*, *The Debate on Classes* (London, 1989).

—— *Reconstructing Marxism: Essays on Explanation and the Theory of History* (New York, 1992).

Globalisation and imperialism

G. Arrighi, *The Long Twentieth Century* (London, 1994).
G. Balakrishnan (ed.), *Debating Empire* (London, 2003).
A. Boron, *'Empire' and Imperialism: A Critical Reading of Michael Hardt and Antonio Negri* (London, 2005).
A. Brewer, *Marxist Theories of Imperialism*, 2nd edn (London, 1991).
S. Burchill and A. Linklater, *Theories of International Relations*, 3rd edn (London, 2004), ch. 5.
R. Brenner, *The Boom and the Bubble* (New York, 2002).
—— *The Economics of Global Turbulence* (New York, 2005).
D. Harvey, *The New Imperialism* (Oxford, 2003).
E. Wood, *Empire of Capital*, 2nd edn (London, 2005).

25
Postmodern Marxism

Postmodernism is a way (or ways) of thinking about postmodernity which, according to some, is a new mode of social production emerging in the 1970s. What is new here consists in at least four elements. First, there is the ever-increasing impact of electronic communication, beginning with television and continuing with information technology and its effect on the globalisation of economic relations and communication. The second is the changing mode of economic production. This has been called a change from Fordism to post-Fordism. The innovations of Henry Ford, among others, gave rise to the economic dominance of mass production, mass consumption, and massified semi-skilled labour with national bargaining between large-scale capital and wage labour with a concomitant Keynesian welfare state. Following the crises of the 1970s and increasing economic internationalisation with huge transnational transfers of capital and floating exchange rates came the perceived necessity for a more flexible approach to production and labour markets. This was accompanied by an explosion of sophisticated advertising, concentration on niche markets, and consumerism as a way of life, all based not on mass industrial production but on systematic theoretical research as the driving force of economic growth. Third, and less tangibly, there was the experience of the rolling back of the emancipatory forces unleashed in the 1960s by the neo-liberal agenda of Thatcher and Reagan. The consequent political disillusionment of the now middle-aged and socially mobile intelligentsia of the 1960s, many of whom had started off at least as Marxists, encouraged an analysis of the present surfaces of society rather than one based on the defeated aspirations of the past or opaque hopes for the future. Finally, in the realm of philosophy, there was the impact of structuralism, particularly in linguistics where it aimed to go below the surface phenomena of language to reveal the underlying structure of concealed signifying systems. The active human subject of (say) Sartre was ousted in favour of the impersonal structure which determined individual action. Post-structuralists such as Derrida, Foucault, and Deleuze then proceeded to do away with the distinction between surface and depth at the expense of the latter. They thereby jettisoned claims to objectivity and truth that were still characteristic of structuralism.

Out of these variegated contexts emerged the style of thought known as postmodernism. Postmodernism is in strong opposition to what is called a 'metanarrative' – any view which aims to give a unified, consistent, and objective account of the world by unifying the different narratives in one overarching framework. Postmodern thought rejects the legacy of the Enlightenment which attempted to ground its approach to the world ideas of universal applicability – common human nature, reason – which would reveal the way the world actually was. In postmodernism, by contrast, the emphasis is on diversification, particularity, and difference. Of course, postmodernism itself is very varied: some thinkers, such as Derrida, concentrate on language and the deconstruction of texts which have, so it is said, no determinate meaning but consist solely of an infinite variety of interpretations. Others, such as Foucault, give us a form of social theory, but one in which, again, nothing exists outside discourse emerging from a method which has no centre.

It will be obvious from the above that postmodernism, like socialism itself, is a French invention. It may also seem that postmodernism has little in common with Marxism. Indeed, in opposition to classical Marxism where (to put it crudely) the economic base determines the superstructure, postmodernism seems to dissolve everything into an indeterminable cultural superstructure. However, a closer inspection shows that several postmodernist thinkers have not rejected the Marxist roots from which many of them sprang. And, of course, there are several Marxist accounts of postmodernism itself. Before considering this, we will look in more detail at some of the leading postmodernists.

The influence of postmodern thought can be dated from Jean-François Lyotard's *The Postmodern Condition* published in 1979. Rejecting the Trotskyist position he had adopted in the 1950s, he here defines the postmodern as 'incredulity towards metanarratives'. In the modern world, science had increasingly come to dominate other forms of knowledge which Lyotard called 'narratives'. Science had partly done this by appealing to a 'metanarrative' which recounted the values of transcendent and universal truths – reason, progress, freedom and so on. However, science could not legitimise itself since it 'cannot know and make known that it is the true knowledge without resorting to the other, narrative, kind of knowledge, which from its point of view is no knowledge at all'.[1] What Lyotard is giving us here is a dressed up combination of, first, the is/ought distinction prominent in Anglo-Saxon analytical philosophy since Hume, and, second, the critique of instrumental reason by Horkheimer and Adorno[2] and, third, the philosophy of the later Wittgenstein to whom Lyotard makes repeated reference. Since it is impossible to 'legitimate' science,

> the road is then open for an important current of postmodernity: science plays its own game; it is incapable of legitimating the other language games. The game of prescription, for example escapes it. But above all, it is incapable of legitimating itself, as speculation assumed it could. The social subject itself seems to dissolve in this dissemination of language games. The social bond is linguistic, but it is not woven with a single thread. It is a fabric formed by the intersection of at least two (and in reality an indeterminate number) of language games obeying different rules.[3]

The result was a free-for-all in which different language games competed for power: 'the State and/or company must abandon the idealist and humanist narratives of legitimation in order to justify the new goal: in the discourse of today's financial backers of research, the only credible goal is power. Scientists, technicians and instruments are purchased not to find truth, but to augment power.'[4] In all this, Lyotard has not quite given up on Marxism. But he has at best a rather ethereal version when he says that Marxism could develop into a form of critical knowledge 'by declaring that socialism is nothing other than the constitution of the autonomous subject'.[5] Lyotard's *The Postmodern Condition* had its origin in a report he was commissioned to write for Quebec's University Council on the status of knowledge in contemporary society. As such, although it proved widely influential, it was a suggestive, rather than a detailed, analysis.

The same cannot be said of Michel Foucault whose analyses of the origins of psychiatry, the birth of the modern prison, and the history of sexuality elaborate on the concept of power mentioned by Lyotard. Like all postmodernists, Foucault is anti-system: 'to imagine another system is to extend our participation in the present system'.[6] Foucault described his method of historical investigation as 'archaeological': sifting through the layers on the surface of history to uncover the deep underlying structures and rules that produce and govern the lives of individuals. In this, at least, like Althusser, Foucault rejects all neo-Hegelian humanism in that 'experience has shown that the human sciences, in their development, led to the disappearance of man rather than his apotheosis'.[7] Foucault argues that the basis for disciplines such as clinical medicine, psychiatry, and criminology lie in various forms of discourse. A discourse, for example in psychiatry, is defined by Foucault as 'the group of statements that belong to a single system of formation'[8] and places limits on what can be said and by whom. And Foucault's aim was to investigate the hidden rules that underlay the various disciplinary practices. What concerned him above all was the idea of power. For Foucault, power was not something that resided self-evidently in, for example, the state or police force. Power was dispersed intangibly throughout society such that it was impossible to locate it in any one individual's hands. The only way to get any sort of a grip on this elusive power was to analyse the different sites where power had been exercised historically, for example the prison, and uncover the knowledge or discourse employed by the particular discipline to exercise control and obtain conformity.

Foucault was not optimistic about the future: 'against ... usurpations by the disciplinary mechanisms, against this ascent of power that is tied to scientific knowledge, we find that there is no solid recourse available to us today'.[9] Nevertheless, Foucault's attempt to show that in the past (and present) there was conflict where there had seemed to be order did encourage the voices of marginalised groups and was received with enthusiasm by the new social movements of the 1980s and beyond.

Foucault started his academic career as a psychologist – and it is arguable that these origins influenced the subsequent evolution of his thought. But of all the postmodernist thinkers, the one most in tune with a psychological approach is Gilles Deleuze whose two volume magnum opus (co-authored with Felix Guattari) is entitled *Capitalism and Schizophrenia* and the more influential first volume *Anti-Oedipus*. The work of Deleuze is exceptionally difficult to summarise as he is deliberately anti-systematic and makes a virtue out of allusive incoherence. Nevertheless (and in this he is similar to Foucault who wrote the Preface to *Anti-Oedipus*) it is clear that one of Deleuze's main targets is Freud and orthodox psychoanalysis. Like Laing and Foucault, Deleuze and Guattari are part of an anti-psychiatry movement. Thus the title of their book is well explained by Wolfenstein: 'Desire is not, in the first instance, familiar and oedipal. It is social and an-oedipal. It only becomes familiarized and oedipalised in specific historical instances. Psychoanalysis mistakes the deformation of desire for desire itself'.[10]

In general, Deleuze, inspired like many postmodernists by Nietzsche, seeks to liberate individuals from the constraints of traditional ideas of what constitutes knowledge. Whereas traditional thought concentrated on a unified fundamental structure, Deleuze emphasised diversity and difference. In particular, Deleuze aimed to achieve this through the evocation of the concept of desire and a celebration of the creative power of schizophrenia. Deleuze widens Foucault's perspective: whereas Foucault examined the codes and discourses operative in particular contexts, Deleuze broadens this to society as a whole and the forces at work to challenge them. He aims to locate and intensify the sites where desire can escape from the pervasive re-coding of restrictive discourses in late capitalist society. Whereas for Foucault power was central, for Deleuze and Guattari it is desire. For them 'the flux of desire, assembling the organic and the inorganic, the human and the natural, the discursive and the social, into contingent and changing unities, constantly breaking down the boundaries which these unities constitute, is primary.'[11] Deleuze's concept of desire is radically indeterminate – hence 'schizophrenic' – and is distorted if subject to any linguistic or social codes. Foucault's desire is negative, being caused by a lack which is never fulfilled: Deleuze's is a positive force like a flow of energy or of information. It is social and not individual: 'social production is purely and simply desiring – production itself under determinate conditions ... There is only desire and the social, and nothing else.'[12]

This extreme vitalism, which reads sometimes like a psychoanalytic version of Bergson's *elan vital*, is supplemented by a concept of territory. For example, capitalism destroys social codes and territories, but replaces them with different codes – laws of the market – and thus establishes its own territory. In opposition to this, Deleuze and Guattari extol the figure of the nomad who rejects the territorialisation of land, labour, and money by the state. The state is sedentary and fixed; the nomad has an approach which is shifting, exploratory and radically pluralist.

It can be argued that Deleuze, unlike most postmodernists who emphasise what in traditional Marxist terms would be the cultural superstructure as opposed to the productive base, is keen to re-emphasise production, which he takes to be coterminous with desire. Deleuze is certainly keen on abolishing certain distinctions; centrally, he deals with the apparent opposition between Freud and Marx by fusing them in the concept of desire-production. In this he goes well beyond Marcuse's attempts to reconcile Freud and Marx in his *Eros and Civilization*.[13] But for all that Deleuze appears to be a perspectivist insisting on diversity and polemicising against 'totalising' systems of thought, his conception of desire-production and its all-pervasive schizophrenic flow can itself be seen as a sort of universal principle.

A rather different reaction to Foucault is present in the work of Jacques Derrida with whose name principally the 'deconstructionist' current in postmodernism has become associated. For Derrida, Foucault's archaeological approach still adhered to the Western philosophical tradition in that it purported to be constructing an alternative history but one that still had some claim to objectivity.[14] Derrida was influenced by the structural linguistics of Saussure in which words got their meaning through relation to other words rather than by virtue of referring to objects. He was also drawn to Heidegger's attack on Western philosophy as concealing the Being to which, though hidden, humanity could lay itself open. In his foundational work *Of Grammatology*, Derrida contrasts the traditional metaphysics of sameness (identity) and presence with the deconstructivist ideas of difference and absence. These two latter ideas were united in the central concept of *différence* which combines the meanings of the words 'differ' and 'defer'. Whereas traditional philosophy had set great store by logic, coherence, and verifiability, the practitioner of *différence* operated in a world where meaning was always postponed. Derrida concentrates on presentation, rhetoric, metaphor, and the unconscious. He thereby deconstructs texts to show failure in their attempts at representation. He claims that we cannot step outside language to see whether it adequately represents some 'real' world. Famously, he declared that 'there is no outside-text'[15] meaning not that there was nothing outside the text but only that we could never know this to be the case. It followed that any apparently coherent piece of writing can be read in many conflicting ways and is subject to an infinite number of interpretations. Derrida thus breaks down the traditional boundaries between disciplines, in particular between philosophy and literary criticism. This levelling of the playing field by looking at all disciplines as a form of literature accounts for the enthusiastic reception he has received in departments of literature in American universities. Derrida's work can be seen as the *ne plus ultra* of the general move within philosophy and social science towards a greater preoccupation with language, from Wittenstein and Habermas to critical discourse analysis.[16]

One of the most striking features of postmodernism is its emphasis on difference. Whereas classical Marxism offered a united front of opposition to capitalism based on the working class, many of the proponents of postmodernism have moved from the revolutionary hopes for global transformation of the 1960s to enthusiasm for single issues and the new social movements of, for example, feminists, ecologists, or anti-racists.

The postmodern trend of the writers mentioned above has thus been buttressed by, and in turn influenced, the so-called new social movements. As Foucault has written:

if it is against *power* that one struggles, then all those who acknowledge it as intolerable can begin the struggle wherever they find themselves and in terms of their own activity (or passivity). In engaging in this struggle that is *their own*, whose objective they clearly understand and whose methods they can determine, they enter into the revolutionary process. As allies of the proletariat, to be sure, because power is exercised the way it is in order to maintain capitalist exploitation. They genuinely serve the cause of the proletariat by fighting in those places where they find themselves oppressed. Women, prisoners, conscripted soldiers, hospital patients, and homosexuals have now begun a specific struggle against the particular form of power, the constraints and controls, that are exercised over them.[17]

Many early feminists, for example, had difficulty with the centrality of class to the explanation of exploitation and struggled to account for gender relations using Marxist concepts. Of course, Marxist writers such as Engels and Bebel had pioneered theories of the origins of sexual exploitation.[18] But later theorists found the combination more difficult. Throughout the 1970s, for example, there was an extended debate on whether and how women's domestic labour fitted Marx's account of value and labour.[19] But it proved difficult, simply in these terms, to see why men and women should not be equally exploited in capitalist society. More promisingly, some who still had strong Marxist sympathies explored the role of capitalism and patriarchy in controlling labour markets and thus access to economic resources.[20] Others built on Engels to stress the role of biological processes in the emergence of male domination.[21] By contrast, writers such as Mackinnon saw feminism as superseding Marxism.[22] By the 1980s, with Foucault replacing Althusser as a central theoretical influence, many feminist writers embraced postmodernism to explore the subjectivity and cultural specificity in which gender relations were constructed,[23] though others such as Hennessey maintained a staunchly materialist approach to explaining structural inequalities.[24]

Although the move from traditional Marxism to an interest in the idea of difference and new social movements was most noticeable in France (partly due to the rapid collapse of the French Communist Party), perhaps the best example of the postmodernist approach to Marxism is the work of Ernesto Laclau and Chantal Mouffe whose *Hegemony and Socialist Strategy* caused widespread debate on its publication in 1985. For Laclau and Mouffe, the impact of new social movements is 'the *novel* role they play in articulating that rapid diffusion of social conflictuality to more and more numerous relations which is characteristic today of advanced industrial societies'.[25] By 'operating deconstructively within Marxist categories', Laclau and Mouffe identify Marxism as one of the central strands in the 'democratic revolution' towards freedom and equality for all stemming from the Enlightenment.[26] Marxism is here one emancipatory discourse amongst others and thus combinable with feminism, anti-racism and so on. Indeed, Laclau and Mouffe find a tension within traditional Marxist thought between activist political struggle and a more determinist view of the economic basis of society. They see in the development of twentieth-century Marxism what Mouffe has called 'the return of the political'[27]. Central here is the concept of hegemony: while Laclau and Mouffe draw heavily on Gramsci, they find in him a residual economism. They give no primacy to the sphere of production since 'the logic of hegemony, as a logic of articulation and contingency, has come to determine the very identify of the hegemonic subjects'[28]. Indeed, in a sentence more reminiscent of Foucault than of Gramsci, they state that 'every object is constituted as an object of discourse'.[29] The role of hegemonic practice is to purpose a struggle for radical democracy involving competition between different discourses and interpretations none of which can ever claim final closure because objectivity, like democracy itself, is something which can never be completely achieved.

Laclau and Mouffe are not alone in claiming some sort of Marxist heritage. Lyotard himself, although critical of Marxism,[30] admits that Frankfurt School Marxism could 'develop into a form of critical knowledge by declaring that socialism is nothing other than the constitution of the autonomous subject and that the only justification for the sciences is if they give the empirical subject (the proletariat) the means to emancipate itself from alienation and repression'.[31] Foucault tells us that he employs Marx as a toolbox, using, for example, Volume Two of *Capital* in his analysis of power.[32] And Deleuze and Guattari in their *Anti-Oedipus* take up Marx's account of primitive accumulation in Volume One of *Capital* in order to illustrate their concept of de-territorialisation both in the flows of labour following rural enclosures and in the parallel flows of money now become capital. But it is Derrida, the master of deconstruction, who has spent most time rethinking Marx. In his *Spectres of Marx* he deconstructs the 'end of history' thesis by referring to the legacy of Marx. He trawls through Marx's work – particularly the *Communist Manifesto, Eighteenth Brumaire, Germany Ideology, Critique of Political Economy,* and the passage on the fetishism of commodities in Volume One of *Capital* – to find the ghostly legacy that is still around to haunt those who believe *à la* Fukuyama that history has ended in the triumph of neo-liberal economics and the Western conception of democracy. For Derrida, 'it will always be a fault not to read and reread and discuss Marx ... There will be no future without this. Not without Marx. No future without Marx, without the memory and inheritance of Marx.'[33]

But if postmodernists have been at times willing to incorporate certain elements of Marxism in their approach, some writing from a Marxist perspective have not always been so tolerant. Perhaps the mildest, as well as the most profound, has been Fredric Jameson who sees postmodernism, in the words of the title of his book on the subject, as the cultural logic of late capitalism. Jameson turns the tables on postmodernism: for its adherents, Marxism is one (sometimes useful, though not in its all-embracing, totalising aims) perspective among others; for Jameson, postmodernism is but the most recent cultural phenomenon in the unfolding of history and not likely to prove less ephemeral than its predecessors. As a Marxist, Jameson links postmodernism firmly to the developing needs of the capitalist economy and is influenced by Mandel's *Late Capitalism*.[34] Here Mandel analyses the 'long waves' of capitalist development and claims that capitalism goes through different stages from competition inside the nation through international competition and imperialism to a late capitalism characterised by the international centralisation of capitalism and the dominance of multinational corporations and banks. He examines the laws of accumulation that govern the transition from one state to another and sees capitalism as contradictory and crisis-prone. In Jameson's view, postmodern culture has fused with the economic developments described by Mandel. Capitalism is everywhere. The production of culture 'has become integrated into commodity production generally: the frantic urgency of producing fresh waves of ever more novel seeming goods (from clothes to airplanes), at ever greater rates of turnover, now assigns an increasingly structural function to aesthetic innovation and experimentation'.[35] The result is that art tends to be levelled down and merely accompanies, and does not oppose, the economic order. This has a consequent effect on the psyche of individuals who begin to lack any sense of history and even feel their own selves to be shifting and ephemeral. In all this, Jameson is concerned not to issue any moral judgement on postmodernism but to absorb it into a totalising account of human development.

David Harvey's book on the same topic is not so reticent. He sees postmodernism as supportive of capitalism in that 'precisely because capitalism is expansionary and imperialistic, cultural life in more and more areas gets brought within the grasp of the cash nexus and the logic of capital circulation'.[36] Postmodernism arises with the demise of Fordism in the 1970s through growing international competition and falling corporate profits. In response to this crisis of overaccumulation, capitalism has relied on a temporal fix by speeding up the continuous and state-backed growth of indebtedness and a spatial fix by relocating production to areas of the world where labour is cheaper. For Harvey, it is this restless, flexible, speculative capitalism which had given rise to postmodernism:

> the experience of time and space has changed, the confidence in the association between scientific and moral judgements has collapsed, aesthetics has triumphed over ethics as a prime focus of social and intellectual concern, images dominate narratives, ephemerality and fragmentation take precedence over eternal truths and unified politics, and explanation has shifted from the realm of political-economic groundings towards a consideration of autonomous cultural and political practices.[37]

While agreeing that postmodernism can be progressive in its emphasis on respect for otherness and support for social movements, Harvey believes that a historical materialist approach is necessary to understand postmodernism as a historical-geographical condition. 'On that critical basis', he writes, 'it becomes possible to launch a counter-attack of narrative against image, of ethics against aesthetics, of a project of Becoming rather than Being, and to search for unity within difference, albeit in a context where the power of the image and of aesthetics, the problems of time-space compression, and the significance of geopolitics and otherness are clearly understood'.[38] In short, a renewal of historical-geographical materialism can promote a regeneration of the Enlightenment project.

A similar reference to the Enlightenment project, although in a more philosophical vein, has been offered by Habermas. He deplores the relativism and defeatism espoused by postmodernists. In particular, he takes issue with Derrida's thought as being, paradoxically, too foundational in what he calls Derrida's 'world-constituting performance of subjectivity'[39] rather than the more procedural production of meaning in intersubjective terms that he himself advocates. And Derrida's perception of rhetoric as all-persuasive elides the difference between philosophy and literary criticism. With regard to Foucault, Habermas argues similarly that 'if the truth claim that Foucault himself raises for his genealogy of knowledge were in fact illusory and amounted to no more than the effects that this theory is capable of releasing within the circle of its adherents, then the entire undertaking of a critical unmasking of the human sciences would lose its point'.[40] Although Habermas admitted that the contrast between German rationalism and French post-structuralism may have been exaggerated, what concerned him most was the support, as he saw it, that postmodernism gave to neo-conservative elements in German society.

From a more sociological perspective, Lash and Urry have connected postmodernism with what they call the disorganised nature of contemporary capitalism.[41] For them, the nation-state can no longer organise its own economy, a globalised economy leads to the decline of manufacturing industry in the West, and the rise of a 'service class' undermines the strength and coherence of the labour movement. Drawing on the work of Bourdieu and Baudrillard, they see the effect of these changes as the consumption of images rather than production, the new importance of spectacle at the expense of meaning, and the developing service class as the consumer *par excellence* of postmodern cultural products.

To those whose Marxism was of a more robust variety, there is little to be welcomed in postmodernism. Harvey's sharp critique has already been mentioned. For Eagleton, postmodernism is part of the problem rather than of the solution. For him, although a lot of postmodernism is politically oppositional, it is economically compliant. But even its political opposition is based on shifting sands. In the face of the authoritarian right, postmodernism is unequal to the struggle: 'its cultural relativism and moral conventionalism, its scepticism, pragmatism and localism, its distaste for solidarity and disciplined organization, its lack of any adequate theory of political agency: all these would tell heavily against it'.[42] Alex Callinicos is even more rejectionist. For him, the whole concept of 'postmodernism' rests on the misconception that the 1970s saw a radical break between the modern and the postmodern whether in art or in economics. In the latter, Callinicos claims that the ideas of a post-industrial society or a new phase of capitalism are mostly the consequences of much longer-term trends with the consequent conclusion that a Marxist approach is just as relevant as ever.[43]

Notes

1. J.-F. Lyotard, *The Postmodern Condition* (Manchester, 1984), p. 29.
2. See pp. 302 f. above.
3. Lyotard, op. cit., p. 40.
4. Lyotard, op. cit., p. 46.
5. Lyotard, op. cit., p. 37.
6. M. Foucault, *Language, Counter-Memory, Practice* (Ithaca, 1977), p. 230.
7. Quoted in M. Drolet (ed.), *The Postmodernism Reader* (London, 2004), p. 70.
8. M. Foucault, *The Archaeology of Knowledge* (New York, 1972), p. 107.
9. M. Foucault, *Power/Knowledge* (New York, 1972), p. 107.
10. E. Wolfenstein, *Psychoanalytic Marxism: Groundwork* (New York, 1993), p. 120.
11. A. Callinicos, *Against Postmodernism: A Marxist Critique* (Cambridge, 1989), p. 84.
12. G. Deleuze and F. Guattari, *Anti-Oedipus: Capitalism and Schizophrenia* (Minneapolis, 1972), p. 29. See further P. Hallward, *Out of this World: Deleuze and the Philosophy of Creation* (London, 2006).
13. See p. 312 above.
14. See here his lecture on Foucault's *Madness and Civilization*, in J. Derrida, *Writing and Difference* (London, 2002).
15. J. Derrida, *Of Grammatology* (Baltimore, 1976), p. 158.
16. See further N. Fairclough and R. Wodak, 'Critical Discourse Analysis', in *Introduction to Discourse Analysis: Discourse as Social Interaction*, ed. T. Van Dijk (Newbury Park, 1997).
17. M. Foucault, *Language, Counter-Memory, Practice: Selected Essays and Interviews* (Ithaca, 1977), p. 216.
18. See p. 13 above.
19. See S. Walby, *Patriarchy at Work* (Cambridge, 1986).
20. See H. Hartmann, 'The Unhappy Marriage of Marxism and Feminism: Towards a More Progressive Union', in L. Sargent (ed.), *Women and Revolution: The Unhappy Marriage of Marxism and Feminism* (London, 1981).
21. For example, M. O'Brien, *The Politics of Reproduction* (London, 1981).
22. See C. Mackinnon, 'Feminism, Marxism, Method and the State: Towards Feminist Jurisprudence', *Signs* (1982), vol. 4.
23. See here the contributions of Barrett and Walby to M. Barrett and A. Phillips (eds) *Destabilizing Theory: Contemporary Feminist Debates* (Oxford, 1992).
24. R. Hennessey, *Materialist Feminism and the Politics of Discourse* (New York, 1993).
25. E. Laclau and S. Mouffe, *Hegemony and Socialist Strategy* (London, 1985), pp. 159 f.
26. Op. cit., p. 3.
27. C. Mouffe, *The Return of the Political* (London, 1993).
28. E. Laclau and C. Mouffe, *Hegemony and Socialist Strategy* (London, 1985), p. 85.
29. Op. cit., p. 107.
30. J.-F. Lyotard, *The Postmodern Condition*, in *The Postmodernism Reader*, ed. M. Drolet (London, 2004), p. 131.
31. J.-F. Lyotard, op. cit., in L. Cahoune, ed., *From Modernism to Post Modernism: An Anthology* (Cambridge, 1996), p. 488.

32. M. Foucault, *Dits et Ecrits*, Vol. 4, Paris, 1994, p. 186.
33. J. Derrida, *Spectres of Marx* (London, 1994), p. 13.
34. E. Mandel, *Late Capitalism* (London, 1975).
35. F. Jameson, *Postmodernism, or, the Cultural Logic of Late Capitalism* (Durham, 1991).
36. D. Harvey, *The Condition of Postmodernity* (Oxford, 1991), p. 344. See also Chapter 3 for an excellent summary of the nature of postmodernity.
37. D. Harvey, op. cit., p. 328.
38. D. Harvey, op. cit., p. 354. See further here Harvey's impressively original application of Marx's theory of crisis to contemporary capitalism in his *Limits to Capital* (Oxford, 1982) and his more recent *The New Imperialism* (Oxford, 2005).
39. J. Habermas, *The Philosophical Discourse of Modernity* (Cambridge, 1990), p. 172.
40. J. Habermas, op. cit., p. 279.
41. See Ch. 9 of S. Lash and J. Urry, *The End of Organized Capitalism* (Oxford, 1987).
42. T. Eagleton, *The Illusions of Postmodernism* (Oxford, 1996), p. 134.
43. A. Callinicos, *Against Postmodernism: A Marxist Critique* (Cambridge, 1989). See also the rather more focused E. Wood, *The Retreat from Class* (London, 1986).

Further reading

For individual works by postmodern thinkers, see references in the notes above. There are good collections by Cahoune and by Drolet. The leading work in this area is Laclau and Mouffe: see the chapter by Daly which is effectively an exposition. Nelson and Grossberg provide a large, rambling *tour d'horizon* of their title and Carver finds the postmodern in Marx himself. For Marxist critiques of postmodernity, see Harvey's sharp analysis and Jameson's more Hegelian approach. On the latter see also Anderson. Hostile dissections of postmodernism are provided by Eagleton and by Callinicos.

Bibliography

P. Anderson, *The Origins of Postmodernity* (New York, 1998).
J. Aune, *Rhetoric and Marxism* (Boulder, 1994).
P. Beilharz, *Postmodern Socialism: Romanticism, City, and State* (Melbourne, 1994).
T. Bennett, *Formalism and Marxism* (London, 2005).
G. Browning, 'Lyotard: After and With Marx, Within and Against Capital', *Contemporary Politics*, Vol. 8, No. 2 (2002).
L. Cahoune (ed.), *From Modernism to Postmodernism* (Cambridge, 1996).
A. Callari *et al.* (eds), *Marxism in the Postmodern Age: Confronting the New World Order* (New York, 1995).
A. Callinicos, *Against Postmodernism: A Marxist Critique* (Cambridge, 1989).
T. Carver, *The Postmodern Marx* (Manchester, 1998).

G. Daly, 'Marxism and Postmodernism', in A. Gamble *et al.* (eds), *Marxism and Social Science* (London, 1999).

M. Drolet (ed.), *The Postmodernism Reader* (London, 2004).

T. Eagleton, *The Illusions of Postmodernism* (Oxford, 1996).

K. Gibson-Graham *et al.* (eds), *Re/presenting Class: Essays in Postmodern Marxism* (Durham, 2001).

D. Goldstein, *Post-Marxist Theory* (Albany, 2005).

D. Harvey, *The Condition of Postmodernity* (Oxford, 1990).

D. Hill *et al.* (eds), *Marxism against Postmodernism in Education Theory* (Oxford, 2002).

R. Hollinger, *Postmodernism and the Social Sciences: A Thematic Approach* (Thousand Oaks, 1994).

J. Hutnyk, *Bad Marxism: Capitalism and Cultural Studies* (London, 2004).

F. Jameson, *Postmodernism, or, the Cultural Logic of Late Capitalism* (Durham, 1991).

D. Kellner, *Jean Baudrillard: From Marxism to Postmodernism and Beyond* (Palo Alto, 1989).

E. Laclau, *A Critical Reader* (London, 2004).

—— *On Populist Reason* (London, 2005).

—— and C. Mouffe, *Hegemony and Socialist Strategy* (London, 1985).

L. Landry, *Marx and the Postmodernism Debates: An Agenda for Critical Theory,* (Westport, 2000).

S. Makdisi *et al.* (eds), *Marxism beyond Marxism* (New York, 1996).

G. McLennan, *Marxism, Pluralism and Beyond* (Oxford, 1989).

R. Munck, *Marx @ 2000: Late Marxist Perspectives* (London, 2000).

C. Nelson and L. Grossberg, *Marxism and the Interpretation of Culture* (Basingstoke, 1988).

S. Sim (ed.), *Post-Marxism: A Reader* (Edinburgh, 1998).

S. Sim, *Post-Marxism. An Intellectual History* (London, 2000).

E. Wolfenstein, *Psychoanalytic-Marxism: Groundwork* (New York, 1993).

N. Thoburn, *Deleuze, Marx, and Politics* (London, 2003).

M. Wayne, *Marxism and Media Studies: Key Concepts and Contemporary Trends* (London, 2003).

M. Zavarzadeh *et al.* (eds), *Post-Ality: Marxism and Postmodernism* (Washington DC, 1995).

Conclusion

The above survey has adequately demonstrated the varied nature of Marxist thought over the past century. Interpretations of Marx have always been strongly influenced by broader shifts in intellectual paradigms. Thus a useful way of looking at the history of the interpretation of Marx in the West is as a history of the attempts to come to terms with, and even incorporate, the successively dominant intellectual trends in these societies. After all, Marx himself evolved his ideas in the shadow of the great Hegel, and his later work, and even more that of Engels, was marked by the nineteenth-century enthusiasm for positivism and science. This scientistic outlook continued to dominate the theoretical output of the German SPD, then the centre of Marxist theory, in the two decades before World War I. The spirit of Hegel was revived by the flux and change that followed the war, with its theoretical counterpart in the late writings of Lenin and, particularly, of the early Lukács. The impact of Freud's theories was felt in the work of the Frankfurt School, in Reich, Marcuse and the early Habermas. The rise of Nazism and its consequences shifted the centre of Marxist theory in the West to France and saw the advent of existentialism as the dominant mode of philosophising and a Sartrean Marxism appeared, to be succeeded by the rapid rise and fall of structuralism with its Althusserian version of Marxism and then the systematic anarchy of postmodernism and the various attempts of Marxists to come to terms with its attack on their 'grand narrative'. In the 1980s the rise of neo-liberalism was accompanied by the emergence of a distinctly Anglo-Saxon Marxism in the shape of an apparently oxymoronic 'rational choice' Marxism with strongly individualistic overtones. With the collapse of the Soviet Union leaving the United States as the world's only superpower and with the increasing importance of international electronic communication, 'globalisation'

419

becomes the centre of attention. And reflecting the real distribution of economic and military power, globalisation came to be viewed in terms of imperialism and empire.

We will briefly survey this intellectual evolution in the three major areas of economics, politics and philosophy.

In *economics*, the central question was how and when capitalism would collapse. Among leaders of the SPD, such as Engels, Bebel and Kautsky, a rather superficial reading of what Marx had said about the falling rate of profit had led them to the view that the breakdown of capitalism was imminent and would proceed automatically, at least in the sense that it did not require the active intervention of the proletariat. The economic case for capitalist collapse was given refinement by Luxemburg's work on imperialism (as also by Lenin's), although in the work of other economists – Hilferding for example – imperialism could appear as a reason for supposing the demise of capitalism to be very far from imminent.

With the success of the Bolshevik Revolution, the hitherto little regarded question of the economic transition from capitalism to Communism became paramount. After the varied experiences of War Communism and the New Economic Policy, the debate lay between Bukharin's idea that the gradual progress of the peasantry would provide an expanding market for industry and Trotsky's view that more energetic measures were needed to transfer surplus from the peasantry for immediate investment in heavy industry – a policy which Stalin eventually applied, though in a most brutal form. The Soviet approach was rejected by Mao, who allotted a leading role to agriculture and emphasised relations of production over forces of production.

While socialism was being constructed (or misconstructed) in the East, the resilience of the capitalist system in the West led to a decline of interest in Marxist economics. This decline was reversed, particularly in the Anglo-Saxon world, only in the 1970s. This was due both to the development of a crisis in the capitalist West and to a serious interest in the problem of world inequality and development. The turn of the century saw this interest concentrating on the economic underpinnings of globalisation and the connections between global capitalism and the vagaries of US imperialist ambitions.

In *politics*, the ongoing debate centred on the relationship of the Party to the proletariat and the development of a revolutionary consciousness among the working class. Even those who seemed to believe in a semi-automatic breakdown of capitalism – Kautsky and Luxemburg in their different ways – were enthusiastic about party organisation (Kautsky) or

such tactics as the mass strike (Luxemburg). But with the growing reformism of large sections of the working class in the West, including the Trade Union leadership, and the lack of the clear polarisation of society, Lenin's idea of a 'vanguard' party which world instil revolutionary ideas into the working class became attractive. With the success of 1917, the Leninist model in which the Party incarnated the consciousness of the working class (as theorised by Lukács) became dominant. In the Soviet Union under Stalin, this conception was used to implement a violent revolution from above. In China the Party, claiming to embody the consciousness of a largely non-existent proletariat, tended to become equally divorced from the people, in spite of such efforts as the Cultural Revolution. Those in the West, like Korsch and the Council Communists, who retained their commitment to workers' self-emancipation, were disillusioned. The Frankfurt School and the structuralists both reflected this lack of faith in the revolutionary potential of the working class. The only thinker to unite predominant interest in the superstructure with active commitment to politics was Gramsci.

In *philosophy*, the development of Marxist thought has again been heterogeneous. Engels said that the German working class was the inheritor of German classical philosophy as recapitulated in Hegel. The debate on Marxist philosophy revolved around the allied questions of in what sense, if any, Marxism is a science and the precise nature of the debt it owes to Hegel. The answers to these questions correlate to an interesting extent with the different views of economics and politics outlined above. For example, those who considered Marxism to be some sort of science akin to natural science, and consequently showed little interest in Hegel, could not take seriously the idea of the self-emancipation of the working class. Either, like Kautsky, they left it to a Darwinian evolutionary process or – like Lenin sometimes and Stalin always – they remanded the task of liberation to the Party or the individual (a process repeated by the Chinese Communist Party with regard to the 'poor and blank' peasants of China). Characteristic of those who thought Marxism was something more than science was an emphasis on the subjective activity of the individual, as in Lukács, Korsch and the early Frankfurt School. Nevertheless, as the prospects for revolution ebbed in the West, many Marxists turned their attention to philosophy almost as an end in itself and to subjects – such as aesthetics – far removed from politics. Indeed, it is a measure of how far Marxist thought has travelled over the last century that the two areas in which currently the most interesting theoretical work is being done are the imperatives of global capitalism and the neo-Hegelian approach of writers such as Fredric Jameson.

Thus the very variety of Marxism shows that the ambivalences inherent in Marx's legacy have indeed been fully explored by his followers.

What, then, is the future for Marxism at the millennium? Some consider the collapse of Communism in the Soviet Union and Eastern Europe to mean the end of Marxism, and indeed history itself.[1] The original sin was traced back to Marx himself and his dangerously utopian aspirations.[2] Others considered Lenin the chief culprit and saw the force of Weber's warning in 1920 to his friend Lukács who had recently joined the Bolshevik camp: 'I am absolutely convinced that these experiments can only have and will have the consequence of discrediting socialism for the next hundred years.'[3] The more stout-hearted could take comfort in the view that:

> from the perspective of *classical* Marxism, the collapse of these regimes and their return to a 'normal' path of capitalist development is eminently predictable. If anything, the long detour from the Bolshevik Revolution to *perestroika* was a challenging anomaly to historical materialism. The restoration of capitalist property relations in relatively underdeveloped industrial economies, on the other hand, actually corroborates the theory. *If* Marx was right, socialism is not achievable until the forces of production have developed massively under capitalism, and further development is fettered by capitalist property relations. The attempt to construct revolutionary socialism by an act of will in violation of this 'law of history' was therefore doomed from the start.[4]

Thus the seventy-year history of the Soviet Union could be seen as a kind of developmental short-cut which telescoped the slower growth of productive forces in the West and whose demise put Russia painfully back into the mainstream of world history.[5] Those of a somewhat more sectarian bent who had always claimed that the Soviet Union and its satellites were really capitalist societies (albeit state ones) could justifiably claim that the same old people still owned and controlled the forces of production except that now they called themselves managing directors of capitalist enterprises instead of Communist *apparatchiks*.[6] In any event, looking back now over more than a century of Marx interpretation it is becoming clearer what is living and what is dead in Marxism. There are three aspects that it is tempting to consign to the mortuary and two that still seem to have considerable life in them.

In the former category, the first and most obvious is Marxism in the sense of an intellectual system which offered a total interpretation of the

world in a metaphysical, philosophical sense: that is, Marxism as traditionally preached by the Soviet Union and written up in umpteen hack-
neyed text-books under the rubric of dialectical materialism.[7] Here the
laws of dialectical materialism governed everything from the change of
quantity to quality right up to the date of the next revolution. This all-
encompassing metaphysic based upon a crude materialist interpretation
of the world was never taken terribly seriously by most thinking people.
But nevertheless it was something which – as rather more simplistic versions of religion have been – was widely propagated, and presumably
accepted to a certain extent by millions upon millions of people. This
aspect of Marxism has (and had) very little validity.

Secondly, and more strictly politically, what recent events have shown
us is that Marxism/Leninism, in the industrialised world at least, has
very little future, at least in the medium term. Marxism/Leninism
emphasises two ideas which Lenin added to the canon of Marxist theory
and practice that he inherited from the previous century. The first of
those two ideas is that of a vanguard party, a party which could propose
and put into action ideas based on theories that were not generated in
the working class itself, a party which had plans and policies that were
its own. This party was vanguard in the sense that it was in advance of –
and acting for the future benefit of – the workers, who were as yet ignorant of where their true interest lay. The second new idea of Lenin was
the theory of imperialism which explained the expansion of the industrial West into Africa and Asia according to the changing needs of capitalist expansion. Those two aspects, the Party and imperialism, which
Lenin added to nineteenth-century Marxism, are the two reasons why, if
there are any parts of the world in which Marxism/Leninism (and specifically the Leninist part) could be still alive, it would be Africa, Asia and
Southern America. That is because the idea of a vanguard party appeals
and has appealed over the decades to elites in these countries, who wish
to use their elite status to modernise and catch up with the developed
West. And the notion of imperialism of course explains to these countries why they are in the parlous state in which they find themselves:
namely, they are being exploited by the advanced capitalist countries.
These two aspects mean that, although Leninism has no conceivable
future in Europe and in North America, it has enjoyed better fortunes in
the less developed parts of the world.

Thirdly, economically, the notion that a command economy, a highly
centralised, highly planned economy, can (at least at the present level of
development) provide answers to social and economic problems has
been shown to be a hollow promise. That is not to deny of course that

with regard to the Soviet Union these same sorts of command economy can deliver an enormous amount of progress in certain areas: putting the first satellite up in space or increasing at an impressive rate the Gross National Product during the 1930s, 1940s and 1950s, or creating societies arguably more egalitarian in important aspects than many in the West.[8] (The demise of these command system has been followed by a degree of justified nostalgia that is understandable.) Nevertheless, the level of authoritarianism in the Eastern European and Soviet societies, the fact that they were so much less efficient at the present level of the development of the productive forces and the fact that they were less (as far as one can gather) desirable in terms of their own citizens have spelt the end of this form of Marxism. These three factors, the factor of efficiency, the factor of authoritarian political relations, and just general discontent among their own citizens, tend to mean that this statist form of Marxism is no longer viable.

Nevertheless, Marxism is not reducible to these three aspects and, therefore, their demise does not imply that Marxism as a whole is now irrelevant. For if you look at the influence of Marxism over the last few decades, there is almost no branch of intellectual (taken in the very widest sense) activity that has not benefited from it. From the liberation theology of Central and Southern America,[9] to some of the classic major contributions to English historiography over the last few decades[10] and certain areas of literary criticism,[11] the fruitful interaction of all these disciplines with Marxism is striking. More precisely, there are two or three areas in which there is still quite a lot that is relevant in the Marxist tradition. The first of these areas is what Marx himself called the materialist conception of history. This is the idea that, if you want to understand what is going on in history, the best starting point is to look at the economic relations of production in that society and try to fit everything else into that. This is, of course, just a very general point. As a vision of history this still seems to make considerable sense as a kind of map on which you can locate various things. As a reading of history, as a way of looking at history, this can be illuminating: the first thing you look at is how people in any society go about satisfying their material needs. For it is on the basis of getting material needs that people engage in other activities – political activities, building legal systems, painting paintings, or praying prayers. This sort of cultural materialist approach seems to be still as valid as ever as against the fashion during recent decades of historians to oscillate wildly between a kind of idealism which tends to explain historical movements by reference almost exclusively to changes in ideas, and the most cynical form of individualism where historical development is analysed in terms of the self-interest of individuals. Against that kind of writing of history it seems that, generally speaking, the Marxist way of looking at these things is living, with recent work on the connections between capitalist development and imperialism being a good example.

There are, of course, difficulties in this approach: the difficulty of the general Marxist conception of history is that it is not terribly good at prediction and implicit in its original formulation by Marx tends to be the view that capitalism in the West will be short-lived. It may be the case that capitalism as a method of organizing society is morally and spiritually bankrupt: but unfortunately it is most certainly not *economically* bankrupt and it is here, in the area precisely of economics and material life, that Marxism claims to have its priority. (If you ask about the morality and the spirituality of Marxism then there are possible answers,[12] but these topics are certainly not to the fore in most of the Marxist tradition.) Indeed, as Simone Weil said: 'Marxist analysis of the mechanism of capitalist oppression is excellent, indeed it is so good that it is difficult to see why that oppression should ever be ended',[13] and in this respect she was more clear-sighted than most of the followers of Marx. This is reflected in the paucity of Marxist political proposals to effect a radical change in society. Of course, there has always been some disjunction between Marxist theory and Marxist practical attempts at radical change.[14] In contemporary debates, this classical problem of the relation of theory to practice is illustrated by the attitude of Marxists to the market. Given the undeniable tendency of the market to promote inequality and frustrate genuine democracy, various alternative socialist methods of organizing the economy have been proposed without, moreover, much indication of how such an organization might be maintained in face of the inevitably undermining efforts of concomitant societies not organised along these lines. There are attractive descriptions of the possible economics and politics of socialist societies but little account of how we can get from here to there. It is striking, for example, that in Hardt and Negri's voluminous books the only specific (and rather modest) proposals are for the abolition of immigration controls and a guaranteed income for all. Perhaps this is because of their determinist view of history: as with Kautsky and the German SPD a century ago, if your theory shows the outcome to be inevitable, then you don't need too much practice to achieve it. But for those whose analyses are less sanguine, the problem remains. Some, such as Callinicos or Wood, stick with classical emphasis on class and on the revolutionary potential of the international proletariat. Others point to economic polarisation, argue for redistribution, and plead for global democracy but fail to go much beyond (to go back again a century) Bernstein's view of democracy as 'at the same time means and end'.[15] Others, such as Holloway, sidestep the problem altogether with a grand refusal to have anything to do with capitalism and advocate a fresh start outside history.[16]

Another difficulty, increasingly coming to the fore, is that the whole strength of the Marxist conception of history is that it points to the forces of production – the tools and instruments that people have at their disposal – and the way they organise themselves together as the carriers of future social progress. Inherent in a lot of traditional Marxism is the view that it is the growth of the forces of production that will bring about a new and a better society – a view which it shares (as Simone Weil also points out[17]) with capitalism. We often forget that liberal capitalism and Marxism are products of the same society and share many of the assumptions of that society. And capitalism also proclaims, in one of its forms anyway, that if you let market forces develop freely, then we shall all – trickling down and so forth – get better in the end. This view shares with Marxism the same confidence that unfettered development of the productive forces will eventually solve the problems which confront us. And it is evident that that sort of view has come under severe question, particularly over the last ten or fifteen years as the noxious ecological consequences (quite apart from the moral and spiritual consequences) of this kind of faith in the development of the productive forces has been brought home to virtually everybody. If climate change is only half as serious as most informed commentators predict, then a drastic re-organisation of the world's economy is inevitable. It will not so much be the proletariat but nature itself which will prove to be the gravedigger of capitalism.[18]

The third difficulty with the Marxist view of history is its emphasis on the economic as the determining factor. If you wanted to isolate something which tends to be the most typical of the Marxist method of analysis, it is (to put it in very simplistic terms) that the economic factor is the most important one; more important than politics, more important than law, more important than religion and so forth. Now this approach also has come under severe strain in three areas. The first of these areas is obviously the continuing virulence of nationalism. The workers of the world were supposed to have no fatherland according to the *Communist Manifesto*; the workers of the world were supposed to be uniting as a single class across national boundaries. The First World War and subsequent events in the twentieth century have put paid to that optimism, and nationalism is as strong now as it ever has been.[19] A second area is the persistence of religion which, according to Marxism, was a spent force. So far from religion disappearing from the world scene, if you read the newspaper or listen to the news, and consider the world at this moment, you will see that it is absolutely *awash* with religion, for better or (often I fear) for worse. So here again is an area in which the medium-term expectations of Marxism have not been borne out.[20] A third, and perhaps even more fundamental, difficulty is that if you are looking at the economic factor in society then you are inclined to divide people up, as Marxism does, in terms of the class they belong to, and generally speaking, at least *start* there in explaining their attitudes and activities. But there are alternative methods of dividing up society, and it seems often that these alternatives are more powerful explanatorily than classes. One of them is obviously race: the real divide is between black and white rather than between worker and capitalist. Another might be nation as mentioned earlier. Or, even more profoundly: the real division in human society is one of gender and not of proletarian and bourgeois. It is the difference and the struggle between men and women and the exploitation of the latter by the former that is the underlying thread that runs through history. Some of the most interesting work in Marxism over the last couple of decades has been done on the interaction between various forms of Marxism and various forms of feminism: books by Juliet Mitchell and Michèle Barrett have asked about the underlying dialectic: is it one of labour or is it one of sex? Or can the two be interlinked through notions of patriarchy? Or, more specifically, what role does the domestic labour of women play in sustaining capitalist relations of production?[21] (It should be said, to its credit, that the Marxist tradition already has, in the shape of the work of Engels on the *Origin of the Family, Private Property and the State*, produced some pioneering historical work in precisely this kind of area.)

Thus there are difficulties in Marx's explanation of history: its lack of predictive ability; its enthusiasm for the growth of the forces of production and concomitant relative lack of sensibility to environmental issues; and its comparative neglect of other factors apart from economics, such as nationalism or religion. And Marx's theory of class, however much it emphasises the economic exploitation of some by others, draws attention away from inequalities of gender and race, factors which seem to influence very strongly people's social and political activities. Nevertheless, the power of the Marxist tradition does indeed reside in its emphasis on material forces, on the economy, and in Marx's insistence that if you want at all to reform society in the sorts of ways that most of us would probably agree to be desirable, then you have to take into account the economy in the sense of the distribution of material resources in our society.[22] And any reform which relies either simply on moral rhetoric or on the law, or on the widening of political rights alone is unlikely to get down to the basis of the problem since, in the Marxist view, the basis of most of these problems is economic and particularly the lack of economic power of a large proportion of individuals in society and the atomisation and anomie that capitalism produces and reproduces. And that emphasis on economics is fundamental to an understanding both of the working of the state and the ways in which these workings are legitimised, both nationally and globally. It is no accident that it is in the two latter areas that Marx's twentieth-century followers in the West have flourished.

In addition to the materialist conception of history, the second area of strength is the way in which Marxism examines the roots of social and political ideas and produces a critique of ideology which asks where do ideas come from and whom do they serve? Marx has been called in this area 'one of the three masters of suspicion' along with Nietzsche and Freud; 'masters of suspicion' in the sense that all three of these thinkers are saying to us: 'Don't take at its face value the description which people – individuals or societies – give of themselves. There is something underneath this. There is something more fundamental which they are concealing, whether consciously or unconsciously.' It is in the developing of this critical theory of society that Marxist ideas are possibly at their strongest. For of those three masters of suspicion, Freud is too much of an individualist to give the rather larger explanations of social and political phenomena that we may be looking for. And Nietzsche, at least in the works of his latter-day followers, is too much of a relativist and an anarchist to serve as any reliable guide. But Marx in this respect is probably the best of all three. It is not accident, therefore, that two of the best books written about the very elusive but all-pervasive concept of postmodernism, by Harvey and by Jameson, are both from a Marxist perspective.[23] What Marx is saying about ideology is that if you take universal concepts like human rights or the national interest, and all the phrases that politicians of every stripe tend to come out with (but some more frequently than others!), you will find that these concepts in fact redound to the benefit of a particular and restricted group in society. Ideology masks the asymmetrical distribution of power and goods in society. Normally speaking these goods will be highly differentially distributed, if not absolutely barred from quite a large section of the population, who cannot afford to pay the piper and still less to call the tune. Marx and his followers may not be good at composing new hits but he will help you work out why you keep on hearing the golden oldies.

Is Marxism currently in crisis? Of course it is. Marxism has been said to be in crisis for well over a century: Thomas Masaryk, later to become first president of the Czechoslovakian Republic, wrote an article saying so in 1898. Indeed, Marxism is itself, among other things, a theory of crisis and inherently, because dialectical, self-critical. One does not need to accept wholly Lukács's view that Marx's method could survive the refutation of all his theses[24] to see that reports of Marxism's death have been exaggerated. What is clear is that, particularly with the collapse of the Soviet Union, Marxism is no longer tied to any party or state. Marxism no longer has a geographical or institutional location. Thus the distinction between orthodoxy and heresy or revisionism has disappeared. The 'short twentieth century' has moved from capitalism to capitalism. But the current neo-liberal world disorder may prove no less fragile than its pre-1914 predecessor. If diagnosis precedes cure, if naming is essential for overcoming, then Marxism's contribution is going to continue to be necessary. Marxism has always been, *pace* Marx, better at interpreting the world than at changing it. But at least it is a start.

Notes

1. See the works of Fukuyama, especially *The End of History, and the Last Man* (Harmondsworth, 1992).
2. See K. Popper, *The Open Society and Its Enemies* (London, 1940), vol. 2, and, more thoroughly, A Walicki, *Marxism and the Leap to the Kingdom of Freedom: The Rise and Fall of the Communist Utopia* (Stanford, 1995).
3. Quoted in A. Kadarky, *George Lukács* (Oxford, 1991), p. 257. Anyone who has a look at such publications as *The Black Book of Communism* (Boston, 1999) will see the force of Weber's remark.
4. E. Wright, A. Levine and E. Sober, *Reconstructing Marxism: Essays on Explanation and the Theory of History* (New York, 1992), p. 190.
5. For an elaboration of this view with close attention to Marx, see Zhongqiao Duan, *Marx's Theory of Social Formation* (Aldershot, 1996).
6. See A. Callinicos, *The Revenge of History: Marxism and the East European Revolutions* (Cambridge, 1991), ch. 2.
7. The classic example here is *The History of the Communist Party of the Soviet Union (Short Course)* (Moscow, 1935).
8. For a balanced assessment, see M. Ellman, *Socialist Planning*, 2nd edn (Cambridge, 1989).
9. For example, A. Fierro, *The Militant Gospel* (London, 1977).
10. See the work of C. Hill, E. Thompson and E. Hobsbawm.
11. For example, T. Eagleton, *The Ideology of the Aesthetic* (Oxford, 1990).
12. See, for example, the discussions in D. McLellan and S. Sayers (eds), *Socialism and Morality* (London, 1990).

13. S. Weil, *Oppression and Liberty*, London, 1988, p. 58.
14. J. Holloway, *Change the World without Taking Power* (London, 2002).
15. See pp. 24 ff. above. Indeed, for those conversant with the debates between writers such as Kautsky, Hilferding and Bernstein, there is more than an element of *plus ça change* about contemporary discussion.
16. See J. Holloway, *Change the World Without Taking Power: The Meaning of Revolution Today*, 2nd edn (London, 2005).
17. Cf. D. McLellan, *Simone Weil: Utopian Pessimist* (New York, 1990), pp. 67ff.
18. For Marxist perspectives on this see J. Foster, *Marx's Ecology: Materialism and Nature* (New York, 2000) and J. Hughes, *Ecology and Historical Materialism* (Cambridge, 2000). Also R. Grundmann, *Marxism and Ecology* (New York, 1991).
19. See E. Hobsbawm, *Nations and Nationalism since 1780: Programme, Myth, Reality* (Cambridge, 1990).
20. See further D. McLellan, *Marxism and Religion* (New York, 1986), pp. 157ff.
21. J. Mitchell, *Women's Estate* (Harmondsworth, 1971) and M. Barrett, *Women's Oppression Today: The Marxist/Feminist Encounter* (New York, 1980). For the domestic labour debate, see D. Coole, *Women in Political Theory* (Brighton, 1988). Also, from a fairly traditional Marxist viewpoint, L. Vogel, *Marxism and Oppression of Women* (London, 1983), and the good general survey by V. Bryson, *Feminist Political Theory: An Introduction* (London, 1992), ch. 13.
22. For a robust defence of this view from a historical point of view, see Z. Duan, *Marx's Theory of Social Formation* (Aldershot, 1995). Also the views of Ellen Wood collected in *Capiltalism versus Democracy* (Cambridge, 1995).
23. See D. Harvey, *The Condition of Postmodernism* (Oxford, 1990), and F. Jameson, *Postmodernism, or the Cultural Logic of Late Capitalism* (Berkeley, 1991). The intellectual excitement of Marx's concept of ideology is well conveyed in the recent and magisterial J. Torrance, *Karl Marx's Theory of Ideas* (Cambridge, 1995).
24. See p. 176 above.

Bibliography

Walter Adamson, *Marx and the Disillusionment of Marxism* (Berkeley, 1985).

Terence Ball and James Farr (eds), *After Marx* (Cambridge, 1984).

Ted Benton, 'Marxism and Natural Limits: An Ecological Critique and Reconstruction', *New Left Review*, vol. 178 (1989).

Axel van der Berg, *The Immanent Utopia: From Marxism on the State to the State of Marxism* (Princeton, N.J., 1988).

Robin Blackburn (ed.), *After the Fall: The Failure of Communism and the Future* (London, 1991).

Robin Blackburn, 'Fin de Siècle: Socialism after the Crash', in R. Blackburn, *After the Fall* (London, 1991).

Alex Callinicos, *The Revenge of History: Marxism and the East European Revolutions* (Cambridge, 1991).

Alex Callinicos, *Is There a Future for Marxism?* (London, 1982).

David Campbell, *The Failure of Marxism: The Concept of Inversion in Marx's Critique of Capitalism* (Aldershot, 1996).

Gøsta Esping-Anderson, *Politics against Markets: The Social Democratic Road to Power* (Princeton, N.J., 1985).

Roger Gottlieb, *Marxism, 1844–1990: Origins, Betrayal, Rebirth* (London, 1992).

Reiner Grundmann, *Marxism and Ecology* (New York, 1991).

Richard Heilbronner, *Marxism: For and Against* (New York, 1980).

James O'Connor, 'Capitalism, Nature, Socialism: A Theoretical Introduction', *Capitalism, Nature, Socialism*, vol. 1 (1988).

Ken Post, *Regaining Marxism* (London, 1996).

Edward Reiss, *Marx: A Clear Guide* (London, 1997).

Lydia Sargeant (ed.), *The Unhappy Marriage of Marxism and Feminism* (London, 1981).

Gary Teeple, *Globalization and the Decline of Social Reform* (Atlantic Highlands, 1995).

Lise Vogel, *Marxism and the Oppression of Women* (London, 1983).

Suke Wolton (ed.), *Marxism, Mysticism and Modern Theory* (London, 1996).

Ellen Meiksins Wood, *Capitalism versus Democracy* (Cambridge, 1995).

Chronological Table

	HISTORY	THEORY
1883	Death of Marx: foundation of SDF	Bebel: *Woman under Socialism* Plekhanov: *Socialism and the Political Struggle*
1884		
1885	Fabian Society founded	Plekhanov: *Our Differences*
1886		
1887	ILP formed	
1888		Engels: *Ludwig Feuerbach*
1889	Foundation of Second International	
1890		
1891	Erfurt Congress of SPD	*Erfurt Programme*
1892		
1893		
1894	Succession of Nicholas II in Russia	Plekhanov: *On the Development of the Monist Conception of History*
1895	Death of Engels: China-Japan war	Engels: *Preface to Class Struggles*
1896		
1897		
1898	Foundation of RSDLP	
1899	SPD Congress rejects Bernstein	Lenin: *Development of Capitalism in Russia* Bernstein: *Evolutionary Socialism* Kautsky: *Agrarian Question*
1900	British Labour Party founded: Boxer rebellion in China	Luxemburg: *Social Reform or Revolution*
1901	Foundation of Socialist Party of America	
1902	2nd Congress of RSDLP: Bolshevik-Menshevik split	Lenin: *What Is to be Done?*
1903		
1904	Russo-Japanese War	
1905	Revolution in Russia: Jena Congress of SPD	
1906		Kautsky: *Ethics* Luxemburg: *Mass Strike* Trotsky: *Results and Prospects*

1907	Stuttgart Congress of International	Bauer: *The Nationalities Question*
1908		Plekhanov: *Fundamental Problems of Marxism*
		Lenin: *Materialism and Empiriocriticism*
1909		Kautsky: *Road to Power*
1910		Hilferding: *Finance Capital*
1911		
1912	Republic proclaimed in China	
1913		Luxemburg: *Accumulation of Capital*
		Stalin: *National Question*
1914	Outbreak of First World War	
1915		Lenin: *Philosophical Notebooks*
		Bukharin: *Imperialism and the World Economy*
1916		Lenin: *Imperialism*
1917	February and October Revolution in Russia: USA enter war	Lenin: *State and Revolution*
1918	Treaty of Brest-Litovsk	
1919	Abortive revolution in Germany	Bukharin and Preobrazhensky: *ABC of Communism*
1920	Treaty of Versailles	
1921	Kronstadt revolt: beginning of NEP	Bukharin: *Historical Materialism*
1922		
1923	USSR established: triumph of Fascism in Italy	Trotsky: *New Course*
		Lukács: *History and Class Consciousness*
		Korsch: *Marxism and Philosophy*
1924	Death of Lenin: Northern Expedition of Chiang Kai-shek	Stalin: *Foundations of Leninism*
1925		
1926		Gramsci: *On the Southern Question*
1927	Trotsky and Zinoviev expelled from Party	Mao: *Peasant Question in Hunan*
1928		
1929	Trotsky expelled from Russia: beginning of Great Depression	Gramsci: *Prison Notebooks* (until 1935)
1930	Collectivisation of agriculture in Russia	
1931		
1932		
1933	Accession to power of Hitler	
1934		
1935	The Long March	Lukács: *Studies in European Realism*
1936		

1937		Trotsky: *Revolution Betrayed*
		Mao: *On Practice: On Contradiction*
1938		Stalin: *Dialectical and Historical Materialism*
1939	Outbreak of Second World War	
1940		Mao: *On New Democracy*
1941		Marcuse: *Reason and Revolution*
1942	Battle of Stalingrad	Sweezy: *Theory of Capitalist Development*
1943		
1944		
1945	End of Second World War	
1946		
1947		Lukács: *The Historical Novel*
		Adorno and Horkheimer: *Dialectic of Enlightenment*
1948	Yugoslavia's break with Soviet Union	
1949	People's Republic of China Proclaimed	Stalin: *Marxism and Linguistics*
		Adorno *et al.*, *Authoritarian Personality*
1950	Korean War	
1951	McCarthyism in USA	
1952		Stalin: *Economic Problems of USSR*
		Sartre: *Communists and the Peace*
1953	Death of Stalin	
1954		
1955		Marcuse: *Eros and Civilization*
1956	Condemnation of Stalin at 20th Congress: Soviet invasion of Hungary	
1957		Baran: *Political Economy of Growth*
		Sartre: *Search for a Method*
		Mao: *Correct Handling of Contradictions*
1958	Great Leap Forward in China	
1959	Cuban revolution	
1960	Sino-Soviet Split	Sartre: *Critique of Dialectical Reason*
1961		
1962	Cuban missile crisis	
1963		

1964	Downfall of Krushchev	Marcuse: *One-Dimensional Man*
		Togliatti's *Testament*
1965		Althusser: *For Marx*
		Guevara: *Socialism and Man in Cuba*
1966	Beginning of Cultural Revolution	Baran and Sweezy: *Monopoly Capital*
1967		Debray: *Revolution in the Revolution*
1968	Soviet invasion of Czechoslovakia: May events in Paris	Althusser: *Reading Capital*
1969		Frank: *Capitalism and Underdevelopment in Latin America*
1970		
1971	Fall of Lin Piao	
1972	US withdrawal from Vietnam	
1973	Allende Government overturned in Chile	Althusser: *Essays in Self Criticism*
		O'Connor: *Fiscal Crisis*
1974		Braverman: *Labour and Monopoly Capital*
1975		
1976	Death of Mao	
1977		
1978		Cohen: *Karl Marx's Theory of History*
1991	Collapse of Soviet Union	
1997	Death of Deng	

A Marxist Genealogy
(the placings below are highly approximate)

Further Publications

Dictionaries

T. Bottomore (ed.), *Dictionary of Marxism*, 2nd edn (Oxford, 1991).
J. Doherty, *Historical Dictionary of Socialism* (Lanham, 1997).
D. Gray and D. Walker, *An Historical Dictionary of Marxism* (Lanham, 2006).
J. Bidet and E. Kouvalakis (eds), *Dictionnaire de Marx Contemporain* (Paris, 2001).
W. Haag (ed.), *Historisches-Kritisches Wörterbuch des Marxismus* (Berlin, 1995–).

Journals

Against the Current

US journal coming from a revolutionary Marxist tradition aimed at those active in anti-globalisation struggles. Address: cfc@igc.org.

Arena Journal

Australian review applying Marx's method to cultural questions and the tensions between instrumental rationality and humanism. Address: PO Box 18, North Carlton, 3054 Australia.

Capital and Class

British journal of political economy incorporating a Marxist analysis of capitalism and its consequences. Publishes a number of special issues. Address: 25 Horsell Road, London, N5 1XL, UK.

Capitalism, Nature, Socialism

A Californian journal dealing with political ecology. It has a strong Marxist tendency mixed with approaches from critical theory and post-modernism. Address: PO Box 8467, Santa Cruz, California 95061, USA.

Critical Sociology

An American journal which used to be called *Insurgent Sociologist*. Still fairly orthodox, it analyses the social bases of contemporary capitalism. Address: 656 West, Kirby, Detroit, Michigan 48202, USA.

Contemporary Marxism Review

A Chinese journal produced by the Centre for Contemporary Marxism at the University of Fudan. It looks at classical Marxist texts and their interpretation by contemporary scholars of Marxism. Address: Centre for Contemporary Marxism Abroad, Fudan University, 220 Handan Road, Shanghai, 200433, China.

Historical Materialism

A British journal with substantial articles and reviews following a strongly Marxist approach. Looks well beyond the anglophone sphere to deal with social transformation on a world-wide scale. Address: Faculty of Law and Social Sciences, SOAS, Thornhaugh Street, London, WC1H 0XG, UK.

Imprints

A British journal drawing on analytical philosophy to promote equality and democracy. Its philosophical approach means that the Marxist input is not substantial. Address: 58 Wilmer Drive, Bradford, BD9 4AS, UK.

International Socialism

A British journal of Trotskyist provenance and relatively wide diffusion. Resolutely traditional Marxist, it is intended more for militants than universities. Address: PO Box 82, London, E3, UK.

Left Curve

A Californian review with only a peripheral interest in mainstream Marxism and a strongly postmodern outlook. Address: PO Box 472, Oakland, California 94604, USA.

Links

Australian journal subtitled 'International Journal of Socialist Renewal'. It aims to provide a forum for discussing political strategies to oppose neo-liberal globalisation. Address: PO Box 515, Broadway, NSW 2007, Australia.

Monthly Review

Main American Marxist journal, founded in 1949. Although based on traditional Marxism and strongly anti-postmodern, it contains discussion of new social movements and anti-globalisation struggles. Address: 122 West 27th Street, New York, NY 10001, USA.

New Left Review

Main British Marxist journal, founded in 1960. Its heavyweight articles are strong on theory and culture with an international anti-capitalist perspective. Address: 6 Meard Street, London, W1V 3HR, UK.

Radical Philosophy

British review founded in 1972 and subtitled 'A Journal of Socialist and Feminist Philosophy'. Its interest centres on Continental European Philosophy (as opposed to Anglo-Saxon analytic) in areas sometimes well beyond the scope of Marxism. Address: http://www.radicalphilosophy.com.

Rethinking Marxism

American review founded in the late 1980s. As its title suggests, its aim is to interpret Marxism in the light of other critical theoretical traditions of more recent provenance. Address: http://www.rethinkingmarxism.org/.

Science and Society

Founded in 1936, this American quarterly is the oldest continuously published review. Originally close to orthodox Marxism, it became more inclusive after the 1960s and contains substantial articles across the board. Address: 445 West 59th Street, Rm 4331, New York, NY 10019, USA.

Social Sciences in China

A review based in the Chinese Academy of Social Sciences. Orthodox in its approach, it gives a good guide to mainstream Chinese debates on philosophy, economics, sociology and history. Address: 158 Gulouxidajie, Beijing 10072, China.

Socialism and Democracy

A radical American journal founded in 1985. It is international in perspective and concentrates on contemporary political struggles. Address: 411 Highland Avenue, Sommerville, MA 02144, USA.

Socialist Register

A British annual dating from 1964. Each volume groups essays around a theme, international in scope and authorship, usually concentrating on economics and politics. Address: The Merlin Press, PO Box 30705, London, WC2E 8JT, UK.

Studies in Political Economy

A Canadian review which concentrates on critical perspectives on capitalist development both in Canada and the world at large. Address: Carleton University, 1125 Colonel By Drive, Ottawa, Ontario KIS 5B6, Canada.

Thesis Eleven

An Australian journal of critical theory founded in 1980. It is particularly interested in European post-Marxist theory. Address: School of Social Sciences, La Trobe University, Bundoora, Victoria 3086, Australia.

Transformation: Marxist Boundary Work in Theory Economics, Politics, and Culture

An American journal with a no-nonsense revolutionary Marxist approach. It deals primarily with classical Marxism and contemporary class struggle. Address: PO Box 4523, Schenectady, NY 12309-0523, USA.

General bibliography

P. Anderson, *Spectrum* (London, 2005).

R. Aronson, *After Marxism* (New York, 1995).

Z. Baranski and J. Short (eds), *Developing Contemporary Marxism* (London, 1985).

R. Bellofiore (ed.), *Marxian Economics: A Reappraisal. Essays on Volume 3 of Capital* (New York, 1998).

E. Benner, *Really Existing Nationalisms: A Post-Communist View from Marx and Engels* (Oxford, 1995).

C. Bertram and A. Chitty (eds), *Has History Ended? Fukuyama, Marx and Modernity* (Aldershot, 1994).

W. Bonefeld and S. Visqueria, *What is to be Done?: Leninism, Anti-Leninist Marxism and the Question of Revolution Today* (Aldershot, 2002).

C. Boggs, *The Socialist Tradition: From Crisis to Decline* (New York, 1995).

A. Callari *et al.* (eds), *Marxism in the Postmodern Age: Confronting the New World Order* (New York, 1995).

A. Callinicos, *Making History: Agency, Structure and Change in Social Theory*, 2nd edn (Leiden, 2004).

M. Cowling and P. Reynolds (eds), *Marxism, the Millennium and Beyond* (Basingstoke, 2000).

S. Cullenberg, *The Falling Rate of Profit: Recasting the Marxian Debate* (London, 1994).

D. Debb, *Marx, Marxism and Utopia* (Aldershot, 2000).

M. Desai, *Marx's Revenge: The Resurgence of Capitalism and the Death of Statist Socialism* (Cambridge, 2002).

J. Doherty, *Historical Dictionary of Socialism* (Lanham, 1997).

J. Foster, *Marx's Ecology: Materialism and Nature* (New York, 2000).

A. Gamble, 'Marxism after Communism', *Review of International Studies*, vol. 25, (December, 1999).

Andrew Gamble *et al.* (eds), *Marxism and Social Science* (Basingstoke, 1999).

P. Guttfried, *The Strange Death of Marxism: The European Left in the New Millennium* (Columbia, 2005).

C. M. Hann (ed.), *Socialism: Ideals, Ideologies and Local Practice* (London, 1993).

M. Howard and J. King, *A History of Marxian Economics, Vol II, 1929–1990* (Basingstoke, 1992).

B. Hudelson, *Marxism and Philosophy in the Twentieth Century* (New York, 1990).

J. Hughes, *Ecology and Historical Materialism* (Cambridge, 2000).

B. Jessop and C. Malcolm-Brown (eds), *Karl Marx: Social and Political Thought, Critical Assessments*, 4 vols (London, 1999).

B. Kagarlitsky, *New Realism, New Barbarism: Socialist Theory in the Age of Globalization* (London, 1999).

R. Miliband, *Socialism for a Sceptical Age* (London, 1994).

F. Moseley and M. Campbell (eds), *New Investigations of Marx's Method* (New Jersey, 1997).

C. Munford, *Production Relations, Class and Black Liberation* (Amsterdam, 1978).

M. Perry, *Marxism and History* (Basingstoke, 2002).

J. Pike, *From Aristotle to Marx* (Aldershot, 1998).

C. Robinson, *An Anthropology of Marxism* (Aldershot, 2001).

T. Rockmore, *Marx after Marxism: The Philosophy of Karl Marx* (Oxford, 2002).

S. Sayers, *Marxism and Human Nature* (London, 1998).

J. Townshend, *The Politics of Marxism: The Critical Debates* (London, 1996).

W. Truitt, *Marxist Ethics: A Short Introduction* (New York, 2005).

D. Walker, *Marx, Methodology and Science: Marx's Science of Politics* (Aldershot, 2001).

D. Walker et al. (eds), *Twentieth Century Marxism* (London, 2007).

P. Wetherly, *Marxism and the State: An Analytical Approach* (Basingstoke, 2005).

L. Wilde, *Marxism's Ethical Thinkers* (Basingstoke, 2001).

R. Woodfin et al., *Introducing Marxism*, Royston, 2004.

Index

443

CPSIA information can be obtained at www.ICGtesting.com
Printed in the USA
LVOW06s1235251113

362741LV00010B/16/P